BUILD THE WORDS
THAT WILL MAKE YOU A CHAMP!

Confound your opponents with:

- The 10 three-letter words you can make from **GO** and the 16 three-letter words you can make from **YE**
- One-letter additions to high-scoring words like **QUART, QUIP, QUIRK, SQUAW, VOW,** and **YOW**
- Two-letter zingers like **KA, JO, AW** and **XI**
- Words they *can't* expand with only one letter—like **HEX, HALF, LACY, RACY, NUMEN, NUTTY,** and **NTH**
- The eight words and their plurals that contain a Q but don't require a U—**FAQIR, QAID, QANAT, QAT, QINDAR, QINTAR, QOPH,** and **TRANQ**

And much more!

Every word you need is here—in the guide that can improve every fan's level of play!

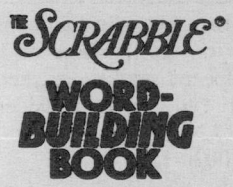

THE **SCRABBLE** ®
WORD-BUILDING BOOK

THE SCRABBLE®
WORD-BUILDING BOOK

Compiled by
SALEEM AHMED
**with Carol "Yasmin," Aisha
and Seema Ahmed**

A Family Project

POCKET BOOKS
New York   London   Toronto   Sydney   Singapore

An *Original* Publication of POCKET BOOKS

POCKET BOOKS, a division of Simon & Schuster Inc.
1230 Avenue of the Americas, New York, NY 10020

Copyright © 1991 by Saleem Ahmed

ISBN: 0-671-73456-3

First Pocket Books printing October 1991

10

POCKET and colophon are registered trademarks of
Simon & Schuster Inc.

SCRABBLE ® is a registered trademark of Hasbro, Inc.
© 1991 Milton Bradley Company, a division of Hasbro, Inc.

Printed in the U.S.A.

*Dedicated to both Grannies
(one in Pakistan, the other in Hawaii)
for their love and support as this project progressed,*

and to

*the small but powerful
University Laboratory School, Honolulu
(graduating class under 50),
for the fine training
they provided
our girls*

CONTENTS

PREFACE

The book you are holding has been a family project and a labor of love for more than seven years, but the conceptual seed was sown more than twenty-five years ago, when I was an agronomist in Pakistan. With leisure-time activities scarce, my Hawaiian-born *sansei* (third generation Japanese) wife, Yasmin, and I often played SCRABBLE®.

In Sukkar, a small town 350 miles north of Karachi, Pakistan, the competition was fierce (I usually lost). How many times I wished some little angel would come to my rescue—especially late in the game, when openings were few, "choice" spots were already taken, and the desperation level was at an all-time high. The brain would race in all directions, the mind would turn to mush, and I would feverishly try to recall nursery rhymes and musical notes to find that two- or three-letter word that could help me win the game. Did the black sheep go **ba-ba** or **baa-baa**; and is the third musical note **me** or **mi**? Other questions that came up as my game improved: Does any letter come before **KA** (the spiritual self in old Egyptian religion)? Answer: **OKA**, a Turkish unit of weight. Or after **OX**? Answer: **OXY**, containing oxygen.

We permitted ourselves to consult the dictionary in our games, because this made the game a learning process also; but flipping through all alphabets to find a suitable connecting letter can be very time-consuming! Thus, secretly, we began to compile our own lists of important two- and three-letter words having high point values, such as **JO** and **XIS** (respectively a Scottish sweetheart and the plural of the fourteenth letter of the Greek alphabet). Still I usually lost.

As our lives became more hectic, we stopped playing SCRABBLE® until our daughters, Aisha and Seema, were old enough to play with us. As competitiveness returned, the thought of expanding our word lists into a book came to mind. When we acquired a computer seven years ago, the project was born.

Had we any notion then of the magnitude of the task we were embarking upon, we probably would have nipped the project in the bud. At first I envisioned our book to list only two- and three-letter words. So, Aisha and Seema pored over dictionaries and made a list of all such words. Then we sorted out 94 two-letter words and about 800 three-letter words commonly accepted in English. Of the latter, about 550 are "built up" by adding a letter to either the front or back of the two-letter words listed. We entered all in the computer, and Yasmin helped with proofreading. Thus, our separate lists of two-letter and three-letter words came into being.

We then realized these were handy lists, but they certainly did not constitute a reference book. So, we decided to include four-, five-, six-, seven-, and buildable eight-letter words also. And with each new listing, our entries expanded in geometric proportions. After two years, when we were celebrating the completion of our task, it dawned on us that it would be highly irritating to the book's users to look at each list separately. Reluctantly we consolidated these separate listings into one alphabetical list. We used the seven-letter list as our base (it was the longest) and entered words from each of the other lists—word by word—in their proper alphabetical sequence. This took another year.

When we got down to celebrating again, another realization struck us: Our book listed only those words from which other words can be made, but what about words standing by themselves, from which no other word could be made? For example, can any letter be added either to the front or back of the common word **QUIZ**? Our book did not include this word at that time, since nothing can be added. Well, the reader would not know whether this was an oversight or whether nothing could be added to either its front or back. Then the stark realization gripped us: The only way to prevent the reader from having to use another dictionary to ensure that nothing could be added to **QUIZ**—or that a word such as **ZYMURGY** (the branch of chemistry dealing with fermentation) existed in English—would be to include in our book all words in the English language, even those standing by themselves.

So, back to the drawing board we went. This time we added *all* other words up to seven letters long which we had previously omitted. Another year's work. All together, more than 70,000 words are listed.

Anyway, here we are, seven years later, proud of our family project. The memory of the family having worked together over these years will certainly be treasured by all of us.

We hope using this book helps draw your family and friends closer together also.

We thank the National SCRABBLE® Association for examining sample sections of this book and offering useful suggestions.

To join the NSA, send $15.00 (foreign fee is $20.00 in U.S. funds) to:

> National SCRABBLE® Association
> Box 700
> Greenport, NY 11944
> USA

You'll receive a year's subscription to the SCRABBLE® NEWS (8 issues), a roster of official SCRABBLE® clubs throughout the U.S. and Canada, a membership card and information about local and regional SCRABBLE® tournaments.

We will appreciate your bringing to our attention any typos you detect, or other words you would like to suggest for inclusion in future editions of The SCRABBLE® Word-Building Book. Please send your comments to:

> Saleem Ahmed
> 781 Eleele Place
> Honolulu, HI 96825
> USA

> Aloha!

> Saleem Ahmed
> Honolulu
> January 1990

INTRODUCTION

How to Use
The SCRABBLE® Word-Building Book

This book is designed primarily as an educational tool to improve your SCRABBLE® and other word-game skills. It is also a reference book listing all words in English containing up to seven letters (the number of tiles each player has on a rack in SCRABBLE®) and all "buildable" eight-letter words.

The book is divided into three sections. Given the importance in SCRABBLE® of using small words in making the most effective use of bonus squares, two special sections—one containing all 94 two-letter words, the other containing the more than 800 three-letter words—have been created. These invaluable words should be memorized over time. Your game will be greatly improved. The main section contains all 70,000 words.

The SCRABBLE® Word-Building Book is the only reference book for SCRABBLE® and other word games that exclusively shows how to build words from both the front and back of existing words by simply adding a letter. All others show how to build only from the back. *The Word-Building Book* works as follows:

	WORD	NEW WORD
1	SPIC	aspic; spice, spick, spics, spicy
2	QUART	–; quarte, quarto, quarts, quartz
3	QUARE	square; –
4	QUIZ	–; –

Example 1 shows that **a** can be added to **SPIC** in front; and **e**, **k**, **s**, and **y** at the back. The semicolon (;) separates "front" and ''back'' words. Example 2 shows that no letter can be added in front of **QUART**; but **e**, **o**, **s**, and **z** can be added at the back. Example 3 shows **s** can be added in front of **QUARE**; but nothing can be added at the back. And Example 4 shows that nothing can be added either in front or back of **QUIZ**.

To economize on space, when a non-expandable word is formed by adding a letter to another word, it is generally not listed again. However, some high-scoring words, such as **QUARTZ**, have also been listed separately, although no other word can be formed from it.

Finally, the English language is growing by ''adopting'' words from other languages and by the creation of new words. For example, since **fax** is now accepted in some dictionaries, we have included it. Other words will be added to future editions of *The SCRABBLE® Word-Building Book* as they become more commonly accepted.

THE SCRABBLE®

WORD-BUILDING BOOK

TWO-LETTER WORD LIST

A *must* for good SCRABBLE® players is a knowledge of two-letter words. Very often these are invaluable word linkers. Listed below are 94 such words. We have omitted some words such as **ja**, which is actually German but is listed in some dictionaries. Memorize them all. Note: each word appears under both alphabets. For example, **ba** appears under both **A** and **B**. Don't think that 188 words are listed.

A: aa, ba, da, fa, ha, ka, la, ma, na, pa, ta, ya; aa, ad, ae, ag, ah, ai, al, am, an, ar, as, at, aw, ax, ay

B: –; ba, be, bi, bo, by

C: –; –

D: ad, id, od; da, de, do

E: ae, be, de, he, me, ne, oe, pe, re, we, ye; ef, eh, el, em, en, er, es, et, ex

F: ef, if, of; fa

G: ag; go

H: ah, eh, oh, sh, uh; ha, he, hi, hm, ho

I: ai, bi, hi, li, mi, pi, si, ti, xi; id, if, in, is, it

J: –; jo

K: –; ka

L: al, el; la, li, lo

M: am, em, hm, mm, om, um; ma, me, mi, mm, mo, mu, my

N: an, en, in, on, un; na, ne, no, nu

O: bo, do, go, ho, jo, lo, mo, no, so, to, wo; od, oe, of, oh, om, on, op, or, os, ow, ox, oy

P: op, up; pa, pe, pi

Q: –; –

R: ar, er, or; re

S: as, es, is, os, us; sh, si, so

T: at, et, it, ut; ta, ti, to

U: mu, nu, xu; uh, um, un, up, us, ut

V: –; –

W: aw, ow; we, wo

X: ax, ex, ox; xi, xu

Y: ay, by, my, oy; ya, ye

Z: –; –

THREE-LETTER WORD LIST

Listed below are about 800 three-letter words. Of these about 550 are "built up" from two-letter words by adding a letter to the front or back; and the remaining 250 are "independent." The latter ones are listed in capital letters, as in **ACT**. Memorize all of these also—with time. As with two-letter words, there are many three-letter words which are also listed twice (for example, **ADO**, which is built up from both **AD** and **DO**). Thus, the total number of entries below is near 1250.

A

AA: baa; aah, aal, aas
ABA
ABO
ABY
ACE
ACT

AD: bad, cad, dad, fad, gad, had, lad, mad, pad, rad, sad, tad, wad; add, ado, ads, adz

AE: gae, hae, kae, mae, nae, sae, tae, wae; — AFF
AFT

AG: bag, dag, fag, gag, hag, jag, lag, mag, nag, rag, sag, tag, wag, zag; aga, age, ago

AH: aah, bah, dah, hah, pah, rah, yah; aha

AI: —; aid, ail, aim, ain, air, ais, ait

AL: bal, gal, pal, sal; ala, alb, ale, all, alp, als, alt

AM: cam, dam, gam, ham, jam, lam, pam, ram, tam, yam; ama, ami, amp, amu

AN: ban, can, dan, fan, gan, man, pan, ran, tan, van, wan; ana, and, ane, ani, ant, any
APE
APT

AR: bar, car, ear, far, gar, jar, lar, mar, oar, par, tar, war, yar; arc, are, arf, ark, arm, ars, art

AS: bas, fas, gas, has, kas, las, mas, pas, ras, tas, vas, was; ash, ask, asp, ass

AT: bat, cat, eat, fat, gat, hat, kat, lat, mat, oat, pat, qat, rat, sat, tat, vat, wat; ate
AUK
AVA

AVE
AVO

AW: caw, daw, haw, jaw,
law, maw, paw, raw,
saw, taw, vaw, waw,
yaw; awa, awe, awl,
awn

AX: fax, lax, pax, rax,
sax, tax, wax, zax;
axe

AY: bay, cay, day, fay,
gay, hay, jay, kay,
lay, may, nay, pay,
ray, say, way, yay;
aye, ays
AZO

B

BA: aba; baa, bad, bag,
bah, bal, ban, bar,
bas, bat, bay

BE: obe; bed, bee, beg,
bel, ben, bet, bey

BI: obi; bib, bid, big, bin,
bio, bis, bit

BO: abo; boa, bob, bod,
bog, boo, bop, bos,
bot, bow, box, boy
BRA
BUB
BUD
BUG
BUM
BUN
BUR
BUS
BUT
BUY

BY: aby; bye, bys

C

CAB
CAD
CAM
CAN
CAP
CAR
CAT
CAW
CAY
CEE
CHI
COB
COD
COG
COL
CON
COO
COP
COS
COT
COW
COX
COY
COZ
CRY
CUB
CUD
CUE
CUM
CUP
CUR
CUT
CWM

D

DA: —; dab, dad, dag,
dah, dak, dam, dan,

DE: dap, daw, day
ode; deb, dee, dei, del, den, des, dev, dew, dex, dey
DIB
DID
DIE
DIG
DIM
DIN
DIP
DIT

DO: ado, udo; doc, doe, dog, dol, dom, don, dor, dos, dot, dow
DRY
DUB
DUC
DUD
DUE
DUG
DUI
DUN
DUO
DUP
DYE

E

EAR
EAT
EAU
EBB
ECU
EDH
EEL

EF: kef, ref; eff, efs, eft
EGG
EGO

EH: peh, yeh; –
EKE

EL: bel, del, eel, gel, mel, sel; eld, elf, elk, ell, elm, els

EM: gem, hem, mem, rem; eme, ems, emu

EN: ben, den, fen, hen, ken, men, pen, sen, ten, wen, yen; end, eng, ens
EON

ER: fer, her, per, ser; era, ere, erg, ern, err, ers

ES: des, hes, pes, res, yes; ess

ET: bet, fet, get, het, jet, let, met, net, pet, ret, set, vet, wet, yet; eta, eth
EVE
EWE

EX: dex, hex, kex, lex, rex, sex, vex; –
EYE

F

FA: –; fad, fag, fan, far, fas, fat, fax, fay
FED
FEE
FEN
FER
FET
FEU
FEW
FEY
FEZ
FIB
FID
FIE

FIG
FIL
FIN
FIR
FIT
FIX
FIZ
FLU
FLY
FOB
FOE
FOG
FOH
FON
FOP
FOR
FOU
FOX
FOY
FRO
FRY
FUB
FUD
FUG
FUN
FUR

GAY
GED
GEE
GEL
GEM
GET
GEY
GHI
GIB
GID
GIE
GIG
GIN
GIP
GIT
GNU

GO: ago, ego; goa, gob, god, goo, gor, got, gox, goy

GUL
GUM
GUN
GUT
GUY
GYM
GYP

G

GAB
GAD
GAE
GAG
GAL
GAM
GAN
GAP
GAR
GAS
GAT

H

HA: aha, wha; had, hae, hag, hah, haj, ham, hap, has, hat, haw, hay

HE: she, the; hem, hen, hep, her, hes, het, hew, hex, hey

HI: chi, ghi, khi, phi; hic, hid, hie, him, hin, hip, his, hit

HM: ohm; –

HO: mho, oho, rho, tho,
who· hnh, hod, hoe,
hog, hop, hot, how,
hoy
HUB
HUE
HUG
HUH
HUM
HUN
HUP
HUT
HYP

I

ICE
ICH
ICY
ID: aid, bid, did, fid, gid,
hid, kid, lid, mid, rid,
yid; ids
IF: kif; ifs
ILK
ILL
IMP
IN: ain, bin, din, fin, gin,
hin, jin, kin, lin, pin,
rin, sin, tin, vin, win,
yin; ink, inn, ins
ION
IRE
IRK
IS: ais, bis, his, lis, mis,
pis, sis, tis, vis, wis,
xis; ism
IT: ait, bit, dit, fit, git, hit,
kit, lit, nit, pit, sit, tit,
uit, wit; its
IVY

J

JAB
JAG
JAM
JAR
JAW
JAY
JEE
JET
JEU
JEW
JIB
JIG
JIN
JO: –; job, joe, jog, jot,
low, joy
JUG
JUN
JUS
JUT

K

KA: oka; kab, kae, kas,
kat, kay
KEA
KEF
KEG
KEN
KEP
KEX
KEY
KHI
KID
KIF
KIN
KIP
KIT
KOA
KOP

KOR
KOS
KUE

L

LA: ala; lab, lac, lad, lag, lam, lap, lar, las, lat, law, lax, lay
LEA
LED
LEE
LEG
LEI
LEK
LET
LEU
LEV
LEX
LEY
LI: –; lib, lid, lie, lin, lip, lis, lit
LO: –; lob, log, loo, lop, lot, low, lox
LUG
LUM
LYE

M

MA: ama; mac, mad, mae, mag, man, map, mar, mas, mat, maw, may
ME: eme; mel, mem, men, met, mew
MHO
MI: ami; mib, mid, mig, mil, mim, mir, mis, mix
MO: –; moa, mob, mod, mog, mol, mom, mon, moo, mop, mor, mos, mot, mow
MU: amu, emu; mud, mug, mum, mun, mus, mut

N

NA: ana; nab, nae, nag, nap, nay
NE: ane, one; neb, nee, net, new
NIB
NIL
NIM
NIP
NIT
NIX
NO: –; nob, nod, nog, noh, nom, noo, nor, nos, not, now
NTH
NU: gnu; nub, nun, nus, nut

O

OAF
OAK
OAR
OAT
OBE
OBI
OCA
OD: bod, cod, god, hod, mod, nod, pod, rod, sod, tod, yod; odd, ode, ods
OE: doe, foe, hoe, joe, roe, toe, voe, woe; oes

OF: —; off, oft
OH: foh, noh, ooh, poh;
      ohm, oho, ohs
      OIL
      OKA
      OKE
      OLD
      OLE
OM: dom, mom, nom, tom,
      yom; oms
ON: con, don, eon, fon,
      ion, mon, son, ton,
      von, won, yon; one,
      ons
      OOH
      OOT
OP: bop, cop, fop, hop,
      kop, lop, mop, pop,
      sop, top, wop; ope,
      ops, opt
OR: dor, for, gor, kor,
      mor, nor, tor; ora,
      orb, orc, ore, ors, ort
OS: bos, cos, dos, kos,
      nos, wos; ose
      OUD
      OUR
      OUT
      OVA
OW: bow, cow, dow, how,
      jow, low, mow, now,
      pow, row, sow, tow,
      vow, wow, yow; owe,
      owl, own
OX: box, cox, fox, gox,
      lox, pox, sox, vox;
      oxy
OY: boy, coy, foy, goy,
      hoy, joy, soy, toy; —

P

PA: spa; pac, pad, pah,
      pal, pam, pan, pap,
      par, pas, pat, paw,
      pax, pay
PE: ape, ope; pea, ped,
      pee, peg, peh, pen,
      pep, per, pes, pet,
      pew
      PHI
      PHT
PI: —; pia, pic, pie, pig,
      pin, pip, pis, pit, piu,
      pix
      PLY
      POD
      POH
      POI
      POL
      POP
      POT
      POW
      POX
      PRO
      PRY
      PSI
      PUB
      PUD
      PUG
      PUL
      PUN
      PUP
      PUR
      PUS
      PUT
      PYA
      PYE
      PYX

Q

QAT
QUA

RUM
RUN
RUT
RYA
RYE

R

RAD
RAG
RAH
RAJ
RAM
RAN
RAP
RAS
RAT
RAW
RAX
RAY

RE: are, ere, ire, ore;
reb, rec, red, ree,
ref, rei, rem, rep,
res, ret, rev, rex

RHO
RIB
RID
RIG
RIM
RIN
RIP
ROB
ROC
ROD
ROE
ROT
ROW
RUB
RUE
RUG

S

SAB
SAC
SAD
SAE
SAG
SAL
SAP
SAT
SAU
SAW
SAX
SAY
SEA
SEC
SEE
SEI
SEL
SEN
SER
SET
SEW
SEX

SH: ash; she, shh, shy
SI: psi; sib, sic, sim, sin,
sip, sir, sis, sit, six
SKI
SKY
SLY

SO: −; sob, sod, sol, son,
sop, sot, sou, sow,
sox, soy

SPA
SPY
SRI
STY
SUB
SUE
SUM
SUN
SUP
SYN

T

TA: eta, uta; tab, tad, tae, tag, taj, tam, tan, tao, tap, tar, tas, tat, tau, tav, taw, tax
TEA
TED
TEE
TEG
TEN
TEW
THE
THO
THY
TI: –; tic, tie, til, tin, tip, tis, tit
TO: –; tod, toe, tog, tom, ton, too, top, tor, tot, tow, toy
TRY
TSK
TUB
TUG
TUI
TUN
TUP
TUT

TUX
TWA
TWO
TYE

U

UDO
UGH
UH: huh; –
UIT
UKE
UM: bum, cum, gum, hum, lum, mum, rum, sum; ump
UN: bun, dun, fun, gun, hun, jun, mun, nun, pun, run, sun, tun; uns
UP: cup, dup, hup, pup, sup, tup, yup; upo, ups
URD
URN
US: bus, jus, mus, nus, pus; use
UT: but, cut, gut, hut, jut, mut, nut, out, put, rut, tut; uta, uts

V

VAN
VAS
VAT
VAV
VAW
VEE
VEG
VET

VEX
VIA
VIE
VIM
VIN
VIS
VOE
VON
VOW
VOX
VUG

W

WAB
WAD
WAE
WAG
WAN
WAP
WAR
WAS
WAT
WAW
WAX
WAY
WE: awe, ewe, owe; web, wed, wee, wen, wet
WHA
WHO
WHY
WIG
WIN
WIS
WIT
WIZ
WO: two; woe, wok, won, woo, wop, wos, wot, wow

WRY
WUD
WYE

X

XI: –; xis

Y

YA: pya, rya; yah, yak, yam, yap, yar, yaw, yay
YE: aye, bye, dye, eye, lye, pye, rye, tye, wye; yea, yeh, yen, yep, yes, yet, yew
YID
YIN
YIP
YOD
YOM
YON
YOU
YOW
YUK
YUP

Z

ZAG
ZAP
ZAX
ZED
ZEE
ZIG
ZIP
ZOA
ZOO

THE MAIN LIST

Listed in this section are the 70,000 words that constitute this book. These include all two- and three-letter words listed in the earlier sections as well as all words in the English language up to seven letters long. This list also contains all eight-letter words that can be built from those seven-letter words.

A

A	aa, ba, da, fa, ha, ka, la, ma, na, pa, ta, ya; aa, ad, ae, ag, ah, ai, al, am, an, ar, as, at, aw, ax, ay	**ABAKAS**	kabakas; −
		ABALONE	−; abalones
		ABAMP	−; ubamps
		ABANDON	−; abandons
		ABAS	babas; −
		ABASE	−; abased, abaser, abases
AA	baa; aah, aal, aas	**ABASER**	−; abasers
AAH	−; aahs	**ABASH**	−; −
AAHED	;	**ABASHED**	−; −
AAHING	−; −	**ABASHES**	−; −
AAL	baal; aals	**ABASING**	−; −
AALII	−; aaliis	**ABATE**	−; abated, abater, abates
AALS	baals; −		
AAS	baas, kaas; −	**ABATER**	−; abaters
ABA	baba; abas	**ABATING**	−; −
		ABATIS	−; −
ABACA	−; abacas	**ABATOR**	−; abators
ABACI	−; −	**ABATTIS**	−; −
ABACK	−; −	**ABAXIAL**	−; −
ABACUS	−; −	**ABAXILE**	−; −
ABAFT	−; −	**ABBACY**	−; −
ABAKA	kabaka; abakas	**ABBE**	−; abbes, abbey
		ABBES	−; abbess

ABBEY	–; abbeys		table; abler,
ABBOT	–; abbots		ables
ABBOTCY	–; –	**ABLER**	fabler; –
ABDOMEN	–; abdomens	**ABLES**	cables, fables,
ABDUCE	–; abduced, abduces		gables, sables, tables;
ABDUCT	–; abducts		ablest
ABEAM	–; –		
ABED	sabed; –	**ABLINGS**	–; –
ABELE	–; abeles	**ABLINS**	–; –
ABET	–; abets	**ABLOOM**	–; –
ABETTAL	–; abettals	**ABLUENT**	–; abluents
ABETTED	–; –	**ABLUSH**	–; –
ABETTER	–; abetters	**ABLUTED**	–; –
ABETTOR	–; abettors	**ABLY**	–; –
ABEYANT	–; –	**ABMHO**	–; abmhos
ABFARAD	–; abfarads	**ABO**	–; abos
ABHENRY	–; abhenrys	**ABOARD**	–; –
ABHOR	–; abhors	**ABODE**	–; aboded, abodes
ABIDE	–; abided, abider, abides	**ABODING**	–; –
ABIDER	–; abiders	**ABOHM**	–; abohms
ABIGAIL	–; abigails	**ABOIL**	–; –
ABILITY	–; –	**ABOLISH**	–; –
ABIOSES	–; –	**ABOLLA**	–; abollae
ABIOSIS	–; –	**ABOMA**	–; abomas
ABIOTIC	–; –	**ABOMASI**	–; –
ABJECT	–; –	**ABOON**	baboon, gaboon; –
ABJURE	–; abjured, abjurer, abjures	**ABORAL**	–; –
		ABORT	–; aborts
		ABORTED	–; –
ABJURER	–; abjurers	**ABORTER**	–; aborters
ABLATE	–; ablated, ablates	**ABOUGHT**	–; –
		ABOULIA	–; aboulias
ABLAUT	–; ablauts	**ABOULIC**	–; –
ABLAZE	–; –	**ABOUND**	–; abounds
ABLE	cable, fable, gable, sable,	**ABOUT**	–; –
		ABOVE	–; aboves

ABRADE	–; abraded, abrader, abrades	**ABUZZ**	–; –
		ABVOLT	–; abvolts
		ABWATT	–; abwatts
ABRADER	–; abraders	**ABY**	baby, gaby; abye, abys
ABREACT	–; abreacts		
ABREAST	–; –	**ABYE**	–; abyes
ABRI	–; abris	**ABYING**	babying; –
ABRIDGE	–; abridged, abridger, abridges	**ABYSM**	–; abysms
		ABYSMAL	–; –
		ABYS	–; abyss
ABROACH	–; –	**ABYSSAL**	–; –
ABROAD	–; –	**ABYSSES**	–; –
ABRUPT	–; –	**ACACIA**	–; acacias
ABSCESS	–; –	**ACADEME**	–; academes
ABSCISE	–; abscised, abscises		
		ACADEMY	–; –
ABSCOND	–; absconds	**ACAJOU**	–; acajous
ABSENCE	–; absences	**ACALEPH**	–; acalephe, acalephs
ABSENT	–; absents		
ABSINTH	–; absinthe, absinths	**ACARI**	–; acarid
		ACARID	–; acarids
ABSOLVE	–; absolved, absolver, absolves	**ACARINE**	–; acarines
		ACAROID	–; –
		ACARUS	–; –
ABSORB	–; absorbs	**ACAUDAL**	–; –
ABSTAIN	–; abstains	**ACCEDE**	–; acceded, acceder, accedes
ABSURD	–; absurds		
ABUBBLE	–; –		
ABULIA	–; abulias	**ACCEDER**	–; acceders
ABULIC	–; –	**ACCENT**	–; accents
ABUSE	–; abused, abuser, abuses	**ACCEPT**	–; accepts
		ACCESS	–; –
		ACCIDIE	–; accidies
ABUSER	–; abusers	**ACCLAIM**	–; acclaims
ABUSING	–; –	**ACCORD**	–; accords
ABUSIVE	–; –	**ACCOST**	–; accosts
ABUT	–; abuts	**ACCOUNT**	–; accounts
ABUTTAL	–; abuttals	**ACCRETE**	–; accreted, accretes
ABUTTED	–; –		
ABUTTER	–; abutters	**ACCRUAL**	–; accruals

ACCRUE	–; accrued, accrues	**ACETOUS**	–; –
		ACETUM	–; –
ACCURST	–; –	**ACETYL**	–; acetyls
ACCUSAL	–; accusals	**ACHE**	cache,
ACCUSE	–; accused, accuser, accuses		tache; ached, aches
ACCUSER	–; accusers	**ACHED**	bached, cached; –
ACE	dace, face, lace, mace, pace, race, tace; aced, aces	**ACHENE**	–; achenes
		ACHES	baches, caches, laches, taches; –
ACED	faced, laced, maced, paced, raced; –	**ACHIER**	–; –
		ACHIEST	–; –
		ACHIEVE	–; achieved, achiever, achieves
ACEDIA	–; acedias		
ACEQUIA	–; acequias	**ACHING**	baching, caching; –
ACERATE	–; acerated		
ACERB	–; –	**ACHIOTE**	–; achiotes
ACERBIC	–; –	**ACHOO**	–; –
ACEROLA	–; acerolas	**ACHY**	–; –
ACEROSE	–; –	**ACICULA**	–; aciculae, acicular, aciculas
ACEROUS	–; –		
ACES	daces, faces, laces, maces, paces, races, taces; –	**ACID**	–; acids, acidy
		ACIDIC	–; –
		ACIDIFY	–; –
ACETA	–; acetal	**ACIDITY**	–; –
ACETAL	–; acetals	**ACIDLY**	–; –
ACETATE	–; acetated, acetates	**ACIFORM**	–; –
		ACINAR	–; –
ACETIC	–; –	**ACING**	facing, lacing, macing, pacing, racing; –
ACETIFY	–; –		
ACETONE	–; acetones		
ACETOSE	–; –		

ACINI	–; acinic		tact; acta, acts
ACINOSE	–; –		
ACINOUS	–; –	**ACTED**	–; –
ACINUS	–; –	**ACTIN**	–; acting, actins
ACLINIC	–; –		
ACMATIC	–; –	**ACTINAL**	–; –
ACME	–; acmes	**ACTING**	–; actings
ACMIC	–; –	**ACTINIA**	–; actiniae, actinian, actinias
ACNE	–; acned, acnes		
ACNODE	tacnode; acnodes	**ACTINIC**	–; –
		ACTINON	–; actinons
ACNODES	tacnodes; –	**ACTION**	faction, paction, taction; actions
ACOCK	–; –		
ACOLD	–; –		
ACOLYTE	–; acolytes		
ACONITE	–; aconites	**ACTIONS**	factions, pactions, tactions; –
ACORN	–; acorns		
ACQUEST	–; acquests		
ACQUIRE	–; acquired, acquirer, acquires	**ACTIVE**	–; actives
		ACTOR	factor; actors
ACQUIT	–; acquits	**ACTORS**	factors; –
ACRASIN	–; acrasins	**ACTRESS**	–; –
ACRE	nacre; acred, acres	**ACTS**	facts, pacts, tacts; –
ACREAGE	–; acreages	**ACTUAL**	factual, tactual; –
ACRED	nacred, sacred; –		
		ACTUARY	–; –
ACRES	nacres; –	**ACTUATE**	–; actuated, actuates
ACRID	–; –		
ACRIDER	–; –	**ACUATE**	–; –
ACRIDLY	–; –	**ACUITY**	vacuity; –
ACROBAT	–; acrobats	**ACUMEN**	–; acumens
ACROGEN	–; acrogens	**ACUTE**	–; acuter, acutes
ACRONIC	–; –		
ACRONYM	–; acronyms	**ACUTELY**	–; –
ACROSS	–; –	**ACUTES**	–; acutest
ACRYLIC	–; acrylics	**ACYCLIC**	–; –
ACT	fact, pact,	**ACYL**	–; acyls

ACYLATE	–; acylated, acylates	**ADDIBLE**	–; –
		ADDICT	–; addicts
AD	bad, cad, dad, fad, gad, had, lad, mad, pad, rad, sad, tad, wad; add, ado, ads, adz	**ADDING**	gadding, madding, padding, radding, wadding; –
		ADDLE	daddle, paddle, raddle, saddle, waddle; addled, addles
ADAGE	–; adages		
ADAGIAL	–; –		
ADAGIO	–; adagios		
ADAMANT	–; adamants		
ADAPT	–; adapts	**ADDLED**	daddled, paddled, raddled, saddled, waddled; –
ADAPTED	–; –		
ADAPTER	–; adapters		
ADAPTOR	–; adaptors		
ADAXIAL	–; –		
ADD	–; adds	**ADDLES**	daddles, paddles, raddles, saddles, waddles; –
ADDABLE	–; –		
ADDAX	–; –		
ADDAXES	–; –		
ADDED	gadded, madded, padded, radded, wadded; –	**ADDLING**	paddling, raddling, saddling, waddling; –
ADDEDLY	–; –	**ADDRESS**	–; –
ADDEND	–; addends	**ADDREST**	–; –
ADDER	gadder, ladder, madder, sadder, wadder; adders	**ADDUCE**	–; adduced, adducer, adduces
		ADDUCER	–; adducers
		ADDUCT	–; adducts
		ADEEM	–; adeems
ADDERS	gadders, ladders, madders, wadders; –	**ADEEMED**	–; –
		ADENINE	–; adenines
		ADENOID	–; adenoids

ADENOMA	–; adenomas		admirer, admires
ADENYL	–; adenyls	**ADMIRER**	–; admirers
ADEPT	–; adepts	**ADMIT**	–; admits
ADEPTER	–; –	**ADMIX**	–; admixt
ADEPTLY	–; –	**ADMIXED**	–; –
ADHERE	–; adhered, adherer, adheres	**ADMIXES**	–; –
		ADNATE	–; –
ADHERER	–; adherers	**ADNEXA**	–; adnexal
ADHIBIT	–; adhibits	**ADNOUN**	–; adnouns
ADIEU	–; adieus, adieux	**ADO**	dado, fado; ados
ADIOS	radios; –	**ADOBE**	–; adobes
ADIPIC	–; –	**ADOPT**	–; adopts
ADIPOSE	–; adiposes	**ADOPTED**	–; –
ADIPOUS	–; –	**ADOPTEE**	–; adoptees
ADIT	–; adits	**ADOPTER**	–; adopters
ADJOIN	–; adjoins, adjoint	**ADORE**	–; adored, adorer, adores
ADJOINT	–; adjoints	**ADORER**	–; adorers
ADJOURN	–; adjourns	**ADORING**	–; –
ADJUDGE	–; adjudged, adjudges	**ADORN**	–; adorns
		ADORNED	–; –
		ADORNER	–; adorners
ADJUNCT	–; adjuncts	**ADOS**	dados, fados; –
ADJURE	–; adjured, adjurer, adjures	**ADOWN**	–; –
		ADOZE	–; –
ADJURER	–; adjurers	**ADRENAL**	–; adrenals
ADJUROR	–; adjurors	**ADRIFT**	–; –
ADJUST	–; adjusts	**ADROIT**	–; –
ADMAN	badman, madman; –	**ADS**	bads, cads, dads, fads, gads, lads, mads, pads, rads, tads, wads; –
ADMEN	badmen, madmen; –		
ADMASS	–; –		
ADMIRAL	–; admirals		
ADMIRE	–; admired,	**ADSORB**	–; adsorbs

ADULATE	–; adulated, adulates	**AEOLIAN**	–; –
ADULT	–; adults	**AEON**	paeon; aeons
ADULTLY	–; –	**AEONIAN**	–; –
ADUNC	–; –	**AEONIC**	–; –
ADUST	–; –	**AEONS**	paeons; –
ADVANCE	–; advanced, advancer, advances	**AERATE**	–; aerated, aerates
ADVENT	–; advents	**AERATOR**	–; aerators
ADVERB	–; adverbs	**AERIAL**	–; aerials
ADVERSE	–; –	**AERIE**	faerie; aeried, aerier, aeries
ADVERT	–; adverts		
ADVICE	–; advices		
ADVISE	–; advised, advisee, adviser, advises	**AERIES**	faeries; aeriest
ADVISEE	–; advisees	**AERIFY**	–; –
ADVISER	–; advisers	**AERILY**	–; –
ADVISOR	–; advisors, advisory	**AERO**	–; –
		AEROBE	–; aerobes
ADYTA	–; –	**AEROBIC**	–; –
ADYTUM	–; –	**AEROGEL**	–; aerogels
ADZ	–; adze	**AEROSOL**	–; aerosols
ADZE	–; adzes	**AERUGO**	–; aerugos
AE	gae, hae, kae, mae, nae, sae, tae, wae; –	**AERY**	faery; –
		AETHER	–; aethers
		AFAR	–; afars
AECIA	–; aecial	**AFEARD**	–; –
AECIUM	–; –	**AFEARED**	–; –
AEDES	–; –	**AFF**	baff, daff, gaff, raff, waff, yaff; –
AEDILE	–; aediles		
AEDINE	–; –	**AFFABLE**	–; –
AEGIS	–; –	**AFFABLY**	–; –
AEGISES	–; –	**AFFAIR**	–; affaire, affairs
AENEOUS	–; –	**AFFAIRE**	–; affaires
AENEUS	–; –	**AFFECT**	–; affects
		AFFIANT	–; affiants
		AFFICHE	–; affiches

AFFINE	–; affined, affines	fag, gag, hag, jag, lag, mag, nag, rag, sag, tag, wag, zag; aga, age, ago
AFFIRM	–; affirms	
AFFIX	–; –	
AFFIXAL	–; –	
AFFIXED	–; –	
AFFIXER	–; affixers	
AFFIXES	–; –	
AFFLICT	–; afflicts	**AGA**
AFFLUX	–; –	gaga, raga, saga; agar, agas
AFFORD	–; affords	
AFFRAY	–; affrays	
AFFRONT	–; affronts	**AGAIN**	–; –
AFGHAN	–; afghani, afghans	**AGAINST**	–; –
		AGAMA	–; agamas
AFIELD	–; –	**AGAMETE**	–; agametes
AFIRE	–; –	**AGAMIC**	–; –
AFLAME	–; –	**AGAMOUS**	–; –
AFLOAT	–; –	**AGAPAE**	–; –
AFOOT	–; –	**AGAPAI**	–; –
AFORE	–; –	**AGAPE**	–; –
AFOUL	-; –	**AGAPEIC**	–; –
AFRAID	–; -	**AGAR**	–; agars
AFREET	–; afreets	**AGARIC**	–; agarics
AFRESH	–; -	**AGAS**	ragas, sagas; –
AFRIT	–; afrits	
AFT	baft, daft, haft, raft, waft; –	**AGATE**	–; agates
		AGATIZE	–; agatized, agatizes
AFTER	dafter, hafter, rafter, wafter; afters	**AGATOID**	–; –
		AGAVE	–; agaves
		AGAZE	–; –
AFTERS	hafters, rafters, wafters; –	**AGE**	cage, gage, mage, page, rage, sage, wage; aged, agee, ager, ages
AFTMOST	–; –	**AGED**	caged, gaged, paged,
AFTOSA	–; aftosas	
AG	bag, dag,	

	raged, waged; –		nagger, sagger,
AGEDLY	–; –		tagger,
AGEE	ragee; –		wagger;
AGEING	–; ageings		aggers
AGELESS	–; –	**AGGERS**	daggers,
AGELONG	–; –		gaggers,
AGENCY	–; –		jaggers,
AGENDA	–; agendas		laggers,
AGENDUM	–; agendums		naggers,
AGENE	–; agenes		saggers,
AGENIZE	–; agenized, agenizes		taggers, waggers; –
AGENT	–; agents	**AGGIE**	baggie;
AGENTRY	–; –		aggies
AGER	cager,	**AGGIES**	baggies; –
	eager,	**AGHA**	–; aghas
	gager,	**AGHAS**	–; aghast
	jager, lager,	**AGILE**	vagile; –
	sager,	**AGILELY**	–; –
	wager,	**AGILITY**	–; –
	yager; agers	**AGIN**	fagin; aging
AGERS	cagers,	**AGING**	caging,
	eagers,		gaging,
	gagers,		paging,
	jagers,		raging,
	lagers,		waging;
	wagers,		agings
	yagers; –	**AGIO**	–; agios
AGES	cages,	**AGIST**	–; agists
	gages,	**AGISTED**	–; –
	mages,	**AGITATE**	–; agitated,
	pages,		agitates
	rages,	**AGITATO**	–; agitator
	sages,	**AGLARE**	–; –
	wages; –	**AGLEAM**	–; –
AGGER	dagger,	**AGLEE**	–; –
	gagger,	**AGLET**	eaglet;
	jagger,		aglets
	lagger,	**AGLETS**	eaglets; –

AGLEY	–; –	**AGREE**	–; agreed,
AGLOW	–; –		agrees
AGLY	–; –	**AGROUND**	–; –
AGLYCON	–; aglycone,	**AGUE**	vague;
	aglycons		agues
AGMA	magma;	**AGUISH**	–; –
	agmas	**AH**	aah, bah,
AGMAS	magmas; –		dah, hah,
AGNAIL	–; agnails		pah, rah,
AGNATE	–; agnates		yah; aha
AGNATIC	–; –	**AHCHOO**	–; –
AGNIZE	–; agnized,	**AHEAD**	–; –
	agnizes	**AHEAP**	–; –
AGNOMEN	–;	**AHEM**	–; –
	agnomens	**AHIMSA**	–; ahimsas
AGO	dago, sago;	**AHOLD**	–; aholds
	agog, agon	**AHORSE**	–; –
AGON	wagon;	**AHOY**	–; –
	agone,	**AHULL**	–; –
	agons,	**AI**	–; aid, ail,
	agony		aim, ain, air,
AGONAL	–; –		ais, ait
AGONE	–; agones	**AIBLINS**	–; –
AGONIC	–; –	**AID**	caid, laid,
AGONIES	–; –		maid, paid,
AGONISE	–; agonised,		qaid, raid,
	agonises		said; aide,
AGONIST	–; agonists		aids
AGONIZE	–; agonized,	**AIDE**	–; aider,
	agonizes		aides
AGONS	wagons; –	**AIDED**	raided; –
AGORA	–; agorae,	**AIDER**	raider;
	agoras		aiders
AGOROT	–; agoroth	**AIDERS**	raiders; –
AGOUTI	–; agoutis	**AIDFUL**	–; –
AGOUTY	–; –	**AIDING**	raiding; –
AGRAFE	–; agrafes	**AIDLESS**	–; –
AGRAFFE	–; agraffes	**AIDMAN**	–; –
AGRAPHA	–; –	**AIDMEN**	–; –
		AIDS	caids, maids,

	qaids, raids,	**AILERON**	–; ailerons
	saids; –	**AILMENT**	–; ailments
AIGLET	–; aiglets	**AIM**	maim; aims
AIGRET	–; aigrets	**AIMED**	maimed; –
AIKIDO	–; aikidos	**AIMER**	maimer;
AIL	bail, fail,		aimers
	hail, jail, kail,	**AIMERS**	maimers; –
	mail, nail,	**AIMFUL**	–; –
	pail, rail,	**AIMING**	maiming; –
	sail, tail, vail,	**AIMLESS**	–; –
	wail; ails	**AIMS**	maims; –
AILED	bailed,	**AIN**	cain, fain,
	failed,		gain, kain,
	hailed,		lain, main,
	jailed,		pain, rain,
	mailed,		sain, tain,
	nailed,		vain, wain;
	railed,		aine, ains
	sailed,	**AINS**	cains, gains,
	tailed,		kains, mains,
	vailed,		pains, rains,
	wailed; –		sains, tains,
AILING	bailing,		vains,
	failing,		wains; –
	hailing,	**AINSELL**	–; ainsells
	jailing,	**AIR**	fair, hair,
	mailing,		lair, mair,
	nailing,		pair, vair,
	railing,		wair; airn,
	sailing,		airs, airt,
	tailing,		airy
	vailing,	**AIRBOAT**	–; airboats
	wailing; –	**AIRBUS**	–; –
AILS	bails, fails,	**AIRCREW**	–; aircrews
	hails, jails,	**AIRDROP**	–; airdrops
	kails, mails,	**AIRED**	faired,
	nails, pails,		haired,
	rails, sails,		laired,
	tails, vails,		paired,
	wails; –		waired; –

AIRER	fairer; –	**AIRTING**	–; –
AIREST	fairest; –	**AIRWARD**	–; –
AIRFLOW	–; airflows	**AIRWAVE**	–; airwaves
AIRFOIL	–; airfoils	**AIRWAY**	fairway;
AIRGLOW	–; airglows		airways
AIRHEAD	–; airheads	**AIRWISE**	–; –
AIRIER	hairier; –	**AIRY**	dairy, fairy,
AIRIEST	hairiest; –		hairy; –
AIRILY	–; –	**AISLE**	–; aisled,
AIRING	fairing,		aisles
	lairing,	**AIT**	bait, gait,
	pairing,		wait; aits
	wairing;	**AITCH**	–; –
	airings	**AITCHES**	–; –
AIRLESS	hairless; –	**AITS**	baits, gaits,
AIRLIFT	–; airlifts		waits; –
AIRLIKE	hairlike; –	**AIVER**	waiver;
AIRLINE	hairline;		aivers
	airliner,	**AJAR**	–; –
	airlines	**AJEE**	–; –
AIRMAIL	–; airmails	**AJIVA**	–; ajivas
AIRMAN	–; –	**AJOG**	–; –
AIRMEN	–; –	**AJOWAN**	–; ajowans
AIRN	bairn, cairn;	**AKEE**	rakee; akees
	airns	**AKEES**	rakees; –
AIRNS	bairns,	**AKELA**	–; akelas
	cairns; –	**AKENE**	–; akenes
AIRPARK	–; airparks	**AKIMBO**	–; –
AIRPORT	–; airports	**AKIN**	takin; –
AIRPOST	–; airposts	**AKVAVIT**	–; akvavits
AIRS	fairs, hairs,	**AL**	bal, gal, pal,
	lairs, mairs,		sal; ala, alb,
	pairs, vairs,		ale, all, alp,
	wairs; –		als, alt
AIRSHIP	–; airships	**ALA**	gala, tala;
AIRSICK	–; –		alae, alan,
AIRT	–; airth, airts		alar, alas
AIRTED	–; –	**ALACK**	–; –
AIRTH	–; airths	**ALAMEDA**	–; alamedas
AIRTHED	–; –	**ALAMO**	–; alamos

ALAMODE	−; alamodes	**ALCALDE**	−; alcaldes
ALAN	−; aland,	**ALCAYDE**	−; alcaydes
	alane,	**ALCAZAR**	−; alcazars
	alang, alans	**ALCHEMY**	−; −
ALAND	−; alands	**ALCHYMY**	−; −
ALANIN	−; alanine,	**ALCOHOL**	−; alcohols
	alanins	**ALCOVE**	−; alcoved,
ALANINE	−; alanines		alcoves
ALANT	−; alants	**ALDER**	balder;
ALANYL	−; alanyls		alders
ALAR	malar, talar;	**ALDOL**	−; aldols
	alarm, alary	**ALDOSE**	−; aldoses
ALARM	−; alarms	**ALDRIN**	−; aldrins
ALARMED	−; −	**ALE**	bale, dale,
ALARUM	−; alarums		gale, hale,
ALARY	salary; −		kale, male,
ALAS	balas, galas,		pale, rale,
	talas; −		sale, tale,
ALASKA	−; alaskas		vale, wale;
ALASTOR	−; alastors		alec, alee,
ALATE	malate,		alef, ales
	palate;	**ALEC**	−; alecs
	alated	**ALEF**	−; alefs
ALATION	−; alations	**ALEGAR**	−; alegars
ALB	−; alba, albs	**ALEMBIC**	−; alembics
ALBA	−; albas	**ALEPH**	−; alephs
ALBATA	−; albatas	**ALERT**	−; alerts
ALBEDO	−; albedos	**ALERTED**	−; −
ALBEIT	−; −	**ALERTER**	−; −
ALBINAL	−; −	**ALERTLY**	−; −
ALBINIC	−; −	**ALES**	bales, dales,
ALBINO	−; albinos		gales, hales,
ALBITE	−; albites		kales, males,
ALBITIC	−; −		pales, rales,
ALBUM	−; albums		sales, tales,
ALBUMEN	−; albumens		vales,
ALBUMIN	−; albumins		wales; −
ALCADE	−; alcades	**ALEURON**	−; aleurone,
ALCAIC	−; alcaics		aleurons
ALCAIDE	−; alcaides	**ALEVIN**	−; alevins

ALEWIFE	–; –	**ALIGN**	malign;
ALEXIA	–; alexins		aligns
ALEXIN	–; alexine,	**ALIGNED**	maligned; –
	alexins	**ALIGNER**	maligner;
ALEXINE	–; alexines		aligners
ALFA	–; alfas	**ALIGNS**	maligns; –
ALFAKI	–; alfakis	**ALIKE**	–; –
ALFALFA	–; alfalfas	**ALIMENT**	–; aliments
ALFAQUI	–; alfaquin,	**ALIMONY**	–; –
	alfaquis	**ALINE**	maline,
ALFORJA	–; alforjas		saline,
ALGA	–; algae,		valine;
	algal, algas		alined,
ALGEBRA	–; algebras		aliner, alines
ALGID	–; –	**ALINER**	–; aliners
ALGIN	–; algins	**ALINES**	malines,
ALGOID	valgoid; –		salines,
ALGOR	–; algors		valines; –
ALGUM	–; algums	**ALINING**	–; –
ALIAS	–; –	**ALIPED**	–; alipeds
ALIASES	–; –	**ALIQUOT**	–; aliquots
ALIBI	–; alibis	**ALIST**	–; –
ALIBIED	–; –	**ALIT**	–; –
ALIBIES	–; –	**ALIUNDE**	–; –
ALIBLE	–; –	**ALIVE**	–; –
ALIDAD	–; alidade,	**ALIYAH**	–; aliyahs
	alidads	**ALKALI**	–; alkalic,
ALIDADE	–; alidades		alkalin,
ALIEN	–; aliens		alkalis
ALIENED	–; –	**ALKALIN**	–; alkaline
ALIENEE	–; alienees	**ALKANE**	–; alkanes,
ALIENER	–; alieners		alkanet
ALIENLY	–; –	**ALKANET**	–; alkanets
ALIENOR	–; alienors	**ALKENE**	–; alkenes
ALIF	calif, kalif;	**ALKINE**	–; alkines
	alifs	**ALKOXY**	–; –
ALIFORM	–; –	**ALKYD**	–; alkyds
ALIFS	califs,	**ALKYL**	–; alkyls
	kalifs; –	**ALKYLIC**	–; –
ALIGHT	–; alights	**ALKYNE**	–; alkynes

ALL	ball, call, fall, gall, hall, lall, mall, pall, sall, tall, wall; alls, ally	**ALLONYM**	–; allonyms
		ALLOT	ballot, hallot; allots
		ALLOTS	ballots; –
		ALLOVER	–; allovers
		ALLOW	callow, fallow, hallow, mallow, sallow, tallow, wallow; allows
ALLAY	–; allays		
ALLAYED	–; –		
ALLAYER	–; allayers		
ALLEGE	–; alleged, alleger, alleges		
ALLEGER	–; allegers	**ALLOWED**	fallowed, hallowed, sallowed, tallowed; –
ALLEGRO	–; allegros		
ALLELE	–; alleles		
ALLELIC	–; –		
ALLERGY	–; –	**ALLOWS**	fallows, gallows, hallows, mallows, sallows, tallows, wallows; –
ALLEY	galley, valley; alleys		
ALLEYS	galleys, valleys; –		
ALLHEAL	–; allheals		
ALLIED	dallied, gallied, rallied, sallied, tallied; –		
		ALLOXAN	–; alloxans
		ALLOY	–; alloys
		ALLOYED	–; –
ALLIES	dallies, gallies, rallies, sallies, tallies, wallies; –	**ALLS**	balls, calls, falls, galls, halls, lalls, malls, palls, walls; –
		ALLSEED	–; allseeds
		ALLUDE	–; alluded, alludes
ALLIUM	pallium; alliums	**ALLURE**	–; allured, allurer, allures
ALLIUMS	palliums; –		
ALLOBAR	–; allobars		
ALLOD	–; allods	**ALLURER**	–; allurers
ALLONGE	–; allonges	**ALLUVIA**	–; alluvial

ALLY	bally, dally, gally, pally, rally, sally, tally, wally; allyl	**ALOHA**	–; alohas
		ALOIN	=; aloins
		ALONE	–; –
		ALONG	kalong; –
		ALOOF	–; –
ALLYING	gallying, rallying; –	**ALOOFLY**	–; –
		ALOUD	–; –
ALLYL	–; allyls	**ALOW**	–; –
ALLYLIC	–; –	**ALP**	palp, salp; alps
ALMA	–; almah, almas		
		ALPACA	–; alpacas
ALMAH	–; almahs	**ALPHA**	–; alphas
ALMANAC	–; almanacs	**ALPHORN**	–; alphorns
ALME	–; almeh, almes	**ALPHYL**	–; alphyls
		ALPINE	–; alpines
ALMEH	–; almehs	**ALPS**	palps, salps; –
ALMEMAR	–; almemars		
ALMNER	–; almners	**ALREADY**	–; –
ALMOND	–; almonds	**ALRIGHT**	–; –
ALMONER	–; almoners	**ALSIKE**	–; alsikes
ALMONRY	–; –	**ALSO**	–; –
ALMOST	–; –	**ALT**	halt, malt, salt; alto, alts
ALMS	balms, calms, halms, malms, palms; –		
		ALTAR	–; altars
		ALTER	falter, halter, palter, salter; alters
ALMSMAN	–; –		
ALMSMEN	–; –	**ALTERED**	faltered, haltered, paltered; –
ALMUCE	–; almuces		
ALMUD	–; almude, almuds		
		ALTERER	falterer, alterers
ALMUDE	–; almudes		
ALMUG	–; almugs	**ALTERS**	falters, halters, palters, salters; –
ALNICO	–; –		
ALODIUM	–; –		
ALOE	–; aloes		
ALOES	haloes; –	**ALTHAEA**	–; althaeas
ALOETIC	–; –	**ALTHEA**	–; altheas
ALOFT	–; –	**ALTHO**	–; –

ALTHORN	–; althorns	**AMASSED**	–; –
ALTO	–; altos	**AMASSER**	–; amassers
ALTS	halts, malts, salts; –	**AMASSES**	–; –
		AMATEUR	–; amateurs
ALUDEL	–; aludels	**AMATIVE**	–; –
ALULA	–; alulae, alular	**AMATOL**	–; amatols
		AMATORY	–; –
ALUM	–; alums	**AMAZE**	–; amazed, amazes
ALUMIN	–; alumina, alumine	**AMAZING**	–; –
ALUMINA	–; aluminas	**AMAZON**	–; amazons
ALUMINE	–; alumines	**AMBAGE**	–; ambages
ALUMNA	–; alumnae	**AMBARI**	–; ambaris
ALUMNI	–; –	**AMBARY**	–; –
ALUMNUS	–; –	**AMBEER**	–; ambeers
ALUNITE	–; alunites	**AMBER**	camber, lamber; ambers, ambery
ALVINE	–; –		
ALWAY	–; always		
ALYSSUM	–; alyssums		
AM	cam, dam, gam, ham, jam, lam, pam, ram, tam, yam; ama, ami, amp, amu	**AMBERS**	cambers, lambers; –
		AMBIENT	–; ambients
		AMBIT	gambit; ambits
		AMBITS	gambits; –
AMA	lama, mama; amah, amas	**AMBLE**	gamble, ramble, wamble; ambled, ambler, ambles
AMADOU	–; amadous		
AMAH	–; amahs		
AMAIN	–; –		
AMALGAM	–; amalgams	**AMBLED**	gambled, rambled, wambled; –
AMANITA	–; amanitas		
AMARNA	–; –		
AMAS	camas, lamas, mamas; amass	**AMBLER**	gambler, rambler; amblers
AMASS	camass; –	**AMBLERS**	gamblers, ramblers; –

AMBLES gambles, rambles, wambles; –

AMBLING gambling, rambling; –

AMBO mambo, sambo; ambos

AMBOINA –; amboinas

AMBONES –; –

AMBOS mambos, sambos; –

AMBOYNA –; amboynas

AMBRIES –; –

AMBROID –; ambroids

AMBRY –; –

AMBSACE –; ambsaces

AMBUSH –; –

AMEBA –; amebae, ameban, amebas

AMEBEAN –; –

AMEBIC –; –

AMEBOID –; –

AMEER –; ameers

AMEN yamen; amend, amens, ament

AMEND –; amends

AMENDED –; –

AMENDER –; amenders

AMENITY –; –

AMENS yamens; –

AMENT lament; aments

AMENTIA –; amentias

AMENTS lament; –

AMERCE –; amerced,

AMERCER –; amercers

AMESACE –; amesaces

AMI kami, rami; amia, amid, amie, amin, amir, amis

AMIA lamia, zamia; amias

AMIABLE –; –

AMIABLY –; –

AMIAS lamias, zamias; –

AMICE –; amices

AMID –; amide, amido, amids

AMIDASE –; amidases

AMIDE –; amides

AMIDIC –; –

AMIDIN –; amidins

AMIDO –; amidol

AMIDOL –; amidols

AMIDST –; –

AMIE mamie, ramie; amies

AMIES mamies, ramies; –

AMIGA –; amigas

AMIGO –; amigos

AMIN gamin; amine, amino, amins

AMINE famine, gamine; amines

AMINES famines, gamines; –

AMINIC –; –

amercer, amercer

AMINITY	–; –	**AMOTION**	–; amotions
AMINO	–; –	**AMOUNT**	–; amounts
AMINS	gamins; –	**AMOUR**	–; amours
AMIR	–; amirs	**AMP**	camp, damp,
AMIRATE	–; amirates		gamp, lamp,
AMIS	tamis; amiss		ramp, samp,
AMITY	–; –		tamp, vamp;
AMMETER	–; ammeters		amps
AMMINE	–; ammines	**AMPERE**	–; amperes
AMMINO	–; –	**AMPHORA**	–;
AMMO	–; ammos		amphorae,
AMMONAL	–; ammonals		amphora,
AMMONIA	–;		amphoras
	ammoniac,	**AMPLE**	sample;
	ammonias		ampler
AMMONIC	–; –	**AMPLER**	sampler; –
AMNESIA	–; amnesiac,	**AMPLEST**	–; –
	amnesias	**AMPLIFY**	–; –
AMNESIC	–; amnesics	**AMPLY**	damply; –
AMNESTY	–; –	**AMPOULE**	–; ampoules
AMNIA	–; –	**AMPS**	camps,
AMNIC	–; –		damps,
AMNION	–; amnions		gamps,
AMNIOTE	–; amniotes		lamps,
AMOEBA	–;		ramps,
	amoebae,		samps,
	amoeban,		tamps,
	amoebas		vamps; –
AMOEBIC	–; –	**AMPUL**	–; ampule,
AMOK	–; amoks		ampuls
AMOLE	–; amoles	**AMPULE**	–; ampules
AMONG	–; –	**AMPULLA**	–; ampullae,
AMONGST	–; –		ampullar
AMORAL	–; –	**AMPUTEE**	–; amputees
AMORINI	–; –	**AMREETA**	–; amreetas
AMORINO	–; –	**AMRITA**	–; amritas
AMORIST	–; amorists	**AMTRAC**	–; amtrack,
AMOROSO	–; –		amtracs
AMOROUS	–; –	**AMTRACK**	–; amtracks
AMORT	–; –	**AMU**	–; amus

AMUCK	–; amucks	**ANALITY**	–; –
AMULET	–; amulets	**ANALLY**	banally; –
AMUS	wamus; amuse	**ANALOG**	–; analogs, analogy
AMUSE	–; amused, amuser, amuses	**ANALYSE**	–; analysed, analyser, analyses
AMUSER	–; amusers	**ANALYST**	–; analysts
AMUSES	wamuses; –	**ANALYZE**	–; analyzed,
AMUSING	–; –		analyzer,
AMUSIVE	–; –		analyzes
AMYL	–; amyls	**ANANKE**	–; anankes
AMYLASE	–; amylases	**ANAPEST**	–; anapests
AMYLENE	–; amylenes	**ANARCH**	–; anarchs,
AMYLIC	–; –		anarchy
AMYLOID	–; amyloids	**ANAS**	kanas,
AMYLOSE	–; amyloses		manas,
AMYLUM	–; amylums		nanas; –
AN	ban, can, dan, fan,	**ANATASE**	–; anatases
	gan, man,	**ANATOMY**	–; –
	pan, ran,	**ANATTO**	–; anattos
	tan, van,	**ANCHOR**	–; anchors
	wan; ana,	**ANCHOVY**	–; –
	and, ane,	**ANCHUSA**	–; anchusas
	ani, ant, any	**ANCIENT**	–; ancients
ANA	kana, mana,	**ANCILLA**	–; ancillae,
	nana; anal,		ancillas
	anas	**ANCON**	–; ancone
ANABAS	–; –	**ANCONAL**	–; –
ANADEM	–; anadems	**ANCONE**	–; ancones
ANAEMIA	–; anaemias	**ANCRESS**	–; –
ANAEMIC	–; –	**AND**	band, hand,
ANAGOGE	–; anagoges		land, rand,
ANAGOGY	–; –		sand, wand;
			ands
ANAGRAM	–; anagrams	**ANDANTE**	–; andantes
ANAL	banal, canal; –	**ANDIRON**	–; andirons
		ANDROID	–; androids
ANALGIA	–; analgias	**ANDS**	bands, hands,

	lands, rands, sands, wands; –	ANGARY	–; –
		ANGAS	fangas, pangas, sangas; –
ANE	bane, cane, fane, gane, jane, kane, lane, mane, pane, sane, vane, wane; anes, anew	ANGEL	mangel; angels
		ANGELIC	–; –
ANEAR	–; anears	ANGELS	mangels; –
ANEARED	–; –	ANGELUS	–; –
ANELE	–; aneled, aneles	ANGER	banger, danger, ganger, hanger, manger, ranger, sanger; angers
ANEMIA	–; anemias		
ANEMIC	–; –		
ANEMONE	–; anemones		
ANENST	–; –	ANGERED	dangered; –
ANENT	–; –	ANGERLY	–; –
ANERGIA	–; anergias	ANGERS	bangers, dangers, gangers, hangers, mangers, rangers, sangers; –
ANERGIC	–; –		
ANERGY	–; –		
ANEROID	–; aneroids		
ANES	banes, canes, fanes, janes, kanes, lanes, manes, panes, sanes, vanes, wanes; –		
		ANGINA	–; anginal, anginas
		ANGIOMA	–; angiomas
		ANGLE	bangle, dangle, jangle, mangle, tangle, wangle; angled, angler, angles
ANETHOL	–; anethole, anethols		
ANEW	–; –		
ANGA	fanga, panga, sanga; angas	ANGLED	dangled, jangled,
ANGARIA	–; angarias		

	mangled, tangled, wangled; –	ANIL ANILIN	–; anile, anila –; aniline,
ANGLER	dangler, jangler, mangler, tangler, wangler;	ANILINE ANILITY ANIMA	anilins –; anilines –; – –; animal, animas
	anglers	ANIMAL	–; animals
ANGLERS	danglers, janglers, manglers,	ANIMATE	–; animated, animater, animates
	tanglers, wanglers; –	ANIMATO ANIME	–; animator –; animes
ANGLES	bangles, dangles, jangles, mangles,	ANIMI ANIMISM ANIMIST	–; animis –; animisms –; animists
	tangles, wangles; –	ANIMUS ANION	–; – fanion, wanion;
ANGLICE	–; –		anions
ANGLING	dangling, gangling,	ANIONIC ANIONS	–; – fanions,
	jangling, mangling,	ANIS	wanions; – ranis; anise
	tangling, wangling;	ANISE ANISEED	–; anises –; aniseeds
	anglings	ANISIC	–; –
ANGORA	–; angoras	ANISOLE	–; anisoles
ANGRIER	–; –	ANKH	–; ankhs
ANGRILY	–; –	ANKLE	rankle;
ANGRY	–; –		ankles,
ANGST	–; angsts		anklets
ANGUINE	–; –	ANKLES	rankles; –
ANGUISH	–; –	ANKLET	–; anklets
ANGULAR	–; –	ANKUS	–; ankush
ANHINGA	–; anhingas	ANKUSES	–; –
ANI	bani, rani; anil, anis	ANKUSH ANLACE	–; – –; anlaces

ANLAGE	–; anlagen, anlages	**ANOMY**	–; –
		ANON	canon,
ANLAS	–; –		fanon; –
ANLASES	–; –	**ANONYM**	–; anonyms
ANNA	canna,	**ANOPIA**	–; anopias
	manna;	**ANOPSIA**	–; anopsias
	annal, annas	**ANORAK**	–; anoraks
ANNAL	–; annals	**ANOREXY**	–; –
ANNAS	cannas,	**ANOSMIA**	–; anosmias
	mannas; –	**ANOSMIC**	–; –
ANNATES	–; –	**ANOTHER**	–; –
ANNATTO	–; annattos	**ANOXIA**	–; anoxias
ANNEAL	–; anneals	**ANOXIC**	–; –
ANNELID	–; annelids	**ANSA**	–; ansae
ANNEX	–; annexe	**ANSATE**	–; ansated
ANNEXE	–; annexed,	**ANSWER**	–; answers
	annexes	**ANT**	cant, hant,
ANNOY	–; annoys		pant, rant,
ANNOYED	–; –		want; anta,
ANNOYER	–; annoyers		ante, anti,
ANNUAL	–; annuals		ants
ANNUITY	–; –	**ANTA**	manta;
ANNUL	–; annuls		antae, antas
ANNULAR	–; –	**ANTACID**	–; antacids
ANNULET	–; annulets	**ANTAS**	mantas; –
ANNULI	–; –	**ANTE**	–; anted,
ANNULUS	–; –		antes
ANOA	–; anoas	**ANTED**	canted,
ANODAL	–; –		hanted,
ANODE	–; anodes		panted,
ANODIC	–; –		ranted,
ANODIZE	–; anodized,		wanted; –
	anodizes	**ANTEED**	–; –
ANODYNE	–; anodynes	**ANTEING**	–; –
ANOINT	–; anoints	**ANTEFIX**	–; –
ANOLE	–; anoles	**ANTENNA**	–; antennae,
ANOLYTE	–; anolytes		antennal,
ANOMALY	–; –		antennas
ANOMIE	–; anomies	**ANTES**	mantes; –
ANOMIC	–; –	**ANTHEM**	–; anthems

ANTHER	panther; anthers	**ANTS**	cants, hants, pants, rants, wants; –
ANTHERS	panthers; –		
ANTHILL	–; anthills	**ANURAN**	–; anurans
ANTHOID	–; –	**ANURIA**	–; anurias
ANTHRAX	–; –	**ANURIC**	–; –
ANTI	–; antic, antis	**ANUROUS**	–; –
		ANUS	manus; –
ANTIAR	–; antiars	**ANUSES**	–; –
ANTIC	cantic, mantic; antick, antics	**ANVIL**	–; anvils
		ANVILED	–; –
		ANXIETY	–; –
ANTICK	–; anticks	**ANXIOUS**	–; –
ANTICLY	–; –	**ANY**	many, wany, zany; –
ANTIFAT	–; –		
ANTIGEN	–; antigene, antigens	**ANYBODY**	–; –
		ANYHOW	–; –
ANTILOG	–; antilogs, antilogy	**ANYMORE**	–; –
		ANYONE	–; –
ANTING	canting, hanting, panting, ranting, wanting; antings	**ANYTIME**	–; –
		ANYWAY	–; anyways
		ANYWISE	–; –
		AORTA	–; aortae, aortal, aortas
ANTIQUE	–; antiqued, antiquer, antiques		
		AORTIC	–; –
		AORIST	–; aorists
ANTIS	mantis; –	**AOUDAD**	–; aoudads
ANTITAX	–; –	**APACE**	–; –
ANTIWAR	–; –	**APACHE**	–; apaches
ANTLER	–; antlers	**APAGOGE**	–; apagoges
ANTLIKE	–; –		
ANTLION	–; antlions	**APANAGE**	–; apanages
ANTONYM	–; antonyms, antonymy	**APAREJO**	–; aparejos
		APART	–; –
ANTRA	mantra, tantra; antral	**APATHY**	–; –
		APATITE	–; apatites
ANTRE	–; antres	**APE**	cape, gape, jape, nape, rape, tape;
ANTRUM	–; –		

	aped, aper, apes, apex	**APHESIS** **APHETIC**	–; – –; –
APEAK	–; –	**APHID**	–; aphids
APED	caped, gaped, japed, raped, taped; –	**APHIDES** **APHIS** **APHONIA** **APHONIC** **APHOTIC**	raphides; – raphis; – –; aphonias –; aphonics –; –
APEEK	–; –	**APHTHA**	naphtha;
APELIKE	–; –		aphthae
APER	caper, gaper, japer, paper, raper, taper; apers, apery	**APHYLLY** **APIAN** **APIARY** **APICAL** **APICES** **APIECE**	–; – –; – –; – –; – –; – –; –
APERCU	–; apercus	**APING**	gaping,
APERIES	naperies; –		japing,
APERS	capers, gapers, japers, papers, rapers, tapers; –		naping, raping, taping; –
		APISH	–; –
		APISHLY	–; –
		APLASIA	–; aplasias
APERY	japery, napery, papery; –	**APLENTY** **APLITE**	–; – haplite; aplites
APES	capes, gapes, japes, napes, rapes, tapes; –	**APLITES** **APLITIC** **APLOMB** **APNEA**	haplites; – –; – –; aplombs –; apneal, apneas
APETALY	–; –	**APNEIC**	–; –
APEX	–; –	**APNOEA**	–; apnoeal,
APEXES	–; –		apnoeas
APHAGIA	–; aphagias	**APNOEIC**	–; –
APHASIA	–; aphasiac, aphasias	**APOCARP**	–; apocarps, apocarpy
APHASIC	–; aphasics	**APOCOPE**	–; apocopes

APODAL	–; –	**APPOSE**	–; apposed,
APODOUS	–; –		apposer,
APOGAMY	–; –		apposes
APOGEAL	–; –	**APPOSER**	–; apposers
APOGEAN	–; –	**APPRISE**	–; apprised,
APOGEE	–; apogees		appriser,
APOGEIC	–; –		apprises
APOLLO	–; apollos	**APPRIZE**	–; apprized,
APOLOG	–; apologs,		apprizer,
	apology		apprizes
APOLUNE	–; apolunes	**APPROVE**	–;
APOMICT	–; apomicts		approved,
APORT	–; –		approver,
APOSTIL	–; apostile,		approves
	apostils	**APPULSE**	–; appulses
APOTHEM	–; apothems	**APRAXIA**	–; apraxias
APPAL	–; appall,	**APRAXIC**	–; –
	appals	**APRICOT**	–; apricots
APPALL	–; appalls	**APRON**	–; aprons
APPARAT	–; apparats	**APRONED**	–; –
APPAREL	–; apparels	**APROPOS**	–; –
APPEAL	–; appeals	**APSE**	lapse; apses
APPEAR	–; appears	**APSES**	lapses; –
APPEASE	–;	**APSIDAL**	–; –
	appeased,	**APSIDES**	–; –
	appeaser,	**APSIS**	–; –
	appeases	**APT**	rapt; –
APPEL	rappel;	**APTER**	–; –
	appels	**APTERAL**	–; –
APPELS	rappels; –	**APTERYX**	–; –
APPEND	–; appends	**APTEST**	–; –
APPLAUD	–; applauds	**APTLY**	raptly; –
APPLE	dapple;	**APTNESS**	–; –
	apples	**APYRASE**	–; apyrases
APPLES	dapples; –	**AQUA**	–; aquae,
APPLIED	–; –		aquas
APPLIER	–; appliers	**AQUARIA**	–; aquarial,
APPLIES	–; –		aquarian
APPLY	–; –	**AQUATIC**	–; aquatics
APPOINT	–; appoints	**AQUAVIT**	–; aquavits

AQUEOUS	–; –	**ARCANUM**	–; –
AQUIFER	–; aquifers	**ARCED**	farced; –
AQUIVER	–; –	**ARCH**	larch, march, parch; –
AR	bar, car, ear, far, gar, jar, lar, mar, oar, par, tar, war, yar; arc, are, arf, ark, arm, ars, art	**ARCHAIC**	–; –
		ARCHED	marched, parched; –
		ARCHER	marcher; archers, archery
ARABESK	–; arabesks	**ARCHERS**	marchers; –
ARABIZE	–; arabized, arabizes	**ARCHES**	larches, marches, parches; –
ARABLE	parable; arables	**ARCHIL**	–; archils
ARABLES	parables; –	**ARCHINE**	–; archines
ARAK	–; araks	**ARCHING**	marching, parching; archings
ARANEID	–; araneids		
ARAROBA	–; ararobas		
ARBITER	–; arbiters	**ARCHIVE**	–; archived, archives
ARBOR	harbor; arbors	**ARCHLY**	–; –
ARBORED	–; –	**ARCHON**	–; archons
ARBORES	–; –	**ARCING**	farcing; –
ARBORS	harbors; –	**ARCKED**	–; –
ARBOUR	harbour; arbours	**ARCKING**	–; –
		ARCO	narco; –
ARBOURS	harbours; –	**ARCS**	marcs, narcs; –
ARBUTE	–; arbutes		
ARBUTUS	–; –	**ARCTIC**	–; arctics
ARC	marc, narc; arch, arco, arcs	**ARCUATE**	–; arcuated
		ARCUS	–; –
		ARCUSES	–; –
ARCADE	–; arcaded, arcades	**ARDEB**	–; ardebs
		ARDENCY	–; –
ARCADIA	–; arcadian, arcadias	**ARDENT**	–; –
		ARDOR	–; ardors
ARCANA	–; –	**ARDOUR**	–; ardours
ARCANE	–; –	**ARE**	bare, care, dare, fare,

	hare, mare,	ARGOL	–; argols
	pare, rare,	ARGON	jargon,
	tare, ware,		argons
	yare; area,	ARGONS	jargons; –
	ares	ARGOSY	–; –
AREA	–; areae,	ARGOT	–; argots
	areal, areas	ARGOTIC	–; –
AREALLY	–; –	ARGUE	–; argued,
AREAWAY	–; areaways		arguer,
ARECA	–; arecas		argues
AREIC	–; –	ARGUER	–; arguers
ARENA	–; arenas	ARGUFY	–; –
ARENOSE	–; –	ARGUING	–; –
ARENOUS	–; –	ARGUS	–; –
AREOLA	–; areolae,	ARGUSES	–; –
	areolar,	ARGYLE	–; argyles
	areolas	ARGYLL	–; argylls
AREOLE	–; areoles	ARHAT	–; arhats
ARES	bares, cares,	ARIA	maria, varia;
	dares, fares,		arias
	hares, lares,	ARID	–; –
	mares, nares,	ARIDER	–; –
	pares, tares,	ARIDEST	–; –
	wares; –	ARIDLY	–; –
ARETE	–; aretes	ARIDITY	–; –
ARF	barf, zarf; –	ARIEL	–; ariels
ARGAL	–; argali,	ARIETTA	–; ariettas
	argals	ARIETTE	–; ariettes
ARGALI	–; argalis	ARIGHT	–; –
ARGENT	margent;	ARIL	–; arils
	argents	ARILED	–; –
ARGENTS	margents; –	ARIOSE	–; –
ARGIL	–; argils	ARIOSI	–; –
ARGLE	gargle;	ARIOSO	–; ariosos
	argled,	ARISE	–; arisen,
	argles		arises
ARGLED	gargled; –	ARISING	–; –
ARGLES	gargles; –	ARISTA	–; aristae,
ARGLING	gargling; –		aristas

ARK	bark, cark, dark, hark, lark, mark, nark, park, sark, wark; arks	warming; armings
		ARMINGS -; farmings
		ARMLESS harmless; -
		ARMLET -; armlets
		ARMLIKE -; -
ARKS	barks, carks, darks, harks, larks, marks, narks, parks, sarks, warks; -	**ARMLOAD** -; armloads
		ARMOIRE -; armoires
		ARMOR -; armors, armory
		ARMORED -; -
		ARMORER -; armorers
ARLES	carles, farles, parles; -	**ARMOUR** -; armours, armoury
		ARMPIT -; armpits
ARM	barm, farm, harm, warm; arms, army	**ARMREST** -; armrests
		ARMS barms, farms, harms, warms; -
ARMADA	-; armadas	
ARMBAND	-; armbands	
ARMED	farmed, harmed, warmed; -	**ARMSFUL** -; -
		ARMURE -; armures
		ARMY barmy; -
ARMER	farmer, harmer, warmer; armers	**ARNATTO** -; arnattos
		ARNICA -; arnicas
		ARNOTTO -; arnottos
		AROID -; aroids
ARMERS	farmers, harmers, warmers; -	**AROINT** -; aroints
		AROMA -; aromas
		AROSE -; -
ARMET	-; armets	**AROUND** -; -
ARMFUL	harmful; armfuls	**AROUSAL** -; arousals
		AROUSE carouse; aroused, arouser, arouses
ARMHOLE	-; armholes	
ARMIES	-; -	
ARMIGER	-; armigers	
ARMILLA	-; armillae, armillas	**AROUSED** caroused; -
		AROUSER carouser; arousers
ARMING	farming, harming,	**AROUSES** carouses; -

AROYNT	–; aroynts	**ARROWS**	barrows,
ARPEN	; arpons,		farrows,
	arpent		harrows,
ARPENT	–; arpents		marrows,
ARRACK	barrack,		narrows,
	carrack;		yarrows; –
	arracks	**ARROWY**	marrowy; –
ARRACKS	–; barracks,	**ARROYO**	–; arroyos
	carracks	**ARS**	bars, cars,
ARRAIGN	–; arraigns		ears, gars,
ARRANGE	–; arranged,		jars, lars,
	arranger,		mars, oars,
	arranges		pars, tars,
ARRANT	–; –		wars; arse
ARRAS	–; –	**ARSE**	carse,
ARRASED	–; –		marse,
ARRAY	–; arrays		parse; arses
ARRAYAL	–; arrayals	**ARSENAL**	–; arsenals
ARRAYED	–; –	**ARSENIC**	–; arsenics
ARRAYER	–; arrayers	**ARSENO**	–; –
ARREAR	–; arrears	**ARSES**	carses,
ARREST	–; arrests		marses,
ARRIS	–; –		parses; –
ARRISES	–; –	**ARSHIN**	–; arshins
ARRIVAL	–; arrivals	**ARSINE**	–; arsines
ARRIVE	; arrived,	**ARSINO**	–; –
	arriver,	**ARSIS**	–; –
	arrives	**ARSON**	parson;
ARROBA	–; arrobas		arsons
ARROW	barrow,	**ART**	cart, dart,
	farrow,		fart, hart,
	harrow,		kart, mart,
	marrow,		part, tart,
	narrow,		wart; arts,
	yarrow;		arty
	arrows,	**ARTAL**	hartal; –
	arrowy	**ARTEL**	cartel; artels
ARROWED	farrowed,	**ARTELS**	cartels; –
	harrowed,	**ARTERY**	–; –
	marrowed; –	**ARTFUL**	cartful; –

ARTICLE	–; articled, articles	**ASCI**	–; –
ARTIER	wartier; –	**ASCITES**	–; –
ARTIEST	–; –	**ASCITIC**	–; –
ARTILY	–; –	**ASCOT**	mascot; ascots
ARTISAN	bartisan, partisan; artisans	**ASCOTS**	mascots; –
		ASCRIBE	–; ascribed, ascribes
ARTIST	–; artiste, artists	**ASCUS**	–; –
		ASDIC	–; asdics
ARTISTE	–; artistes	**ASEA**	–; –
ARTLESS	–; –	**ASEPSES**	–; –
ARTS	carts, darts, farts, harts, karts, marts, parts, tarts, warts; –	**ASEPSIS**	–; –
		ASEPTIC	–; –
		ASEXUAL	–; –
		ASH	bash, cash, dash, fash, gash, hash, lash, mash, pash, rash, sash, wash; ashy
ARTWORK	–; artworks		
ARTY	party, warty; –		
ARUM	larum; arums		
ARUMS	larums; –		
ARUSPEX	–; –	**ASHAMED**	–; –
ARVAL	–; –	**ASHCAN**	–; ashcans
ARVO	–; arvos	**ASHED**	bashed, cashed, dashed, fashed, gashed, hashed, lashed, mashed, pashed, rashed, sashed, washed; –
ARYL	–; aryls		
AS	bas, fas, gas, has, kas, las, mas, pas, ras, tas, vas, was; ash, ask, asp, ass		
ASARUM	–; asarums		
ASCARID	–; ascarids		
ASCARIS	–; –		
ASCEND	–; ascends		
ASCENT	nascent; ascents	**ASHEN**	–; –
		ASHES	bashes, cashes, dashes,
ASCESIS	–; –		
ASCETIC	–; ascetics		

	fashes,	**ASKANCE**	–; –
	gashes,	**ASKANT**	,
	hashes,	**ASKED**	basked,
	lashes,		casked,
	mashes,		masked,
	pashes,		tasked; –
	rashes,	**ASKER**	masker;
	sashes,		askers
	washes; –	**ASKERS**	maskers; –
ASHIER	cashier,	**ASKESES**	–; –
	dashier,	**ASKESIS**	–; –
	washier; –	**ASKEW**	–; –
ASHIEST	–; –	**ASKING**	basking,
ASHING	bashing,		casking,
	cashing,		gasking,
	dashing,		masking,
	fashing,		tasking;
	gashing,		askings
	hashing,	**ASKINGS**	gaskings,
	lashing,		maskings; –
	mashing,	**ASKS**	basks, casks,
	pashing,		masks,
	sashing,		tasks; –
	washing; –	**ASLANT**	–; –
ASHLAR	–; ashlars	**ASLEEP**	–; –
ASHLER	–; ashlors	**ASLOPE**	–; –
ASHLESS	cashless; –	**ASOCIAL**	–; –
ASHMAN	–; –	**ASP**	gasp, hasp,
ASHMEN	–; –		rasp, wasp;
ASHORE	–; –		asps
ASHRAM	–; ashrams	**ASPECT**	–; aspects
ASHTRAY	–; ashtrays	**ASPEN**	–; aspens
ASHY	dashy,	**ASPER**	gasper,
	mashy,		jasper,
	washy; –		rasper;
ASIDE	–; asides		aspers
ASININE	–; –	**ASPERS**	gaspers,
ASK	bask, cask,		jaspers,
	mask, task;		raspers;
	asks		asperse

ASPERSE	–; aspersed, asperser, asperses		sasses, tasses; assess
ASPHALT	–; asphalts	**ASSET**	basset,
ASPHYXY	–; –		tasset;
ASPIC	–; aspics		assets
ASPIRE	–; aspired, aspirer, aspires	**ASSETS**	bassets, tassets; –
		ASSIGN	–; assigns
ASPIRER	–; aspirers	**ASSIST**	bassist;
ASPIRIN	–; aspirings, aspirins		assists
		ASSISTS	bassists; -
ASPIS	–; aspish	**ASSIZE**	–; assizes
ASPISH	raspish; –	**ASSLIKE**	–; –
ASPS	gasps, hasps, rasps, wasps; –	**ASSOIL**	–; assoils
		ASSORT	–; assorts
		ASSUAGE	–;
ASQUINT	–; –		assuaged,
ASRAMA	–; asramas		assuages
ASS	bass, lass, mass, pass, sass, tass; –	**ASSUME**	–; assumed, assumer, assumes
ASSAGAI	–; assagais	**ASSUMER**	–; assumers
ASSAI	–; assail, assais	**ASSURE**	–; assured, assurer, assures
ASSAIL	wassail; assails	**ASSURED**	–; assureds
ASSAULT	–; assaults	**ASSURER**	–; assurers
ASSAY	–; assays	**ASSUROR**	–; assurors
ASSAYED	–; –	**ASSWAGE**	–;
ASSAYER	–; assayers		asswaged,
ASSEGAI	–; assegais		asswages
ASSENT	–; assents	**ASTASIA**	–; astasias
ASSERT	–; asserts	**ASTATIC**	–; –
ASSES	basses, gasses, lasses, masses, passes,	**ASTER**	baster, caster, easter, faster, laster,

	master,		kat, lat, mat,
	paster,		oat, pat,
	raster,		qat, rat, sat,
	taster,		tat, vat, wat;
	vaster,		ate
	waster;	**ATABAL**	–; atabals
	astern,	**ATAGHAN**	–; ataghans
	asters	**ATALAYA**	–; atalayas
ASTERIA	–; asterias	**ATAMAN**	–; atamans
ASTERN	eastern,	**ATARAXY**	–; –
	pastern; –	**ATAVIC**	–; –
ASTERS	basters,	**ATAVISM**	–; atavisms
	casters,	**ATAVIST**	–; atavists
	easters,	**ATAXIA**	–; ataxias
	lasters,	**ATAXIC**	–; ataxics
	masters,	**ATAXIES**	–; –
	pasters,	**ATAXY**	–; –
	rasters,	**ATE**	bate, cate,
	tasters,		date, fate,
	wasters; –		gate, hate,
ASTHENY	–; –		late, mate,
ASTHMA	–; asthmas		pate, rate,
ASTIR	–; –		sate, tate;
ASTONY	–; –		ates
ASTOUND	–; astounds	**ATELIC**	–; –
ASTRAL	gastral;	**ATELIER**	–; ateliers
	astrals	**ATES**	bates, cates,
ASTRAY	–; –		dates, fates,
ASTRICT	–; astricts		gates, hates,
ASTRIDE	–; –		lates, mates,
ASTUTE	–; –		nates, pates,
ASTYLAR	–; –		rates, sates,
ASUNDER	–; –		tates; –
ASWARM	–; –	**ATHEISM**	–; atheisms
ASWIRL	–; –	**ATHEIST**	–; atheists
ASWOON	–; –	**ATHIRST**	–; –
ASYLA	–; –	**ATHLETE**	–; athletes
ASYLUM	–; asylums	**ATHODYD**	–; athodyds
AT	bat, cat, eat,	**ATHWART**	–; –
	fat, gat, hat,	**ATILT**	–; –

ATINGLE	–; –	**ATROPIN**	–; atropine, atropins
ATLAS	–; –		
ATLASES	–; –	**ATTACH**	–; attache
ATLATL	–; atlatls	**ATTACHE**	–; attached, attacher, attaches
ATMA	–; atman, atmas		
ATMAN	batman; atmans	**ATTACK**	–; attacks
		ATTAIN	–; attains, attaint
ATOLL	–; atolls		
ATOM	–; atoms, atomy	**ATTAINT**	–; attaints
		ATTAR	–; attars
ATOMIC	–; atomics	**ATTEMPT**	–; attempts
ATOMIES	–; –	**ATTEND**	–; attends
ATOMISE	–; atomised, atomises	**ATTENT**	–; –
		ATTEST	fattest, wattest; attests
ATOMISM	–; atomisms		
ATOMIST	–; atomists		
ATOMIZE	–; atomized, atomizer, atomizes	**ATTIC**	–; attics
		ATTIRE	–; attired, attires
ATONAL	–; –		
ATONE	–; atoned, atoner, atones	**ATTORN**	–; attorns
		ATTRACT	–; attracts
		ATTRITE	–; attrited
ATONER	–; atoners	**ATTUNE**	–; attuned, attunes
ATONIC	–; atonics		
ATONIES	–; –	**ATWAIN**	–; –
ATONING	–; –	**ATWEEN**	–; –
ATONY	–; –	**ATYPIC**	–; –
ATOP	–; atopy	**AUBADE**	–; aubades
ATOPIC	–; –	**AUBERGE**	–; auberges
ATOPIES	–; –	**AUBURN**	–; auburns
ATRESIA	–; atresias	**AUCTION**	–; auctions
ATRIA	latria; atrial	**AUDAD**	caudad; audads
ATRIP	–; –		
ATRIUM	natrium; atriums	**AUDIBLE**	–; audibles
		AUDIBLY	–; audibly
ATRIUMS	natriums; –	**AUDIENT**	–; audients
ATROPHY	–; –	**AUDILE**	–; audiles
		AUDING	–; audings

AUDIO	–; audios	vaunt; aunts,
AUDIT	–; audits	aunty
AUDITED	–; –	**AUNTIE** vauntie;
AUDITOR	–; auditors,	aunties
	auditory	**AUNTLY** –; –
AUGEND	–; augends	**AUNTS** daunts,
AUGER	gauger,	haunts,
	mauger,	jaunts,
	sauger;	taunts,
	augers	vaunts; –
AUGERS	gaugers,	**AUNTY** jaunty,
	saugers; –	vaunty; –
AUGHT	caught,	**AURA** laura; aurae,
	naught,	aural, aurar,
	taught,	auras
	waught;	**AURAE** laurae; –
	aughts	**AURAL** laural; –
AUGHTS	naughts,	**AURALLY** –; –
	waughts; –	**AURAS** lauras; –
AUGITE	–; augites	**AURATE** –; aurated
AUGITIC	–; –	**AUREATE** –; –
AUGMENT	–; augments	**AUREI** –; –
AUGUR	–; augurs,	**AUREOLA** –; aureolae,
	augury	aureolas
AUGURAL	–; –	**AUREOLE** –; aureoled,
AUGERER	–; augerers	aureoles
AUGUST	–; –	**AURES** –; –
AUK	jauk, wauk;	**AUREUS** –; –
	auks	**AURIC** –; –
AUKLET	–; auklets	**AURICLE** –; auricled,
AUKS	jauks,	auricles
	wauks; –	**AURIS** kauris; aurist
AULD	cauld, fauld,	**AURIST** –; aurists
	yauld; –	**AUROCH** –; aurochs
AULDER	–; –	**AURORA** –; aurorae,
AULDEST	–; –	auroral,
AULIC	–; –	auroras
AUNT	daunt,	**AUROUS** –; –
	gaunt, haunt,	**AURUM** –; aurums
	jaunt, taunt,	**AUSPEX** –; –

AUSPICE	–; auspices	AVENUE	–; avenues
AUSTERE	–; austerer	AVER	caver, haver,
AUSTRAL	–; –		laver, paver,
AUTARKY	–; –		raver, saver,
AUTHOR	–; authors		waver;
AUTISM	–; autisms		avers, avert
AUTO	–; autos	AVERAGE	–;
AUTOBUS	–; –		averaged,
AUTOED	–; –		averages
AUTOING	–; –	AVERRED	–; –
AUTOPSY	–; –	AVERS	cavers,
AUTUMN	–; autumns		havers,
AUXESES	–; –		lavers,
AUXESIS	–; –		pavers,
AUXETIC	–; auxetics		ravers,
AUXIN	–; auxins		savers,
AUXINIC	–; –		wavers;
AVA	java, kava,		averse
	lava; –	AVERT	–; averts
AVAIL	–; avails	AVERTED	–;
AVAILED	–; –	AVES	caves,
AVARICE	–; avarices		eaves,
AVAST	–; –		haves, laves,
AVATAR	–; avatars		naves,
AVAUNT	–; –		oaves,
AVE	cave, eave,		paves,
	gave, have,		raves, saves,
	lave, nave,		waves; –
	pave, rave,	AVGAS	–; –
	save, wave;	AVGASES	–; –
	aver, aves	AVIAN	–; avians
AVELLAN	–; avellane	AVIARY	–; –
AVENGE	–; avenged,	AVIATE	–; aviated,
	avenger,		aviates
	avenges	AVIATOR	–; aviators
AVENGER	–; avengers	AVID	pavid; –
AVENS	davens,	AVIDIN	–; avidins
	havens,	AVIDITY	–; –
	mavens,	AVIDLY	–; –
	ravens; –	AVION	–; avions

AVIONIC	–; avionics	**AWARDER**	–; awarders
AVISO	–; avisos	**AWARDS**	vawards,
AVO	–; avos,	**AWARE**	–; –
	avow	**AWASH**	–; –
AVOCADO	–; avocados	**AWAY**	–; –
AVOCET	–; avocets	**AWE**	–; awed,
AVODIRE	–; avodires		awee, awes
AVOID	–; avoids	**AWEARY**	–; –
AVOIDED	–; –	**AWED**	cawed,
AVOIDER	–; avoiders		dawed,
AVOSET	–; avosets		hawed,
AVOUCH	–; –		jawed,
AVOW	–; avows		lawed,
AVOWAL	–; avowals		mawed,
AVOWED	–; –		pawed,
AVOWER	–; avowers		sawed,
AVULSE	–; avulsed,		tawed; –
	avulses	**AWEE**	–; –
AW	caw, daw,	**AWEIGH**	–; –
	haw, jaw,	**AWEING**	–; –
	law, maw,	**AWELESS**	–; –
	paw, raw,	**AWESOME**	–; –
	saw, taw,	**AWFUL**	lawful; –
	vaw, waw,	**AWFULLY**	lawfully; –
	yaw; awa,	**AWHILE**	–; –
	awe, awl,	**AWHIRL**	, –
	awn	**AWING**	cawing,
AWA	–; –		dawing,
AWAIT	–; awaits		hawing,
AWAITED	–; –		jawing,
AWAITER	–; awaiters		lawing,
AWAKE	–; awaked,		mawing,
	awaken,		pawing,
	awakes		sawing,
AWAKEN	–; awakens		tawing; –
AWAKING	–; –	**AWL**	bawl, pawl,
AWARD	vaward;		wawl, yawl;
	awards		awls
AWARDED	–; –	**AWLESS**	lawless; –
AWARDEE	–; awardees	**AWLS**	bawls,

	pawls,		taxed,
	wawls,		waxed; –
	yawls; –	AXEL	–; axels
AWLWORT	–; –	AXEMAN	–; –
AWMOUS	–; –	AXEMEN	–; –
AWN	dawn, fawn,	AXENIC	–; –
	lawn, mawn,	AXES	faxes,
	pawn, sawn,		paxes,
	yawn; awns,		raxes, saxes,
	awny		taxes,
AWNED	dawned,		waxes,
	fawned,		zaxes; –
	pawned,	AXIAL	–; –
	yawned; –	AXIALLY	–; –
AWNING	dawning,	AXIL	–; axile,
	fawning,		axils
	pawning,	AXILLA	maxilla;
	yawning;		axillae,
	awnings		axillar,
AWNLESS	–; –		axillas
AWNS	dawns,	AXILLAE	maxillae; –
	fawns,	AXILLAR	–; axillars,
	lawns,		axillary
	pawns,	AXILLAS	maxillas; –
	yawns; –	AXING	faxing,
AWNY	fawny,		raxing,
	tawny; –		taxing,
AWOKE	–; awoken		waxing; –
AWOL	–; awols	AXIOM	–; axioms
AWRY	–; –	AXIS	maxis,
AX	fax, lax,		taxis; –
	pax, rax,	AXISED	–; –
	sax, tax,	AXISES	–; –
	wax, zax;	AXITE	taxite; axites
	axe	AXLE	–; axled,
AXAL	–; –		axles
AXE	–; axed,	AXLIKE	waxlike; –
	axes	AXMAN	taxman; –
AXED	faxed,	AXMEN	taxmen; –
	raxed,	AXOLOTL	–; axolotls

AXON	taxon;	rays, says,
	axone,	ways, —
	axons	**AZALEA**	—; azaleas
AXONAL	—; —	**AZAN**	hazan;
AXONE	—; axones		azans
AXONIC	—; —	**AZANS**	hazans; —
AXONS	taxons; —	**AZIDE**	—; azides
AXSEED	—; axseeds	**AZIDO**	—; —
AY	bay, cay,	**AZIMUTH**	—; azimuths
	day, fay,	**AZINE**	—; azines
	gay, hay,	**AZO**	—; azon
	jay, kay, lay,	**AZOIC**	—; —
	may, nay,	**AZOLE**	—; azoles
	pay, ray,	**AZON**	—; azons
	say, way,	**AZONAL**	—;
	yay; aye,	**AZONIC**	—;
	ays	**AZOTE**	—; azoted,
AYAH	rayah; ayahs		azotes
AYAHS	rayahs; —	**AZOTH**	—; azoths
AYE	—; ayes	**AZOTIC**	—; —
AYIN	zayin; ayins	**AZOTISE**	—; azotised,
AYINS	zayins; —		azotises
AYS	bays, cays,	**AZOTIZE**	—; azotized,
	days, fays,		azotizes
	gays, hays,	**AZURE**	—; azures
	jays, kays,	**AZURITE**	—; azurites
	lays, mays,	**AZYGOS**	—; —
	nays, pays,	**AZYGOUS**	—; —

B

B	—; ba, be,	**BAA**	—; baas,
	bi, bo, by		baal
BA	aba; baa,	**BAAED**	—; —
	bad, bag,	**BAAING**	—; —
	bah, bal,	**BAAL**	—; baals
	ban, bar,	**BAALIM**	—; —
	bas, bat,	**BAALISM**	—; baalisms
	bay	**BABA**	—; babas

BABASSU	–; babassus	**BACKING**	–; backings
BABBITT	–; babbitts	**BACKLIT**	–; –
BABBLE	–; babbled, babbler, babbles	**BACKLOG**	–; backlogs
		BACKOUT	–; backouts
		BACKSAW	–; backsaws
BABBLER	–; babblers	**BACKSET**	–; backsets
BABBOOL	–; babbools	**BACKUP**	–; backups
BABE	–; babel, babes	**BACON**	–; bacons
		BAD	–; bade, bads
BABEL	–; babels		
BABESIA	–; babesias	**BADDIE**	–; baddies
BABICHE	–; babiches	**BADDY**	–; –
BABIED	–; –	**BADE**	–; –
BABIES	–; –	**BADGE**	–; badged, badger, badges
BABKA	–; babkas		
BABOO	–; babool, baboon, baboos	**BADGED**	–; –
		BADGER	–; badgers
BABOOL	–; babools	**BADGING**	–; –
BABOON	–; baboons	**BADLAND**	–; badlands
BABU	–; babul, babus	**BADLY**	–; –
		BADMAN	–; –
BABUL	–; babuls	**BADMEN**	–; –
BABY	–; –	**BADNESS**	–; –
BABYING	–; –	**BAFF**	–; baffs, baffy
BABYISH	–; –		
BACCA	–; baccae	**BAFFED**	–; –
BACCARA	–; baccaras, baccarat	**BAFFIES**	–; –
		BAFFING	–; –
BACCATE	–; baccated	**BAFFLE**	–; baffled, baffler, baffles
BACCHIC	–; –		
BACH	–; –		
BACHED	–; –	**BAFFLER**	–; bafflers
BACHES	–; –	**BAFFY**	–; –
BACHING	–; –	**BAG**	–; bags
BACK	aback; backs	**BAGASS**	–; bagasse
		BAGASSE	–; bagasses
BACKED	–; –	**BAGEL**	–; bagels
BACKER	–; backers	**BAGFUL**	–; bagfuls
BACKHOE	–; backhoes		

BAGGAGE	–; baggages	**BAIZE**	–; baizes
BAGGED	–; –	**BAKE**	, baked, baker, bakes
BAGGIE	–; baggier, baggies	**BAKER**	–; bakers, bakery
BAGGIES	–; baggiest	**BAKING**	–; bakings
BAGGILY	–; –	**BAKLAVA**	–; baklavas
BAGGING	–; baggings	**BAKLAWA**	–; baklawas
BAGGY	–; –	**BAL**	–; bald, bale, balk, ball, balm, bals
BAGMAN	–; –		
BAGMEN	–; –		
BAGNIO	–; bagnios		
BAGPIPE	–; bagpiper, bagpipes	**BALANCE**	–; balanced, balancer, balances
BAGSFUL	–; –		
BAGUET	–; baguets	**BALAS**	–; –
BAGWIG	–; bagwigs	**BALASES**	–; –
BAGWORM	–; bagworms	**BALATA**	–; balatas
		BALBOA	–; balboas
BAH	–; baht	**BALCONY**	–; –
BAHADUR	–; bahadurs	**BALD**	–; balds
BAHT	–; bahts	**BALDED**	–; –
BAIL	–; bails	**BALDER**	–; –
BAILED	–; –	**BALDEST**	–; –
BAILEE	–; bailees	**BALDING**	–; –
BAILER	–; bailers	**BALDISH**	–; –
BAILEY	–; baileys	**BALDLY**	–; –
BAILIE	–; bailies	**BALDRIC**	–; baldrick, baldrics
BAILIFF	–; bailiffs		
BAILING	–; –	**BALE**	–; baled, baler, bales
BAILOR	–; bailors		
BAILOUT	–; bailouts	**BALEEN**	–; baleens
BAIRN	–; bairns	**BALEFUL**	–; –
BAIRNLY	–; –	**BALER**	–; balers
BAIT	–; baith, baits	**BALING**	–; –
		BALK	–; balks, balky
BAITED	–; –		
BAITER	–; baiters	**BALKED**	–; –
BAITING	–; –	**BALKER**	–; balkers
BAIZA	–; baizas	**BALKIER**	–; –

BALKILY	–; –	**BANDBOX**	–; –
BALKING	–; –	**BANDEAU**	–;
BALKY	–; –		bandeaus,
BALL	–; balls,		bandeaux
	bally	**BANDED**	–; –
BALLAD	–; ballade,	**BANDER**	–; banders
	ballads	**BANDIED**	–; –
BALLADE	–; ballades	**BANDIES**	–; –
BALLAST	–; ballasts	**BANDING**	–; –
BALLED	–; –	**BANDIT**	–; bandits
BALLER	–; ballers	**BANDOG**	–; bandogs
BALLET	–; ballets	**BANDORA**	–; bandoras
BALLING	–; –	**BANDORE**	–; bandores
BALLON	–; ballons	**BANE**	–; baned,
BALLOT	–; ballots		banes
BALM	–; balms,	**BANEFUL**	–; –
	balmy	**BANG**	–; bangs
BALMIER	–; –	**BANGED**	–; –
BALMILY	–; –	**BANGER**	–; bangers
BALNEAL	–; –	**BANGING**	–; –
BALONEY	–; baloneys	**BANGKOK**	–; bangkoks
BALSA	–; balsam,	**BANGLE**	–; bangles
	balsas	**BANIAN**	–; banians
BALSAM	–; balsams	**BANING**	–; –
BAMBINO	–; bambinos	**BANISH**	–; –
BAMBOO	–; bamboos	**BANJO**	–; banjos
BAN	–; band,	**BANJOES**	–; –
	bane, bang,	**BANK**	–; banks
	bani, bank,	**BANKED**	–; –
	bans	**BANKER**	–; bankers
BANAL	–; –	**BANKING**	–; bankings
BANALLY	–; –	**BANKSIA**	–; banksias
BANANA	–; bananas	**BANNED**	–; –
BANCO	–; bancos	**BANNER**	–; banners
BAND	–; bands,	**BANNET**	–; bannets
	bandy	**BANNING**	–; –
BANDAGE	–; bandaged,	**BANNOCK**	–; bannocks
	bandager,	**BANNS**	–; –
	bandages	**BANQUET**	–; banquets
BANDANA	–; bandanas	**BANSHEE**	–; banshees

BANSHIE	–; banshies	**BAREFIT**	–; –
BANTAM	–; bantams	**BAREGE**	–; bareges
BANTER	–; banters	**BARELY**	–; –
BANYAN	–; banyans	**BARER**	–; –
BANZAI	–; banzais	**BARES**	–; barest
BAOBAB	–; baobabs	**BARF**	–; barfs
BAPTISE	–; baptised, baptises	**BARFED**	–; –
BAPTISM	–; baptisms	**BARFING**	–; –
BAPTIST	–; baptists	**BARFLY**	–; –
BAPTIZE	–; baptized, baptizer, baptizes	**BARGAIN**	–; bargains
		BARGE	–; barged, bargee, barges
BAR	–; barb, bard, bare, barf, bark, barm, barn, bars	**BARGEE**	–; bargees
		BARGING	–; –
		BARHOP	–; barhops
		BARIC	–; –
		BARILLA	–; barillas
BARBAL	–; –	**BARING**	–; –
BARBATE	–; –	**BARITE**	–; barites
BARBE	–; barbed, barbel, barbes	**BARIUM**	–; bariums
		BARK	–; barks, barky
BARBEL	–; barbell, barbels	**BARKED**	–; –
		BARKER	–; barkers
BARBELL	–; barbells	**BARKIER**	–; –
BARBER	–; barbers	**BARKING**	–; –
BARBET	–; barbets	**BARLESS**	–; –
BARBING	–; –	**BARLEY**	–; barleys
BARBULE	–; barbules	**BARLOW**	–; barlows
BARBUT	–; barbuts	**BARM**	–; barms, barmy
BARD	–; barde, bards		
		BARMAID	–; barmaids
BARDE	–; barded, bardes	**BARMAN**	–; –
		BARMEN	–; –
BARDIC	–; –	**BARMIE**	–; barmier
BARDING	–; –	**BARN**	–; barns, barny
BARE	–; bared, barer, bares		
		BARNIER	–; –
		BARON	–; barong,

	barons,	**BASELY**	–; –
	barony	**BASENJI**	–; basenjis
BARONET	–; baronets	**BASER**	abaser;
BARONG	–; barongs		basers
BARONNE	–; baronnes	**BASERS**	abasers; –
BAROQUE	–; baroques	**BASES**	abases;
BARQUE	–; barques		basest
BARRACK	–; barracks	**BASH**	abash; –
BARRAGE	–; barraged,	**BASHAW**	–; bashaws
	barrages	**BASHED**	abashed; –
BARRE	–; barred,	**BASHER**	–; bashers
	barrel,	**BASHES**	abashes; –
	barren,	**BASHFUL**	–; –
	barres,	**BASHING**	abashing; –
	barret	**BASHLYK**	–; bashlyks
BARREL	–; barrels	**BASIC**	–; basics
BARREN	–; barrens	**BASIFY**	–; –
BARRET	–; barrets	**BASIL**	–; basils
BARRIER	–; barriers	**BASILAR**	–; basilary
BARRING	–; –	**BASILIC**	–; basilica
BARRIO	–; barrios	**BASIN**	–; basins
BARROOM	–; barrooms	**BASINAL**	–; –
BARROW	–; barrows	**BASINED**	–; –
BARTEND	–; bartends	**BASINET**	–; basinets
BARTER	–; barters	**BASING**	abasing; –
BARWARE	–; barwares	**BASION**	–; basions
BARYE	–; baryes	**BASIS**	–; –
BARYON	–; baryons	**BASK**	–; basks
BARYTA	–; barytas	**BASKED**	–; –
BARYTE	–; barytes	**BASKET**	–; baskets
BARYTIC	–; –	**BASKING**	–; –
BAS	abas; –	**BASKS**	–; –
BASAL	–; basalt	**BASQUE**	–; basques
BASALLY	–; –	**BASS**	–; bassi,
BASALT	–; basalts		basso, bassy
BASCULE	–; bascules	**BASSES**	–; –
BASE	abase;	**BASSET**	–; bassets
	based,	**BASSIST**	–; bassists
	baser, bases	**BASSLY**	–; –
BASED	abased; –	**BASSO**	–; bassos

BASSOON	–; bassoons	BATLIKE	–; –
BAST	–; baste, basts	BATMAN	–; –
		BATMEN	–; –
BASTARD	–; bastards, bastardy	BATON	–; batons
		BATSMAN	–; –
BASTE	–; basted, baster, bastes	BATSMEN	–; –
		BATT	–; batts, battu, batty
BASTER	–; basters	BATTEAU	–; batteaux
BASTILE	–; bastiles	BATTED	–; –
BASTING	–; bastings	BATTEN	–; battens
BASTION	–; bastions	BATTER	–; batters, battery
BAT	–; bate, bath, bats, batt	BATTIER	–; –
		BATTIK	–; battiks
BATBOY	–; batboys	BATTING	–; battings
BATCH	–; –	BATTLE	–; battled, battler, battles
BATCHED	–; –		
BATCHER	–; batchers		
BATCHES	–; –	BATTLER	–; battlers
BATE	abate; bated, bates	BATTU	–; battue
		BATTUE	–; battues
BATEAU	–; bateaux	BATTY	–; –
BATED	abated; –	BATWING	–; –
BATES	abates; –	BAUBEE	–; baubees
BATFISH	–; –	BAUBLE	–; baubles
BATFOWL	–; batfowls	BAUD	–; bauds
BATH	–; bathe, baths	BAULK	–; baulks, baulky
BATHE	–; bathed, bather, bathes	BAULKED	–; –
		BAUSOND	–; –
		BAUXITE	–; bauxites
BATHER	–; bathers	BAWBEE	–; bawbees
BATHING	–; –	BAWCOCK	–; bawcocks
BATHOS	–; –	BAWD	–; bawds, bawdy
BATHTUB	–; bathtubs		
BATHYAL	–; –	BAWDIER	–; –
BATIK	–; batiks	BAWDIES	–; bawdiest
BATING	abating; –	BAWDILY	–; –
BATISTE	–; batistes	BAWDRIC	·; bawdrics

BAWDRY	–; –	BEAKIER	–; –
BAWL	–; bawls	BEAM	abeam;
BAWLED	–; –		beams,
BAWLER	–; bawlers		beamy
BAWLING	–; –	BEAMED	–; –
BAWSUNT	–; –	BEAMIER	–; –
BAWTIE	–; bawties	BEAMILY	–; –
BAWTY	–; –	BEAMING	–; –
BAY	–; bays	BEAMISH	–; –
BAYAMO	–; bayamos	BEAN	–; beano,
BAYARD	–; bayards		beans
BAYED	–; –	BEANBAG	–; beanbags
BAYING	–; –	BEANED	–; –
BAYONET	–; bayonets	BEANERY	–; –
BAYOU	–; bayous	BEANIE	–; beanies
BAYWOOD	–;	BEANING	–; –
	baywoods	BEANO	–; beanos
BAZAAR	–; bazaars	BEAR	–; beard,
BAZAR	–; bazars		bears
BAZOOKA	–; bazookas	BEARCAT	–; bearcats
BE	obe; bed,	BEARD	–; beards
	bee, beg,	BEARDED	–; –
	bel, ben,	BEARER	–; bearers
	bet, bey	BEARING	–; bearings
BEACH	–; beachy	BEARISH	–; –
BEACHED	–; –	BEAST	–; beasts
BEACHES	–; –	BEASTIE	–; beasties
BEACON	–; beacons	BEASTLY	–; –
BEAD	–; beads,	BEAT	–; beats
	beady	BEATEN	–; –
BEADED	–; –	BEATER	–; beaters
BEADIER	–; –	BEATIFY	–; –
BEADILY	–; –	BEATING	–; beatings
BEADING	–; beadings	BEATNIK	–; beatniks
BEADLE	–; beadles	BEAU	–; beaus,
BEAGLE	–; beagles		beaut,
BEAK	–; beaks,		beaux
	beaky	BEAUISH	–; –
BEAKED	–; –	BEAUT	–; beauts,
BEAKER	–; beakers		beauty

BEAVER	–; beavers	**BEDEMAN**	–; –
BEBEERU	; bebeerus	**BEDEMEN**	;
BEBLOOD	–; bebloods	**BEDEVIL**	–; bedevils
BEBOP	–; bebops	**BEDEW**	–; bedews
BECALM	–; becalms	**BEDEWED**	–; –
BECAME	–; –	**BEDFAST**	–; –
BECAP	–; becaps	**BEDGOWN**	–;
BECAUSE	–; –		bedgowns
BECHALK	–; bechalks	**BEDIGHT**	–; bedights
BECHARM	–; becharms	**BEDIM**	–; bedims
BECK	–; becks	**BEDIRTY**	–; –
BECKED	–; –	**BEDIZEN**	–; bedizens
BECKET	–; beckets	**BEDLAM**	–; bedlamp,
BECKING	–; –		bedlams
BECKON	–; beckons	**BEDLAMP**	–; bedlamps
BECLASP	–; beclasps	**BEDLESS**	–; –
BECLOAK	–; becloaks	**BEDLIKE**	–; –
BECLOG	–; beclogs	**BEDMATE**	–; bedmates
BECLOUD	–; beclouds	**BEDOUIN**	–; bedouins
BECLOWN	–; beclowns	**BEDPAN**	–; bedpans
BECOME	–; becomes	**BEDPOST**	–; bedposts
BECRAWL	–; becrawls	**BEDRAIL**	–; bedrails
BECRIME	–; becrimed,	**BEDRAPE**	–;
	becrimes		bedraped,
BECROWD	–; becrowds		bedrapes
BECRUST	–; becrusts	**BEDRID**	–; –
BECURSE	–; becursed,	**BEDROCK**	–; bedrocks
	becurses	**BEDROLL**	–; bedrolls
BECURST	; –	**BEDROOM**	–; bedrooms
BED	abed; beds	**BEDRUG**	–; bedrugs
BEDAMN	–; bedamns	**BEDSIDE**	–; bedsides
BEDAUB	–; bedaubs	**BEDSORE**	–; bedsores
BEDBUG	–; bedbugs	**BEDTICK**	–; bedticks
BEDDED	–; –	**BEDTIME**	–; bedtimes
BEDDER	–; bedders	**BEDUIN**	–; beduins
BEDDING	–; beddings	**BEDUMB**	–; bedumbs
BEDECK	–; bedecks	**BEDUNCE**	–;
BEDEL	–; bedell,		bedunced,
	bedels		bedunces
BEDELL	–; bedells	**BEDWARD**	–; bedwards

BEDWARF	–; bedwarfs	**BEFRET**	–; befrets
BEE	–; beef,	**BEG**	–; begs
	been, beep,	**BEGALL**	–; begalls
	beer, bees,	**BEGAN**	–; –
	beet	**BEGAT**	–; –
BEEBEE	–; beebees	**BEGAZE**	–; begazed,
BEECH	–; beechy		begazes
BEECHEN	–; –	**BEGET**	–; begets
BEECHES	–; –	**BEGGAR**	–; beggars,
BEEF	–; beefs,		beggary
	beefy	**BEGGED**	–; –
BEEFED	–; –	**BEGGING**	–; –
BEEFIER	–; –	**BEGIN**	–; begins
BEEFILY	–; –	**BEGIRD**	–; begirds
BEEFING	–; –	**BEGIRT**	–; –
BEEHIVE	–; beehives	**BEGLAD**	–; beglads
BEELIKE	–; –	**BEGLOOM**	–; beglooms
BEELINE	–; beelines	**BEGONE**	–; –
BEEN	–; –	**BEGONIA**	–; begonias
BEEP	–; beeps	**BEGORAH**	–; –
BEEPED	–; –	**BEGORRA**	–; begorrah
BEEPER	–; beepers	**BEGOT**	–; –
BEEPING	–; –	**BEGRIM**	–; begrime,
BEER	–; beers,		begrims
	beery	**BEGRIME**	–; begrimed,
BEERIER	–; –		begrimes
BEET	–; beets	**BEGROAN**	–; begroans
BEETLE	–; beetled,	**BEGUILE**	–; beguiled,
	beetles		beguiler,
BEEVES	–; –		beguiles
BEFALL	–; befalls	**BEGUINE**	–; beguines
BEFELL	–; –	**BEGULF**	–; begulfs
BEFIT	–; befits	**BEGUM**	–; begums
BEFLAG	–; beflags	**BEGUN**	–; –
BEFLEA	–; befleas	**BEHALF**	–; –
BEFLECK	–; beflecks	**BEHAVE**	–; behaved,
BEFOG	–; befogs		behaver,
BEFOOL	–; befools		behaves
BEFORE	–; –	**BEHAVER**	–; behavers
BEFOUL	–; befouls	**BEHEAD**	–; beheads

BEHELD	–; –	**BELIER**	–; beliers
BEHEST	–; behests	**BELIEVE**	–; believed,
BEHIND	–; behinds		believer,
BEHOLD	–; beholds		believes
BEHOOF	–; –	**BELIKE**	–; –
BEHOOVE	–;	**BELIVE**	–; –
	behooved,	**BELL**	–; belle,
	behooves		belly
BEHOVE	–; behoved,	**BELLBOY**	–; bellboys
	behoves	**BELLE**	–; belled,
BEHOWL	–; behowls		belles
BEIGE	–; beiges	**BELLEEK**	–; belleeks
BEIGY	–; –	**BELLHOP**	–; bellhops
BEING	–; beings	**BELLIED**	–; –
BEJEWEL	; bejewels	**BELLIES**	–; –
BEKISS	–; –	**BELLING**	–; –
BEKNOT	–; beknots	**BELLMAN**	–; –
BEL	–; bell, bels,	**BELLMEN**	–; –
	belt	**BELLOW**	–; bellows
BELABOR	–; belabors	**BELONG**	–; belongs
BELACED	–; –	**BELOVED**	–; beloveds
BELADY	–; –	**BELOW**	–; belows
BELATED	–; –	**BELT**	–; belts
BELAUD	–; belauds	**BELTED**	–; –
BELAY	–; belays	**BELTING**	–; beltings
BELCH	–; –	**BELTWAY**	–; beltways
BELCHED	–; –	**BELUGA**	–; belugas
BELCHER	–; belchers	**BELYING**	–; –
BELCHES	–; –	**BEMA**	–; bemas
BELDAM	–; beldame,	**BEMATA**	–; –
	beldams	**BEMEAN**	–; bemeans
BELDAME	–; beldames	**BEMIRE**	–; bemired,
BELEAP	–; beleaps,		bemires
	beleapt	**BEMIST**	–; bemists
BELFRY	–; –	**BEMIX**	–; bemixt
BELGA	–; belgas	**BEMIXED**	–; –
BELIE	–; belied,	**BEMIXES**	–; –
	belief,	**BEMOAN**	–; bemoans
	belier, belies	**BEMOCK**	–; bemocks
BELIEF	–; beliefs		

BEMUSE	–; bemused, bemuses	**BENZIN**	–; benzine, benzins
BEN	–; bend, bene, bens, bent	**BENZINE**	–; benzines
		BENZOIC	–; benzoic
		BENZOIN	–; benzoins
BENAME	–; benamed, benames	**BENZOL**	–; benzole, benzols
BENCH	–; –	**BENZOLE**	–; benzoles
BENCHED	–; –	**BENZOYL**	–; benzoyls
BENCHER	–; benchers	**BENZYL**	–; benzyls
BENCHES	–; –	**BEPAINT**	–; bepaints
BEND	–; bends, bendy	**BEQUEST**	–; bequests
		BERAKE	–; beraked, berakes
BENDAY	–; bendays	**BERATE**	–; berated, berates
BENDED	–; –		
BENDEE	–; bendees	**BEREAVE**	–; bereaved, bereaver, bereaves
BENDER	–; benders		
BENDING	–; –		
BENDY	–; bendys		
BENE	–; benes	**BEREFT**	–; –
BENEATH	–; –	**BERET**	–; berets
BENEFIC	–; –	**BERETTA**	–; berettas
BENEFIT	–; benefits	**BERG**	–; bergs
BENEMPT	–; –	**BERHYME**	–; berhymed, berhymes
BENIGN	–; –		
BENISON	–; benisons		
BENNE	–; bennes, bennet	**BERIME**	–; berimed, berimes
BENNET	–; bennets		
BENNI	–; bennis	**BERLIN**	–; berline, berlins
BENNIES	–; –		
BENNY	–; –	**BERLINE**	–; berlines
BENT	–; bents	**BERM**	–; berme, berms
BENTHAL	–; –		
BENTHIC	–; –	**BERME**	–; bermes
BENTHOS	–; –	**BERRIED**	–; –
BENUMB	–; benumbs	**BERRIES**	–; –
BENZAL	–; –	**BERRY**	–; –
BENZENE	–; benzenes	**BERSEEM**	–; berseems
		BERSERK	–; berserks

BERTH	–; bertha, berths	**BESTREW**	–; bestrewn, bestrews
BERTHA	–; berthas	**BESTROW**	–; bestrown,
BERTHED	–; –		bestrows
BERYL	–; beryls	**BESTUD**	–; bestuds
BESCOUR	–; bescours	**BESWARM**	–; beswarms
BESEECH	–; –	**BET**	abet; beta,
BESEEM	–; beseems		beth, bets
BESET	–; besets	**BETA**	–; betas
BESHAME	–; beshamed, beshames	**BETAINE**	–; betaines
		BETAKE	–; betaken, betakes
BESHOUT	–; beshouts	**BETAXED**	–; –
BESHREW	–; beshrews	**BETEL**	–; betels
BESIDE	–; besides	**BETH**	–; beths
BESIEGE	–; besieged, besieger, besieges	**BETHANK**	–; bethanks
		BETHEL	–; bethels
		BETHINK	–; bethinks
BESLIME	–; beslimed, beslimes	**BETHORN**	–; bethorns
		BETHUMP	–; bethumps
BESMEAR	–; besmears	**BETIDE**	–; betided, betides
BESMILE	–; besmiled, besmiles		
		BETIME	–; betimes
BESMOKE	–; besmoked, besmokes	**BETISE**	–; betises
		BETOKEN	–; betokens
		BETON	–; betons, botony
BESMUT	–; besmuts		
BESNOW	–; besnows	**BETOOK**	–; –
BESOM	–; besoms	**BETRAY**	–; betrays
BESOT	–; besots	**BETROTH**	–; betroths
BESPAKE	–; –	**BETS**	abets; –
BESPEAK	–; bespeaks	**BETTA**	–; bettas
BEST	–; bests	**BETTED**	abetted; –
BESTEAD	–; besteads	**BETTER**	abetter; betters
BESTED	–; –		
BESTIAL	–; –	**BETTERS**	abetters;
BESTING	–; –	**BETTING**	abetting;
BESTIR	–; bestirs	**BETTOR**	abettor; bettors
BESTOW	–; bestows		
		BETTORS	abettors;

BETWEEN	–; –	BI	obi; bib, bid,
BETWIXT	–; –		big, bin, bio,
BEVEL	–; bevels		bis, bit
BEVELED	–; –	BIALY	–; bialys
BEVELER	–; bevelers	BIAS	obias; –
BEVIES	–; –	BIASED	–; –
BEVOMIT	–; bevomits	BIASES	–; –
BEVOR	–; bevors	BIASING	–; –
BEVY	–; –	BIAXAL	–; –
BEWAIL	–; bewails	BIAXIAL	–; –
BEWARE	–; bewared,	BIB	–; bibb, bibs
	bewares	BIBASIC	–; –
BEWEARY	–; –	BIBB	–; bibbs
BEWEEP	–; beweeps	BIBBED	–; –
BEWEPT	–; –	BIBBER	–; bibbers,
BEWIG	–; bewigs		bibbery
BEWITCH	–; –	BIBBING	–; –
BEWORM	–; beworms	BIBCOCK	–; bibcocks
BEWORRY	–; –	BIBELOT	–; bibelots
BEWRAP	–; bewraps,	BIBLE	–; bibles
	bewrapt	BIBLES	–; bibless
BEWRAY	–; bewrays	BIBLIKE	–; –
BEY	obey; beys	BICARB	–; bicarbs
BEYLIC	–; beylics	BICE	–; bices
BEYLIK	–; beyliks	BICEPS	–; –
BEYOND	–; beyonds	BICES	ibices; –
BEYS	obeys; –	BICKER	–; bickers
BEZANT	–; bezants	BICOLOR	–; bicolors
BEZEL	–; bezels	BICORN	–; bicorne
BEZIL	–; bezils	BICORNE	–; bicornes
BEZIQUE	–; beziques	BICRON	–; bicrons
BEZOAR	–; bezoars	BICYCLE	–; bicycled,
BEZZANT	–; bezzants		bicycler,
BHAKTA	–; bhaktas		bicycles
BHAKTI	–; bhaktis	BID	–; bide, bids
BHANG	–; bhangs	BIDARKA	–; bidarkas
BHEESTY	–; –	BIDDEN	–; –
BHISTIE	–; bhisties	BIDDER	–; bidders
BHOOT	–; bhoots	BIDDING	–; –
BHUT	–; bhuts	BIDDY	–; –

BIDE	abide;	BIGNESS	–; –
	bided, bider,	BIGOT	–; bigots
	bides, bidet	BIGOTED	–; –
BIDED	abided; –	BIGOTRY	–; –
BIDER	abider;	BIGWIG	–; bigwigs
	biders	BIJOU	–; bijous,
BIDERS	abiders; –		bijoux
BIDES	abides; –		
BIDET	–; bidets	BIKE	–; biked,
BIDING	abiding; –		biker, bikes
BIELD	–; bields	BIKER	–; bikers
BIELDED	–; –	BIKEWAY	–; bikeways
BIER	–; biers	BIKING	–; –
BIFF	–; biffs, biffy	BIKINI	–; bikinis
BIFFED	–; –	BILBO	–; bilboa,
BIFFIES	–; –		bilbos
BIFFIN	–; biffing,	BILBOA	–; bilboas
	biffins	BILBOES	–; –
BIFID	–; –	BILE	–; biles
BIFIDLY	–; –	BILGE	–; bilged,
BIFILAR	–; –		bilges
BIFLEX	–; –	BILGIER	–; –
BIFOCAL	–; bifocals	BILGING	–; –
BIFOLD	–; –	BILGY	–; –
BIFORM	–; –	BILIARY	–; –
BIG	–; –	BILIOUS	–; –
BIGAMY	–; –	BILK	–; bilks
BIGEYE	–; bigeyes	BILKED	–; –
BIGGER	–; –	BILKER	–; bilkers
BIGGEST	–; –	BILKING	–; –
BIGGETY	–; –	BILL	–; bills, billy
BIGGIN	–; bigging,	BILLBUG	–; billbugs
	biggins	BILLED	–; –
BIGGISH	–; –	BILLER	–; billers
BIGGITY	–; –	BILLET	–; billets
BIGHEAD	–; bigheads	BILLIE	–; billies
BIGHORN	–; bighorns	BILLING	–; billings
BIGHT	–; bights	BILLION	–; billions
BIGHTED	–; –	BILLON	–; billons,
BIGLY	–; –	BILLOW	–; billows,
			billowy

BILOBED	–; –	BIOPSY	–; –
BILSTED	–; bilsteds	BIOPTIC	–; –
BILTONG	–; biltongs	BIOTA	–; biotas
BIMA	–; bimah, bimas	BIOTIC	abiotic; biotics
BIMAH	–; bimahs	BIOTIN	–; biotins
BIMETAL	–; bimetals	BIOTITE	–; biotites
BIMODAL	–; –	BIOTOPE	–; biotopes
BIN	–; bind, bine, bins, bint	BIOTRON	–; biotrons
		BIOTYPE	–; biotypes
BINAL	–; –	BIPACK	–; bipacks
BINARY	–; –	BIPARTY	–; –
BINATE	–; –	BIPED	–; bipeds
BIND	–; binds	BIPEDAL	–; –
BINDER	–; binders, bindery	BIPLANE	–; biplanes
		BIPOD	–; bipods
BINDING	–; bindings	BIPOLAR	–; –
BINDLE	–; bindles	BIRCH	–; –
BINE	–; bines	BIRCHED	–; –
BINGE	–; binges	BIRCHEN	–; –
BINGO	–; bingos	BIRCHES	–; –
BINIT	–; binits	BIRD	–; birds
BINNED	–; –	BIRDED	–; –
BINNING	–; –	BIRDER	–; birders
BINOCLE	–; binocles	BIRDIE	–; birdied, birdies
BINT	–; bints		
BIO	–; bios	BIREME	–; biremes
BIOCIDE	–; biocides	BIRETTA	–; birettas
BIOGEN	–; biogens, biogeny	BIRK	–; birks
		BIRKIE	–; birkies
BIOHERM	–; bioherms	BIRL	–; birls
BIOLOGY	–; –	BIRLE	–; birled, birler, birles
BIOMASS	–; –		
BIOME	–; biomes	BIRLER	–; birlers
BIONIC	–; bionics	BIRLING	–; birlings
BIONOMY	–; –	BIRR	–; birrs
BIONT	–; bionts	BIRRED	–; –
BIONTIC	–; –	BIRRING	–; –
BIOPSIC	–; –	BIRSE	–; birses
		BIRTH	–; births

BIRTHED	–; –	**BIVALVE**	–; bivalved,
BIS	ibis, obis,		bivalves
	bise, bisk	**BIVINYL**	–; bivinyls
BISCUIT	–; biscuits	**BIVOUAC**	–; bivouacs
BISE	–; bises	**BIZARRE**	–; bizarres
BISECT	–; bisects	**BIZE**	–; bizes
BISHOP	–; bishops	**BIZNAGA**	–; biznagas
BISK	–; bisks	**BIZONAL**	–; –
BISMUTH	–; bismuths	**BIZONE**	–; bizones
BISNAGA	–; bisnagas	**BLAB**	–; blabs
BISON	–; bisons	**BLABBED**	–; –
BISQUE	–; bisques	**BLABBER**	–; blabbers
BISTATE	–; –	**BLABBY**	–; –
BISTER	–; bisters	**BLACK**	–; blacks
BISTORT	–; bistorts	**BLACKED**	–; –
BISTRE	–; bistred,	**BLACKEN**	–; blackens
	bistres	**BLACKER**	–; –
BISTRO	–; bistros	**BLACKLY**	–; –
BIT	obit; bite,	**BLADDER**	–; bladders,
	bits, bitt		bladdery
BITABLE	–; –	**BLADE**	–; bladed,
BITCH	–; bitchy		blades
BITCHED	–; –	**BLAE**	–; –
BITCHES	–; –	**BLAH**	–; blahs
BITE	–; biter,	**BLAIN**	–; blains
	bites	**BLAME**	–; blamed,
BITER	–; biters		blamer,
BITING	–; –		blames
BITS	obits; bitsy	**BLAMER**	–; blamers
BITT	–; bitte,	**BLAMING**	–; –
	bitts, bitty	**BLANCH**	–; –
BITTE	–; bitted,	**BLAND**	–; –
	bitten, bitter	**BLANDER**	–; –
BITTER	–; bittern,	**BLANDLY**	–; –
	bitters	**BLANK**	–; blanks
BITTIER	–; –	**BLANKED**	–; –
BITTING	–; bittings	**BLANKER**	–; –
BITTOCK	–; bittocks	**BLANKET**	–; blankets
BITUMEN	–; bitumens	**BLANKLY**	–; –

BLARE	–; blared, blares	**BLEATER**	–; bleaters
		BLEB	–; blebs
BLARNEY	–; blarneys	**BLEBBY**	–; –
BLASE	–; –	**BLED**	–; –
BLAST	oblast; blasts, blasty	**BLEED**	–; bleeds
		BLEEDER	–; bleeders
BLASTED	–; –	**BLELLUM**	–; blellums
BLASTER	–; blasters	**BLEMISH**	–; –
BLASTIE	–; blastier, blasties	**BLENCH**	–; –
		BLEND	–; blende, blends
BLASTS	oblasts; –		
BLAT	–; blate, blats	**BLENDE**	–; blended, blender, blendes
BLATANT	–; –		
BLATE	ablate, oblate; –	**BLENDER**	–; blenders
		BLENNY	–; –
BLATHER	–; blathers	**BLENT**	–; –
BLATTED	–; –	**BLESBOK**	–; blesboks
BLATTER	–; blatters	**BLESS**	–; –
BLAUBOK	–; blauboks	**BLESSED**	–; –
BLAW	–; blawn, blaws	**BLESSER**	–; blessers
		BLEST	–; –
BLAWED	–; –	**BLET**	–; blets
BLAWING	–; –	**BLETHER**	–; blethers
BLAZE	ablaze; blazed, blazer, blazes	**BLEW**	–; –
		BLIGHT	–; blights, blighty
BLAZER	–; blazers	**BLIMEY**	–; –
BLAZING	–; –	**BLIMP**	–; blimps
BLAZON	–; blazons	**BLIMY**	–; –
BLEACH	–; –	**BLIN**	–; blind, blini
BLEAK	–; bleaks	**BLIND**	–; blinds
BLEAKER	–; –	**BLINDED**	–; –
BLEAKLY	–; –	**BLINDER**	–; blinders
BLEAR	–; blears, bleary	**BLINDLY**	–; –
		BLINI	–; blinis
BLEARED	–; –	**BLINK**	–; blinks
BLEAT	–; bleats	**BLINKED**	–; –
BLEATED	; –	**BLINKER**	–; blinkers
		BLINTZ	–; blintze

BLINTZE	–; blintzes	**BLOOPER**	–; bloopers
BLIP	; blips	**BLOSSOM**	, blossoms,
BLIPPED	–; –		blossomy
BLISS	–; –	**BLOT**	–; blots
BLISSES	–; –	**BLOTCH**	–; blotchy
BLISTER	–; blisters,	**BLOTTED**	–; –
	blistery	**BLOTTER**	–; blotters
BLITE	–; blites	**BLOTTO**	–; –
BLITHE	–; blither	**BLOTTY**	–; –
BLITHER	–; blithers	**BLOUSE**	–; bloused,
BLITZ	–; –		blouses
BLITZED	–; –	**BLOUSON**	–; blousons
BLITZES	–; –	**BLOUSY**	–; –
BLOAT	–; bloats	**BLOW**	–; blown,
BLOATED	–; –		blows, blowy
BLOATER	–; bloaters	**BLOWBY**	–; blowbys
BLOB	–; blobs	**BLOWER**	–; blowers
BLOBBED	–; –	**BLOWFLY**	–; –
BLOC	–; block,	**BLOWGUN**	–; blowguns
	blocs	**BLOWIER**	–; –
BLOCK	–; blocks,	**BLOWING**	–; –
	blocky	**BLOWN**	–; –
BLOCKED	–; –	**BLOWOFF**	–; blowoffs
BLOCKER	–; blockers	**BLOWOUT**	–; blowouts
BLOKE	–; blokes	**BLOWSED**	–; –
BLOND	–; blonde,	**BLOWS**	–; blowsy
	blonds	**BLOWUP**	–; blowups
BLONDE	–; blonder,	**BLOWZED**	–; –
	blondes	**BLOWZY**	–; –
BLOOD	–; bloods,	**BLUBBER**	–; blubbers,
	bloody		blubbery
BLOODED	–; –	**BLUCHER**	–; bluchers
BLOOM	abloom;	**BLUE**	–; blued,
	blooms,		bluer, blues,
	bloomy		bluet, bluey
BLOOMED	–; –	**BLUECAP**	–; bluecaps
BLOOMER	–; bloomers,	**BLUEFIN**	–; bluefins
	bloomery	**BLUEGUM**	–; bluegums
BLOOP	–; bloops	**BLUEING**	–; blueings
BLOOPED	–; –	**BLUEJAY**	–; bluejays

BLUELY	–; –	bog, boo,
BLUES	–; bluest,	bop, bos,
	bluesy	bot, bow,
BLUET	–; bluets	box, boy
BLUEY	–; blueys	**BOA** –; boar,
BLUFF	–; bluffs	boas, boat
BLUFFED	–; –	**BOAR** –; board,
BLUFFER	–; bluffers	boars, boart
BLUFFLY	–; –	**BOARD** aboard;
BLUING	–; bluings	boards
BLUISH	–; –	**BOARDED** –; –
BLUME	–; blumed,	**BOARDER** –; boarders
	blumes	**BOARISH** –; –
BLUMING	–; –	**BOART** –; boarts
BLUNDER	–; blunders	**BOAST** –; boasts
BLUNGE	–; blunged,	**BOASTED** –; –
	blunger,	**BOASTER** –; boasters
	blunges	**BOAT** –; boats
BLUNGER	–; blungers	**BOATED** –; –
BLUNT	–; blunts	**BOATEL** –; boatels
BLUNTED	–; –	**BOATER** –; boaters
BLUNTER	–; –	**BOATING** –; boatings
BLUNTLY	–; –	**BOATMAN** –; –
BLUR	–; blurb,	**BOATMEN** –; –
	blurs, blurt	**BOB** –; bobs
BLURB	–; blurbs	**BOBBED** –; –
BLURRED	–; –	**BOBBER** –; bobbers,
BLURRY	–; –	bobbery
BLURT	–; blurts	**BOBBIES** –; –
BLURTED	–; –	**BOBBIN** –; bobbing
BLURTER	–; blurters	**BOBBLE** –; bobbled,
BLUSH	ablush; –	bobbles
BLUSHED	–; –	**BOBBY** –; –
BLUSHER	–; blushers	**BOBCAT** –; bobcats
BLUSHES	–; –	**BOBECHE** –; bobeches
BLUSTER	–; blusters,	**BOBSLED** –; bobsleds
	blustery	**BOBSTAY** –; bobstays
BLYPE	–; blypes	**BOBTAIL** –; bobtails
BO	abo; boa,	**BOCCE** –; bocces
	bob, bod,	

BOCCI	–; boccia, boccis	**BOGLE**	–; bogles
		BOGUS	–; –
BOCCIA	–; boccias	**BOGWOOD**	–;
BOCCIE	–; boccies		bogwoods
BOCHE	–; boches	**BOGYISM**	–; bogyisms
BOCK	–; bocks	**BOGYMAN**	–; –
BOD	–; bode, bods, body	**BOGYMEN**	–; –
		BOHEA	–; boheas
BODE	abode; boded, bodes	**BOHEMIA**	–; bohemian, bohemias
BODED	aboded; –	**BOHUNK**	–; bohunks
BODEGA	–; bodegas	**BOIL**	aboil; boils
BODES	abodes; –	**BOILED**	–; –
BODICE	–; bodices	**BOILER**	–; boilers
BODIED	–; –	**BOILING**	–; –
BODIES	–; –	**BOITE**	–; boites
BODILY	–; –	**BOLA**	–; bolar, bolas
BODING	aboding; bodings	**BOLASES**	–; –
BODKIN	–; bodkins	**BOLD**	–; –
BOFF	–; boffs	**BOLDER**	–; –
BOFFIN	–; boffins	**BOLDEST**	–; –
BOFFO	–; boffos	**BOLDLY**	–; –
BOFFOLA	–; boffolas	**BOLE**	obole; boles
BOG	–; bogs, bogy	**BOLERO**	–; boleros
		BOLES	oboles; –
BOGAN	–; bogans	**BOLETE**	–; boletes
BOGBEAN	–; bogbeans	**BOLETI**	–; –
BOGEY	–; bogeys	**BOLETUS**	–; –
BOGEYED	–; –	**BOLIDE**	–; bolides
BOGGED	–; –	**BOLIVAR**	–; bolivars
BOGGIER	–; –	**BOLIVIA**	–; bolivias
BOGGING	–; –	**BOLL**	–; bolls
BOGGISH	–; –	**BOLLARD**	–; bollards
BOGGLE	–; boggled, boggles	**BOLLED**	–; –
		BOLLING	–; –
BOGGLER	–; bogglers	**BOLLIX**	–; –
BOGGY	–; –	**BOLLOX**	–; –
BOGIE	–; bogies	**BOLO**	–; bolos

BOLOGNA	−; bolognas	**BONGING**	−; −
BOLONEY	−; boloneys	**BONGO**	−; bongos
BOLSON	−; bolsons	**BONGOES**	−; −
BOLSTER	−; bolsters	**BONIER**	−; −
BOLT	−; bolts	**BONIEST**	−; −
BOLTED	−; −	**BONING**	−; −
BOLTER	−; bolters	**BONITA**	−; bonitas
BOLTING	−; −	**BONITO**	−; bonitos
BOLUS	obolus; −	**BONKERS**	−; −
BOLUSES	−; −	**BONNE**	−; bonnes, bonnet
BOMB	−; bombe, bombs	
		BONNET	−; bonnets
BOMBARD	−; bombards	**BONNIE**	−; bonnier
BOMBAST	−; bombasts	**BONNILY**	−; −
BOMBE	−; bombed, bomber, bombes	**BONNOCK**	−; bonnocks
		BONNY	−; −
		BONSAI	−; bonsais
~~BOMBER~~	−; bombers	**BONUS**	−; −
~~BOMBING~~	−; bombings	**BONUSES**	−; −
BOMBYX	−; −	**BONY**	ebony; −
BONACI	−; bonacis	**BONZE**	−; bonzer, bonzes
BONANZA	−; bonanzas	
BONBON	−; bonbons	**BOO**	−; boob, book, boom, boon, boor, boos, boot
BOND	−; bonds	
BONDAGE	−; bondages	
BONDED	−; −	
BONDER	−; bonders	**BOOB**	−; boobs, booby
BONDING	−; −	
BONDMAN	−; −	
BONDMEN	−; −	**BOOBIES**	−; −
BONDUC	−; bonducs	**BOOBOO**	−; booboos
BONE	−; boned, boner, bones, boney	**BOODLE**	−; boodled, boodler, boodles
		BOODLER	−; boodlers
		BOOED	−; −
BONER	−; boners	**BOOGER**	−; boogers
BONFIRE	−; bonfires	**BOOGIE**	−; boogies
BONG	−; bongo, bongs	**BOOHOO**	−; boohoos
		BOOING	−; −
BONGED	−; −	**BOOK**	−; books

BOOKED	–; –	**BOOZILY**	–; –
BOOKEND	–; bookends	**BOOZING**	–; –
BOOKER	–; bookers	**BOOZY**	–; –
BOOKIE	–; bookies	**BOP**	–; bops
BOOKING	–; bookings	**BOPPED**	–; –
BOOKISH	–; –	**BOPPER**	–; boppers
BOOKLET	–; booklets	**BOPPING**	–; –
BOOKMAN	–; –	**BORA**	–; boras
BOOKMEN	–; –	**BORACES**	–; –
BOOM	–; booms, boomy	**BORACIC**	–; –
		BORAGE	–; borages
BOOMED	–; –	**BORANE**	–; boranes
BOOMER	–; boomers	**BORATE**	–; borated, borates
BOOMIER	–; –		
BOOMING	–; –	**BORAX**	–; –
BOOMKIN	–; boomkins	**BORAXES**	;
BOOMLET	–; boomlets	**BORAZON**	–; borazons
BOON	aboon; boons	**BORDEL**	–; bordels
		BORDER	–; borders
BOONS	aboons; –	**BORDURE**	–; bordures
BOONIES	–; –	**BORE**	–; bored, borer, bores
BOOR	–; boors		
BOORISH	–; –	**BOREAL**	–; –
BOOST	–; boosts	**BOREDOM**	–; boredoms
BOOSTED	–; –	**BORER**	–; borers
BOOSTER	–; boosters	**BORIC**	–; –
BOOT	–; booth, boots, booty	**BORIDE**	–; borides
		BORING	aboring; borings
BOOTED	–; –		
BOOTEE	–; bootees	**BORN**	–; borne
BOOTERY	–; –	**BORNEOL**	–; borneols
BOOTH	–; booths	**BORNITE**	–; bornites
BOOTIE	–; booties	**BORON**	–; borons
BOOTING	–; –	**BORONIC**	–; –
BOOTLEG	–; bootlegs	**BOROUGH**	–; boroughs
BOOZE	–; boozed, boozer, boozes	**BORROW**	–; borrows
		BORSCH	–; borscht
		BORSHT	–; borshts
BOOZER	–; boozers	**BORSTAL**	–; borstals
BOOZIER	–; –		

BORT	abort; borts, borty, bortz	**BOTCHER**	–; botchers, botchery
BORTS	aborts; –	**BOTCHES**	–; –
BORTZ	–; –	**BOTEL**	–; botels
BORTZES	–; –	**BOTFLY**	–; –
BORZOI	–; borzois	**BOTH**	–; –
BOS	abos; bosh, bosk, boss	**BOTHER**	–; bothers
		BOTONEE	–; botoneee
BOSCAGE	–; boscages	**BOTT**	–; botts
BOSHBOK	–; boshboks	**BOTTLE**	–; bottled, bottler, bottles
BOSHES	–; –		
BOSK	–; bosks, bosky		
		BOTTLER	–; bottlers
BOSKAGE	–; boskages	**BOTTOM**	–; bottoms
BOSKER	–; –	**BOTULIN**	–; botulins
BOSKET	–; boskets	**BOUCLE**	–; boucles
BOSKIER	–; –	**BOUDOIR**	–; boudoirs
BOSOM	–; bosoms, bosomy	**BOUFFE**	–; bouffes
		BOUGH	–; boughs, bought
BOSOMED	–; –		
BOSON	–; bosons	**BOUGHED**	–; –
BOSQUE	–; bosques, bosquet	**BOUGHT**	abought; –
		BOUGIE	–; bougies
BOSQUET	–; bosquets	**BOULDER**	–; boulders, bouldery
BOSS	–; bossy		
BOSSDOM	–; bossdoms	**BOULE**	–; boules
BOSSED	–; –	**BOULLE**	–; boulles
BOSSES	–; –	**BOUNCE**	–; bounced, bouncer, bounces
BOSSIER	–; –		
BOSSIES	–; bossiest		
BOSSILY	–; –	**BOUNCER**	–; bouncers
BOSSING	–; –	**BOUNCY**	–; –
BOSTON	–; bostons	**BOUND**	abound; bounds
BOSUN	–; bosuns		
BOT	–; both, bots, bott	**BOUNDED**	–; –
		BOUNDEN	–; –
BOTANIC	–; –	**BOUNDER**	–; bounders
BOTANY	–; –	**BOUNDS**	abounds; –
BOTCH	–; botchy	**BOUNTY**	–; –
BOTCHED	–; –	**BOUQUET**	–· bouquets

BOURBON	–; bourbons	**BOWMEN**	–; –
BOURDON	, bourdons	**BOWPOT**	, bowpots
BOURG	–; bourgs	**BOWSE**	–; bowsed,
BOURN	–; bourne,		bowses
	bourns	**BOWSHOT**	–; bowshots
BOURNE	–; bournee,	**BOWSING**	–; –
	bournes	**BOWWOW**	–; bowwow
BOURNEE	–; bournees	**BOWYER**	–; bowyers
BOURSE	–; bourses	**BOX**	–; boxy
BOUSE	–; boused,	**BOXCAR**	–; boxcars
	bouses	**BOXED**	–; –
BOUSING	–; –	**BOXER**	–; boxers
BOUSY	–; –	**BOXES**	–; –
BOUT	about; bouts	**BOXFISH**	–; –
BOVID	–; bovids	**BOXFUL**	–; boxfuls
BOVINE	–; bovines	**BOXHAUL**	–; boxhauls
BOW	–; bowl,	**BOXIER**	–; –
	bows	**BOXIEST**	–; –
BOWED	–; –	**BOXING**	–; boxings
BOWEL	–; bowels	**BOXLIKE**	–; –
BOWELED	–; –	**BOXWOOD**	–;
BOWER	–; bowers,		boxwoods
	bowery	**BOXY**	–; –
BOWERED	–; –	**BOY**	–; boyo,
BOWFIN	–; bowfins		boys
BOWHEAD	–;	**BOYAR**	–; boyard,
	bowheads		boyars
BOWING	–; bowings	**BOYARD**	–; boyards
BOWKNOT	–; bowknots	**BOYCOTT**	–; boycotts
BOWL	–; bowls	**BOYHOOD**	–; boyhoods
BOWLDER	–; bowlders	**BOYISH**	–; –
BOWLED	–; –	**BOYLA**	–; boylas
BOWLEG	–; bowlegs	**BOYO**	–; boyos
BOWLER	–; bowlers	**BOZO**	–; bozos
BOWLESS	–; –	**BRA**	–; brad,
BOWLFUL	–; bowlfuls		brae, brag,
BOWLIKE	–; –		bran, bras,
BOWLINE	–; bowlines		brat, braw,
BOWLING	–; bowlings		bray
BOWMAN	–; –	**BRABBLE**	–; brabbled,

brabbler,
brabbles

BRACE   –; braced,
bracer,
braces

BRACER   –; bracero,
bracers

BRACERO   –; braceros

BRACH   –; –

BRACHES   –; –

BRACHET   –; brachets

BRACING   –; bracings

BRACKEN   –; brackens

BRACKET   –; brackets

BRACT   –; bracts

BRACTED   –; –

BRAD   –; brads

BRADAWL   –; bradawls

BRADDED   –; –

BRADOON   –; bradoons

BRAE   –; braes

BRAG   –; brags

BRAGGED   –; –

BRAGGER   –; braggers

BRAGGY   –; –

BRAHMA   –; brahmas

BRAID   –; braids

BRAIDED   –; –

BRAIDER   –; braiders

BRAIL   –; brails

BRAILED   –; –

BRAILLE   –; brailled,
brailles

BRAIN   –; brains,
brainy

BRAINED   –; –

BRAISE   –; braised,
braises

BRAIZE   –; braizes

BRAKE   –; braked,
brakes

BRAKING   –; –

BRAKY   –; –

BRAMBLE   –; brambled,
brambles

BRAMBLY   –; –

BRAN   –; brand,
brank, brans

BRANCH   –; branchy

BRAND   –; brands,
brandy

BRANDED   –; –

BRANDER   –; branders

BRANK   –; branks

BRANNED   –; –

BRANNER   –; branners

BRANNY   –; –

BRANT   –; brants

BRASH   –; brashy

BRASHER   –; –

BRASHES   –; brashest

BRASHLY   –; –

BRASIER   –; brasiers

BRASIL   –; brasils

BRASS   –; brassy

BRASSES   –; –

BRASSIE   –; brassier,
brassies

BRAT   –; brats

BRATTLE   –; brattled,
brattles

BRATTY   –; –

BRAVA   –; bravas

BRAVADO   –; bravados

BRAVE   –; braved,
braver,
braves

BRAVELY   –; –

BRAVER	—; bravers, bravery	**BREADTH**	—; breadths
BRAVES	—; bravest	**BREAK**	—; breaks
BRAVING	—; —	**BREAKER**	—; breakers
BRAVO	—; bravos	**BREAKUP**	—; breakups
BRAVOED	—; —	**BREAM**	—; breams
BRAVOES	—; —	**BREAMED**	—; —
BRAVURA	—; bravuras	**BREAST**	abreast; breasts
BRAVURE	—; —	**BREATH**	—; breathe,
BRAW	—; brawl, brawn, braws		breaths, breathy
BRAWER	—; —	**BREATHE**	—; breathed, breather,
BRAWEST	—; —		breathes
BRAWL	—; brawls, brawly	**BRECCIA**	—; breccial, breccias
BRAWLED	—; —	**BRECHAM**	—; brechams
BRAWLER	—; brawlers	**BRECHAN**	—; brechans
BRAWLIE	—; —	**BRED**	—; brede
BRAWN	—; brawns, brawny	**BREDE**	—; bredes
		BREE	—; breed, brees
BRAXIES	—; —		
BRAXY	—; —	**BREECH**	—; —
BRAY	—; brays	**BREED**	—; breeds
BRAYED	—; —	**BREEDER**	—; breeders
BRAYER	—; brayers	**BREEKS**	—; —
BRAYING	—; —	**BREEZE**	—; breezed,
BRAZA	—; brazas		breezes
BRAZE	—; brazed, brazen, brazer, brazes	**BREEZY**	—; —
		BREGMA	—; —
		BRENT	—; brents
		BREVE	—; breves, brevet
BRAZEN	—; brazens		
BRAZER	—; brazers	**BREVET**	—; brevets
BRAZIER	—; braziers	**BREVIER**	—; breviers
BRAZIL	—; brazils	**BREVITY**	—; —
BRAZING	—; —	**BREW**	—; brews
BREACH	—; —	**BREWAGE**	—; brewages
BREAD	—; breads	**BREWED**	—; —
BREADED	—; —		

BREWER	–; brewers, brewery	**BRIGADE**	–; brigaded, brigades
BREWING	–; brewings	**BRIGAND**	–; brigands
BREWIS	–; –	**BRIGHT**	–; brights
BRIAR	–; briard, briars, briary	**BRILL**	–; brills
		BRIM	–; brims
BRIARD	–; briards	**BRIMFUL**	–; brimfull
BRIBE	–; bribed, briber, bribes	**BRIMMED**	–; –
		BRIMMER	–; brimmers
BRIBER	–; bribers, bribery	**BRIN**	–; brine, bring, brink, brins, briny
BRIBING	–; –		
BRICK	–; bricks, bricky	**BRINDED**	–; –
		BRINDLE	–; brindled, brindles
BRICKED	–; –		
BRICKLE	–; brickles	**BRINE**	–; brined, briner, brines
BRICOLE	–; bricoles		
BRIDAL	–; bridals	**BRINER**	–; briners
BRIDE	–; brides	**BRINING**	–; –
BRIDGE	abridge; bridged, bridges	**BRING**	–; brings
		BRINGER	–; bringers
		BRINIER	–; –
		BRINIES	–; briniest
BRIDGED	abridged; –	**BRINING**	–; –
BRIDGES	abridges; –	**BRINISH**	–; –
BRIDLE	–; bridled, bridler, bridles	**BRINK**	–; brinks
		BRIO	–; brios
		BRIOCHE	–; brioches
BRIDLER	–; bridlers	**BRIONY**	–; –
BRIDOON	–; bridoons	**BRIQUET**	–; briquets
BRIE	–; brief, brier, bries	**BRISK**	–; brisks
		BRISKED	–; –
BRIEF	–; briefs	**BRISKER**	–; –
BRIEFED	–; –	**BRISKET**	–; briskets
BRIEFER	–; briefers	**BRISKLY**	–; –
BRIEFLY	–; –	**BRISTLE**	–; bristled, bristles
BRIER	–; briers, briery		
		BRISTLY	–; –
BRIG	–; brigs	**BRISTOL**	–; bristols
		BRIT	–; brits, britt

BRITSKA	–; britskas	**BROMIDE**	–; bromides
BRITT	–; britts	**BROMIN**	–; bromine,
BRITTLE	–; brittled,		bromins
	brittler,	**BROMINE**	–; bromines
	brittles	**BROMISM**	–; bromisms
BRITZKA	–; britzkas	**BROMO**	–; bromos
BROACH	abroach; –	**BRONC**	–; bronco,
BROAD	abroad;		broncs
	broads	**BRONCHI**	–; bronchia
BROADAX	–; broadaxe	**BRONCHO**	–; bronchos
BROADEN	–; broadens	**BRONCO**	–; broncos
BROADER	–; –	**BRONZE**	–; bronzed,
BROADLY	–; –		bronzer,
BROCADE	–;		bronzes
	brocaded,	**BRONZER**	–; bronzers
	brocades	**BRONZY**	–; –
BROCHE	–; –	**BROO**	–; brood,
BROCK	–; brocks		brook,
BROCKET	–; brockets		broom,
BROCOLI	–; brocolis		broos
BROGAN	–; brogans	**BROOCH**	–; –
BROGUE	–; brogues	**BROOD**	–; broods,
BROIDER	–; broiders,		broody
	broidery	**BROODED**	–; –
BROIL	–; broils	**BROODER**	–; brooders
BROILED	–; –	**BROOK**	–; brooks
BROILER	–; broilers	**BROOKED**	–; –
BROKAGE	–; brokages	**BROOM**	–; brooms,
BROKE	–; broken,		broomy
	broker	**BROOMED**	–; –
BROKER	–; brokers	**BROSE**	–; broses
BROLLY	–; –	**BROSY**	–; –
BROMAL	–; bromals	**BROTH**	–; broths,
BROMATE	–;		brothy
	bromated,	**BROTHEL**	–; brothels
	bromates	**BROTHER**	–; brothers
BROME	–; bromes	**BROUGHT**	–; –
BROMIC	–; –	**BROW**	–; brown,
BROMID	–; bromide,		brows
	bromids		

BROWN	–; browns, browny	**BRUT**	–; brute
BROWNED	–;	**BRUTAL**	–; –
BROWNER	–; –	**BRUTE**	–; bruted, brutes
BROWNIE	–; brownier, brownies	**BRUTELY**	–; –
BROWSE	–; browsed, browser, browses	**BRUTIFY**	–; –
		BRUTING	–; –
		BRUTISH	–; –
		BRUTISM	–; brutisms
BROWSER	–; browsers	**BRUXISM**	–; bruxisms
BRUCIN	–; brucine, brucins	**BRYONY**	–; –
		BUB	–; bubo, bubs
BRUCINE	–; brucines		
BRUGH	–; brughs	**BUBAL**	–; bubale, bubals
BRUIN	–; bruins		
BRUISE	–; bruised, bruiser, bruises	**BUBALE**	–; bubales
		BUBALIS	–; –
		BUBBIES	–; –
BRUISER	–; bruisers	**BUBBLE**	abubble; bubbled, bubbler, bubbles
BRUIT	–; bruits		
BRUITED	–; –		
BRUITER	–; bruiters		
BRULOT	–; brulots	**BUBBLER**	–; bubblers
BRULYIE	–; brulyies	**BUBBLY**	–; –
BRULZIE	–; brulzies	**BUBBY**	–; –
BRUMAL	–; –	**BUBINGA**	–; bubingas
BRUMBY	–; –	**BUBOED**	–; –
BRUME	–; brumes	**BUBOES**	–; –
BRUMOUS	–; –	**BUBONIC**	–; –
BRUNCH	–; –	**BUCCAL**	–; –
BRUNET	–; brunets	**BUCK**	–; bucks
BRUNT	–; brunts	**BUCKED**	–; –
BRUSH	–; brushy	**BUCKEEN**	–; buckeens
BRUSHED	–; –	**BUCKER**	–; buckers
BRUSHER	–; brushers	**BUCKET**	–; buckets
BRUSHES	–; –	**BUCKEYE**	–; buckeyes
BRUSHUP	–; brushups	**BUCKISH**	–; –
BRUSK	–; –	**BUCKLE**	–; buckled, buckler, buckles
BRUSKER	–; –		
BRUSQUE	–; brusquer		

BUCKLER	–; bucklers	**BUGGER**	–; buggers,
BUCKOES	,		buggory
BUCKRA	–; buckram,	**BUGGIER**	–; –
	buckras	**BUGGIES**	–; buggiest
BUCKRAM	–; buckrams	**BUGGING**	–; –
BUCKSAW	–; bucksaws	**BUGGY**	–; –
BUCOLIC	–; bucolics	**BUGLE**	–; bugled,
BUD	–; buds		bugler,
BUDDED	–; –		bugles
BUDDER	–; budders	**BUGLER**	–; buglers
BUDDIES	–; –	**BUGLING**	–; –
BUDDING	–; –	**BUGLOSS**	–; –
BUDDLE	–; buddles	**BUGSEED**	–; bugseeds
BUDDY	–; –	**BUGSHA**	–; bugshas
BUDGE	–; budged,	**BUHL**	–; buhls
	budger,	**BUHR**	–; buhrs
	budges,	**BUILD**	–; builds
	budget	**BUILDED**	–; –
BUDGER	–; budgers	**BUILDER**	–; builders
BUDGET	–; budgets	**BUILDUP**	–; buildups
BUDGIE	–; budgies	**BUILT**	–; –
BUDGING	–; –	**BUIRDLY**	–; –
BUDLESS	–; –	**BULB**	–; bulbs
BUDLIKE	–; –	**BULBAR**	–; –
BUFF	–; buffi,	**BULBED**	–; –
	buffo, buffs,	**BULBEL**	–; bulbels
	buffy	**BULBIL**	–; bulbils
BUFFALO	–; buffalos	**BULBOUS**	–; –
BUFFED	–; –	**BULBUL**	–; bulbuls
BUFFER	–; buffers	**BULGE**	–; bulged,
BUFFET	–; buffets		bulger,
BUFFIER	–; –		bulges
BUFFO	–; buffos	**BULGER**	–; bulgers
BUFFOON	–; buffoons	**BULGIER**	–; –
BUG	–; bugs	**BULGING**	–; –
BUGABOO	–; bugaboos	**BULGUR**	–; bulgurs
BUGBANE	–; bugbanes	**BULGY**	–; –
BUGBEAR	–; bugbears	**BULIMIA**	–; bulimiac,
BUGEYE	–; bugeyes		bulimias
BUGGED	–; –	**BULIMIC**	–; –

BULK	–; bulks, bulky	**BUMMING**	–; –
		BUMP	–; bumps, bumpy
BULKAGE	–; bulkages		
BULKED	–; –	**BUMPED**	–; –
BULKIER	–; –	**BUMPER**	–; bumpers
BULKILY	–; –	**BUMPIER**	–; –
BULKING	–; –	**BUMPILY**	–; –
BULKY	–; –	**BUMPING**	–; –
BULL	–; bulla, bulls, bully	**BUMPKIN**	–; bumpkins
		BUN	–; bund, bung, bunk, bunn, buns, bunt
BULLA	–; bullae		
BULLACE	–; bullaces		
BULLATE	–; –		
BULLBAT	–; bullbats	**BUNCH**	–; bunchy
BULLDOG	–; bulldogs	**BUNCHED**	–; –
BULLED	–; –	**BUNCHES**	–; –
BULLET	–; bullets	**BUNCO**	–; buncos
BULLING	–; –	**BUNCOED**	–; –
BULLIED	–; –	**BUND**	–; bunds
BULLIER	–; –	**BUNDIST**	–; bundists
BULLIES	–; bulliest	**BUNDLE**	–; bundled, bundler, bundles
BULLION	–; bullions		
BULLISH	–; –		
BULLOCK	–; bullocks, bullocky	**BUNDLER**	–; bundlers
		BUNG	–; bungs
BULLOUS	–; –	**BUNGED**	–; –
BULLPEN	–; bullpens	**BUNGING**	–; –
BULRUSH	–; –	**BUNGLE**	–; bungled, bungler, bungles
BULWARK	–; bulwarks		
BUM	–; bumf, bump, bums		
BUMBLE	–; bumbled, bumbler, bumbles	**BUNGLER**	–; bunglers
		BUNION	–; bunions
		BUNK	–; bunko, bunks
BUMBLER	–; bumblers	**BUNKED**	–; –
BUMBOAT	–; bumboats	**BUNKER**	–; bunkers
BUMF	–; bumfs	**BUNKING**	–; –
BUMKIN	–; bumkins	**BUNKO**	–; bunkos
BUMMED	–; –	**BUNKOED**	–; –
BUMMER	–; bummers	**BUNKUM**	–; bunkums

BUNN	–; bunns, bunny	**BURGEON**	–; burgeons
		BURGER	–; burgers
BUNNIES	–; –	**BURGESS**	–; –
BUNT	–; bunts	**BURGH**	–; burghs
BUNTED	–; –	**BURGHAL**	–; –
BUNTER	–; bunters	**BURGHER**	–; burghers
BUNTING	–; buntings	**BURGLAR**	–; burglars, burglary
BUNYA	–; bunyas		
BUOY	–; buoys	**BURGLE**	–; burgled, burgles
BUOYAGE	–; buoyages		
BUOYANT	–; –	**BURGOO**	–; burgoos
BUOYED	–; –	**BURGOUT**	–; burgouts
BUOYING	–; –	**BURIAL**	–; burials
BUQSHA	–; buqshas	**BURIED**	–; –
BUR	–; bura, burd, burg, burl, burn, burp, burr, burs, bury	**BURIER**	–; buriers
		BURIES	–; –
		BURIN	–; burins
		BURKE	–; burked, burker, burkes
BURA	–; buran, buras		
BURAN	–; burans	**BURKER**	–; burkers
BURBLE	–; burbled, burbler, burbles	**BURKITE**	–; burkites
		BURL	–; burls, burly
BURBLER	–; burblers	**BURLAP**	–; burlaps
BURBLY	–; –	**BURLED**	;
BURBOT	–; burbots	**BURLER**	–; burlers
BURD	–; burds	**BURLESK**	–; burlesks
BURDEN	–; burdens	**BURLEY**	–; burleys
BURDIE	–; burdies	**BURLILY**	–; –
BURDOCK	–; burdocks	**BURLING**	–; –
BUREAU	–; bureaus, bureaux	**BURN**	–; burns, burnt
		BURNED	–; –
BURET	–; burets	**BURNER**	–; burners
BURETTE	–; burettes	**BURNET**	–; burnets
BURG	–; burgh, burgs	**BURNIE**	–; burnies
		BURNING	–; burnings
BURGAGE	–; burgages	**BURNISH**	–; –
BURGEE	–; burgees	**BURNOUT**	–; burnouts

BURP	–; burps	BUSHED	–; –
BURPED	–; –	BUSHEL	–; bushels
BURPING	–; –	BUSHER	–; bushers
BURR	–; burro, burrs, burry	BUSHES	–; bushes
		BUSHIDO	–; bushidos
BURRED	–; –	BUSHIER	–; –
BURRER	–; burrers	BUSHILY	–; –
BURRIER	–; –	BUSHING	–; bushings
BURRIES	–; burriest	BUSHMAN	–; –
BURRING	–; –	BUSHMEN	–; –
BURRO	–; burros, burrow	BUSHTIT	–; bushtits
		BUSIED	–; –
BURROW	–; burrows	BUSIER	–; –
BURRY	–; –	BUSIES	–; busiest
BURS	–; bursa, burse, burst	BUSILY	–; –
		BUSING	abusing; busings
BURSA	–; bursae, bursal, bursar, bursas		
		BUSK	–; busks
		BUSKED	–; –
		BUSKER	–; buskers
BURSAR	–; bursars, bursary	BUSKIN	–; busking, buskins
BURSATE	–; –	BUSMAN	–; –
BURSE	–; burses	BUSMEN	–; –
BURSEED	–; burseeds	BUSS	–; –
BURST	–; bursts	BUSSED	–; –
BURSTED	–; –	BUSSES	–; –
BURSTER	–; bursters	BUSSING	–; bussings
BURTHEN	–; burthens	BUST	–; busts, busty
BURTON	–; burtons		
BURWEED	–; burweeds	BUSTARD	–; bustards
BUS	–; bush, busk, buss, bust, busy	BUSTED	–; –
		BUSTER	–; busters
		BUSTIC	–; bustics
BUSBIES	–; –	BUSTIER	–; –
BUSBOY	–; busboys	BUSTING	–; –
BUSBY	–; –	BUSTLE	–; bustled, bustles
BUSED	abused; –		
BUSES	abuses; –	BUT	abut; buts, butt
BUSH	–; bushy		

BUTANE	–; butanes	**BUYING**	–; –
BUTANOL	–; butanols	**BUZZ**	abuzz; –
BUTCH	–; –	**BUZZARD**	–; buzzards
BUTCHER	–; butchers, butchery	**BUZZED**	–; –
		BUZZER	–; buzzers
BUTCHES	–; –	**BUZZING**	–; –
BUTENE	–; butenes	**BUZZWIG**	–; buzzwigs
BUTEO	–; buteos	**BWANA**	–; bwanas
BUTLER	–; butlers, butlery	**BY**	aby; bye, bys
BUTS	abuts; –	**BYE**	abye; byes
BUTT	–; butte, butts, butty	**BYES**	abyes; –
		BYELAW	–; byelaws
BUTTALS	abuttals; –	**BYGONE**	–; bygones
BUTTE	–; butter, buttes	**BYLAW**	–; bylaws
		BYLINE	–; bylined, byliner, bylines
BUTTED	abutted; –		
BUTTER	abutter; butters, buttery	**BYLINER**	–; byliners
		BYNAME	–; bynames
BUTTERS	abutters; –	**BYPASS**	–; –
BUTTIES	–; –	**BYPAST**	–; –
BUTTING	abutting; –	**BYPATH**	–; bypaths
BUTTOCK	–; buttocks	**BYPLAY**	–; byplays
BUTTON	–; buttons, buttony	**BYRE**	–; byres
		BYRL	–; byrls
BUTUT	–; bututs	**BYRLED**	–; –
BUTYL	–; butyls	**BYRLING**	–; –
BUTYRAL	–; butyrals	**BYRNIE**	–; byrnies
BUTYRIC	–; –	**BYROAD**	–; byroads
BUTYRIN	–; butyrins	**BYS**	abys; –
BUTYRYL	–; butyryls	**BYSSUS**	–; –
BUXOM	–; –	**BYTALK**	–; bytalks
BUXOMER	–; –	**BYTE**	–; bytes
BUXOMLY	–; –	**BYWAY**	–; byways
BUY	–; buys	**BYWORD**	–; bywords
BUYABLE	–; –	**BYWORK**	–; byworks
BUYER	–; buyers	**BYZANT**	–; byzants

C

CAB	scab; cabs	CACHING	–; –
CABAL	–; cabala, cabals	CACHOU	–; cachous
		CACIQUE	–; caciques
CABALA	–; cabalas	CACKLE	–; cackled, cackler, cackles
CABANA	–; cabanas		
CABARET	–; cabarets		
CABBAGE	–; cabbaged, cabbages	CACKLER	–; cacklers
		CACODYL	–; cacodyls
		CACTI	–; –
CABBALA	–; cabalah, cabbalas	CACTOID	–; –
		CACTUS	–; –
CABBIE	–; cabbies	CAD	scad; cade, cadi, cads
CABBY	scabby; –		
CABER	–; cabers	CADAVER	–; cadavers
CABEZON	–; cabezone, cabezons	CADDICE	–; caddices
		CADDIE	–; caddied, caddies
CABILDO	–; cabildos		
CABIN	–; cabins	CADDIS	–; caddish
CABINED	–; –	CADDIED	–; –
CABINET	–; cabinets	CADDIES	–; –
CABLE	–; cabled, cables, cablet	CADDY	–; –
		CADE	–; cades, cadet
CABLET	–; cablets	CADELLE	–; cadelles
CABMAN	–; –	CADENCE	–; cadenced, cadences
CABMEN	–; –		
CABOB	–; cabobs	CADENCY	–; –
CABOOSE	–; cabooses	CADENT	–; –
CABS	scabs; –	CADENZA	–; cadenzas
CACAO	–; cacaos	CADET	–; cadets
CACHE	–; cached, caches, cachet	CADGE	–; cadged, cadger, cadget
CACHET	–; cachets	CADGER	–; cadgers
CACHEXY	–; –		

CADGING	–; –	**CAISSON**	–; caissons
CADGY	–; –	**CAITIFF**	–; caitiffs
CADI	–; cadis	**CAJAPUT**	–; cajaputs
CADMIC	–; –	**CAJOLE**	–; cajoled,
CADMIUM	–; cadmiums		cajoler,
CADRE	–; cadres		cajoles
CADS	scads; –	**CAJOLER**	–; cajolers,
CAECA	–; caecal		cajolery
CAECUM	–; –	**CAJON**	–; –
CAEOMA	–; caeomas	**CAJONES**	–; –
CAESIUM	–; caesiums	**CAJUPUT**	–; cajuputs
CAESTUS	–; –	**CAKE**	–; caked,
CAESURA	–; caesurae,		cakes
	caesural,	**CAKING**	–; –
	caesuras	**CALAMAR**	–; calamars,
CAFE	–; cafes		calamary
CAFFEIN	–; caffeine,	**CALAMI**	–; –
	caffeins	**CALAMUS**	–; –
CAFTAN	–; caftans	**CALANDO**	–; –
CAGE	–; caged,	**CALASH**	–; –
	cager,	**CALCAR**	–; calcars
	cages,	**CALCES**	–; –
	cagey	**CALCIC**	–; –
CAGER	–; cagers	**CALCIFY**	;
CAGIER	–; –	**CALCINE**	–; calcined,
CAGIEST	–; –		calcines
CAGILY	–; –	**CALCITE**	–; calcites
CAGING	–; –	**CALCIUM**	–; calciums
CAGY	–; –	**CALDERA**	–; calderas
CAHIER	–; cahiers	**CALDRON**	–; caldrons
CAHOOT	–; cahoots	**CALECHE**	–; caleches
CAHOW	–; cahows	**CALENDS**	–; –
CAID	–; caids	**CALESA**	–; calesas
CAIMAN	–; caimans	**CALF**	–; calfs
CAIN	–; cains	**CALIBER**	–; calibers
CAIQUE	–; caiques	**CALIBRE**	–; calibred,
CAIRD	–; cairds		calibres
CAIRN	–; cairns,	**CALICES**	–; –
	cairny	**CALICHE**	–; caliches
CAIRNED	–; –	**CALICLE**	–; calicles

CALICO	-; calicos	**CALPAC**	-; calpack, calpacs
CALIF	-; califs		
CALIPEE	-; calipees	**CALPACK**	-; calpacks
CALIPER	-; calipers	**CALQUE**	-; calqued, calques
CALIPH	-; caliphs		
CALIX	-; -	**CALTRAP**	-; caltraps
CALK	-; calks	**CALTROP**	-; caltrops
CALKED	-; -	**CALUMET**	-; calumets
CALKER	-; calkers	**CALUMNY**	-; -
CALKIN	-; calking, calkins	**CALVARY**	-; -
		CALVE	-; calved, calves
CALL	scall; calla, calls		
		CALVING	-; -
CALLA	-; callas	**CALX**	-; -
CALLAN	-; callans, callant	**CALXES**	-; -
		CALYCES	-; -
CALLANT	-; callants	**CALYCLE**	-; calycles
CALLBOY	-; callboys	**CALYPSO**	-; calypsos
CALLED	-; -	**CALYX**	-; -
CALLER	-; callers	**CALYXES**	-; -
CALLET	-; callets	**CAM**	scam; came, camp, cams
CALLING	-; callings		
CALLOSE	-; calloses	**CAMAIL**	-; camails
CALLOUS	-; -	**CAMAS**	-; camass
CALLOW	-; -	**CAMASES**	-; -
CALLS	scalls; -	**CAMBER**	-; cambers
CALLUS	-; -	**CAMBIA**	-; cambial
CALM	-; calms	**CAMBISM**	-; cambisms
CALMED	-; -	**CAMBIST**	-; cambists
CALMER	-; -	**CAMBIUM**	-; cambiums
CALMEST	-; -	**CAMBRIC**	-; cambrics
CALMING	-; -	**CAME**	-; camel, cameo, cames
CALMLY	-; -		
CALOMEL	-; calomels		
CALORIC	-; calorics	**CAMEL**	-; camels
CALORIE	-; calories	**CAMELIA**	-; camelias
CALORY	-; -	**CAMEO**	-; cameos
CALOTTE	-; calottes	**CAMEOED**	-; -
CALOYER	-; caloyers	**CAMERA**	-; camerae,

	cameral, cameras	CANCEL	–; cancels
CAMION	–; camions	CANCER	–; cancers
CAMISA	–; camisas	CANCHA	–; canchas
CAMISE	–; camises	CANDELA	–; candelas
CAMISIA	–; camisias	CANDENT	–; –
CAMLET	–; camlets	CANDID	–; candida, candids
CAMORRA	–; camorras		
CAMP	scamp; campi, campo, camps, campy	CANDIDA	–; candidas
		CANDIED	–; –
		CANDIES	–; –
		CANDLE	–; candled, candler, candles
CAMPED	scamped; –	CANDLER	–; candlers
CAMPER	scamper; campers	CANDOR	–; candors
		CANDOUR	–; candours
CAMPERS	scampers; –	CANDY	–; –
CAMPHOL	–; camphols	CANE	–; caned, caner, canes
CAMPHOR	–; camphors		
CAMPI	scampi; –	CANELLA	–; canellas
CAMPIER	–; –	CANER	–; caners
CAMPILY	–; –	CANFUL	–; canfuls
CAMPING	–; campings	CANGUE	–; cangues
CAMPION	; campions	CANIKIN	–; canikins
CAMPO	–; campos	CANINE	–; canines
CAMPONG	–; campongs	CANING	–; –
		CANKER	–; cankers
CAMPS	scamps; –	CANNA	–; cannas
CAMPUS	–; –	CANNED	scanned; –
CAMS	scams; –	CANNEL	–; cannels
CAN	scan; cane, cans, cant	CANNER	scanner; canners, cannery
CANAKIN	–; canakins		
CANAL	–; canals	CANNERS	scanners; –
CANALED	–; –	CANNIE	–; cannier
CANAPE	–; canapes	CANNILY	–; –
CANARD	–; canards	CANNING	scanning; cannings
CANARY	–; –		
CANASTA	–; canastas	CANNON	–; cannons
CANCAN	–; cancans	CANNOT	–; –

CANNULA	–; cannulae, cannular, cannulas	**CANULA**	–; canulae, canulas
		CANVAS	–; canvass
CANNY	–; –	**CANYON**	–; canyons
CANOE	–; canoed, canoes	**CANZONA**	–; canzonas
		CANZONE	–; canzones, canzonet
CANON	–; canons		
CANONIC	–; –	**CANZONI**	–; –
CANOPY	–; –	**CAP**	–; cape, caph, capo, caps
CANS	scans; canso, canst		
		CAPABLE	–; capabler
CANSFUL	–; –	**CAPABLY**	–; –
CANSO	–; cansos	**CAPE**	scape; caped, caper, capes
CANT	scant; canto, cants, canty		
CANTALA	–; cantalas		
CANTATA	–; cantatas		
CANTDOG	–; cantdogs	**CAPED**	scaped; –
CANTED	scanted; –	**CAPELAN**	–; capelans
CANTEEN	–; canteens	**CAPELET**	–; capelets
CANTER	scanter; canters	**CAPELIN**	–; capelins
		CAPER	–; capers
CANTHAL	–; –	**CAPERED**	–; –
CANTHI	–; –	**CAPERER**	–; caperers
CANTHUS	acanthus; –	**CAPES**	scapes; –
CANTIC	–; –	**CAPFUL**	–; capfuls
CANTINA	–; cantinas	**CAPH**	–; caphs
CANTING	scanting; –	**CAPIAS**	–; –
CANTLE	–; cantles	**CAPITA**	–; capital
CANTO	–; canton, cantor, cantos	**CAPITAL**	–; capitals
		CAPITOL	–; capitols
		CAPLESS	–; –
CANTON	–; cantons	**CAPLIN**	–; caplins
CANTOR	–; cantors	**CAPO**	–; capon, capos
CANTRAP	–; cantraps		
CANTRIP	–; cantrips	**CAPON**	–; capons
CANTS	scants; –	**CAPORAL**	–; caporals
CANTUS	–; –	**CAPOTE**	–; capotes
CANTY	scanty; –	**CAPOUCH**	–; –
		CAPPED	–; –

CAPPER	–; cappers	CARAT	–; carate, carats
CAPPING	–; cappings		
CAPRIC	–; caprice	CARATE	–; carates
CAPRICE	–; caprices	CARAVAN	–; caravans
CAPRINE	–; –	CARAVEL	–; caravels
CAPSID	–; capsids	CARAWAY	–; caraways
CAPSIZE	–; capsized, capsizes	CARBARN	–; carbarns
		CARBIDE	–; carbides
CAPSTAN	–; capstans	CARBINE	–; carbines
CAPSULE	–; capsuled, capsules	CARBON	–; carbons
		CARBORA	–; carboras
CAPTAIN	–; captains	CARBOY	–; carboys
CAPTAN	–; captans	CARCASE	–; carcases
CAPTION	–; captions	CARCASS	–; –
CAPTIVE	–; captives	CARCEL	–; carcels
CAPTOR	–; captors	CARD	–; cards
CAPTURE	–; captured, capturer, captures	CARDED	–; –
		CARDER	–; carders
		CARDIA	–; cardiac, cardiae, cardias
CAPUCHE	–; capuched, capuches		
		CARDING	–; cardings
CAPUT	–; –	CARDOON	–; cardoons
CAR	scar; card, care, cark, curl, carn, carp, cart	CARE	scare; cared, carer, cares, carex scared; –
CARABAO	–; carabaos	CAREEN	–; careens
CARABID	–; carabids	CAREER	–; careers
CARABIN	–; carabine, carabins	CAREFUL	–; –
		CARER	scarer; carers
CARACAL	–; caracals		
CARACK	–; caracks	CARERS	scarers; –
CARACOL	–; caracole, caracols	CARES	scares; caress
CARACUL	–; caraculs	CARET	–; carets
CARAFE	–; carafes	CAREX	–; –
CARAMEL	–; caramels	CARFARE	–; carfares
CARAPAX	–; –	CARFUL	–; carfuls
		CARGO	–; cargos

CARGOES	–; –	**CARNIE**	–; carnies
CARHOP	–; carhops	**CAROB**	–; carobs
CARIBE	–; caribes	**CAROCH**	–; caroche
CARIBOU	–; caribous	**CAROCHE**	–; caroches
CARICES	–; –	**CAROL**	–; caroli, carols
CARIED	–; –		
CARIES	–; –	**CAROLED**	–; –
CARINA	ocarina; carinae, carinal, carinas	**CAROLER**	–; carolers
		CAROLUS	–; –
		CAROM	–; caroms
		CAROMED	–; –
CARINAS	ocarinas; –	**CAROTID**	–; carotids
CARING	scaring; –	**CAROTIN**	–; carotins
CARIOCA	–; cariocas	**CAROUSE**	–; caroused, carousel, carouser, carouses
CARIOLE	–; carioles		
CARIOUS	–; –		
CARK	–; carks		
CARKED	–; –	**CARP**	scarp; carpi, carps
CARKING	–; –		
CARL	–; carle, carls	**CARPAL**	–; carpale, carpals
CARLE	–; carles	**CARPED**	scarped; –
CARLES	–; carless	**CARPEL**	–; carpels
CARLESS	scarless; –	**CARPER**	scarper; carpers
CARLIN	–; carline, carling, carlins	**CARPERS**	scarpers; –
		CARPET	–; carpets
CARLINE	–; carlines	**CARPING**	scarping; carpings
CARLING	–; carlings		
CARLISH	–; –	**CARPORT**	–; carports
CARLOAD	–; carloads	**CARPS**	scarps; –
CARMAN	–; –	**CARPUS**	–; –
CARMEN	–; –	**CARRACK**	–; carracks
CARMINE	–; carmines	**CARREL**	–; carrell, carrels
CARN	–; carns, carny		
		CARRELL	–; carrells
CARNAGE	–; carnages	**CARRIED**	–; –
CARNAL	–; –	**CARRIER**	·; carriers
CARNEY	–; carneys	**CARRIES**	–; –

CARRION	–; carrions	CASCADE	–;
CARROCH	–; –		cascaded,
CARROM	–; carroms		cascades
CARROT	–; carrots,	CASCARA	–; cascaras
	carroty	CASE	–; cased,
CARRY	scarry; –		cases
CARRYON	–; carryons	CASEASE	–; caseases
CARS	scars; carse	CASEATE	–; caseated,
CARSE	–; carses		caseates
CARSICK	–; –	CASEFY	–; –
CART	scart; carte,	CASEIN	–; caseins
	carts	CASEOSE	–; caseoses
CARTAGE	–; cartages	CASEOUS	–; –
CARTE	ecarte;	CASERN	–; caserne,
	carted,		caserns
	cartel,	CASERNE	–; casernes
	carter,	CASETTE	–; casettes
	cartes	CASH	–;
CARTED	scarted; –	CASHAW	–; cashaws
CARTEL	–; cartels	CASHBOX	–; –
CARTER	–; carters	CASHED	–; –
CARTES	ecartes; –	CASHES	–; –
CARTING	scarting; –	CASHEW	–; cashews
CARTON	–; cartons	CASHIER	–; cashiers
CARTOON	–; cartoons	CASHING	–; –
CARTOP	–; –	CASHOO	–; cashoos
CARTS	scarts; –	CASING	–; casings
CARVE	–; carved,	CASINO	–; casinos
	carvel,	CASK	–; casks,
	carven,		casky
	carver,	CASKED	–; –
	carves	CASKET	–; caskets
CARVED	–; –	CASKING	–; –
CARVEL	–; carvels	CASQUE	–; casqued,
CARVER	–; carvers		casques
CARVES	scarves; –	CASSABA	–; cassabas
CARVING	–; carvings	CASSAVA	–; cassavas
CASA	–; casas	CASSIA	–; cassias
CASABA	–; casabas	CASSINO	–; cassinos
CASAVA	–; casavas	CASSOCK	–; cassocks

CAST	–; caste, casts	**CATHECT**	–; cathects
CASTE	–; caster, castes	**CATHODE**	–; cathodes
		CATION	–; cations
CASTER	–; casters	**CATKIN**	–; catkins
CASTING	–; castings	**CATLIKE**	–; –
CASTLE	–; castled, castles	**CATLIN**	–; catling, catlins
CASTOFF	–; castoffs	**CATLING**	–; catlings
CASTOR	–; castors	**CATMINT**	–; catmints
CASUAL	–; casuals	**CATNAP**	–; catnaps
CASUIST	–; casuists	**CATNIP**	–; catnips
CASUS	–; –	**CATS**	scats; –
CAT	scat; cate, cats	**CATSPAW**	–; catspaws
		CATSUP	–; catsups
CATALO	–; catalog, catalos	**CATTAIL**	–; cattails
		CATTALO	–; cattalos
CATALOG	–; catalogs	**CATTED**	scatted; –
CATALPA	–; catalpas	**CATTIE**	–; cattier, catties
CATARRH	–; catarrhs	
CATBIRD	–; catbirds	**CATTIES**	–; cattiest
CATBOAT	–; catboats	**CATTILY**	–; –
CATCALL	–; catcalls	**CATTING**	scatting; –
CATCH	–; catchy	**CATTISH**	–; –
CATCHER	–; catchers	**CATTLE**	–; –
CATCHES	–; –	**CATTY**	scatty; –
CATCHUP	–; catchups	**CATWALK**	–; catwalks
CATE	–; cater, cates	**CAUCUS**	–; –
		CAUDAD	–; –
CATECHU	–; catechus	**CAUDAL**	acaudal; –
CATENA	–; catenae, catenas	**CAUDATE**	acaudate, ecaudate; –
CATER	–; caters	
CATERAN	–; caterans	**CAUDEX**	–; –
CATERER	–; caterers	**CAUDLE**	–; caudles
CATFACE	–; catfaces	**CAUGHT**	–; –
CATFALL	–; catfalls	**CAUL**	–; cauld, caulk, cauls
CATFISH	–; –	
CATGUT	–; catguts	**CAULD**	–; caulds
CATHEAD	–; catheads	**CAULES**	–; –
		CAULINE	–; –
		CAULIS	–; –

CAULK	–; caulks	**CAWING**	–; –
CAULKED	–; –	**CAY**	–; cays
CAULKER	–; caulkers	**CAYENNE**	–;
CAUSAL	–; causals		cayenned,
CAUSE	–; caused,		cayennes
	causer,	**CAYMAN**	–; caymans
	causes,	**CAYUSE**	–; cayuses
	causey	**CAZIQUE**	–; caziques
CAUSER	–; causers	**CEASE**	–; ceased,
CAUSEY	–; causeys		ceases
CAUSING	–; –	**CEASING**	–; –
CAUSTIC	–; caustics	**CEBID**	–; cebids
CAUTERY	–; –	**CEBOID**	–; ceboids
CAUTION	–; cautions	**CECA**	–; cecal
CAVALLA	–; cavallas	**CECALLY**	–; –
CAVALLY	–; –	**CECUM**	–; –
CAVALRY	–; –	**CEDAR**	–; cedarn,
CAVE	–; caved,		cedars
	caver, caves	**CEDE**	–; ceded,
CAVEAT	–; caveats		ceder, cedes
CAVEMAN	–; –	**CEDER**	–; ceders
CAVEMEN	–; –	**CEDI**	–; cedis
CAVER	–; cavern,	**CEDILLA**	–; cedillas
	cavers	**CEDING**	–; –
CAVERN	–; caverns	**CEDULA**	–; cedulas
CAVETTI	–; –	**CEE**	–; cees
CAVETTO	–; cavettos	**CEIBA**	–; ceibas
CAVIAR	–; caviare,	**CEIL**	–; ceils
	caviars	**CEILED**	–; –
CAVIARE	–; caviares	**CEILER**	–; ceilers
CAVIE	–; cavies	**CEILING**	–; ceilings
CAVIL	–; cavils	**CELADON**	–; celadons
CAVILED	–; –	**CELEB**	–; celebs
CAVILER	–; cavilers	**CELERY**	–; –
CAVING	–; –	**CELESTA**	–; celestas
CAVITY	–; –	**CELESTE**	–; celestes
CAVORT	–; cavorts	**CELIAC**	–; –
CAVY	–; –	**CELL**	–; cella,
CAW	–; caws		celli, cello,
CAWED	–; –		cells

CELLA	–; cellae, cellar, cellas	**CENTRA**	–; central
		CENTRAL	–; centrals
CELLAR	ocellar; cellars	**CENTRE**	–; centred, centres
CELLED	–; –	**CENTRIC**	acentric; –
CELLING	–; –	**CENTRUM**	–; centrums
CELLIST	–; cellists	**CENTS**	scents; –
CELLO	–; cellos	**CENTUM**	–; centums
CELLULE	–; cellules	**CENTURY**	–; –
CELOM	–; celoms	**CEORL**	–; ceorls
CELT	–; celts	**CERAMAL**	–; ceramals
CEMBALI	–; –	**CERAMIC**	–; ceramics
CEMBALO	–; cembalos	**CERATE**	acerate; cerated, cerates
CEMENT	–; cements		
CENACLE	–; cenacles		
CENOTE	–; cenotes	**CERATED**	acerated; –
CENSE	–; censed, censer, censes	**CERATIN**	–; ceratins
		CERCI	–; cercis
		CERCUS	–; –
CENSER	–; censers	**CERE**	–; cered, ceres
CENSING	–; –		
CENSOR	–; censors	**CEREAL**	–; cereals
CENSUAL	–; –	**CEREUS**	–; –
CENSURE	–; censured, censurer, censures	**CERIA**	–; cerias
		CERIC	–; –
		CERING	–; –
CENSUS	–; –	**CERIPH**	–; ceriphs
CENT	scent; cento, cents	**CERISE**	–; cerises
		CERITE	–; cerites
CENTAL	–; centals	**CERIUM**	–; ceriums
CENTARE	–; centares	**CERMET**	–; cermets
CENTAUR	–; centaurs, centaury	**CERO**	–; ceros
		CEROTIC	–; –
CENTAVO	–; centavos	**CEROUS**	acerous; –
CENTER	–; centers	**CERTAIN**	–; –
CENTILE	–; centiles	**CERTES**	–; –
CENTIME	–; centimes	**CERTIFY**	–; –
CENTIMO	–; centimos	**CERUMEN**	–; cerumens
CENTNER	–; centners	**CERUSE**	–; ceruses
CENTO	–; centos	**CERVINE**	–;

CERVIX	–; –	CHAIR	–; chairs
CESIUM	, cesiums	CHAIRED	;
CESS	–; –	CHAISE	–; chaises
CESSED	–; –	CHALAH	–; chalahs
CESSES	–; –	CHALAZA	–; chalazae,
CESSING	–; –		chalazal,
CESSION	–; cessions		chalazas
CESSPIT	–; cesspits	CHALCID	–; chalcids
CESTA	–; cestas	CHALEH	–; chalehs
CESTI	–; –	CHALET	–; chalets
CESTODE	–; cestodes	CHALICE	–; chaliced,
CESTOI	–; cestoid		chalices
CESTOID	–; cestoids	CHALK	–; chalks,
CESTOS	–; –		chalky
CESTUS	–; –	CHALKED	–; –
CESURA	–; cesurae,	CHALLAH	–; challahs
	cesuras	CHALLIE	–; challies
CETANE	–; cetanes	CHALLIS	–; –
CETE	–; cetes	CHALLOT	–; challoth
CHABOUK	–; chabouks	CHALLY	–; –
CHABUK	–; chabuks	CHALONE	–; chalones
CHACMA	–; chacmas	CHALOT	–; chaloth
CHAD	–; chads	CHALUTZ	–; –
CHAETA	–; chaetae,	CHAM	–; champ,
	chaetal		chams
CHAFE	–; chafed,	CHAMADE	–; chamades
	chafer,	CHAMBER	–; chambers
	chafes	CHAMFER	–; chamfers
CHAFER	–; chafers	CHAMISE	–; chamises
CHAFF	–; chaffs,	CHAMISO	–; chamisos
	chaffy	CHAMMY	–; –
CHAFFED	–; –	CHAMOIS	–; –
CHAFFER	–; chaffers	CHAMOIX	–; –
CHAFING	–; –	CHAMP	–; champs,
CHAGRIN	–; chagrins		champy
CHAIN	–; chaine,	CHAMPAC	–; champacs
	chains	CHAMPAK	–; champaks
CHAINE	–; chained,	CHAMPED	–; –
	chaines	CHAMPER	–; champers

CHANCE	–; chanced, chancel, chances		chars, chart, chary
		CHARADE	–; charades
CHANCEL	–; chancels	**CHARAS**	–; –
CHANCRE	–; chancres	**CHARD**	echard; chards
CHANCY	–; –		
CHANG	–; change, changs	**CHARDS**	echards; –
		CHARE	–; chared, chares
CHANGE	–; changed, changer, changes	**CHARGE**	–; charged, charger, charges
CHANGER	–; changers		
CHANNEL	–; channels	**CHARGER**	–; chargers
CHANSON	–; chansons	**CHARIER**	–; –
CHANT	–; chants, chanty	**CHARILY**	–; –
		CHARING	–; –
CHANTED	–; –	**CHARIOT**	–; chariots
CHANTER	–; chanters	**CHARISM**	–; charisma, charisms
CHANTEY	–; chanteys		
CHANTOR	–; chantors	**CHARITY**	–; –
CHANTRY	–; –	**CHARK**	–; charka, charks
CHAOS	–; –		
CHAOSES	–; –	**CHARKA**	–; charkas
CHAOTIC	–; –	**CHARKED**	–; –
CHAP	–; chape, chaps, chapt	**CHARKHA**	–; charkhas
		CHARM	–; charms
CHAPE	–; chapel, chapes	**CHARMED**	–; –
		CHARMER	–; charmers
CHAPEAU	–; chapeaus, chapeaux	**CHARNEL**	–; charnels
		CHARPAI	–; charpais
		CHARPOY	–; charpoys
CHAPEL	–; chapels	**CHARQUI**	–; charquid, charquis
CHAPLET	–; chaplets		
CHAPMAN	–; –	**CHARR**	–; charro, charrs, charry
CHAPMEN	–; –		
CHAPPED	–; –		
CHAPTER	–; chapters	**CHARRED**	–; –
CHAR	–; chard, chare, chark, charm, charr,	**CHART**	–; charts
		CHARTED	–; –
		CHARTER	–; charters

CHASE	–; chased, chasor, chases	CHEATER	–; cheaters
CHASER	–; chasers	CHEBEC	–; chebecs
CHASING	–; chasings	CHECK	–; checks
CHASM	–; chasms, chasmy	CHECKED	–; –
CHASMAL	–; –	CHECKER	–; checkers
CHASMED	–; –	CHECKUP	–; checkups
CHASMIC	–; –	CHEDDAR	–; cheddars
CHASSE	–; chassed, chasses	CHEDER	–; cheders
		CHEDITE	–; chedites
CHASSIS	–; –	CHEEK	–; cheeks, cheeky
CHASTE	–; chasten, chaster	CHEEKED	–; –
		CHEEP	–; cheeps
CHASTEN	–; chastens	CHEEPED	–; –
CHAT	–; chats	CHEEPER	–; cheepers
CHATEAU	–; chateaus, chateaux	CHEER	–; cheero, cheers, cheery
CHATTEL	–; chattels	CHEERED	–; –
CHATTED	–; –	CHEERER	–; cheerers
CHATTER	–; chatters, chattery	CHEERIO	–; cheerios
		CHEERO	–; cheeros
CHATTY	–; –	CHEESE	–; cheesed, cheeses
CHAUFER	–; chaufers	CHEESY	–; –
CHAUNT	–; chaunts	CHEETAH	–; cheetahs
CHAW	–; chaws	CHEF	–; chefs
CHAWED	–; –	CHEFDOM	–; chefdoms
CHAWER	–; chawers	CHEGOE	–; chegoes
CHAWING	–; –	CHELA	–; chelae, chelas
CHAYOTE	–; chayotes		
CHAZAN	–; chazans	CHELATE	–; chelated, chelates
CHAZZEN	–; chazzens		
CHEAP	–; cheaps	CHELOID	–; cheloids
CHEAPEN	–; cheapens	CHEMIC	–; chemics
CHEAPER	–; –	CHEMISE	–; chemises
CHEAPIE	–; cheapies	CHEMISM	–; chemisms
CHEAPLY	–; –	CHEMIST	–; chemists
CHEAT	–; cheats	CHEQUE	–; chequer, cheques
CHEATED	–; –		

CHEQUER	–; chequers		chicaner,
CHERISH	–; –		chicanes
CHEROOT	–; cheroots	**CHICHI**	–; chichis
CHERRY	–; –	**CHICK**	–; chicks
CHERT	–; cherts,	**CHICKEN**	–; chickens
	cherty	**CHICLE**	–; chicles
CHERUB	–; cherubs	**CHICLY**	–; –
CHERVIL	–; chervils	**CHICO**	–; chicos
CHESS	–; –	**CHICORY**	–; –
CHESSES	–; –	**CHID**	–; chide
CHEST	–; chests,	**CHIDDEN**	–; –
	chesty	**CHIDE**	–; chided,
CHESTED	–; –		chider,
CHETAH	–; chetahs		chides
CHETH	–; cheths	**CHIDER**	–; chiders
CHEVIED	–; –	**CHIDING**	–; –
CHEVIES	–; –	**CHIEF**	–; chiefs
CHEVIOT	–; cheviots	**CHIEFER**	–; –
CHEVRON	–; chevrons	**CHIEFLY**	–; –
CHEVY	–; –	**CHIEL**	–; chield,
CHEW	–; chews,		chiels
	chewy	**CHIELD**	–; chields
CHEWED	–; -	**CHIFFON**	–; chiffons
CHEWER	–; chewers	**CHIGGER**	–; chiggers
CHEWING	–; –	**CHIGNON**	–; chignons
CHEWINK	–; chewinks	**CHIGOE**	–; chigoes
CHEZ	–; –	**CHILD**	–; childe
CHI	–; chia, chis	**CHILDE**	–; childes
CHIA	–; chiao,	**CHILDLY**	–; –
	chias	**CHILE**	–; chiles
CHIASM	–; chiasma,	**CHILI**	–; –
	chiasms	**CHILIAD**	–; chiliads
CHIASMA	–; chiasmal,	**CHILIES**	–; –
	chiasmas	**CHILL**	–; chilli,
CHIAUS	–; –		chills, chilly
CHIBOUK	–; chibouks	**CHILLED**	–; –
CHIC	–; chick,	**CHILLER**	–; chillers
	chico, chics	**CHILLI**	–, chillis
CHICANE	–; chicaned,	**CHILLUM**	–; chillums

CHIMAR	–; chimars	**CHIRMED**	–; –
CHIMB	, chimbs	**CHIRO**	, chiros
CHIMBLY	–; –	**CHIRP**	–; chirps,
CHIME	–; chimed,		chirpy
	chimer, chimes	**CHIRPED**	–; –
CHIMER	–; chimera,	**CHIRPER**	–; chirpers
	chimere,	**CHIRR**	–; chirre,
	chimers		chirrs
CHIMERA	–; chimeras	**CHIRRE**	–; chirred,
CHIMERE	–; chimeres		chirres
CHIMING	–; –	**CHIRRUP**	–; chirrups,
CHIMLA	–; chimlas		chirrupy
CHIMLEY	–; chimleys	**CHISEL**	–; chisels
CHIMNEY	–; chimneys	**CHIT**	–; chits
CHIMP	–; chimps	**CHITAL**	–; –
CHIN	–; china,	**CHITIN**	–; chitins
	chine, chink,	**CHITLIN**	–; chitling,
	chino, chins		chitlins
CHINA	–; chinas	**CHITON**	–; chitons
CHINCH	–; chinchy	**CHITTER**	–; chitters
CHINE	–; chined,	**CHITTY**	–; –
	chines	**CHIVARI**	–; chivaris
CHINK	–; chinks,	**CHIVE**	–; chives
	chinky	**CHIVIED**	–; –
CHINKED	–; –	**CHIVIES**	–; –
CHINNED	–; –	**CHIVVY**	–; –
CHINO	–; chinos	**CHIVY**	–; –
CHINONE	–; chinones	**CHLAMYS**	–; –
CHINOOK	–; chinooks	**CHLORAL**	–; chlorals
CHINTS	–; –	**CHLORIC**	–; –
CHINTZ	–; chintzy	**CHLORID**	–; chloride,
CHIP	–; chips		chlorids
CHIPPED	–; –	**CHLORIN**	–; chlorine,
CHIPPER	–; chippers		chlorins
CHIPPIE	–; chippies	**CHOCK**	–; chocks,
CHIPPY	–; –		chocky
CHIRK	–; chirks	**CHOCKED**	–; –
CHIRKED	–; –	**CHOICE**	–; choicer,
CHIRKER	–; –		choices
CHIRM	–; chirms	**CHOIR**	–; choirs

CHOIRED	–; –	**CHOREA**	–; choreal,
CHOKE	–; choked,		choreas
	choker,	**CHOREIC**	–; –
	chokes,	**CHORIAL**	–; –
	chokey	**CHORIC**	–; –
CHOKER	–; chokers	**CHORINE**	–; chorines
CHOKIER	–; –	**CHORING**	–; –
CHOKING	–; –	**CHORION**	–; chorions
CHOKY	–; –	**CHORIZO**	–; chorizos
CHOLATE	–; cholates	**CHOROID**	–; choroids
CHOLER	–; cholera,	**CHORTLE**	–; chortled,
	cholers		chortler,
CHOLERA	–; choleras		chortles
CHOLINE	–; cholines	**CHORUS**	ichorus; –
CHOLLA	–; chollas	**CHOSE**	–; chosen,
CHOMP	–; chomps		choses
CHOMPED	–; –	**CHOTT**	–; chotts
CHON	–; –	**CHOUGH**	–; choughs
CHOOSE	–; chooser,	**CHOUSE**	–; choused,
	chooses,		chouser,
	choosey		chouses
CHOOSER	–; choosers	**CHOUSH**	–; –
CHOOSEY	–; –	**CHOW**	–; chows
CHOOSY	–; –	**CHOWDER**	–; chowders
CHOP	–; chops	**CHOWED**	–; –
CHOPIN	–; chopine,	**CHOWSE**	–; chowsed,
	chopins		chowses
CHOPINE	–; chopines	**CHRISM**	–; chrisms
CHOPPED	–; –	**CHRISOM**	–; chrisoms
CHOPPER	–; choppers	**CHRISTY**	–; –
CHOPPY	–; –	**CHROMA**	–; chromas
CHORAL	–; chorale,	**CHROME**	–; chromed,
	chorals		chromes
CHORALE	–; chorales	**CHROMIC**	achromic; –
CHORD	–; chords	**CHROMO**	–; chromos
CHORDAL	–; –	**CHROMYL**	–; –
CHORDED	–; –	**CHRONIC**	–; chronics
CHORE	–; chorea,	**CHRONON**	–; chronons
	chored,	**CHUB**	–; chubs
	chores	**CHUBBY**	–; –

CHUCK	−; chucks, chucky	CHUTE	−; chuted, chutes
CHUCKED	−; −	CHUTING	−; −
CHUCKLE	−; chuckled, chuckler, chuckles	CHUTIST	−; chutists
		CHUTNEE	−; chutnees
		CHUTNEY	−; chutneys
CHUDDAH	−; chuddahs	CHUTZPA	−; chutzpah, chutzpas
CHUDDAR	−; chuddars		
CHUDDER	−; chudders	CHYLE	−; chyles
CHUFA	−; chufas	CHYLOUS	−; −
CHUFF	−; chuffs, chuffy	CHYME	−; chymes
		CHYMIC	−; chymics
CHUFFED	−; −	CHYMIST	−; chymists
CHUFFER	−; −	CHYMOUS	−; −
CHUG	−; chugs	CIAO	−; −
CHUGGED	−; −	CIBOL	−; cibols
CHUGGER	−; chuggers	CIBOULE	−; ciboules
CHUKAR	−; chukars	CICADA	−; cicadae, cicadas
CHUKKA	−; chukkar, chukkas		
		CICALA	−; cicalas
CHUKKAR	−; chukkars	CICALE	−; −
CHUKKER	−; chukkers	CICELY	−; −
CHUM	−; chump, chums	CICERO	−; ciceros
		CICHLID	−; cichlids
CHUMMED	−; −	CICOREE	; cicorees
CHUMMY	−; −	CIDER	−; ciders
CHUMP	−; chumps	CIGAR	−; cigars
CHUMPED	−; −	CIGARET	−; cigarets
CHUNK	−; chunks, chunky	CILCIUM	−; −
		CILIA	−; −
CHUNKED	−; −	CILIARY	−; −
CHUNTER	−; chunters	CILIATE	−; ciliated, ciliates
CHURCH	−; churchy		
CHURL	−; churls	CILICE	−; cilices
CHURN	−; churns	CIMEX	−; −
CHURNED	−; −	CIMICES	−; −
CHURNER	−; churners	CINCH	−; −
CHURR	−; churrs	CINCHED	−; −
CHURRED	−; −	CINCHES	−; −

CINDER	–; cinders, cindery	**CITABLE**	–; –
		CITADEL	–; citadels
CINE	–; cines	**CITE**	–; cited,
CINEAST	–; cineaste,		citer, cites
	cineasts	**CITER**	–; citers
CINEMA	–; cinemas	**CITHARA**	–; citharas
CINEOL	–; cineole,	**CITHER**	–; cithern,
	cineols		cithers
CINEOLE	–; cineoles	**CITHERN**	–; citherns
CINERIN	–; cinerins	**CITHREN**	–; cithrens
CINQUE	–; cinques	**CITIED**	–; –
CION	scion; cions	**CITIES**	–; –
CIONS	scions; –	**CITIFY**	–; –
CIPHER	–; ciphers	**CITING**	–; –
CIPHONY	–; –	**CITIZEN**	–; citizens
CIPOLIN	–; cipolins	**CITOLA**	–; citolas
CIRCA	–; –	**CITOLE**	–; citoles
CIRCLE	–; circled,	**CITRAL**	–; citrals
	circler,	**CITRATE**	–; citrated
	circles,		citrates
	circlet	**CITRIC**	–; –
CIRCLER	–; circlers	**CITRIN**	–; citrine
CIRCLET	–; circlets		citrins
CIRCUIT	–; circuits,	**CITRINE**	–; citrines
	circuity	**CITRON**	–; citrons
CIRCUS	–; circusy	**CITROUS**	–; –
CIRQUE	–; cirques	**CITRUS**	–; –
CIRRATE	–; –	**CITTERN**	–; citterns
CIRRI	–; –	**CITY**	–; –
CIRROSE	–; –	**CIVET**	–; civets
CIRROUS	–; –	**CIVIC**	–; civics
CIRRUS	–; –	**CIVIE**	–; civies
CIRSOID	–; –	**CIVIL**	–; –
CISCO	–; ciscos	**CIVILLY**	–; –
CISCOES	–; –	**CIVISM**	–; civisms
CISSOID	–; cissoids	**CIVVY**	–; –
CIST	–; cists	**CLABBER**	–; clabbers
CISTERN	–; cisterna,	**CLACH**	–; clachs
	cisterns	**CLACHAN**	–; clachans
CISTRON	–; cistrons	**CLACK**	–; clacks

CLACKED	–; –	**CLARO**	–; claros
CLACKER	, clackers	**CLARY**	–; –
CLAD	–; clads	**CLASH**	–; –
CLADODE	–; cladodes	**CLASHED**	–; –
CLAG	–; clags	**CLASHER**	–; clashers
CLAGGED	–; –	**CLASHES**	–; –
CLAIM	–; claims	**CLASP**	–; clasps,
CLAIMED	–; –		claspt
CLAIMER	–; claimers	**CLASPED**	–; –
CLAM	–; clamp,	**CLASPER**	–; claspers
	clams	**CLASS**	–; classy
CLAMANT	–; –	**CLASSED**	–; –
CLAMBER	–; clambers	**CLASSER**	–; classers
CLAMMED	–; –	**CLASSES**	–; –
CLAMMY	–; –	**CLASSIC**	–; classics
CLAMOR	–; clamors	**CLASSIS**	–; –
CLAMOUR	–; clamours	**CLAST**	–; clasts
CLAMP	–; clamps	**CLASTIC**	–; clastics
CLAMPED	–; –	**CLATTER**	–; clatters,
CLAMPER	–; clampers		clattery
CLAN	–; clang,	**CLAUCHT**	–; –
	clank, clans	**CLAUGHT**	–; claughts
CLANG	–; clangs	**CLAUSAL**	–; –
CLANGED	–; –	**CLAUSE**	–; clauses
CLANGOR	–; clangors	**CLAVATE**	–; –
CLANK	–; clanks	**CLAVE**	–; claver
CLANKED	,	**CLAVER**	–; clavers
CLAP	–; claps,	**CLAVIER**	–; claviers
	clapt	**CLAW**	–; claws
CLAPPED	–; –	**CLAWED**	–; –
CLAPPER	–; clappers	**CLAWER**	–; clawers
CLAQUE	–; claquer,	**CLAXON**	–; claxons
	claques	**CLAY**	–; clays
CLAQUER	–; claquers	**CLAYED**	–; –
CLARET	–; clarets	**CLAYEY**	–; –
CLARIES	–; –	**CLAYIER**	–; –
CLARIFY	–; –	**CLAYING**	–; –
CLARION	–; clarions	**CLAYISH**	–; –
CLARITY	–; –	**CLAYPAN**	–; claypans
CLARKIA	–; clarkias	**CLEAN**	–; cleans

CLEANED	–; –	**CLEWED**	–; –
CLEANER	–; cleaners	**CLICHE**	–; cliched
CLEANLY	–; –		cliches
CLEANS	–; cleanse	**CLICK**	–; clicks
CLEANSE	–; cleansed,	**CLICKED**	–; –
	cleanser,	**CLICKER**	–; clicker.
	cleanses	**CLIENT**	–; clients
CLEANUP	–; cleanups	**CLIFF**	–; cliffs,
CLEAR	–; clears		cliffy
CLEARED	–; –	**CLIFT**	–; clifts
CLEARER	–; clearers	**CLIMATE**	–; climate
CLEARLY	–; –	**CLIMAX**	–; –
CLEAT	–; cleats	**CLIMB**	–; climbs
CLEATED	–; –	**CLIMBED**	–; –
CLEAVE	–; cleaved,	**CLIMBER**	–; climbe.
	cleaver,	**CLIME**	–; climes
	cleaves	**CLINAL**	–; –
CLEAVER	–; cleavers	**CLINCH**	–; –
CLEEK	–; cleeks	**CLINE**	–; clines
CLEEKED	–; –	**CLING**	–; clings
CLEF	–; clefs, cleft		clingy
CLEFT	–; clefts	**CLINGED**	–; –
CLEMENT	–; –	**CLINGER**	–; clingers
CLENCH	–; –	**CLINIC**	aclinic;
CLEOME	–; cleomes		clinics
CLEPE	–; cleped,	**CLINK**	–; clinks
	clepes	**CLINKED**	–; –
CLEPED	ycleped; –	**CLINKER**	–; clinkers
CLEPING	–; –	**CLIP**	–; clips, clip.
CLEPT	yclept; –	**CLIPPED**	–; –
CLERGY	–; –	**CLIPPER**	–; clippers
CLERIC	–; clerics	**CLIQUE**	–; cliqued
CLERID	–; clerids		cliques,
CLERISY	–; –		cliquey
CLERK	–; clerks	**CLIQUY**	–; –
CLERKED	–; –	**CLIVERS**	–; –
CLERKLY	–; –	**CLOACA**	–; cloacae
CLEVER	–; –		cloacal
CLEVIS	–; –	**CLOAK**	–; cloaks
CLEW	–; clews	**CLOAKED**	·; –

CLOBBER	–; clobbers	**CLOTH**	–; clothe,
CLOCHE	–; cloches		cloths
CLOCK	–; clocks	**CLOTHE**	–; clothed,
CLOCKED	–; –		clothes
CLOCKER	–; clockers	**CLOTTED**	–; –
CLOD	–; clods	**CLOTTY**	–; –
CLODDY	–; –	**CLOTURE**	–; clotured,
CLOG	–; clogs		clotures
CLOGGED	–; –	**CLOUD**	–; clouds,
CLOGGY	–; –		cloudy
CLOMB	–; –	**CLOUDED**	–; –
CLOMP	–; clomps	**CLOUGH**	–; cloughs
CLOMPED	–; –	**CLOUR**	–; clours
CLON	–; clone,	**CLOURED**	–; –
	clonk, clons	**CLOUT**	–; clouts
CLONAL	–; –	**CLOUTED**	–; –
CLONE	–; cloned,	**CLOUTER**	–; clouters
	clones	**CLOVE**	–; cloven,
CLONIC	–; –		clover,
CLONISM	–; clonisms		cloves
CLONK	–; clonks	**CLOVER**	–; clovers
CLONKED	–; –	**CLOWDER**	–; clowders
CLONUS	–; –	**CLOWN**	–; clowns
CLOOT	–; cloots	**CLOWNED**	–; –
CLOP	–; clops	**CLOY**	–; cloys
CLOPPED	;	**CLOYED**	–; –
CLOSE	–; closed,	**CLOYING**	–; –
	closer,	**CLOZE**	–; –
	closes,	**CLUB**	–; clubs
	closet	**CLUBBED**	–; –
CLOSELY	–; –	**CLUBBER**	–; clubbers
CLOSER	–; closers	**CLUBBY**	–; –
CLOSES	–; closest	**CLUBMAN**	–; –
CLOSET	–; closets	**CLUBMEN**	–; –
CLOSING	–; closings	**CLUCK**	–; clucks
CLOSURE	–; closured,	**CLUCKED**	–; –
	closures	**CLUE**	–; clued,
CLOT	–; cloth,		clues
	clots	**CLUEING**	–; –
		CLUING	–; –

CLUMBER	–; clumbers	**COAPTED**	–; –
CLUMP	–; clumps, clumpy	**COARSE**	–; coarsen, coarser
CLUMPED	–; –	**COARSEN**	–; coarsens
CLUMSY	–; –	**COAST**	–; coasts
CLUNG	–; –	**COASTAL**	–; –
CLUNK	–; clunks	**COASTED**	–; –
CLUNKED	–; –	**COASTER**	–; coasters
CLUNKER	–; clunkers	**COAT**	–; coati, coats
CLUPEID	–; clupeids		
CLUSTER	–; clusters, clustery	**COATED**	–; –
		COATEE	–; coatees
CLUTCH	–; clutchy	**COATER**	–; coaters
CLUTTER	–; clutters	**COATI**	–; coatis
CLYPEAL	–; –	**COATING**	–; coatings
CLYPEI	–; –	**COAX**	–; –
CLYPEUS	–; –	**COAXAL**	–; –
CLYSTER	–; clysters	**COAXED**	–; –
COACH	–; –	**COAXER**	–; coaxers
COACHED	–; –	**COAXES**	–; –
COACHER	–; coachers	**COAXIAL**	–; –
COACHES	–; –	**COAXING**	–; –
COACT	–; coacts	**COB**	–; cobb, cobs
COACTED	–; –		
COADMIT	–; coadmits	**COBALT**	–; cobalts
COAEVAL	–; coaevals	**COBB**	–; cobbs, cobby
COAGENT	–; coagents		
COAL	–; coala, coals	**COBBER**	–; cobbers
		COBBIER	–; –
COALA	–; coalas	**COBBLE**	–; cobbled, cobbler, cobbles
COALBIN	–; coalbins		
COALBOX	–; –		
COALED	–; –	**COBBLER**	–; cobblers
COALER	–; coalers	**COBIA**	–; cobias
COALIFY	–; –	**COBLE**	–; cobles
COALING	–; –	**COBNUT**	–; cobnuts
COALPIT	–; coalpits	**COBRA**	–; cobras
COAMING	–; coamings	**COBWEB**	–; cobwebs
COANNEX	–; –	**COCA**	–; cocas
COAPT	–; coapts		

COCAIN	–; cocaine, cocains	**COCONUT**	–; coconuts
		COCOON	–; cocoons
COCAINE	–; cocaines	**COCOTTE**	–; cocottes
COCCAL	–; –	**COD**	–; coda, code, cods
COCCI	–; coccic, coccid		
		CODA	–; codas
COCCID	–; coccids	**CODABLE**	–; –
COCCOID	–; coccoids	**CODDER**	–; codders
COCCOUS	–; –	**CODDLE**	–; coddled, coddler, coddles
COCCUS	–; –		
COCCYX	–; –		
COCHAIR	–; cochairs	**CODDLER**	–; coddlers
COCHIN	–; cochins	**CODE**	–; coded, coden, coder, codes, codex
COCHLEA	–; cochleae, cochlear, cochleas		
COCK	acock; cocks, cocky		
		CODEIA	–; codeias
COCKADE	–; cockaded, cockades	**CODEIN**	–; codeina, codeine, codeins
COCKED	–; –	**CODEINA**	–; codeinas
COCKER	–; cockers	**CODEINE**	–; codeines
COCKEYE	–; cockeyed, cockeyes	**CODEN**	–; codens
		CODER	–; coders
		CODEX	–; –
COCKIER	–; –	**CODFISH**	–; –
COCKING	–; –	**CODGER**	–; codgers
COCKILY	–; –	**CODICES**	–; –
COCKISH	–; –	**CODICIL**	–; codicils
COCKLE	–; cockled, cockles	**CODIFY**	–; –
		CODING	–; –
COCKNEY	–; cockneys	**CODLIN**	–; codling, codlins
COCKPIT	–; cockpits		
COCKSHY	–; –	**CODLING**	–; codlings
COCKUP	–; cockups	**CODON**	–; codons
COCO	–; cocoa, cocos	**COED**	–; coeds
		COELIAC	–; –
COCOA	–; cocoas	**COELOM**	–; coelome coeloms
COCOMAT	·; cocomats		

COELOME	–; coelomes	COHABIT	–; cohabits
COEMPT	–; coempts	COHEIR	–; coheirs
COENACT	–; coenacts	COHERE	–; cohered.
COENURE	–; coenures		coherer,
COEQUAL	–; coequals		coheres
COERCE	–; coerced,	COHERER	–; coherers
	coercer,	COHO	–; cohog,
	coerces		cohos
COERCER	–; coercers	COHOG	–; cohogs
COERECT	–; coerects	COHORT	–; cohorts
COEVAL	–; coevals	COHOSH	–; –
COEXERT	–; coexerts	COHUNE	–; cohunes
COEXIST	–; coexists	COIF	–; coifs
COFF	scoff; coffs	COIFED	–; –
COFFEE	–; coffees	COIFFE	–; coiffed,
COFFER	scoffer;		coiffes
	coffers	COIFING	–; –
COFFERS	scoffers; –	COIGN	–; coigne,
COFFIN	–; coffing,		coigns
	coffins	COIGNE	–; coigned,
COFFLE	–; coffled,		coignes
	coffles	COIL	–; coils
COFFRET	–; coffrets	COILED	–; –
COFFS	scoffs; –	COILER	–; coilers
COFT	–; –	COILING	–; –
COG	–; cogs	COIN	–; coins
COGENCY	–; –	COINAGE	–; coinages
COGENT	–; –	COINED	–; –
COGGED	–; –	COINER	–; coiners
COGGING	–; –	COINFER	–; coinfers
COGITO	–; cogitos	COINING	–; –
COGNAC	–; cognacs	COINTER	–; cointers
COGNATE	–; cognates	COIR	–; coirs
COGNISE	–; cognised,	COITAL	–; –
	cognises	COITION	–; coitions
COGNIZE	–; cognized,	COITUS	–; –
	cognizer,	COKE	–; coked,
	cognizes		cokes
COGON	–; cogons	COKING	–; –
COGWAY	–; cogways	COI'	–. cola

cold, cole, cols, colt, coly

COLA	–; colas
COLD	acold, scold; colds
COLDER	scolder; –
COLDEST	–; –
COLDISH	–; –
COLDLY	–; –
COLDS	scolds; –
COLE	ecole; coles
COLES	ecoles; –
COLEUS	–; –
COLIC	–; colics
COLICIN	–; colicine, colicins
COLICKY	–; –
COLIES	–; –
COLIN	–; colins
COLITIC	–; –
COLITIS	–; –
COLLAGE	–; collagen, collages
COLLAR	–; collard, collars
COLLARD	–; collards
COLLATE	–; collated, collates
COLLECT	–; collects
COLLEEN	–; colleens
COLLEGE	–; colleger, colleges
COLLET	–; collets
COLLIDE	–; collided, collides
COLLIE	–; collied, collier, collies
COLLIER	–; colliers, colliery
COLLINS	–; –
COLLOID	–; colloids
COLLOP	scollop; collops
COLLOPS	scollops; –
COLLUDE	–; colluded, colluder, colludes
COLLY	–; –
COLOG	–; cologs
COLOGNE	–; cologned, colognes
COLON	–; coloni, colons, colony
COLONEL	–; colonels
COLONI	–; colonic
COLOR	–; colors
COLORED	–; coloreds
COLORER	–; colorers
COLOUR	–; colours
COLT	–; colts
COLTER	–; colters
COLTISH	–; –
COLUGO	–; colugos
COLUMEL	–; columels
COLUMN	–; columns
COLURE	–; colures
COLY	–; –
COLZA	–; colzas
COMA	–; comae, comal, comas
COMAKER	–; comakers
COMAL	–; –
COMATE	–; comates
COMATIC	–; –
COMATIK	–; comatiks

COMB	–; combe, combo, combs	**COMMATA**	–; –
		COMMEND	–; commends
COMBAT	–; combats		
COMBE	–; combed, comber, combes	**COMMENT**	–; comments
		COMMIE	–; commies
		COMMIT	–; commits
COMBER	–; combers	**COMMIX**	–; commixt
COMBINE	–; combined, combiner, combines	**COMMODE**	–; commodes
		COMMON	–; commons
		COMMOVE	–; commoved, commoves
COMBING	–; combings		
COMBO	–; combos		
COMBUST	–; –	**COMMUNE**	–; communed, communes
COME	–; comer, comes, comet		
		COMMUTE	–; commuted, commuter, commutes
COMEDIC	–; –		
COMEDO	–; comedos		
COMEDY	–; –		
COMELY	–; –	**COMMY**	–; –
COMER	–; comers	**COMOSE**	–; –
COMET	–; cometh, comets	**COMOUS**	–; –
		COMP	–; compo, comps, compt
COMETIC	–; –		
COMFIER	–; –		
COMFIT	–; comfits	**COMPACT**	–; compacts
COMFORT	–; comforts	**COMPANY**	–; –
COMFREY	–; comfreys	**COMPARE**	–; compared, comparer, compares
COMFY	–; –		
COMIC	–; comics		
COMICAL	–; –		
COMING	–; comings	**COMPART**	–; comparts
COMITIA	–; comitial	**COMPASS**	–; –
COMITY	–; –	**COMPED**	–; –
COMMA	–; commas	**COMPEER**	–; compeers
COMMAND	–; commando, commands	**COMPEL**	–; compels
		COMPEND	–; compends
		COMPERE	–; comperes

COMPETE	–; competed, competes		conceder, concedes
COMPILE	–; compiled, compiler, compiles	**CONCEIT**	–; conceits
		CONCENT	–; concents
		CONCEPT	–; concepts
COMPING	–; –	**CONCERN**	–; concerns
COMPLEX	–; –	**CONCERT**	–; concerto, concerts
COMPLIN	–; compline, complins	**CONCH**	–; concha, conchs, conchy
COMPLOT	–; complots		
COMPLY	–; –		
COMPO	–; compos	**CONCHA**	–; conchae, conchal
COMPONE	–; –		
COMPONY	–; –	**CONCHES**	–; –
COMPORT	–; comports	**CONCISE**	–; conciser
COMPOSE	–; composed, composer, composes	**CONCOCT**	–; concocts
		CONCORD	–; concords
		CONCUR	–; concurs
		CONCUSS	–; –
COMPOST	–; composts	**CONDEMN**	–; condemns
COMPOTE	–; compotes	**CONDIGN**	–; –
COMPT	–; compts	**CONDOLE**	–; condoled, condoler, condoles
COMPTED	–; –		
COMPUTE	–; computed, computer, computes	**CONDOM**	–; condoms
		CONDONE	–; condoned, condoner, condones
COMRADE	–; comrades		
COMTE	–; comtes		
CON	icon; cone, coni, conk, conn, cons, cony	**CONDOR**	–; condors
		CONDUCE	–; conduced, conducer, conduces
CONATUS	–; –		
CONCAVE	–; concaved, concaves	**CONDUCT**	–; conducts
		CONDUIT	–; conduits
CONCEAL	–; conceals	**CONDYLE**	–; condyles
CONCEDE	–; conceded,	**CONE**	scone; coned,

	cones, coney
CONES	icones, scones; –
CONEY	–; coneys
CONFAB	–; confabs
CONFECT	–; confects
CONFER	–; confers
CONFESS	–; –
CONFIDE	–; confided, confider, confides
CONFINE	–; confined, confiner, confines
CONFIRM	–; confirms
CONFLUX	–; –
CONFORM	–; conforms
CONFUSE	–; confused, confuses
CONFUTE	–; confuted, confuter, confutes
CONGA	–; congas
CONGAED	–; –
CONGE	–; congee, conger, conges
CONGEAL	–; congeals
CONGEE	–; congeed, congees
CONGER	–; congers
CONGEST	–; congests
CONGIUS	–; –
CONGO	–; congos, congou
CONGOES	–; –
CONGOU	–; congous
CONI	–; conic, conin

CONIC	iconic; conics
CONICAL	iconical; –
CONIES	–; –
CONIFER	–; conifers
CONIINE	–; coniines
CONIN	–; conine, coning, conins
CONINE	–; conines
CONING	–; –
CONIUM	–; coniums
CONJOIN	–; conjoins, conjoint
CONJURE	–; conjured, conjurer, conjures
CONK	–; conks, conky
CONKED	–; –
CONKER	–; conkers
CONKING	–; –
CONN	–; conns
CONNATE	–; –
CONNECT	–; connects
CONNED	–; –
CONNER	–; conners
CONNING	–; –
CONNIVE	–; connived, conniver, connives
CONNOTE	–; connoted, connotes
CONOID	–; conoids
CONQUER	–; conquers
CONS	econs, icons; –
CONSENT	–; consents
CONSIGN	–; consigns
CONSIST	–; consists

CONSOL	–; console, consols		convoker, convokes
CONSOLE	–; consoled, consoler, consoles	**CONVOY**	–; convoys
		COO	–; coof, cook, cool, coon, coop, coos, coot
CONSORT	–; consorts		
CONSUL	–; consuls, consult		
CONSULT	–; consults	**COOCH**	–; –
CONSUME	–; consumed, consumer, consumes	**COOCHES**	–; –
		COOEE	–; cooeed, cooees
CONTACT	–; contacts	**COOER**	–; cooers
CONTAIN	–; contains	**COOEY**	–; cooeys
CONTE	–; contes	**COOEYED**	–; –
CONTEMN	–; contemns	**COOF**	–; coofs
CONTEND	–; contends	**COOING**	–; –
CONTENT	–; contents	**COOK**	–; cooks, cooky
CONTEST	–; contests		
CONTEXT	–; contexts	**COOKED**	–; –
CONTO	–; contos	**COOKER**	–; cookers, cookery
CONTORT	–; contorts		
CONTOUR	–; contours	**COOKEY**	–; cookeys
CONTRA	–; –	**COOKIE**	–; cookies
CONTROL	–; controls	**COOKING**	–; cookings
CONTUSE	–; contused, contuses	**COOKOUT**	–; cookouts
		COOL	–; cools, cooly
CONUS	–; –	**COOLANT**	–; coolants
CONVECT	–; convects	**COOLED**	–; –
CONVENE	–; convened, convener, convenes	**COOLER**	–; coolers
		COOLEST	–; –
		COOLIE	–; coolies
		COOLING	–; –
		COOLISH	–; –
CONVENT	–; convents	**COOLLY**	–; –
CONVERT	–; converts	**COOMB**	–; coombe, coombs
CONVEX	–; –		
CONVEY	–; conveys	**COOMBE**	–; coombes
CONVICT	–; convicts	**COON**	–; coons
CONVOKE	–; convoked,	**COONCAN**	–; cooncans

COONTIE	–; coonties	**COPPED**	–; –
COOP	scoop; coops, coopt	**COPPER**	–; coppers, coppery
COOPED	scooped; –	**COPPICE**	–; coppiced, coppices
COOPER	scooper; coopers, coopery	**COPPING**	–; –
COOPERS	scoopers; –	**COPPRA**	–; coppras
COOPING	scooping; –	**COPRA**	–; coprah, copras
COOPS	scoops; –	**COPRAH**	–; coprahs
COOPT	–; coopts	**COPS**	scops; copse
COOPTED	–; –	**COPSE**	–; copses
COOT	scoot; coots	**COPTER**	–; copters
COOTIE	–; cooties	**COPULA**	scopula; copulae, copular, copulas
COOTS	scoots; –		
COP	scop; cope, cops, copy		
COPAIBA	–; copaibas	**COPULAE**	scopulae; –
COPAL	–; copalm, copals	**COPULAS**	scopulas; –
		COPYBOY	–; copyboys
COPALM	–; copalms	**COPYCAT**	–; copycats
COPE	scope; coped, copen, coper, copes	**COPYIST**	–; copyists
		COQUET	–; coquets
		COQUINA	–; coquinas
		COQUITO	–; coquitos
		CORACLE	–; coracles
		CORAL	–; corals
COPECK	–; copecks	**CORANTO**	–; corantos
COPEN	–; copens	**CORBAN**	–; corbans
COPEPOD	–; copepods	**CORBEIL**	–; corbeils
COPER	–; copers	**CORBEL**	–; corbels
COPES	scopes; –	**CORBIE**	–; corbies
COPIED	–; –	**CORBINA**	–; corbinas
COPIER	–; copiers	**CORBY**	–; –
COPIES	–; –	**CORD**	–; cords
COPIHUE	–; copihues	**CORDAGE**	–; cordages
COPILOT	–; copilots	**CORDATE**	–; –
COPING	–; copings	**CORDED**	–; –
COPIOUS	–; –	**CORDER**	–; corders
COPLOT	–; coplots	**CORDIAL**	–; cordials

CORDING	–; –	CORNET	–; cornets
CORDITE	, cordites	CORNFED	–; –
CORDOBA	–; cordobas	CORNICE	–; corniced,
CORDON	–; cordons		cornices
CORE	score;	CORNIER	–; –
	cored, corer,	CORNILY	–; –
	cores	CORNING	scorning; –
CORED	scored; –	CORNS	acorns,
COREIGN	–; coreigns		scorns; –
CORER	scorer;	CORNU	–; cornua,
	corers		cornus
CORERS	scorers; –	CORNUAL	–; –
CORES	scores; –	CORNUTE	–; cornuted
CORF	–; –	CORNUTO	–; cornutos
CORGI	–; corgis	CORODY	–; –
CORIA	scoria; –	COROLLA	–; corollas
CORING	scoring; –	CORONA	–; coronae,
CORIUM	–; –		coronal,
CORK	–; corks,		coronas
	corky	CORONAL	–; coronals
CORKAGE	–; corkages	CORONEL	–; coronels
CORKED	–; –	CORONER	–; coroners
CORKER	–; corkers	CORONET	–; coronets
CORKIER	–; –	CORPORA	–; corporal
CORKING	–; –	CORPS	–; corpse
CORM	–; corms	CORPSE	–; corpses
CORMEL	–; cormels	CORPUS	–; –
CORMOID	–; –	CORRADE	–; corraded,
CORMOUS	–; –		corrades
CORN	acorn, scorn;	CORRAL	–; corrals
	corns, corny	CORRECT	–; corrects
CORNCOB	–; corncobs	CORRIDA	–; corridas
CORNEA	–; corneal,	CORRIE	–; corries
	corneas	CORRODE	–; corroded,
CORNED	scorned; –		corrodes
CORNEL	–; cornels	CORRODY	–; –
CORNER	scorner;	CORRUPT	–; corrupts
	corners	CORSAC	–; corsacs
CORNERS	scorners; –	CORSAGE	–; corsages
		CORSAIR	–; corsairs

CORSE	–; corses, corset	**COSTA**	–; costae, costal, costar
CORSET	–; corsets		
CORSLET	–; corslets	**COSTAR**	–; costard, costars
CORTEGE	–; corteges		
CORTEX	–; –	**COSTARD**	–; costards
CORTIN	–; cortins	**COSTATE**	–; –
CORVEE	–; corvees	**COSTED**	–; –
CORVES	–; –	**COSTER**	–; costers
CORVET	–; corvets	**COSTING**	–; –
CORVINA	–; corvinas	**COSTIVE**	–; –
CORVINE	–; –	**COSTLY**	–; –
CORYMB	–; corymbs	**COSTREL**	–; costrels
CORYZA	–; coryzal, coryzas	**COSTUME**	–; costumed, costumer, costumes, costumey
COS	–; cosh, coss, cost, cosy		
		COT	scot; cote, cots
COSEC	–; cosecs		
COSES	–; –	**COTAN**	–; cotans
COSET	–; cosets	**COTE**	–; coted, cotes
COSEY	–; coseys		
COSHED	–; –	**COTEAU**	–; coteaux
COSHER	–; coshers	**COTERIE**	–; coteries
COSHES	–; –	**COTHURN**	–; cothurni, cothurns
COSHING	–; –		
COSIE	–; cosier, cosies	**COTIDAL**	–; –
		COTING	–; –
COSIES	–; cosiest	**COTS**	scots; –
COSIGN	–; cosigns	**COTTA**	–; cottae, cottar, cottas
COSILY	–; –		
COSINE	–; cosines		
COSMIC	–; –	**COTTAGE**	–; cottager, cottages, cottagey
COSMISM	–; cosmisms		
COSMIST	–; cosmists		
COSMOS	–; –	**COTTAR**	–; cottars
COSSACK	–; cossacks	**COTTER**	–; cotters
COSSET	–; cossets	**COTTIER**	–; cottiers
COST	–; costa, costs	**COTTON**	–; cottons, cottony

COTYPE	ecotype; cotypes		couranto, courants
COTYPES	ecotypes; –	**COURIER**	–; couriers
COUCH	–; –	**COURLAN**	–; courlans
COUCHED	–; –	**COURSE**	–; coursed, courser, courses
COUCHER	–; couchers		
COUCHES	–; –		
COUDE	–; –	**COURSER**	–; coursers
COUGAR	–; cougars	**COURT**	–; courts
COUGH	–; coughs	**COURTED**	–; –
COUGHED	–; –	**COURTER**	–; courters
COUGHER	–; coughers	**COURTLY**	–; –
COULD	–; –	**COUSIN**	–; cousins
COULDST	–; –	**COUTEAU**	–; couteaux
COULEE	–; coulees	**COUTER**	scouter; couters
COULOIR	–; couloirs		
COULOMB	–; coulombs	**COUTERS**	scouters; –
COULTER	–; coulters	**COUTH**	scouth; couths
COUNCIL	–; councils		
COUNSEL	–; counsels		
COUNT	–; counts, county	**COUTHER**	–; –
		COUTHIE	–; couthier
COUNTED	–; –	**COUTHS**	scouths; –
COUNTER	–; counters	**COUTURE**	–; coutures
COUNTRY	–; –	**COUVADE**	–; couvades
COUNTY	–; –	**COVE**	–; coved, coven, cover, coves, covet, covey
COUP	–; coupe		
COUPE	–; couped, coupes		
		COVEN	–; covens
COUPING	–; –	**COVER**	–; covers, covert
COUPLE	–; coupled, coupler, couples, couplet		
		COVERED	–; –
		COVERER	–; coverers
COUPLER	–; couplers	**COVERT**	–; coverts
COUPLET	–; couplets	**COVET**	–; covets
COUPON	–; coupons	**COVETED**	–; –
COURAGE	–; courages	**COVETER**	–; coveters
COURANT	–; courante,	**COVEY**	–; coveys
		COVING	–; covings

COW	scow; cowl, cows, cowy	COWSHED	–; cowsheds
		COWSKIN	–; cowskins
COWAGE	–; cowages	COWSLIP	–; cowslips
COWARD	–; cowards	COX	–; coxa
COWBANE	–; cowbanes	COXA	–; coxae, coxal
COWBELL	–; cowbells		
COWBIND	–; cowbinds	COXALGY	–; –
COWBIRD	–; cowbirds	COXCOMB	–; coxcombs
COWBOY	–; cowboys	COXED	–; –
COWED	scowed; –	COXES	–; –
COWEDLY	–; –	COXING	–; –
COWER	–; cowers	COY	–; coys
COWERED	–; –	COYED	–; –
COWFISH	–; –	COYER	–; –
COWGIRL	–; cowgirls	COYEST	–; –
COWHAGE	–; cowhages	COYING	–; –
COWHAND	–; cowhands	COYISH	–; –
COWHERB	–; cowherbs	COYLY	–; –
COWHERD	–; cowherds	COYNESS	–; –
COWHIDE	–; cowhided, cowhides	COYOTE	–; coyotes
		COYPOU	–; coypous
		COYPU	–; coypus
COWIER	–; –	COZ	–; cozy
COWIEST	–; –	COZEN	–; cozens
COWING	scowing; –	COZENED	–; –
COWL	scowl; cowls	COZENER	–; cozeners
COWLED	scowled; –	COZES	–; –
COWLICK	–; –	COZEY	–; cozeys
COWLING	scowling; cowlings	COZIE	–; cozier, cozies
COWLS	scowls; –	COZIES	–; coziest
COWMAN	–; –	COZILY	–; –
COWMEN	–; –	COZZES	–; –
COWPAT	–; cowpats	CRAAL	–; craals
COWPEA	–; cowpeas	CRAALED	–; –
COWPOKE	–; cowpokes	CRAB	–; crabs
COWPOX	–; –	CRABBED	–; –
COWRIE	–; cowries	CRABBER	–; crabbers
COWRY	–; –	CRABBY	–; –
COWS	scows; –		

CRACK	–; cracks, cracky	**CRANKED**	–; –
CRACKED	–; –	**CRANKER**	–; –
CRACKER	–; crackers	**CRANKLE**	–; crankled, crankles
CRACKLE	–; crackled, crackles	**CRANKLY**	–; –
CRACKLY	–; –	**CRANNOG**	–; crannoge, crannogs
CRACKUP	–; crackups	**CRANNY**	–; –
CRADLE	–; cradled, cradler, cradles	**CRAP**	scrap; crape, craps
CRADLER	–; cradlers	**CRAPE**	scrape; craped, crapes
CRAFT	–; crafts, crafty	**CRAPED**	scraped; –
CRAFTED	–; –	**CRAPES**	scrapes; –
CRAG	scrag; crags	**CRAPIE**	scrapie; crapies
CRAGGED	scragged; –		
CRAGGY	scraggy; –	**CRAPIES**	scrapies; –
CRAGS	scrags; –	**CRAPING**	scraping; –
CRAKE	–; crakes	**CRAPPED**	scrapped; –
CRAM	scram; cramp, crams	**CRAPPER**	scrapper; crappers
CRAMBE	–; crambes	**CRAPPIE**	–; crappies
CRAMBO	–; crambos	**CRAPPY**	scrappy; –
CRAMMED	scrammed; –	**CRAPS**	scraps; –
CRAMMER	–; crammers	**CRASES**	–; –
CRAMP	–; cramps	**CRASH**	–; –
CRAMPED	–; –	**CRASHED**	–; –
CRAMPIT	–; crampits	**CRASHER**	–; crashers
CRAMPON	–; crampons	**CRASHES**	–; –
CRAMS	scrams; –	**CRASIS**	–; –
CRANCH	–; –	**CRASS**	–; –
CRANE	–; craned, cranes	**CRASSER**	–; –
		CRASSLY	–; –
CRANIA	–; cranial	**CRATCH**	scratch; –
CRANING	–; –	**CRATE**	–; crated, crater, crates
CRANIUM	–; craniums		
CRANK	–; cranks, cranky	**CRATER**	–; craters
		CRATING	–; –

CRATON	–; cratons	**CREAMS**	screams; –
CRAUNCH	–; –	**CREASE**	–; creased,
CRAVAT	–; cravats		creaser,
CRAVE	–; craved,		creases
	craven,	**CREASER**	–; creasers
	craver,	**CREASY**	–; –
	craves	**CREATE**	ocreate;
CRAVEN	–; cravens		created,
CRAVER	–; cravers		creates
CRAVING	–; cravings	**CREATIN**	–; creatine,
CRAW	–; crawl,		creating,
	craws		creatins
CRAWDAD	–; crawdads	**CREATOR**	–; creators
CRAWL	scrawl;	**CRECHE**	–; creches
	crawls,	**CREDAL**	–; –
	crawly	**CREDENT**	–; –
CRAWLED	scrawled; –	**CREDIT**	–; credits
CRAWLER	scrawler;	**CREDO**	–; credos
	crawlers	**CREED**	screed;
CRAWLS	scrawls; –		creeds
CRAWLY	scrawly; –	**CREEDAL**	–; –
CRAYON	–; crayons	**CREEDS**	screeds; –
CRAZE	–; crazed,	**CREEK**	–; creeks
	crazes	**CREEL**	–; creels
CRAZIER	–; –	**CREEP**	–; creeps,
CRAZILY	–; –		creepy
CRAZING	–; –	**CREEPER**	–; creepers
CRAZY	–; –	**CREEPIE**	–; creepies
CREAK	screak;	**CREESE**	–; creeses
	creaks, creaky	**CREESH**	–; –
CREAKED	screaked; –	**CREMATE**	–; cremated,
CREAKS	screaks; –		cremates
CREAKY	screaky; –	**CREME**	–; cremes
CREAM	scream;	**CRENATE**	–; crenated
	creams,	**CRENEL**	–; crenels
	creamy	**CREOLE**	–; creoles
CREAMED	screamed; –	**CREOSOL**	–; creosols
CREAMER	screamer;	**CREPE**	–; creped,
	creamers,		crepes,
	creamery		crepey

CREPING	–; –	CRIMPER	–; crimpers
CREPIER	–; –	CRIMPLE	–; crimpled,
CREPT	–; –		crimples
CREPY	–; –	CRIMPS	scrimps; –
CRESOL	–; cresols	CRIMPY	scrimpy; –
CRESS	–; –	CRIMSON	–; crimsons
CRESSES	–; –	CRINGE	–; cringed,
CRESSET	–; cressets		cringer,
CREST	–; crests		cringes
CRESTAL	–; –	CRINGER	–; cringers
CRESTED	–; –	CRINGLE	–; cringles
CRESYL	–; cresyls	CRINITE	–; crinites
CRETIC	–; cretics	CRINKLE	–; crinkled,
CRETIN	–; cretins		crinkles
CREVICE	–; creviced,	CRINKLY	–; –
	crevices	CRINOID	–; crinoids
CREW	screw; crews	CRINUM	–; crinums
CREWED	screwed; –	CRIOLLO	–; criollos
CREWEL	–; crewels	CRIPPLE	–; crippled,
CREWMAN	–; –		crippler,
CREWMEN	–; –		cripples
CREWING	screwing; –	CRIS	–; crisp
CREWS	screws; –	CRISES	–; –
CRIB	–; cribs	CRISIC	–; –
CRIBBED	–; –	CRISIS	–; –
CRIBBER	–; cribbers	CRISP	–; crisps,
CRICK	–; cricks		crispy
CRICKED	–; –	CRISPED	–; –
CRICKET	–; crickets	CRISPEN	–; crispens
CRICOID	–; cricoids	CRISPER	–; crispers
CRIED	–; –	CRISPLY	–; –
CRIER	–; criers	CRISSA	–; crissal
CRIES	–; –	CRISSUM	–; –
CRIME	–; crimes	CRISTA	–; cristae
CRIMMER	–; crimmers	CRITIC	–; critics
CRIMP	scrimp;	CRITTER	–; critters
	crimps,	CRITTUR	–; critturs
	crimpy	CROAK	–; croaks,
CRIMPED	scrimped; –		croaky

CROAKED	–; –	CROUP	–; croupe,
CROAKER	–; croakers		croups,
CROCEIN	–; croceine,		croupy
	croceins	CROUPE	–; croupes
CROCHET	–; crochets	CROUSE	–; –
CROCI	–; –	CROUTON	–; croutons
CROCINE	–; –	CROW	–; crowd,
CROCK	–; crocks		crown, crows
CROCKED	–; –		
CROCKET	–; crockets	CROWBAR	–; crowbars
CROCUS	–; –	CROWD	–; crowds,
			crowdy
CROFT	–; crofts		
CROFTER	–; crofters	CROWDER	–; crowders
CROJIK	–; crojiks	CROWDIE	–; crowdies
CRONE	–; crones	CROWED	–; –
CRONIES	–; –	CROWER	–; crowers
CRONY	–; –	CROWING	–; –
CROOK	–; crooks	CROWN	–; crowns
CROOKED	–; –	CROWNED	–; –
CROON	–; croons	CROWNER	–; crowners
CROONED	–; –	CROWNET	–; crownets
CROONER	–; crooners	CROZE	–; crozer,
CROP	–; crops		crozes
CROPPED	–; –		
CROPPER	–; croppers	CROZER	–; crozers
CROQUET	–; croquets	CROZIER	–; croziers
CROQUIS	–; –	CRUCES	–; –
CRORE	–; crores	CRUCIAL	–; –
CROSIER	–; crosiers	CRUCIAN	–; crucians
CROSS	across;	CRUCIFY	–; –
	crosse	CRUD	–; crude,
CROSSE	–; crossed,		cruds
	crosser,	CRUDDED	–; –
	crosses	CRUDDY	–; –
CROSSER	–; crossers	CRUDE	–; cruder,
CROSSES	–; crossest		crudes
CROSSLY	–; –	CRUDELY	–; –
CROTCH	–; –	CRUDES	–; crudest
CROTON	–; crotons	CRUDITY	–; –
CROUCH	–; –	CRUEL	–; –
		CRUELER	–; –
		CRUELLY	–; –

CRUELTY	–; –	**CRUSHES**	–; –
CRUET	–; cruets	**CRUSILY**	–; –
CRUISE	–; cruised, cruiser, cruises	**CRUST**	–; crusts, crusty
		CRUSTAL	–; –
CRUISER	–; cruisers	**CRUSTED**	–; –
CRULLER	–; crullers	**CRUTCH**	–; –
CRUMB	–; crumbs, crumby	**CRUX**	–; –
		CRUXES	–; –
CRUMBED	–; –	**CRUZADO**	–; cruzados
CRUMBER	–; crumbers	**CRWTH**	–; crwths
CRUMBLE	–; crumbled, crumbles	**CRY**	–; –
		CRYBABY	–; –
CRUMBLY	–; –	**CRYING**	–; –
CRUMMIE	–; crummies	**CRYOGEN**	–; cryogens, cryogeny
CRUMMY	–; –		
CRUMP	–; crumps	**CRYONIC**	–; cryonics
CRUMPED	–; –	**CRYPT**	–; crypto, crypts
CRUMPET	–; crumpets		
CRUMPLE	–; crumpled, crumples	**CRYPTAL**	–; –
		CRYPTIC	–; –
CRUMPLY	–; –	**CRYPTO**	–; cryptos
CRUNCH	scrunch; crunchy	**CRYSTAL**	–; crystals
		CTENOID	–; –
CRUNODE	–; crunodes	**CUB**	–; cube, cubs
CRUOR	–; cruors		
CRUPPER	–; cruppers	**CUBAGE**	–; cubages
CRURA	–; crural	**CUBBIES**	–; –
CRUS	–; cruse, crush, crust	**CUBBISH**	–; –
		CUBBY	–; –
CRUSADE	–; crusaded, crusader, crusades	**CUBE**	–; cubeb, cubed, cuber, cubes
CRUSADO	–; crusados	**CUBEB**	–; cubebs
CRUSE	–; cruses, cruset	**CUBER**	–; cubers
		CUBIC	–; cubics
CRUSET	–; crusets	**CUBICAL**	–; –
CRUSH	–; –	**CUBICLE**	–; cubicles
CRUSHED	–; –	**CUBICLY**	–; –
CRUSHER	–; crushers	**CUBING**	–; –

CUBISM	–; cubisms	**CULICID**	–; culicids
CUBIST	–; cubists	**CULL**	scull; culls, cully
CUBIT	–; cubits		
CUBITAL	–; –	**CULLAY**	–; cullays
CUBOID	–; cuboids	**CULLED**	sculled; –
CUCKOLD	–; cuckolds	**CULLER**	sculler; cullers
CUCKOO	–; cuckoos		
CUD	scud; cuds	**CULLERS**	scullers; –
CUDBEAR	–; cudbears	**CULLET**	–; cullets
CUDDIE	–; cuddies	**CULLIED**	–; –
CUDDLE	–; cuddled, cuddles	**CULLIES**	–; –
		CULLING	sculling; –
CUDDLY	–; –	**CULLION**	–; cullions
CUDDY	–; –	**CULLIS**	–; –
CUDGEL	–; cudgels	**CULLS**	sculls; –
CUDS	scuds; –	**CULM**	–; culms
CUDWEED	–; cudweeds	**CULMED**	–; –
CUE	–; cued, cues	**CULMING**	–; –
		CULOTTE	–; culottes
CUEING	–; –	**CULPA**	–; culpae
CUESTA	–; cuestas	**CULPRIT**	–; culprits
CUFF	scuff; cuffs	**CULT**	–; culti, cults
CUFFED	scuffed; –	**CULTCH**	–; –
CUFFING	scuffing; –	**CULTI**	–; cultic
CUFFS	scuffs; –	**CULTISM**	–; cultisms
CUIF	–; cuifs	**CULTIST**	–; cultists
CUING	–; –	**CULTURE**	–; cultured, cultures
CUIRASS	–; –		
CUISH	–; –	**CULTUS**	–; –
CUISHES	–; –	**CULVER**	–; culvers, culvert
CUISINE	–; cuisines		
CUISSE	–; cuisses	**CULVERT**	–; culverts
CUITTLE	–; cuittled, cuittles	**CUM**	scum; –
		CUMARIN	–; cumarins
CUKE	–; cukes	**CUMBER**	–; cumbers
CULCH	–; –	**CUMIN**	–; cumins
CULCHES	–; –	**CUMMER**	scummer; cummers
CULET	–; culets		
CULEX	–; –	**CUMMERS**	scummers; –
CULICES	–; –	**CUMMIN**	–; cummins

CUMQUAT	–; cumquats	**CURABLE**	–; –
CUMSHAW	–; cumshaws	**CURABLY**	–; –
CUMULI	–; –	**CURACAO**	–; curacaos
CUMULUS	–; –	**CURACOA**	–; curacoas
CUNDUM	–; cundums	**CURACY**	–; –
CUNEAL	–; –	**CURAGH**	–; curaghs
CUNEATE	–; cuneated	**CURARA**	–; curaras
CUNNER	scunner; cunners	**CURARE**	–; curares
		CURARI	–; curaris
CUNNING	–; cunnings	**CURATE**	–; curates
CUP	scup; cups	**CURATOR**	–; curators
CUPCAKE	–; cupcakes	**CURB**	–; curbs
CUPEL	–; cupels	**CURBED**	–; –
CUPELED	–; cupeled	**CURBER**	–; curbers
CUPELER	–; cupelers	**CURBING**	–; curbings
CUPFUL	–; cupfuls	**CURCH**	–; –
CUPID	–; cupids	**CURCHES**	–; –
CUPLIKE	–; –	**CURCUMA**	–; curcumas
CUPOLA	–; cupolas	**CURD**	–; curds, curdy
CUPPA	–; cuppas		
CUPPED	–; –	**CURDED**	–; –
CUPPER	scupper; cuppers	**CURDING**	–; –
		CURDIER	–; –
CUPPERS	scuppers; –	**CURDLE**	–; curdled, curdler, curdles
CUPPING	–; cuppings		
CUPPY	–; –		
CUPRIC	–;	**CURDLER**	–; curdlers
CUPRITE	–; cuprites	**CURE**	–; cured, curer, cures, curet
CUPROUS	–; –		
CUPRUM	–; cuprums		
CUPS	scups; –	**CURER**	–; curers
CUPSFUL	–; –	**CURET**	–; curets
CUPULA	–; cupulae, cupular	**CURETTE**	–; curetted, curettes
CUPULE	–; cupules	**CURF**	scurf; curfs
CUR	–; curb, curd, cure, curf, curl, curn, curr, curs, curt	**CURFEW**	–; curfews
		CURFS	scurfs; –
		CURIA	–; curiae, curial
		CURIE	–; curies

CURING	–; –	**CURSOR**	–; cursors, cursory
CURIO	–; curios		
CURIOSA	–; –	**CURSORY**	–; –
CURIOUS	–; –	**CURST**	–; –
CURITE	–; curites	**CURT**	–; –
CURIUM	–; curiums	**CURTAIL**	–; curtails
CURL	–; curls, curly	**CURTAIN**	–; curtains
		CURTAL	–; curtals
CURLED	–; –	**CURTATE**	–; –
CURLER	–; curlers	**CURTER**	–; –
CURLEW	–; curlews	**CURTEST**	–; –
CURLIER	–; –	**CURTLY**	–; –
CURLILY	–; –	**CURTSEY**	–; curtseys
CURLING	–; curlings	**CURTSY**	–; –
CURN	–; curns	**CURULE**	–; –
CURR	–; currs, curry	**CURVE**	–; curved, curves, curvet, curvey
CURRACH	–; currachs		
CURRAGH	–; curraghs		
CURRAN	–; currans, currant	**CURVET**	–; curvets
CURRANT	–; currants	**CURVEY**	–; –
CURRED	–; –	**CURVIER**	–; –
CURRENT	–; currents	**CURVING**	–; –
CURRIE	–; curried, currier, curries	**CURVY**	scurvy; –
		CUSCUS	–; –
		CUSEC	–; cusecs
CURRIED	scurried; –	**CUSHAT**	–; cushats
CURRIER	–; curriers, curriery	**CUSHAW**	–; cushaws
		CUSHIER	–; –
CURRIES	scurries; –	**CUSHILY**	–; –
CURRING	–; –	**CUSHION**	–; cushions, cushiony
CURRISH	–; –		
CURRY	scurry; –	**CUSHY**	–; –
CURSE	–; cursed, curser, curses	**CUSK**	–; cusks
		CUSP	–; cusps
		CUSPATE	–; –
CURSER	–; cursers	**CUSPED**	–; –
CURSING	–; –	**CUSPID**	–; cuspids
CURSIVE	–; cursives	**CUSPIS**	–; –
		CUSS	–; cusso

CUSSED	–; –	**CUTTAGE**	–; cuttages
CUSSER	–; cussers	**CUTTER**	scutter;
CUSSING	–; –		cutters
CUSSO	–; cussos	**CUTTERS**	scutters; –
CUSTARD	–; custards	**CUTTIES**	–; –
CUSTODY	–; –	**CUTTING**	–; cuttings
CUSTOM	–; customs	**CUTTLE**	scuttle;
CUSTOS	–; –		cuttled,
CUT	scut; cute,		cuttles
	cuts	**CUTTLED**	scuttled; –
CUTAWAY	–; cutaways	**CUTTLES**	scuttles; –
CUTBACK	–; cutbacks	**CUTTY**	–; –
CUTCH	scutch; –	**CUTUP**	–; cutups
CUTCHES	scutches; –	**CUTWORK**	–; cutworks
CUTDOWN	–; cutdowns	**CUTWORM**	–; cutworms
CUTE	acuto, acute,	**CUVETTE**	–; cuvettes
	cuter, cutes,	**CWM**	–; cwms
	cutey	**CYAN**	–; cyans
CUTELY	acutely; –	**CYANATE**	–; cyanates
CUTER	acuter; –	**CYANIC**	–; –
CUTES	acutes,	**CYANID**	–; cyanide,
	scutes;		cyanids
	cutest,	**CYANIDE**	–; cyanided,
	cutesy		cyanides
CUTEST	acutest; –	**CYANIN**	–; cyanine,
CUTEY	–; cuteys		cyanins
CUTICLE	–; cuticles	**CYANINE**	–; cyanines
CUTIE	–; cuties	**CYANITE**	–; cyanites
CUTIN	–; cutins	**CYANO**	–; –
CUTIS	–; –	**CYBORG**	–; cyborgs
CUTISES	–; –	**CYCAD**	–; cycads
CUTLAS	–; cutlass	**CYCAS**	–; –
CUTLER	–; cutlers,	**CYCASES**	–; –
	cutlery	**CYCASIN**	–; cycasins
CUTLET	–; cutlets	**CYCLASE**	–; cyclases
CUTLINE	–; cutlines	**CYCLE**	–; cycled,
CUTOFF	–; cutoffs		cycler,
CUTOUT	–; cutouts		cycles
CUTOVER	–; –	**CYCLER**	–; cyclers
CUTS	scuts; –	**CYCLIC**	acyclic; –

CYCLING	–; cyclings	**CYMOID**	–; –
CYCLIST	–; cyclists	**CYMOL**	–; cymols
CYCLIZE	–; cyclized, cyclizes	**CYMOSE**	–; –
		CYMOUS	–; –
CYCLO	–; cyclos	**CYNIC**	–; cynics
CYCLOID	–; cycloids	**CYNICAL**	–; –
CYCLONE	–; cyclones	**CYPHER**	–; cyphers
CYCLOPS	–; –	**CYPRES**	–; cypress
CYDER	–; cyders	**CYPRIAN**	–; cyprians
CYESES	–; –	**CYPRUS**	–; –
CYESIS	–; –	**CYPSELA**	–; cypselae
CYGNET	–; cygnets	**CYST**	–; cysts
CYLICES	–; –	**CYSTEIN**	–; cysteine, cysteins
CYLIX	–; –		
CYMA	–; cymae, cymar, cymas	**CYSTIC**	–; –
		CYSTINE	–; cystines
		CYSTOID	–; cystoids
CYMAR	–; cymars	**CYTON**	–; cytons
CYMBAL	–; cymbals	**CZAR**	–; czars
CYME	–; cymes	**CZARDAS**	–; –
CYMENE	–; cymenes	**CZARDOM**	–; czardoms
CYMLIN	–; cymling, cymlins	**CZARINA**	–; czarinas
		CZARISM	–; czarisms
CYMLING	–; cymlings	**CZARIST**	–; czarists

D

D	ad, id, od; da, de, di, do	**DABBING**	–; –
		DABBLE	–; dabbled, dabbler, dabbles
DA	–; dab, dad, dag, dah, dak, dam, dan, dap, daw, day		
		DABBLER	–; dabblers
		DABSTER	–; dabsters
		DACE	–; daces
		DACHA	–; dachas
		DACKER	–; dackers
DAB	–; dabs	**DACOIT**	–; dacoits, dacoity
DABBED	–; –		
DABBER	–; dabbers		

DACTYL	–; dactyls	**DAIMEN**	–; –
DAD	, dada, dado, dads	**DAIMIO**	; daimios
		DAIMON	–; daimons
DADA	–; dadas	**DAIMYO**	–; daimyos
DADAISM	–; dadaisms	**DAINTY**	–; –
DADAIST	–; dadaists	**DAIRIES**	–; –
DADDIES	–; –	**DAIRY**	–; –
DADDLE	–; daddled, daddles	**DAIS**	–; daisy
		DAISES	–; –
DADDY	–; –	**DAISIED**	–; –
DADO	–; dados	**DAISIES**	–; –
DADOED	–; –	**DAK**	–; daks
DADOES	–; –	**DAKOIT**	–; dakoits, dakoity
DADOING	–; –		
DAEDAL	–; –	**DALAPON**	–; dalapons
DAEMON	–; daemons	**DALASI**	–; dalasis
DAFF	–; daffs, daffy	**DALE**	–; dales
		DALETH	–; daleths
DAFFED	–; –	**DALLES**	–; –
DAFFIER	–; –	**DALLIED**	–; –
DAFFING	–; –	**DALLIER**	–; dalliers
DAFT	–; –	**DALLIES**	–; –
DAFTER	–; –	**DALLY**	–; –
DAFTEST	–; –	**DAM**	–; dame, damn, damp, dams
DAFTLY	–; –		
DAG	–; dago, dags		
		DAMAGE	–; damaged, damager, damages
DAGGER	–; daggers		
DAGGLE	–; daggled, daggles		
DAGLOCK	–; daglocks	**DAMAGER**	–; damagers
DAGO	–; dagos	**DAMAN**	–; damans
DAGOBA	–; dagobas	**DAMAR**	–; damars
DAGOES	–; –	**DAMASK**	–; damasks
DAH	–; dahs	**DAME**	–; dames
DAHLIA	–; dahlias	**DAMMAR**	–; dammars
DAHOON	–; dahoons	**DAMMED**	–; –
DAIKER	–; daikers	**DAMMER**	–; dammers
DAILY	–; –	**DAMMING**	–; –
DAILIES	–; –	**DAMN**	–; damns

DAMNED	–; –	**DANGLER**	–; danglers
DAMNER	–; damners	**DANIO**	–; danios
DAMNIFY	–; –	**DANK**	–; –
DAMNING	–; –	**DANKER**	–; –
DAMOSEL	–; damosels	**DANKEST**	–; –
DAMOZEL	–; damozels	**DANKLY**	–; –
DAMP	–; damps	**DANSEUR**	–; danseurs
DAMPED	–; –	**DAP**	–; daps
DAMPEN	–; dampens	**DAPHNE**	–; daphnes
DAMPER	–; dampers	**DAPHNIA**	–; daphnias
DAMPEST	–; –	**DAPPED**	–; –
DAMPING	–; –	**DAPPER**	–; –
DAMPISH	–; –	**DAPPING**	–; –
DAMPLY	–; –	**DAPPLE**	–; dappled, dapples
DAMSEL	–; damsels		
DAMSON	–; damsons	**DARB**	–; darbs
DAN	–; dang, dank, dans	**DARBIES**	–; –
		DARE	–; dared, darer, dares
DANCE	–; danced, dancer, dances		
		DAREFUL	–; –
		DARER	–; darers
DANCER	–; dancers	**DARESAY**	–; –
DANCING	–; –	**DARIC**	–; darics
DANDER	–; danders	**DARING**	–; darings
DANDIER	–; –	**DARIOLE**	–; darioles
DANDIES	–; dandiest	**DARK**	–; darks, darky
DANDIFY	–; –		
DANDILY	–; –	**DARKED**	–; –
DANDLE	–; dandled, dandler, dandles	**DARKEN**	–; darkens
		DARKER	–; –
		DARKEST	–; –
DANDLER	–; dandlers	**DARKEY**	–; darkeys
DANDY	–; –	**DARKIE**	–; darkies
DANG	–; dangs	**DARKING**	–; –
DANGED	–; –	**DARKISH**	–; –
DANGER	–; dangers	**DARKLE**	–; darkled, darkles
DANGING	–; –		
DANGLE	–; dangled, dangler, dangles	**DARKLY**	–; –
		DARLING	–; darlings
		DARN	–; darns

DARNED	–; –	**DAUBE**	–; daubed,
DARNEL	–; darnels		dauber,
DARNER	–; darners		daubes
DARNING	–; darnings	**DAUBER**	–; daubers,
DART	–; darts		daubery
DARTED	–; –	**DAUBIER**	–; –
DARTER	–; darters	**DAUBING**	–; –
DARTING	–; –	**DAUBRY**	–; –
DARTLE	–; dartled,	**DAUNDER**	–; daunders
	dartles	**DAUNT**	–; daunts
DASH	–; dashy	**DAUNTED**	–; –
DASHED	–; –	**DAUNTER**	–; daunters
DASHEEN	–; dasheens	**DAUPHIN**	–; dauphine,
DASHER	–; dashers		dauphins
DASHIER	–; –	**DAUT**	–; dauts
DASHING	–; –	**DAUTED**	–; –
DASHIKI	–; dashikis	**DAUTIE**	–; dauties
DASHPOT	–; dashpots	**DAUTING**	–; –
DASSIE	–; dassies	**DAVEN**	–; davens
DASTARD	–; dastards	**DAVENED**	–; –
DASYURE	–; dasyures	**DAVIES**	–; –
DATA	–; –	**DAVIT**	–; davits
DATABLE	–; –	**DAVY**	–; –
DATARY	–; –	**DAW**	–; dawk,
DATCHA	–; datchas		dawn, daws,
DATE	–; dated,		dawt
	dater, dates	**DAWDLE**	–; dawdled,
DATEDLY	–; –		dawdler,
DATER	–; daters		dawdles
DATING	–; –	**DAWDLER**	–; dawdlers
DATIVAL	–; –	**DAWED**	–; –
DATIVE	–; datives	**DAWEN**	–; –
DATO	–; datos	**DAWING**	–; –
DATTO	–; dattos	**DAWK**	–; dawks
DATUM	–; datums	**DAWN**	–; dawns
DATURA	–; daturas	**DAWNED**	–; –
DATURIC	–; –	**DAWNING**	–; –
DAUB	–; daube,	**DAWT**	–; dawts
	daubs,	**DAWTED**	–; –
	dauby	**DAWTIE**	–; dawties

DAWTING	–; –	**DEAFEST**	–; –
DAY	–; days	**DEAFISH**	–; –
DAYBED	–; daybeds	**DEAFLY**	–; –
DAYBOOK	–; daybooks	**DEAIR**	–; deairs
DAYFLY	–; –	**DEAIRED**	–; –
DAYGLOW	–; –	**DEAL**	ideal; deals, dealt
DAYLILY	–; –		
DAYLONG	–; –	**DEALATE**	–; dealated, dealates
DAYMARE	–; daymares		
DAYROOM	–; dayrooms	**DEALER**	–; dealers
DAYSIDE	–; daysides	**DEALING**	–; dealings
DAYSMAN	–; –	**DEALS**	ideals; –
DAYSMEN	–; –	**DEAN**	–; deans
DAYSTAR	–; daystars	**DEANED**	–; –
DAYTIME	–; daytimes	**DEANING**	–; –
DAZE	–; dazed, dazes	**DEAR**	–; dears, deary
DAZEDLY	–; –	**DEARER**	–; –
DAZING	–; –	**DEAREST**	–; –
DAZZLE	–; dazzled, dazzler, dazzles	**DEARIE**	–; dearies
		DEARLY	–; –
		DEARTH	–; dearths
DAZZLER	–; dazzlers	**DEASH**	–; –
DE	ode; deb, dee, dei, del, den, des, dev, dew, dex, dey	**DEASHED**	–; –
		DEASHES	–; –
		DEASIL	–; –
		DEATH	–; deaths, deathy
DEACON	–; deacons	**DEATHLY**	–; –
DEAD	–; deads	**DEAVE**	–; deaved, deaves
DEADEN	–; deadens		
DEADER	–; –	**DEAVING**	–; –
DEADEST	–; –	**DEB**	–; debs, debt
DEADEYE	–; deadeyes		
DEADLY	–; –	**DEBACLE**	–; debacles
DEADPAN	–; deadpans	**DEBAR**	–; debark, debars
DEAF	–; –		
DEAFEN	–; deafens	**DEBARK**	–; debarks
DEAFER	–; –	**DEBASE**	–; debased,

	debaser, debuses	**DECEIVE**	–; deceived, docoivor, deceives
DEBASER	–; debasers		
DEBATE	–; debated, debater, debates	**DECENCY**	–; –
		DECENT	–; –
		DECERN	–; decerns
DEBATER	–; debaters	**DECIARE**	–; deciares
DEBAUCH	–; –	**DECIBEL**	–; decibels
DEBIT	–; debits	**DECIDE**	–; decided, decider, decides
DEBONE	–; deboned, deboner, debones		
		DECIDER	–; deciders
DEBONER	–; deboners	**DECIDUA**	–; deciduae, decidual, deciduas
DEBOUCH	–; debouche		
DEBRIEF	–; debriefs		
DEBRIS	–; –	**DECILE**	–; deciles
DEBT	–; debts	**DECIMAL**	–; decimals
DEBTOR	–; debtors	**DECK**	–; decks
DEBUG	–; debugs	**DECKED**	–; –
DEBUNK	–; debunks	**DECKEL**	–; deckels
DEBUT	–; debuts	**DECKER**	–; deckers
DEBUTED	–; –	**DECKING**	–; deckings
DEBYE	–; debyes	**DECKLE**	–; deckles
DECADAL	; –	**DECLAIM**	–; declaims
DECADE	; decades	**DECLARE**	–; declared, declarer, declares
DECAGON	–; decagons		
DECAL	–; decals		
DECAMP	–; decamps	**DECLASS**	–; declasse
DECANAL	–; –	**DECLINE**	–; declined, decliner, declines
DECANE	–; decanes		
DECANT	–; decants		
DECAPOD	–; decapods	**DECOCT**	–; decocts
DECARE	–; decares	**DECODE**	–; decoded, decoder, decodes
DECAY	–; decays		
DECAYED	–; –		
DECAYER	–; decayers	**DECODER**	–; decoders
DECEASE	–; deceased, deceases	**DECOLOR**	–; decolors
		DECOR	–; decors
		DECORUM	–; decorums
DECEIT	–; deceits	**DECOY**	–; decoys

DECOYED	–; –	**DEEPER**	–; –
DECOYER	–; decoyers	**DEEPEST**	–; –
DECREE	–; decreed,	**DEEPLY**	–; –
	decreer,	**DEER**	–; deers
	decrees	**DEERFLY**	–; –
DECREER	–; decreers	**DEEWAN**	–; deewans
DECRIAL	–; decrials	**DEFACE**	–; defaced,
DECRIED	–; –		defacer,
DECRIER	–; decriers		defaces
DECROWN	–; decrowns	**DEFACER**	–; defacers
DECRY	–; –	**DEFAME**	–; defamed,
DECRYPT	–; decrypts		defamer,
DECUMAN	–; –		defames
DECUPLE	–; decupled,	**DEFAMER**	–; defamers
	decuples	**DEFAT**	–; defats
DECURVE	–; decurved,	**DEFAULT**	–; defaults
	decurves	**DEFEAT**	–; defeats
DECURY	–; –	**DEFECT**	–; defects
DEDAL	–; –	**DEFENCE**	–; defences
DEDANS	–; –	**DEFEND**	–; defends
DEDUCE	–; deduced,	**DEFENSE**	–; defensed,
	deduces		defenses
DEDUCT	–; deducts	**DEFER**	–; defers
DEE	–; deed,	**DEFI**	–; defis
	deem, deep,	**DEFICIT**	–; deficits
	deer, dees,	**DEFIED**	–; –
	deet	**DEFIER**	–; defiers
DEED	–; deeds,	**DEFIES**	–; –
	deedy	**DEFILE**	–; defiled,
DEEDED	–; –		defiler,
DEEDIER	–; –		defiles
DEEDING	–; –	**DEFILER**	–; defilers
DEEJAY	–; deejays	**DEFINE**	–; defined,
DEEM	adeem;		definer,
	deems		defines
DEEMED	adeemed; –	**DEFINER**	–; definers
DEEMING	–; –	**DEFLATE**	–; deflated,
DEEMS	adeems; –		deflates
DEEP	–; deeps	**DEFLEA**	–; defleas
DEEPEN	–; deepens	**DEFLECT**	–; deflects

DEFOAM	–; defoams	**DEHORT**	–; dehorts
DEFOG	–; defogs	**DEI**	–; deil
DEFORCE	–; deforced, deforces	**DEICE**	–; deiced, deicer, deices
DEFORM	–; deforms		
DEFRAUD	–; defrauds	**DEICER**	–; deicers
DEFRAY	–; defrays	**DEICIDE**	–; deicides
DEFROCK	–; defrocks	**DEICING**	–; –
DEFROST	–; defrosts	**DEICTIC**	–; –
DEFT	–; –	**DEIFIC**	–; –
DEFTER	–; –	**DEIFIED**	–; –
DEFTEST	–; –	**DEIFIER**	–; deifiers
DEFTLY	–; –	**DEIFIES**	–; –
DEFUNCT	–; –	**DEIFORM**	–; –
DEFUSE	–; defused, defuses	**DEIFY**	–; –
		DEIGN	–; deigns
DEFUZE	–; defuzed, defuzes	**DEIGNED**	–; –
		DEIL	–; deils
DEFY	–; –	**DEISM**	–; deisms
DEGAGE	–; –	**DEIST**	–; deists
DEGAME	–; degames	**DEISTIC**	–; –
DEGAMI	–; degamis	**DEITIES**	–; –
DEGAS	–; –	**DEITY**	–; –
DEGASES	–; –	**DEJECT**	–; dejecta, dejects
DEGAUSS	–; –		
DEGERM	–; degerms	**DEKARE**	–; dekares
DEGLAZE	–; deglazed, deglazes	**DEKE**	–; deked, dekes
		DEKING	–; –
DEGRADE	–; degraded, degrader, degrades	**DEL**	–; dele, delf, deli, dell, dels
		DELAINE	–; delaines
DEGREE	–; degreed, degrees	**DELATE**	–; delated, delates
DEGUM	–; degums	**DELATOR**	–; delators
DEGUST	–; degusts	**DELAY**	–; delays
DEHISCE	–; dehisced, dehisces	**DELAYED**	–; –
		DELAYER	–; delayers
DEHORN	–; dehorns		

DELE	–; deled, deles	**DEMAND**	–; demands
DELEAD	–; deleads	**DEMARK**	–; demarks
DELEING	–; –	**DEMAST**	–; demasts
DELETE	–; deleted, deletes	**DEME**	–; demes
		DEMEAN	–; demeans
DELF	–; delfs, delft	**DEMENT**	–; dements
		DEMERIT	–; demerits
DELFT	–; delfts	**DEMESNE**	–; demesnes
DELI	–; delis	**DEMIES**	–; –
DELICT	–; delicts	**DEMIGOD**	–; demigods
DELIGHT	–; delights	**DEMIREP**	–; demireps
DELIME	–; delimed, delimes	**DEMISE**	–; demised, demises
DELIMIT	–; delimits	**DEMIT**	–; demits
DELIST	–; delists	**DEMO**	–; demob, demon, demos
DELIVER	–; delivers, delivery		
DELL	–; dells, delly	**DEMOB**	–; demobs
		DEMODE	–; demoded
DELLIES	–; –	**DEMON**	–; demons
DELOUSE	–; deloused, delouses	**DEMONIC**	–; –
		DEMOSES	–; –
DELTA	–; deltas	**DEMOTE**	–; demoted, demotes
DELTAIC	–; –		
DELTIC	–; –	**DEMOTIC**	–; demotics
DELTOID	–; deltoids	**DEMOUNT**	–; demounts
DELUDE	–; deluded, deluder, deludes	**DEMUR**	–; demure, demurs
DELUDER	–; deluders	**DEMURE**	–; demurer
DELUGE	–; deluged, deluges	**DEMY**	–; –
		DEN	–; dene, dens, dent, deny
DELUXE	–; –	**DENARY**	–; –
DELVE	–; delved, delver, delves	**DENE**	–; denes
		DENGUE	–; dengues
		DENIAL	–; denials
DELVER	–; delvers	**DENIED**	–;
DEMAGOG	–; demagogs, demagogy	**DENIER**	–; deniers
		DENIES	–; –

DENIM	–; denims	**DEPLORE**	–; deplored,
DENIZEN	–; denizens		deplorer,
DENNED	–; –		deplores
DENNING	–; –	**DEPLOY**	–; deploys
DENOTE	–; denoted,	**DEPLUME**	–;
	denotes		deplumed,
DENSE	–; denser		deplumes
DENSELY	–; –	**DEPONE**	–; deponed,
DENSIFY	–; –		depones
DENSITY	–; –	**DEPORT**	–; deports
DENT	–; dents	**DEPOSAL**	–; deposals
DENTAL	–; dentals	**DEPOSE**	–; deposed,
DENTATE	–; dentated		deposer,
DENTED	–; –		deposes
DENTIL	–; dentils	**DEPOSER**	–; deposers
DENTIN	–; dentine,	**DEPOSIT**	–; deposits
	denting,	**DEPOT**	–; depots
	dentins	**DEPRAVE**	–;
DENTINE	–; dentines		depraved,
DENTIST	–; dentists		depraver,
DENTOID	–; –		depraves
DENTURE	–; dentures	**DEPRESS**	–; –
DENUDE	–; denuded,	**DEPRIVE**	–; deprived,
	denuder,		depriver,
	denudes		deprives
DENUDER	–; denuders	**DEPSIDE**	–; depsides
DEODAND	–; deodands	**DEPTH**	–; depths
DEODAR	–; deodara,	**DEPUTE**	–; deputed,
	deodars		deputes
DEODARA	–; deodaras	**DEPUTY**	–; –
DEPAINT	–; depaints	**DERAIGN**	–; deraigns
DEPART	–; departs	**DERAIL**	–; derails
DEPEND	–; depends	**DERANGE**	–;
DEPERM	–; deperms		deranged,
DEPICT	–; depicts		deranges
DEPLANE	–;	**DERAT**	–; derats
	deplaned,	**DERAY**	–; derays
	deplanes	**DERBIES**	–; –
DEPLETE	–; depleted,	**DERBY**	–; –
	depletes	**DERE**	–; –

DERIDE	–; derided, derider, derides	**DESIST**	–; desists
		DESK	–; desks
DERIDER	–; deriders	**DESKMAN**	–; –
DERIVE	–; derived, deriver, derives	**DESKMEN**	–; –
		DESMAN	–; desmans
		DESMID	–; desmids
DERIVER	–; derivers	**DESMOID**	–; desmoids
DERM	–; derma, derms	**DESORB**	–; desorbs
		DESPAIR	–; despairs
DERMA	–; dermal, dermas	**DESPISE**	–; despised, despiser, despises
DERMIS	–; –	**DESPITE**	–; despited, despites
DERMOID	–; –		
DERNIER	–; –	**DESPOIL**	–; despoils
DERRICK	–; derricks	**DESPOND**	–; desponds
DERRIES	–; –	**DESPOT**	–; despots
DERRIS	–; –	**DESSERT**	–; desserts
DERRY	–; –	**DESTAIN**	–; destains
DERVISH	–; –	**DESTINE**	–; destined, destines
DES	ides, odes; desk		
		DESTINY	–; –
DESALT	–; desalts	**DESTROY**	–; destroys
DESAND	–; desands	**DESUGAR**	–; desugars
DESCANT	–; descants	**DETACH**	–; –
DESCEND	–; descends	**DETAIL**	–; details
DESCENT	–; descents	**DETAIN**	–; detains
DESCRY	–; –	**DETECT**	–; detects
DESERT	–; deserts	**DETENT**	–; detente, detents
DESERVE	–; deserved, deserver, deserves	**DETENTE**	–; detentes
		DETER	–; deters
DESEX	–; –	**DETERGE**	–; deterged, deterger, deterges
DESEXED	–; –		
DESEXES	–; –		
DESIGN	–; designs	**DETEST**	–; detests
DESIRE	–; desired, desirer, desires	**DETICK**	–; deticks
		DETINUE	–; detinues
		DETOUR	–; detours
DESIRER	–; desirers	**DETRACT**	–; detracts

DETRAIN	–; detrains	devotee,
DETRUDE	–; detruded,	devotes
	detrudes	**DEVOTEE**	–; devotees
DEUCE	–; deuced,	**DEVOUR**	–; devours
	deuces	**DEVOUT**	–; –
DEUTZIA	–; deutzias	**DEW**	–; dews,
DEV	–; deva,	dewy
	devs	**DEWAN**	–; dewans
DEVA	–; devas	**DEWATER**	–; dewaters
DEVALUE	–; devalued,	**DEWAX**	–; –
	devalues	**DEWAXED**	–; –
DEVEIN	–; deveins	**DEWAXES**	–; –
DEVEL	–; devels	**DEWCLAW**	–; dewclaws
DEVELOP	–; develope,	**DEWDROP**	–; dewdrops
	develops	**DEWED**	–; –
DEVEST	–; devests	**DEWFALL**	–; dewfalls
DEVIANT	–; deviants	**DEWIER**	–; –
DEVIATE	–; deviated,	**DEWIEST**	–; –
	deviates	**DEWILY**	–; –
DEVICE	–; devices	**DEWING**	–; –
DEVIL	–; devils	**DEWLAP**	–; dewlaps
DEVILED	–; –	**DEWLESS**	–; –
DEVILRY	–; –	**DEWOOL**	–; dewools
DEVIOUS	–; –	**DEWORM**	–; deworms
DEVISAL	–; devisals	**DEX**	–; –
DEVISE	–; devised,	**DEXES**	–; –
	devisee,	**DEXIES**	–; –
	deviser,	**DEXTER**	–; –
	devises	**DEXTRAL**	–; –
DEVISEE	–; devisees	**DEXTRAN**	–; dextrans
DEVISER	–; devisers	**DEXTRIN**	–; dextrine,
DEVISOR	–; devisors	dextrins
DEVOICE	–; devoiced,	**DEXTRO**	–; –
	devoices	**DEY**	–; deys
DEVOID	–; –	**DEZINC**	–; dezincs
DEVOIR	–; devoirs	**DHAK**	–; dhaks
DEVOLVE	–; devolved,	**DHARMA**	–; dharmas
	devolves	**DHARMIC**	–; –
DEVON	–; devons	**DHARNA**	–; dharnas
DEVOTE	–; devoted,	**DHOLE**	–; dholes

DHOOLY	–; –	**DIARIES**	–; –
DHOORA	–; dhooras	**DIARIST**	–; diarists
DHOOTI	–; dhootie, dhootis	**DIARY**	–; –
		DIASTER	–; diasters
DHOOTIE	–; dhooties	**DIATOM**	–; diatoms
DHOTI	–; dhotis	**DIAZIN**	–; diazine, diazins
DHOURRA	–; dhourras		
DHOW	–; dhows	**DIAZINE**	–; diazines
DHURNA	–; dhurnas	**DIAZO**	–; –
DHUTI	–; dhutis	**DIAZOLE**	–; diazoles
DIABASE	–; diabases	**DIB**	–; dibs
DIABOLO	–; diabolos	**DIBASIC**	–; –
DIACID	–; diacids	**DIBBED**	–; –
DIADEM	–; diadems	**DIBBER**	–; dibbers
DIAGRAM	–; diagrams	**DIBBING**	–; –
DIAL	–; dials	**DIBBLE**	–; dibbled, dibbler, dibbles
DIALED	–; –		
DIALECT	–; dialects		
DIALER	–; dialers	**DIBBLER**	–; dibblers
DIALING	–; dialings	**DIBBUK**	–; dibbuks
DIALIST	–; dialists	**DICAST**	–; dicasts
DIALLED	–; –	**DICE**	–; diced, dicer, dices, dicey
DIALLEL	–; –		
DIALLER	–; diallers		
DIALOG	–; dialogs	**DICER**	–; dicers
DIALYSE	–; dialysed, dialyser, dialyses	**DICIER**	–; –
		DICIEST	–; –
		DICING	–; –
DIALYZE	–; dialyzed, dialyzer, dialyzes	**DICK**	–; dicks, dicky
		DICKENS	–; –
DIAMIDE	–; diamides	**DICKER**	–; dickers
DIAMIN	–; diamine, diamins	**DICKEY**	–; dickeys
		DICKIE	–; dickies
DIAMINE	–; diamines	**DICLINY**	–; –
DIAMOND	–; diamonds	**DICOT**	–; dicots
DIAPER	–; diapers	**DICOTYL**	–; dicotyls
DIAPIR	–; diapirs	**DICTA**	–; –
DIAPSID	–; –	**DICTATE**	–; dictated, dictates
DIARCHY	–; –		

DICTION	–; dictions	**DIGHT**	–; dights
DICTUM	–; dictums	**DIGHTED**	–; –
DICYCLY	–; –	**DIGIT**	–; digits
DID	–; dido, didy	**DIGITAL**	–; digitals
		DIGLOT	–; diglots
DIDACT	–; didacts	**DIGNIFY**	–; –
DIDDLE	–; diddled, diddler, diddles	**DIGNITY**	–; –
		DIGOXIN	–; digoxins
DIDDLER	–; diddlers	**DIGRAPH**	–; digraphs
DIDIE	–; didies	**DIGRESS**	–; –
DIDO	–; didos	**DIKDIK**	–; dikdiks
DIDOES	–; –	**DIKE**	–; diked, diker, dikes
DIDST	–; –		
DIE	; diod, diel, dies, diet	**DIKER**	–; dikers
		DIKING	–; –
DIEBACK	–; diebacks	**DIKTAT**	–; diktats
DIEHARD	–; diehards	**DILATE**	–; dilated, dilater, dilates
DIEING	–; –		
DIENE	–; dienes	**DILATER**	–; dilaters
DIESEL	–; diesels	**DILATOR**	–; dilators, dilatory
DIESES	–; –		
DIESIS	–; –	**DILDO**	–; dildoe, dildos
DIESTER	–; diesters		
DIET	–; diets	**DILDOE**	–; dildoes
DIETARY	–; –	**DILEMMA**	–; dilemmas
DIETED	–; –	**DILL**	–; dills, dilly
DIETER	–; dieters	**DILLIES**	–; –
DIETING	–; –	**DILUENT**	–; diluents
DIFFER	–; differs	**DILUTE**	–; diluted, diluter, dilutes
DIFFUSE	–; diffused, diffuser, diffuses		
		DILUTER	–; diluters
DIG	–; digs	**DILUTOR**	–; dilutors
DIGAMMA	–; digammas	**DILUVIA**	–; diluvial, diluvian
DIGAMY	–; –		
DIGEST	–; digests	**DIM**	–; dime, dims
DIGGED	–; –		
DIGGER	–; diggers	**DIME**	–; dimer, dimes
DIGGING	–; diggings		

DIMER	–; dimers	**DINGOES**	–; –
DIMERIC	–; –	**DINGUS**	–; –
DIMETER	–; dimeters	**DINING**	–; –
DIMITY	–; –	**DINK**	–; dinks,
DIMLY	–; –		dinky
DIMMED	–; –	**DINKED**	–; –
DIMMER	–; dimmers	**DINKEY**	–; dinkeys
DIMMEST	–; –	**DINKIER**	–; –
DIMMING	–; –	**DINKIES**	–; dinkiest
DIMNESS	–; –	**DINKING**	–; –
DIMORPH	–; dimorphs	**DINKLY**	–; –
DIMOUT	–; dimouts	**DINKUM**	–; –
DIMPLE	–; dimpled,	**DINNED**	–; –
	dimples	**DINNER**	–; dinners
DIMPLY	–; –	**DINNING**	–; –
DIMWIT	–; dimwits	**DINT**	–; dints
DIN	–; dine,	**DINTED**	–; –
	ding, dink,	**DINTING**	–; –
	dins, dint	**DIOBOL**	–; diobols
DINAR	–; dinars	**DIOCESE**	–; dioceses
DINDLE	–; dindled,	**DIODE**	–; diodes
	dindles	**DIOL**	–; diols
DINE	–; dined,	**DIOPTER**	–; diopters
	diner, dines	**DIOPTRE**	–; dioptres
DINER	–; dinero,	**DIORAMA**	–; dioramas
	diners	**DIORITE**	–; diorites
DINERIC	–; –	**DIOXANE**	–; dioxanes
DINERO	–; dineros	**DIOXID**	–; dioxide,
DINETTE	–; dinettes		dioxids
DING	–; dingo,	**DIOXIDE**	–; dioxides
	dings, dingy	**DIP**	–; dips, dipt
DINGBAT	–; dingbats	**DIPHASE**	–; –
DINGE	–; dinged	**DIPLEX**	–; –
DINGEY	–; dingeys	**DIPLOE**	–; diploes
DINGHY	–; –	**DIPLOIC**	–; –
DINGIER	–; –	**DIPLOID**	–; diploids,
DINGIES	–; dingiest		diploidy
DINGILY	–; –	**DIPLOMA**	–; diplomas,
DINGING	–; –		diplomat
DINGLE	–; dingles	**DIPLONT**	–; diplonts

DIPNOAN	–; dipnoans	**DISAVOW**	–; disavows
DIPODIC	–; –	**DISBAND**	–; disbands
DIPODY	–; –	**DISBAR**	–; disbars
DIPOLAR	–; –	**DISBUD**	–; disbuds
DIPOLE	–; dipoles	**DISC**	–; disci,
DIPPED	–; –		disco, discs
DIPPER	–; dippers	**DISCANT**	–; discants
DIPPIER	–; –	**DISCARD**	–; discards
DIPPING	–; –	**DISCASE**	–; discased,
DIPPY	–; –		discases
DIPSAS	–; –	**DISCEPT**	–; discepts
DIPTERA	–; dipteral,	**DISCERN**	–; discerns
	dipteran	**DISCO**	–; discos
DIPTYCA	–; diptycas	**DISCOID**	–; discoids
DIPTYCH	–; diptychs	**DISCORD**	–; discords
DIQUAT	–; diquats	**DISCUS**	–; discuss
DIRDUM	–; dirdums	**DISDAIN**	–; disdains
DIRE	–; direr	**DISEASE**	–; diseased,
DIRECT	–; directs		diseases
DIREFUL	–; –	**DISEUSE**	–; diseuses
DIRELY	–; –	**DISGUST**	–; disgusts
DIREST	–; –	**DISH**	–; dishy
DIRGE	–; dirges	**DISHED**	–; –
DIRHAM	–; dirhams	**DISHELM**	–; dishelms
DIRK	–; dirks	**DISHES**	–; –
DIRKED	–; –	**DISHFUL**	–; dishfuls
DIRKING	–; –	**DISHIER**	–; –
DIRL	–; dirls	**DISHING**	–; –
DIRLED	–; –	**DISHPAN**	–; dishpans
DIRLING	–; –	**DISHRAG**	–; dishrags
DIRNDL	–; dirndls	**DISJECT**	–; disjects
DIRT	–; dirts,	**DISJOIN**	–; disjoins,
	dirty		disjoint
DIRTIED	–; –	**DISK**	–; disks
DIRTIER	–; –	**DISKED**	–; –
DIRTIES	–; dirtiest	**DISKING**	–; –
DIRTILY	–; –	**DISLIKE**	–; disliked,
DISABLE	–; disabled,		disliker,
	disables		dislikes
DISARM	–; disarms	**DISLIMN**	–; dislimns

DISMAL	–; dismals	**DISTIL**	–; distill, distils
DISMAST	–; dismasts		
DISMAY	–; dismays	**DISTILL**	–; distills
DISME	–; dismes	**DISTOME**	–; distomes
DISMISS	–; –	**DISTORT**	–; distorts
DISOBEY	–; disobeys	**DISTURB**	–; disturbs
DISOMIC	–; –	**DISUSE**	–; disused, disuses
DISOWN	–; disowns		
DISPART	–; disparts	**DISYOKE**	–; disyoked, disyokes
DISPEL	–; dispels		
DISPEND	–; dispends	**DIT**	adit, edit; dita, dite, dits
DISPLAY	–; displays		
DISPORT	–; disports		
DISPOSE	–; disposed, disposer, disposes	**DITA**	–; ditas
		DITCH	–; –
		DITCHED	–; –
DISPUTE	–; disputed, disputer, disputes	**DITCHER**	–; ditchers
		DITE	–; dites
		DITHER	–; dithers, dithery
DISRATE	–; disrated, disrates		
		DITHIOL	–; –
DISROBE	–; disrobed, disrober, disrobes	**DITS**	adits, edits; –
		DITTANY	–; –
		DITTIES	–; –
DISROOT	–; disroots	**DITTO**	–; dittos
DISRUPT	–; disrupts	**DITTOED**	–; –
DISSAVE	–; dissaved, dissaves	**DITTY**	–; –
		DIURNAL	–; diurnals
DISSEAT	–; disseats	**DIURON**	–; diurons
DISSECT	–; dissects	**DIVA**	–; divan, divas
DISSENT	–; dissents		
DISSERT	–; disserts	**DIVAN**	–; divans
DISTAFF	–; distaffs	**DIVE**	–; dived, diver, dives
DISTAIN	–; distains		
DISTAL	–; –	**DIVER**	–; divers, divert
DISTANT	–; –		
DISTEND	–; distends	**DIVERGE**	–; diverged, diverges
DISTENT	–; –		
DISTICH	–; distichs	**DIVERSE**	–; –
		DIVERT	–; diverts

DIVEST	–; divests	dom, don,
DIVIDE	–; divided,	dor, dos,
	divider,	dot, dow
	divides	**DOABLE**	–; –
DIVIDER	–; dividers	**DOAT**	–; doats
DIVINE	–; divined,	**DOATED**	–; –
	diviner,	**DOATING**	–; –
	divines	**DOBBER**	–; dobbers
DIVINER	–; diviners	**DOBBIES**	–; –
DIVINES	–; divinest	**DOBBIN**	–; dobbins
DIVING	–; –	**DOBBY**	–; –
DIVISOR	–; divisors	**DOBIE**	–; dobies
DIVORCE	–; divorced,	**DOBLA**	–; doblas
	divorcee,	**DOBLON**	–; doblons
	divorcer,	**DOBRA**	–; dobras
	divorces	**DOBSON**	–; dobsons
DIVOT	–; divots	**DOBY**	–; –
DIVULGE	–; divulged,	**DOC**	–; dock,
	divulger,		docs
	divulges	**DOCENT**	–; docents
DIVVIED	–; –	**DOCETIC**	–; –
DIVVIES	–; –	**DOCILE**	–; –
DIVVY	–; –	**DOCK**	–; docks
DIWAN	–; diwans	**DOCKAGE**	–; dockages
DIXIT	–; dixits	**DOCKED**	–; –
DIZEN	–; dizens	**DOCKER**	–; dockers
DIZENED	–; –	**DOCKET**	–; dockets
DIZZIED	–; –	**DOCKING**	–; –
DIZZIER	–; –	**DOCTOR**	–; doctors
DIZZIES	–; dizziest	**DODDER**	–; dodders,
DIZZILY	–; –		doddery
DIZZY	–; –	**DODGE**	–; dodged,
DJEBEL	–; djebels		dodger,
DJIN	–; djinn,		dodges
	djins	**DODGER**	–; dodgers,
DJINN	–; djinni,		dodgery
	djinns, djinny	**DODGIER**	–; –
DO	ado, udo;	**DODGING**	–; –
	doc, doe,	**DODGY**	–; –
	dog, dol,	**DODO**	–; dodos

DODOES	–; dodoes	**DOGIE**	–; dogies
DODOISM	–; dodoisms	**DOGLEG**	–; doglegs
DOE	–; doer, does	**DOGLIKE**	–; –
		DOGMA	–; dogmas
DOER	–; doers	**DOGMATA**	–; –
DOES	–; doest	**DOGNAP**	–; dognaps
DOESKIN	–; doeskins	**DOGSLED**	–; dogsleds
DOEST	–; –	**DOGTROT**	–; dogtrots
DOETH	–; –	**DOGVANE**	–; dogvanes
DOFF	–; doffs	**DOGWOOD**	–; dogwoods
DOFFED	–; –		
DOFFER	–; doffers	**DOILED**	–; –
DOFFING	–; –	**DOILIES**	–; –
DOG	–; doge, dogs, dogy	**DOILY**	–; –
		DOING	–; doings
DOGBANE	–; dogbanes	**DOIT**	–; doits
DOGCART	–; dogcarts	**DOITED**	–; –
DOGDOM	–; dogdoms	**DOJO**	–; dojos
DOGE	–; doges, dogey	**DOL**	idol; dole, doll, dols
DOGEDOM	–; dogedoms	**DOLCE**	–; –
		DOLCI	–; –
DOGEY	–; dogeys	**DOLE**	–; doled, doles
DOGFACE	–; dogfaces		
DOGFISH	–; –	**DOLEFUL**	–; –
DOGGED	–; –	**DOLING**	–; –
DOGGER	–; doggers, doggery	**DOLL**	–; dolls, dolly
DOGGIE	–; doggier, doggies	**DOLLAR**	–; dollars
		DOLLED	–; –
DOGGIES	–; doggiest	**DOLLIED**	–; –
DOGGING	–; –	**DOLLIES**	–; –
DOGGISH	–; –	**DOLLING**	–; –
DOGGO	–; –	**DOLLISH**	–; –
DOGGONE	–; doggoned, doggoner, doggones	**DOLLOP**	–; dollops
		DOLMAN	–; dolmans
		DOLMEN	–; dolmens
		DOLOR	–; dolors
DOGGREL	–; doggrels	**DOLOUR**	–; dolours
DOGGY	–; –	**DOLPHIN**	–; dolphins

DOLS	idols; –	**DONOR**	–; donors
DOLT	, dolts	**DONSIE**	–; –
DOLTISH	–; –	**DONSY**	–; –
DOM	–; dome, doms	**DONUT**	–; donuts
DOMAIN	–; domains	**DONZEL**	–; donzels
DOMAL	–; –	**DOODAD**	–; doodads
DOME	–; domed, domes	**DOODLE**	–; doodled, doodler, doodles
DOMIC	–; –	**DOODLER**	–; doodlers
DOMICAL	–; –	**DOOLEE**	–; doolees
DOMICIL	–; domicile, domicils	**DOOLIE**	–; doolies
DOMINE	–; domines	**DOOLY**	–; –
DOMING	–; –	**DOOM**	–; dooms
DOMINIE	–; dominies	**DOOMED**	–; –
DOMINO	–; dominos	**DOOMING**	–; –
DON	–; dona, done, dong, dons	**DOOMFUL**	–; –
		DOOR	–; doors
DONA	–; donas	**DOORMAN**	–; –
DONATE	odonate; donated, donates	**DOORMEN**	–; –
		DOORMAT	–; doormats
		DOORWAY	–; doorways
DONATES	odonates; –	**DOOZER**	–; doozers
DONATOR	–; donators	**DOOZIES**	–; –
DONE	–; donee	**DOOZY**	–; –
DONEE	–; donees	**DOPA**	–; dopas
DONG	–; dongs	**DOPANT**	–; dopants
DONGOLA	–; dongolas	**DOPE**	–; doped, doper, dopes, dopey
DONJON	–; donjons		
DONKEY	–; donkeys	**DOPER**	–; dopers
DONNA	–; donnas	**DOPIER**	–; –
DONNE	–; donned, donnee	**DOPIEST**	–; –
		DOPING	–; –
DONNEE	–; donnees	**DOPY**	–; –
DONNERD	–; –	**DOR**	odor; dorm, dorp, dorr, dors, dory
DONNERT	–; –		
DONNING	–; –		
DONNISH	–; –	**DORADO**	–; dorados

DORBUG	–; dorbugs	doth, dots,
DORHAWK	–; dorhawks	doty
DORIES	–; –	**DOTAGE** –; dotages
DORM	–; dorms,	**DOTAL** –; –
	dormy	**DOTARD** –; dotards
DORMANT	–; –	**DOTE** –; doted,
DORMER	–; dormers	doter, dotes
DORMICE	–; –	**DOTER** –; doters
DORMIE	–; –	**DOTIER** –; –
DORMIN	–; dormins	**DOTIEST** –; –
DORNECK	–; dornecks	**DOTING** –; –
DORNICK	–; dornicks	**DOTTED** –; –
DORNOCK	–; dornocks	**DOTTEL** –; dottels
DORP	–; dorps	**DOTTER** –; dotters
DORPER	–; dorpers	**DOTTIER** –; –
DORR	–; dorrs	**DOTTILY** –; –
DORS	odors; dorsa	**DOTTING** –; –
DORSA	–; dorsad,	**DOTTLE** –; dottles
	dorsal	**DOTTREL** –; dottrels
DORSAL	–; dorsals	**DOTTY** –; –
DORSER	–; dorsers	**DOUBLE** –; doubled,
DORSUM	–; –	doubler,
DORTY	–; –	doubles,
DOS	ados, udos;	doublet
	dose, doss,	**DOUBLER** –; doublers
	dost	**DOUBLET** –; doublets
DOSAGE	–; dosages	**DOUBLY** –; –
DOSE	–; dosed,	**DOUBT** –; doubts
	doser, doses	**DOUBTED** –; –
DOSER	–; dosers	**DOUBTER** –; doubters
DOSING	–; –	**DOUCE** –; –
DOSSAL	–; dossals	**DOUCELY** –; –
DOSSED	–; –	**DOUCEUR** –; douceurs
DOSSEL	–; dossels	**DOUCHE** –; douched,
DOSSER	–; dossers	douches
DOSSES	–; –	**DOUGH** –; doughs,
DOSSIER	–; dossiers	dought,
DOSSIL	–; dossils	doughy
DOSSING	–; –	**DOUGHT** –; doughty
DOT	–; dote,	**DOUMA** –; doumas

DOUR	odour; doura	**DOWNIER**	–; –
DOURA	–; dourah, douras	**DOWNING**	–; –
		DOWRIES	–; –
DOURAH	–; dourahs	**DOWRY**	–; –
DOURER	–; –	**DOWSE**	–; dowsed, dowser, dowses
DOUREST	–; –		
DOURINE	–; dourines		
DOURLY	–; –	**DOWSER**	–; dowsers
DOUSE	–; doused, douser, douses	**DOXIE**	–; doxies
		DOXY	–; –
		DOYEN	–; doyens
DOUSER	–; dousers	**DOYLEY**	–; doyleys
DOUSING	–; –	**DOYLY**	–; –
DOVE	–; doven, doves	**DOZE**	adoze; dozed, dozen, dozer, dozes
DOVECOT	–; dovecote, dovecots		
DOVEKEY	–; dovekeys		
DOVEKIE	–; dovekies	**DOZEN**	–; dozens
DOVEN	–; dovens	**DOZENED**	–; –
DOVENED	–; –	**DOZENTH**	–; dozenths
DOVISH	–; –	**DOZER**	–; dozers
DOW	–; down, dows	**DOZIER**	–; –
		DOZIEST	–; –
DOWABLE	–; –	**DOZILY**	–; –
DOWAGER	–; dowagers	**DOZING**	–; –
DOWDIER	–; –	**DOZY**	–; –
DOWDIES	–; dowdiest	**DRAB**	–; drabs
DOWDILY	–; –	**DRABBED**	–; –
DOWDY	–; –	**DRABBER**	–; –
DOWEL	–; dowels	**DRABBET**	–; drabbets
DOWELED	–; –	**DRABBLE**	–; drabbled, drabbles
DOWER	–; dowers, dowery		
		DRABLY	–; –
DOWIE	–; –	**DRACHM**	–; drachma, drachms
DOWN	adown; downs, downy		
		DRACHMA	–; drachmae, drachmai, drachmas
DOWNED	–; –		
DOWNER	–; downers		

DRAFF	–; draffs, draffy	drawn, draws
DRAFT	–; drafts, drafty	**DRAWBAR** –; drawbars
		DRAWEE –; drawees
DRAFTED	–; –	**DRAWER** –; drawers
DRAFTEE	–; draftees	**DRAWING** –; drawings
DRAFTER	–; drafters	**DRAWL** –; drawls, drawly
DRAG	–; drags	
DRAGEE	–; dragees	**DRAWLED** –; –
DRAGGED	–; –	**DRAWLER** –; drawlers
DRAGGER	–; draggers	**DRAY** –; drays
DRAGGLE	–; draggled, draggles	**DRAYAGE** –; drayages
		DRAYED –; –
DRAGGY	–; –	**DRAYING** –; –
DRAGNET	–; dragnets	**DREAD** –; dreads
DRAGON	–; dragons	**DREADED** –; –
DRAGOON	–; dragoons	**DREAM** –; dreams, dreamt, dreamy
DRAIL	–; drails	
DRAIN	–; drains	
DRAINED	–; –	**DREAMED** –; –
DRAINER	–; drainers	**DREAMER** –; dreamers
DRAKE	–; drakes	**DREAR** –; dreary
DRAM	–; drama, drams	**DRECK** –; drecks
		DREDGE –; dredged, dredger, dredges
DRAMA	–; dramas	
DRAMMED	–; –	
DRANK	–; –	**DREDGER** –; dredgers
DRAPE	–; draped, draper, drapes	**DREE** –; dreed, drees
		DREEING –; –
DRAPER	–; drapers, drapery	**DREG** –; dregs
		DREGGY –; –
DRAPING	–; –	**DREICH** –; –
DRASTIC	–; –	**DREIDEL** –; dreidels
DRAT	–; drats	**DREIDL** –; dreidls
DRATTED	–; –	**DREIGH** –; –
DRAUGHT	–; draughts, draughty	**DREK** –; dreks
		DRENCH –; –
DRAVE	–; –	**DRESS** –; dressy
DRAW	–; drawl,	**DRESSED** –; –

DRESSER	–; dressers	**DROLL**	–; drolls,
DRESSES	–,		drolly
DREST	–; –	**DROLLED**	–; –
DREW	–; –	**DROLLER**	–; drollery
DRIB	–; dribs	**DROMON**	–; dromond,
DRIBBED	–; –		dromons
DRIBBLE	–; dribbled,	**DROMOND**	–; dromonds
	dribbler,	**DRONE**	–; droned,
	dribbles,		droner,
	dribblet		drones
DRIBLET	–; driblets	**DRONER**	–; droners
DRIED	–; –	**DRONGO**	–; drongos
DRIER	–; driers	**DRONING**	–; –
DRIES	–; driest	**DRONISH**	–; –
DRIFT	adrift; drifts,	**DROOL**	–; drools
	drifty	**DROOLED**	–; –
DRIFTED	–; –	**DROOP**	–; droops,
DRIFTER	–; drifters		droopy
DRILL	–; drills	**DROOPED**	–; –
DRILLED	–; –	**DROP**	–; drops,
DRILLER	–; drillers		dropt
DRILY	–; –	**DROPLET**	–; droplets
DRINK	–; drinks	**DROPOUT**	–; dropouts
DRINKER	–; drinkers	**DROPPED**	–; –
DRIP	–; drips,	**DROPPER**	–; droppers
	dript	**DROPS**	–; dropsy
DRIPPED	–; –	**DROSERA**	–; droseras
DRIPPER	–; drippers	**DROSHKY**	–; –
DRIPPY	–; –	**DROSKY**	–; –
DRIVE	–; drivel,	**DROSS**	–; drossy
	driven,	**DROSSES**	–; –
	driver, drives	**DROUGHT**	–; droughts,
DRIVEL	–; drivels		droughty
DRIVER	–; drivers	**DROUK**	–; drouks
DRIVING	–; –	**DROUKED**	–; –
DRIZZLE	–; drizzled,	**DROUTH**	–; drouths,
	drizzles		drouthy
DRIZZLY	–; –	**DROVE**	–; droved,
DROGUE	–; drogues		drover,
DROIT	adroit; droits		droves

DROVER	–; drovers	**DRYEST**	–; –
DROVING	–; –	**DRYING**	–; –
DROWN	–; drownd, drowns	**DRYLOT**	–; drylots
		DRYLY	–; –
DROWNED	–; –	**DRYNESS**	–; –
DROWNER	–; drowners	**DUAD**	–; duads
DROWSE	–; drowsed, drowses	**DUAL**	–; duals
		DUALISM	–; dualisms
DROWSY	–; –	**DUALIST**	–; dualists
DRUB	–; drubs	**DUALITY**	–; –
DRUBBED	–; –	**DUALIZE**	–; dualized, dualizes
DRUBBER	–; drubbers		
DRUDGE	–; drudged, drudger, drudges	**DUALLY**	–; –
		DUB	–; dubs
		DUBBED	–; –
DRUDGER	–; drudgers, drudgery	**DUBBER**	–; dubbers
		DUBBIN	–; dubbing, dubbins
DRUG	–; drugs		
DRUGGED	–; –	**DUBBING**	–; dubbings
DRUGGET	–; druggets	**DUBIETY**	–; –
DRUID	–; druids	**DUBIOUS**	–; –
DRUIDIC	–; –	**DUC**	–; duce, duci, duck, ducs, duct
DRUM	–; drums		
DRUMBLE	–; drumbled, drumbles		
		DUCAL	–; –
DRUMLIN	–; drumlins	**DUCALLY**	–; –
DRUMLY	–; –	**DUCAT**	–; ducats
DRUMMED	–; –	**DUCE**	educe; duces
DRUMMER	–; drummers		
DRUNK	–; drunks	**DUCES**	educes; –
DRUNKEN	–; –	**DUCHESS**	–; –
DRUNKER	–; –	**DUCHIES**	–; –
DRUPE	–; drupes	**DUCHY**	–; –
DRUSE	–; druses	**DUCI**	–; –
DRY	–; drys	**DUCK**	–; ducks, ducky
DRYABLE	–; –		
DRYAD	–; dryads	**DUCKED**	–; –
DRYADES	–; –	**DUCKER**	–; duckers
DRYADIC	–; –	**DUCKIE**	–; duckier, duckies
DRYER	–; dryers		

DUCKIES	–; duckiest	DUI	–; duit
DUCKING	–; –	DUIKER	–; duikers
DUCKPIN	–; duckpins	DUIT	–; duits
DUCT	educt; ducts	DUKE	–; dukes
DUCTED	–; –	DUKEDOM	–; dukedoms
DUCTILE	–; –	DULCET	–; dulcets
DUCTING	–; ductings	DULCIFY	–; –
DUCTS	educts; –	DULIA	–; dulias
DUCTULE	–; ductules	DULL	–; dulls, dully
DUD	–; dude, duds		
		DULLARD	–; dullards
DUDDIE	–; –	DULLED	–; –
DUDDY	–; –	DULLER	–; –
DUDE	–; dudes	DULLEST	–; –
DUDEEN	–; dudeens	DULLING	–; –
DUDGEON	–; dudgeons	DULLISH	–; –
DUDISH	–; –	DULNESS	–; –
DUE	–; duel, dues, duet	DULSE	–; dulses
		DULY	–; –
DUEL	–; duels	DUMA	–; dumas
DUELED	–; –	DUMB	–; dumbs
DUELER	–; duelers	DUMBED	–; –
DUELING	–; –	DUMBER	–; –
DUELIST	–; duelists	DUMBEST	–; –
DUELLED	–; –	DUMBING	–; –
DUELLER	–; duellers	DUMBLY	–; –
DUELLI	–; –	DUMDUM	–; dumdums
DUELLO	–; duellos	DUMKA	–; –
DUENDE	–; duendes	DUMKY	–; –
DUENESS	–; –	DUMMIED	–; –
DUENNA	–; duennas	DUMMIES	–; –
DUET	–; duets	DUMMY	–; –
DUETTED	–; –	DUMP	–; dumps, dumpy
DUFF	–; duffs		
DUFFEL	–; duffels	DUMPED	–; –
DUFFER	–; duffers	DUMPER	–; dumpers
DUFFLE	–; duffles	DUMPIER	–; –
DUG	–; dugs	DUMPILY	–; –
DUGONG	–; dugongs	DUMPING	–; dumpings
DUGOUT	–; dugouts	DUMPISH	–; –

DUN	–; dune, dung, dunk, duns, dunt	**DUPER**	–; dupers, dupery
DUNCE	–; dunces	**DUPING**	–; –
DUNCISH	–; –	**DUPLE**	–; duplex
DUNCH	–; –	**DUPPED**	–; –
DUNCHES	–; –	**DUPPING**	–; –
DUNE	–; dunes	**DURA**	–; dural, duras
DUNG	–; dungs, dungy	**DURABLE**	–; durables
DUNGED	–; –	**DURABLY**	–; –
DUNGING	–; –	**DURAMEN**	–; duramens
DUNITE	–; dunites	**DURANCE**	–; durances
DUNITIC	–; –	**DURBAR**	–; durbars
DUNK	–; dunks	**DURE**	–; dured, dures
DUNKED	–; –		
DUNKER	–; dunkers	**DURES**	–; duress
DUNKING	–; –	**DURIAN**	–; durians
DUNLIN	–; dunlins	**DURING**	–; –
DUNNAGE	–; dunnages	**DURION**	–; durions
DUNNED	–; –	**DURMAST**	–; durmasts
DUNNER	–; –	**DURN**	–; durns
DUNNESS	–; –	**DURNED**	–; –
DUNNEST	–; –	**DURNING**	–; –
DUNNING	–; –	**DURO**	–; duroc, duros
DUNNITE	–; dunnites		
DUNT	–; dunts	**DUROC**	–; durocs
DUNTED	–; –	**DURR**	–; durra, durrs
DUNTING	–; –	**DURRA**	–; durras
DUO	–; duos	**DURST**	–; –
DUOLOG	–; duologs	**DURUM**	–; durums
DUOMI	–; –	**DUSK**	–; dusks, dusky
DUOMO	–; duomos		
DUOPOLY	–; –	**DUSKED**	–; –
DUOTONE	–; duotones	**DUSKIER**	–; –
DUP	–; dupe, dups	**DUSKILY**	–; –
		DUSKING	–; –
DUPE	–; duped, duper, dupes	**DUSKISH**	–; –
		DUST	adust; dusts, dusty

DUSTBIN	–; dustbins	DWINE	–; dwined, dwines
DUSTED	–; –		
DUSTER	–; dusters	DWINING	–; –
DUSTIER	–; –	DYABLE	–; –
DUSTILY	–; –	DYAD	–; dyads
DUSTING	–; –	DYADIC	–; dyadics
DUSTMAN	–; –	DYARCHY	–; –
DUSTMEN	–; –	DYBBUK	–; dybbuks
DUSTPAN	–; dustpans	DYE	–; dyed, dyer, dyes
DUSTRAG	–; dustrags		
DUSTUP	–; dustups	DYEABLE	–; –
DUTCH	–; –	DYEING	–; dyeings
DUTEOUS	–; –	DYER	–; dyers
DUTIES	–; –	DYEWEED	–; dyeweeds
DUTIFUL	–; –	DYEWOOD	–; dyewoods
DUTY	–; –		
DUUMVIR	–; duumviri, duumvirs	DYING	–; dyings
		DYKE	–; dyked, dykes
DUVETYN	–; duvetyne, duvetyns		
		DYKING	–; –
DWARF	–; dwarfs	DYNAMIC	–; dynamics
DWARFED	–; –	DYNAMO	–; dynamos
DWARFER	–; –	DYNAST	–; dynasts, dynasty
DWARVES	–; –		
DWELL	–; dwells	DYNE	–; dynes
DWELLED	–; –	DYNODE	–; dynodes
DWELLER	–; dwellers	DYSPNEA	–; dyspneal, dyspneas
DWELT	–; –		
DWINDLE	–; dwindled, dwindles	DYSURIA	–; dysurias
		DYSURIC	–; –
		DYVOUR	–; dyvours

E

| E | ae, be, de, he, me, ne, oe, pe, re, we, ye; ef, eh, el, em, | | en, er, es, et, ex |
| | | EACH | beach, leach, peach, |

	reach, teach; –		tearing, wearing;
EAGER	meager; eagers	**EARINGS**	earings bearings; –
EAGERER	–; –	**EARL**	pearl; earls,
EAGERLY	meagerly; –		early
EAGLE	beagle; eagles, eaglet	**EARLAP** **EARLDOM**	–; earlaps –; earldoms
EAGLES	beagles; –	**EARLESS**	fearless, gearless; –
EAGLET	–; eaglets	**EARLIER**	–; –
EAGRE	meagre; eagres	**EARLOBE** **EARLOCK**	–; earlobes –; earlocks
EANLING	–; eanlings	**EARLS**	pearls; –
EAR	bear, dear, fear, gear, hear, lear, near, pear, rear, sear, tear, wear, year; earl, earn, ears	**EARLY**	dearly, nearly, pearly, yearly, –
		EARMARK **EARMUFF**	–; earmarks –; earmuffs
		EARN	learn, yearn; earns
EARACHE	–; earaches	**EARNED**	learned,
EARDROP	–; eardrops		yearned; –
EARDRUM	–; eardrums	**EARNER**	learner,
EARED	feared, geared, neared, reared, seared, teared; –		yearner; earners
		EARNERS	learners, yearners; –
		EARNEST	–; earnests
		EARNING	learning, yearning; earnings
EARFLAP	–; earflaps		
EARFUL	–; earfuls	**EARNS**	learns, yearns; –
EARING	bearing, fearing, gearing, hearing, nearing, rearing, searing,	**EARPLUG**	–; earplugs
		EARRING	–; earrings
		EARS	bears, dears, fears, gears, hears,

	lears, nears,	**EASIER**	–; –
	pears, rears,	**EASIES**	–; easiest
	sears, tears,	**EASILY**	–; –
	wears,	**EASING**	ceasing,
	years; –		feasing,
EARSHOT	–; earshots		leasing,
EARTH	dearth,		teasing; –
	hearth;	**EAST**	beast, feast,
	earths,		least, yeast;
	earthy		easts
EARTHED	–; –	**EASTER**	feaster;
EARTHEN	–; –		eastern,
EARTHLY	–; –		easters
EARTHS	dearths,	**EASTERS**	feasters; –
	hearths; –	**EASTING**	foasting;
EARWAX	–; –		eastings
EARWIG	–; earwigs	**EASTS**	beasts,
EARWORM	–; earworms		feasts,
EASE	cease,		leasts,
	fease, lease,		yeasts; –
	pease,	**EASY**	–; –
	tease;	**EAT**	beat, feat,
	eased,		heat, meat,
	easel, eases		neat, peat,
EASED	ceased,		seat, teat;
	feased,		eats, eath
	leased,	**EATABLE**	beatable;
	teased; –		eatables
EASEFUL	–; –	**EATEN**	beaten,
EASEL	teasel,		neaten; –
	weasel;	**EATER**	beater,
	easels		feater,
EASELS	teasels,		heater,
	weasels; –		neater,
EASES	ceases,		seater;
	feases,		eaters,
	leases,		eatery
	peases,	**EATERS**	beaters,
	teases; –		heaters,
			seaters; –

EATH	death, heath, neath; –	**EBONISE**	–; ebonised, ebonises
EATING	beating, heating, seating; eatings	**EBONITE**	–; ebonites
		EBONIZE	–; ebonized, ebonizes
EATINGS	beatings, seatings; –	**ECARTE**	–; ecartes
		ECBOLIC	–; ecbolics
EATS	beats, feats, heats, meats, neats, peats, seats, teats; –	**ECCRINE**	–; –
		ECDYSES	–; –
		ECDYSIS	–; –
		ECDYSON	–; ecdysone, ecdysons
EAU	beau; eaux	**ECESES**	–; –
EAUX	beaux; –	**ECESIS**	–; –
EAVE	deave, heave, leave, reave, weave; eaved, eaves	**ECHARD**	–; echards
		ECHE	–; eched, eches
		ECHED	peched, teched; –
		ECHES	leches; –
		ECHELON	–; echelons
EAVED	deaved, heaved, leaved, reaved, weaved; –	**ECHIDNA**	–; echidnae, echidnas
		ECHING	peching; –
		ECHNI	–; –
		ECHINUS	–; –
EAVES	deaves, heaves, leaves, reaves, weaves; –	**ECHO**	–; –
		ECHOED	–; –
		ECHOER	–; echoers
		ECHOES	–; –
		ECHOEY	–; –
EBB	–; ebbs	**ECHOIC**	–; –
EBBED	webbed; –	**ECHOING**	–; –
EBBET	–; ebbets	**ECHOISM**	–; echoisms
EBBING	webbing; –	**ECLAIR**	–; eclairs
EBON	–; ebons, ebony	**ECLAT**	–; eclats
		ECLIPSE	–; eclipsed, eclipses
EBONIES	–; –		
		ECLOGUE	–; eclogues

ECOLE	–; ecoles	**EDGER**	hedger,
ECOLOGY	–; –		ledger,
ECONOMY	–; –		sedger;
ECOTONE	–; ecotones		edgers
ECOTYPE	–; ecotypes	**EDGERS**	hedgers,
ECRU	–; ecrus		ledgers; –
ECSTASY	–; –	**EDGES**	hedges,
ECTASES	pectases; –		kedges,
ECTASIS	–; –		ledges,
ECTATIC	–; –		sedges,
ECTHYMA	–; –		wedges; –
ECTOPIA	–; ectopias	**EDGIER**	hedgier,
ECTOPIC	–; –		sedgier,
ECTYPAL	–; –		wedgier; –
ECTYPE	–; ectypes	**EDGIEST**	hedgiest,
ECU	–; ecus		wedgiest; –
ECZEMA	–; eczemas	**EDGILY**	–; –
EDACITY	–; –	**EDGING**	hedging,
EDAPHIC	–; –		kedging,
EDDIED	–; –		wedging;
EDDIES	–; –		edgings
EDDO	–; –	**EDGINGS**	–; –
EDDOES	–; –	**EDGY**	hedgy,
EDDY	teddy; –		ledgy,
EDDYING	–; –		sedgy,
EDEMA	oedema;		wedgy; –
	edemas	**EDH**	–; edhs
EDEMAS	oedemas; –	**EDIBLE**	–; edibles
EDEMATA	oedemata; –	**EDICT**	–; edicts
EDGE	hedge,	**EDIFICE**	–; edifices
	kedge,	**EDIFIED**	–; –
	ledge,	**EDIFIER**	–; edifiers
	sedge,	**EDIFIES**	–; –
	wedge;	**EDIFY**	–; –
	edged,	**EDILE**	aedile,
	edger,		sedile; ediles
	edges	**EDILES**	aediles; –
EDGED	hedged,	**EDIT**	–; edits
	kedged,	**EDITED**	–; –
	wedged; –	**EDITING**	–; –

EDITION	–; editions	**EERILY**	–; –
EDITOR	–; editors	**EERY**	beery, leery,
EDUCATE	–; educated,		peery,
	educates		veery; –
EDUCE	deduce,	**EF**	kef, ref; eff,
	reduce,		efs, eft
	seduce;	**EFF**	teff; effs
	educed,	**EFFABLE**	–; –
	educes	**EFFACE**	–; effaced,
EDUCED	deduced,		effacer,
	reduced,		effaces
	seduced; –	**EFFACER**	–; effacers
EDUCES	deduces,	**EFFECT**	–; effects
	reduces,	**EFFENDI**	–; effendis
	seduces; –	**EFFETE**	–; –
EDUCING	deducing,	**EFFIGY**	–; –
	reducing,	**EFFLUX**	–; –
	seducing; –	**EFFORT**	–; efforts
EDUCT	deduct;	**EFFS**	teffs
	educts	**EFFULGE**	–; effulged,
EDUCTOR	–; eductors		effulges
EDUCTS	deducts; –	**EFFUSE**	–; effused,
EEL	feel, heel,		effuses
	keel, peel,	**EFS**	kefs, refs; –
	reel, seel,	**EFT**	deft, heft,
	weel; eels,		left, reft,
	eely		weft; efts
EELIER	–; –	**EFTS**	hefts, lefts,
EELIEST	–; –		wefts; –
EELLIKE	–; –	**EFTSOON**	–; –
EELPOUT	–; eelpouts	**EGAD**	–; egads
EELS	feels, heels,	**EGAL**	legal,
	keels, peels,		regal; –
	reels,	**EGALITE**	–; egalites
	seels; –	**EGER**	leger; egers
EELWORM	–; eelworms	**EGERS**	legers; –
EERIE	peerie;	**EGEST**	–; egesta,
	eerier		egests
EERIER	beerier; –	**EGESTED**	–; –
EERIEST	beeriest; –	**EGG**	yegg; eggs

EGGARS	beggars, seggars;	**EIGHTS**	heights, weights; –
EGGCUP	–; eggcups	**EIGHTVO**	–; eightvos
EGGED	begged, legged, pegged; –	**EIGHTY**	weighty; –
		EIKON	–; eikons
		EIKONES	–; –
EGGER	–; eggers	**EINKORN**	–; einkorns
EGGHEAD	–; eggheads	**EIRENIC**	–; –
EGGING	begging, legging, pegging; –	**EITHER**	neither; –
		EJECT	deject, reject; ejecta, ejects
EGGNOG	–; eggnogs		
EGGS	yeggs; –	**EJECTA**	dejecta; –
EGIS	aegis; –	**EJECTED**	dejected, rejected; –
EGISES	–; –		
EGO	sego; egos	**EJECTOR**	–; ejectors
EGOS	segos; –	**EJECTS**	dejects, rejects; –
EGOISM	–; egoisms		
EGOIST	–; egoists	**EKE**	deke, peke; eked, ekes
EGOS	segos; –		
EGOTISM	–; egotisms	**EKES**	dekes, pekes; –
EGOTIST	–; egotists		
EGRESS	regress; –	**EKING**	deking; –
EGRET	regret; egrets	**EKISTIC**	–; –
		EL	bel, del, eel, gel, mel, sel; eld, elf, elk, ell, elm, els
EGRETS	regrets; –		
EH	peh, yeh; –		
EIDE	–; eider		
EIDER	–; eiders	**ELAIN**	–; elains
EIDETIC	–; –	**ELAN**	–; eland, elans
EIDOLA	–; –		
EIDOLON	–; eidolons	**ELAND**	–; elands
EIDOS	–; –	**ELAPID**	–; elapids
EIGHT	height, weight; eighth, eights, eighty	**ELAPINE**	–; –
		ELAPSE	relapse; elapsed, elapses
EIGHTH	heighth; eighths	**ELAPSED**	relapsed; –
		ELAPSES	relapses; –
		ELASTIC	–; elastics

ELASTIN	–; elastins	**ELDS**	gelds, melds,
ELATE	delate,		velds,
	gelate,		welds; –
	relate,	**ELECT**	select; elects
	velate;	**ELECTED**	selected; –
	elated,	**ELECTOR**	–; electors
	elater, elates	**ELECTRO**	–; electron,
ELATED	belated,		electros
	delated,	**ELECTS**	selects; –
	gelated,	**ELEGANT**	–; –
	related; –	**ELEGIAC**	–; elegiacs
ELATER	relater;	**ELEGIES**	–; –
	elaters	**ELEGISE**	–; elegised,
ELATES	delates,		elegises
	gelates,	**ELEGIST**	–; elegists
	relates; –	**ELEGIT**	–; elegits
ELATING	delating,	**ELEGIZE**	–; elegized,
	gelating,		elegizes
	relating; –	**ELEGY**	–; –
ELATION	delation,	**ELEMENT**	–; elements
	gelation,	**ELEMI**	–; elemis
	relation;	**ELEVATE**	–; elevated,
	elations		elevates
ELATIVE	relative;	**ELEVEN**	–; elevens
	elatives	**ELEVON**	–; elevons
ELBOW	–; elbows	**ELF**	delf, pelf,
ELBOWED	–; –		self; –
ELD	geld, held,	**ELFIN**	–; elfins
	meld, veld,	**ELFISH**	selfish; –
	yeld; elds	**ELFLOCK**	–; elflocks
ELDER	gelder,	**ELHI**	–; –
	melder,	**ELICIT**	–; elicits
	welder;	**ELIDE**	–; elided,
	elders		elides
ELDERLY	–; –	**ELIDING**	–; –
ELDERS	gelders,	**ELISION**	–; elisions
	melders,	**ELITE**	pelite; elites
	welders; –	**ELITES**	pelites,
ELDEST	–; –		velites; –
ELDRICH	–; –		

ELITISM	–; elitisms		eluder,
ELITIST	–; elitists		eludes
ELIXIR	–; elixirs	**ELUDED**	deluded; –
ELK	yelk; elks	**ELUDER**	deluder;
ELKS	yelks; –		eluders
ELL	bell, cell,	**ELUDERS**	deluders; –
	dell, fell,	**ELUDES**	deludes; –
	hell, jell,	**ELUDING**	deluding; –
	mell, sell,	**ELUENT**	–; eluents
	tell, well,	**ELUSION**	delusion;
	yell; ells		elusions
ELLIPSE	–; ellipses	**ELUSIVE**	delusive; –
ELLS	bells, cells,	**ELUSORY**	delusory; –
	dells, fells,	**ELUTE**	–; eluted,
	hells, jells,		elutes
	mells, sells,	**ELUTING**	–; –
	tells, wells,	**ELUTION**	–; elutions
	yells; –	**ELUVIA**	–; eluvial
ELM	helm; elms,	**ELUVIUM**	–; eluviums
	elmy	**ELVER**	delver;
ELMIER	–; –		elvers
ELMIEST	–; –	**ELVERS**	delvers; –
ELMS	helms; –	**ELVES**	delves,
ELODEA	–; elodeas		helves,
ELOIGN	–; eloigns		pelves,
ELOIN	–; eloins		selves; –
ELOINED	–; –	**ELVISH**	–; –
ELOINER	–; eloiners	**ELYSIAN**	–; –
ELOPE	–; eloped,	**ELYTRA**	–; –
	eloper,	**ELYTRON**	–; –
	elopes	**ELYTRUM**	–; –
ELOPER	; elopers	**EM**	gem, hem,
ELOPING	–; –		mem, rem;
ELS	bels, dels,		eme, ems,
	gels, mels,		emu
	sels; else	**EMANATE**	–;
ELUANT	–; eluants		emanated,
ELUATE	–; eluates		emanates
ELUDE	delude;	**EMBALM**	–; embalms
	eluded,	**EMBANK**	–; embanks

EMBAR	–; embark, embars	**EMBRYON**	–; embroyns
EMBARGO	–; –	**EMCEE**	–; emceed, emcees
EMBARK	–; embarks	**EME**	deme, feme,
EMBASSY	–; –		heme, seme;
EMBAY	–; embays		emes, emeu
EMBAYED	–; –	**EMEER**	–; emeers
EMBED	–; embeds	**EMEND**	remend;
EMBER	member; embers		emends
EMBERS	members; –	**EMENDED**	–; –
EMBLAZE	–; emblazed, emblazer, emblazes	**EMENDER**	–; emenders
		EMENDS	remends; –
		EMERALD	–; emeralds
		EMERGE	remerge; emerged, emerges
EMBLEM	–; emblems		
EMBODY	–; –	**EMERGED**	remerged; –
EMBOLI	–; embolic	**EMERGES**	remerges; –
EMBOLUS	–; –	**EMERIES**	–; –
EMBOLY	–; –	**EMERITA**	–; –
EMBOSK	–; embosks	**EMEROD**	–; emerods
EMBOSOM	–; embosoms	**EMEROID**	–; emeroids
		EMERY	–; –
EMBOSS	–; –	**EMES**	demes, femes, hemes, semes; –
EMBOW	–; embows		
EMBOWED	–; –		
EMBOWEL	–; embowels		
EMBOWER	–; embowers	**EMESES**	nemeses; –
EMBRACE	–; embraced, embracer, embraces	**EMESIS**	nemesis; –
		EMETIC	–; emetics
		EMETIN	–; emetine, emetins
EMBROIL	–; embroils	**EMETINE**	–; emetines
EMBROWN	–; embrowns	**EMEU**	–; emeus
EMBRUE	–; embrued, embrues	**EMEUTE**	–; emeutes
		EMIGRE	–; emigres
EMBRUTE	–; embruted, embrutes	**EMINENT**	–; –
		EMIR	–; emirs
EMBRYO	–; embryon, embryos	**EMIRATE**	–; emirates

EMIT	demit, remit; emits		emplaced, emplaces
EMITS	demits, remits; –	EMPLANE	–; emplaned, emplanes
EMITTED	demitted, remitted; –	EMPLOY	–; employe, employs
EMITTER	remitter; emitters	EMPLOYE	–; employed, employee, employer, employes
EMMER	hemmer; emmers		
EMMERS	hemmers; –		
EMMET	–; emmets		
EMODIN	–; emodins	EMPOWER	–; empowers
EMOTE	demote, gemote, remote; emoted, emoter, emotes	EMPRESS	–; –
		EMPRISE	–; emprises
		EMPRIZE	–; emprizes
		EMPTIED	–; –
EMOTED	demoted; –	EMPTIER	–; emptiers
EMOTER	remoter; emoters	EMPTIES	–; emptiest
EMOTES	demotes, gemotes; –	EMPTILY	–; –
		EMPTINS	–; –
EMOTING	demoting; –	EMPTY	–; –
EMOTION	demotion; emotions	EMPYEMA	–; empyemas
		EMS	gems, hems, mems, rems; –
EMOTIVE	–; –	EMU	–; emus
EMPALE	–; empaled, empaler, empales	EMULATE	–; emulated, emulates
		EMULOUS	–; –
EMPALER	–; empalers	EMYD	–; emyde, emyds
EMPANEL	–; empanels		
EMPATHY	–; –	EMYDE	–; emydes
EMPEROR	–; emperors	EN	ben, den, fen, hen, ken, men, pen, sen, ten, wen,
EMPERY	–; –		
EMPIRE	–; empires		
EMPIRIC	–; empirics		
EMPLACE	–;		

	yen; end, eng, ens
ENABLE	tenable; enabled, enabler, enables
ENABLER	–; enablers
ENACT	–; enacts
ENACTED	–; –
ENACTOR	–; enactors, enactory
ENAMEL	–; enamels
ENAMINE	–; enamines
ENAMOR	–; enamors
ENAMOUR	–; enamours
ENATE	penate, senate; enates
ENATES	senates; –
ENATIC	venatic; –
ENATION	–; enations
ENCAGE	–; encaged, encages
ENCAMP	–; encamps
ENCASE	–; encased, encases
ENCASH	–; –
ENCHAIN	–; enchains
ENCHANT	–; enchants
ENCHASE	–; enchased, enchaser, enchases
ENCINA	–; encinal, encinas
ENCLASP	–; enclasps
ENCLAVE	–; enclaves
ENCLOSE	–; enclosed, encloser, encloses

ENCODE	–; encoded, encoder, encodes
ENCODER	–; encoders
ENCORE	–; encored, encores
ENCRUST	–; encrusts
ENCRYPT	–; encrypts
ENCYST	–; encysts
END	bend, fend, lend, mend, pend, rend, send, tend, vend, wend; ends
ENDARCH	–; endarchy
ENDEAR	–; endears
ENDED	bended, fended, mended, pended, rended, tended, vended, wended; –
ENDEMIC	–; endemics
ENDER	bender, fender, gender, lender, mender, render, sender, tender, vender; enders
ENDERS	benders, fenders, genders, lenders,

	menders,		rends,
	renders,		sends, tends,
	senders,		vends,
	tenders,		wends; –
	venders; –	ENDUE	vendue;
ENDING	bending,		endued,
	fending,		endues
	lending,	ENDUES	vendues; –
	mending,	ENDURE	–; endured,
	pending,		endures
	rending,	ENDURO	–; enduros
	sending,	ENDWAYS	–; –
	tending,	ENDWISE	–; –
	vending,	ENEMA	–; enemas
	wending;	ENEMATA	–; –
	endings	ENEMIES	–; –
ENDINGS	mendings; –	ENEMY	–; –
ENDITE	–; endited,	ENERGID	–; energids
	endites	ENERGY	–; –
ENDIVE	–; endives	ENFACE	–; enfaced,
ENDLEAF	–; –		enfaces
ENDLESS	–; –	ENFEOFF	–; enfeoffs
ENDLONG	–; –	ENFEVER	–; enfevers
ENDMOST	–; –	ENFIN	–; –
ENDOGEN	–;	ENFLAME	–; enflamed,
	endogens,		enflames
	endogeny	ENFOLD	tenfold;
ENDOPOD	–; endopods		enfolds
ENDORSE	–; endorsed,	ENFOLDS	tenfolds; –
	endorsee,	ENFORCE	–; enforced,
	endorser,		enforcer,
	endorses		enforces
ENDOW	–; endows	ENFRAME	–; enframed,
ENDOWED	–; –		enframes
ENDOWER	–; endowers	ENG	–; engs
ENDRIN	–; endrins	ENGAGE	–; engaged,
ENDS	bends,		engager,
	fends, lends,		engages
	mends,	ENGAGER	–; engagers
	pends,	ENGILD	–; engilds

ENGINE	–; engined, engines	**ENNOBLE**	–; ennobled, ennobler, ennobles
ENGIRD	–; engirds		
ENGIRT	–; –	**ENNUI**	–; ennuis
ENGLISH	–; –	**ENNUYE**	–; ennuyee
ENGLUT	–; engluts	**ENOL**	–; enols
ENGORGE	–; engorged, engorges	**ENOLASE**	–; enolases
		ENOLIC	–; –
		ENOLOGY	–; –
ENGRAFT	–; engrafts	**ENORM**	–; –
ENGRAIL	–; engrails	**ENOSIS**	–; –
ENGRAIN	–; engrains	**ENOUGH**	–; enoughs
ENGRAM	–; engrams	**ENOUNCE**	–; enounced, enounces
ENGRAVE	–; engraved, engraver, engraves		
		ENOW	–; enows
ENGROSS	–; –	**ENPLANE**	–; enplaned, enplanes
ENGULF	–; engulfs		
ENHALO	–; –	**ENQUIRE**	–; enquired, enquires
ENHANCE	–; enhanced, enhancer, enhances		
		ENQUIRY	–; –
		ENRAGE	–; enraged, enrages
ENIGMA	–; enigmas		
ENISLE	–; enisled, enisles	**ENRAPT**	–; –
		ENRICH	–; –
		ENROBE	–; enrobed, enrober, enrobes
ENJOIN	–; enjoins		
ENJOY	–; enjoys		
ENJOYED	–; –	**ENROBER**	–; enrobers
ENJOYER	–; enjoyers	**ENROL**	–; enroll, enrols
ENLACE	–; enlaced, enlaces		
		ENROLL	–; enrolls
ENLARGE	–; enlarged, enlarger, enlarges	**ENROOT**	–; enroots
		ENS	bens, dens, fens, gens, hens, kens, lens, pens, tens, wens, yens; –
ENLIST	–; enlists		
ENLIVEN	–; enlivens		
ENMESH	–; –		
ENMITY	–; –		
ENNEAD	–; enneads		

ENSERF	−; enserfs		entera,
ENSIGN	−; ensigns		enters
ENSILE	pensile,	ENTERA	−; enteral
	tensile;	ENTERED	centered; −
	ensiled,	ENTERER	centerer;
	ensiles		enterers
ENSKIED	−; −	ENTERS	centers,
ENSKIES	−; −		renters,
ENSKY	−; −		tenters,
ENSKYED	−; −		venters; −
ENSLAVE	−; enslaved,	ENTERIC	−; −
	enslaver,	ENTERON	−; enterons
	enslaves	ENTHRAL	−; enthrall,
ENSNARE	−; ensnared,		enthrals
	ensnarer,	ENTHUSE	−; enthused,
	ensnares		enthuses
ENSNARL	−; ensnarls	ENTIA	−; −
ENSOUL	−; ensouls	ENTICE	−; enticed,
ENSUE	−; ensued,		enticer,
	ensues		entices
ENSUING	−; −	ENTICER	−; enticers
ENSURE	censure;	ENTIRE	−; entires
	ensured,	ENTITLE	−; entitled,
	ensurer,		entitles
	ensures	ENTITY	−; −
ENSURED	censured; −	ENTOIL	−; entoils
ENSURER	censurer;	ENTOMB	−; entombs
	ensurers	ENTOPIC	−; −
ENSURES	censures; −	ENTOZOA	−; entozoal,
ENTAIL	ventail;		entozoan
	entails	ENTRAIN	−; entrains
ENTAILS	ventails; −	ENTRANT	−; entrants
ENTASES	−; −	ENTRAP	−; entraps
ENTASIA	−; entasias	ENTREAT	−; entreats,
ENTASIS	−; −		entreaty
ENTENTE	−; ententes	ENTREE	−; entrees
ENTER	center,	ENTRIES	gentries,
	renter,		sentries; −
	tenter,	ENTROPY	−; −
	venter;	ENTRUST	−; entrusts

ENTRY	gentry, sentry; –	**EONIAN**	aeonian; –
		EONISM	peonism; eonisms
ENTWINE	–; entwined, entwines	**EONS**	aeons, neons, peons; –
ENTWIST	–; entwists		
ENURE	tenure; enured, enures	**EOSIN**	–; eosine, eosins
ENURED	tenured; –	**EOSINE**	–; eosines
ENURES	tenures; –	**EOSINIC**	–; –
ENVELOP	–; envelope, envelops	**EPACT**	–; epacts
		EPARCH	–; eparchs, eparchy
ENVENOM	–; envenoms		
ENVIED	–; –	**EPAULET**	–; epaulets
ENVIER	–; enviers	**EPEE**	tepee; epees
ENVIES	–; –		
ENVIOUS	–; –	**EPEEIST**	–; epeeists
ENVIRON	–; environs	**EPEES**	tepees; –
ENVOI	renvoi; envois	**EPEIRIC**	–; –
		EPERGNE	–; epergnes
ENVOIS	renvois; –	**EPHA**	–; ephah, ephas
ENVOY	–; envoys		
ENVY	–; –	**EPHAH**	–; ephahs
ENWHEEL	–; enwheels	**EPHEBE**	–; ephebes
ENWIND	–; enwinds	**EPHEBI**	–; ephebic
ENWOMB	–; enwombs	**EPHEBOI**	–; –
ENWOUND	–; –	**EPHEBOS**	–; –
ENWRAP	–; enwraps	**EPHEBUS**	–; –
ENZYM	–; enzyme, enzyms	**EPHEDRA**	–; ephedras
		EPHOD	–; ephods
ENZYME	–; enzymes	**EPHOR**	–; ephori, ehpors
ENZYMIC	–; –		
EOBIONT	–; eobionts	**EPHORAL**	–; –
EOLIAN	aeolian; –	**EPIBOLY**	–; –
EOLITH	neolith; eoliths	**EPIC**	sepic; epics
		EPICAL	–; –
EOLITHS	neoliths; –	**EPICARP**	–; epicarps
EON	aeon, geon, neon, peon; eons	**EPICENE**	–; epicenes
		EPICURE	–; epicures
		EPIDERM	–; epiderms

EPIDOTE	–; epidotes	**EQUABLE**	–; –
EPIGEAL	–; –	**EQUABLY**	–; –
EPIGEAN	–; –	**EQUAL**	–; equals
EPIGENE	–; –	**EQUALED**	–; –
EPIGON	–; epigone, epigons	**EQUALLY**	–; –
		EQUATE	–; equated, equates
EPIGONE	–; epigones		
EPIGRAM	–; epigrams	**EQUATOR**	–; equators
EPIGYNY	–; –	**EQUERRY**	–; –
EPILOG	–; epilogs	**EQUINE**	–; equines
EPIMER	–; epimere, epimers	**EQUINOX**	–; –
		EQUIP	–; equips
EPIMERE	–; epimeres	**EQUITES**	requites; –
EPINAOS	–; –	**EQUITY**	–; –
EPISCIA	–; episcias	**ER**	fer, her, per, ser; era, ere, erg, ern, err, ers
EPISODE	–; episodes		
EPISOME	–; episomes		
EPISTLE	–; epistler, epistles	**ERA**	sera, vera; eras
EPITAPH	–; epitaphs		
EPITAXY	–; –	**ERAS**	–; erase
EPITHET	–; epithets	**ERASE**	–; erased, eraser, erases
EPITOME	–; epitomes		
EPIZOA	–; –		
EPIZOIC	–; –	**ERASER**	–; erasers
EPIZOON	–; –	**ERASION**	–; erasions
EPOCH	–; epochs	**ERASURE**	–; erasures
EPOCHAL	–; –	**ERBIUM**	–; erbiums
EPODE	–; epodes	**ERE**	cere, dere, fere, here, mere, pere, sere, were; –
EPONYM	–; eponyms, eponymy		
EPOPEE	–; epopees		
EPOS	pepos; –		
EPOSES	deposes, reposes; –	**ERECT**	–; erects
		ERECTED	–; –
EPOXIDE	–; epoxides	**ERECTER**	–; –
EPOXIED	–; –	**ERECTLY**	–; –
EPOXIES	–; –	**ERECTOR**	–; erectors
EPOXY	–; –	**ERELONG**	–; –
EPSILON	–; epsilons	**EREMITE**	–; eremites

ERENOW	–; –	**EROTIC**	cerotic, xerotic; erotica, erotics
EREPSIN	–; erepsins		
ERG	berg; ergo, ergs		
ERGATE	–; ergates	**EROTICA**	–; erotical
ERGO	–; ergot	**EROTISM**	–; erotisms
ERGODIC	–; –	**ERR**	–; errs
ERGOT	–; ergots	**ERRANCY**	–; –
ERGOTIC	–; –	**ERRAND**	–; errands
ERGS	bergs; –	**ERRANT**	–; errants
ERICA	–; ericas	**ERRATA**	–; erratas
ERICOID	–; –	**ERRATIC**	–; erratics
ERINGO	–; eringos	**ERRATUM**	–; –
ERISTIC	–; eristics	**ERRED**	–; –
ERKLING	–; erklings	**ERRHINE**	–; errhines
ERMINE	–; ermined, ermines	**ERRING**	herring; –
		ERROR	terror; errors
ERN	fern, hern, kern, tern; erne, erns	**ERRORS**	terrors; –
		ERS	hers, sers; erst
ERNE	kerne, terne; ernes	**ERSATZ**	–; –
		ERSES	perses, verses; –
ERNES	kernes, ternes; –	**ERST**	verst; –
		ERUCT	–; eructs
ERNS	ferns, herns, kerns, terns; –	**ERUCTED**	–; –
		ERUDITE	–; –
ERODE	–; eroded, erodes	**ERUGO**	aerugo; erugos
ERODENT	–; –	**ERUGOS**	aerugos; –
ERODING	–; –	**ERUPT**	–; erupts
EROS	ceros, heros, zeros; erose	**ERUPTED**	–; –
		ERVIL	–; ervils
EROSE	reroses; eroses	**ERYNGO**	–; eryngos
		ES	des, hes, pes, res, yes; ess
EROSELY	–; –		
EROSES	xeroses; –		
EROSION	–; erosions	**ESCALOP**	–; escalops
EROSIVE	–; –	**ESCAPE**	–; escaped, escapee,

	escaper, escapes		
ESCAPEE	–; escapees	ESSAYER	–; essayers
ESCAPER	–; escapers	ESSENCE	–; essences
ESCAR	–; escarp, escars	ESSES	cesses, fesses, jesses, messes, nesses, yesses; –
ESCARP	–; escarps		
ESCHAR	–; eschars		
ESCHEAT	–; escheats	ESSOIN	–; essoins
ESCHEW	–; eschews	ESTATE	gestate, restate, testate; estated, estates
ESCOLAR	–; escolars		
ESCORT	–; escorts		
ESCOT	–; escots		
ESCOTED	–; –		
ESCROW	–; escrows	ESTATED	gestated, restated; –
ESCUAGE	–; escuages		
ESCUDO	–; escudos	ESTATES	gestates, restates
ESERINE	–; eserines		
ESES	–; –	ESTEEM	–; esteems
ESKAR	–; eskars	ESTER	fester, jester, nester, pester, rester, tester, wester, yester; esters
ESKER	–; eskers		
ESPANOL	–; –		
ESPARTO	–; espartos		
ESPIAL	–; espials		
ESPIED	–; –		
ESPIES	–; –		
ESPOUSE	–; espoused, espouser, espouses	ESTERS	festers, jesters, nesters, pesters, resters, testers, westers; –
ESPRIT	–; esprits		
ESPY	–; –		
ESQUIRE	–; esquired, esquires	ESTHETE	–; esthetes
ESS	cess, fess, jess, less, mess, ness; –	ESTIVAL	aestival, festival; –
		ESTOP	–; estops
ESSAY	–; essays	ESTRAL	vestral; –
ESSAYED	–; –	ESTRAY	–; estrays

ESTREAT	–; estreats	**ETCHES**	fetches,
ESTRIN	oestrin;		ketches,
	estrins		letches,
ESTRINS	oestrins; –		retches,
ESTRIOL	–; estriols		vetches; –
ESTRONE	–; estrones	**ETCHING**	fetching,
ESTROUS	–; –		retching;
ESTRUAL	–; –		etchings
ESTRUM	oestrum;	**ETERNAL**	–; eternals
	estrums	**ETERNE**	–; –
ESTRUMS	oestrums; –	**ETESIAN**	–; etesians
ESTRUS	oestrus; –	**ETH**	beth, heth,
ESTUARY	–; –		teth; eths
ET	bet, fet, get,	**ETHANE**	methane;
	het, jet, let,		ethanes
	met, net,	**ETHANES**	methanes
	pet, ret, set,	**ETHANOL**	–; ethanols
	vet, wet, yet;	**ETHENE**	–; ethenes
	eta, eth	**ETHER**	aether,
ETA	beta, feta,		nether,
	meta, seta,		tether,
	zeta; etas		wether;
ETAGERE	–; etageres		ethers
ETAMIN	–; etamine,	**ETHERIC**	–; –
	etamins	**ETHERS**	aethers,
ETAMINE	–; etamines		tethers,
ETAPE	–; etapes		wethers; –
ETAS	betas, fetas,	**ETHIC**	–; ethics
	zetas; –	**ETHICAL**	–; ethicals
ETATISM	–; etatisms	**ETHINYL**	–; ethinyls
ETATIST	–; –	**ETHION**	–; ethions
ETCH	fetch, ketch,	**ETHMOID**	–; ethmoids
	letch, retch,	**ETHNIC**	–; ethnics
	vetch; –	**ETHNOS**	–; –
ETCHED	fetched,	**ETHOS**	–; –
	retched,	**ETHOSES**	–; –
	tetched; –	**ETHOXY**	methoxy;
ETCHER	fetcher;		ethoxyl
	etchers	**ETHOXYL**	–; ethoxyls
ETCHERS	fetchers; –		

ETHS	beths, heths, teths; –	**EUSTACY**	–; –
		EUSTELE	–; eusteles
ETHYL	methyl; ethyls	**EUTAXY**	–; –
		EVACUEE	–; evacuees
ETHYLIC	–; –	**EVADE**	–; evaded, evader, evades
ETHYLS	methyls; –		
ETHYNE	–; ethynes		
ETHYNYL	–; ethynyls	**EVADER**	–; evaders
ETNA	–; etnas	**EVANGEL**	–; evangels
ETOILE	–; etoiles	**EVANISH**	–; –
ETUDE	–; etudes	**EVASION**	–; evasions
ETUI	–; etuis	**EVASIVE**	–; –
ETWEE	–; etwees	**EVE**	jeves, neve; even, ever, eves
ETYMA	–; –		
ETYMON	–; etymons		
EUCAINE	–; eucaines	**EVEN**	seven; evens, event
EUCHRE	–; euchred, euchres		
		EVENED	–; –
EUCLASE	–; euclases	**EVENER**	–; eveners
EUCRITE	–; eucrites	**EVENEST**	–; –
EUDEMON	–; –	**EVENING**	–; evenings
EUGENIC	–; eugenics	**EVENLY**	–; –
EUGENOL	–; eugenols	**EVENS**	sevens; –
EUGLENA	–; euglenas	**EVENT**	–; events
EULOGIA	–; eulogiae, eulogias	**EVER**	fever, lever, never, sever, evert, every
EULOGY	–; –		
EUNUCH	–; eunuchs	**EVERT**	revert; everts
EUPEPSY	–; –	**EVERTED**	–; –
EUPHONY	–; –	**EVERTOR**	–; evertors
EUPHROE	–; euphroes	**EVERTS**	reverts; –
EUPLOID	–; euploids, euploidy	**EVERY**	revery; –
		EVES	jeves, neves; –
EUPNEA	–; eupneas		
EUPNEIC	–; –	**EVICT**	–; evicts
EUPNOEA	–; eupnoeas	**EVICTED**	–; –
EUREKA	–; –	**EVICTEE**	–; evictees
EURIPI	–; –	**EVICTOR**	–; evictors
EURIPUS	–; –	**EVIDENT**	–; –
EURO	–; euros		

EVIL	devil, kevil; evils	EWERS	hewers, sewers; –
EVILER	reviler; –	EX	dex, hex,
EVILEST	–; –		kex, lex, rex,
EVILLER	–; –		sex, vex; –
EVILLY	–; –	EXACT	–; exacta,
EVILS	devils, kevils; –		exacts
EVINCE	–; evinced, evinces	EXACTA	–; exactas
		EXACTED	–; –
EVITE	–; evited, evites	EXACTER	–; exacters
		EXACTLY	–; –
EVITING	–; –	EXACTOR	–; exactors
EVOKE	revoke; evoked, evoker, evokes	EXALT	–; exalts
		EXALTED	–; –
		EXALTER	–; exalters
		EXAM	–; exams
EVOKED	revoked; –	EXAMEN	–; examens
EVOKER	revoker; evokers	EXAMINE	–; examined, examinee, examiner, examines
EVOKES	revokes; –	
EVOKING	–; –	
EVOLUTE	–; evolutes	EXAMPLE	–; exampled, examples
EVOLVE	devolve, revolve; evolved, evolver, evolves	
		EXARCH	–; exarchs, exarchy
		EXCEED	–; exceeds
EVOLVED	revolved; –	EXCEL	–; excels
EVOLVER	revolver; evolvers	EXCEPT	–; excepts
		EXCERPT	–; excerpts
EVOLVES	revolves; –	EXCESS	–; –
EVZONE	–; evzones	EXCIDE	–; excided, excides
EWE	–; ewer, ewes	
		EXCIPLE	–; exciples
EWER	fewer, hewer, newer, sewer; ewers	EXCISE	–; excised, excises
		EXCITE	–; excited, exciter, excites

EXCITER	–; exciters		exhumer,
EXCITON	–; excitons		exhumes
EXCITOR	–; excitors	**EXHUMER**	–; exhumers
EXCLAIM	–; exclaims	**EXIGENT**	–; –
EXCLAVE	–; exclaves	**EXILE**	–; exiled,
EXCLUDE	–; excluded,		exiles
	excluder,	**EXILIAN**	–; –
	excludes	**EXILIC**	–; –
EXCRETA	–; excretal	**EXILING**	–; –
EXCRETE	–; excreted,	**EXINE**	–; exines
	excreter,	**EXIST**	sexist; exists
	excretes	**EXISTED**	–; –
EXCUSE	–; excused,	**EXISTS**	sexists; –
	excuser,	**EXIT**	–; exits
	excuses	**EXITED**	–; –
EXCUSER	–; excusers	**EXITING**	–; –
EXEC	–; execs	**EXOCARP**	–; exocarps
EXECUTE	–; executed,	**EXODERM**	–; exoderms
	executer,	**EXODOI**	–; –
	executes	**EXODOS**	–; –
EXEDRA	–; exedrae	**EXODUS**	–; –
EXEGETE	–; exegetes	**EXOGAMY**	–; –
EXEMPT	–; exempts	**EXOGEN**	–; exogens
EXEQUY	–; –	**EXOTIC**	–; exotica,
EXERGUE	–; exergues		exotics
EXERT	–; exerts	**EXOTISM**	–; exotisms
EXERTED	–; –	**EXPAND**	–; expands
EXES	dexes,	**EXPANSE**	–; expanses
	hexes,	**EXPECT**	–; expects
	kexes, rexes,	**EXPEL**	–; expels
	sexes,	**EXPEND**	–; expends
	vexes; –	**EXPENSE**	–; expensed,
EXEUNT	–; –		expenses
EXHALE	–; exhaled,	**EXPERT**	–; experts
	exhales	**EXPIATE**	–; expiated,
EXHAUST	–; exhausts		expiates
EXHIBIT	–; exhibits	**EXPIRE**	–; expired,
EXHORT	–; exhorts		expirer,
EXHUME	–; exhumed,		expires

EXPIRER	–; expirers	**EXTOLL**	–; extolls
EXPIRY	–; –	**EXTORT**	–; extorts
EXPLAIN	–; explains	**EXTRA**	–; extras
EXPLANT	–; explants	**EXTRACT**	–; extracts
EXPLODE	–;	**EXTREMA**	–; –
	exploded,	**EXTREME**	–; extremer,
	exploder,		extremes
	explodes	**EXTRUDE**	–; extruded,
EXPLOIT	–; exploits		extruder,
EXPLORE	–; explored,		extrudes
	explorer,	**EXUDATE**	–; exudates
	explores	**EXUDE**	–; exuded,
EXPO	–; expos		exudes
EXPORT	–; exports	**EXULT**	–; exults
EXPOSAL	–; exposals	**EXULTED**	–; –
EXPOSE	–; exposed,	**EXURB**	–; exurbs
	exposer,	**EXURBAN**	–; –
	exposes	**EXUDATE**	–; exudates
EXPOSER	–; exposers	**EXURBIA**	–; exurbias
EXPOSIT	–; exposits	**EXUVIA**	–; exuviae,
EXPOUND	–; expounds		exuvial
EXPRESS	–; –	**EXUVIUM**	–; –
EXPULSE	–; expulsed,	**EYAS**	–; –
	expulses	**EYASES**	–; –
EXPUNGE	–;	**EYE**	–; eyed,
	expunged,		eyen, eyer,
	expunger,		eyes
	expunges	**EYEABLE**	–; –
EXSCIND	–; exscinds	**EYEBALL**	–; eyeballs
EXSECT	–; exsects	**EYEBEAM**	–;
EXSERT	–; exserts		eyebeams
EXTANT	sextant; –	**EYEBOLT**	–; eyebolts
EXTEND	–; extends	**EYEBROW**	–; eyebrows
EXTENT	–; extents	**EYECUP**	–; eyecups
EXTERN	–; externe,	**EYEFUL**	–; eyefuls
	externs	**EYEHOLE**	–; eyeholes
EXTERNE	–; externes	**EYEHOOK**	–; eyehooks
EXTINCT	–; extincts	**EYEING**	–; –
EXTOL	–; extoll,	**EYELASH**	–; –
	extols	**EYELESS**	–; –

EYELET	–; eyelets	**EYEWINK**	–; eyewinks
EYELID	–; eyelids	**EYING**	keying; –
EYELIKE	–; –	**EYNE**	–; –
EYER	feyer; eyers	**EYRA**	–; eyras
EYESHOT	–; eyeshots	**EYRE**	–; eyres
EYESOME	–; –	**EYRIE**	–; eyries
EYESORE	–; eyesores	**EYRIR**	–; –
EYESPOT	–; eyespots	**EYRY**	–; –
EYEWASH	–; –		

F

F	ef, if, of; fa	**FACILE**	–; –
FA	–; fad, fag,	**FACING**	–; facings
	fan, far, fas,	**FACT**	–; facts
	fat, fax, fay	**FACTFUL**	–; –
FABLE	–; fabled,	**FACTION**	–; factions
	fabler,	**FACTIVE**	–; –
	fables	**FACTOR**	–; factors,
FABLER	–; fablers		factory
FABLIAU	–; fabliaux	**FACTUAL**	–; –
FABLING	–; –	**FACTURE**	–; factures
FABRIC	–; fabrics	**FACULA**	–; faculae,
FABULAR	–; –		facular
FACADE	–; facades	**FACULTY**	–; –
FACE	–; faced,	**FAD**	–; fade,
	facer, faces,		fado, fads
	facet	**FADABLE**	–; –
FACER	–; facers	**FADDIER**	–; –
FACET	–; facete,	**FADDISH**	–; –
	facets	**FADDISM**	–; faddisms
FACETE	–; faceted	**FADDIST**	–; faddists
FACEUP	–; –	**FADDY**	–; –
FACIA	–; facial,	**FADE**	–; faded,
	facias		fader, fades
FACIAL	–; facials	**FADELY**	–; –
FACIEND	–; faciends	**FADER**	–; faders
FACIENT	–; –	**FADGE**	–; fadged,
FACIES	–; –		fadges

FADING	–; fadings	**FAITOUR**	–; faitours
FADO	–; fados	**FAKE**	–; faked,
FAECAL	–; –		faker, fakes
FAECES	–; –	**FAKEER**	–; fakeers
FAENA	–; faenas	**FAKER**	–; fakers,
FAERIE	–; faeries		fakery
FAERY	–; –	**FAKING**	–; –
FAG	–; fags	**FAKIR**	–; fakirs
FAGGED	–; –	**FALBALA**	–; falbalas
FAGGING	–; –	**FALCATE**	–; falcated
FAGGOT	–; faggots	**FALCON**	–; falcons
FAGIN	–; fagins	**FALL**	–; falls
FAGOT	–; fagots	**FALLACY**	–; –
FAGOTED	–; –	**FALLAL**	–; fallals
FAGOTER	–; fagoters	**FALLEN**	–; –
FAIENCE	–; faiences	**FALLER**	–; fallers
FAIL	–; fails	**FALLING**	–; –
FAILED	–; –	**FALLOFF**	–; falloffs
FAILING	–; failings	**FALLOUT**	–; fallouts
FAILLE	–; failles	**FALLOW**	–; fallows
FAILURE	–; failures	**FALSE**	–; falser
FAIN	–; faint	**FALSELY**	–; –
FAINER	–; –	**FALSEST**	–; –
FAINEST	–; –	**FALSIE**	–; falsies
FAINT	–; faints	**FALSIFY**	–; –
FAINTED	–; –	**FALSITY**	–; –
FAINTER	–; fainters	**FALTER**	–; falters
FAINTLY	–; –	**FAME**	–; famed,
FAIR	–; fairs,		fames
	fairy	**FAMILY**	–; –
FAIRED	–; –	**FAMINE**	–; famines
FAIRER	–; –	**FAMING**	–; –
FAIREST	–; –	**FAMISH**	–; –
FAIRIES	–; –	**FAMOUS**	–; –
FAIRING	–; fairings	**FAMULI**	–; –
FAIRISH	–; –	**FAMULUS**	–; –
FAIRLY	–; –	**FAN**	–; fane,
FAIRWAY	–; fairways		fang, fano,
FAITH	–; faiths		fans
FAITHED	–; –	**FANATIC**	–; fanatics

FANCIED	–; –	FARADAY	–; faradays
FANCIER	–; fanciers	FARADIC	–; –
FANCIES	–; fanciest	FARAWAY	–; –
FANCILY	–; –	FARCE	–; farced, farcer, farces
FANCY	–; –		
FANDOM	–; fandoms		
FANE	–; fanes	FARCER	–; farcers
FANEGA	–; fanegas	FARCEUR	–; farceurs
FANFARE	–; fanfares	FARCI	–; farcie
FANFOLD	–; fanfolds	FARCIE	–; farcies
FANG	–; fanga, fangs	FARCING	–; –
		FARCY	–; –
FANGA	–; fangas	FARD	–; fards
FANGED	; –	FARDED	–; –
FANION	–; fanions	FARDEL	–; fardels
FANJET	–; fanjets	FARDING	–; –
FANLIKE	–; –	FARE	–; fared, farer, fares
FANNED	–; –		
FANNER	–; fanners	FARER	–; farers
FANNING	–; –	FARFAL	–; –
FANNY	–; –	FARFEL	–; farfels
FANO	–; fanon, fanos	FARINA	–; farinas
		FARING	–; –
FANON	–; fanons	FARINHA	–; farinhas
FANTAIL	–; fantails	FARL	–; farle, farls
FANTASM	–; fantasms		
FANTAST	–; fantasts	FARLE	–; farles
FANTASY	–; –	FARM	–; farms
FANTOD	–; fantods	FARMED	–; –
FANTOM	–; fantoms	FARMER	–; farmers
FANUM	–; fanums	FARMING	–; farmings
FANWISE	–; –	FARNESS	–; –
FANWORT	–; fanworts	FARO	–; faros
FAQIR	–; faqirs	FARRAGO	–; –
FAQUIR	–; faquirs	FARRIER	–; farriers, farriery
FAR	afar; fard, fare, farl, farm, faro, fart		
		FARROW	–; farrows
		FART	–; farts
		FARTED	–; –
FARAD	–; farads	FARTHER	–; –

FARTING	–; –	**FATSO**	–; fatsos
FAS	–; fash, fast	**FATSOES**	–; –
FASCES	–; –	**FATTED**	–; –
FASCIA	–; fasciae, fascial, fascias	**FATTEN**	–; fattens
		FATTER	–; –
		FATTEST	–; –
FASCINE	–; fascines	**FATTIER**	–; –
FASCISM	–; fascisms	**FATTIES**	–; fattiest
FASCIST	–; fascists	**FATTILY**	–; –
FASH	–; –	**FATTING**	–; –
FASHED	–; –	**FATTISH**	–; –
FASHES	–; –	**FATTY**	–; –
FASHING	–; –	**FATUITY**	–; –
FASHION	–; fashions	**FATUOUS**	–; –
FAST	–; fasts	**FAUCAL**	–; faucals
FASTED	–; –	**FAUCES**	–; –
FASTEN	–; fastens	**FAUCET**	–; faucets
FASTER	–; –	**FAUCIAL**	–; –
FASTEST	–; –	**FAUGH**	–; –
FASTING	–; fastings	**FAULD**	–; faulds
FAT	–; fate, fats	**FAULT**	–; faults, faulty
FATAL	–; –		
FATALLY	–; –	**FAULTED**	–; –
FATBACK	–; fatbacks	**FAUN**	–; fauna, fauns
FATBIRD	–; fatbirds		
FATE	–; fated, fates	**FAUNA**	–; faunae, faunal, faunas
FATEFUL	–; –		
FATHEAD	–; fatheads	**FAUVE**	–; fauves
FATHER	–; fathers	**FAUVISM**	–; fauvisms
FATHOM	–; fathoms	**FAUVIST**	–; fauvists
FATIDIC	–; –	**FAVELA**	–; favelas
FATIGUE	–; fatigued, fatigues	**FAVOR**	–; favors
		FAVORED	–; –
FATING	–; –	**FAVORER**	–; favorers
FATLESS	–; –	**FAVOUR**	–; favours
FATLIKE	–; –	**FAVUS**	–; –
FATLING	–; fatlings	**FAVUSES**	–; –
FATLY	–; –	**FAWN**	–; fawns, fawny
FATNESS	–; –		

FAWNED	–; –	FEBRILE	–; –
FAWNER	–; fawners	FECAL	–; –
FAWNIER	–; –	FECES	–; –
FAWNING	–; –	FECIAL	–; fecials
FAX	–; –	FECK	–; fecks
FAXED	–; –	FECKLY	–; –
FAXES	–; –	FECULA	–; feculae
FAXING	–; –	FECUND	–; –
FAY	ofay; fays	FED	–; feds
FAYED	–;	FEDAYEE	–; fedayeen
FAYING	–; –	FEDERAL	–; federals
FAYS	ofays; –	FEDORA	–; fedoras
FAZE	–; fazed, fazes	FEE	–; feed, feel, fees, feet
FAZENDA	–; fazendas		
FAZING	–; –	FEEBLE	–; feebler
FEAL	–; –	FEEBLY	–; –
FEALTY	–; –	FEED	–; feeds
FEAR	–; fears	FEEDBAG	–; feedbags
FEARED	afeared; –	FEEDBOX	–; –
FEARER	–; fearers	FEEDER	–; feeders
FEARFUL	–; –	FEEDING	–; –
FEARING	–; –	FEEDLOT	–; feedlots
FEASE	–; feased, feases	FEEING	–; –
FEASING	–; –	FEEL	–; feels
FEAST	–; feasts	FEELER	–; feelers
FEASTED	–; –	FEELESS	–; –
FEASTER	–; feasters	FEELING	–; feelings
FEAT	–; feats	FEET	–; –
FEATER	–; –	FEEZE	–; feezed, feezes
FEATEST	–; –		
FEATHER	–; feathers, feathery	FEEZING	–; –
		FEIGN	–; feigns
FEATLY	–; –	FEIGNED	–; –
FEATURE	–; featured, features	FEIGNER	–; feigners
		FEINT	–; feints
FEAZE	–; feazed, feazes	FEINTED	–; –
		FEIRIE	–; –
FEAZING	–; –	FEIST	–; feists, feisty

FELID	–; felids	**FENDING**	–; –
FELINE	–; felines	**FENNEC**	–; fennecs
FELL	–; fella,	**FENNEL**	–; fennels
	fells, felly	**FENNY**	–; –
FELLA	–; fellah,	**FEOD**	–; feods
	fellas	**FEODARY**	–; –
FELLAH	–; fellahs	**FEOFF**	–; feoffs
FELLED	–; –	**FEOFFED**	–; –
FELLER	–; fellers	**FEOFFEE**	–; feoffees
FELLIES	–; –	**FEOFFER**	–; feoffer
FELLING	–; –	**FER**	–; fere, fern
FELLOE	–; felloes	**FERAL**	–; –
FELLOW	–; fellows	**FERBAM**	–; ferbams
FELON	–; felons,	**FERE**	–; feres
	felony	**FERIA**	–; feriae,
FELONRY	–; –		ferial, ferias
FELSITE	–; felsites	**FERINE**	–; –
FELSPAR	–; felspars	**FERITY**	–; –
FELT	–; felts	**FERLIE**	–; ferlies
FELTED	–; –	**FERLY**	–; –
FELTING	–; feltings	**FERMATA**	–; fermatas
FELUCCA	–; feluccas	**FERMATE**	–; –
FELWORT	–; felworts	**FERMENT**	–; ferments
FEMALE	–; females	**FERMI**	–; fermis
FEME	–; femes	**FERMION**	–; fermions
FEMINIE	–; –	**FERMIUM**	–; fermiums
FEMME	–; femmes	**FERN**	–; ferns,
FEMORA	–; femoral		ferny
FEMUR	–; femurs	**FERNERY**	–; –
FEN	–; fend, fens	**FERNIER**	–; –
FENAGLE	–; fenagled,	**FERRATE**	–; ferrates
	fenagles	**FERREL**	–; ferrels
FENCE	–; fenced,	**FERRET**	–; ferrets,
	fencer,		ferrety
	fences	**FERRIC**	–; –
FENCER	–; fencers	**FERRIED**	–; –
FENCING	–; fencings	**FERRIES**	–; –
FEND	–; fends	**FERRITE**	–; ferrites
FENDED	–; –	**FERROUS**	–; –
FENDER	–; fenders		

FERRULE	–; ferruled, ferrules	**FETTED**	–; –
FERRUM	–; ferrums	**FETTER**	–; fetters
FERRY	–; –	**FETTING**	–; –
FERTILE	–; –	**FETTLE**	–; fettled, fettles
FERULA	–; ferulae, ferulas		
		FETUS	–; –
		FETUSES	–; –
FERULE	–; feruled, ferules	**FEU**	–; feud, feus
		FEUAR	–; feuars
FERVENT	–; –	**FEUD**	–; feuds
FERVID	–; –	**FEUDAL**	–; –
FERVOR	–; fervors	**FEUDARY**	–; –
FERVOUR	–; fervours	**FEUDED**	–; –
FESCUE	–; fescues	**FEUDING**	–; –
FESS	–; fesse	**FEUDIST**	–; feudists
FESSE	–; fessed, fesses	**FEUED**	–; –
		FEUING	–; –
FESSING	–; –	**FEVER**	–; fevers
FESTAL	–; –	**FEVERED**	–; –
FESTER	–; festers	**FEW**	–; –
FESTIVE	–; –	**FEWER**	–; –
FESTOON	–; festoons	**FEWEST**	–; –
FET	–; feta, fete, fets	**FEWNESS**	–; –
		FEY	–; –
FETA	–; fetal, fetas	**FEYER**	–; –
		FEYEST	–; –
FETCH	–; –	**FEYNESS**	–; –
FETCHED	–; –	**FEZ**	–; –
FETCHER	–; fetchers	**FEZES**	–; –
FETCHES	–; –	**FEZZED**	–; –
FETE	–; feted, fetes	**FEZZES**	–; –
		FIACRE	–; fiacres
FETIAL	–; fetials	**FIANCE**	–; fiancee, fiances
FETICH	–; –		
FETID	–; –	**FIANCEE**	–; fiancees
FETIDLY	–; –	**FIAR**	–; fiars
FETING	–; –	**FIASCHI**	–; –
FETISH	–; –	**FIASCO**	–; fiascos
FETLOCK	–; fetlocks	**FIAT**	–; fiats
FETOR	–; fetors	**FIB**	–; fibs

FIBBED	–; –	FIELD	afield; fields
FIBBER	–; fibbers	FIELDED	–; –
FIBBING	–; –	FIELDER	–; fielders
FIBER	–; fibers	FIEND	–; fiends
FIBERED	–; –	FIERCE	–; fiercer
FIBRE	–; fibres	FIERIER	–; –
FIBRIL	–; fibrils	FIERILY	–; –
FIBRIN	–; fibrins	FIERY	–; –
FIBROID	–; fibroids	FIESTA	–; fiestas
FIBROIN	–; fibroins	FIFE	–; fifed,
FIBROMA	–; fibromas		fifer, fifes
FIBROUS	–; –	FIFER	–; fifers
FIBULA	–; fibulae,	FIFTEEN	–; fifteens
	fibular,	FIFTH	–; fifths
	fibulas	FIFTHLY	–; –
FICE	–; fices	FIFTIES	–; –
FICHE	–; fiches	FIFTY	–; –
FICHU	–; fichus	FIG	–; figs
FICIN	–; ficins	FIGGED	–; –
FICKLE	–; fickler	FIGGING	–; –
FICO	–; –	FIGHT	–; fights
FICOES	–; –	FIGHTER	–; fighters
FICTILE	–; –	FIGMENT	–; figments
FICTION	–; fictions	FIGURAL	–; –
FICTIVE	–; –	FIGURE	–; figured,
FID	–; fido, fids		figurer,
FIDDLE	–; fiddled,		figures
	fiddler,	FIGURER	–; figurers
	fiddles	FIGWORT	–; figworts
FIDDLER	–; fiddlers	FIL	–; fila, file,
FIDEISM	–; fideisms		fils
FIDEIST	–; fideists	FILA	–; filar
FIDGE	–; fidged,	FILAREE	–; filarees
	fidges, fidget	FILARIA	–; filariae,
FIDGET	–; fidgety		filarial,
FIDGING	–; –		filarian
FIDO	–; fidos	FILBERT	–; filberts
FIE	–; fief	FILCH	–; –
FIEF	–; fiefs	FILCHED	–; –
FIEFDOM	–; fiefdoms		

FILCHER	–; filchers		fink, finn,
FILCHES	–; –		fins;
FILE	–; filed, filer,	**FINABLE**	–; –
	files, filet	**FINAGLE**	–; finagled,
FILEMOT	–; –		finagler,
FILER	–; filers		finagles
FILET	–; filets	**FINAL**	–; finale,
FILETED	–; –		finals
FILIAL	–; –	**FINALE**	–; finales
FILIATE	–; filiated,	**FINALIS**	–; finalism,
	filiates		finalist
FILIBEG	–; filibegs	**FINALLY**	–; –
FILING	–; filings	**FINANCE**	–; financed,
FILL	–; fille, fills,		finances
	filly	**FINBACK**	–; finbacks
FILLE	–; filled,	**FINCH**	;
	filler, filles,	**FINCHES**	–; –
	fillet	**FIND**	–; finds
FILLER	–; fillers	**FINDER**	–; finders
FILLET	–; fillets	**FINDING**	–; findings
FILLIES	–; –	**FINE**	–; fined,
FILLING	–; fillings		finer, fines
FILLIP	–; fillips	**FINELY**	–; –
FILM	–; films, filmy	**FINER**	–; finery
FILMDOM	–; filmdoms	**FINES**	–; finest
FILMED	–; –	**FINESSE**	–; finessed,
FILMIC	–; –		finesses
FILMIER	–; –	**FINFISH**	–; –
FILMILY	–; –	**FINFOOT**	–; finfoots
FILMING	–; –	**FINGER**	–; fingers
FILMSET	–; filmsets	**FINIAL**	–; finials
FILOSE	–; –	**FINICAL**	–; –
FILTER	–; filters	**FINICKY**	–; –
FILTH	–; filths,	**FINIKIN**	–; finiking
	filthy	**FINING**	–; finings
FILUM	–; –	**FINIS**	–; finish
FIMBLE	–; fimbles	**FINISES**	–; –
FIMBRIA	–; fimbriae,	**FINITE**	–; finites
	fimbrial	**FINK**	–; finks
FIN	–; find, fine,	**FINKED**	–; –

FINKING	–; –	**FISHER**	–; fishers,
FINLESS	–; –		fishery
FINLIKE	–; –	**FISHEYE**	–; fisheyes
FINMARK	–; finmarks	**FISHGIG**	–; fishgigs
FINNED	–; –	**FISHIER**	–; –
FINNIER	–; –	**FISHILY**	–; –
FINNING	–; –	**FISHING**	–; fishings
FINNY	–; –	**FISHNET**	–; fishnets
FIORD	–; fiords	**FISHWAY**	–; fishways
FIPPLE	–; fipples	**FISSATE**	–; –
FIQUE	–; fiques	**FISSILE**	–; –
FIR	–; fire, firm,	**FISSION**	–; fissions
	firn, firs	**FISSURE**	–; fissured,
FIRE	afire; fired,		fissures
	firer, fires	**FIST**	–; fists
FIREARM	–; firearms	**FISTED**	–; –
FIREBOX	–; –	**FISTING**	–; –
FIREBUG	–; firebugs	**FISTFUL**	–; fistfuls
FIREDOG	–; firedogs	**FISTIC**	–; –
FIREFLY	–; –	**FISTULA**	–; fistulae,
FIREMAN	–; –		fistular,
FIREMEN	–; –		fistulas
FIREPAN	–; firepans	**FIT**	–; fits
FIRER	–; firers	**FITCH**	–; fitchy
FIRING	–; firings	**FITCHEE**	–; –
FIRKIN	–; firkins	**FITCHES**	–; –
FIRM	–; firms	**FITCHET**	–; fitchets
FIRMAN	–; firmans	**FITCHEW**	–; fitchews
FIRMED	–; –	**FITFUL**	–; –
FIRMER	–; firmers	**FITLY**	–; –
FIRMLY	–; –	**FITMENT**	–; fitments
FIRN	–; firns	**FITNESS**	–; –
FIRRY	–; –	**FITTED**	–; –
FIRST	–; firsts	**FITTER**	–; fitters
FIRSTLY	–; –	**FITTEST**	–; –
FIRTH	–; firths	**FITTING**	–; fittings
FISC	–; fiscs	**FIVE**	–; fiver, fives
FISCAL	–; fiscals	**FIVER**	–; fivers
FISH	–; fishy	**FIX**	–; fixt
FISHED	–; –	**FIXABLE**	–; –

FIXATE	–; fixated, fixates	**FLAKE**	–; flaked, flaker, flakes
FIXATIF	–; fixatifs	**FLAKER**	–; flakers
FIXED	–; –	**FLAKIER**	–; –
FIXEDLY	–; –	**FLAKILY**	–; –
FIXER	–; fixers	**FLAKING**	–; –
FIXES	–; –	**FLAM**	–; flame, flams, flamy
FIXING	–; fixings		
FIXITY	–; –	**FLAMBE**	–; flambee, flambes
FIXTURE	–; fixtures		
FIXURE	–; fixures	**FLAMBEE**	–; flambeed, flambees
FIZ	–; fizz		
FIZGIG	–; fizgigs	**FLAME**	aflame; flamed, flamen, flamor, flames
FIZZ	–; fizzy		
FIZZED	–; –		
FIZZER	–; fizzers		
FIZZES	–; –		
FIZZING	;	**FLAMEN**	–; flamens
FIZZLE	–; fizzled, fizzles	**FLAMER**	–; flamers
		FLAMIER	–; –
FJELD	–; fjelds	**FLAMING**	–; flamingo
FJORD	–; fjords	**FLAMMED**	–; –
FLAB	–; flabs	**FLAN**	–; flank, flans
FLABBY	–;		
FLACCID	–; –	**FLANES**	–; –
FLACK	–; flacks	**FLANEUR**	–; flaneurs
FLACON	–; flacons	**FLANGE**	–; flanged, flanger, flanges
FLAG	–; flags		
FLAGGED	–; –		
FLAGGER	–; flaggers	**FLANGER**	–; flangers
FLAGGY	–; –	**FLANK**	–; flanks
FLAGMAN	–; –	**FLANKED**	–; –
FLAGMEN	–; –	**FLANKER**	–; flankers
FLAGON	–; flagons	**FLANNEL**	–; flannels
FLAIL	–; flails	**FLAP**	–; flaps
FLAILED	–; –	**FLAPPED**	–; –
FLAIR	–; flairs	**FLAPPER**	–; flappers
FLAK	–; flake, flaky	**FLAPPY**	–; –
		FLARE	–; flared, flares

FLARING	–; –	**FLAYER**	–; flayers
FLASH	–; flashy	**FLAYING**	–; –
FLASHED	–; –	**FLEA**	–; fleam, fleas
FLASHER	–; flashers		
FLASHES	–; –	**FLEABUG**	–; fleabugs
FLASK	–; flasks	**FLEAM**	–; fleams
FLASKET	–; flaskets	**FLECHE**	–; fleches
FLAT	–; flats	**FLECK**	–; flecks, flecky
FLATBED	–; flatbeds		
FLATCAP	–; flatcaps	**FLECKED**	–; –
FLATCAR	–; flatcars	**FLED**	–; –
FLATLET	–; flatlets	**FLEDGE**	–; fledged, fledges
FLATLY	–; –		
FLATTED	–; –	**FLEDGY**	–; –
FLATTEN	–; flattens	**FLEE**	–; fleer, flees, fleet
FLATTER	–; flatters, flattery		
		FLEECE	–; fleeced, fleecer, fleeces
FLATTOP	–; flattops		
FLATUS	–; –		
FLAUNT	–; flaunts, flaunty	**FLEECER**	–; fleecers
		FLEECH	–; –
FLAVIN	–; flavine, flavins	**FLEECY**	–; –
		FLEER	–; fleers
FLAVINE	–; flavines	**FLEERED**	–; –
FLAVONE	–; flavones	**FLEET**	–; fleets
FLAVOR	–; flavors, flavory	**FLEETED**	–; –
		FLEEING	–; –
FLAVOUR	–; flavours, flavoury	**FLEMISH**	–; –
		FLENCH	–; –
FLAW	–; flaws, flawy	**FLENSE**	–; flensed, flenser, flenses
FLAWED	–; –		
FLAWIER	–; –	**FLENSER**	–; flensers
FLAWING	–; –	**FLESH**	–; fleshy
FLAX	–; flaxy	**FLESHED**	–; –
FLAXEN	–; –	**FLESHER**	–; fleshers
FLAXES	–; –	**FLESHLY**	–; –
FLAXIER	–; –	**FLETCH**	–; –
FLAY	–; flays	**FLEURY**	–; –
FLAYED	–; –	**FLEW**	–; flews

FLEX	–; –	FLITTED	–; –
FLEXED	–; –	FLITTER	–; flitters
FLEXES	–; –	FLIVVER	–; flivvers
FLEXILE	–; –	FLOAT	afloat;
FLEXING	–; –		floats, floaty
FLEXION	–; flexions	FLOATED	–; –
FLEXOR	–; flexors	FLOATER	–; floaters
FLEXURE	–; flexures	FLOC	–; flock,
FLEY	–; fleys		flocs
FLEYED	–; –	FLOCCED	–; –
FLEYING	–; –	FLOCCI	–; –
FLIC	–; flick, flics	FLOCCUS	–; –
FLICK	–; flicks	FLOCK	–; flocks,
FLICKED	–; –		flocky
FLICKER	–; flickers,	FLOCKED	–; –
	flickery	FLOE	–; floes
FLIED	–; –	FLOG	–; flogs
FLIER	–; fliers	FLOGGED	–; –
FLIES	–; fliest	FLOGGER	–; floggers
FLIGHT	–; flights,	FLONG	–; flongs
	flighty	FLOOD	–; floods
FLIMSY	–; –	FLOODED	–; –
FLINCH	–; –	FLOODER	–; flooders
FLINDER	–; flinders	FLOOEY	–; –
FLING	–; flings	FLOOR	–; floors
FLINGER	, flingers	FLOORED	,
FLINT	–; flints,	FLOORER	–; floorers
	flinty	FLOOSY	–; –
FLINTED	–; –	FLOOZIE	–; floozies
FLIP	–; flips	FLOOZY	–; –
FLIPPED	–; –	FLOP	–; flops
FLIPPER	–; flippers	FLOPPED	–; –
FLIRT	–; flirts, flirty	FLOPPER	–; floppers
FLIRTED	–; –	FLOPPY	–; –
FLIRTER	–; flirters	FLORA	–; florae,
FLIT	–; flite, flits		floral, flora
FLITCH	–; –	FLORET	–; florets
FLITE	–; flited,	FLORID	–; –
	flites	FLORIN	–; florins
FLITING	–; –	FLORIST	; florists

FLORUIT	–; floruits	FLUKY	–; –
FLOSS	–; flossy	FLUME	–; flumed, flumes
FLOSSIE	–; flossies		
FLOTA	–; flotas	FLUMING	–; –
FLOTAGE	–; flotages	FLUMMOX	–; –
FLOTSAM	–; flotsams	FLUMP	–; flumps
FLOUNCE	–; flounced, flounces	FLUMPED	–; –
		FLUNG	–; –
FLOUNCY	–; –	FLUNK	–; flunks, flunky
FLOUR	–; flours, floury		
		FLUNKED	–; –
FLOURED	–; –	FLUNKER	–; flunkers
FLOUT	–; flouts	FLUNKEY	–; flunkeys
FLOUTED	–; –	FLUOR	–; fluors
FLOUTER	–; flouters	FLUORIC	–; –
FLOW	–; flown, flows	FLUORID	–; fluoride, fluorids
FLOWAGE	–; flowages	FLUORIN	–; fluorine, fluorins
FLOWER	–; flowers, flowery		
		FLURRY	–; –
FLU	–; flub, flue, flus, flux	FLUSH	–; –
		FLUSHED	–; –
FLUB	–; flubs	FLUSHER	–; flushers
FLUBBED	–; –	FLUSHES	–; –
FLUBDUB	–; flubdubs	FLUSTER	–; flusters
FLUE	–; flued, flues	FLUTE	–; fluted, fluter, flutes
FLUENCY	–; –	FLUTER	–; fluters
FLUENT	–; –	FLUTIER	–; –
FLUERIC	–; fluerics	FLUTING	–; flutings
FLUFF	–; fluffs, fluffy	FLUTIST	–; flutists
		FLUTTER	aflutter; flutters, fluttery
FLUFFED	–; –		
FLUID	–; fluids		
FLUIDAL	–; –	FLUTY	–; –
FLUIDIC	–; fluidics	FLUVIAL	–; –
FLUIDLY	–; –	FLUX	–; –
FLUKE	–; fluked, flukes, flukey	FLUXED	–. –
		FLUXES	–; –
FLUKIER	–; –	FLUXING	–:

FLUXION	–; fluxions	FOCI	–; –
FLUYT	–; fluyts	FOCUS	–; –
FLY	–; –	FOCUSED	–; –
FLYABLE	–; –	FOCUSER	–; focusers
FLYAWAY	–; flyaways	FOCUSES	–; –
FLYBELT	–; flybelts	FODDER	–; fodders
FLYBLEW	–; –	FODGEL	–; –
FLYBLOW	–; flyblown, flyblows	FOE	–; foes
		FOEHN	–; foehns
FLYBOAT	–; flyboats	FOEMAN	–; –
FLYBY	–; flybys	FOEMEN	–; –
FLYER	–; flyers	FOETAL	–; –
FLYING	–; flyings	FOETID	–; –
FLYLEAF	–; –	FOETOR	–; foetors
FLYMAN	–; –	FOETUS	–; –
FLYMEN	–; –	FOG	–; fogs, fogy
FLYOVER	–; flyovers		
FLYPAST	–; flypasts	FOGBOW	–; fogbows
FLYSCH	–; –	FOGDOG	–; fogdogs
FLYTE	–; flyted, flytes	FOGEY	–; fogeys
		FOGGAGE	–; foggages
FLYTIER	–; flytiers	FOGGED	–; –
FLYTING	–; flytings	FOGGER	–; foggers
FLYTRAP	–; flytraps	FOGGIER	–; –
FLYWAY	–; flyways	FOGGILY	–; –
FOAL	–; foals	FOGGING	–; –
FOALED	–; –	FOGGY	–; –
FOALING	–; –	FOGHORN	–; foghorns
FOAM	–; foams, foamy	FOGIE	–; fogies
		FOGLESS	–; –
FOAMED	–; –	FOGYISM	–; fogyisms
FOAMER	–; foamers	FOH	–; fohn
FOAMIER	–; –	FOHN	–; fohns
FOAMING	–; –	FOIBLE	–; foibles
FOAMILY	–; –	FOIL	–; foils
FOB	–; fobs	FOILED	–; –
FOBBED	–; –	FOILING	–; –
FOBBING	–; –	FOIN	–; foins
FOCAL	–; –	FOINED	–; –
FOCALLY	–; –	FOINING	; –

FOISON	–; foisons	fondler,
FOIST	–; foists	fondles
FOISTED	–; –	**FONDLER**	–; fondlers
FOLACIN	–; folacins	**FONDLY**	–; –
FOLATE	–; folates	**FONDU**	–; fondue,
FOLD	–; folds	fondus
FOLDED	–; –	**FONDUE**	–; fondues
FOLDER	–; folders	**FONT**	–; fonts
FOLDING	–; –	**FONTAL**	–; –
FOLDOUT	–; foldouts	**FONTINA**	–; fontinas
FOLIA	–; foliar	**FOOD**	–; foods
FOLIAGE	–; foliaged,	**FOOL**	–; fools
	foliages	**FOOLED**	–; –
FOLIATE	–; foliated,	**FOOLERY**	–; –
	foliates	**FOOLING**	–; –
FOLIO	–; folios	**FOOLISH**	–; –
FOLIOED	–; –	**FOOT**	afoot; foots,
FOLIOSE	–; –	footy
FOLIOUS	–; –	**FOOTAGE**	–; footages
FOLIUM	–; foliums	**FOOTBOY**	–; footboys
FOLK	–; folks	**FOOTED**	–; –
FOLKISH	–; –	**FOOTER**	–; footers
FOLKMOT	–; folkmots	**FOOTIE**	–; footier,
FOLKS	–; folksy	footies
FOLKWAY	–; folkways	**FOOTING**	–; footings
FOLLIES	–; –	**FOOTLE**	–; footled,
FOLLIS	–; –	footler,
FOLLOW	–; follows	footles
FOLLY	–; –	**FOOTLER**	–; footlers
FOMENT	–; foments	**FOOTMAN**	–; –
FON	–; fond,	**FOOTMEN**	–; –
	fons, font	**FOOTPAD**	–; footpads
FOND	–; fonds,	**FOOTSIE**	–; footsies
	fondu	**FOOTWAY**	–; footways
FONDANT	–; fondants	**FOOZLE**	–; foozled,
FONDED	–; –	foozler,
FONDER	–; –	foozles
FONDEST	–; –	**FOOZLER**	–; foozlers
FONDING	–; –	**FOP**	–; fops
FONDLE	–; fondled,	**FOPPED**	–; –

FOPPERY	–; –	**FOREBY**	–; forebye
FOPPING	–; –	**FOREDID**	–; –
FOPPISH	–; –	**FOREDO**	–; –
FOR	–; fora,	**FOREGO**	–; –
	forb, ford,	**FOREGUT**	–; foreguts
	fore, fork,	**FOREIGN**	–; –
	form, fort	**FORELEG**	–; forelegs
FORA	–; foram	**FOREMAN**	–; –
FORAGE	–; foraged,	**FOREMEN**	–; –
	forager,	**FOREPAW**	–; forepaws
	forages	**FORERUN**	–; foreruns
FORAGER	–; foragers	**FORESAW**	–; –
FORAM	–; forams	**FORESEE**	–; foreseen,
FORAMEN	–; foramens		foreseer,
FORAY	–; forays		foresees
FORAYED	–; –	**FOREST**	–; forests
FORAYER	–; forayers	**FORETOP**	–; foretops
FORB	–; forbs,	**FOREVER**	–; forevers
	forby	**FORFEIT**	–; forfeits
FORBAD	–; forbade	**FORFEND**	–; forfends
FORBEAR	–; forbears	**FORGAT**	–; –
FORBID	–; forbids	**FORGAVE**	–; –
FORBODE	–; forboded,	**FORGE**	–; forged,
	forbodes		forger,
FORBORE	–; –		forges,
FORBY	–; forbye		forget
FORCE	–; forced,	**FORGER**	–; forgers,
	forcer,		forgery
	forces	**FORGET**	–; forgets
FORCEPS	–; –	**FORGING**	–; forgings
FORCER	–; forcers	**FORGIVE**	–; forgiven,
FORCING	–; –		forgiver,
FORD	–; fordo,		forgives
	fords	**FORGO**	–; forgot
FORDID	–; –	**FORGOER**	–; forgoers
FORDOES	–; –	**FORGOES**	–; –
FORDONE	–; –	**FORGONE**	–; –
FORE	afore; fores	**FORINT**	–; forints
FOREARM	–; forearms	**FORK**	–; forks,
FOREBAY	–; forebays		forky

FORKED	–; –	**FORUM**	–; forums
FORKER	–; forkers	**FORWARD**	–; forwards
FORKFUL	–; forkfuls	**FORWENT**	–; –
FORKIER	–; –	**FORWHY**	–; –
FORKING	–; –	**FORWORN**	–; –
FORLORN	–; –	**FOSS**	–; fossa, fosse
FORM	–; forme, forms		
		FOSSA	–; fossae
FORMAL	–; formals	**FOSSATE**	–; –
FORMANT	–; formants	**FOSSE**	–; fosses
FORMAT	–; formate, formats	**FOSSICK**	–; fossicks
		FOSSIL	–; fossils
FORMATE	–; formates	**FOSTER**	–; fosters
FORME	–; formed, formee, former, formes	**FOU**	–; foul, four
		FOUGHT	–; –
		FOUL	afoul; fouls
		FOULARD	–; foulards
FORMER	–; formers	**FOULER**	–; –
FORMFUL	–; –	**FOULEST**	–; –
FORMIC	–; –	**FOULING**	–; foulings
FORMING	–; –	**FOULLY**	–; –
FORMOL	–; formols	**FOUND**	–; founds
FORMULA	–; formulae, formulas	**FOUNDED**	–; –
		FOUNDER	–; founders
FORMYL	–; formyls	**FOUNDRY**	–; –
FORNIX	–; –	**FOUNT**	–; founts
FORRIT	–; –	**FOUR**	–; fours
FORSAKE	–; forsaken, forsaker, forsakes	**FOURGON**	–; fourgons
		FOURTH	–; fourths
		FOVEA	–; foveae, foveal
FORSOOK	–; –		
FORT	–; forte, forth, forts, forty	**FOVEATE**	–; foveated
		FOVEOLA	–; foveolae, foveolar, foveolas
FORTE	–; fortes		
FORTIES	–; –	**FOVEOLE**	–; foveoles, foveolet
FORTIFY	–; –		
FORTIS	–; –	**FOWL**	–; fowls
FORTUNE	–; fortuned, fortunes	**FOWLED**	–; –
		FOWLER	–; fowlers

FOWLING	-; fowlings	FRAMER	-; framers
FOWLPOX	-; -	FRAMING	-; -
FOX	-; foxy	FRANC	-; francs
FOXED	-; -	FRANK	-; franks
FOXES	-; -	FRANKED	-; -
FOXFIRE	-; foxfires	FRANKER	-; frankers
FOXFISH	-; -	FRANKLY	-; -
FOXHOLE	-; foxholes	FRANTIC	-; -
FOXIER	-; -	FRAP	-; fraps
FOXIEST	-; -	FRAPPE	-; frapped,
FOXILY	-; -		frappes
FOXING	-; foxings	FRAT	-; frats
FOXLIKE	-; -	FRATER	-; fraters
FOXSKIN	; foxskins	FRAUD	-; frauds
FOXTAIL	-; foxtails	FRAUGHT	-; fraughts
FOY	-; foys	FRAY	-; frays
FOYER	-; foyers	FRAYED	-; -
FOZIER	-; -	FRAYING	-; frayings
FOZIEST	-; -	FRAZZLE	-; frazzled,
FOZY	-; -		frazzles
FRACAS	-; -	FREAK	-; freaks,
FRACTED	-; -		freaky
FRACTUR	-; fracture,	FREAKED	-; -
	tracturs	FRECKLE	-; freckled,
FRAE	-; -		freckles
FRAENA	-; -	FRECKLY	-; -
FRAENUM	-; fraenums	FREE	-; freed,
FRAG	-; frags		freer, frees
FRAGGED	-; -	FREEBEE	-; freebees
FRAGILE	-; -	FREEBIE	-; freebies
FRAIL	-; frails,	FREEDOM	-; freedoms
	fraily	FREELY	-; -
FRAILER	-; -	FREEMAN	-; -
FRAILLY	-; -	FREEMEN	-; -
FRAILTY	-; -	FREER	-; freers
FRAISE	-; fraises	FREES	-; freest
FRAKTUR	-; frakturs	FREESIA	-; freesias
FRAME	-; framed,	FREEWAY	-; freeways
	framer,	FREEZE	-; freezer,
	frames		freezes

FREEZER	–; freezers	**FRIJOL**	–; frijole
FREIGHT	–; freights	**FRIJOLE**	–; frijoles
FREMD	–; –	**FRILL**	–; frills, frilly
FRENA	–; –	**FRILLED**	–; –
FRENCH	–; –	**FRILLER**	–; frillers
FRENUM	–; frenums	**FRINGE**	–; fringed,
FRENZY	–; –		fringes
FRERE	–; freres	**FRINGY**	–; –
FRESCO	–; frescos	**FRISE**	–; frises
FRESH	afresh; –	**FRISEUR**	–; friseurs
FRESHED	–; –	**FRISK**	–; frisks,
FRESHEN	–; freshens		frisky
FRESHER	–; –	**FRISKED**	–; –
FRESHES	–; freshest	**FRISKER**	–; friskers
FRESHET	–; freshets	**FRISKET**	–; friskets
FRESHLY	–; –	**FRISSON**	–; frissons
FRESNEL	–; fresnels	**FRIT**	afrit; frith,
FRET	–; frets		frits, fritt
FRETFUL	–; –	**FRITH**	–; friths
FRETSAW	–; fretsaws	**FRITS**	afrits; –
FRETTED	–; –	**FRITT**	–; fritts
FRETTY	–; –	**FRITTED**	–; –
FRIABLE	–; –	**FRITTER**	–; fritters
FRIAR	–; friars,	**FRIVOL**	–; frivols
	friary	**FRIZ**	–; frizz
FRIARLY	–; –	**FRIZED**	–; –
FRIBBLE	–; fribbled,	**FRIZER**	–; frizers
	fribbler,	**FRIZES**	–; –
	fribbles	**FRIZING**	–; –
FRIDGE	–; fridges	**FRIZZ**	–; frizzy
FRIED	–; –	**FRIZZED**	–; –
FRIEND	–; friends	**FRIZZER**	–; frizzers
FRIER	–; friers	**FRIZZES**	–; –
FRIES	–; –	**FRIZZLE**	–; frizzled,
FRIEZE	–; friezes		frizzler,
FRIG	–; frigs		frizzles
FRIGATE	–; frigates	**FRIZZLY**	–; –
FRIGGED	–; –	**FRO**	–; froe,
FRIGHT	–; frights		frog, from,
FRIGID	–; –		frow

FROCK	–; frocks	**FROWZY**	–; –
FROCKED	–; –	**FROZE**	–; frozen
FROE	–; froes	**FRUG**	–; frugs
FROG	–; frogs	**FRUGAL**	–; –
FROGEYE	–; frogeyed,	**FRUGGED**	–; –
	frogeyes	**FRUIT**	–; fruits,
FROGGED	–; –		fruity
FROGGY	–; –	**FRUITED**	–; –
FROGMAN	–; –	**FRUITER**	–; fruiters
FROGMEN	–; –	**FRUMP**	–; frumps,
FROLIC	–; frolics		frumpy
FROM	–; –	**FRUSTA**	–;
FROMAGE	–; fromages	**FRUSTUM**	–; frustums
FROND	–; fronds	**FRY**	–; –
FRONDED	–; –	**FRYER**	–; fryers
FRONS	–; –	**FRYING**	–; –
FRONT	–; fronts	**FRYPAN**	–; frypans
FRONTAL	–; frontals	**FUB**	–; fubs
FRONTED	–; –	**FUBBED**	–; –
FRONTER	–; –	**FUBBING**	–; –
FRONTES	–; –	**FUBSIER**	–; –
FRONTON	–; frontons	**FUBSY**	–; –
FRORE	–; –	**FUCHSIA**	–; fuchsias
FROSH	–; –	**FUCHSIN**	–; fuchsine,
FROST	–; frosts,		fuchsins
	frosty		
FROSTED	–; frosteds	**FUCI**	–; –
FROTH	–; froths,	**FUCOID**	–; fucoids
	frothy	**FUCOSE**	–; fucoses
		FUCOUS	–; –
FROTHED	–; –	**FOCUS**	–; –
FROUNCE	–; frounced,	**FOCUSES**	–; –
	frounces	**FUD**	–; fuds
FROUZY	–; –	**FUDDLE**	–; fuddled,
FROW	–; frown,		fuddles
	frows	**FUDGE**	–; fudged,
FROWN	–; frowns		fudges
FROWNED	–; –	**FUEHRER**	–; fuehrers
FROWNER	–; frowners	**FUEL**	–; fuels
FROWS	–; frowsy	**FUELED**	–; –
FROWSTY	–; –	**FUELER**	–; fuelers

FUELING	–; –	**FULSOME**	–; –
FUELLED	–; –	**FULVOUS**	–; –
FUELLER	–; fuellers	**FUMARIC**	–; –
FUG	–; fugs	**FUMBLE**	–; fumbled, fumbler, fumbles
FUGAL	–; –		
FUGALLY	–; –		
FUGATO	–; fugatos	**FUMBLER**	–; fumblers
FUGGED	–; –	**FUME**	–; fumed, fumer, fumes, fumet
FUGGIER	–; –		
FUGGING	–; –		
FUGGY	–; –	**FUMER**	–; fumers
FUGIO	–; fugios	**FUMET**	–; fumets
FUGLE	–; fugled, fugles	**FUMETTE**	–; fumettes
FUGLING	–; –	**FUMIER**	–; –
FUGUE	–; fugued, fugues	**FUMIEST**	–; –
		FUMING	–; –
FUGUING	–; –	**FUMULI**	–; –
FUGUIST	–; fuguists	**FUMULUS**	–; –
FUHRER	–; fuhrers	**FUMY**	–; –
FUJI	–; fujis	**FUN**	–; fund, funk, funs
FULCRA	–; –		
FULCRUM	–; fulcrums	**FUNCTOR**	–; functors
FULFIL	–; fulfill, fulfils	**FUND**	–; fundi, funds
FULFILL	–; fulfills	**FUNDED**	–; –
FULGENT	–; –	**FUNDI**	–; fundic
FULGID	–; –	**FUNDING**	–; –
FULHAM	–; fulhams	**FUNDUS**	–; –
FULL	–; fulls, fully	**FUNERAL**	–; funerals
FULLAM	–; fullams	**FUNEST**	–; –
FULLED	–; –	**FUNFAIR**	–; funfairs
FULLER	–; fullers, fullery	**FUNGAL**	–; fungals
		FUNGI	–; fungic
FULLEST	–; –	**FUNGO**	–; –
FULLING	–; –	**FUNGOES**	–; –
FULMAR	–; fulmars	**FUNGOID**	–; fungoids
FULMINE	–; fulmined, fulmines	**FUNGOUS**	–; –
		FUNGUS	–; –
FULNESS	–; –	**FUNICLE**	–; funicles

FUNK	–; funks, funky	**FUROR**	–; furore, furors
FUNKED	–; –	**FURORE**	–; furores
FUNKER	–; funkers	**FURRED**	–; –
FUNKIA	–; funkias	**FURRIER**	–; furriers, furriery
FUNKIER	–; –		
FUNKING	–; –	**FURRILY**	–; –
FUNNED	–; –	**FURRING**	–; furrings
FUNNEL	–; funnels	**FURROW**	–; furrows, furrowy
FUNNIER	–; –		
FUNNIES	–; funniest	**FURRY**	–; –
FUNNILY	–; –	**FURTHER**	–; furthers
FUNNING	–; –	**FURTIVE**	–; –
FUNNY	–; –	**FURZE**	–; furzes
FUR	–; furl, furs, fury	**FURZIER**	–; –
		FURZY	–; –
FURAN	–; furane, furans	**FUSAIN**	–; fusains
		FUSCOUS	–; –
FURANE	–; furanes	**FUSE**	–; fused, fusee, fusel, fuses
FURBISH	–; –		
FURCATE	–; furcated, furcates		
		FUSEE	–; fusees
FURCULA	–; furculae, furcular	**FUSEL**	–; fusels
		FUSIBLE	–; –
FURFUR	–; –	**FUSIBLY**	–; –
FURIES	–; –	**FUSIL**	–; fusile, fusils
FURIOSO	–; –		
FURIOUS	–; –	**FUSING**	–; –
FURL	–; furls	**FUSION**	–; fusions
FURLED	–; –	**FUSS**	–; fussy
FURLER	–; furlers	**FUSSED**	–; –
FURLESS	–; –	**FUSSER**	–; fussers
FURLING	–; –	**FUSSES**	–; –
FURLONG	–; furlongs	**FUSSIER**	–; –
FURMETY	–; –	**FUSSILY**	–; –
FURMITY	–; –	**FUSSING**	–; –
FURNACE	–; furnaced, furnaces	**FUSSPOT**	–; fusspots
		FUSTIAN	–; fustians
FURNISH	–; –	**FUSTIC**	–; fustics
		FUSTIER	–; –

FUSTILY	–; –	**FUZIL**	–; fuzils
FUSTY	–; –	**FUZING**	–; –
FUTHARC	–; futharcs	**FUZZ**	–; fuzzy
FUTHARK	–; futharks	**FUZZED**	–; –
FUTHORC	–; futhorcs	**FUZZES**	–; –
FUTHORK	–; futhorks	**FUZZIER**	–; –
FUTILE	–; –	**FUZZILY**	–; –
FUTTOCK	–; futtocks	**FUZZING**	–; –
FUTURAL	–; –	**FYCE**	–; fyces
FUTURE	–; futures	**FYKE**	–; fykes
FUZE	–; fuzed, fuzee, fuzes	**FYLFOT**	–; fylfots
		FYTTE	–; fyttes
FUZEE	–; fuzees		

G

G	–; go	**GABLING**	–; –
GAB	–; gabs, gaby	**GABOON**	–; gaboons
		GAD	egad; gads, gadi
GABBARD	–; gabbards		
GABBART	–; gabbarts	**GADDED**	–; –
GABBED	–; –	**GADDER**	–; gadders
GABBER	–; gabbers	**GADDI**	–; gaddis
GABBIER	–; –	**GADDING**	–; –
GABBING	–; –	**GADFLY**	–; –
GABBLE	–; gabbled, gabbler, gabbles	**GADGET**	–; gadgets, gadgety
		GADI	–; gadid, gadis
GABBLER	–; gabblers		
GABBRO	–; gabbros	**GADID**	–; gadids
GABBY	–; –	**GADOID**	–; gadoids
GABELLE	–; gabelled, gabelles	**GADROON**	–; gadroons
		GADS	egads; –
GABFEST	–; gabfests	**GADWALL**	–; gadwalls
GABIES	–; –	**GAE**	–; gaed, gaes
GABION	–; gabions		
GABLE	–; gabled, gables	**GAFF**	–; gaffe, gaffs

GAFFE	–; gaffed, gaffer, gaffes	GALAGO	–; galagos
GAFFER	–; gaffers	GALAH	–; galahs
GAFFING	–; –	GALATEA	–; galateas
GAG	–; gaga, gage, gags	GALAX	–; galaxy
		GALAXES	–; –
GAGE	–; gaged, gager, gages	GALE	–; galea, gales
		GALEA	–; galeae, galeas
GAGER	–; gagers	GALEATE	–; galeated
GAGGED	–; –	GALENA	–; galenas
GAGGER	–; gaggers	GALENIC	–; –
GAGGING	–; –	GALERE	–; galeres
GAGGLE	–; gaggled, gaggles	GALILEE	–; galilees
		GALIOT	; galiots
GAGING	–; –	GALIPOT	–; galipots
GAGMAN	–; –	GALL	–; galls, gally
GAGMEN	–; –		
GAGSTER	–; gagsters	GALLANT	–; gallants
GAHNITE	–; gahnites	GALLATE	–; gallates
GAIETY	–; –	GALLED	–; –
GAILY	–; –	GALLEIN	–; galleins
GAIN	again; gains	GALLEON	–; galleons
GAINED	–; –	GALLERY	–; –
GAINER	–; gainers	GALLETA	–; galletas
GAINFUL	–; –	GALLEY	–; galleys
GAINING	–; –	GALLFLY	–; –
GAINLY	–; –	GALLIC	–; –
GAINS	–; gainst	GALLIED	–; –
GAINSAY	–; gainsays	GALLIES	–; –
GAINST	against; –	GALLING	–; –
GAIT	–; gaits	GALLIOT	–; galliots
GAITED	–; –	GALLIUM	–; galliums
GAITER	–; gaiters	GALLNUT	–; gallnuts
GAITING	–; –	GALLON	–; gallons
GAL	egal; gala, gale, gall, gals	GALLOON	–; galloons
		GALLOOT	–; galloots
		GALLOP	–; gallops
GALA	–; galah, galas	GALLOUS	–; –
		GALLOWS	–; –

GALLUS	–; –	GAMETE	agamete;
GALOOT	–; galoots		gametes
GALOP	–; galops	GAMETES	agametes; –
GALORE	–; galores	GAMETIC	–; –
GALOSH	–; galoshe	GAMIC	agamic; –
GALOSHE	–; galoshed,	GAMIER	–; –
	galoshes	GAMIEST	–; –
GALUMPH	–; galumphs	GAMILY	–; –
GALYAC	–; galyacs	GAMIN	–; gamine,
GALYAK	–; galyaks		gaming,
GAM	ogam;		gamins
	gamb,		
	game,	GAMINE	–; gamines
	gamp, gams,	GAMING	–; gamings
	gamy	GAMMA	–; gammas
GAMB	–; gamba,	GAMMED	–; –
	gambe,	GAMMER	–; gammers
	gambs	GAMMING	–; –
GAMBA	–; gambas	GAMMON	–; gammons
GAMBADE	–; gambades	GAMP	–; gamps
GAMBADO	–; gambados	GAMS	ogams; –
GAMBE	–; gambes	GAMUT	–; gamuts
GAMBIA	–; gambias	GAN	–; gane,
GAMBIER	–; gambiers		gang
GAMBIR	–; gambirs	GANDER	–; ganders
GAMBIT	–; gambits	GANE	–; ganef,
GAMBLE	–; gambled,		ganev
	gambler,	GANEF	–; ganefs
	gambles	GANEV	–; ganevs
GAMBLER	–; gamblers	GANG	–; gangs
GAMBOGE	–; gamboges	GANGED	–; –
GAMBOL	–; gambols	GANGER	–; gangers
GAMBREL	–; gambrels	GANGING	–; –
GAME	–; gamed,	GANGLIA	–; ganglial,
	gamer,		gangliar
	games,	GANGLY	–; –
	gamey	GANGREL	–; gangrels
GAMELAN	–; gamelans	GANGUE	–; gangues
GAMELY	–; –	GANGWAY	–;
GAMES	–; gamest		gangways
		GANJA	–; ganjas

GANNET	–; gannets	**GARGET**	–; gargets,
GANOF	–; ganofs		gargety
GANOID	–; ganoids	**GARGLE**	–; gargled,
GANTLET	–; gantlets		gargler,
GANTRY	–; –		gargles
GAOL	–; gaols	**GARGLER**	–; garglers
GAOLED	–; –	**GARISH**	–; –
GAOLER	–; gaolers	**GARLAND**	–; garlands
GAOLING	–; –	**GARLIC**	–; garlics
GAP	–; gape,	**GARMENT**	–; garments
	gaps, gapy	**GARNER**	–; garners
GAPE	agape;	**GARNET**	–; garnets
	gaped,	**GARNISH**	–; –
	gaper,	**GAROTE**	–; garoted,
	gapes		garotes
GAPER	–; gapers	**GAROTTE**	–; garotted,
GAPING	–; –		garotter,
GAPOSES	–; –		garottes
GAPOSIS	–; –	**GARPIKE**	–; garpikes
GAPPED	–; –	**GARRED**	–; –
GAPPIER	–; –	**GARRET**	–; garrets
GAPPING	–; –	**GARRING**	–; –
GAPPY	–; –	**GARRON**	–; garrons
GAR	agar; garb,	**GARROTE**	–; garroted,
	gars		garroter,
GARAGE	–; garaged,		garrotes
	garages	**GARS**	agars; –
GARB	–; garbs	**GARTER**	–; garters
GARBAGE	–; garbages	**GARTH**	–; garths
GARBED	–; –	**GARVEY**	–; garveys
GARBING	–; –	**GAS**	agas; gash,
GARBLE	–; garbled,		gasp, gast
	garbler,	**GASBAG**	–; gasbags
	garbles	**GASCON**	–; gascons
GARBLER	–; garblers	**GASEOUS**	–; –
GARBOIL	–; garboils	**GASES**	–; –
GARCON	–; garcons	**GASHED**	–; –
GARDANT	–; –	**GASHER**	–; –
GARDEN	–; gardens	**GASHES**	–; gashest
GARFISH	–; –	**GASHING**	–; –

GASIFY	–; –	**GAUDERY**	–; –
GASKET	–; gaskets	**GAUDIER**	–; –
GASKIN	–; gasking, gaskins	**GAUDIES**	–; gaudiest
		GAUDILY	–; –
GASKING	–; gaskings	**GAUDY**	–; –
GASLESS	–; –	**GAUFFER**	–; gauffers
GASLIT	–; –	**GAUGE**	–; gauged, gauger, gauges
GASMAN	–; –		
GASMEN	–; –		
GASP	–; gasps	**GAUGER**	–; gaugers
GASPED	–; –	**GAUGING**	–; –
GASPER	–; gaspers	**GAULT**	–; gaults
GASPING	–; –	**GAUM**	–; gaums
GASSED	–; –	**GAUMED**	–; –
GASSER	–; gassers	**GAUMING**	–; –
GASSES	–; –	**GAUN**	–; gaunt
GASSIER	–; –	**GAUNTER**	–; –
GASSING	–; gassings	**GAUNTLY**	–; –
GASSY	–; –	**GAUNTRY**	–; –
GAST	–; gasts	**GAUR**	–; gaurs
GASTED	–; –	**GAUSS**	–; –
GASTING	–; –	**GAUSSES**	–; –
GASTRAL	–; –	**GAUZE**	–; gauzes
GASTREA	–; gastreas	**GAUZIER**	–; –
GASTRIC	–; –	**GAUZILY**	–; –
GASTRIN	–; gastrins	**GAUZY**	–; –
GAT	–; gate, gats	**GAVAGE**	–; gavages
		GAVE	agave; gavel
GATE	agate; gated, gates	**GAVEL**	–; gavels
		GAVELED	–; –
GATEMAN	–; –	**GAVIAL**	–; gavials
GATEMEN	–; –	**GAVOT**	–; gavots
GATES	agates; –	**GAVOTTE**	–; gavotted, gavottes
GATEWAY	–; gateways		
GATHER	–; gathers	**GAWK**	–; gawks, gawky
GATING	–; –		
GAUCHE	–; gaucher	**GAWKED**	–; –
GAUCHO	–; gauchos	**GAWKER**	–; gawkers
GAUD	–; gauds, gaudy	**GAWKIER**	–; –
		GAWKIES	–· gawkiest

GAWKILY	–; –	GEES	ogees;
GAWKING	–; –		geese, geest
GAWKISH	–; –	GEEST	–; geests
GAWSIE	–; –	GEEZER	–; geezers
GAWSY	–; –	GEISHA	–; geishas
GAY	–; gays	GEL	–; geld,
GAYAL	–; gayals		gels, gelt
GAYER	–; –	GELABLE	–; –
GAYEST	–; –	GELADA	–; gelada
GAYETY	–; –	GELANT	–; gelants
GAYLY	–; –	GELATE	–; gelated,
GAYNESS	–; –		gelates
GAZABO	–; gazabos	GELATIN	–; gelatine,
GAZE	agaze;		gelatins
	gazed,	GELD	–; gelds
	gazer,	GELDED	–; –
	gazes	GELDER	–; gelders
GAZEBO	–; gazebos	GELDING	–; geldings
GAZELLE	–; gazelles	GELEE	–; gelees
GAZER	–; gazers	GELID	–; –
GAZETTE	–; gazetted,	GELIDLY	–; –
	gazettes	GELLANT	–; gellants
GAZING	–; –	GELLED	–; –
GEAR	–; gears	GELLING	–; –
GEARBOX	–; –	GELT	–; gelts
GEARED	–; –	GEM	–; gems
GEARING	–; gearings	GEMINAL	–; –
GECK	–; gecko,	GEMLIKE	–; –
	gecks	GEMMA	–; gemmae
GECKED	–; –	GEMMATE	–;
GECKING	–; –		gemmated,
GECKO	–; geckos		gemmates
GECKOES	–; –	GEMMED	–; –
GED	aged; geds	GEMMIER	–; –
GEE	agee, ogee;	GEMMILY	–; –
	geed, geek,	GEMMING	–; –
	gees	GEMMULE	–; gemmules
GEEGAW	–; geegaws	GEMMY	–; –
GEEING	–; –	GEMOT	–; gemote,
GEEK	–; geeks		gemots

GEMOTE	–; gemotes		gentler,
GEMSBOK	–; gemsboks		gentles
GENDER	–; genders	**GENTLY**	–; –
GENE	agene;	**GENTRY**	agentry; -
	genes, genet	**GENTS**	agents; –
GENERA	–; general	**GENU**	–; genua.
GENERAL	–; generals		genus
GENERIC	–; generics	**GENUSES**	–; –
GENES	agenes; –	**GENUINE**	–; –
GENESES	–; –	**GEODE**	–; geodes
GENESIS	agenesis; –	**GEODESY**	–; –
GENET	–; genets	**GEODIC**	–; –
GENETIC	–; genetics	**GEOID**	–; geoids
GENETTE	–; genettes	**GEODUCK**	–; geoducks
GENEVA	–; genevas	**GEOID**	–; geoids
GENIAL	–; –	**GEOIDAL**	–; –
GENIC	–; –	**GEOLOGY**	–; –
GENIE	–; genies	**GEORGIC**	–; georgics
GENII	–; –	**GERAH**	–; gerahs
GENIP	–; genips	**GERBERA**	–; gerberas
GENIPAP	–; genipaps	**GERBIL**	–; gerbils
GENITAL	–; genitals	**GERENT**	–; gerents
GENITOR	–; genitors	**GERENUK**	–; gerenuks
GENIUS	–; –	**GERM**	–; germs.
GENOA	–; genoas		germy
GENOM	–; genome,	**GERMAN**	–; germane
	genoms		germans
GENOME	–; genomes	**GERMEN**	–; germens
GENOMIC	–; –	**GERMIER**	–; –
GENRE	–; genres	**GERMINA**	–; germinal
GENRO	–; genros	**GERUND**	–; gerunds
GENS	–; –	**GESSO**	–; –
GENSENG	–; gensengs	**GESSOES**	–; –
GENT	agent; gents	**GEST**	egest; geste
GENTEEL	–; –		gests
GENTES	–; –	**GESTALT**	–; gestalts
GENTIAN	–; gentians	**GESTAPO**	–; gestapos
GENTIL	–; gentile	**GESTATE**	–; gestated.
GENTILE	–; gentiles		gestates
GENTLE	–; gentled,	**GESTE**	–· gestes

GESTIC	–; –	GIBBER	–; gibbers
GESTS	egests; –	GIBBET	–; gibbets
GESTURE	–; gestured, gesturer, gestures	GIBBING	–; –
		GIBBON	–; gibbons
		GIBBOSE	–; –
GET	–; gets	GIBBOUS	–; –
GETABLE	–; –	GIBE	–; gibed, giber, gibes
GETAWAY	–; getaways		
GETTER	–; getters	GIBER	–; gibers
GETTING	–; –	GIBING	–; –
GETUP	–; getups	GIBLET	–; giblets
GEUM	–; geums	GID	–; gids
GEWGAW	–; gewgaws	GIDDAP	–; –
GEY	–; –	GIDDIED	–; –
GEYSER	–; geysers	GIDDIER	–; –
GHARRI	–; gharris	GIDDIES	–; giddiest
GHARRY	–; –	GIDDILY	–; –
GHAST	aghast; –	GIDDY	–; –
GHASTLY	–; –	GIE	–; gied, gien, gies
GHAT	–; ghats		
GHAUT	–; ghauts	GIEING	–; –
GHAZI	–; ghazis	GIFT	–; gifts
GHAZIES	–; –	GIFTED	–; –
GHEE	–; ghees	GIFTING	–; –
GHERAO	–; –	GIG	–; giga, gigs
GHERKIN	–; gherkins	GIGA	–; gigas
GHETTO	–; ghettos	GIGABIT	–; gigabits
GHI	–; ghis	GIGATON	–; gigatons
GHIBLI	–; ghiblis	GIGGED	–; –
GHILLIE	–; ghillies	GIGGING	–; –
GHOST	–; ghosts, ghosty	GIGGLE	–; giggled, giggler, giggles
GHOSTED	–; –		
GHOSTLY	–; –	GIGGLER	–; gigglers
GHOUL	–; ghouls	GIGGLY	–; –
GHYLL	–; ghylls	GIGHE	–; –
GIANT	–; giants	GIGLET	–; giglets
GIAOUR	–; giaours	GIGLOT	–; giglots
GIB	–; gibe, gibs	GIGOLO	–; gigolos
GIBBED	–; –	GIGOT	–; gigots

GIGUE	–; gigues	**GINK**	–; ginks
GILBERT	–; gilberts	**GINKGO**	–; ginkgos
GILD	–; gilds	**GINNED**	–; –
GILDED	–; –	**GINNER**	aginner;
GILDER	–; gilders		ginners
GILDING	–; gildings	**GINNERS**	aginners; –
GILL	–; gills, gilly	**GINNIER**	–; –
GILLED	–; –	**GINNING**	–; ginnings
GILLER	–; gillers	**GINNY**	–; –
GILLIE	–; gillied,	**GINSENG**	–; ginsengs
	gillies	**GIP**	–; gips
GILLING	–; –	**GIPON**	–; gipons
GILLNET	–; gillnets	**GIPPED**	–; –
GILT	–; gilts	**GIPPER**	–; gippers
GIMBAL	–; gimbals	**GIPPING**	–; –
GIMEL	–; gimels	**GIPS**	–; gipsy
GIMLET	–; gimlets	**GIPSIED**	–; –
GIMMAL	–; gimmals	**GIPSIES**	–; –
GIMMICK	–; gimmicks,	**GIRAFFE**	–; giraffes
	gimmicky	**GIRASOL**	–; girasole,
GIMP	–; gimps,		girasols
	gimpy	**GIRD**	–; girds
GIMPED	–; –	**GIRDED**	–; –
GIMPIER	–; –	**GIRDER**	–; girders
GIMPING	–; –	**GIRDING**	–; –
GIN	agin; gink,	**GIRDLE**	–; girdled,
	gins		girdler,
GINGAL	–; gingall,		girdles
	gingals	**GIRDLER**	–; girdlers
GINGALL	–; gingalls	**GIRL**	–; girls, girly
GINGELI	–; gingelis	**GIRLIE**	–; girlies
GINGELY	–; –	**GIRLISH**	–; –
GINGER	aginger;	**GIRN**	–; girns
	gingers,	**GIRNED**	–; –
	gingery	**GIRNING**	–; –
GINGHAM	–; ginghams	**GIRO**	–; giron,
GINGILI	–; gingilis		giros
GINGIVA	–; gingivae,	**GIRON**	–; girons
	gingival	**GIROSOL**	–; girosols
GINGKO	–; gingkos	**GIRSH**	–; –

GIRSHES	–; –	**GLAIRE**	–; glaired,
GIRT	–; girth, girts		glaires
GIRTED	–; –	**GLAIRY**	–; –
GIRTH	–; girths	**GLAIVE**	–; glaived,
GIRTHED	–; –		glaives
GIRTING	–; –	**GLAMOR**	–; glamors
GISARME	–; gisarmes	**GLAMOUR**	–; glamours
GISMO	–; gismos	**GLANCE**	–; glanced,
GIST	agist; gists		glances
GISTS	agists; –	**GLAND**	–; glands
GIT	–; –	**GLANDES**	–; –
GITANO	–; gitanos	**GLANS**	–; –
GITTERN	–; gitterns	**GLARE**	aglare;
GIVE	ogive; given,		glared,
	giver, gives		glares
GIVEN	–; givens	**GLARIER**	–; –
GIVER	–; givers	**GLARING**	–; –
GIVES	ogives; –	**GLARY**	–; –
GIVING	–; –	**GLASS**	–; glassy
GIZMO	–; gizmos	**GLASSED**	–; –
GIZZARD	–; gizzards	**GLASSES**	–; –
GJETOST	–; gjetosts	**GLASSIE**	–; glassier
GLACE	–; glaces		glassies
GLACEED	–; –	**GLAZE**	–; glazed,
GLACIAL	–; –		glazer,
GLACIER	–; glaciers		glazes
GLACIS	–; –	**GLAZER**	–; glazers
GLAD	–; glade,	**GLAZIER**	–; glaziers,
	glads, glady		glaziery
GLADDED	–; –	**GLAZING**	–; glazings
GLADDEN	–; gladdens	**GLAZY**	–; –
GLADDER	–; –	**GLEAM**	agleam;
GLADE	–; glades		gleams,
GLADIER	–; –		gleamy
GLADLY	–; –	**GLEAMED**	–; –
GLAIKET	–; –	**GLEAN**	–; gleans
GLAIKIT	–; –	**GLEANED**	–; –
GLAIR	–; glaire,	**GLEANER**	–; gleaners
	glairs, glairy	**GLEBA**	–; glebae
		GLEBE	–; glebes

GLED	–; glede, gleds	glimpser, glimpses
GLEDE	–; gledes	**GLINT**	–; glints
GLEE	aglee; gleed, gleek, glees, gleet	**GLINTED**	–; –
		GLIOMA	–; gliomas
		GLISTEN	–; glistens
GLEED	–; gleeds	**GLISTER**	–; glisters
GLEEFUL	–; –	**GLITCH**	–; –
GLEEK	–; gleeks	**GLITTER**	aglitter; glitters, glittery
GLEEKED	–; –		
GLEEMAN	–; –		
GLEEMEN	–; –	**GLOAM**	–; gloams
GLEET	–; gleets, gleety	**GLOAT**	–; gloats
		GLOATED	–; –
GLEETED	–; –	**GLOATER**	–; gloaters
GLEG	–; –	**GLOB**	–; globe globs
GLEGLY	–; –		
GLEN	–; glens	**GLOBAL**	–; –
GLENOID	–; –	**GLOBATE**	–; globatea
GLEY	agley; gleys	**GLOBE**	–; globed, globes
GLIADIN	–; gliadine, gliadins		
		GLOBIN	–; globing, globins
GLIAL	–; –		
GLIB	–; –	**GLOBOID**	–; globoids
GLIBBER	–; –	**GLOBOSE**	–; –
GLIBLY	–; –	**GLOBOUS**	–; –
GLIDE	–; glided, glider, glides	**GLOBULE**	–; globules
		GLOCHID	–; glochids
GLIDER	–; gliders	**GLOGG**	–; gloggs
GLIDING	–; –	**GLOM**	–; gloms
GLIFF	–; gliffs	**GLOMERA**	–; –
GLIM	–; glime, glims	**GLOMMED**	–; –
		GLOMUS	–; –
GLIME	–; glimed, glimes	**GLOOM**	–; glooms gloomy
GLIMING	–; –	**GLOOMED**	–; –
GLIMMER	aglimmer; glimmers	**GLOP**	–; glops
		GLORIA	–; glorias
GLIMPSE	–; glimpsed,	**GLORIED**	–; –

GLORIES	–; –	GLUMLY	–; –
GLORIFY	–; –	GLUMMER	–; –
GLORY	–; –	GLUMPY	–; –
GLOSS	–; glossa, glossy	GLUNCH	–; -
		GLUT	–; gluts
GLOSSA	–; glossae, glossal, glossas	GLUTEAL	–; –
		GLUTEI	–; –
		GLUTEN	–; glutens
GLOSSED	–; –	GLUTEUS	–; –
GLOSSER	–; glossers	GLUTTED	–; –
GLOSSES	–; –	GLUTTON	–; gluttons gluttony
GLOST	–; glosts	
GLOTTAL	–; –	GLYCAN	–; glycans
GLOTTIC	–; –	GLYCIN	–; glycine, glycins
GLOTTIS	–; –	
GLOUT	–; glouts	GLYCINE	–; glycines
GLOUTED	–;	GLYCOL	–; glycols
GLOVE	–; gloved, glover, gloves	GLYCYL	–; glycyls
		GLYPH	–; glyphs
GLOVER	–; glovers	GLYPHIC	–; –
GLOVING	–; –	GLYPTIC	–; glyptics
GLOW	aglow; glows	GNAR	–; gnarl, gnars
GLOWED	–;	
GLOWER	–; glowers	GNARL	–; gnarls, gnarly
GLOWFLY	–; –	
GLOWING	–; –	GNARLED	–; –
GLOZE	–; glozed, glozes	GNARR	–; gnarrs
		GNARRED	–; –
GLOZING	–; –	GNASH	–; –
GLUCOSE	–; glucoses	GNASHED	–; –
GLUE	–; glued, gluer, glues, gluey	GNASHES	–; –
		GNAT	–; gnats
		GNATHAL	–; –
GLUER	–; gluers	GNATHIC	–; –
GLUIER	–; –	GNATTY	–; –
GLUIEST	–; –	GNAW	–; gnawn, gnaws
GLUILY	–; –	
GLUING	–; –	GNAWED	–; –
GLUM	–; glume	GNAWER	–; gnawers
GLUME	–; glumes	GNAWING	–; gnawings

GNEISS	–; –		gobbler,
GNOCCHI	–; –		gobbles
GNOME	–; gnomes	GOBBLER	–; gobblers
GNOMIC	–; –	GOBIES	–; –
GNOMISH	–; –	GOBIOID	–; gobioids
GNOMIST	–; gnomists	GOBLET	–; goblets
GNOMON	–; gnomons	GOBLIN	–; goblins
GNOSES	–; –	GOBO	–; gobos
GNOSIS	–; –	GOBOES	–; –
GNOSTIC	agnostic; –	GOBONEE	–; –
GNU	–; gnus	GOBONY	–; –
GO	ago, ego;	GOD	–; gods
	goa, gob,	GODDED	–; –
	god, goo,	GODDESS	–; –
	gor, got,	GODDING	–; –
	gox, goy	GODHEAD	–; godheads
GOA	–; goad,	GODHOOD	–; godhoods
	goal, goas,	GODLESS	–; –
	goat	GODLIER	–; –
GOAD	–; goads	GODLIKE	–; –
GOADED	–; –	GODLING	–; godlings
GOADING	–; –	GODLILY	–; –
GOAL	–; goals	GODLY	–; –
GOALED	–; –	GODOWN	–; godowns
GOALIE	–; goalies	GODROON	–; godroons
GOALING	–; –	GODSEND	–; godsends
GOAT	–; goats	GODSHIP	–; godships
GOATEE	–; goateed,	GODSON	–; godsons
	goatees	GODWIT	–; godwits
GOATISH	–; –	GOER	–; goers
GOB	–; gobo,	GOES	–; –
	gobs, goby	GOFFER	–; goffers
GOBAN	–; gobang,	GOGGLE	–; goggled,
	gobans		goggler,
GOBANG	–; gobangs		goggles
GOBBED	–; –	GOGGLER	–; gogglers
GOBBET	–; gobbets	GOGGLY	–; –
GOBBING	–; –	GOGLET	–; goglets
GOBBLE	–; gobbled,	GOGO	–; gogos

GOING	–; goings	**GOO**	–; good,
GOITER	–; goiters		goof, gook,
GOITRE	–; goitres		goon, goop,
GOLD	–; golds		goos
GOLDARN	–; goldarns	**GOOBER**	–; goobers
GOLDBUG	–; goldbugs	**GOOD**	–; goods,
GOLDEN	–; –		goody
GOLDER	–; –	**GOODBY**	–; goodbye,
GOLDEST	–; –		goodbys
GOLDEYE	–; goldeyes	**GOODBYE**	–; goodbyes
GOLDURN	–; goldurns	**GOODIES**	–; –
GOLEM	–; golems	**GOODISH**	–; –
GOLF	–; golfs	**GOODLY**	–; –
GOLFED	–; –	**GOODMAN**	–; –
GOLFER	–; golfers	**GOODMEN**	–; –
GOLFING	–; golfings	**GOOEY**	–; –
GOLIARD	–; goliards	**GOOF**	–; goofs,
GOLLY	–; –		goofy
GOLOSH	–; –	**GOOFED**	–; –
GOMBO	–; gombos	**GOFFIER**	–; –
GOMERAL	–; gomerals	**GOOFILY**	–; –
GOMEREL	–; gomerels	**GOOFING**	–; –
GOMERIL	–; gomerils	**GOOGLY**	–; –
GOMUTI	–; gomutis	**GOOGOL**	–; googols
GONAD	–; gonads	**GOOIER**	–; –
GONADAL	–; –	**GOOIEST**	–; –
GONADIC	;	**GOOK**	–; gooks,
GONDOLA	–; gondolas		gooky
GONE	agone; goner	**GOON**	–; goons,
GONER	–; goners		goony
GONG	–; gongs	**GOONEY**	–; gooneys
GONGED	–; –	**GOONIE**	–; goonies
GONGING	–; –	**GOOP**	–; goops
GONIA	–; –	**GOORAL**	–; goorals
GONIDIC	–; –	**GOOSE**	–; goosed,
GONIF	–; gonifs		gooses,
GONION	–; –		goosey
GONIUM	–; –	**GOOSIER**	–; –
GONOF	–; gonofs	**GOOSING**	–; –
GONOPH	–; gonophs	**GOOSY**	–; –

GOPHER	–; gophers		gouger,
GOR	–; gore,		gouges
	gory	**GOUGER**	–; gougers
GORAL	–; gorals	**GOUGING**	–; –
GORCOCK	–; gorcocks	**GOULASH**	–; –
GORE	–; gored,	**GOURAMI**	–; gouramis
	gores	**GOURD**	–; gourde,
GORGE	–; gorged,		gourds
	gorger,	**GOURDE**	–; gourdes
	gorges,	**GOURMET**	–; gourmets
	gorget	**GOUT**	–; gouts,
GORGER	–; gorgers		gouty
GORGET	–; gorgets	**GOUTIER**	–; –
GORGING	–; –	**GOUTILY**	–; –
GORGON	–; gorgons	**GOUTY**	agouty; –
GORHEN	–; gorhens	**GOVERN**	–; governs
GORIER	–; –	**GOWAN**	–; gowans,
GORIEST	–; –		gowany
GORILLA	–; gorillas	**GOWANED**	–; –
GORILY	–; –	**GOWD**	–; gowds
GORING	–; –	**GOWK**	–; gowks
GORMAND	–; gormands	**GOWN**	–; gowns
GORSE	–; gorses	**GOWNED**	–; –
GORSIER	–; –	**GOWNING**	–; –
GORSY	–; –	**GOX**	–; –
GOSH	–; –	**GOXES**	–; –
GOSHAWK	–; goshawks	**GOY**	–; goys
GOSLING	–; goslings	**GOYIM**	–; –
GOSPEL	–; gospels	**GOYISH**	–; –
GOSPORT	–; gosports	**GRAAL**	–; graals
GOSSAN	–; gossans	**GRAB**	–; grabs
GOSSIP	–; gossips,	**GRABBED**	–; –
	gossipy	**GRABBER**	–; grabbers
GOSSOON	–; gossoons	**GRABBLE**	–; grabbled,
GOT	–; –		grabbler,
GOTHIC	–; gothics		grabbles
GOTHITE	–; gothites	**GRABBY**	–; –
GOTTEN	–; –	**GRABEN**	–; grabens
GOUACHE	–; gouaches	**GRACE**	–; graced,
GOUGE	–; gouged,		graces

GRACILE	–; –	**GRANDAM**	–; grandame,
GRACING	–; –		grandams
GRACKLE	–; grackles	**GRANDEE**	–; grandees
GRAD	–; grade,	**GRANDER**	–; –
	grads	**GRANDLY**	–; –
GRADATE	–; gradated,	**GRANDMA**	–; grandmas
	gradates	**GRANDPA**	–; grandpas
GRADE	–; graded,	**GRANGE**	–; granger,
	grader,		granges
	grades	**GRANGER**	–; grangers
GRADER	–; graders	**GRANITE**	–; granites
GRADIN	–; gradine,	**GRANNIE**	–; grannies
	grading,	**GRANNY**	–; –
	gradins	**GRANT**	–; grants
GRADINE	–; gradines	**GRANTED**	–; –
GRADUAL	–; graduals	**GRANTEE**	–; grantees
GRADUS	–; –	**GRANTER**	–; granters
GRAFT	–; grafts	**GRANTOR**	–; grantors
GRAFTED	–; –	**GRANULE**	–; granules
GRAFTER	–; grafters	**GRANUM**	–; –
GRAHAM	–; –	**GRAPE**	–; grapes
GRAIL	–; grails	**GRAPERY**	–; –
GRAIN	–; grains,	**GRAPH**	–; graphs
	grainy	**GRAPHED**	–; –
GRAINED	–; –	**GRAPHIC**	–; graphics
GRAINER	–; grainers	**GRAPIER**	–; –
GRAM	–; grama,	**GRAPLIN**	–; grapline,
	gramp,		graplins
	grams	**GRAPNEL**	–; grapnels
GRAMA	–; gramas	**GRAPPA**	–; grappas
GRAMARY	–; –	**GRAPPLE**	–; grappled,
GRAMMAR	–; grammars		grappler,
GRAMME	–; grammes		grapples
GRAMP	–; gramps	**GRAPY**	–; –
GRAMPUS	–; –	**GRASP**	–; grasps
GRANA	–; –	**GRASPED**	–; –
GRANARY	–; –	**GRASPER**	–; graspers
GRAND	–; grands	**GRASS**	–; grassy
GRANDAD	–; grandads	**GRASSED**	–; –
		GRASSES	–; –

GRAT	–; grate
GRATE	–; grated, grater, grates
GRATER	–; graters
GRATIFY	–; –
GRATIN	–; grating, gratins
GRATING	–; gratings
GRATIS	–; –
GRAUPEL	–; graupels
GRAVE	–; graved, gravel, graven, graver, graves
GRAVEL	–; gravels, gravely
GRAVER	–; gravers
GRAVES	–; gravest
GRAVID	–; gravida
GRAVIDA	–; gravidae, gravidas
GRAVIES	–; –
GRAVING	–; –
GRAVITY	–; –
GRAVURE	–; gravures
GRAVY	–; –
GRAY	–; grays
GRAYED	–; –
GRAYER	–; –
GRAYEST	–; –
GRAYING	–; –
GRAYISH	–; –
GRAYLAG	–; graylags
GRAYLY	–; –
GRAYOUT	–; grayouts
GRAZE	–; grazed, grazer, grazes

GRAZER	–; grazers
GRAZIER	–; graziers
GRAZING	–; grazings
GREASE	–; greased, greaser, greases
GREASER	–; greasers
GREASY	–; –
GREAT	–; greats
GREATEN	–; greatens
GREATER	–; –
GREATLY	–; –
GREAVE	–; greaved, greaves
GREBE	–; grebes
GRECIZE	–; grecized, grecizes
GREE	agree; greed, greek, green, grees, greet
GREED	agreed; greeds, greedy
GREEING	–; –
GREEK	–; –
GREEN	–; greens, greeny
GREENED	–; –
GREENER	–; –
GREENLY	–; –
GREENTH	–; greenths
GREES	agrees; –
GREET	–; greets
GREETED	–; –
GREETER	–; greeters
GREGO	–; gregos
GREIGE	–; greiges
GREISEN	–; greisens

GREMIAL	–; gremials	**GRILLE**	–; grilled, griller, grilles
GREMLIN	–; gremlins		
GREMMIE	–; gremmies	**GRILLER**	–; grillers
GREMMY	–; –	**GRILSE**	–; grilses
GRENADE	–; grenades	**GRIM**	–; grime, grimy
GREW	–; –		
GREY	–; greys	**GRIMACE**	–; grimaced, grimacer, grimaces
GREYED	–; –		
GREYER	–; –		
GREYEST	–; –	**GRIME**	–; grimed, grimes
GREYHEN	–; greyhens		
GREYING	–; –	**GRIMIER**	–; –
GREYISH	–; –	**GRIMILY**	–; –
GREYLAG	–; greylags	**GRIMING**	–; –
GREYLY	–; –	**GRIMLY**	–; –
GRIBBLE	–; gribbles	**GRIMMER**	–; –
GRID	–; gride, grids	**GRIN**	–; grind, grins
GRIDDLE	–; griddled, griddles	**GRIND**	–; grinds
		GRINDED	–; –
GRIDE	–; grided, grides	**GRINDER**	–; grinders, grindery
GRIDING	–; –	**GRINGO**	–; gringos
GRIEF	–; griefs	**GRINNED**	–; –
GRIEVE	–; grieved, griever, grieves	**GRINNER**	–; grinners
		GRIP	–; gripe, grips, gript, gripy
GRIEVER	–; grievers		
GRIFF	–; griffe, griffs	**GRIPE**	–; griped, griper, gripes, gripey
GRIFFE	–; griffes		
GRIFFIN	–; griffins		
GRIFFON	–; griffons	**GRIPER**	–; gripers
GRIFT	–; grifts	**GRIPIER**	–; –
GRIFTED	–; –	**GRIPING**	–; –
GRIFTER	–; grifters	**GRIPPE**	–; gripped, gripper, grippes
GRIG	–; grigs		
GRIGRI	–; grigris		
GRILL	–; grille, grills	**GRIPPER**	–; grippers
		GRIPPLE	–; –

GRIPPY	–; –	**GROPING**	–; –
GRISKIN	–; griskins	**GROSS**	–; –
GRISLY	–; –	**GROSSED**	–; –
GRISON	–; grisons	**GROSSER**	–; grossers
GRIST	–; grists	**GROSSES**	–; grossest
GRISTLE	–; gristles	**GROSSLY**	–; –
GRISTLY	–; –	**GROSZ**	–; groszy
GRIT	–; grith, grits	**GROT**	–; grots
GRITH	–; griths	**GROTTO**	–; grottos
GRITTED	–; –	**GROUCH**	–; grouchy
GRITTY	–; –	**GROUND**	aground;
GRIVET	–; grivets		grounds
GRIZZLE	–; grizzled,	**GROUP**	–; groups
	grizzler,	**GROUPED**	–; –
	grizzles	**GROUPER**	–; groupers
GRIZZLY	–; –	**GROUPIE**	–; groupies
GROAN	–; groans	**GROUSE**	–; groused,
GROANED	–; –		grouser,
GROANER	–; groaners		grouses
GROAT	–; groats	**GROUSER**	–; grousers
GROCER	–; grocers,	**GROUT**	–; grouts,
	grocery		grouty
GROG	–; grogs	**GROUTED**	–; –
GROGGY	–; –	**GROUTER**	–; grouters
GROGRAM	–; grograms	**GROVE**	–; groved,
GROIN	–; groins		grovel,
GROINED	–; groined		groves
GROMMET	–; grommets	**GROVEL**	–; grovels
GROOM	–; grooms	**GROW**	–; growl,
GROOMED	–; –		grown,
GROOMER	–; groomers		grows
GROOVE	–; grooved,	**GROWER**	–; growers
	groover,	**GROWING**	–; –
	grooves	**GROWL**	–; growls,
GROOVER	–; groovers		growly
GROOVY	–; –	**GROWLED**	–; –
GROPE	–; groped,	**GROWLER**	–; growlers
	groper,	**GROWNUP**	–; grownups
	gropes	**GROWTH**	–; growths
GROPER	–; gropers	**GROYNE**	–; groynes

GRUB	–; grubs	**GUACO**	–; guacos
GRUBBED	–; –	**GUAIAC**	–; guaiac
GRUBBER	–; grubbers	**GUAN**	–; guans
GRUBBY	–; –	**GUANACO**	–; guanacos
GRUDGE	–; grudged, grudger, grudges	**GUANASE**	–; guanases
		GUANIN	–; guanine, guanins
GRUDGER	–; grudgers	**GUANINE**	–; guanines
GRUEL	–; gruels	**GUANO**	–; guanos
GRUELED	–; –	**GUAR**	–; guard, guars
GRUELER	–; gruelers		
GRUFF	–; gruffs, gruffy	**GUARANI**	–; guaranis
		GUARD	–; guards
GRUFFED	–; –	**GUARDED**	–; –
GRUFFER	–; –	**GUARDER**	–; guarders
GRUFFLY	–; –	**GUAVA**	–; guavas
GRUGRU	–; grugrus	**GUAYULE**	–; guayules
GRUM	–; grume	**GUCK**	–; gucks
GRUMBLE	–; grumbled, grumbler, grumbles	**GUDE**	–; gudes
		GUDGEON	–; gudgeons
		GUENON	–; guenons
GRUME	–; grumes	**GUERDON**	–; guerdons
GRUMMER	–; –	**GUESS**	–; –
GRUMMET	–; grummets	**GUESSED**	–; –
GRUMOSE	–; –	**GUESSER**	–; guessers
GRUMOUS	–; –	**GUESSES**	–; –
GRUMP	–; grumps, grumpy	**GUEST**	–; guests
		GUESTED	–; –
GRUMPED	–; –	**GUFF**	–; guffs
GRUMPHY	–; –	**GUFFAW**	–; guffaws
GRUNION	–; grunions	**GUGGLE**	–; guggled, guggles
GRUNT	–; grunts		
GRUNTED	–; –	**GUGLET**	–; guglets
GRUNTER	–; grunters	**GUID**	–; guide, guids
GRUNTLE	–; gruntled, gruntles		
		GUIDE	–; guided, guider, guides
GRUSHIE	–; –		
GRUTCH	–; –		
GRUTTEN	–; –	**GUIDER**	–; guiders
GRYPHON	–; gryphons	**GUIDING**	–; –

GUIDON	–; guidons	**GULPING**	–; –
GUILD	–; guilds	**GUM**	–; gums
GUILDER	–; guilders	**GUMBO**	–; gumbos
GUILE	–; guiled, guiles	**GUMBOIL**	–; gumboils
		GUMDROP	–; gumdrops
GUILT	–; guilts, guilty	**GUMLESS**	–; –
		GUMLIKE	–; –
GUIMPE	–; guimpes	**GUMMA**	–; gummas
GUINEA	–; guineas	**GUMMATA**	–; –
GUIPURE	–; guipures	**GUMMED**	–; –
GUIRO	–; –	**GUMMER**	–; gummers
GUISARD	–; guisards	**GUMMIER**	–; –
GUISE	–; guised, guises	**GUMMING**	–; –
		GUMMITE	–; gummites
GUITAR	–; guitar	**GUMMOSE**	–; –
GUL	–; gulf, gull, gulp, guls	**GUMMOUS**	–; –
		GUMMY	–; –
GULAR	–; –	**GUMSHOE**	–; gumshoed, gumshoes
GULCH	–; –		
GULCHES	–; –	**GUMTREE**	–; gumtrees
GULDEN	–; guldens	**GUMWEED**	–; gumweeds
GULES	–; –		
GULF	–; gulfs, gulfy	**GUMWOOD**	–; gumwoods
GULFED	–; –	**GUN**	–; gunk, guns
GULFIER	–; –		
GULFING	–; –	**GUNBOAT**	–; gunboats
GULL	–; gulls, gully	**GUNDOG**	–; gundogs
		GUNFIRE	–; gunfires
GULLED	–; –	**GUNK**	–; gunks
GULLET	–; gullets	**GUNLESS**	–; –
GULLEY	–; gulleys	**GUNLOCK**	–; gunlocks
GULLIED	–; –	**GUNMAN**	–; –
GULLIES	–; –	**GUNMEN**	–; –
GULLING	–; –	**GUNNED**	–; –
GULP	–; gulps, gulpy	**GUNNEL**	–; gunnels
		GUNNEN	–; –
GULPED	–; –	**GUNNER**	–; gunners, gunnery
GULPER	–; gulpers		
GULPIER	–; –	**GUNNIES**	–; –

GUNNING	–; gunnings	GUT	–; guts
GUNNY	–; –	GUTLESS	–; –
GUNPLAY	–; gunplays	GUTLIKE	–; –
GUNROOM	–; gunrooms	GUTS	–; gutsy
GUNSEL	–; gunsels	GUTSIER	–; –
GUNSHIP	–; gunships	GUTTA	–; guttae
GUNSHOT	–; gunshots	GUTTATE	–; guttated
GUNWALE	–; gunwales	GUTTED	–; –
GUPPIES	–; –	GUTTER	–; gutters, guttery
GUPPY	–; –		
GURGE	–; gurged, gurges	GUTTIER	–; –
		GUTTING	–; –
GURGING	–; –	GUTTLE	–; guttled, guttler, guttles
GURGLE	–; gurgled, gurgles, gurglet		
		GUTTLER	–; guttlers
GURGLET	–; gurglets	GUTTY	–; –
GURNARD	–; gurnards	GUY	–; guys
GURNET	–; gurnets	GUYED	–; –
GURNEY	–; gurneys	GUYING	–; –
GURRIES	–; –	GUYOT	–; guyots
GURRY	–; –	GUZZLE	–; guzzled, guzzler, guzzles
GURSH	–; –		
GURSHES	;		
GURU	–; gurus	GUZZLER	–; guzzlers
GUSH	–; gushy	GWEDUC	–; gweduck, gweducs
GUSHED	–; –		
GUSHER	–; gushers	GWEDUCK	–; gweducks
GUSHES	–; –	GYBE	–; gybed, gybes
GUSHIER	–; –		
GUSHILY	–; –	GYBING	–; –
GUSHING	–; –	GYM	–; gyms
GUSSET	–; gussets	GYMNAST	–; gymnasts
GUST	–; gusto, gusts, gusty	GYNECIA	–; –
		GYNECIC	–; –
GUSTED	–; –	GYP	–; gyps
GUSTIER	–; –	GYPPED	–; –
GUSTILY	–; –	GYPPER	–; gyppers
GUSTING	–; –	GYPPING	–; –
GUSTOES	–; –	GYPS	–; gypsy

GYPSIED	–; –	**GYRENE**	–; gyrenes
GYPSIES	–; –	**GYRI**	–; –
GYPSUM	–; gypsums	**GYRING**	–; –
GYRAL	–; –	**GYRO**	–; gyron,
GYRALLY	–; –		gyros
GYRATE	–; gyrated,	**GYRON**	–; gyrons
	gyrates	**GYROSE**	–; –
GYRATOR	–; gyrators,	**GYRUS**	–; –
	gryatory	**GYVE**	–; gyved,
GYRE	–; gyred,		gyves
	gyres	**GYVING**	–; –

H

H	ah, eh, oh,	**HACK**	shack, thack,
	sh, uh; ha,		whack;
	he, hi, hm,		hacks
	ho	**HACKBUT**	–; hackbuts
HA	aha, wha;	**HACKED**	thacked,
	had, hae,		whacked; –
	hag, hah,	**HACKEE**	–; hackees
	haj, ham,	**HACKER**	whacker; –
	hap, has,	**HACKIE**	–; hackies
	hat, haw,	**HACKING**	thacking,
	hay		whacking; –
HAAF	–; haafs	**HACKLE**	shackle;
HAAR	–; haars		hackled,
HABILE	–; –		hackler,
HABIT	–; habits		hackles
HABITAN	–; habitans,	**HACKLED**	shackled; –
	habitant	**HACKLER**	shackler;
HABITAT	–; habitats		hacklers
HABITED	–; –	**HACKLES**	shackles; –
HABITUE	–; habitues	**HACKLY**	–; –
HABITUS	–; –	**HACKMAN**	–; –
HABU	–; habus	**HACKMEN**	–; –
HACEK	–; haceks	**HACKNEY**	–; hackneys
HACHURE	–; hachured,	**HACKSAW**	–; hacksaws
	hachures	**HACKS**	shacks,

	thacks, whacks; –	**HAFTS**	shafts; –
HAD	chad, shad; hade, hadj	**HAG**	shag; hags
		HAGADIC	–; –
HADAL	–; –	**HAGBORN**	–; –
HADARIM	chadarim; –	**HAGBUSH**	–; –
HADDEST	–; –	**HAGBUT**	–; hagbuts
HADDOCK	–; haddocks	**HAGDON**	–; hagdons
HADE	shade; haded, hades	**HAGFISH**	–; –
		HAGGARD	–; haggards
HADED	shaded; –	**HAGGED**	shagged; –
HADES	shades; –	**HAGGING**	shagging; –
HADING	shading; –	**HAGGIS**	–; haggish
HADJ	–; hadji	**HAGGLE**	–; haggled, haggler, haggles
HADJEE	–; hadjees		
HADJES	–; –		
HADJI	–; hadjis	**HAGGLER**	–; hagglers
HADRON	–; hadrons	**HAGRIDE**	–; hagrides
HADST	–; –	**HAGRODE**	–; –
HAE	thae; haed, haem, haen, haes, haet	**HAGS**	shags; –
		HAH	shah; hahs
		HAHS	shahs; –
		HAIK	–; haika, haiks, haiku
HAEING	–; –	**HAIL**	–; hails
HAEM	–; haems	**HAILED**	–; –
HAEMAL	–; –	**HAILER**	–; hailers
HAEMIC	–; –	**HAILING**	–; –
HAEMIN	–; haemins	**HAIR**	chair; hairs, hairy
HAEMOID	–; –		
HAERES	–; –	**HAIRCAP**	–; haircaps
HAET	–; haets	**HAIRCUT**	–; haircuts
HAFFET	–; haffets	**HAIRDO**	–; hairdos
HAFFIT	–; haffits	**HAIRED**	chaired; –
HAFIS	–; –	**HAIRIER**	–; –
HAFIZ	–; –	**HAIRPIN**	–; hairpins
HAFNIUM	–; hafniums	**HAIRS**	chairs; –
HAFT	shaft; hafts	**HAJ**	–; haji, hajj
HAFTED	shafted; –	**HAJES**	–; –
HAFTER	–; hafters	**HAJI**	–; hajis
HAFTING	shafting; –	**HAJJI**	–; hajjis

HAKE	shake; hakes	**HALL**	shall; hallo, halls
HAKEEM	–; hakeems		
HAKES	shakes; –	**HALLAH**	challah; hallahs
HAKIM	–; hakims		
HALAKAH	–; halakahs	**HALLAHS**	challahs; –
HALAKIC	–; –	**HALLEL**	–; hallels
HALALA	–; halalah, halalas	**HALLO**	–; halloa, halloo, hallos, hallot, hallow
HALALAH	halalahs		
HALAVAH	–; halavahs		
HALBERD	–; halberds		
HALBERT	–; halberts	**HALLOA**	–; halloas
HALCYON	–; halcyons	**HALLOED**	–; –
HALE	shale, whale; haled, haler, hales	**HALLOES**	–; –
		HALLOO	–; halloos
		HALLOT	challot, shallot; halloth
HALED	shaled, whaled; –		
HALER	thaler, whaler; halers, haleru	**HALLOTH**	challoth; –
		HALLOW	shallow; hallows
HALERS	thalers, whalers; –	**HALLOWS**	shallows; –
		HALLS	shalls; –
HALES	shales, whales; halest	**HALLUX**	–; –
		HALLWAY	–; hallways
HALF	–; –	**HALM**	–; halms
HALFWAY	–; –	**HALO**	–; halos
HALFWIT	–; halfwits	**HALOED**	–; –
HALIBUT	–; halibuts	**HALOES**	–; –
HALID	–; halide, halids	**HALOGEN**	–; halogens
		HALOID	–; haloids
HALIDE	–; halides	**HALOING**	–; –
HALIDOM	–; halidome, halidoms	**HALT**	shalt; halts
		HALTED	–; –
HALING	whaling; –	**HALTER**	–; haltere, halters
HALITE	–; halites	**HALTERE**	–; haltered, halteres
HALITUS	–; –		
		HALTING	–; –
		HALUTZ	chalutz; –

HALVA	-; halvah, halvas	HAMSTER	-; hamsters
HALVAH	-; halvahs	HAMULAR	-; -
HALVE	-; halved, halves	HAMULI	-; -
		HAMULUS	-; -
HALVERS	-; -	HAMZA	-; hamzah, hamzas
HALVING	-; -		
HALYARD	-; halyards	HAMZAH	-; hamzahs
HAM	cham, sham, wham; hame, hams	HANAPER	-; hanapers
		HANCE	chance; hances
HAMAL	-; hamals	HANCES	chances; -
HAMATE	-; hamates	HAND	-; hands, handy
HAMAUL	-; hamauls		
HAMBURG	-; hamburgs	HANDBAG	-; handbags
HAME	shame; hames	HANDCAR	-; handcars, handcart
HAMES	shames; -	HANDED	-; -
HAMLET	-; hamlets	HANDFUL	-; handfuls
HAMMAL	-; hammals	HANDGUN	-; handguns
HAMMED	shammed, whammed; -	HANDIER	-; -
		HANDILY	-; -
HAMMER	shammer; hammers	HANDING	-; -
		HANDLE	-; handled, handler, handles
HAMMERS	shammers; -		
HAMMIER	-; -	HANDLER	-; handlers
HAMMILY	-; -	HANDOFF	-; handoffs
HAMMING	shamming, whamming; -	HANDOUT	-; handouts
		HANDSAW	-; handsaws
HAMMOCK	-; hammocks	HANDSEL	-; handsels
		HANDSET	-; handsets
HAMMY	chammy, shammy, whammy; -	HANDY	shandy; -
		HANG	bhang, chang, whang; hangs
HAMPER	champer; hampers		
HAMPERS	champers; -	HANGAR	-; hangars
HAMS	chams, shams, whams; -	HANGDOG	-; hangdogs
		HANGED	changed, whanged; -

HANGER	changer; hangers	**HAPAX**	–; –
		HAPAXES	–; –
HANGERS	changers; –	**HAPLESS**	–; –
HANGING	changing, whanging; hangings	**HAPLITE**	–; haplites
		HAPLOID	–; haploids, haploidy
HANGMAN	–; –	**HAPLONT**	–; haplonts
HANGMEN	–; –	**HAPLY**	–; –
HANGOUT	–; hangouts	**HAPPED**	chapped, whapped; –
HANGS	bhangs, changs, whangs; –	**HAPPEN**	–; happens
		HAPPIER	–; –
HANGTAG	–; hangtags	**HAPPILY**	–; –
HANGUP	–; hangups	**HAPPING**	chapping, whapping; –
HANK	shank, thank; hanks, hanky	**HAPPY**	–; –
HANKED	shanked, thanked; –	**HAPS**	chaps, whaps; –
HANKER	thanker; hankers	**HAPTEN**	–; haptene, haptens
HANKERS	thankers; –	**HAPTENE**	–; haptenes
HANKIE	–; hankies	**HAPTIC**	–; –
HANKING	shanking, thanking; –	**HARASS**	–; –
		HARBOR	–; harbors
HANKS	shanks, thanks; –	**HARBOUR**	–; harbours
HANSE	–; hansel, hanses	**HARD**	chard, shard; hards, hardy
HANSEL	–; hansels	**HARDEN**	–; hardens
HANSOM	–; hansoms	**HARDER**	–; –
HANT	chant; hants	**HARDEST**	–; –
HANTED	chanted; –	**HARDHAT**	–; hardhats
HANTING	chanting; –	**HARDIER**	–; –
HANTLE	–; hantles	**HARDIES**	–; hardiest
HANTS	chants; –	**HARDILY**	–; –
HANUMAN	–; hanumans	**HARDLY**	–; –
HAOLE	–; haoles	**HARDPAN**	–; hardpans
HAP	chap, whap; chaps	**HARDS**	chards, shards; –

HARDSET	–; –	**HARMINE**	–; harmines
HARDTOP	–; hardtops	**HARMING**	charming; –
HARE	chare, share; hared, harem, hares	**HARMONY**	–; –
		HARMS	charms, tharms; –
HARED	chared, shared; –	**HARNESS**	–; –
HAREEM	–; hareems	**HARP**	sharp; harps, harpy
HARELIP	–; harelips	**HARPED**	sharped; –
HAREM	–; harems	**HARPER**	sharper; harpers
HARES	chares, shares; –	**HARPERS**	sharpers; –
HARIANA	–; harianas	**HARPIES**	sharpies; –
HARICOT	–; haricots	**HARPIN**	–; harping, harpins
HARIJAN	–; harijans		
HARING	–; charing, sharing	**HARPING**	sharping; –
		HARPIST	–; harpists
HARK	chark, shark; harks	**HARPOON**	–; harpoons
		HARPS	sharps; –
HARKED	charked, sharked; –	**HARPY**	sharpy; –
		HARRIED	–; –
HARKEN	–; harkens	**HARRIER**	charrier; –
HARKING	charking, sharking; –	**HARRIES**	–; –
		HARROW	–; harrows
HARKS	charks, sharks; –	**HARRY**	charry, gharry; –
HARL	–; harls	**HARSH**	–; –
HARLOT	charlot; harlots	**HARSHEN**	–; harshens
		HARSHER	–; –
HARLOTS	charlots; –	**HARSHLY**	–; –
HARM	charm, tharm; harms	**HARSLET**	–; harslets
		HART	chart; harts
HARMED	charmed; –	**HARTAL**	–; hartals
HARMER	charmer; harmers	**HARTS**	charts; –
		HARVEST	–; harvests
HARMERS	charmers; –	**HAS**	–; hash, hasp, hast
HARMFUL	–; –		
HARMIN	–; harmine, harming, harmins	**HASHED**	–; –
		HASHES	–; –

HASHING	–; –	**HATE**	–; hated,
HASHISH	–; –		hater, hates
HASLET	–; haslets	**HATEFUL**	–; –
HASP	–; hasps	**HATER**	–; haters
HASPED	–; –	**HATFUL**	–; hatfuls
HASPING	–; –	**HATING**	–; –
HASSEL	–; hassels	**HATLESS**	–; –
HASSLE	–; hassled,	**HATLIKE**	–; –
	hassles	**HATPIN**	–; hatpins
HASSOCK	–; –	**HATRACK**	–; hatracks
HAST	ghast; haste,	**HATRED**	–; hatreds
	hasty	**HATS**	chats, ghats
HASTATE	–; –		khats,
HASTE	chaste;		whats; –
	hasted,	**HATSFUL**	–; –
	hasten,	**HATTED**	chatted; -
	hastes	**HATTER**	chatter,
HASTEN	chasten;		shatter;
	hastens		hatters
HASTENS	chastens; –	**HATTERS**	chatters,
HASTIER	–; –		shatters; –
HASTILY	–; –	**HATTING**	chatting; –
HASTING	–; –	**HAUBERK**	–; hauberks
HAT	chat, ghat,	**HAUGH**	shaugh;
	khat, phat,		haughs
	shat, that,	**HAUGHS**	shaughs; –
	what; hate,	**HAUGHTY**	–; –
	hath, hats	**HAUL**	shaul; haulm
HATABLE	–; –		hauls
HATBAND	–; hatbands	**HAULAGE**	–; haulages
HATBOX	–; –	**HAULED**	shauled; –
HATCH	thatch; –	**HAULER**	–; haulers
HATCHED	thatched; –	**HAULIER**	–; hauliers
HATCHEL	–; hatchels	**HAULING**	shauling; -
HATCHER	thatcher;	**HAULM**	–; haulms
	hatchers,		haulmy
	hatchery	**HAULS**	shauls; -
HATCHES	thatches; –	**HAUNCH**	–; –
HATCHET	–; hatchets	**HAUNT**	chaunt;
			haunts

HAUNTED	chaunted; –	**HAWS**	chaws,
HAUNTER	chaunter;		shaws,
	haunters		thaws; –
HAUNTS	chaunts; –	**HAWSE**	–; hawser,
HAUSEN	–; hausens		hawses
HAUTBOY	–; hautboys	**HAWSER**	–; hawsers
HAUTEUR	–; hauteurs	**HAY**	shay; hays
HAVE	shave;	**HAYCOCK**	–; haycocks
	haven,	**HAYED**	–; –
	haver, haves	**HAYER**	–; hayers
HAVEN	shaven;	**HAYFORK**	–; hayforks
	havens	**HAYING**	–; hayings
HAVENED	–; –	**HAYLAGE**	–; haylages
HAVER	shaver;	**HAYLOFT**	–; haylofts
	havers	**HAYMOW**	–; haymows
HAVERED	–; –	**HAYRACK**	–; hayracks
HAVEREL	–; haverels	**HAYRICK**	–; hayricks
HAVERS	shavers; –	**HAYRIDE**	–; hayrides
HAVES	shaves; –	**HAYSEED**	–; hayseeds
HAVING	shaving; –	**HAYWARD**	–; haywards
HAVIOR	–; haviors	**HAYWIRE**	–; haywires
HAVIOUR	–; haviours	**HAYS**	shays; –
HAVOC	–; havocs	**HAZAN**	chazan;
HAW	chaw, shaw,		hazans
	thaw; hawk,	**HAZANS**	chazans; –
	haws	**HAZARD**	–; hazards
HAWED	chawed,	**HAZE**	–; hazed,
	shawed,		hazel,
	thawed; –		hazer, hazes
HAWING	chawing,	**HAZEL**	–; hazels
	shawing,	**HAZELLY**	–; –
	thawing; –	**HAZER**	–; hazers
HAWK	–; hawks	**HAZIER**	–; –
HAWKED	–; –	**HAZIEST**	–; –
HAWKER	–; hawkers	**HAZILY**	–; –
HAWKEY	–; hawkeys	**HAZING**	–; hazings
HAWKIE	–; hawkies	**HAZY**	–; –
HAWING	thawing; –	**HAZZAN**	–; hazzans
HAWKING	–; hawkings	**HE**	she, the;
HAWKISH	–; –		hem, hen,

	hep, her,	**HEARS**	shears;
	hes, het,		hearse
	hex, hew,	**HEARSE**	–; hearsed
	hey		hearses
HEAD	ahead;	**HEART**	–; hearth,
	heads,		hearts,
	heady		hearty
HEADED	–; –	**HEARTED**	–; –
HEADER	–; headers	**HEARTEN**	–; heartens
HEADIER	–; –	**HEARTH**	–; hearths
HEADILY	–; –	**HEAT**	cheat,
HEADING	–; headings		wheat;
HEADMAN	–; –		heath, heats
HEADMEN	–; –	**HEATED**	cheated; –
HEADPIN	–; headpins	**HEATER**	cheater,
HEADSET	–; headsets		theater;
HEADWAY	–; headways		heaters
HEAL	sheal, wheal;	**HEATERS**	cheaters,
	heals		theaters; –
HEALED	–; –	**HEATH**	sheath;
HEALER	–; healers		heaths,
HEALING	shealing; –		heathy
HEALS	sheals,	**HEATHEN**	–; heathens
	wheals; –	**HEATHER**	sheather;
HEALTH	–; healths,		heathers,
	healthy		heathery
HEAP	cheap;	**HEATHS**	sheaths; –
	heaps	**HEATING**	cheating;
HEAPED	–; –	**HEATS**	cheats,
HEAPING	–; –		wheats; –
HEAPS	cheaps; –	**HEAUME**	–; heaumes
HEAR	shear;	**HEAVE**	sheave;
	heard,		heaved,
	hears, heart		heaven,
			heaves
HEARER	–; hearers	**HEAVED**	sheaved; –
HEARING	shearing;	**HEAVEN**	–; heavens
	hearings	**HEAVER**	–; heavers
HEARKEN	–; hearkens	**HEAVES**	sheaves; –
HEARSAY	–; hearsays	**HEAVIER**	–; –

HEAVIES	–; heaviest	**HEEZE**	wheeze;
HEAVILY	–; –		heezed,
HEAVING	sheaving; –		heezes
HEAVY	–; –	**HEEZES**	wheezes; –
HEBETIC	–; –	**HEEZING**	wheezing; –
HECK	check; hecks	**HEFT**	theft; hefts,
HECKLE	–; heckled,		hefty
	heckler,	**HEFTED**	–; –
	heckles	**HEFTER**	–; hefters
HECKLER	–; hecklers	**HEFTIER**	–; –
HECKS	checks; –	**HEFTILY**	–; –
HECTARE	–; hectares	**HEFTING**	–; –
HECTIC	–; –	**HEFTS**	thefts; –
HECTOR	–; hectors	**HEGARI**	–; hegaris
HEDDLE	–; heddles	**HEGIRA**	–; hegiras
HEDER	cheder;	**HEGUMEN**	–;
	heders		hegumene,
HEDERS	cheders; –		hegumens,
HEDGE	–; hedged,		hegumeny
	hedger,	**HEIFER**	–; heifers
	hedges	**HEIGH**	–; height
HEDGER	–; hedgers	**HEIGHT**	–; heighth.
HEDGIER	–; –		heights
HEDGING	–; –	**HEIGHTH**	–; heighths
HEDGY	–; –	**HEIL**	–; heils
HEDONIC	–; hedonics	**HEILED**	–; –
HEED	–; heeds	**HEILING**	–; –
HEEDED	–; –	**HEINIE**	–; heinies
HEEDER	–; heeders	**HEINOUS**	–; –
HEEDFUL	–; –	**HEIR**	their; heirs
HEEDING	–; –	**HEIRDOM**	–; heirdoms
HEEHAW	–; heehaws	**HEIRED**	–; –
HEEL	wheel; heels	**HEIRESS**	–; –
HEELED	wheeled; –	**HEIRING**	–; –
HEELER	wheeler;	**HEIRS**	theirs; –
	heelers	**HEIST**	theist; heists
HEELERS	wheelers; –	**HEISTED**	–; –
HEELING	wheeling; –	**HEISTER**	–; heisters
HEELS	wheels; –	**HEISTS**	theists; –
HEELTAP	–; heeltaps	**HEJIRA**	–; hejiras

HEKTARE	–; hektares	**HELPING**	whelping; –
HELD	–; –	**HELPS**	whelps; –
HELIAC	–; –	**HELVE**	shelve;
HELIAST	–; heliasts		helved,
HELICAL	–; –		helves
HELICES	–; –	**HELVED**	shelved; –
HELICON	–; helicons	**HELVES**	shelves; –
HELIO	–; helios	**HELVING**	shelving; –
HELIPAD	–; helipads	**HEM**	ahem, them;
HELIUM	–; heliums		heme, hemp,
HELIX	–; –		hems
HELIXES	–; –	**HEMAGOG**	–;
HELL	shell; hells		hemagogs
HELLBOX	–; –	**HEMAL**	–; –
HELLCAT	–; hellcats	**HEMATAL**	–; –
HELLED	shelled; –	**HEMATIC**	rhematic;
HELLER	sheller;		hematics
	helleri,	**HEMATIN**	–; hematine,
	hellers,		hematins
	hellery	**HEME**	theme;
HELLERS	shellers; –		hemes
HELLING	shelling; –	**HEMES**	themes; –
HELLION	–; hellions	**HEMIC**	chemic; –
HELLISH	–; –	**HEMIN**	–; hemins
HELLO	–; hellos	**HEMIOLA**	–; hemiolas
HELLOED	–; –	**HEMLINE**	–; hemlines
HELLOES	–; –	**HEMLOCK**	–; hemlocks
HELLS	shells; –	**HEMMED**	–; –
HELLUVA	–; –	**HEMMER**	–; hemmers
HELM	whelm; helms	**HEMMING**	–; –
HELMED	whelmed; –	**HEMOID**	–; –
HELMET	–; helmets	**HEMP**	–; hemps,
HELMING	whelming; –		hempy
HELMS	whelms; –	**HEMPEN**	–; –
HELOT	–; helots	**HEMPIE**	–; hempier
HELOTRY	–; –	**HEN**	then, when;
HELP	whelp; helps		hens, hent
HELPED	whelped; –	**HENBANE**	–; henbanes
HELPER	–; helpers	**HENBIT**	–; henbits
HELPFUL	–; –		

HENCE	thence, whence; –	**HERDS**	sherds; –
HENCOOP	–; hencoops	**HERE**	there, where; heres
HENNA	–; hennas		
HENNAED	–; –	**HEREAT**	thereat, whereat; –
HENNERY	–; –		
HENPECK	–; henpecks	**HEREBY**	thereby, whereby; –
HENRIES	–; –		
HENRY	–; henrys	**HEREDES**	–; –
HENS	thens, whens; –	**HEREIN**	therein, wherein; –
HENT	shent; hents	**HEREOF**	thereof, whereof; –
HENTED	–; –		
HENTING	–; –	**HEREON**	thereon, whereon; –
HEP	–; –	**HERES**	theres, wheres; heresy
HEPARIN	–; heparins		
HEPATIC	–; hepatica, hepatics		
		HERETIC	–; heretics
HEPCAT	–; hepcats	**HERETO**	thereto, whereto; –
HEPTAD	–; heptads		
HEPTANE	–; heptanes	**HERIOT**	–; heriots
HEPTOSE	–; heptoses	**HERITOR**	–; heritors
HER	–; herb, herd, here, herl, herm, hern, hero, hers	**HERL**	–; herls
		HERM	therm; herma, herms
		HERMA	–; hermae, hermai
HERALD	–; heralds		
HERB	–; herbs, herby	**HERMAE**	thermae; –
		HERMIT	thermit; hermits
HERBAGE	–; herbages		
HERBAL	–; herbals	**HERMITS**	thermits; –
HERBIER	–; –	**HERMS**	therms; –
HERD	sherd; herds	**HERN**	–; herns
HERDED	–; –	**HERNIA**	–; herniae, hernial, hernias
HERDER	–; herders		
HERDIC	–; herdics		
HERDING	–; –	**HERO**	–; heron, heros
HERDMAN	–;		
HERDMEN	–; –	**HEROES**	–; –

HEROIC	–; heroics	**HEUGHS**	sheughs; –
HEROIN	–; heroine, heroins	**HEW**	chew, phew, shew, thew, whew; hewn hews
HEROINE	–; heroines		
HEROISM	–; heroisms		
HEROIZE	–; heroized, heroizes	**HEWABLE**	chewable; -
		HEWED	chewed, shewed; –
HERON	–; herons		
HERONRY	–; –	**HEWER**	chewer, shewer; –
HERPES	–; –		
HERRIED	wherried; –	**HEWERS**	chewers, shewers; –
HERRIES	cherries, sherries, wherries; –		
		HEWING	chewing, shewing; –
HERRING	–; herrings	**HEWN**	shewn; –
HERRY	cherry, sherry, wherry; –	**HEWS**	chews, shews, thews, whews; -
HERSELF	–; –		
HERTZ	–; –	**HEX**	–; –
HERTZES	–; –	**HEXAD**	–; hexade, hexads
HES	shes; –		
HESSIAN	–; hessians	**HEXADE**	–; hexades
HESSITE	–; hessites	**HEXADIC**	–; –
HEST	chest; hests	**HEXAGON**	–; hexagons
HESTS	chests; –	**HEXANE**	–; hexanes
HET	whet; heth	**HEXAPLA**	–; hexaplar hexaplas
HETAERA	–; hetaerae, hetaeras		
		HEXAPOD	–; hexapods, hexapody
HETAIRA	–; hetairai, hetairas		
		HEXED	–; –
HETERO	–; heteros	**HEXER**	–; hexers
HETH	cheth; heths	**HEXEREI**	–; hexereis
HETHS	cheths; –	**HEXES**	–; –
HETMAN	–; hetmans	**HEXING**	–; –
HEUCH	sheuch; heuchs	**HEXONE**	–; hexones
		HEXOSAN	–; hexosans
HEUCHS	sheuchs; –	**HEXOSE**	–; hexoses
HEUGH	sheugh; heughs	**HEXYL**	–; hexyls

HEY	they, whey; –	**HIGGLE**	–; higgled, higgler, higgles
HEYDAY	–; heydays		
HEYDEY	–; heydeys	**HIGGLER**	–; higglers
HI	chi, ghi, khi, phi; hic, hid, hie, him, hin, hip, his, hit	**HIGH**	thigh; highs, hight
		HIGHBOY	–; highboys
		HIGHER	–; –
HIATAL	–; –	**HIGHEST**	–; –
HIATUS	–; –	**HIGHLY**	–; –
HIBACHI	–; hibachis	**HIGHS**	thighs; –
HIC	chic; hick	**HIGHT**	–; highth, hights
HICCUP	–; hiccups		
HICK	chick, thick; hicks	**HIGHTED**	–; –
		HIGHTH	–; highths
HICKEY	–; hickeys	**HIGHWAY**	–; highways
HICKORY	–; –	**HIJACK**	–; hijacks
HICKS	chicks, thicks; –	**HIJINKS**	–; –
		HIKE	–; hiked, hiker, hikes
HID	chid, whid; hide		
		HIKER	–; hikers
HIDABLE	–; –	**HIKING**	–; –
HIDALGO	–; hidalgos	**HILA**	–; hilar
HIDDEN	chidden; –	**HILDING**	–; hildings
HIDE	chide; hided, hider, hides	**HILI**	chili; –
		HILL	chill, shill, thill; hillo, hills, hilly
HIDED	chided; –		
HIDEOUS	–; –		
HIDEOUT	–; hideouts	**HILLED**	chilled, shilled; –
HIDER	chider; hiders		
		HILLER	chiller; hillers
HIDERS	chiders; –	**HILLERS**	chillers
HIDES	chides; –	**HILLIER**	–; –
HIDING	chiding; hidings	**HILLING**	chilling, shilling; –
HIE	–; hied, hies	**HILLO**	–; hilloa, hillos
HIED	shied; –		
HIEING	–; –	**HILLOA**	–; hilloas
HIEMAL	–; –	**HILLOCK**	–; hillocks, hillocky
HIES	shies; –		

HILLOED	–; –	**HIPLIKE**	–; –
HILLS	chills, shills,	**HIPNESS**	–; –
	thills; –	**HIPPED**	chipped,
HILLTOP	–; hilltops		shipped,
HILLY	chilly, shilly; –		whipped; –
HILT	–; hilts	**HIPPER**	chipper,
HILTED	–; –		shipper,
HILTING	–; –		whipper; –
HILUM	–; –	**HIPPEST**	–; –
HILUS	–; –	**HIPPIE**	chippie;
HIM	shim,		hippier,
	whim; –		hippies
HIMSELF	–; –	**HIPPIER**	whippier; –
HIN	chin, shin,	**HIPPIES**	chippies;
	thin, whin;		hippiest
	hind, hins,	**HIPPING**	chipping,
	hint		shipping,
HIND	–; hinds		whipping; –
HINDER	–; hinders	**HIPPISH**	–; –
HINDGUT	–; hindguts	**HIPPO**	–; hippos
HINGE	–; hinged,	**HIPPY**	chippy,
	hinger,		whippy; –
	hinges	**HIPS**	chips, ships,
HINGER	–; hingers		whips; –
HINGING	–; –	**HIPSHOT**	–; –
HINNIED	shinnied; –	**HIPSTER**	–; hipsters
HINNIES	shinnies; –	**HIRABLE**	–; –
HINNY	shinny,	**HIRCINE**	–; –
	whinny; –	**HIRE**	ahire, shire;
HINS	chins, shins,		hired, hirer,
	thins, whins; –		hires
HINT	–; hints	**HIRER**	–; hirers
HINTED	–; –	**HIRES**	shires; –
HINTER	–; hinters	**HIRING**	–; –
HINTING	–; –	**HIRPLE**	–; hirpled,
HINTS	chints; –		hirples
HIP	chip, ship,	**HIRSEL**	–; hirsels
	whip; hips	**HIRSLE**	–; hirsled,
HIPBONE	–; hipbones		hirsles
HIPLESS	–; –	**HIRSUTE**	–; –

HIRUDIN	–; hirudins	**HIVES**	chives,
HIS	chis, ghis,		shives; –
	khis, phis,	**HIVING**	–; –
	this; hisn,	**HM**	ohm; –
	hiss, hist	**HO**	mho, oho,
HISPID	–; –		rho, tho,
HISSED	–; –		who; hob,
HISSELF	–; –		hod, hoe,
HISSER	–; hissers		hog, hop,
HISSES	–; –		hot, how,
HISSING	–; hissings		hoy
HIST	shist, whist;	**HOAGIE**	–; hoagies
	hists	**HOAGY**	–; –
HISTED	whisted; –	**HOAR**	–; hoard,
HISTING	whisting; –		hoars, hoary
HISTOID	–; –	**HOARD**	–; hoards
HISTONE	–; histones	**HOARDED**	–; –
HISTORY	–; –	**HOARDER**	–; hoarders
HISTS	shists,	**HOARIER**	–; –
	whists; –	**HOARILY**	–; –
HIT	chit, whit;	**HOARSE**	–; hoarsen,
	hits		hoarses
HITCH	–; –	**HOARSEN**	–; hoarsens
HITCHED	–; –	**HOATZIN**	–; hoatzins
HITCHER	–; hitchers	**HOAX**	–; –
HITCHES	–; –	**HOAXED**	–; –
HITHER	thither,	**HOAXER**	–; hoaxers
	whither; –	**HOAXES**	–; –
HITLESS	–; –	**HOAXING**	–; –
HITS	chits,	**HOB**	–; hobo,
	whits; –		hobs
HITTER	chitter,	**HOBBED**	–; –
	whitter;	**HOBBIES**	–; –
	hitters	**HOBBING**	–; –
HITTERS	chitters,	**HOBBLE**	–; hobbled,
	whitters; –		hobbler,
HITTING	–; –		hobbles
HIVE	chive, shive;	**HOBBLER**	–; hobblers
	hived, hives	**HOBBY**	–; –
		HOBLIKE	–; –

HOBNAIL	–; hobnails	**HOG**	shog; hogg, hogs
HOBNOB	–; hobnobs		
HOBO	–; hobos	**HOGAN**	–; hogans
HOBOED	–; –	**HOGBACK**	–; hogbacks
HOBOES	–; –	**HOGFISH**	–; –
HOBOING	–; –	**HOGG**	–; hoggs
HOBOISM	–; hoboisms	**HOGGED**	shogged; –
HOCK	chock, shock; hocks	**HOGGER**	–; hoggers
		HOGGING	shogging; –
HOCKED	chocked, shocked; –	**HOGGISH**	–; –
		HOGLIKE	–; –
HOCKER	shocker; hockers	**HOGMANE**	–; hogmanes
HOCKERS	shockers; –	**HOGNOSE**	–; hognoses
HOCKEY	–; hockeys	**HOGNUT**	–; hognuts
HOCKING	chocking, shocking; –	**HOGS**	shogs; –
		HOGTIE	–; hogtied, hogties
HOCKS	chocks, shocks; –	**HOGWASH**	–; –
HOCUS	–; –	**HOGWEED**	–; hogweeds
HOCUSED	–; –		
HOCUSES	–; –	**HOICK**	–; hoicks
HOD	shod; hods	**HOICKED**	–; –
HODAD	–; hodads	**HOIDEN**	–; hoidens
HODADDY	–; –	**HOISE**	–; hoised, hoises
HODDEN	shodden; hoddens		
HODDIN	–; hoddins	**HOISING**	–; –
HOE	shoe; hoed, hoer, hoes	**HOIST**	–; hoists
		HOISTED	–; –
HOECAKE	–; hoecakes	**HOISTER**	–; hoisters
HOED	shoed; –	**HOKE**	choke; hoked, hokes, hokey
HOEDOWN	–; hoedowns		
HOEING	shoeing; –	**HOKED**	choked; –
HOELIKE	–; –	**HOKES**	chokes; –
HOER	shoer; hoers	**HOKEY**	chokey; –
HOERS	shoers; –	**HOKING**	choking; –
HOES	shoes; –	**HOKKU**	–; –
		HOKUM	–; hokums
		HOLARD	–; holards

HOLD	ahold; holds	HOLLOO	–; holloos
HOLDALL	–; holdalls	HOLLOW	–; hollows
HOLDEN	–; –	HOLLY	wholly; –
HOLDER	–; holders	HOLM	–; holms
HOLDING	–; holdings	HOLMIC	–; –
HOLDOUT	–; holdouts	HOLMIUM	–; holmiums
HOLDS	aholds; –	HOLP	–; –
HOLDUP	–; holdups	HOLPEN	–; –
HOLE	ahole,	HOLSTER	–; holsters
	dhole, thole,	HOLT	–; holts
	whole;	HOLY	–; –
	holed, holes,	HOLYDAY	–; holydays
	holey	HOMAGE	–; homaged,
HOLED	tholed; –		homager,
HOLES	dholes,		homages
	tholes,	HOMAGER	–; homagers
	wholes; –	HOMBRE	–; hombres
HOLIBUT	–; holibuts	HOMBURG	–; homburgs
HOLIDAY	–; holidays	HOME	–; homed,
HOLIER	–; –		homen,
HOLIES	–; holiest		homer,
HOLILY	–; –		homes,
HOLING	tholing; –		homey
HOLISM	–; holisms	HOMELY	–; –
HOLIST	–; holists	HOMER	–; homers
HOLK	–; holks	HOMERED	–; –
HOLKED	–; –	HOMIER	–; –
HOLKING	–; –	HOMIEST	–; –
HOLLA	cholla; hollas	HOMILY	–; –
HOLLAED	–; –	HOMING	–; –
HOLLAND	–; hollands	HOMINID	–; hominids
HOLLAS	chollas; –	HOMINY	–; –
HOLLER	–; hollers	HOMMOCK	–;
HOLLIES	–; –		hommocks
HOLLO	–; holloa,	HOMO	–; homos
	holloo,	HOMOLOG	–;
	hollos,		homologs,
	hollow		homology
HOLLOA	–; holloas	HOMONYM	–; homonyms,
HOLLOED	–; –		homonymy

HOMY	–; –	HOODING	–; –
HONAN	–; honans	HOODLUM	–; hoodlums
HONCHO	–; honchos	HOODOO	–; hoodoos
HONDA	–; hondas	HOOEY	phooey;
HONE	phone,		hooeys
	shone;	HOOF	–; hoofs
	honed,	HOOFED	–; –
	honer,	HOOFER	–; hoofers
	hones,	HOOFING	–; –
	honey	HOOK	shook;
HONED	phoned; –		hooks, hooky
HONER	–; honers	HOOKA	–; hookah,
HONES	phones;		hookas
	honest	HOOKAH	–; hookahs
HONEST	–; honesty	HOOKED	–; –
HONEY	phoney;	HOOKER	–; –
	honeys	HOOKEY	–; hookeys
HONEYED	–; –	HOOKIER	–; –
HONEYS	phoneys; –	HOOKIES	–; hookiest
HONG	thong; hongs	HOOKING	–; –
HONGS	thongs; –	HOOKLET	–; hooklets
HONIED	–; –	HOOKS	shooks; –
HONING	phoning; –	HOOKUP	–; hookups
HONK	–; honks,	HOOLIE	–; –
	honky	HOOLY	dhooly; –
HONKED	–; –	HOOP	whoop;
HONKER	–; honkers		hoops
HONKEY	–; honkeys	HOOPED	whooped; –
HONKIE	–; honkies	HOOPER	whooper;
HONKING	–; –		hoopers
HONOR	–; honors	HOOPING	whooping; –
HONORED	–; –	HOOPLA	whoopla;
HONOREE	–; honorees		hooplas
HONORER	–; honorers	HOOPLAS	whooplas; –
HONOUR	–; honours	HOOPOE	–; hoopoes
HOOCH	–; –	HOOPOO	–; hoopoos
HOOCHES	–; –	HOOPS	whoops; –
HOOD	–; hoods	HOORAH	–; hoorahs
HOODED	–; –	HOORAY	–; hoorays
HOODIE	–; hoodies	HOOSGOW	–; hoosgows

HOOT	bhoot, shoot; hoots	**HOPSACK**	–; hopsacks
HOOTCH	–; –	**HOPTOAD**	–; hoptoads
HOOTED	–; –	**HORA**	–; horae, horah, horal, horas
HOOTER	shooter; hooters		
HOOTERS	shooters; –	**HORAH**	–; horahs
HOOTING	shooting; –	**HORAL**	choral; –
HOOTS	bhoots, shoots; –	**HORARY**	–; –
		HORDE	–; horded, hordes
HOOVES	–; –		
HOP	chop, shop, whop; hope, hops	**HORDED**	chorded; –
		HORDEIN	–; hordeins
HOPE	–; hoped, hoper, hopes	**HORDING**	–; –
		HORIZON	–; horizons
		HORMONE	–; hormones
		HORN	shorn, thorn; horns, horny
HOPEFUL	–; hopefuls		
HOPER	–; hopers	**HORNED**	thorned; –
HOPHEAD	–; hopheads	**HORNET**	–; hornets
HOPING	–; –	**HORNIER**	–; –
HOPLITE	–; hoplites	**HORNILY**	–; –
HOPPED	chopped, shopped, whopped; –	**HORNING**	thorning; –
		HORNITO	–; hornitos
		HORNS	thorns; –
HOPPER	chopper, shopper, whopper; hoppers	**HORNY**	thorny; –
		HORRENT	–; –
		HORRID	–; –
		HORRIFY	–; –
		HORROR	–; horrors
HOPPERS	choppers, shoppers, whoppers; –	**HORSE**	ahorse; horsed, horses, horsey
HOPPING	chopping, shopping, whopping; –	**HORSIER**	–; –
		HORSILY	–; –
HOPPLE	–; hoppled, hopples	**HORSING**	–; –
		HORST	–; horste, horsts
HOPS	chops, shops, whops; –	**HORSTE**	–; horstes
		HORSY	–; –

HOSANNA	–; hosannas	**HOTSHOT**	–; hotshots
HOSE	chose,	**HOTSPUR**	–; hotspurs
	those,	**HOTTED**	shotted; –
	whose;	**HOTTER**	–; –
	hosed,	**HOTTEST**	–; –
	hosel,	**HOTTING**	shotting; –
	hosen, hoses	**HOTTISH**	–; –
HOSEL	–; hosels	**HOUDAH**	–; houdan,
HOSES	choses; –		houdahs
HOSIER	–; hosiers,	**HOUND**	–; hounds
	hosiery	**HOUNDED**	–; –
HOSING	–; –	**HOUNDER**	–; hounders
HOSPICE	–; hospices	**HOUR**	–; houri,
HOST	ghost; hosts		hours
HOSTAGE	–; hostages	**HOURI**	–; houris
HOSTED	ghosted; –	**HOURLY**	–; –
HOSTEL	–; hostels	**HOUSE**	chouse;
HOSTESS	–; –		housed,
HOSTILE	–; hostiles		housel,
HOSTING	–; –		houser,
HOSTLER	–; hostlers		houses
HOSTS	ghosts; –	**HOUSED**	choused; –
HOSTLY	ghostly; –	**HOUSEL**	–; housels
HOT	phot, shot;	**HOUSER**	chouser;
	hots		housers
HOTBED	–; hotbeds	**HOUSES**	chouses; –
HOTBOX	–; –	**HOUSING**	chousing;
HOTCAKE	–; hotcakes		housings
HOTCH	–; –	**HOVE**	shove; hovel,
HOTCHED	–; –		hover
HOTCHES	–; –	**HOVEL**	shovel;
HOTDOG	–; hotdogs		hovels
HOTEL	–; hotels	**HOVELS**	shovels; –
HOTFOOT	–; hotfoots	**HOVER**	shover;
HOTHEAD	–; hotheads		hovers
HOTLY	–; –	**HOVERED**	–; –
HOTNESS	–; –	**HOVERER**	–; hoverers
HOTROD	–; hotrods	**HOVERS**	shovers; –
HOTS	phots,	**HOW**	chow, dhow,
	shots; –		show; howe,

	howf, howk, howl, hows		huddler, huddles
HOWBEIT	–; –	HUDDLER	–; huddlers
HOWDAH	–; howdahs	HUE	–; hued, hues
HOWDIE	–; howdies		
HOWDY	–; –	HUELESS	–; –
HOWE	–; howes	HUFF	chuff; huffs, huffy
HOWEVER	–; –		
HOWF	–; howff, howfs	HUFFED	chuffed; –
		HUFFIER	chuffier; –
HOWFF	–; howffs	HUFFILY	–; –
HOWK	–; howks	HUFFING	–; –
HOWKED	–; –	HUFFISH	;
HOWKING	–; –	HUFFS	chuffs; –
HOWL	–; howls	HUFFY	chuffy; –
HOWLED	–; –	HUG	chug, thug; huge, hugs
HOWLER	–; howlers		
HOWLET	–; howlets	HUGE	–; huger
HOWLING	–; –	HUGELY	–; –
HOWS	chows, dhows, shows; –	HUGEOUS	–; –
		HUGER	–; –
		HUGEST	–; –
HOY	ahoy; hoys	HUGGED	chugged; –
HOYDEN	–; hoydens	HUGGER	chugger; huggers
HOYLE	–; hoyles		
HUB	chub; hubs	HUGGERS	chuggers; –
HUBBIES	–; –	HUGGING	chugging; –
HUBBUB	–; hubbubs	HUGS	chugs, thugs; –
HUBBY	chubby; –		
HUBCAP	–; hubcaps	HUH	–; –
HUBRIS	–; –	HUIC	–; –
HUBS	chubs; –	HULA	–; hulas
HUCK	chuck, shuck; hucks	HULK	–; hulks, hulky
HUCKLE	chuckle; huckles	HULKED	–; –
		HULKIER	–; –
HUCKLES	chuckles; –	HULKING	–; –
HUCKS	chucks, shucks; –	HULL	ahull; hullo, hulls
HUDDLE	–; huddled,	HULLED	–; –

HULLER	–; hullers		thump,
HULLING	–; –		whump;
HULLO	–; hulloa, hullos		humph, humps,
HULLOA	–; hulloas		humpy
HULLOED	–; –	**HUMPED**	chumped,
HULLOES	–; –		thumped,
HUM	chum; hump, hums		whumped; –
		HUMPH	–; humphs
HUMAN	–; humane, humans	**HUMPHED**	–; –
		HUMPIER	–; –
HUMANE	–; humaner	**HUMPING**	chumping,
HUMANLY	–; –		thumping,
HUMATE	–; humates		whumping; –
HUMBLE	–; humbled, humbler, humbles	**HUMPS**	chumps, thumps, whumps; –
HUMBLER	–; humblers	**HUMS**	chums; –
HUMBLES	–; humblest	**HUMUS**	–; –
HUMBLY	–; –	**HUMUSES**	–; –
HUMBUG	–; humbugs	**HUN**	shun; hung, hunk, huns, hunt
HUMDRUM	–; humdrums		
HUMERAL	–; humerals		
HUMERI	–; –	**HUNCH**	–; –
HUMERUS	–; –	**HUNCHED**	–; –
HUMIC	–; –	**HUNCHES**	–; –
HUMID	–; –	**HUNDRED**	–; hundreds
HUMIDLY	–; –	**HUNG**	–; –
HUMIDOR	–; humidors	**HUNGER**	–; hungers
HUMMED	chummed; –	**HUNGRY**	–; –
HUMMER	–; hummers	**HUNK**	chunk; hunks, hunky
HUMMING	chumming; –		
HUMMOCK	–; hummocks, hummocky	**HUNKER**	–; hunkers
		HUNKIES	–; –
		HUNKS	chunks; –
HUMOR	–; humors	**HUNKY**	chunky; –
HUMORAL	–; –	**HUNNISH**	–; –
HUMORED	–; –	**HUNS**	shuns; –
HUMOUR	–; humours	**HUNT**	shunt; hunts
HUMP	chump,	**HUNTED**	shunted; –

HUNTER	chunter, shunter; hunters	**HUSHFUL**	–; –
		HUSHING	shushing; –
HUNTERS	chunters, shunters; –	**HUSK**	–; husks, husky
HUNTING	shunting; huntings	**HUSKED**	–; –
		HUSKER	–; huskers
HUNTS	shunts; –	**HUSKIER**	–; –
HUP	–; –	**HUSKIES**	–; huskiest
HURDIES	–; –	**HUSKILY**	–; –
HURDLE	–; hurdled, hurdler, hurdles	**HUSKING**	–; huskings
		HUSSAR	–; hussars
		HUSSIES	–; –
HURDLER	–; hurdlers	**HUSSY**	–; –
HURDS	–; –	**HUSTLE**	–; hustled, hustler, hustles
HURL	churl, thurl; hurls, hurly		
		HUSTLER	–; hustlers
HURLED	–; –	**HUSWIFE**	–; huswifes
HURLER	–; hurlers	**HUT**	bhut, shut; huts
HURLEY	–; hurleys		
HURLIES	–; –	**HUTCH**	–; –
HURLING	–; hurlings	**HUTCHED**	–; –
HURLS	churls, thurls; –	**HUTCHES**	–; –
		HUTLIKE	–; –
HURRAH	–; hurrahs	**HUTMENT**	–; hutments
HURRAY	–; hurrays	**HUTS**	bhuts, shuts; –
HURRIED	–; –		
HURRIER	–; hurriers	**HUTTED**	–; –
HURRY	–; –	**HUTTING**	shutting; –
HURT	–; hurts	**HUTZPA**	chutzpa; hutzpah, hutzpas
HURTER	–; hurters		
HURTFUL	–; –		
HURTING	–; –	**HUTZPAH**	chutzpah; hutzpahs
HURTLE	–; hurtled, hurtles	**HUTZPAS**	chutzpas; –
HUSBAND	–; husbands	**HUZZA**	–; huzzah, huzzas
HUSH	shush; –		
HUSHABY	–; –	**HUZZAH**	–; huzzahs
HUSHED	shushed; –	**HUZZAED**	–; –
HUSHES	shushes; –	**HWAN**	–; –

HYAENA	–; hyaenas	**HYING**	shying; –
HYAENIC	–; –	**HYLA**	phyla; hylas
HYALIN	–; hyaline, hyalins	**HYMEN**	–; hymens
		HYMENAL	–; –
HYALINE	–; hyalines	**HYMN**	–; hymns
HYALITE	–; hyalites	**HYMNAL**	–; hymnals
HYALOID	–; hyaloids	**HYMNARY**	–; –
HYBRID	–; hybrids	**HYMNED**	–; –
HYBRIS	–; –	**HYMNING**	–; –
HYDATID	–; hydatids	**HYMNIST**	–; hymnists
HYDRA	–; hydrae, hydras	**HYMNODY**	–; –
		HYOID	–; hyoids
HYDRANT	–; hydranth, hydrants	**HYOIDAL**	–; –
		HYP	–; hype, hyps
HYDRASE	–; hydrases		
HYDRATE	–; hydrated, hydrates	**HYPE**	–; hypes
		HYPERON	–; hyperons
HYDRIA	–; hydriae	**HYPHA**	–; hyphae, hyphal
HYDRIC	–; –		
HYDRID	–; hydride, hydrids	**HYPHEN**	–; hyphens
		HYPNIC	–; –
HYDRIDE	–; hydrides	**HYPNOID**	–; –
HYDRO	–; hydros	**HYPO**	–; hypos
HYDROID	–; hydroids	**HYPOED**	–; –
HYDROPS	–; hydropsy	**HYPOING**	–; –
HYDROUS	–; –	**HYPONEA**	–; hyponeas
HYDROXY	–; hydroxyl	**HYPOXIA**	–; hypoxias
HYENA	–; hyenas	**HYPOXIC**	–; –
HYENIC	–; –	**HYRACES**	–; –
HYENINE	–; –	**HYRAX**	–; –
HYENOID	–; –	**HYRAXES**	–; –
HYETAL	–; –	**HYSON**	–; hysons
HYGEIST	–; hygeists	**HYSSOP**	–; hyssops
HYGIENE	–; hygienes	**HYTE**	–; –

I

I	ai, bi, hi, li, mi, pi, si, ti, xi; id, if, in, is, it

IAMB	–; iambi, iambs	**ICIER**	dicier; –
		ICIEST	diciest; –
IAMBIC	–; iambics	**ICILY**	–; –
IAMBUS	–; –	**ICINESS**	–; –
IATRIC	–; –	**ICING**	dicing,
IBEX	–; –		ricing,
IBEXES	–; –		vicing;
IBICES	–; –		icings
IBIDEM	–; –	**ICKER**	bicker,
IBIS	–; –		dicker,
ICE	bice, dice,		kicker, licker,
	fice, lice,		nicker,
	mice, nice,		picker,
	pice, rice,		sicker, ticker,
	sice, vice;		wicker; ickers
	iced, ices	**ICKERS**	bickers,
ICEBERG	–; icebergs		dickers,
ICEBOAT	–; iceboats		kickers,
ICEBOX	–; –		lickers,
ICECAP	–; icecaps		nickers,
ICED	diced, riced,		pickers,
	viced; –		tickers,
ICEFALL	–; icefalls		wickers; –
ICELESS	–; –	**ICKIER**	pickier; –
ICELIKE	–; –	**ICKIEST**	pickiest; –
ICEMAN	–; –	**ICTERIC**	–; icterics
ICEMEN	–; –	**ICTERUS**	–; –
ICES	bices,	**ICKY**	dicky,
	dices,		picky; –
	fices,	**ICON**	–; icons
	rices,	**ICONES**	–; –
	sices,	**ICONIC**	–; –
	vices; –	**ICTERIC**	–; icterics
ICH	rich, wich;	**ICTERUS**	–; –
	ichs	**ICTIC**	–; –
ICHNITE	–; ichnites	**ICTUS**	–; –
ICHOR	–; ichors	**ICTUSES**	–; –
ICHORUS	–; –	**ICY**	–; –
ICICLE	–; icicled,	**ID**	aid, bid, did,
	icicles		fid, gid, hid,

	kid, lid, mid,	**IDYL**	–; idyll, idyls
	rid, yid; ids	**IDYLIST**	–; idylists
IDEA	–; ideal,	**IDYLL**	–; idylls
	ideas	**IDYLLIC**	–; –
IDEAL	–; ideals	**IF**	kif; ifs
IDEALLY	–; –	**IFFIER**	miffier; –
IDEATE	–; ideated,	**IFFIEST**	–; –
	ideates	**IFFY**	biffy, jiffy,
IDEM	–; –		miffy; –
IDENTIC	–; –	**IFS**	kifs; –
IDES	bides, hides,	**IGLOO**	–; igloos
	nides, rides,	**IGLU**	–; iglus
	sides, tides,	**IGNATIA**	–; ignatias
	wides; –	**IGNEOUS**	–; –
IDIOCY	–; –	**IGNIFY**	lignify; –
IDIOM	–; idioms	**IGNITE**	lignite;
IDIOT	–; idiots		ignited,
IDIOTIC	–; –		igniter,
IDLE	sidle; idled,		ignites
	idler, idles	**IGNITER**	–; igniters
IDLED	sidled; –	**IGNITES**	lignites; –
IDLER	sidler; idlers	**IGNITOR**	–; ignitors
IDLERS	sidlers; –	**IGNOBLE**	–; –
IDLES	sidles; idlest	**IGNOBLY**	–; –
IDLESSE	–; idlesses	**IGNORE**	signore;
IDLING	sidling; –		ignored,
IDLY	–; –		ignorer,
IDOL	–; idols		ignores
IDOLISE	–; idolised,	**IGNORER**	–; ignorers
	idoliser,	**IGUANA**	–; iguanas
	idolises	**IHRAM**	–; ihrams
IDOLISM	–; idolisms	**IKEBANA**	–; ikebanas
IDOLIZE	–; idolized,	**IKON**	eikon; ikons
	idolizer,	**IKONS**	eikons; –
	idolizes	**ILEA**	pilea; ileac,
IDS	aids, bids,		ileal
	fids, gids,	**ILEITIS**	–; –
	hids, kids,	**ILEUM**	pileum; –
	lids, mids,	**ILEUS**	–; –
	rids, yids; –	**ILEUSES**	–; –

ILEX	silex; –	**IMAGERY**	–; –
ILEXES	silexes; –	**IMAGINE**	, imagined,
ILIA	cilia, milia;		imaginer,
	iliac, iliad,		imagines
	ilial	**IMAGING**	–; –
ILIAL	filial; –	**IMAGISM**	–; imagisms
ILIAD	–; iliads	**IMAGIST**	–; imagists
ILIUM	milium; –	**IMAGO**	–; –
ILK	bilk, milk,	**IMAGOES**	–; –
	silk; ilka, ilks	**IMAM**	–; imams
ILKS	bilks, milks,	**IMAMATE**	–; imamates
	silks; –	**IMARET**	–; imarets
ILL	bill, dill, fill,	**IMAUM**	–; imaums
	gill, hill, jill,	**IMBALM**	–; imbalms
	kill, mill, nill,	**IMBARK**	–; imbarks
	pill, rill, sill,	**IMBED**	limbed;
	till, vill, will,		imbeds
	yill; ills, illy	**IMBIBE**	–; imbibed,
ILLEGAL	–; –		imbiber,
ILLICIT	–; –		imbibes
ILLITE	–; illites	**IMBIBER**	–; imbibers
ILLITIC	–; –	**IMBLAZE**	–; imblazed,
ILLNESS	–; –		imblazes
ILLOGIC	–; illogics	**IMBODY**	–; –
ILLS	bills, dills,	**IMBOSOM**	–; imbosoms
	fills, gills,	**IMBOWER**	–; imbowers
	hills, jills,	**IMBROWN**	–; imbrowns
	kills, mills,	**IMBRUE**	–; imbrued,
	nills, pills,		imbrues
	rills, sills, tills,	**IMBRUTE**	–; imbruted,
	vills, wills,		imbrutes
	yills; –	**IMBUE**	–; imbued,
ILLUME	–; illumed,		imbues
	illumes	**IMBUING**	–; –
ILLY	billy, dilly,	**IMID**	timid; imide,
	filly, gilly,		imido, imids
	hilly, silly,	**IMIDE**	–; imides
	willy; –	**IMIDIC**	–; –
IMAGE	–; imaged,	**IMIDO**	–; –
	images	**IMINE**	–; imines

IMINO	–; –	**IMPAVID**	–; –
IMITATE	–; imitated, imitates	**IMPAWN**	–; impawns
		IMPEACH	–; –
IMMANE	–; –	**IMPEARL**	–; impearls
IMMENSE	–; immenser	**IMPED**	gimped,
IMMERGE	–; immerged, immerges		limped, pimped; –
		IMPEDE	–; impeded, impeder, impedes
IMMERSE	–; immersed, immerses		
IMMESH	–; –	**IMPEDER**	–; impeders
IMMIES	jimmies; –	**IMPEL**	–; impels
IMMIX	–; –	**IMPEND**	–; impends
IMMIXED	–; immixed	**IMPERIA**	–; imperial
IMMIXES	–; –	**IMPERIL**	–; imperils
IMMORAL	–; –	**IMPETUS**	–; –
IMMUNE	–; immunes	**IMPHEE**	–; imphees
IMMURE	–; immured, immures	**IMPI**	–; impis
		IMPIETY	–; –
IMMY	jimmy; –	**IMPING**	gimping,
IMP	gimp, jimp, limp, pimp, simp; impi, imps		limping, pimping; impinge, impings
IMPACT	–; impacts	**IMPINGE**	–; impinged, impinger, impinges
IMPAINT	–; impaints		
IMPAIR	–; impairs		
IMPALA	–; impalas	**IMPIOUS**	–; –
IMPALE	–; impaled, impaler, impales	**IMPIS**	–; impish
		IMPLANT	–; implants
		IMPLEAD	–; impleads
IMPALER	–; impalers	**IMPLIED**	–; –
IMPANEL	–; impanels	**IMPLIES**	–; –
IMPARK	–; imparks	**IMPLODE**	–; imploded, implodes
IMPART	–; imparts		
IMPASSE	–; impasses	**IMPLORE**	–; implored, implorer, implores
IMPASTE	–; impasted, impastes		
IMPASTO	–; impastos	**IMPLY**	jimply,

	limply, pimply, simply; –	**INANE**	–; inaner, inanes
IMPONE	–; imponed, impones	**INANELY**	–; –
		INANES	–; inanest
IMPORT	–; imports	**INANITY**	–; –
IMPOSE	–; imposed, imposer, imposes	**INAPT**	–; –
		INAPTLY	–; –
		INARCH	–; –
		INARM	–; inarms
IMPOSER	–; imposers	**INARMED**	–; –
IMPOST	–; imposts	**INBEING**	–; inbeings
IMPOUND	–; impounds	**INBOARD**	–; inboards
IMPOWER	–; impowers	**INBORN**	–; –
IMPREGN	–; impregns	**INBOUND**	–; inbounds
IMPRESA	–; impresas	**INBRED**	–; –
IMPRESE	–; impreses	**INBREED**	–; inbreeds
IMPRESS	–; –	**INBUILT**	–; –
IMPREST	–; imprests	**INBURST**	–; inbursts
IMPRINT	–; imprints	**INBY**	–; inbye
IMPROVE	–; improved, improver, improves	**INCAGE**	–; incaged, incages
IMPS	gimps, jimps, limps, pimps, simps; –	**INCASE**	–; incased, incases
		INCENSE	–; incensed, incenses
IMPUGN	–; impugns	**INCEPT**	–; incepts
IMPULSE	–; impulsed, impulses	**INCEST**	–; incests
		INCH	cinch, finch, pinch, winch; –
IMPURE	–; –		
IMPUTE	–; imputed, imputer, imputes	**INCHED**	cinched, pinched, winched; –
IMPUTER	–; imputers		
IN	ain, bin, din, fin, gin, hin, jin, kin, lin, pin, rin, sin, tin, vin, win, yin; ink, inn, ins	**INCHES**	cinches, finches, pinches, winches; –
		INCHING	cinching, pinching, winching; –

INCIPIT	–; incipits	**INDAMIN**	–; indamine, indamins
INCISE	–; incised, incises	**INDEED**	–; –
INCISOR	–; incisors, incisory	**INDENE**	–; indenes
INCITE	–; incited, inciter, incites	**INDENT**	–; indents
		INDEX	–; –
		INDEXED	–; –
INCITER	–; inciters	**INDEXER**	–; indexers
INCIVIL	–; –	**INDEXES**	–; –
INCLASP	–; inclasps	**INDICAN**	–; indicans, indicant
INCLINE	–; inclined, incliner, inclines	**INDICES**	–; –
		INDICIA	–; indicias
INCLIP	–; inclips	**INDICT**	–; indicts
INCLOSE	–; inclosed, incloser, incloses	**INDIGEN**	–; indigene, indigens, indigent
INCLUDE	–; included, includes	**INDIGN**	–; –
INCOG	–; incogs	**INDIGO**	windigo; indigos
INCOME	–; incomer, incomes	**INDIGOS**	windigos; –
		INDITE	–; indited, inditer, indites
INCOMER	–; incomers		
INCONNU	–; inconnus	**INDITER**	–; inditers
INCONY	–; –	**INDIUM**	–; indiums
INCROSS	–; –	**INDOL**	–; indole, indols
INCRUST	–; incrusts		
INCUBI	–; –	**INDOLE**	–; indoles
INCUBUS	–; –	**INDOOR**	–; indoors
INCUDAL	–; –	**INDORSE**	–; indorsed, indorsee, indorser, indorses
INCUDES	–; –		
INCULT	–; –		
INCUR	–; incurs		
INCURVE	–; incurved, incurves	**INDOW**	window; indows
INCUS	–; incuse	**INDOWED**	–; –
INCUSE	–; incused, incuses	**INDOWS**	windows; –
		INDOXYL	–; indoxyls
INDABA	–; indabas	**INDRAFT**	–; indrafts

INDRAWN	–; –	INFEOFF	–; infeoffs
INDRI	–; indris	INFER	–; infers
INDUCE	–; induced, induger, induces	INFERNO	–; infernos
		INFEST	–; infests
		INFIDEL	–; infidels
INDUCER	–; inducers	INFIELD	–; infields
INDUCT	–; inducts	INFIRM	–; infirms
INDUE	–; indued, indues	INFIX	–; –
		INFIXED	–; –
INDULGE	–; indulged, indulger, indulges	INFIXES	–; –
		INFLAME	–; inflamed, inflamer, inflames
INDULIN	–; induline, indulins	INFLATE	–; inflated, inflater, inflates
INDULT	–; indults		
INDWELL	–; indwells		
INDWELT	–; –	INFLECT	–; inflects
INEARTH	–; inearths	INFLICT	–; inflicts
INEDITA	–; –	INFLOW	–; inflows
INEPT	–; –	INFLUX	–; –
INEPTLY	–; –	INFO	–; infos
INERT	–; inerts	INFOLD	pinfold; infolds
INERTIA	–; inertiae, inertial, inertias		
		INFOLDS	pinfolds; –
		INFORM	–; informs
INERTLY	–; –	INFRA	–; –
INEXACT	–; –	INFRACT	–; infracts
INFAMY	–; –	INFUSE	–; infused, infuser, infuses
INFANCY	–; –		
INFANT	–; infanta, infante, infants		
		INFUSER	–; infusers
		INGATE	–; ingates
INFANTA	–; infantas	INGENUE	–; ingenues
INFANTE	–; infantes	INGEST	–; ingesta, ingests
INFARCT	–; infarcts		
INFARE	–; infares	INGLE	dingle, jingle, mingle, single, tingle; ingles
INFAUNA	–; infaunae, infaunal, infaunas		
INFECT	–; infects		

INGLES	dingles, jingles, mingles, singles, tingles; –	**INK**	dink, fink, gink, jink, kink, link, mink, oink, pink, rink, sink, wink; inks, inky
INGOING	–; –		
INGOT	–; ingots		
INGOTED	–; –	**INKBLOT**	–; inkblots
INGRAFT	–; ingrafts	**INKED**	dinked, finked, jinked, kinked, linked, oinked, pinked, winked; –
INGRAIN	–; ingrains		
INGRATE	–; ingrates		
INGRESS	–; –		
INGROUP	–; ingroups		
INGROWN	–; –		
INGULF	–; ingulfs		
INHABIT	–; inhabits		
INHALE	–; inhaled, inhaler, inhales	**INKER**	jinker, linker, pinker, sinker, tinker, winker; inkers
INHALER	–; inhalers		
INHAUL	–; inhauls	**INKERS**	jinkers, linkers, sinkers, tinkers, winkers; –
INHERE	–; inhered, inheres		
INHERIT	–; inherits		
INHIBIT	–; inhibits		
INHUMAN	–; inhumane	**INKHORN**	–; inkhorns
INHUME	–; inhumed, inhumer, inhumes	**INKIER**	dinkier, kinkier; –
		INKIEST	dinkiest; –
INHUMER	–; inhumers	**INKING**	finking, jinking, kinking, linking, oinking, pinking, sinking, winking; –
INIA	–; –		
INION	minion, pinion; –		
INITIAL	–; initials		
INJECT	–; injects		
INJURE	–; injured, injurer, injures		
		INKLE	tinkle, winkle; inkles
INJURER	–; injurers		
INJURY	–; –		

INKLES	tinkles, winkles; inkless	**INNER**	dinner, ginner, pinner, sinner, tinner, winner; inners
INKLIKE	–; –		
INKLING	–; inklings		
INKPOT	–; inkpots		
INKS	dinks, finks, ginks, jinks, kinks, links, minks, oinks, pinks, rinks, sinks, winks; –	**INNERLY**	–; –
		INNERS	dinners, ginners, pinners, sinners, tinners, winners; –
INKWELL	–; inkwells		
INKWOOD	–; inkwoods		
INKY	dinky, kinky, linky, pinky, zinky; –	**INNERVE**	–; innerved, innerves
		INNING	binning, dinning, finning, ginning, pinning, rinning, sinning, tinning, winning; innings
INLACE	–; inlaced, inlaces		
INLAID	–; –		
INLAND	–; inlands		
INLAY	–; inlays		
INLAYER	–; inlayers		
INLET	–; inlets		
INLIER	–; inliers		
INLY	–; –		
INMATE	–; inmates	**INNINGS**	ginnings, winnings; –
INMESH	–; –		
INMOST	–; –	**INNLESS**	–; –
INN	jinn, linn; inns	**INNS**	jinns, linns; –
INNARDS	–; –	**INOSITE**	–; inosites
INNATE	–; –	**INPHASE**	–; –
INNED	binned, dinned, finned, ginned, pinned, sinned, tinned, winned; –	**INPOUR**	–; inpours
		INPUT	–; inputs
		INQUEST	–; inquests
		INQUIET	–; inquiets
		INQUIRE	–; inquired, inquirer, inquires
		INQUIRY	–; –

INROAD	–; inroads	**INSTATE**	–; instated, instates
INRUSH	–; –		
INS	ains, bins, dins, fins, gins, hins, jins, kins, lins, pins, rins, sins, tins, wins, yins; –	**INSTEAD**	–; –
		INSTEP	–; insteps
		INSTIL	–; instill, instils
		INSTILL	–; instills
		INSULAR	–; insulars
		INSULIN	–; insulins
		INSULT	–; insults
INSANE	–; insaner	**INSURE**	–; insured, insurer, insures
INSCULP	–; insculps		
INSEAM	–; inseams		
INSECT	–; insects		
INSERT	–; inserts	**INSURED**	–; insureds
INSET	–; insets	**INSURER**	–; insurers
INSHORE	–; –	**INSWEPT**	–; –
INSIDE	–; insider, insides	**INTACT**	–; –
		INTAKE	–; intakes
INSIDER	–; insiders	**INTEGER**	–; integers
INSIGHT	–; insights	**INTEND**	–; intends
INSIGNE	–; –	**INTENSE**	–; intenser
INSIPID	–; –	**INTENT**	–; intents
INSIST	–; insists	**INTER**	hinter, linter, minter, sinter, tinter, winter; intern, inters
INSNARE	–; insnared, insnarer, insnares		
INSOFAR	–; –	**INTERIM**	–; interims
INSOLE	–; insoles	**INTERN**	–; interne, interns
INSOUL	–; insouls		
INSPAN	–; inspans	**INTERNE**	–; interned, internee, internes
INSPECT	–; inspects		
INSPIRE	–; inspired, inspirer, inspires		
		INTERS	hinters, linters, minters, sinters, tinters, winters; –
INSTAL	–; install, instals		
INSTALL	–; installs		
INSTANT	–; instants		
INSTAR	–; instars		

INTHRAL	—; inthrall, inthrals	invader, invadoo
INTIMA	—; intimae, intimal, intimas	
		INVADER —; invaders
		INVALID —; invalids
		INVAR —; invars
INTIME	—; —	**INVEIGH** —; inveighs
INTINE	—; intines	**INVENT** —; invents
INTITLE	—; intitled, intitles	**INVERSE** —; inverses
		INVERT —; inverts
INTO	pinto; —	**INVEST** —; invests
INTOMB	—; intombs	**INVITAL** —; —
INTONE	—; intoned, intoner, Intones	**INVITE** —; invited, invitee, inviter, invites
INTONER	—; intoners	
INTORT	—; intorts	**INVITEE** —; invitees
INTOWN	—; —	**INVITER** —; inviters
INTRANT	—; intrants	**INVOICE** —; invoiced, invoices
INTREAT	—; intreats	
INTRO	—; intros	**INVOKE** —; invoked, invoker, invokes
INTROFY	—; —	
INTROIT	—; introits	**INVOKER** —; invokers
INTRUDE	—; intruded, intruder, intrudes	**INVOLVE** —; involved, involver, involves
INTRUST	—; intrusts	**INWALL** —; inwalls
INTUIT	—; intuits	**INWARD** —; inwards
INTURN	—; inturns	**INWEAVE** —; inweaved, inweaves
INTWINE	—; intwined, intwines	
		INWIND —; inwinds
INTWIST	—; intwists	**INWOUND** —; —
INULASE	—; inulases	**INWOVE** —; inwoven
INULIN	—; inulins	**INWRAP** —; inwraps
INURE	—; inured, inures	**IODATE** —; iodated, iodates
INURN	—; inurn	**IODIC** —; —
INURNED	—; —	**IODID** —; iodide, iodids
INUTILE	—; —	
INVADE	—; invaded,	

IODIDE	–; iodides	**IRADE**	tirade; irades
IODIN	–; iodine, iodins	**IRADES**	tirades; –
IODINE	–; iodines	**IRATE**	pirate; irater
IODISM	–; iodisms	**IRATELY**	–; –
IODIZE	–; iodized, iodizer, iodizes	**IRATEST**	–; –
		IRE	dire, fire, hire, lire, mire, sire, tire, wire; ired, ires
IODIZER	–; iodizers		
IODOL	–; iodols		
IODOUS	–; –		
IOLITE	–; iolites	**IRED**	aired, fired, hired, mired, sired, tired, wired; –
ION	cion, lion, pion; ions		
IONIC	bionic, pionic; ionics		
		IREFUL	direful; –
IONICS	bionics; –	**IRELESS**	wireless; –
IONISE	lionise; ionised, ionises	**IRENIC**	eirenic; irenics
		IRES	fires, hires, mires, sires, tires, vires, wires; –
IONISED	lionised; –		
IONISES	lionises; –		
IONIUM	ioniums; –		
IONIZE	lionize; ionized, ionizer, ionizes	**IRIDES**	–; –
		IRIDIC	–; –
		IRIDIUM	–; iridiums
IONIZED	lionized; –	**IRING**	airing, firing, hiring, miring, siring, tiring, wiring; –
IONIZES	lionizes; –		
IONIZER	lionizer; ionizers		
		IRIS	–; –
IONOMER	–; ionomers	**IRISED**	–; –
IONONE	–; ionones	**IRISES**	–; –
IONS	cions, lions, pions; –	**IRISING**	–; –
		IRITIC	–; –
IOTA	biota; iotas	**IRITIS**	–; –
IOTAS	biotas; –	**IRK**	birk, dirk, kirk, mirk; irks
IPECAC	–; ipecacs		
IPOMOEA	–; ipomoeas		
IRACUND	–; –	**IRKED**	–; –

IRKING	–; –	ISOCHOR	–; isochore,
IRKS	birks, dirks,		isochors
	kirks, mirks; –	ISODOSE	–; –
IRKSOME	–; –	ISOGAMY	–; –
IRON	giron; irone,	ISOGENY	–; –
	irons, irony	ISOGON	–; isogone,
IRONE	–; ironed,		isogons,
	ironer, irones		isogony
IRONER	–; ironers	ISOGONE	–; isogones
IRONIC	–; –	ISOGRAM	–; isograms
IRONIES	–; –	ISOGRIV	–; isogrivs
IRONING	–; ironings	ISOHEL	–; isohels
IRONIST	–; ironists	ISOHYET	–; isohyets
IRONS	girons; –	ISOLATE	–; isolated,
IRREAL	–; –		isolates
IRRUPT	–; irrupts	ISOLEAD	–; isoleads
IS	ais, bis, his,	ISOLINE	–; isolines
	lis, mis, pis,	ISOLOG	–; isologs
	sis, tis, vis,	ISOMER	–; isomers
	wis, xis; ism	ISONOMY	–; –
ISAGOGE	–; isagoges	ISOPOD	–; isopods
ISATIN	–; isatine,	ISOSPIN	–; isospins
	isatins	ISOTACH	–; isotachs
ISATINE	–; isatines	ISOTONE	–; isotones
ISBA	–; isbas	ISOTOPE	–; isotopes
ISCHIA	–; ischial	ISOTOPY	–; –
ISCHIUM	–; –	ISOTYPE	–; isotypes
ISLAND	–; islands	ISOZYME	–; isozymes
ISLE	aisle, lisle;	ISSEI	–; isseis
	isled, isles,	ISSUANT	–; –
	islet	ISSUE	tissue;
ISLED	misled; –		issued,
ISLES	aisles, lisles; –		issuer, issues
ISLET	–; islets	ISSUED	tissued; –
ISLING	–; –	ISSUER	–; issuers
ISM	–; isms	ISSUES	tissues; –
ISOBAR	–; isobare,	ISTHMI	–; isthmic
	isobars	ISTHMUS	–; –
ISOBARE	–; isobares	ISTLE	–; istles
ISOBATH	–; isobaths	IT	ait, bit, dit,

	fit, git, hit, kit, lit, mit, nit, pit, sit, tit, uit, wit; its	**ITEMING**	–; –
		ITEMIZE	–; itemized, itemizer, itemizes
ITALIC	–; italics	**ITERANT**	–; –
ITCH	aitch, bitch, ditch, fitch, hitch, pitch, witch; itchy	**ITERATE**	–; iterated, iterates
		ITERUM	–; –
ITCHED	bitched, ditched, hitched, pitched, witched; –	**ITHER**	cither, dither, either, hither, lither, mither, tither, wither, zither; –
ITCHES	aitches, bitches, ditches, fitches, hitches, pitches, witches; –	**ITS**	aits, bits, dits, fits, gits, hits, kits, lits, nits, pits, sits, tits, wits; –
		ITSELF	–; –
		IVIED	–; –
ITCHIER	–; –	**IVIES**	civies; –
ITCHING	bitching, ditching, hitching, pitching, witching; itchings	**IVORIES**	–; –
		IVORY	–; –
		IVY	tivy; –
		IVYLIKE	–; –
		IWIS	kiwis; –
		IXIA	–; ixias
ITCHY	bitchy, fitchy, pitchy, witchy; –	**IXODID**	–; ixodids
		IXTLE	–; ixtles
		IZAR	sizar; izars
ITEM	–; items	**IZARS**	sizars; –
ITEMED	–; –	**IZZARD**	gizzard, lizzard; izzards

J

J	–; jo	**JABBED**	–; –
JAB	–; jabs	**JABBER**	–; jabbers

JABBING	-; -	JAGGIER	-; -
JABIRU	-; jabirus	JAGGING	-; -
JABOT	-; jabots	JAGLESS	-; -
JACAL	-; jacals	JAGRA	-; jagras
JACALES	-; -	JAGUAR	-; jaguars
JACAMAR	-; jacamars	JAIL	-; jails
JACANA	-; jacanas	JAILED	-; -
JACINTH	-; jacinthe, jacinths	JAILER	-; jailers
		JAILING	-; -
JACK	-; jacks, jacky	JAILOR	-; jailors
		JAKE	-; jakes
JACKAL	-; jackals	JALAP	-; jalaps
JACKASS	-; -	JALAPIC	-; -
JACKDAW	-; jackdaws	JALAPIN	-; jalapins
JACKED	-; -	JALOP	-; jalops, jalopy
JACKER	-; jackers		
JACKET	-; jackets	JALOPPY	-; -
JACKIES	-; -	JAM	-; jamb, jams
JACKING	-; -		
JACKLEG	-; jacklegs	JAMB	-; jambe, jambs
JACKPOT	-; jackpots		
JACOBIN	-; jacobins	JAMBE	-; jambed, jambes
JACOBUS	-; -		
JACONET	-; jaconets	JAMBEAU	-; jambeaux
JADE	-; jaded, jades	JAMBING	-; -
		JAMMED	-; -
JADEDLY	-; -	JAMMER	-; jammers
JADEITE	-; jadeites	JAMMING	-; -
JADING	-; -	JANE	-; janes
JADISH	-; -	JANGLE	-; jangled, jangler, jangles
JADITIC	-; -		
JAEGER	-; jaegers		
JAG	-; jagg; jags	JANGLER	-; janglers
JAGER	-; jagers	JANITOR	-; janitors
JAGG	-; jaggs, jaggy	JANTY	-; -
		JAPAN	-; japans
JAGGARY	-; -	JAPE	-; japed, japer, japes
JAGGED	-; -		
JAGGER	-; jaggers, jaggery	JAPER	-; japers, japery

JAPING	–; –	**JAWING**	–; –
JAR	ajar; jarl, jars	**JAWLIKE**	–; –
		JAWLINE	–; jawlines
JARFUL	–; jarfuls	**JAY**	–; jays
JARGON	–; jargons	**JAYBIRD**	–; jaybirds
JARGOON	–; jargoons	**JAYGEE**	–; jaygees
JARINA	–; jarinas	**JAYVEE**	–; jayvees
JARL	–; jarls	**JAYWALK**	–; jaywalks
JARLDOM	–; jarldoms	**JAZZ**	–; jazzy
JARRAH	–; jarrahs	**JAZZED**	–; –
JARRED	–; –	**JAZZER**	–; jazzers
JARRING	–; –	**JAZZES**	–; –
JARSFUL	–; –	**JAZZIER**	–; –
JARVEY	–; jarveys	**JAZZILY**	–; –
JASMINE	–; jasmines	**JAZZING**	–; –
JASPER	–; jaspers, jaspery	**JAZZMAN**	–; –
		JAZZMEN	–; –
JASSID	–; jassids	**JEALOUS**	–; jealousy
JATO	–; jatos	**JEAN**	–; jeans
JAUK	–; jauks	**JEBEL**	djebels; jebels
JAUKED	–; –		
JAUKING	–; –	**JEBELS**	djebels; –
JAUNCE	–; jaunced, jaunces	**JEE**	ajee; jeed, jeep, jeer, jees, jeez
JAUNT	–; jaunts, jaunty		
		JEEING	–; –
JAUNTED	–; –	**JEEP**	–; jeeps
JAUP	–; jaups	**JEER**	–; jeers
JAUPED	–; –	**JEERED**	–; –
JAUPING	–; –	**JEERER**	–; jeerers
JAVA	–; javas	**JEERING**	–; –
JAVELIN	–; javelina, javelins	**JEEZ**	–; –
		JEFE	–; jefes
JAW	–; jaws	**JEHAD**	–; jehads
JAWAN	–; jawans	**JEHU**	–; jehus
JAWBONE	–; jawboned, jawbones	**JEJUNA**	–; jejunal
		JEJUNE	–; –
		JELL	–; jells, jelly
JAWED	–; –	**JELLED**	–; –

JELLIED	–; –	JESTING	–; jestings
JELLIES	–; –	JESUIT	–; jesuits
JELLIFY	–; –	JET	–; jete, jets
JELLING	–; –	JETBEAD	–; jetbeads
JEMADAR	–; jemadars	JETE	–; jetes
JEMIDAR	–; jemidars	JETON	–; jetons
JEMMIED	–; –	JETPORT	–; jetports
JEMMIES	–; –	JETSAM	–; jetsams
JEMMY	–; –	JETSOM	–; jetsoms
JENNET	–; jennets	JETTED	–; –
JENNIES	–; –	JETTIED	–; –
JENNY	–; –	JETTIES	–; –
JEOPARD	–; jeopards, jeopardy	JETTING	–; –
		JETTON	–; jettons
JERBOA	–; jerboas	JETTY	–; –
JEREED	–; jereeds	JEU	–; jeux
JERID	–; jerids	JEW	–; jews
JERK	–; jerks, jerky	JEWED	–; –
		JEWEL	–; jewels
JERKED	–; –	JEWELED	–; –
JERKER	–; jerkers	JEWELER	–; jewelers, jewelry
JERKIER	–; –		
JERKIES	–; jerkiest	JEWING	–; –
JERKILY	–; –	JEWFISH	–; –
JERKIN	–; jerking, jerkins	JEZAIL	–; jezails
		JEZEBEL	–; jezebels
JERREED	–; jerreeds	JIB	; jibb, jibc, jibs
JERRID	–; jerrids		
JERRIES	–; –	JIBB	–; jibbs
JERSEY	–; jerseys	JIBBED	–; –
JERRY	–; –	JIBBER	–; jibbers
JESS	–; jesse	JIBBING	–; –
JESSE	–; jessed, jesses	JIBBOOM	–; jibbooms
		JIBE	–; jibed, jiber, jibes
JESSING	–; –		
JEST	–; jests	JIBER	–; jibers
JESTED	–; –	JIBING	–; –
JESTER	–; jesters	JIFF	–; jiffs, jiffy
JESTFUL	–; –	JIFFIES	–; –

JIG	–; jigs	**JINK**	–; jinks
JIGABOO	–; jigaboos	**JINKED**	–; –
JIGGED	–; –	**JINKER**	–; jinkers
JIGGER	–; jiggers	**JINKING**	–; –
JIGGING	–; –	**JINN**	djinn; jinni, jinns
JIGGLE	–; jiggled, jiggles	**JINNEE**	–; –
JIGGLY	–; –	**JINNI**	djinni; –
JIGSAW	–; jigsawn, jigsaws	**JINNS**	djinns; –
		JINS	djins; –
JIHAD	–; jihads	**JINX**	–; –
JILL	–; jills	**JINXED**	–; –
JILLION	–; jillions	**JINXES**	–; –
JILT	–; jilts	**JINXING**	–; –
JILTED	–; –	**JITNEY**	–; jitneys
JILTER	–; jilters	**JITTER**	–; jitters, jittery
JILTING	–; –		
JIMINY	–; –	**JIVE**	–; jived, jives
JIMJAMS	–; –	**JIVING**	–; –
JIMMIED	–; –	**JNANA**	–; jnanas
JIMMIES	–; –	**JO**	–; job, joe, jog, jot, jow, joy
JIMMINY	–; –		
JIMMY	–; –		
JIMP	–; jimpy	**JOANNES**	–; –
JIMPER	–; –	**JOB**	–; jobs
JIMPEST	–; –	**JOBBED**	–; –
JIMPLY	–; –	**JOBBER**	–; jobbers, jobbery
JIN	djin; jink, jinn, jins, jinx	**JOBBING**	–; –
		JOBLESS	–; –
JINGAL	–; jingall, jingals	**JOCK**	–; jocko, jocks
JINGALL	–; jingalls		
JINGKO	–; –	**JOCKEY**	–; jockeys
JINGLE	–; jingled, jingler, jingles	**JOCKO**	–; jockos
		JOCOSE	–; –
		JOCULAR	–; –
JINGLER	–; jinglers	**JOCUND**	–; –
JINGLY	–; –	**JODHPUR**	–; jodhpurs
JINGO	–; –	**JOE**	–; joel, joes, joey
JINGOES	–; –		

JOEY	–; joeys	JOLTILY	–; –
JOG	ajog; jogs	JOLTING	–; –
JOGGED	–; –	JONQUIL	–; jonquils
JOGGER	–; joggers	JORAM	–; jorams
JOGGING	–; –	JORDAN	–; jordans
JOGGLE	–; joggled, joggler, joggles	JORUM	–; jorums
		JOSEPH	–; josephs
JOGGLER	–; jogglers	JOSH	–; –
JOHN	–; johns	JOSHED	–; –
JOHNNY	–; –	JOSHER	–; joshers
JOIN	–; joins, joint	JOSHES	–; –
JOINDER	–; joinders	JOSHING	–; –
JOINED	–; –	JOSS	–; –
JOINER	–; joiners, joinery	JOSSES	–; –
		JOSTLE	–; jostled, jostler, jostles
JOINING	–; joinings		
JOINT	–; joints	JOSTLER	–; jostlers
JOINTED	–; –	JOT	–; jota, jots
JOINTER	–; jointers	JOTA	–; jotas
JOINTLY	–; –	JOTTED	–; –
JOIST	–; joists	JOTTING	–; jottings
JOISTED	–; –	JOTTY	–; –
JOJOBA	–; jojobas	JOUK	–; jouks
JOKE	–; joked, joker, jokes	JOUKED	–; –
		JOUKING	–; –
JOKER	–; jokers	JOULE	–; joules
JOKING	–; –	JOUNCE	–; jounced, jounces
JOLE	–; joles		
JOLLIED	–; –	JOUNCY	–; –
JOLLIER	–; –	JOURNAL	–; journals
JOLLIES	–; jolliest	JOURNEY	–; journeys
JOLLIFY	–; –	JOUST	–; jousts
JOLLILY	–; –	JOUSTED	–; –
JOLLITY	–; –	JOUSTER	–; jousters
JOLLY	–; –	JOVIAL	–; –
JOLT	–; jolts, jolty	JOW	–; jowl, jows
JOLTED	–; –	JOWED	–; –
JOLTER	–; jolters	JOWING	–; –
JOLTIER	–; –	JOWL	jowls, jowly

JOWLED	–; –	JUGGLER	–; jugglers, jugglery
JOWLIER	–; –		
JOY	–; joys	JUGHEAD	–; jugheads
JOYANCE	–; joyances	JUGSFUL	–; –
JOYED	–; –	JUGULA	–; jugular
JOYFUL	–; –	JUGULAR	–; jugulars
JOYLESS	–; –	JUGULUM	–; –
JOYOUS	–; –	JUGUM	–; jugums
JOYING	–; –	JUICE	–; juiced, juicer, juices
JOYPOP	–; joypops		
JOYRIDE	–; joyrider, joyrides	JUICER	–; juicers
		JUICIER	–; –
JUBA	–; jubas	JUICILY	–; –
JUBBAH	–; jubbahs	JUICING	–; –
JUBE	–; jubes	JUICY	–; –
JUBHAH	–; jubhahs	JUJITSU	–; jujitsus
JUBILE	–; jubilee, jubiles	JUJU	–; jujus
		JUJUBE	–; jujubes
JUBILEE	–; jubilees	JUJUISM	–; jujuisms
JUDAS	–; –	JUJUIST	–; jujuists
JUDASES	–; –	JUJUTSU	–; jujutsus
JUDDER	–; judders	JUKE	–; juked, jukes
JUDGE	–; judged, judger, judges		
		JUKING	–; –
		JUKEBOX	–; –
JUDGER	–; judgers	JULEP	–; juleps
JUDGING	–; –	JUMBLE	–; jumbled, jumbler, jumbles
JUDO	–; judos		
JUDOIST	–; judoists		
JUDOKA	–; judokas	JUMBLER	–; jumblers
JUG	–; juga, jugs	JUMBO	–; jumbos
JUGA	–; jugal	JUMBUCK	–; jumbucks
JUGATE	–; –	JUMP	–; jumps, jumpy
JUGFUL	–; jugfuls		
JUGGED	–; –	JUMPED	–; –
JUGGING	–; –	JUMPER	–; jumpers
JUGGLE	–; juggled, juggler, juggles	JUMPIER	–; –
		JUMPILY	–; –
		JUMPING	–; –
		JUMPOFF	–; jumpoffs

JUN	−; junk	JURIDIC	−; −
JUNCO	−; juncos	JURIES	−; −
JUNCOES	−; −	JURIST	−; jurists
JUNGLE	−; jungles	JUROR	−; jurors
JUNGLY	−; −	JURY	−; −
JUNIOR	−; juniors	JURYMAN	−; −
JUNIPER	−; junipers	JURYMEN	−; −
JUNK	−; junks, junky	JUS	−; just
		JUSSIVE	−; jussives
JUNKED	−; −	JUST	−; justs
JUNKER	−; junkers	JUSTED	−; −
JUNKING	−; −	JUSTER	−; justers
JUNKET	−; junkets	JUSTEST	−; −
JUNKIE	−; junkier, junkies	JUSTICE	−; justices
		JUSTIFY	−; −
JUNKIES	−; junkiest	JUSTLE	−; justled, justles
JUNKMAN	−; −		
JUNKMEN	−; −	JUSTLY	−; −
JUNTA	−; juntas	JUT	−; jute, juts
JUNTO	−; juntos	JUTE	−; jutes
JUPE	−; jupes	JUTTED	−; −
JUPON	−; jupons	JUTTIED	−; −
JURA	−; jural, jurat	JUTTIES	−; −
JURALLY	−; −	JUTTING	−; −
JURANT	−; jurants	JUTTY	−; −
JURAT	−; jurats	JUVENAL	−; juvenals
JUREL	−; jurels		

K

K	−; ka	KABAR	−; kabars
KA	oka; kab, kae, kas, kat, kay	KABAYA	−; kabayas
		KABBALA	−; kabbalah, kabbalas
KAAS	−; −	KABIKI	−; kabikis
KAB	−; kabs	KABOB	−; kabobs
KABAB	−; kababs	KABUKI	−; kabukis
KABAKA	−; kabakas	KACHINA	−; kachinas
KABALA	−; kabalas	KADDISH	−; −

KADI	–; kadis	KANE	–; kanes
KAE	–; kaes	KANJI	–; kanjis
KAFFIR	–; kaffirs	KANTAR	–; kantars
KAFIR	–; kafirs	KANTELE	–; kanteles
KAFTAN	–; kaftans	KAOLIN	–; kaoline,
KAGU	–; kagus		kaolins
KAHUNA	–; kahunas	KAOLINE	–; kaolines
KAIAK	–; kaiaks	KAON	–; kaons
KAIF	–; kaifs	KAPA	–; kapas
KAIL	–; kails	KAPH	–; kaphs
KAIN	–; kains	KAPOK	–; kapoks
KAINIT	–; kainite,	KAPPA	–; kappas
	kainits	KAPUT	–; kaputt
KAINITE	–; kainites	KARAKUL	–; karakuls
KAISER	–; kaisers	KARAT	–; karate,
KAJEPUT	–; kajeputs		karats
KAKA	–; kakas	KARATE	–; karates
KAKAPO	–; kakapos	KARMA	–; karmas
KAKI	–; kakis	KARMIC	–; –
KALAM	–; kalams	KARN	–; karns
KALE	–; kales	KAROO	–; karoos
KALENDS	–; –	KAROSS	–; –
KALIAN	–; kalians	KARROO	–; karroos
KALIF	–; kalifs	KARST	–; karsts
KALIMBA	–; kalimbas	KARSTIC	–; –
KALIPH	–; kaliphs	KART	–; karts
KALIUM	–; kaliums	KARTING	–; kartings
KALMIA	–; kalmias	KAS	okas; –
KALONG	–; kalongs	KASHA	–; kashas
KALPA	–; kalpak,	KASHER	–; kashers
	kalpas	KASHMIR	–; kashmirs
KALPAK	–; kalpaks	KASHRUT	–; kashruth,
KAMALA	–; kamalas		kashruts
KAME	–; kames	KAT	skat; kats
KAMI	–; kamik	KATHODE	–; kathodes
KAMIK	–; kamiks	KATION	–; kations
KAMPONG	–; kampongs	KATS	skats; –
KAMSEEN	–; kamseens	KATYDID	–; katydids
KAMSIN	–; kamsins	KAURI	–; kauris
KANA	–; kanas	KAURIES	–; –

KAURY	–; –	KEENED	–; –
KAVA	–; kavas	KEENER	–; keeners
KAVAS	–; kavass	KEENEST	–; –
KAY	okay; kays	KEENING	–; –
KAYAK	–; kayaks	KEENLY	–; –
KAYAKER	–; kayakers	KEENS	skeens; –
KAYLES	–; –	KEEP	–; keeps
KAYO	–; kayos	KEEPER	–; keepers
KAYOED	–; –	KEEPING	–; keepings
KAYOES	–; –	KEESTER	–; keesters
KAYOING	–; –	KEET	skeet; keets
KAYS	okays; –	KEETS	skeets; –
KAZOO	–; kazoos	KEEVE	–; keeves
KEA	–; keas	KEF	–; kefs
KEBAB	–; kebabs	KEFIR	–; kefirs
KEBAR	–; kebars	KEG	skeg; kegs
KEBBIE	–; kebbies	KEGELER	–; kegelers
KEBBOCK	–; kebbocks	KEGLER	–; keglers
KEBBUCK	–; kebbucks	KEGLING	–; keglings
KEBLAH	–; keblahs	KEGS	skegs; –
KEBOB	–; kebobs	KEIR	–; keirs
KECK	–; kecks	KEISTER	–; keisters
KECKED	–; –	KEITLOA	–; keitloas
KECKING	–; –	KELOID	–; keloids
KECKLE	–; keckled, keckles	KELP	skelp; kelps, kelpy
KEDDAH	–; keddahs	KELPED	skelped; –
KEDGE	–; kedged, kedges	KELPIE	–; kelpies
		KELPING	skelping; –
KEDGING	–; –	KELPS	skelps; –
KEEF	–; keefs	KELSON	–; kelsons
KEEK	–; keeks	KELTER	skelter; kelters
KEEKED	–; –		
KEEKING	–; –	KELTERS	skelters; –
KEEL	–; keels	KELVIN	–; kelvins
KEELAGE	–; keelages	KEMP	–; kemps, kempt
KEELED	–; –		
KEELING	–; –	KEN	–; keno, kens, kent
KEELSON	–; keelsons		
KEEN	skeen; keens	KENAF	–; kenafs

KENCH	–; –	**KERSEY**	–; kerseys
KENCHES	–; –	**KERYGMA**	–; –
KENDO	–; kendos	**KESTREL**	–; kestrels
KENELED	–; –	**KETCH**	sketch; –
KENNED	–; –	**KETCHES**	sketches; –
KENNEL	–; kennels	**KETCHUP**	–; ketchups
KENNING	–; kennings	**KETENE**	–; ketenes
KENO	–; kenos	**KETO**	–; –
KENOSIS	–; –	**KETONE**	–; ketones
KENOTIC	–; –	**KETONIC**	–; –
KEP	skep; kepi,	**KETOSE**	–; ketoses
	keps, kept	**KETOSIS**	–; –
KEPI	–; kepis	**KETOTIC**	–; –
KEPPED	–; –	**KETTLE**	–; kettles
KEPPEN	–; –	**KEVEL**	–; kevels
KEPPING	–; –	**KEVIL**	–; kevils
KEPS	skeps; –	**KEX**	–; –
KERAMIC	–; keramics	**KEXES**	–; –
KERATIN	–; keratins	**KEY**	–; keys
KERB	–; kerbs	**KEYED**	–; –
KERBED	–; –	**KEYHOLE**	–; keyholes
KERBING	–; –	**KEYING**	–; –
KERCHOO	–; –	**KEYLESS**	–; –
KERF	–; kerfs	**KEYNOTE**	–; keynoted,
KERFED	–; –		keynoter,
KERFING	–; –		keynotes
KERMES	–; kermess	**KEYSET**	–; keysets
KERMIS	–; –	**KEYSTER**	–; keysters
KERN	–; kerne,	**KEYWAY**	–; keyways
	kerns	**KEYWORD**	–; keywords
KERNE	–; kerned,	**KHADDAR**	–; khaddars
	kernel,	**KHADI**	–; khadis
	kernes	**KHAKI**	–; khakis
KERNEL	–; kernels	**KHALIF**	–; khalifa,
KERNING	–; –		khalifs
KERNITE	–; kernites	**KHALIFA**	–; khalifas
KEROGEN	–; kerogens	**KHAMSIN**	–; khamsins
KERRIA	–; kerrias	**KHAN**	–; khans
KERRIES	skerries; –	**KHANATE**	–; khanates
KERRY	skerry; –	**KHAT**	–; khats

KHAZEN	–; khazens	KIDSKIN	–; kidskins
KHEDA	–; khedah, khedas	KIEF	–; kiefs
		KIER	skier; kiers
KHEDAH	–; khedahs	KIERS	skiers; –
KHEDIVE	–; khedives	KIESTER	–; kiesters
KHI	–; khis	KIF	–; kifs
KHIRKAH	–; khirkahs	KIKE	–; kikes
KIANG	–; kiangs	KILIM	–; kilims
KIAUGH	–; kiaughs	KILL	skill; kills
KIBBLE	–; kibbled, kibbles	KILLDEE	–; killdeer, killdees
KIBBUTZ	–; –	KILLED	skilled; –
KIBE	–; kibes	KILLER	–; killers
KIBITZ	–; –	KILLICK	–; killicks
KIBLA	–; kiblah, kiblas	KILLING	–; killings
		KILLJOY	–; killjoys
KIBLAH	–; kiblahs	KILLOCK	–; killocks
KIBOSH	–; –	KILLS	skills; –
KICK	–; kicks	KILN	–; kilns
KICKED	–; –	KILNED	–; –
KICKER	–; kickers	KILNING	–; –
KICKING	–; –	KILO	–; kilos
KICKOFF	–; kickoffs	KILOBAR	–; kilobars
KICKUP	–; kickups	KILOBIT	–; kilobits
KID	skid; kids	KILORAD	–; kilorads
KIDDED	skidded; –	KILOTON	–; kilotons
KIDDER	skidder; kidders	KILT	–; kilts, kilty
		KILTED	–; –
KIDDERS	skidders; –	KILTER	–; kilters
KIDDIE	–; kiddies	KILTIE	–; kilties
KIDDING	skidding; –	KILTING	–; kiltings
KIDDISH	–; –	KIMONO	–; kimonos
KIDDO	–; kiddos	KIN	akin, skin;
KIDDOES	–; –		kind, kine,
KIDDUSH	–; –		king, kink,
KIDDY	skiddy; –		kino, kins
KIDLIKE	–; –	KINASE	–; kinases
KIDNAP	–; kidnaps	KIND	–; kinds
KIDNEY	–; kidneys	KINDER	–; –
KIDS	skids; –	KINDEST	–; –

KINDLE	–; kindled, kindler, kindles	**KIPPERS**	skippers; –
		KIPPING	skipping; –
		KIPS	skips; –
KINDLER	–; kindlers	**KIPSKIN**	–; kipskins
KINDLY	–; –	**KIRK**	–; kirks
KINDRED	–; kindreds	**KIRKMAN**	–; –
KINE	–; kines	**KIRKMEN**	–; –
KINEMA	–; kinemas	**KIRMESS**	–; –
KINESES	–; –	**KIRN**	–; kirns
KINESIS	–; –	**KIRNED**	–; –
KINETIC	–; kinetics	**KIRNING**	–; –
KINETIN	–; kinetins	**KIRSCH**	–; –
KINFOLK	–; kinfolks	**KIRTLE**	–; kirtled, kirtles
KING	eking; kings		
KINGCUP	–; kingcups	**KISHKA**	–; kishkas
KINGDOM	–; kingdoms	**KISHKE**	–; kishkes
KINGED	–; –	**KISMAT**	–; kismats
KINGING	–; –	**KISMET**	–; kismets
KINGLET	–; kinglets	**KISS**	–; –
KINGLY	–; –	**KISSED**	–; –
KINGPIN	–; kingpins	**KISSER**	–; kissers
KININ	–; kinins	**KISSES**	–; –
KINK	skink; kinks, kinky	**KISSING**	–; –
		KIST	–; kists
KINKED	skinked; –	**KISTFUL**	–; kistfuls
KINKIER	–; –	**KIT**	skit; kite, kith, kits
KINKILY	–; –		
KINKING	skinking; –	**KITCHEN**	–; kitchens
KINKS	skinks; –	**KITE**	skite; kited, kiter, kites
KINO	–; kinos		
KINS	skins; –	**KITED**	skited; –
KINSHIP	–; kinships	**KITER**	–; kiters
KINSMAN	–; –	**KITES**	skites; –
KINSMEN	–; –	**KITH**	–; kithe, kiths
KIOSK	–; kiosks		
KIP	skip; kips	**KITHARA**	–; kitharas
KIPPED	skipped; –	**KITHE**	–; kithed, kithes
KIPPEN	–; –		
KIPPER	skipper; kippers	**KITHING**	–; –
		KITING	skiting; –

KITLING	–; kitlings	**KNAWEL**	–; knawels
KITSCH	–; kitschy	**KNEAD**	–; kneads
KITS	skits; –	**KNEADED**	–; –
KITTED	–; –	**KNEADER**	–; kneaders
KITTEL	–; –	**KNEE**	–; kneed,
KITTEN	–; kittens		kneel, knees
KITTIES	–; –	**KNEECAP**	–; kneecaps
KITTING	–; –	**KNEEING**	–; –
KITTLE	skittle;	**KNEEL**	–; kneels
	kittled,	**KNEELED**	–; –
	kittler, kittles	**KNEELER**	–; kneelers
KITTLES	skittles;	**KNEEPAD**	–; kneepads
	kittlest	**KNEEPAN**	–; kneepans
KITTY	–; –	**KNELL**	–; knells
KIVA	–; kivas	**KNELLED**	–; –
KIWI	–; kiwis	**KNELT**	–; –
KLATCH	–; –	**KNEW**	–; –
KLATSCH	–; –	**KNIFE**	–; knifed,
KLAVERN	–; klaverns		knifer, knifes
KLAXON	–; klaxons	**KNIFER**	–; knifers
KLEAGLE	–; kleagles	**KNIFING**	–; –
KLEPHT	–; klephts	**KNIGHT**	–; knights
KLONG	–; klongs	**KNISH**	–; –
KLOOF	–; kloofs	**KNISHES**	–; –
KLUDGE	–; kludges	**KNIT**	–; knits
KLUTZ	–; klutzy	**KNITTED**	–; –
KLUTZES	–; –	**KNITTER**	–; knitters
KNACK	–; knacks	**KNIVES**	–; –
KNACKED	–; –	**KNOB**	–; knobs
KNACKER	–; knackers,	**KNOBBED**	–; –
	knackery	**KNOBBY**	–; –
KNAP	–; knaps	**KNOCK**	–; knocks
KNAPPED	–; –	**KNOCKED**	–; –
KNAPPER	–; knappers	**KNOCKER**	–; knockers
KNAR	–; knars	**KNOLL**	–; knolls,
KNARRED	–; –		knolly
KNARRY	–; –	**KNOLLED**	–; –
KNAVE	–; knaves	**KNOLLER**	–; knollers
KNAVISH	–; –	**KNOP**	–; knops
KNAVERY	–; –	**KNOPPED**	–; –

KNOSP	–; knosps	**KOOK**	–; kooks, kooky
KNOT	–; knots		
KNOTTED	–; –	**KOOKIE**	–; kookier
KNOTTER	–; knotters	**KOP**	–; koph, kops
KNOTTY	–; –		
KNOUT	–; knouts	**KOPECK**	–; kopecks
KNOUTED	–; –	**KOPEK**	–; kopeks
KNOW	–; known, knows	**KOPH**	–; kophs
		KOPJE	–; kopjes
KNOWER	–; knowers	**KOPPA**	–; koppas
KNOWING	–; knowings	**KOPPIE**	–; koppies
KNOWN	–; knowns	**KOR**	–; kors
KNUCKLE	–; knuckled, knuckler, knuckles	**KORUN**	–; koruna, koruny
KNUCKLY	–; –	**KORUNA**	–; korunas
KNUR	–; knurl, knurs	**KOS**	–; koss
		KOSHER	–; koshers
KNURL	–; knurls, knurly	**KOTO**	–; kotos, kotow
KNURLED	–; –	**KOTOW**	–; kotows
KOA	–; koan, koas	**KOTOWED**	–; –
		KOTOWER	–; kotowers
KOALA	–; koalas	**KOUMIS**	–; koumiss
KOAN	–; koans	**KOUMYS**	–; koumyss
KOBOLD	–; kobolds	**KOUSSO**	–; koussos
KOEL	–; koels	**KOWTOW**	–; kowtows
KOHL	–; kohls	**KRAAL**	–; kraals
KOINE	–; koines	**KRAALED**	–; –
KOKANEE	–; kokanees	**KRAFT**	–; krafts
KOLA	–; kolas	**KRAIT**	–; kraits
KOLACKY	–; –	**KRAKEN**	–; krakens
KOLHOZ	–; kolhozy	**KRATER**	–; kraters
KOLKHOS	–; kolkhosy	**KRAUT**	–; krauts
KOLKHOZ	–; kolkhozy	**KREMLIN**	–; kremlins
KOLKOZ	–; kolkozy	**KREUZER**	–; kreuzers
KOLO	–; kolos	**KRILL**	–; krills
KOMATIK	–; komatiks	**KRIMMER**	–; krimmers
KOODOO	–; koodoos	**KRIS**	–;
		KRISES	–; –
		KRONA	–; –

KRONE	–; kronen, kronur	KURGAN	–; kurgans
KRONOR	–; –	KURTA	–; kurtas
KRONUR	–; –	KURU	–; kurus
KROON	–; krooni, kroons	KUSSO	–; kussos
		KVAS	–; kvass
KRUBI	–; krubis	KVASES	–; –
KRUBUT	–; krubuts	KVASSES	–; –
KRULLER	–; krullers	KVETCH	–; –
KRYPTON	–; kryptons	KWACHA	–; –
KUCHEN	–; –	KYACK	–; kyacks
KUDO	–; kudos	KYANISE	–; kyanised, kyanises
KUDU	–; kudus		
KUDZU	–; kudzus	KYANITE	–; kyanites
KUE	–; kues	KYANIZE	–; kyanized, kyanizes
KULAK	–; kulaki, kulaks		
		KYAR	–; kyars
KULTUR	–; kulturs	KYAT	–; kyats
KUMISS	–; –	KYLIKES	–; –
KUMMEL	–; kummels	KYLIX	–; –
KUMQUAT	–; kumquats	KYRIE	–; kyries
KUMYS	–; –	KYTE	–; kytes
KUMYSES	–; –	KYTHE	–; kythed, kythes
KUNZITE	–; kunzites		
KURBASH	–; –	KYTHING	–; –

L

L	el; la, li, lo	LABEL	–; labels
LA	ala; lab, lac, lad, lag, lam, lap, lar, las, lat, law, lax, lay	LABELED	–; –
		LABELER	–; labelers
		LABELLA	glabella; –
		LABIA	–; labial
		LABIAL	–; labials
LAAGER	–; laagers	LABIATE	–; labiated, labiates
LAB	blab, flab, slab; labs		
		LABILE	–; –
LABARA	–; –	LABIUM	–; –
LABARUM	–; labarums	LABOR	–; labors

LABORED	–; –	**LACKERS**	clackers,
LABORER	–; laborers		slackers; –
LABOUR	–; labours	**LACKEY**	–; lackeys
LABRA	–; –	**LACKING**	blacking,
LABRET	–; labrets		clacking; –
LABROID	–; labroids	**LACONIC**	–; –
LABRUM	–; labrums	**LACKS**	blacks,
LABS	blabs, flabs,		clacks,
	slabs; –		flacks,
LAC	–; lace,		placks,
	lack, lacs,		slacks; –
	lacy	**LACQUER**	–; lacquers
LACE	glace, place;	**LACQUEY**	–; lacqueys
	laced, lacer,	**LACTAM**	–; lactams
	laces, lacey	**LACTARY**	–; –
LACED	glaced,	**LACTASE**	–; lactases
	placed; –	**LACTATE**	–; lactated,
LACER	placer;		lactates
	lacers	**LACTEAL**	–; lacteals
LACERS	placers; –	**LACTEAN**	–; –
LACES	glaces,	**LACTIC**	–; –
	places; –	**LACTONE**	–; lactones
LACEY	–; –	**LACTOSE**	–; lactoses
LACHES	–; –	**LACUNA**	–; lacunae,
LACIER	glacier; –		lacunal,
LACIEST	–; –		lacunar,
LACILY	–; –		lacunas
LACING	placing;	**LACUNAR**	–; lacunars,
	lacings		lacunary
LACK	alack, black,	**LACUNE**	–; lacunes
	clack, flack,	**LACY**	–; –
	plack, slack;	**LAD**	clad, glad;
	lacks		lade, lads,
LACKED	blacked,		lady
	clacked,	**LADANUM**	–; ladanums
	slacked; –	**LADDER**	bladder,
LACKER	blacker,		gladder;
	clacker,		ladders
	slacker;	**LADDERS**	bladders; –
	lackers	**LADDIE**	–; laddies

LADE	blade, glade, laded, laden, lader, lades	**LAGGING**	clagging, flagging, slagging; laggings
LADEN	–; ladens	**LAGOON**	–; lagoons
LADENED	–; –	**LAGS**	clags, flags, slags; –
LADER	–; laders		
LADES	blades, glades; –	**LAGUNA**	–; lagunas
		LAGUNE	–; lagunes
LADIES	–; –	**LAIC**	–; laich, laics
LADING	–; ladings	**LAICAL**	–; –
LADINO	–; ladinos	**LAICH**	–; laichs
LADLE	–; ladled, ladler, ladles	**LAICISE**	–; laicised, laicises
LADLER	–; ladlers	**LAICISM**	–; laicisms
LADLING	–; –	**LAICIZE**	–; laicized, laicizes
LADRON	–; ladrone, ladrons		
		LAID	plaid; –
LADRONE	–; ladrones	**LAIGH**	–; laighs
LADS	clads, glads; –	**LAIN**	blain, elain, plain, slain; –
LADY	glady; –		
LADYBUG	–; ladybugs	**LAIR**	flair, gluir; laird, lairs
LADYISH	–; –		
LADYKIN	–; ladykins	**LAIRD**	–; lairds
LAEVO	–; –	**LAIRDLY**	–; –
LAG	clag, flag, slag; lags	**LAIRED**	glaired; –
		LAIRING	glairing; –
LAGAN	–; lagans	**LAIRS**	flairs, glairs; –
LAGEND	–; lagends		
LAGER	–; lagers	**LAITH**	–; –
LAGERED	–; –	**LAITHLY**	–; –
LAGGARD	–; laggards	**LAITIES**	–; –
LAGGED	clagged, flagged, slagged; –	**LAITY**	–; –
		LAKE	flake, slake; laked, laker, lakes
LAGGER	flagger; laggers		
LAGGERS	flaggers; –	**LAKED**	flaked, slaked; –

LAKER	flaker,		flame;
	slaker; lakers		lamed,
LAKERS	flakers,		lamer, lames
	slakers; –	**LAMED**	blamed,
LAKES	flakes,		flamed;
	slakes; –		lamedh,
LAKH	–; lakhs		lameds
LAKIER	flakier; –	**LAMEDH**	–; lamedhs
LAKIEST	flakiest; –	**LAMELLA**	–; lamellae,
LAKING	flaking,		lamellar,
	slaking;		lamellas
	lakings	**LAMELY**	–; –
LAKY	flaky; –	**LAMENT**	–; laments
LALL	–; lalls	**LAMER**	blamer,
LALLAN	–; lalland,		flamer; –
	lallans	**LAMES**	blames,
LALLAND	–; lallands		flames;
LALLED	–; –		lamest
LALLING	–; –	**LAMIA**	–; lamiae,
LAM	clam, flam,		lamias
	slam; lama,	**LAMINA**	–; laminae,
	lamb, lame,		laminal,
	lamp, lams		laminar,
LAMA	ulamas; lamas		laminas
LAMAS	ulamas; –	**LAMINAR**	–; laminary
LAMB	–; lambs	**LAMING**	blaming,
LAMBAST	–; lambaste,		flaming; –
	lambasts	**LAMMED**	clammed,
LAMBDA	–; lambdas		flammed,
LAMBED	–; –		slammed; –
LAMBENT	–; –	**LAMMING**	clamming,
LAMBER	clamber;		flamming,
	lambers,		slamming; –
	lambert	**LAMP**	clamp; lamps
LAMBERS	clambers; –	**LAMPAD**	–; lampads
LAMBERT	–; lamberts	**LAMPAS**	–; –
LAMBIE	–; lambies	**LAMPED**	clamped; –
LAMBING	–; –	**LAMPER**	clamper;
LAMBKIN	–; lambkins		lampers
LAME	blame,	**LAMPERS**	clampers; –

LAMPING	clamping; –	**LANE**	alane,
LAMPION	–; lampions		plane; lanes
LAMPOON	–; lampoons	**LANELY**	–; –
LAMPREY	–; lampreys	**LANES**	flanes,
LAMPS	clamps; –		planes; –
LAMS	clams, flams,	**LANG**	alang, clang,
	slams; –		slang; –
LAMSTER	–; lamsters	**LANGLEY**	–; langleys
LANAI	–; lanais	**LANGREL**	–; langrels
LANATE	planate;	**LANGUE**	–; langues,
	lanated		languet
LANCE	glance;	**LANGUET**	–; languets
	lanced,	**LANGUID**	–; –
	lancer,	**LANGUOR**	–; languors
	lances,	**LANGUR**	–; langurs
	lancet	**LANIARD**	–; laniards
LANCED	glanced; –	**LANIARY**	–; –
LANCER	–; lancers	**LANITAL**	–; lanitals
LANCES	glances; –	**LANK**	blank, clank,
LANCET	–; lancets		flank, plank,
LANCING	glancing; –		slank; lanky
LAND	aland,	**LANKER**	blanker,
	bland,		flanker; –
	eland,	**LANKEST**	blankest; –
	gland; lands	**LANKIER**	–; –
LANDAU	–; landaus	**LANKILY**	–; –
LANDED	–; –	**LANKLY**	blankly; –
LANDER	blander,	**LANNER**	planner;
	slander;		lanners
	landers	**LANNERS**	planners; –
LANDERS	glanders,	**LANOLIN**	–; lanoline,
	slanders; –		lanolins
LANDING	–; landings	**LANOSE**	–; –
LANDLER	–; landlers	**LANTANA**	–; lantanas
LANDMAN	–; –	**LANTERN**	–; lanterns
LANDMEN	–; –	**LANUGO**	–; lanugos
LANDS	alands,	**LANYARD**	–; lanyards
	blands,	**LAP**	clap, flap,
	elands,		slap; laps
	glands; –	**LAPDOG**	–; lapdogs

LAPEL	–; lapels	**LARDER**	–; larders
LAPFUL	–; lapfuls	**LARDIER**	–; –
LAPIDES	–; –	**LARDING**	–; –
LAPIN	–; lapins	**LARDON**	–; lardons
LAPIS	–; –	**LARDOON**	–; lardoons
LAPISES	–; –	**LARES**	blares,
LAPPED	clapped,		flares,
	flapped,		glares; –
	slapped; –	**LARGE**	–; larger,
LAPPER	clapper,		larges
	flapper,	**LARGELY**	–; –
	slapper;	**LARGES**	–; largess,
	lappers		largest
LAPPERS	clappers,	**LARGESS**	–; largesse
	flappers,	**LARGISH**	–; –
	slappers; –	**LARGO**	–; largos
LAPPET	–; lappets	**LARIAT**	–; lariats
LAPPING	clapping,	**LARINE**	–; –
	flapping,	**LARK**	–; larks,
	slapping; –		larky
LAPS	claps, flaps,	**LARKED**	–; –
	slaps; lapse	**LARKER**	–; larkers
LAPSE	elapse;	**LARKIER**	–; –
	lapsed,	**LARKING**	–; –
	lapser,	**LARRUP**	–; larrups
	lapses	**LARUM**	alarum;
LAPSED	elapsed; –		larums
LAPSER	–; lapsers	**LARUMS**	alarums; –
LAPSES	elapses; –	**LARVA**	–; larvae,
LAPSING	elapsing; –		larval, larvas
LAPSUS	–; –	**LARYNX**	–; –
LAPWING	–; lapwings	**LAS**	alas; lase,
LAR	alar; lard,		lash, lass,
	lark, lars		last
LARCENY	–; –	**LASAGNA**	–; lasagnas
LARCH	–; –	**LASAGNE**	–; lasagnes
LARCHES	–; –	**LASCAR**	–; lascars
LARD	–; lards,	**LASE**	blase; lased,
	lardy		laser, lases
LARDED	–; –	**LASER**	–; lasers

LASH   clash, flash, plash, slash· –

LASHED   clashed, flashed, plashed, slashed; –

LASHER   clasher, flasher, plasher, slasher; lashers

LASHERS   clashers, flashers, plashers, slashers;

LASHES   clashes, flashes, plashes, slashes; –

LASHING   clashing, flashing, plashing, slashing; lashings

LASHINS   –; –

LASHKAR   –; lashkars

LASING   –; –

LASS   class, glass; lasso

LASSES   classes, glasses; –

LASSIE   glassie; lassies

LASSIES   glassies; –

LASSO   –; lassos

LASSOED   –; –

LASSOER   –; lassoers

LASSOES   –; –

LAST   blast, clast; lasts

LASTED   blasted; –

LASTER   blaster, plaster; lasters

LASTERS   blasters, plasters; –

LASTING   blasting; lastings

LASTLY   –; –

LASTS   blasts, clasts; –

LAT   blat, flat, plat, slat; lati, lats

LATAKIA   –; latakias

LATCH   klatch, slatch; –

LATCHED   –; –

LATCHES   klatches, slatches; –

LATCHET   –; latchets

LATE   alate, blate, elate, plate, slate, lated, laten, later, lates, latex

LATED   alated, elated, plated, slated; –

LATEEN   –; lateens

LATELY   –; –

LATEN   platen; latens, latent

LATENCY   –; –

LATENED   –; –

LATENS   platens; –

LATENT   –; latents

LATER   elater, plater, slater; –

LATERAD	–; –	**LAUDED**	–; –
LATERAL	–; laterals	**LAUDER**	–; lauders
LATES	elates; latest	**LAUDING**	–; –
LATEST	–; latests	**LAUGH**	–; laughs
LATEX	–; –	**LAUGHED**	–; –
LATEXES	–; –	**LAUGHER**	–; laughers
LATH	–; lathe, laths, lathy	**LAUNCE**	–; launces
		LAUNCH	–; –
LATHE	–; lathed, lather, lathes	**LAUNDER**	–; launders
		LAUNDRY	–; –
LATHER	blather, slather; lathers, lathery	**LAURA**	–; laurae, lauras
		LAUREL	–; laurels
LATHERS	blathers, slathers; –	**LAUWINE**	–; lauwines
		LAVA	–; lavas
LATHIER	–; –	**LAVABO**	–; lavabos
LATHING	–; lathings	**LAVAGE**	–; lavages
LATICES	–; –	**LAVE**	clave, slave; laved, laver, laves
LATIGO	–; latigos		
LATISH	–; –	**LAVED**	slaved; –
LATOSOL	–; latosols	**LAVEER**	–; laveers
LATRIA	–; latrias	**LAVER**	claver, slaver; lavers
LATRINE	–; latrines		
LATS	blats, flats, plats, slats; –	**LAVERS**	clavers, slavers; –
		LAVES	slaves; –
LATTEN	flatten; lattens	**LAVING**	slaving; –
		LAVISH	slavish; –
LATTENS	flattens; –	**LAVROCK**	–; lavrocks
LATTER	blatter, clatter, flatter, platter; –	**LAW**	blaw, claw, flaw, slaw; lawn, laws
LATTICE	–; latticed, lattices	**LAWED**	blawed, clawed, flawed; –
LATTIN	–; lattins	**LAWFUL**	–; –
LAUAN	–; lauans	**LAWINE**	–; lawines
LAUD	–; lauds	**LAWING**	blawing,

	clawing,	**LAYMAN**	–; –
	flawing;	**LAYMEN**	–; –
	luwings	**LAYOFF**	playoff;
LAWLESS	flawless; –		layoffs
LAWLIKE	–; –	**LAYOFFS**	playoffs; –
LAWMAN	–; –	**LAYOUT**	–; layouts
LAWMEN	–; –	**LAYOVER**	–; layovers
LAWN	blawn;	**LAYS**	clays, flays,
	lawns, lawny		plays, slays; –
LAWS	blaws,	**LAZAR**	–; lazars
	claws, flaws,	**LAZARET**	–; lazarets
	slaws; –	**LAZE**	blaze,
LAWSUIT	–; lawsuits		glaze;
LAWYER	–; lawyers		lazed, lazes
LAX	flax; –	**LAZED**	blazed,
LAXER	–; –		glazed; –
LAXEST	–; –	**LAZES**	blazes,
LAXITY	–; –		glazes; –
LAXLY	–; –	**LAZIED**	–; –
LAXNESS	–; –	**LAZIER**	glazier; –
LAY	clay, flay,	**LAZIES**	–; laziest
	play, slay;	**LAZIEST**	glaziest; –
	lays	**LAZILY**	–; –
LAYAWAY	–; layaways	**LAZING**	blazing,
LAYED	clayed,		glazing; –
	flayed,	**LAZULI**	–; lazulis
	played; –	**LAZY**	glazy; –
LAYER	flayer,	**LAZYING**	–; –
	player,	**LAZYISH**	–; –
	slayer;	**LEA**	flea, ilea,
	layers		olea, plea;
LAYERED	–; –		lead, leaf,
LAYERS	flayers,		leak, leal,
	players,		lean, leap,
	slayers; –		lear, leas
LAYETTE	–; layettes	**LEACH**	bleach,
LAYING	claying,		pleach;
	flaying,		leachy
	playing,	**LEACHED**	bleached,
	slaying; –		pleached; –

LEACHER	bleacher; leachers	**LEANED**	cleaned, gleaned; –
LEACHES	bleaches; –	**LEANER**	cleaner,
LEAD	plead; leads, leady	**LEANEST**	gleaner; – cleanest; –
LEADED	pleaded; –	**LEANING**	cleaning,
LEADEN	–; –		gleaning;
LEADER	pleader; leaders		leanings
		LEANLY	cleanly; –
LEADERS	pleaders; –	**LEANS**	cleans,
LEADIER	–; –		gleans; –
LEADING	pleading; leadings	**LEAP**	–; leaps, leapt
LEADOFF	–; leadoffs	**LEAPED**	–; –
LEADS	pleads; –	**LEAPER**	–; leapers
LEAF	–; leafs, leafy	**LEAPING**	–; –
LEAFAGE	–; leafages	**LEAR**	blear, clear;
LEAFED	–; –		learn, lears,
LEAFIER	–; –		leary
LEAFING	–; –	**LEARIER**	blearier; –
LEAFLET	–; leaflets	**LEARN**	–; learns,
LEAGUE	–; leagued,		learnt
	leaguer,	**LEARNED**	–; –
	leagues	**LEARNER**	–; learners
LEAGUER	–; leaguers	**LEARS**	blears,
LEAK	bleak; leaks,		clears; –
	leaky	**LEARY**	bleary; –
LEAKAGE	–; leakages	**LEAS**	fleas, pleas;
LEAKED	–; –		lease, leash,
LEAKER	bleaker;		least
	leakers	**LEASE**	please;
LEAKIER	–; –		leased,
LEAKILY	–; –		leaser,
LEAKING	–; –		leases
LEAKS	bleaks; –	**LEASED**	pleased; –
LEAL	ileal; –	**LEASER**	pleaser;
LEALLY	–; –		leasers
LEALTY	–; –	**LEASERS**	pleasers; –
LEAN	clean, glean;	**LEASES**	pleases; –
	leans, leant	**LEASHED**	–; –

LEASHES	–; –	**LED**	bled, fled,
LEASING	pleasing;		gled, pled,
	leasings		sled; –
LEAST	–; leasts	**LEDGE**	fledge,
LEATHER	–; leathers,		pledge,
	leathern,		sledge;
	leathery		ledges
LEAVE	cleave,	**LEDGER**	pledger;
	sleave;		ledgers
	leaved,	**LEDGERS**	pledgers; –
	leaven,	**LEDGES**	fledges,
	leaver,		pledges,
	leaves		sledges; –
LEAVED	cleaved,	**LEDGIER**	fledgier; –
	sleaved; –	**LEDGY**	fledgy; –
LEAVEN	–; leavens	**LEE**	alee, flee,
LEAVER	cleaver;		glee; leek,
	leavers		leer, lees,
LEAVERS	cleavers; –		leet
LEAVES	cleaves,	**LEECH**	fleech; –
	sleaves	**LEECHED**	fleeched; –
LEAVIER	–; –	**LEECHES**	fleeches; –
LEAVING	cleaving,	**LEEK**	cleek, gleek,
	sleaving;		sleek; leeks
	leavings	**LEEKS**	cleeks,
LEAVY	–; –		gleeks,
LEBEN	–; lebens		sleeks; –
LECH	–; –	**LEER**	fleer; leers,
LECHER	–; lechers,		leery
	lechery	**LEERED**	fleered; –
LECHES	–; –	**LEERIER**	–; –
LECTERN	–; lecterns	**LEERILY**	–; –
LECTION	election;	**LEERING**	fleering; –
	lections	**LEERS**	fleers; –
LECTOR	elector;	**LEES**	flees, glees; –
	lectors	**LEET**	fleet, gleet,
LECTORS	electors; –		sleet; leets
LECTURE	–; lectured,	**LEETS**	fleets, gleets,
	lecturer,		sleets; –
	lectures		

LEEWARD	–; leewards	**LEGLESS**	–; –
LEEWAY	–; leeways	**LEGLIKE**	–; –
LEFT	cleft; lefts, lefty	**LEGMAN**	–; –
		LEGMEN	–; –
LEFTER	–; –	**LEGROOM**	–; legrooms
LEFTEST	–; –	**LEGUME**	–; legumes
LEFTIES	–; –	**LEGUMIN**	–; legumins
LEFTISM	–; leftisms	**LEGWORK**	–; legworks
LEFTIST	–; leftists	**LEHAYIM**	–; lehayims
LEFTS	clefts; –	**LEHR**	–; lehrs
LEG	gleg; legs	**LEI**	–; leis
LEGACY	–; –	**LEISTER**	–; leisters
LEGAL	–; legals	**LEISURE**	–; leisured,
LEGALLY	–; –		leisures
LEGATE	–; legated,	**LEK**	–; leks
	legatee,	**LEMAN**	–; lemans
	legates	**LEMMA**	–; lemmas
LEGATEE	–; legatees	**LEMMATA**	–; –
LEGATO	–; legator,	**LEMMING**	–; lemmings
	legatos	**LEMON**	–; lemons,
LEGATOR	–; legators		lemony
LEGEND	–; legends	**LEMPIRA**	–; lempiras
LEGER	–; legers	**LEMUR**	–; lemurs
LEGES	–; –	**LEMURES**	–; –
LEGGED	–; –	**LEND**	blend; lends
LEGGIER	–; –	**LENDER**	blender,
LEGGIN	–; legging,		slender;
	leggins		lenders
LEGGING	–; leggings	**LENDERS**	blenders; –
LEGGY	–; –	**LENDING**	blending; –
LEGHORN	–; leghorns	**LENDS**	blends; –
LEGIBLE	–; –	**LENES**	–; –
LEGIBLY	–; –	**LENGTH**	–; lengths,
LEGION	–; legions		lengthy
LEGIST	elegist;	**LENIENT**	–; –
	legists	**LENIS**	–; –
LEGISTS	elegists; –	**LENITY**	–; –
LEGIT	elegit; legits	**LENO**	–; lenos
LEGITS	elegits; –	**LENS**	glens; lense

LENSE	flense; lensed, lenses	**LETHE**	–; lethes
		LETS	blets; –
		LETTED	–; –
LENSED	flensed; –	**LETTER**	–; letters
LENSES	flenses; –	**LETTING**	–; –
LENT	blent; lento	**LETTUCE**	–; lettuces
LENTEN	–; –	**LETUP**	–; letups
LENTIC	–; –	**LEU**	–; leud
LENTIGO	–; –	**LEUCIN**	–; leucine, leucins
LENTIL	–; lentils		
LENTISK	–; lentisks	**LEUCINE**	–; leucines
LENTO	–; lentos	**LEUCITE**	–; leucites
LENTOID	–; –	**LEUCOMA**	–; leucomas
LEONE	–; leones	**LEUD**	–; leuds
LEONINE	–; –	**LEUKOMA**	–; leukomas
LEOPARD	–; leopards	**LEUKON**	–; leukons
LEOTARD	–; leotards	**LEV**	–; leva, levo, levy
LEPER	–; lepers		
LEPORID	–; leporids	**LEVANT**	–; levants
LEPROSE	–; –	**LEVATOR**	–; levators
LEPROSY	–; –	**LEVEE**	–; leveed, levees
LEPROUS	–; –		
LEPTA	–; –	**LEVEL**	–; levels
LEPTON	–; leptons	**LEVELED**	–; –
LESBIAN	–; lesbians	**LEVELER**	–; levelers
LESION	–; lesions	**LEVELLY**	–; –
LESS	bless; –	**LEVER**	clever; levers
LESSEE	–; lessees	**LEVERED**	–; –
LESSEN	–; lessens	**LEVERET**	–; leverets
LESSER	blesser; –	**LEVIED**	–; –
LESSON	–; lessons	**LEVIER**	–; leviers
LESSOR	plessor; lessors	**LEVIES**	–; –
		LEVIN	alevin; levins
LESSORS	plessors; –	**LEVINS**	alevins; –
LEST	blest; –	**LEVITY**	–; –
LET	blet; lets	**LEVULIN**	–; levulins
LETCH	fletch; –	**LEVYING**	–; –
LETCHES	fletches; –	**LEWD**	–; –
LETDOWN	–; letdowns	**LEWDER**	–; –
LETHAL	–; lethals	**LEWDEST**	–; –

LEWDLY	–; –	LIBRI	–; –
LEWIS	–; –	LICE	slice; –
LEWISES	–; –	LICENCE	–; licenced,
LEX	flex, ilex; –		licencee,
LEXICA	–; lexical		licencer,
LEXICON	–; lexicons		licences
LEY	fley, gley;	LICENSE	–; licensed,
	leys		licensee,
LEYS	fleys,		licenser,
	gleys; –		licenses
LI	–; lib, lid,	LICHEE	–; lichees
	lie, lin, lip,	LICHEN	–; lichens
	lis, lit	LICHI	–; lichis
LIABLE	pliable; –	LICHT	–; lichts
LIAISE	–; liaised,	LICHTED	–; –
	liaises	LICHTLY	–; –
LIASES	aliases; –	LICIT	elicit; –
LIAISON	–; liaisons	LICITLY	–; –
LIANA	–; lianas	LICK	click, flick,
LIANE	–; lianes		slick; clicks
LIANG	–; liangs	LICKED	clicked,
LIANOID	–; –		flicked,
LIAR	–; liard, liars		slicked; –
LIARD	–; liards	LICKER	clicker,
LIB	glib; libs		flicker,
LIBBER	glibber;		slicker;
	libbers		lickers
LIBEL	–; libels	LICKERS	clickers,
LIBELED	–; –		flickers,
LIBELEE	–; libelees		slickers; –
LIBELER	–; libelers	LICKING	clicking,
LIBER	–; libers		flicking,
LIBERAL	–; liberals		slicking;
LIBERTY	–; –		lickings
LIBIDO	–; libidos	LICKS	clicks, flicks,
LIBRA	–; librae,		slicks; –
	libras	LICTOR	–; lictors
LIBRARY	–; –	LID	slid; lido, lids
LIBRATE	–; librated,	LIDAR	–; lidars
	librates	LIDDED	–; –

LIDDING	–; –	**LIGATE**	–; ligated, ligates
LIDLESS	–; –		
LIDO	–; lidos	**LIGHT**	alight, blight, flight, plight, slight; lights
LIE	plie; lied, lief, lien, lier, lies, lieu		
LIED	flied, plied; –	**LIGHTED**	alighted, blighted, flighted, plighted, slighted; –
LIEDER	–; –		
LIEFER	–; –		
LIEFEST	–; –	**LIGHTEN**	–; lightens
LIEFLY	–; –	**LIGHTER**	blighter, plighter, slighter; lighters
LIEGE	–; lieges		
LIEN	alien; liens		
LIENAL	–; –		
LIENS	aliens; –	**LIGHTLY**	slightly; –
LIER	flier, plier, slier; liers	**LIGHTS**	alights, blights, flights, plights, slights; –
LIERNE	–; liernes		
LIERS	fliers, pliers; –		
LIES	flies, plies; –		
LIEU	–; lieus	**LIGNIFY**	–; –
LIEVE	–; liever	**LIGNIN**	–; lignins
LIEVEST	–; –	**LIGNITE**	–; lignites
LIFE	–; lifer	**LIGROIN**	–; ligroine, ligroins
LIFEFUL	–; –		
LIFER	–; lifers	**LIGULA**	–; ligulae, ligular, ligulas
LIFEWAY	–; lifeways		
LIFT	clift; lifts		
LIFTED	–; –	**LIGULE**	–; ligules
LIFTER	–; lifters	**LIGURE**	–; ligures
LIFTING	–; –	**LIKABLE**	–; –
LIFTMAN	–; –	**LIKE**	alike; liked, liken, liker, likes
LIFTMEN	–; –		
LIFTOFF	–; liftoffs		
LIFTS	clifts; –	**LIKELY**	–; –
LIGAN	–; ligand, ligans	**LIKEN**	–; likens
		LIKENED	–; –
LIGAND	–; ligands	**LIKER**	–; likers
LIGASE	–; ligases	**LIKES**	–; likest

LIKING	–; likings	**LIMEY**	blimey;
LIKUTA	–; –		limeys
LILAC	–; lilacs	**LIMIER**	slimier; –
LILIED	–; –	**LIMIEST**	slimiest; –
LILIES	–; –	**LIMINA**	–; liminal
LILT	–; lilts	**LIMING**	gliming,
LILTED	–; –		sliming; –
LILTING	–; –	**LIMIT**	–; limits
LILY	slily; –	**LIMITED**	–; limiteds
LIMA	–; liman,	**LIMITER**	–; limiters
	limas	**LIMITES**	–; –
LIMACON	–; limacons	**LIMMER**	glimmer,
LIMAN	–; limans		slimmer;
LIMB	climb; limba,		limmers
	limbi, limbo,	**LIMMERS**	glimmers; –
	limbs, limby	**LIMN**	–; limns
LIMBA	–; limbas	**LIMNED**	–; –
LIMBATE	–; –	**LIMNER**	–; limners
LIMBECK	–; limbecks	**LIMNIC**	–; –
LIMBED	climbed; –	**LIMNING**	–; –
LIMBER	climber;	**LIMO**	–; limos
	limbers	**LIMP**	blimp; limps
LIMBERS	climbers; –	**LIMPED**	–; –
LIMBING	climbing; –	**LIMPER**	–; limpers
LIMBI	–; limbic	**LIMPEST**	–; –
LIMBIER	–; –	**LIMPET**	–; limpets
LIMBO	–; limbos	**LIMPID**	–; –
LIMBS	climbs; –	**LIMPING**	–; –
LIMBUS	–; –	**LIMPKIN**	–; limpkins
LIME	clime, glime,	**LIMPLY**	–; –
	slime; limed,	**LIMPS**	blimps; –
	limen, limes,	**LIMPSY**	slimpsy; –
	limey	**LIMULI**	–; –
LIMEADE	–; limeades	**LIMULUS**	–; –
LIMED	glimed,	**LIMY**	blimy,
	slimed; –		slimy; –
LIMEN	–; limens	**LIN**	blin; line,
LIMES	climes,		ling, link,
	glimes,		linn, lino,
	slimes; –		lins, lint, liny

LINABLE	–; –		flingers,
LINAC	–; linacs		slingers; –
LINAGE	–; linages	**LINGIER**	–; –
LINALOL	–; linalols	**LINGOES**	–; –
LINDANE	–; lindanes	**LINGS**	clings, flings,
LINDEN	–; lindens		slings; –
LINDIES	–; –	**LINGUA**	–; linguae,
LINDY	–; –		lingual
LINE	aline, cline;	**LINGUAL**	–; linguals
	lined, linen,	**LINGY**	clingy; –
	liner, lines,	**LINIER**	–; –
	liney	**LINIEST**	–; –
LINEAGE	–; lineages	**LININ**	–; lining,
LINEAL	–; –		linins
LINEAR	–; –	**LINING**	alining;
LINEATE	–; lineated		linings
LINECUT	–; linecuts	**LINK**	blink, clink,
LINED	alined; –		plink, slink;
LINEMAN	–; –		links, linky
LINEMEN	–; –	**LINKAGE**	–; linkages
LINEN	–; linens,	**LINKBOY**	–; linkboys
	lineny	**LINKED**	blinked,
LINER	aliner; liners		clinked,
LINERS	aliners; –		plinked; –
LINES	alines,	**LINKER**	blinker,
	clines; –		clinker,
LINEUP	–; lineups		plinker;
LING	cling, fling,		linkers
	sling, linga,	**LINKERS**	blinkers,
	lingo, lings,		clinkers,
	lingy		plinkers; –
LINGA	–; lingam,	**LINKING**	blinking,
	lingas		clinking,
LINGAM	–; lingams		plinking,
LINGCOD	–; lingcods		slinking; –
LINGER	clinger,	**LINKMAN**	–; –
	flinger,	**LINKMEN**	–; –
	slinger;	**LINKS**	blinks, clinks,
	lingers		plinks,
LINGERS	clingers,		slinks; –

LINKUP	–; linkups	clipped,
LINKY	slinky; –	flipped,
LINN	–; linns	slipped; –
LINNET	–; linnets	**LIPPEN** –; lippens
LINO	–; linos	**LIPPER** clipper,
LINOCUT	–; linocuts	flipper,
LINSANG	–; linsangs	slipper;
LINSEED	–; linseeds	lippers
LINSEY	–; linseys	**LIPPERS** clippers,
LINT	flint, glint;	flippers,
	lints, linty	slippers; –
LINTEL	–; lintels	**LIPPIER** –; –
LINTER	–; linters	**LIPPING** blipping,
LINTIER	–; –	clipping,
LINTOL	–; lintols	flipping,
LINTS	flints,	slipping;
	glints; –	lippings
LINTY	flinty; –	**LIPPY** slippy; –
LINUM	–; linums	**LIPS** blips, clips,
LION	–; lions	flips, slips; –
LIONESS	–; –	**LIQUATE** –; liquated,
LIONISE	–; lionised,	liquates
	lioniser,	
	lionises	**LIQUEFY** –; –
LIONIZE	–; lionized,	**LIQUEUR** –; liqueurs
	lionizer,	**LIQUID** –; liquids
	lionizes	**LIQUIFY** –; –
LIP	blip, clip,	**LIQUOR** –; liquors
	flip, slip; lips	**LIRA** –; liras
LIPASE	–; lipases	**LIRE** –; –
LIPID	–; lipide,	**LIROT** –; liroth
	lipids	**LIS** –; lisp, list
LIPIDE	–; lipides	**LISLE** –; lisles
LIPIDIC	–; –	**LISP** –; lisps
LIPIN	–; lipins	**LISPED** –; –
LIPLESS	–; –	**LISPER** –; lispers
LIPLIKE	–; –	**LISPING** –; –
LIPOID	–; lipoids	**LISSOM** –; lissome
LIPOMA	–; lipomas	**LIST** alist; lists
LIPPED	blipped,	**LISTED** –; –
		LISTEL –; listels

LISTEN	glisten; listens	**LITTLES**	–; littlest
LISTENS	glistens; –	**LITS**	flits, slits; –
LISTER	blister, glister; listers	**LITURGY**	–; –
		LIVABLE	–; –
LISTERS	blisters, glisters; –	**LIVE**	alive, olive; lived, liven, liver, lives
LISTING	–; listings		
LIT	alit, flit, slit; lits, litu	**LIVELY**	–; –
		LIVEN	–; livens
LITAI	–; –	**LIVENED**	–; –
LITANY	–; –	**LIVENER**	–; liveners
LITAS	–; –	**LIVER**	sliver; livers, livery
LITCHI	–; litchis		
LITER	–; liters	**LIVERS**	clivers, slivers, –
LITERAL	–; literals		
LITHE	blithe; lither	**LIVES**	olives, livest
LITHELY	blithely; –	**LIVID**	–; –
LITHER	blither, slither; –	**LIVIDLY**	–; –
		LIVIER	–; liviers
LITHEST	blithest; –	**LIVING**	–; livings
LITHIA	–; lithias	**LIVRE**	–; livres
LITHIC	–; –	**LIVYER**	–; livyers
LITHIUM	–; lithiums	**LIZARD**	–; lizards
LITHO	–; lithos	**LLAMA**	–; llamas
LITHOID	–; lithoids	**LLANO**	–; llanos
LITMUS	–; –	**LO**	–; lob, log, loo, lop, lot, low, lox
LITORAL	clitoral; –		
LITOTES	–;	**LOACH**	–; –
LITRE	–; litres	**LOACHES**	–; –
LITTEN	–; –	**LOAD**	–; loads
LITTER	flitter, glitter, slitter; litters, littery	**LOADED**	–; –
		LOADER	–; loaders
		LOADING	–; loadings
LITTERS	flitters, glitters, slitters; –	**LOAF**	–; loafs
		LOAFED	–; –
		LOAFER	–; loafers
LITTERY	glittery; –	**LOAFING**	–; –
LITTLE	–; littler, littles	**LOAM**	gloam; loams, loamy

LOAMED	–; –	**LOBULE**	globule; lobules
LOAMIER	–; –		
LOAMING	gloaming; –	**LOBULES**	globules; –
LOAMS	gloams; –	**LOBWORM**	–; lobworms
LOAN	–; loans	**LOCA**	–; local
LOANED	–; –	**LOCAL**	–; locale, locals
LOANER	–; loaners		
LOANING	–; loanings	**LOCALE**	–; locales
LOATH	–; loathe	**LOCALLY**	–; –
LOATHE	–; loathed, loather, loathes	**LOCATE**	–; located, locater, locates
LOATHER	–; loathers	**LOCATER**	–; locaters
LOATHLY	–; –	**LOCATOR**	–; locators
LOAVES	–; –	**LOCH**	–; lochs
LOB	blob, glob, slob; lobe, lobo, lobs	**LOCHIA**	–; lochial
		LOCI	–; –
		LOCK	block, clock, flock; locks
LOBAR	–; –		
LOBATE	globate; lobated	**LOCKAGE**	blockage; lockages
LOBATED	globated; –	**LOCKBOX**	–; –
LOBBED	blobbed; –	**LOCKED**	blocked, clocked, flocked; –
LOBBIED	–; –		
LOBBIES	–; –		
LOBBING	blobbing; –	**LOCKER**	blocker, clocker; lockers
LOBBY	–; –		
LOBBYER	–; lobbyers	**LOCKERS**	blockers, clockers; –
LOBE	globe; lobed, lobes		
LOBED	globed; –	**LOCKET**	–; lockets
LOBEFIN	–; lobefins	**LOCKING**	blocking, clocking, flocking; –
LOBELIA	–; lobelias		
LOBES	globes; –		
LOBO	–; lobos	**LOCKJAW**	–; lockjaws
LOBS	blobs, globs, slobs; –	**LOCKNUT**	–; locknuts
		LOCKOUT	–; lockouts
LOBSTER	–; lobsters	**LOCKRAM**	–; lockrams
LOBULAR	globular; –		

LOCKS	blocks, clocks, flocks; –		logo, logs, logy
LOCKUP	–; lockups	**LOGAN**	slogan; logans
LOCO	–; locos	**LOGANS**	slogans; –
LOCOED	–; –	**LOGBOOK**	–; logbooks
LOCOES	–; –	**LOGE**	–; loges
LOCOING	–; –	**LOGGATS**	–; –
LOCOISM	–; locoisms	**LOGGED**	clogged, flogged, slogged; –
LOCULAR	–; –		
LOCULE	–; loculed, locules		
		LOGGER	flogger, slogger; loggers
LOCULI	–; –		
LOCULUS	–; –	**LOGGERS**	floggers, sloggers,
LOCUM	–; locums		
LOCUS	–; locust	**LOGGETS**	–; –
LOCUST	–; locusta, locusts	**LOGGIA**	–; loggiae, loggias
LOCUSTA	–; locustae, locustal		
		LOGGIER	–; –
LODE	–; loden, lodes	**LOGGING**	clogging, flogging, slogging; loggings
LODEN	–; lodens		
LODGE	–; lodged, lodger, lodges		
		LOGGY	cloggy; –
		LOGIA	–; –
LODGER	–; lodgers	**LOGIC**	–; logics
LODGING	–; lodgings	**LOGICAL**	alogical; –
LOESS	–; –	**LOGIER**	–; –
LOESSAL	–; –	**LOGIEST**	–; –
LOESSES	–; –	**LOGILY**	–; –
LOFT	aloft; lofts, lofty	**LOGION**	–; logions
		LOGJAM	–; logjams
LOFTED	–; –	**LOGO**	–; logoi, logos
LOFTER	–; lofters		
LOFTIER	–; –	**LOGROLL**	–; logrolls
LOFTILY	–; –	**LOGWAY**	–; logways
LOFTING	–; –	**LOGWOOD**	–; logwoods
LOG	clog, flog, slog; loge,	**LOGS**	clogs, flogs, slogs; –

LOGY	ology; –	**LOOEY**	flooey;
LOIN	aloin, eloin;		looeys
	loins	**LOOF**	aloof, kloof;
LOINS	aloins,		loofa, loofs
	eloins; –	**LOOFA**	–; loofah,
LOITER	–; loiters		loofas
LOLL	–; lolls, lolly	**LOOFAH**	–; loofahs
LOLLED	–; –	**LOOFS**	kloofs; –
LOLLER	–; lollers	**LOOIE**	–; looies
LOLLIES	–; –	**LOOING**	–; –
LOLLING	–; –	**LOOK**	–; looks
LOLLOP	–; lollops	**LOOKED**	–; –
LOLLY	–; –	**LOOKER**	–; lookers
LOMENT	–; loments	**LOOKING**	–; –
LONE	alone, clone;	**LOOKOUT**	–; lookouts
	loner	**LOOKUP**	–; lookups
LONELY	–; –	**LOOM**	bloom,
LONER	–; loners		gloom;
LONG	along, flong,		looms
	klong; longe,	**LOOMED**	bloomed,
	longs		gloomed; –
LONGAN	–; longans	**LOOMING**	blooming,
LONGBOW	–; longbows		glooming; –
LONGE	–; longed,	**LOOMS**	blooms,
	longer,		glooms;
	longes	**LOON**	–; loons,
LONGER	–; longers		loony
LONGING	–; longings	**LOONIER**	–; –
LONGISH	–; –	**LOONIES**	–; looniest
LONGLY	–; –	**LOONEY**	–; –
LONGS	flongs,	**LOONY**	–; –
	klongs; –	**LOOP**	bloop,
LOO	–; loof,		sloop; loops,
	look, loom,		loopy
	loon, loop,	**LOOPED**	blooped; –
	loos, loot	**LOOPER**	blooper;
LOOBIES	–; –		loopers
LOOBY	–; –	**LOOPERS**	bloopers; –
LOOED	–; –	**LOOPING**	blooping; –

LOOPS	bloops, sloops; –	**LOPPERS**	floppers; –
LOOSE	–; loose	**LOPPIER**	floppier; –
LOOSE	–; loosed, loosen, looser, looses	**LOPPING**	clopping, flopping, plopping, slopping; –
LOOSELY	–; –	**LOPPY**	floppy, sloppy; –
LOOSEN	–; loosens	**LOPS**	clops, flops, glops, plops, slops; –
LOOSES	–; loosest		
LOOSING	–; –		
LOOT	cloot; loots	**LOQUAT**	–; loquats
LOOTED	–; –	**LORAL**	floral; –
LOOTER	–; looters	**LORAN**	–; lorans
LOOTING	–; –	**LORD**	–; lords
LOOTS	cloots; –	**LORDED**	–; –
LOP	clop, flop, glop, plop, slop; lope, lops	**LORDING**	–; lordings
		LORDLY	–; –
		LORDOMA	–; lordomas
LOPE	elope, slope; loped, loper, lopes	**LORE**	–; lores
		LOREAL	–; –
		LORICA	–; loricae
LOPED	eloped, sloped; –	**LORIES**	glories; –
		LORIMER	–; lorimers
LOPER	eloper, sloper; lopers	**LORINER**	–; loriners
		LORIS	–; –
		LORISES	–; –
LOPERS	elopers, slopers; –	**LORN**	–; –
		LORRIES	–; –
LOPES	elopes, slopes; –	**LORRY**	–; –
		LORY	glory; –
LOPING	eloping, sloping; –	**LOSABLE**	closable; –
		LOSE	close; losel, loser, loses
LOPPED	clopped, flopped, plopped, slopped; –		
		LOSEL	–; losels
		LOSER	closer; losers
		LOSERS	closers; –
		LOSES	closes; –
LOPPER	flopper; loppers	**LOSING**	closing; losings

LOSS	floss, gloss; lossy	LOUDEST	–; –
LOSSES	flosses, glosses; –	LOUDISH	–; –
		LOUDLY	–; –
LOSSY	flossy, glossy; –	LOUGH	clough, plough, slough; loughs
LOST	glost; –		
LOT	blot, clot, plot, slot; lota, loth, lots	LOUGHS	cloughs, ploughs, sloughs; –
LOTA	flota; lotah, lotas	LOUIE	–; louies
		LOUIS	–; –
LOTAH	–; lotahs	LOUNGE	–; lounged, lounger, lounges
LOTAS	flotas; –		
LOTH	cloth, sloth; –	LOUNGER	–; loungers
LOTIC	–; –	LOUNGY	–; –
LOTION	–; lotions	LOUP	–; loupe, loups
LOTOS	–; –		
LOTOSES	–; –	LOUPE	–; louped, loupen, loupes
LOTS	blots, clots, plots, slots; –		
LOTTED	blotted, clotted, plotted, slotted; –	LOUPING	–; –
		LOUR	clour, flour; lours, loury
		LOURED	floured; –
LOTTERY	–; –	LOURING	clouring, flouring; –
LOTTING	blotting, clotting, plotting, slotting; –		
		LOURS	clours, flours; –
		LOURY	floury; –
		LOUSE	blouse; loused, louses
LOTTO	blotto; lottos		
LOTUS	–; –	LOUSED	bloused; –
LOTUSES	–; –	LOUSES	blouses; –
LOUD	aloud, cloud; –	LOUSIER	–; –
		LOUSILY	–; –
LOUDEN	–; loudens	LOUSING	blousing; –
LOUDER	–; –	LOUSY	blousy; –

LOUT	clout, flout, glout; louts	**LOWBRED**	–; –
		LOWBROW	–; lowbrows
LOUTED	clouted, flouted, glouted; –	**LOWDOWN**	–; lowdowns
		LOWE	–; lowed, lower, lowes
LOUTING	clouting, flouting, glouting; –	**LOWED**	flowed, glowed, plowed, slowed; –
LOUTISH	–; –		
LOUTS	clouts, flouts, glouts; –	**LOWER**	blower, flower, glower, plower, slower; lowers, lowery
LOUVER	–; louvers		
LOUVRE	–; louvres		
LOVABLE	–; –		
LOVABLY	;		
LOVAGE	–; lovages		
LOVE	clove, glove; loved, lover, loves	**LOWERED**	flowered; –
		LOWERS	blowers, flowers, glowers, plowers; –
LOVED	cloved, gloved; –		
LOVELY	–; –	**LOWERY**	flowery; –
LOVER	clover, glover, plover; lovers	**LOWEST**	slowest; –
		LOWING	blowing, flowing, glowing, plowing, slowing; lowings
LOVERLY	–; –		
LOVERS	clovers, glovers, plovers; –		
		LOWISH	slowish; –
		LOWLAND	plowland; lowlands
LOVES	cloves, gloves; –		
LOVING	gloving; –	**LOWLIER**	–; –
LOW	alow, blow, flow, glow, plow, slow; lowe, lown, lows	**LOWLIFE**	–; lowlifes
		LOWLY	slowly; –
		LOWN	blown, clown, flown; –
LOWBORN	–; –	**LOWNESS**	slowness; –
LOWBOY	–; lowboys	**LOWS**	blows, flows,

	glows,	**LUCKIER**	pluckier; –
	plows, slows;	**LUCKIES**	–; luckiest
	lowse	**LUCKILY**	pluckily; –
LOX	–; –	**LUCKING**	clucking,
LOXED	–; –		plucking; –
LOXES	–; –	**LUCKS**	clucks,
LOXING	–; –		plucks; –
LOYAL	–; –	**LUCKY**	plucky; –
LOYALER	–; –	**LUCRE**	–; lucres
LOYALLY	–; –	**LUES**	blues, clues,
LOYALTY	–; –		flues, glues,
LOZENGE	–; lozenges		slues; –
LUAU	–; luaus	**LUETIC**	–; luetics
LUBBER	blubber,	**LUFF**	bluff, fluff,
	clubber,		sluff; luffa,
	slubber;		luffs
	lubbers	**LUFFA**	–; luffas
LUBBERS	blubbers,	**LUFFED**	bluffed,
	clubbers,		fluffed,
	slubbers; –		sluffed; –
LUBE	–; lubes	**LUFFING**	bluffing,
LUBRIC	–; –		fluffing,
LUCARNE	–; lucarnes		sluffing; –
LUCE	–; luces	**LUFFS**	bluffs, fluffs,
LUCENCE	–; lucences		sluffs; –
LUCENCY	–; –	**LUG**	plug, slug;
LUCENT	–; –		luge, lugs
LUCERN	–; lucerne,	**LUGE**	–; luges
	lucerns	**LUGGAGE**	–; luggages
LUCERNE	–; lucernes	**LUGGED**	plugged,
LUCES	–; –		slugged; –
LUCID	–; –	**LUGGER**	plugger,
LUCIDLY	–; –		slugger;
LUCIFER	–; lucifers		luggers
LUCK	cluck, pluck;	**LUGGERS**	pluggers,
	lucks, lucky		sluggers; –
LUCKED	clucked,	**LUGGIE**	–; luggies
	plucked; –	**LUGGING**	plugging,
LUCKIE	–; luckier,		slugging; –
	luckies		

LUGS	plugs, slugs; –	**LUMPERS**	plumpers; –
LUGSAIL	–; lugsails	**LUMPIER**	clumpier, glumpier; –
LULL	–; lulls	**LUMPILY**	–; –
LULLABY	–; –	**LUMPING**	clumping,
LULLED	–; –		flumping,
LULLING	–; –		plumping,
LULU	–; lulus		slumping; –
LUM	alum, glum, plum, slum; lump, lums	**LUMPISH**	plumpish; –
		LUMPS	clumps, flumps,
LUMBAGO	plumbago; lumbagos		plumps, slumps; –
LUMBAR	–; lumbars	**LUMPY**	clumpy,
LUMBER	clumber, plumber, slumber; lumbers	**LUMS**	glumpy; –
			alums, glums, plums,
LUMBERS	clumbers, plumbers, slumbers; –		slums; –
		LUNA	–; lunar, lunas
LUMEN	–; lumens	**LUNACY**	–; –
LUMENAL	–; –	**LUNAR**	–; lunars
LUMINA	alumina; luminal	**LUNATE**	–; lunated
		LUNATIC	–; lunatics
LUMMOX	–; –	**LUNCH**	glunch; –
LUMP	clump, flump, plump, slump; lumps, lumpy	**LUNCHED**	glunched; –
		LUNCHER	–; lunchers
		LUNCHES	glunches; –
		LUNE	–; lunes, luner
LUMPED	clumped, flumped, plumped, slumped; –	**LUNET**	–; lunets
		LUNETTE	–; lunettes
		LUNG	clung, flung, slung; lunge, lungi, lungs
LUMPEN	plumpen; lumpens		
		LUNGAN	–; lungans
LUMPENS	plumpens; –	**LUNGE**	blunge, plunge; lunged, lungee,
LUMPER	plumper; lumpers		

	lunger, lunges	**LUPIN**	–; lupine, lupins
LUNGED	blunged, plunged; –	**LUPINE**	–; lupines
LUNGEE	–; lungees	**LUPOUS**	–; –
LUNGER	blunger, plunger; lungers	**LUPULIN**	–; lupulins
		LUPUS	–; –
LUNGERS	blungers, plungers; –	**LUPUSES**	–; –
		LURCH	–; –
LUNGES	plunges; –	**LURCHED**	–; –
LUNGI	–; lungis	**LURCHER**	–; lurchers
LUNGING	blunging, plunging; –	**LURCHES**	–; –
		LURDAN	–; lurdane, lurdans
LUNGYI	–; lungyis	**LURDANE**	–; lurdanes
LUNIER	–; –	**LURE**	–; lured, lurer, lures
LUNIES	–; luniest		
LUNK	clunk, flunk, plunk, slunk; lunks	**LURER**	–; lurers
		LURID	–; –
LUNKER	clunker, flunker, plunker; lunkers	**LURIDLY**	–; –
		LURING	–; –
		LURK	–; lurks
		LURKED	–; –
LUNKERS	clunkers, flunkers, plunkers; –	**LURKER**	–; lurkers
		LURKING	–; –
LUNKS	clunks, flunks, plunks; –	**LUSH**	blush, flush, plush, slush; –
LUNT	blunt; lunts	**LUSHED**	blushed, flushed, slushed; –
LUNTED	blunted; –		
LUNTING	blunting; –	**LUSHER**	blusher, flusher, plusher; –
LUNTS	blunts; –		
LUNULA	–; lunulae, lunular	**LUSHES**	blushes, flushes, plushes, slushes; lushest
LUNULE	–; lunules		
LUNY	–; –		
LUPANAR	–; lupanars	**LUSHEST**	flushest, plushest; –

LUSHING	blushing, flushing, slushing; –	**LUTIST**	flutist; lutists
		LUTISTS	flutists; –
		LUX	flux; luxe
LUSHLY	plushly; –	**LUXATE**	–; luxated, luxates
LUST	–; lusts, lusty		
LUSTED	–; –	**LUXE**	–; luxes
LUSTER	bluster, cluster, fluster; lusters	**LUXES**	fluxes; –
		LUXURY	–; –
		LYARD	–; –
		LYART	–; –
LUSTERS	blusters, clusters, flusters; –	**LYASE**	–; lyases
		LYCEA	–; –
		LYCEE	–; lycees
LUSTFUL	–; –	**LYCEUM**	–; lyceums
LUSTIER	–; –	**LYCHEE**	–; lychees
LUSTILY	–; –	**LYCHNIS**	–; –
LUSTING	–; –	**LYCOPOD**	–; lycopods
LUSTRA	–; lustral	**LYDDITE**	–; lyddites
LUSTRE	–; lustred, lustres	**LYE**	–; lyes
		LYING	flying, plying; lyings
LUSTRUM	–; lustrums		
LUSUS	–; –	**LYINGLY**	plyingly; –
LUSUSES	–; –	**LYINGS**	flyings; –
LUTE	elute, flute; lutea, luted, lutes	**LYMPH**	–; lymphs
		LYNCEAN	–; –
		LYNCH	–; –
LUTEA	–; luteal	**LYNCHED**	–; –
LUTEAL	gluteal; –	**LYNCHER**	–; lynchers
LUTED	eluted, fluted; –	**LYNCHES**	–; –
		LYNX	–; –
LUTEIN	–; luteins	**LYNXES**	–; –
LUTEOUS	–; –	**LYRATE**	–; lyrated
LUTES	elutes, flutes; –	**LYRE**	–; lyres
		LYRIC	–; lyrics
LUTEUM	–; –	**LYRICAL**	–; –
LUTHERN	–; lutherns	**LYRISM**	–; lyrisms
LUTING	eluting, fluting; lutings	**LYRIST**	–; lyrists
		LYSATE	–; lysates
		LYSE	–; lysed, lyses
LUTINGS	flutings; –		

LYSIN	–; lysine, lysing, lysins	**LYSSA**	–; lyssas
		LYTIC	–; –
LYSINE	–; lysines	**LYTTA**	–; lyttae,
LYSIS	–; –		lyttas
LYSOGEN	–; lysigens, lysogeny		

M

M	am, em, hm, mm, om, um; ma, me, mi, mm, mo, mu, my	**MACHREE**	–; machrees
		MACHZOR	–; machzors
		MACING	–; –
		MACK	smack; macks
MA	ama; mac, mad, mae, mag, man, map, mar, mas, mat, maw, may	**MACKLE**	–; mackled, mackles
		MACKS	–; smacks; –
		MACLE	–; macled, macles
		MACRAME	–; macrames
MAAR	–; maars	**MACRO**	–; macron, macros
MAC	mace, mach, mack, macs		
		MACRON	–; macrons
MACABER	–; –	**MACULA**	–; maculae, macular, maculas
MACABRE	–; –		
MACACO	–; macacos		
MACADAM	–; macadams	**MACULE**	–; maculed, macules
MACAQUE	–; macaques		
MACAW	–; macaws	**MAD**	–; made, mads
MACCHIA	–; –		
MACCHIE	–; –	**MADAM**	–; madame, madams
MACE	–; maced, macer, maces		
		MADAME	–; madames
		MADCAP	–; madcaps
MACER	–; macers	**MADDED**	–; –
MACH	–; machs	**MADDEN**	–; maddens
MACHETE	–; machetes	**MADDER**	–; madders
MACHINE	–; machined, machines	**MADDEST**	–; –
		MADDING	–; –

MADDISH	–; –	**MAGMA**	–; magmas
MADEIRA	–; madeiras	**MAGMATA**	;
MADLY	–; –	**MAGNATE**	–; magnates
MADMAN	–; –	**MAGNET**	–; magnets
MADMEN	–; –	**MAGNETO**	–; magnetos
MADNESS	–; –	**MAGNIFY**	–; –
MADONNA	–;	**MAGNUM**	–; magnums
	madonnas	**MAGOT**	–; magots
MADRAS	–; –	**MAGPIE**	–; magpies
MADRE	–; madres	**MAGUEY**	–; magueys
MADRONA	–; madronas	**MAGUS**	–; –
MADRONE	–; madrones	**MAHATMA**	–; mahatmas
MADRONO	–; madronos	**MAHJONG**	–; mahjongg,
MADURO	–; maduros		mahjongs
MADWORT	–; madworts	**MAHOE**	–; mahoes
MADZOON	–;	**MAHONIA**	–; mahonias
	madzoons	**MAHOUT**	–; mahouts
MAE	–; maes	**MAHUANG**	–; mahuangs
MAENAD	–; maenads	**MAHZOR**	–; mahzors
MAESTRI	–; –	**MAID**	–; maids
MAESTRO	–; maestros	**MAIDEN**	–; maidens
MAFFIA	–; maffias	**MAIDISH**	–; –
MAFFICK	–; mafficks	**MAIGRE**	–; –
MAFIA	–; mafias	**MAIHEM**	–; maihems
MAFIC	–; –	**MAIL**	–; maile,
MAFIOSI	–; –		maill, mails
MAFIOSO	–; –	**MAILBAG**	–; mailbags
MAFTIR	–; maftirs	**MAILBOX**	–; –
MAG	; mage,	**MAILE**	–; mailed,
	magi, mags		mailer,
MAGE	image;		mailes
	mages	**MAILER**	–; mailers
MAGENTA	–; magentas	**MAILING**	–; mailings
MAGES	images; –	**MAILL**	–; maills
MAGGOT	–; maggots,	**MAILLOT**	–; maillots
	maggoty	**MAILMAN**	–; –
MAGI	–; magic	**MAILMEN**	–; –
MAGIC	–; magics	**MAIM**	–; maims
MAGICAL	–; –	**MAIMED**	–; –
MAGILP	–; magilps		

MAIMER	–; maimers	**MALLARD**	–; mallards
MAIMING	–; –	**MALLED**	–; –
MAIN	amain; mains	**MALLEE**	–; mallees
MAINLY	–; –	**MALLEI**	–; –
MAINTOP	–; maintops	**MALLET**	–; mallets
MAIR	–; mairs	**MALLEUS**	–; –
MAIST	–; maists	**MALLING**	–; –
MAIZE	–; maizes	**MALLOW**	–; mallows
MAJAGUA	–; majaguas	**MALM**	–; malms,
MAJESTY	–; –		malmy
MAJOR	–; majors	**MALMIER**	–; –
MAKABLE	–; –	**MALMSEY**	–; malmseys
MAKAR	–; makars	**MALLS**	smalls; –
MAKE	–; maker,	**MALODOR**	–; malodors
	makes	**MALT**	smalt; malts,
MAKER	–; makers		malty
MAKEUP	–; makeups	**MALTASE**	–; maltases
MAKING	–; makings	**MALTED**	–; malteds
MAKO	–; makos	**MALTHA**	–; malthas
MAKUTA	–; –	**MALTIER**	–; –
MALADY	–; –	**MALTING**	–; –
MALAISE	–; malaises	**MALTOL**	–; maltols
MALAR	–; malars	**MALTOSE**	–; maltoses
MALARIA	–; malarial,	**MALTS**	smalts; –
	malarian,	**MAMA**	–; mamas
	malarias	**MAMBA**	–; mambas
MALARKY	–; –	**MAMBO**	–; mambos
MALATE	–; malates	**MAMBOED**	–; –
MALE	–; males	**MAMBOES**	–; –
MALEATE	–; maleates	**MAMEY**	–; mameys
MALEFIC	–; –	**MAMEYES**	–; –
MALFED	–; –	**MAMIE**	–; mamies
MALGRE	–; –	**MAMLUK**	–; mamluks
MALIC	–; malice	**MAMMA**	–; mammae,
MALICE	–; malices		mammal,
MALIGN	–; maligns		mammas
MALINE	–; malines		
MALISON	–; malisons	**MAMMAL**	–; mammals
MALKIN	–; malkins	**MAMMARY**	–; –
MALL	small; malls	**MAMMATE**	–; –
		MAMMEE	–; mammees

MAMMER	–; mammers		manger,
MAMMET	–; mammets		manges,
MAMMEY	–; mammeys		mangey
MAMMIE	–; mammies	MANGEL	–; mangels
MAMMOCK	–; mammocks	MANGER	–; mangers
MAMMON	–; mammons	MANGEY	–; –
MAMMOTH	–; mammoths	MANGIER	–; –
		MANGILY	–; –
MAMMY	–; –	MANGLE	–; mangled, mangler, mangles
MAN	–; mane, mano, mans, many	
		MANGLER	–; manglers
MANA	–; manas	MANGO	–; mangos
MANACLE	–; manacled, manacles	MANGOES	–; –
		MANGOLD	–; mangolds
		MANGY	–; –
MANAGE	–; managed, manager, manages	MANHOLE	–; manholes
		MANHOOD	–; manhoods
MANAGER	–; managers	MANHUNT	–; manhunts
MANAKIN	–; manakins	MANIA	–; maniac, manias
MANANA	–; mananas	
MANATEE	–; manatees	MANIAC	–; maniacs
MANCHE	–; manches, manchet	MANIC	–; manics
		MANIHOT	–; manihots
MANCHET	–; manchets	MANIKIN	–; manikins
MANDALA	–; mandalas	MANILA	–; manilas
MANDATE	–; mandated, mandates	MANILLA	–; manillas
		MANILLE	–; manilles
		MANIOC	–; manioca, maniocs
MANDOLA	–; mandolas	
MANDREL	–; mandrels	MANIOCA	–; maniocas
MANDRIL	–; mandrill, mandrils	MANIPLE	–; maniples
		MANITO	–; manitos, manitou
MANE	–; maned, manes	
		MANITOU	–; manitous
MANEGE	–; maneges	MANITU	–; manitus
MANFUL	–; –	MANKIND	–; –
MANGABY	–; –	MANLESS	–; –
MANGE	–; mangel,	MANLIER	–; –

MANLIKE	–; –	**MANUMIT**	–; manumits
MANLILY	–; –	**MANURE**	–; manured,
MANLY	–; –		manurer,
MANMADE	–; –		manures
MANNA	–; mannan,	**MANURER**	–; manurers
	mannas	**MANUS**	–; –
MANNAN	–; mannans	**MANWARD**	–; manwards
MANNED	–; –	**MANWISE**	–; –
MANNER	–; manners	**MAP**	–; maps
MANNING	–; –	**MAPLE**	–; maples
MANNISH	–; –	**MAPPED**	–; –
MANNITE	–; mannites	**MAPPER**	–; mappers
MANNOSE	–; mannoses	**MAPPING**	–; mappings
MANO	–; manor,	**MAQUI**	–; maquis
	manos	**MAR**	–; marc,
MANOR	–; manors		mare, mark,
MANPACK	–; –		marl, mars,
MANQUE	–; –		mart
MANROPE	–; manropes	**MARABOU**	–; marabous,
MANSARD	–; mansards		marabout
MANSE	–; manses	**MARACA**	–; maracas
MANSION	–; mansions	**MARANTA**	–; marantas
MANTA	–; mantas	**MARASCA**	–; marascas
MANTEAU	–; manteaus,	**MARAUD**	–; marauds
	manteaux	**MARBLE**	–; marbled,
MANTEL	–; mantels		marbler,
MANTES	–; –		marbles
MANTIC	–; –	**MARBLER**	–; marblers
MANTID	–; mantids	**MARBLY**	–; –
MANTIS	–; –	**MARC**	–; march,
MANTLE	–; mantled,		marcs
	mantles,	**MARCEL**	–; marcels
	mantlet	**MARCH**	–; –
MANTLET	–; mantlets	**MARCHED**	–; –
MANTRA	–; mantrap,	**MARCHEN**	–; –
	mantras	**MARCHER**	–; marchers
MANTRAP	–; mantraps	**MARCHES**	–;
MANTUA	–; mantuas		marchesa,
MANUAL	–; manuals		marchese
MANUARY	–; –	**MARE**	–; mares

MAREMMA	–; –	MARQUES	–; marquess
MAREMME	–; –	MARQUIS	–; marquise
MARGAY	–; margays	MARRAM	–; marrams
MARGE	–; marges	MARRED	–; –
MARGENT	–; margents	MARRER	–; marrers
MARGIN	–; margins	MARRIED	–; –
MARIA	–; –	MARRIER	–; marriers
MARIMBA	–; marimbas	MARRIES	–; –
MARINA	–; marinas	MARRING	–; –
MARINE	–; mariner, marines	MARRON	–; marrons
		MARROW	–; marrows, marrowy
MARINER	–; mariners		
MARISH	–; –	MARRY	–; –
MARITAL	–; –	MARSE	–; marses
MARK	–; marks	MARSH	–; marshy
MARKED	–; –	MARSHAL	–; marshall, marshals
MARKER	–; markers		
MARKET	–; markets	MARSHES	–; –
MARKHOR	–; markhors	MART	smart; marts
MARKING	–; markings	MARTED	smarted; –
MARKKA	–; markkaa, markkas	MARTEN	smarten; martens
MARKUP	–; markups	MARTENS	smartens; –
MARL	–; marls, marly	MARTIAL	–; –
		MARTIAN	–; martians
MARLED	–; –	MARTIN	–; marting, martini, martins
MARLIER	–; –		
MARLIN	–; marline, marling, marlins	MARTING	smarting; –
		MARTINI	–; martinis
MARLINE	–; marlines	MARTLET	–; martlets
MARLING	–; marlings	MARTS	smarts; –
MARLITE	–; marlites	MARTYR	–; martyrs, martyry
MARMITE	–; marmites		
MARMOT	–; marmots	MARVEL	–; marvels
MAROON	–; maroons	MAS	amas; mash, mask, mass, mast
MARPLOT	–; marplots		
MARQUE	–; marquee, marques		
		MASCARA	–; mascaras
MARQUEE	–; marquees	MASCON	–; mascons

MASCOT	–; mascots	**MASSIVE**	–; –
MASER	–; masers	**MASSING**	amassing; –
MASH	smash; mashy	**MAST**	–; masts
		MASTABA	–; mastabah, mastabas
MASHED	smashed; –		
MASHER	smasher; mashers	**MASTED**	–; –
		MASTER	–; masters, mastery
MASHERS	smashers; –		
MASHES	smashes; –	**MASTIC**	–; mastics
MASHIE	–; mashies	**MASTIFF**	–; mastiffs
MASHING	smashing; –	**MASTING**	–; –
MASJID	–; masjids	**MASTIX**	–; –
MASK	–; masks	**MASTOID**	–; mastoids
MASKED	–; –	**MAT**	–; mate, math, mats, matt
MASKEG	–; maskegs		
MASKER	–; maskers		
MASKING	–; maskings	**MATADOR**	–; matadors
MASON	–; masons	**MATCH**	–; –
MASONED	–; –	**MATCHED**	–; –
MASONIC	–; –	**MATCHER**	–; matchers
MASONRY	–; –	**MATCHES**	–; –
MASQUE	–; masquer, masques	**MATE**	–; mated, mater, mates, matey
MASQUER	–; masquers		
MASS	amass; massa, masse, massy		
		MATER	–; maters
		MATEY	–; mateys
MASSA	–; massas	**MATH**	–; maths
MASSAGE	–; massaged, massager, massages	**MATILDA**	–; matildas
		MATIN	–; mating, matins
		MATINAL	–; –
MASSE	–; massed, masses	**MATINEE**	–; matinees
		MATING	–; matings
MASSED	amassed; –	**MATLESS**	–; –
MASSES	amasses; –	**MATRASS**	–; –
MASSEUR	–; masseurs	**MATRES**	–; –
MASSIER	–; –	**MATRIX**	–; –
MASSIF	–; massifs	**MATRON**	–; matrons

MATT	–; matte, matts	**MAUVE**	–; mauves
MATTE	–; matted, matter, mattes	**MAVEN**	–; mavens
		MAVIE	–; mavies
		MAVIN	–; mavins
MATTER	smatter; matters, mattery	**MAVIS**	–; –
		MAVISES	–; –
		MAW	–; mawn, maws
MATTERS	smatters; –	**MAWED**	–; –
MATTIN	–; matting, mattins	**MAWING**	–; –
		MAWKISH	–; –
MATTING	–; mattings	**MAXI**	–; maxim, maxis
MATTOCK	–; mattocks		
MATTOID	–; mattoids	**MAXILLA**	–; maxillae, maxillas
MATURE	–; matured, maturer, matures		
		MAXIM	–; maxima, maxims
MATURES	–; maturest	**MAXIMA**	–; maximal
MATZA	–; matzah, matzas	**MAXIMAL**	–; maximals
		MAXIMIN	–; maximins
MATZAH	–; matzahs	**MAXIMUM**	–; maximums
MATZO	–; matzoh, matzos, matzot	**MAXIXE**	–; maxixes
		MAXWELL	–; maxwells
		MAY	–; maya, mays
MATZOH	–; matzohs		
MATZOON	–; matzoons	**MAYA**	–; mayan, mayas
MATZOT	–; matzoth		
MAUDLIN	–; –	**MAYBE**	–; –
MAUGER	–; –	**MAYBUSH**	–; –
MAUGRE	–; –	**MAYDAY**	–; maydays
MAUL	–; mauls	**MAYED**	–; –
MAULED	–; –	**MAYEST**	–; –
MAULER	–; maulers	**MAYFLY**	–; –
MAULING	–; –	**MAYHAP**	–; –
MAUMET	–; maumets	**MAYHEM**	–; mayhems
MAUN	–; maund	**MAYING**	–; mayings
MAUND	–; maunds, maundy	**MAYOR**	–; mayors
		MAYORAL	–; –
MAUNDER	–; maunders	**MAYPOLE**	–; maypoles
MAUT	–; mauts	**MAYPOP**	–; maypops

MAYS	–; mayst	**MEANDER**	–; meanders
MAYVIN	–; mayvins	**MEANER**	–; meaners
MAYWEED	–; mayweeds	**MEANEST**	–; –
		MEANIE	–; meanies
MAZARD	–; mazards	**MEANING**	–; meanings
MAZE	amaze, smaze; mazed, mazer, mazes	**MEANLY**	–; –
		MEASLE	–; measled, measles
MAZED	amazed; –	**MEASLY**	–; –
MAZEDLY	amazedly; –	**MEASURE**	–; measured, measurer, measures
MAZER	–; mazers		
MAZES	amazes, smazes; –	**MEAT**	–; meats, meaty
MAZIER	–; –	**MEATAL**	–; –
MAZIEST	–; –	**MEATIER**	–; –
MAZILY	–; –	**MEATILY**	–; –
MAZING	amazing; –	**MEATUS**	–; –
MAZUMA	–; mazumas	**MECCA**	–; meccas
MAZURKA	–; mazurkas	**MEDAKA**	–; medakas
MAZY	–; –	**MEDAL**	–; medals
MAZZARD	–; mazzards	**MEDALED**	–; –
MBIRA	–; mbiras	**MEDDLE**	–; meddled, meddler, meddles
ME	eme; mel, mem, men, met		
		MEDIA	–; mediad, mediae, medial, median, medias
MEAD	–; meads		
MEADOW	–; meadows, meadowy		
MEAGER	–; –	**MEDIACY**	–; –
MEAGRE	–; –	**MEDIAL**	–; medials
MEAL	–; meals, mealy	**MEDIAN**	–; medians, mediant
MEALIE	–; mealier, mealies	**MEDIATE**	–; mediated, mediates
MEALIES	–; mealiest	**MEDIC**	–; medics
MEAN	–; means, meant, meany	**MEDICAL**	–; medicals
		MEDICK	–; medicks

MEDICO	–; medicos	**MEL**	–; meld, mell,
MEDII	–; –		mels, melt
MEDIUM	–; mediums	**MELANGE**	–; melanges
MEDIUS	–; –	**MELANIC**	–; melanics
MEDLAR	–; medlars	**MELANIN**	–; melanins
MEDLEY	–; medleys	**MELD**	–; melds
MEDULLA	–; medullae,	**MELDED**	–; –
	medullar,	**MELDER**	–; melders
	medullas	**MELDING**	–; –
MEDUSA	–; medusae,	**MELEE**	–; melees
	medusan,	**MELIC**	–; –
	medusas	**MELILOT**	–; melilots
MEDUSAN	–; medusans	**MELISMA**	–; melismas
MEED	–; meeds	**MELL**	smell; mells
MEEK	smeek; –	**MELLED**	smelled; –
MEEKER	–; –	**MELLING**	smelling; –
MEEKEST	–; –	**MELLOW**	–; mellows
MEEKLY	–; –	**MELLS**	smells; –
MEET	–; meets	**MELODIA**	–; melodias
MEETER	–; meeters	**MELODIC**	–; –
MEETING	–; meetings	**MELODY**	–; –
MEETLY	–; –	**MELOID**	–; meloids
MEGABAR	–; megabars	**MELON**	–; melons
MEGABIT	–; megabits	**MELT**	smelt; melts
MEGAPOD	–;	**MELTAGE**	–; meltages
	megapode	**MELTED**	smelted; –
MEGASS	–; megasse	**MELTER**	smelter;
MEGASSE	–; megasses		melters
MEGATON	–; megatons	**MELTERS**	smelters; –
MEGILP	–; megilph,	**MELTING**	smelting; –
	megilps	**MELTON**	–; meltons
MEGLIPH	–; megliphs	**MELTS**	smelts; –
MEGOHM	–; megohms	**MEM**	–; memo,
MEGRIM	–; megrims		mems
MEIKLE	–; –	**MEMBER**	–; members
MEINIE	–; meinies	**MEMENTO**	–; mementos
MEINY	–; –	**MEMO**	–; memos
MEIOSES	–; –	**MEMOIR**	–; memoirs
MEIOSIS	–; –	**MEMORY**	–; –
MEIOTIC	–; –	**MEN**	amen, omen;

	mend, meno,	**MENTUM**	omentum; –
	menu	**MENU**	–; menus
MENACE	–; menaced,	**MEOW**	–; meows
	menacer,	**MEOWED**	–; –
	menaces	**MEOWING**	–; –
MENACER	–; menacers	**MERCER**	amercer;
MENAD	–; menads		mercers,
MENAGE	–; menages		mercery
MEND	amend,	**MERCERS**	amercers; –
	emend;	**MERCIES**	–; –
	mends	**MERCURY**	–; –
MENDED	amended,	**MERCY**	–; –
	emended; –	**MERE**	–; merer,
MENDER	amender,		meres
	emender;	**MERELY**	–; –
	menders	**MERES**	–; merest
MENDERS	amenders,	**MERGE**	emerge;
	emenders; –		merged,
MENDIGO	–; mendigos		merger
MENDING	amending,	**MERGED**	emerged; –
	emending;	**MERGER**	–; mergers
	mendings	**MERGES**	emerges; –
MENDS	amends,	**MERGING**	emerging; –
	emends; –	**MERINO**	–; merinos
MENFOLK	–; menfolks	**MERISES**	–; –
MENHIR	–; menhirs	**MERISIS**	–; –
MENIAL	–; menials	**MERIT**	–; merits
MENINX	–; –	**MERITED**	–; –
MENORAH	–; menorahs	**MERK**	smerk; merks
MENSA	–; mensae,	**MERKS**	smerks; –
	mensal,	**MERL**	–; merle,
	mensas		merls
MENSCH	–; –	**MERLE**	–; merles
MENSE	–; mensed,	**MERLIN**	–; merlins
	menses	**MERLON**	–; merlons
MENSING	–; –	**MERMAID**	–; mermaids
MENTA	–; mental	**MERMAN**	–; –
MENTHOL	–; menthols	**MERMEN**	–; –
MENTION	–; mentions	**MEROPIA**	–; meropias
MENTOR	–; mentors	**MEROPIC**	–; –

MERRIER	–; –	**METALED**	–; –
MERRILY	–; –	**METAMER**	–; metamere, metamers
MERRY	–; –		
MESA	–; mesas	**METATE**	–; metates
MESALLY	–; –	**METE**	–; meted, meter, metes
MESARCH	–; –		
MESCAL	–; mescals	**METEOR**	–; meteors
MESEEMS	–; –	**METEPA**	–; metepas
MESH	–; meshy	**METER**	–; meters
MESHED	–; –	**METERED**	–; –
MESHES	–; –	**METHANE**	–; methanes
MESHIER	–; –	**METHOD**	–; methods
MESHING	–; –	**METHOXY**	–; methoxyl
MESIAL	–; –	**METHYL**	–; methyls
MESIAN	–; –	**METIER**	–; metiers
MESIC	–; –	**METING**	–; –
MESNE	–; –	**METIS**	–; –
MESON	–; mesons	**METISSE**	–; metisses
MESONIC	–; –	**METONYM**	–; metonyms, metonymy
MESQUIT	–; mesquite, mesquits		
		METOPAE	–; –
MESS	–; messy	**METOPE**	–; metopes
MESSAGE	–; messages	**METOPIC**	–; –
MESSAN	–; messans	**METOPON**	–; metopons
MESSED	–; –	**METRE**	–; metred, metres
MESSES	–; –		
MESSIAH	–; messiahs	**METRIC**	–; metrics
MESSIER	–; –	**METRIFY**	–; –
MESSILY	–; –	**METRING**	–; –
MESSING	–; –	**METRIST**	–; metrists
MESTEE	–; mestees	**METRO**	–; metros
MESTESO	–; mestesos	**METTLE**	–; mettled, mettles
MESTINO	–; mestinos		
MESTIZA	–; mestizas	**METUMP**	–; metumps
MESTIZO	–; mestizos	**MEW**	smew; mewl, mews
MET	–; meta, mete		
		MEWED	–; –
META	–; metal	**MEWING**	–; –
METAGE	–; metages	**MEWL**	–; mewls
METAL	–; metals	**MEWLED**	–; –

MEWLER	–; mewlers	**MICKLES**	–; micklest
MEWLING	–; –	**MICRA**	–; –
MEWS	smews; –	**MICRIFY**	–; –
MEZCAL	–; mezcals	**MICRO**	–; micron
MEZQUIT	–; mezquite,	**MICROBE**	–; microbes
	mezquits	**MICROHM**	–; microhms
MEZUZA	–; mezuzah,	**MICRON**	omicron;
	mezuzas		microns
MEZUZAH	–; mezuzahs	**MICRONS**	omicrons; –
MEZUZOT	–; mezuzoth	**MID**	amid, imid;
MEZZO	–; mezzos		midi, mids
MHO	–; mhos	**MIDAIR**	–; midairs
MI	ami; mib,	**MIDDAY**	–; middays
	mid, mig, mil,	**MIDDEN**	–; middens
	mim, mir,	**MIDDIES**	–; –
	mis, mix	**MIDDLE**	–; middled,
MIAOU	–; miaous		middler,
MIAOUED	–; –		middles
MIAOW	–; miaows	**MIDDLER**	–; middlers
MIAOWED	–; –	**MIDDY**	–; –
MIASM	–; miasma,	**MIDGE**	–; midges,
	miasms		midget
MIASMA	–; miasmal,	**MIDGET**	–; midgets
	miasmas	**MIDGUT**	–; midguts
MIASMIC	–; –	**MIDI**	–; midis
MIAUL	–; miauls	**MIDIRON**	–; midirons
MIAULED	–; –	**MIDLAND**	–; midlands
MIB	–; mibs	**MIDLEG**	–; midlegs
MICA	–; micas	**MIDLINE**	–; midlines
MICE	amice; –	**MIDMOST**	–; midmosts
MICELL	–; micella,	**MIDNOON**	–; midnoons
	micelle,	**MIDRASH**	–; –
	micells	**MIDRIB**	–; midribs
MICELLA	–; micellae,	**MIDRIFF**	–; midriffs
	micellar	**MIDS**	amids,
MICELLE	–; micelles		imids; –
MICK	–; micks	**MIDSHIP**	amidship;
MICKEY	–; mickeys		midships
MICKLE	–; mickler,	**MIDST**	amidst;
	mickles		midsts

MIDTERM	–; midterms	**MILADY**	–; –
MIDTOWN	–; midtowns	**MILAGE**	–; milages
MIDWAY	–; midways	**MILCH**	–; –
MIDWEEK	–; midweeks	**MILCHIG**	–; –
MIDWIFE	–; midwifed, midwifes	**MILD**	–; –
		MILDEN	–; mildens
MIDYEAR	–; midyears	**MILDER**	–; –
MIEN	–; miens	**MILDEST**	–; –
MIFF	–; miffs, miffy	**MILDEW**	–; mildews, mildewy
MIFFED	–; –	**MILDLY**	–; –
MIFFIER	–; –	**MILE**	smile; miler, miles
MIFFING	–; –		
MIFFY	–; –	**MILEAGE**	–; mileages
MIG	–; migg, migs	**MILER**	smiler; milers
		MILERS	smilers; –
MIGG	–; miggs	**MILES**	smiles; –
MIGGLE	–; miggles	**MILFOIL**	–; milfoils
MIGHT	–; mights, mighty	**MILIA**	–; –
		MILIARY	–; –
MIGNON	–; mignons	**MILIEU**	–; milieus, milieux
MIGRANT	emigrant; migrants		
		MILITIA	–; militias
MIGRATE	emigrate; migrated, migrates	**MILIUM**	–; –
		MILK	–; milks, milky
MIKADO	–; mikados	**MILKED**	–; –
MIKE	–; mikes	**MILKER**	–; milkers
MIKRA	–; –	**MILKIER**	–; –
MIKRON	omikron; mikrons	**MILKILY**	–; –
		MILKING	–; –
MIKRONS	omikrons; –	**MILKMAN**	–; –
MIKVAH	–; mikvahs	**MILKMEN**	–; –
MIKVEH	–; mikvehs	**MILKSOP**	–; milksops
MIKVOTH	–; –	**MILL**	–; mille, mills
MIL	–; mild, mile, milk, mill, milo, mils, milt	**MILLAGE**	–; millages
		MILLDAM	–; milldams
		MILLE	–; milled, miller, milles, millet
MILADI	–; miladis		

MILLER	–; millers	**MIND**	–; –
MILLET	–; millets	**MINDED**	–; –
MILLIER	–; milliers	**MINDER**	–; minders
MILLIME	–; millimes	**MINDFUL**	–; –
MILLINE	–; millines	**MINDING**	–; –
MILLING	–; millings	**MINE**	amine, imine;
MILLION	–; millions		mined,
MILLRUN	–; millruns		miner, mines
MILO	–; milos	**MINER**	–; miners
MILORD	–; milords	**MINERAL**	–; minerals
MILPA	–; milpas	**MINES**	amines,
MILREIS	–; –		imines; –
MILT	–; milts, milty	**MINGIER**	–; –
MILTED	–; –	**MINGLE**	–; mingled,
MILTER	–; milters		mingler,
MILTIER	–; –		mingles
MILTING	–; –	**MINGLER**	–; minglers
MIM	–; mime	**MINGY**	–; –
MIMBAR	–; mimbars	**MINI**	–; minim,
MIME	–; mimed,		minis
	mimer, mimes	**MINIBUS**	–; –
MIMER	–; mimers	**MINICAB**	–; minicabs
MIMESIS	–; –	**MINICAR**	–; minicars
MIMETIC	–; –	**MINIFY**	–; –
MIMIC	–; mimics	**MINIKIN**	–; minikins
MIMICAL	–; –	**MINIM**	–; minima,
MIMICRY	–; –		minims
MIMING	–; –	**MINIMA**	–; minimal,
MIMOSA	–; mimosas		minimax
MINA	–; minae,	**MINIMAL**	–; minimals
	minas	**MINIMUM**	–; minimums
MINABLE	–; –	**MINING**	–; minings
MINARET	–; minarets	**MINION**	–; minions
MINCE	–; minced,	**MINISH**	–; –
	mincer,	**MINIUM**	–; miniums
	minces	**MINIVER**	–; minivers
MINCER	–; mincers	**MINK**	–; minks
MINCIER	–; –	**MINNIES**	–; –
MINCING	–; –	**MINNOW**	–; minnows
MINCY	–; –	**MINNY**	–; –

MINOR	–; minors	**MIRING**	–; –
MINORCA	–; minorcas	**MIRK**	smirk, mirks,
MINSTER	–; minsters		mirky
MINT	–; mints,	**MIRKIER**	smirkier; –
	minty	**MIRKILY**	–; –
MINTAGE	–; mintages	**MIRKS**	smirks; –
MINTED	–; –	**MIRKY**	smirky; –
MINTER	–; minters	**MIRROR**	–; mirrors
MINTIER	–; –	**MIRS**	amirs,
MINTING	–; –		emirs; –
MINUEND	–; minuends	**MIRTH**	–; mirths
MINUET	–; minuets	**MIRZA**	–; mirzas
MINUS	–; –	**MIS**	amis; mise,
MINUSES	–; –		miso, miss,
MINUTE	–, minuted,		mist
	minuter,	**MISACT**	–; misacts
	minutes	**MISADD**	–; misadds
MINUTES	–; minutest	**MISAIM**	–; misaims
MINUTIA	–; minutiae,	**MISALLY**	–; –
	minutial	**MISATE**	–; –
MINX	–; –	**MISAVER**	–; misavers
MINXES	–; –	**MISBIAS**	–; –
MINXISH	–; –	**MISBILL**	–; misbills
MINYAN	–; minyans	**MISBIND**	–; misbinds
MIOSES	–; –	**MISCALL**	–; miscalls
MIOSIS	–; –	**MISCAST**	–; miscasts
MIOTIC	–; miotics	**MISCITE**	–; miscited,
MIR	amir, emir;		miscites
	mire, miri,	**MISCOIN**	–; miscoins
	mirk, mirs,	**MISCOOK**	–; miscooks
	miry	**MISCOPY**	–; –
MIRACLE	–; miracles	**MISCUE**	–; miscued,
MIRADOR	–; miradors		miscues
MIRAGE	–; mirages	**MISCUT**	–; miscuts
MIRE	–; mired,	**MISDATE**	–; misdated,
	mires, mirex		misdates
MIREX	–; –	**MISDEAL**	–; misdeals,
MIREXES	–; –		misdealt
MIRIER	–; –	**MISDEED**	–; misdeeds
MIRIEST	–; –	**MISDEEM**	–; misdeems

MISDID	–; –	**MISLEAD**	–; misleads
MISDO	–; –	**MISLED**	–; –
MISDOER	–; misdoers	**MISLIE**	–; mislies
MISDOES	–; –	**MISLIKE**	–; misliked,
MISDONE	–; –		misliker,
MISDRAW	–; misdrawn,		mislikes
	misdraws	**MISLIT**	–; –
MISE	–; miser,	**MISLIVE**	–; mislived,
	mises		mislives
MISEASE	–; miseases	**MISMARK**	–; mismarks
MISEAT	–; miseats	**MISMATE**	–; mismated,
MISEDIT	–; misedits		mismates
MISER	–; misers,	**MISMEET**	–; mismeets
	misery	**MISMOVE**	–;
MISERLY	–; –		mismoved,
MISFILE	–; misfiled,		mismoves
	misfiles	**MISNAME**	–;
MISFIRE	–; misfired,		misnamed,
	misfires		misnames
MISFIT	–; misfits	**MISO**	–; misos
MISFORM	–; misforms	**MISPAGE**	–;
MISGAVE	–; –		mispaged,
MISGIVE	–; misgiven,		mispages
	misgives	**MISPART**	–; misparts
MISGROW	–; misgrown,	**MISPEN**	–; mispens
	misgrows	**MISPLAY**	–; misplays
MISHAP	–; mishaps	**MISRATE**	–; misrated,
MISHEAR	–; misheard,		misrates
	mishears	**MISREAD**	–; misreads
MISHIT	–; mishits	**MISRELY**	–; –
MISJOIN	–; misjoins	**MISRULE**	–; misruled,
MISKAL	–; miskals		misrules
MISKEEP	–; miskeps	**MISS**	amiss; missy
MISKEPT	–; –	**MISSAID**	–; –
MISKNEW	–; –	**MISSAL**	–; missals
MISKNOW	–; misknown,	**MISSAY**	–; missays
	misknows	**MISSEAT**	–; misseats
MISLAID	–; –	**MISSED**	–; –
MISLAIN	–; –	**MISSEL**	–; missels
MISLAY	–; mislays	**MISSEND**	–; missends

MISSES	–; –	**MISUSE**	–; misused,
MISSHOD	–; –		misuser,
MISSIES	–; –		misuses
MISSILE	–; missiles	**MISUSER**	–; misusers
MISSING	–; –	**MISWORD**	–; miswords
MISSION	emission,	**MISYOKE**	–; misyoked,
	omission;		misyokes
	missions	**MITE**	smite; miter,
MISSIS	–; –		mites
MISSIVE	omissive;	**MITER**	smiter; miters
	missives	**MITERED**	–; –
MISSORT	–; missorts	**MITERER**	–; miterers
MISSOUT	–; missouts	**MITERS**	smiters; –
MISSTEP	–; missteps	**MITES**	smites; –
MISSTOP	–; misstops	**MITHER**	–; mithers
MISSUIT	–; missuits	**MITIER**	–; –
MISSUS	–; –	**MITIEST**	–; –
MIST	–; mists,	**MITIS**	;
	misty	**MITISES**	–; –
MISTAKE	–; mistaken,	**MITOGEN**	–; mitogens
	mistaker,	**MITOSES**	amitoses; –
	mistakes	**MITOSIS**	amitosis; –
MISTBOW	–; mistbows	**MITOTIC**	amitotic; –
MISTED	–; –	**MITRAL**	–; –
MISTEND	–; mistends	**MITRE**	–; mitred,
MISTER	–; misterm,		mitres
	misters	**MITSVAH**	–; mitsvahs
MISTERM	–; misterms	**MITT**	–; mitts
MISTEUK	; –	**MITTEN**	smitten,
MISTIER	–; –		mittens
MISTILY	–; –	**MITY**	amity; –
MISTIME	–; mistimed,	**MITZVAH**	–; mitzvahs
	mistimes	**MIX**	–; mixt
MISTING	–; –	**MIXABLE**	–; –
MISTOOK	–; –	**MIXED**	–; –
MISTRAL	–; mistrals	**MIXER**	–; mixers
MISTUNE	–; mistuned,	**MIXES**	–; –
	mistunes	**MIXIBLE**	–; –
MISTYPE	–; mistyped,	**MIXING**	–; –
	mistypes	**MIXTURE**	–; mixtures

MIXUP	–; mixups	**MOCKUP**	–; mockups
MIZEN	–; mizens	**MOD**	–; mode,
MIZZEN	–; mizzens		modi, mods
MIZZLE	–; mizzled,	**MODAL**	–; –
	mizzles	**MODALLY**	–; –
MIZZLY	–; –	**MODE**	–; model,
MM	–; –		modes
MO	–; moa,	**MODEL**	–; models
	mob, mod,	**MODELED**	–; –
	mog, mol,	**MODELER**	–; modelers
	mom, mon,	**MODERN**	–; moderns
	moo, mop,	**MODES**	–; modest
	mor, mos,	**MODEST**	–; modesty
	mot, mow	**MODI**	–; –
MOA	–; moan,	**MODICA**	–; –
	moas, moat	**MODICUM**	–; modicums
MOAN	–; moans	**MODIFY**	–; –
MOANED	–; –	**MODISH**	–; –
MOANING	–; –	**MODISTE**	–; modistes
MOANFUL	–; –	**MODULAR**	–; –
MOAT	–; moats	**MODULE**	–; modules
MOATED	–; –	**MODULI**	–; –
MOATING	–; –	**MODULO**	–; –
MOB	–; mobs	**MODULUS**	–; –
MOBBED	–; –	**MODUS**	–; –
MOBBER	–; mobbers	**MOFETTE**	–; mofettes
MOBBING	–; –	**MOG**	smog; mogs
MOBBISH	–; –	**MOGGED**	–; –
MOBCAP	–; mobcaps	**MOGGING**	–; –
MOBILE	–; mobiles	**MOGS**	smogs; –
MOBSTER	–; mobsters	**MOGUL**	–; moguls
MOCHA	–; mochas	**MOHAIR**	–; mohairs
MOCHILA	–; mochilas	**MOHALIM**	–; –
MOCK	smock;	**MOHEL**	–; mohels
	mocks	**MOHUR**	–; mohurs
MOCKED	smocked; –	**MOIDORE**	–; moidores
MOCKER	–; mockers,	**MOIETY**	–; –
	mockery	**MOIL**	–; moils
MOCKING	smocking; –	**MOILED**	–; –
MOCKS	smocks; –	**MOILER**	–; moilers

MOILING	–; –	**MOLOCH**	–; molochs
MOIRA	–; moirai	**MOLT**	smolt; molto, molts
MOIRE	–; moires		
MOIST	–; –	**MOLTED**	–; –
MOISTEN	–; moistens	**MOLTEN**	–; –
MOISTER	–; –	**MOLTER**	–; molters
MOISTLY	–; –	**MOLTING**	–; –
MOJARRA	–; mojarras	**MOLTS**	smolts; –
MOKE	smoke; mokes	**MOM**	–; mome, momi, moms
MOKES	smokes; –	**MOME**	–; momes
MOL	–; mola, mold, mole, moll, mols, molt, moly	**MOMENT**	–; momenta, momento, moments
MOLA	–; molal, molar, molas	**MOMENTO**	–; momentos
		MOMI	–; –
MOLAR	–; molars	**MOMISH**	–; momisms
MOLD	–; molds, moldy	**MOMMA**	–; mommas
		MOMUS	–; –
MOLDED	–; –	**MOMUSES**	–; –
MOLDER	smolder; molders	**MON**	–; monk, mono, mons, mony
MOLDERS	smolders; –	**MONACID**	–; monacids
MOLDIER	–; –	**MONAD**	–; manads
MOLDING	–; moldings	**MONADAL**	–; –
MOLE	amole; moles	**MONADES**	–; –
MOLES	amoles; molest	**MONADIC**	–; –
		MONARCH	–; monarchs, monarchy
MOLEST	–; molests		
MOLIES	–; –		
MOLINE	–; –	**MONARDA**	–; monardas
MOLL	–; molls, molly	**MONAS**	–; –
		MONDE	–; mondes
MOLLAH	–; mollahs	**MONDO**	–; mondos
MOLLIE	–; mollies	**MONEY**	–; moneys
MOLLIFY	–; –	**MONEYED**	–; –
MOLLUSC	–; molluscs	**MONEYER**	–; moneyers
MOLLUSK	–; mollusks	**MONGER**	–; mongers
		MONGO	–; mongoe,

	mongol,	**MONTHLY**	–; –
	mongos	**MONURON**	–; monurons
MONGOE	–; mongoes	**MOO**	–; mood,
MONGOL	–; mongols		mool, moon,
MONGREL	–; mongrels		moor, moos,
MONGST	amongst; –		moot
MONIE	–; monied,	**MOOCH**	smooch; –
	monies	**MOOCHED**	smooched; –
MONIKER	–; monikers	**MOOCHER**	–; moochers
MONISH	–; –	**MOOCHES**	smooches; –
MONISM	–; monisms	**MOOD**	–; moods,
MONIST	–; monists		moody
MONITOR	–; monitors,	**MOODIER**	–; –
	monitory	**MOODILY**	–; –
MONK	–; monks	**MOOED**	–; –
MONKERY	–; –	**MOOING**	–; –
MONKEY	–; monkeys	**MOOL**	–; moola,
MONKISH	–; –		mools
MONO	–; monos	**MOOLA**	–; moolah,
MONOCLE	–;		moolas
	monocled,	**MOOLAH**	–; moolahs
	monocles	**MOOLEY**	–; mooleys
MONOCOT	–; monocots	**MOON**	–; moons,
MONODIC	–; –		moony
MONODY	–; –	**MOONBOW**	–;
MONOECY	–; –		moonbows
MONOFIL	–; monofils	**MOONED**	–; –
MONOLOG	–;	**MOONEYE**	–; mooneyes
	monologs,	**MOONIER**	–; –
	monology	**MOONILY**	–; –
MONOMER	–; monomers	**MOONING**	–; –
MONSOON	–; monsoons	**MOONISH**	–; –
MONSTER	–; monsters	**MOONLET**	–; moonlets
MONTAGE	–;	**MOONLIT**	–; –
	montaged,	**MOONSET**	–; moonsets
	montages	**MOOR**	–; moors,
MONTANE	–; montanes		moory
MONTE	–; montes	**MOORAGE**	–; moorages
MONTERO	–; –	**MOORED**	–; –
MONTH	–; months	**MOORHEN**	–; moorhens

MOORIER	–; –	**MORE**	–; morel,
MOORING	–; moorings		mores
MOORISH	–; –	**MOREEN**	–; moreens
MOOSE	–; –	**MOREL**	–; morels
MOOT	–; moots	**MORELLE**	–; morelles
MOOTED	–; –	**MORELLO**	–; morellos
MOOTER	–; mooters	**MORGEN**	–; morgens
MOOTING	–; –	**MORGUE**	–; morgues
MOP	–; mope,	**MORION**	–; morions
	mops	**MORN**	–; morns
MOPE	–; moped,	**MORNING**	–; mornings
	moper,	**MOROCCO**	–; moroccos
	mopes	**MORON**	–; morons
MOPED	–; mopeds	**MOROSE**	–; –
MOPER	–; mopers	**MORPH**	; morphs
MOPING	–; –	**MORPHIA**	–; morphias
MOPISH	–; –	**MORPHIC**	–; –
MOPOKE	–; mopokes	**MORPHIN**	–; morphine,
MOPPED	–; –		morphins
MOPPER	–; moppers	**MORPHO**	–; morphos
MOPPET	–; moppets	**MORRION**	–; morrions
MOPPING	–; –	**MORRIS**	–; –
MOR	–; mora,	**MORRO**	–; morros,
	more, morn,		morrow
	mors, mort	**MORROW**	–; morrows
MORA	–; morae,	**MORSEL**	–; morsels
	moral, moras,	**MORT**	amort; morts
	moray	**MORTAL**	–; mortals
MORAINE	–; moraines	**MORTAR**	–; mortars,
MURAL	amoral;		mortary
	morale,	**MORTICE**	–; morticed,
	morals		mortices
MORALE	–; morales	**MORTIFY**	–; –
MORALLY	amorally; –	**MORTISE**	amortise;
MORASS	–; morassy		mortised,
MORAY	–; morays		mortiser,
MORBID	–; –		mortises
MORCEAU	–; morceaux	**MORULA**	–; morulae,
MORDANT	–; mordants		morular,
MORDENT	–; mordents		morulas

MOSAIC	–; mosaics	**MOTIONS**	amotions,
MOSEY	–; moseys		emotions; –
MOSEYED	–; –	**MOTIVE**	emotive;
MOSHAV	–; –		motived,
MOSK	–; mosks		motives
MOSQUE	–; mosques	**MOTIVIC**	–; –
MOSS	–; mosso,	**MOTLEY**	–; motleys
	mossy	**MOTLIER**	–; –
MOSSED	–; –	**MOTMOT**	–; motmots
MOSSER	–; mossers	**MOTOR**	–; motors
MOSSES	–; –	**MOTORED**	–; –
MOSSIER	–; –	**MOTORIC**	–; –
MOSSING	–; –	**MOTT**	–; motte,
MOST	–; moste,		motto, motts
	mosts	**MOTTE**	–; mottes
MOSTLY	–; –	**MOTTLE**	–; mottled,
MOT	–; mote,		mottler,
	moth, mots,		mottles
	mott	**MOTTLER**	–; mottlers
MOTE	emote,	**MOTTO**	–; mottos
	smote;	**MOTTOES**	–; –
	motel,	**MOUCH**	–; –
	motes,	**MOUCHED**	–; –
	motey	**MOUCHES**	–; –
MOTEL	–; motels	**MOUE**	–; moues
MOTES	emotes; –	**MOUFLON**	–; mouflons
MOTET	–; motets	**MOUILLE**	–; –
MOTH	–; moths,	**MOUJIK**	–; moujiks
	mothy	**MOULAGE**	–; moulages
MOTHER	smother;	**MOULD**	–; moulds,
	mothers,		mouldy
	mothery	**MOULDED**	–; –
MOTHERS	smothers; –	**MOULDER**	smoulder;
MOTHERY	smothery; –		moulders
MOTHIER	–; –	**MOULIN**	–; moulins
MOTIF	–; motifs	**MOULT**	–; moults
MOTILE	–; motiles	**MOULTED**	–; –
MOTION	amotion,	**MOULTER**	–; moulters
	emotion;	**MOUND**	–; mounds
	motions	**MOUNDED**	–; –

MOUNT	amount; mounts	**MOZETTE**	–; –
		MOZO	–; mozos
MOUNTED	amounted; –	**MU**	amu, emu;
MOUNTER	–; mounters		mud, mug,
MOUNTS	amounts; –		mum, mun,
MOURN	–; mourns		mus, mut
MOURNED	–; –	**MUCH**	–; –
MOURNER	–; mourners	**MUCHES**	–; –
MOUSE	–; moused,	**MUCID**	–; –
	mouser,	**MUCIN**	–; mucins
	mouses,	**MUCK**	amuck;
	mousey		mucks, mucky
MOUSER	–; mousers	**MUCKED**	–; –
MOUSIER	–; –	**MUCKER**	–; muckers
MOUSILY	–; –	**MUCKIER**	–; –
MOUSING	–; mousings	**MUCKILY**	–; –
MOUSSE	–; mousses	**MUCKING**	–; –
MOUSY	–; –	**MUCKLE**	–; muckles
MOUTH	–; mouths,	**MUCKS**	amucks; –
	mouthy	**MUCLUC**	–; muclucs
MOUTHED	–; –	**MUCOID**	–; mucoids
MOUTHER	–; mouthers	**MUCOR**	–; mucors
MOUTON	–; moutons	**MUCOSA**	–; mucosae,
MOVABLE	–; movables		mucosal,
MOVABLY	–; –		mucosas
MOVE	–; moved,	**MUCOSE**	–; –
	mover,	**MUCOUS**	–; –
	moves	**MUCRO**	–; –
MOVER	–; movers	**MUCUS**	–; –
MOVIE	–; movies	**MUCUSES**	–; –
MOVING	–; –	**MUD**	–; muds
MOW	–; mown,	**MUDCAP**	–; mudcaps
	mows	**MUDDED**	–; –
MOWED	–; –	**MUDDER**	–; mudders
MOWER	–; mowers	**MUDDIED**	–; –
MOWING	–; –	**MUDDIER**	–; –
MOXA	–; moxas	**MUDDIES**	–; muddiest
MOXIE	–; moxies	**MUDDILY**	–; –
MOZETTA	–; mozettas	**MUDDING**	–; –
		MUDDLE	–; muddled,

	muddler, muddles	**MUJIK**	–; mujiks
MUDDLER	–; muddlers	**MUKLUK**	–; mukluks
MUDDY	–; –	**MULATTO**	–; mulattos
MUDFISH	–; –	**MULCH**	–; –
MUDLARK	–; mudlarks	**MULCHED**	–; –
MUDRA	–; mudras	**MULCHES**	–; –
MUDROCK	–; mudrocks	**MULCT**	–; mulcts
MUDROOM	–; mudrooms	**MULCTED**	–; –
MUDSILL	–; mudsills	**MULE**	–; muled, mules, muley
MUEDDIN	–; mueddins	**MULETA**	–; muletas
MUEZZIN	–; muezzins	**MULEY**	–; muleys
MUFF	–; muffs	**MULING**	–; –
MUFFED	–; –	**MULISH**	–; –
MUFFIN	–; muffing, muffins	**MULL**	–; mulla, mulls
MUFFLE	–; muffled, muffler, muffles	**MULLA**	–; mullah, mullas
MUFFLER	–; mufflers	**MULLAH**	–; mullahs
MUFTI	–; muftis	**MULLEIN**	–; mulleins
MUG	smug; mugg, mugs	**MULLED**	–; –
		MULLEN	–; mullens
MUGG	–; muggs, muggy	**MULLER**	–; mullers
		MULLET	–; mullets
MUGGAR	–; muggars	**MULLEY**	–; mulleys
MUGGED	–; –	**MULLING**	–; –
MUGGER	smugger; muggers	**MULLION**	–; mullions
		MULLITE	–; mullites
MUGGIER	–; –	**MULLOCK**	–; mullocks, mullocky
MUGGILY	–; –	**MULTURE**	–; multures
MUGGING	–; –	**MUM**	–; mumm, mump, mums
MUGGING	–; muggings		
MUGGINS	–; –	**MUMBLE**	–; mumbled, mumbler, mumbles
MUGGUR	–; muggurs		
MUGWORT	–; mugworts		
MUGWUMP	–; mugwumps	**MUMBLER**	–; mumblers
		MUMM	–; mumms, mummy
MUHLIES	–; –		
MUHLY	–; –	**MUMMED**	–; –

MUMMER	–; mummers, mummory	MURK	–; murks, murky
MUMMIED	–; –	MURKER	–; –
MUMMIES	–; –	MURKEST	–; –
MUMMIFY	–; –	MURKIER	–; –
MUMMING	–; –	MURKILY	–; –
MUMP	–; mumps	MURKLY	–; –
MUMPED	–; –	MURMUR	–; murmurs
MUMPER	–; mumpers	MURPHY	–; –
MUMPING	–; –	MURR	–; murra, murre, murrs, murry
MUN	–; muns		
MUNCH	–; –		
MUNCHED	–; –	MURRA	–; murras
MUNCHER	–; munchers	MURRAIN	–; murrains
MUNCHES	–; –	MURRE	–; murres, murrey
MUNDANE	–; –		
MUNGO	–; mungos	MURREY	–; murreys
MUNNION	–; munnions	MURRHA	–; murrhas
MUNSTER	–; munsters	MURRIES	–; –
MUNTIN	–; munting, muntins	MURRINE	–; –
		MURTHER	–; murthers
MUNTING	–; muntings	MUS	amus, emus; muse, mush, musk, muss, must
MUNTJAC	–; muntjacs		
MUNTJAK	–; muntjaks		
MUON	–; muons		
MUONIC	–; –	MUSCA	–; muscae, muscat
MURA	–; mural, muras		
		MUSCAT	–; muscats
MURAL	–; murals	MUSCID	–; muscids
MURDER	–; murders	MUSCLE	–; muscled, muscles
MURE	–; mured, mures, murex		
		MUSCLY	–; –
MUREIN	–; mureins	MUSE	amuse; mused, muser, muses
MUREXES	–; –		
MURIATE	–; muriated, muriates		
		MUSED	amused; –
MURICES	–; –	MUSER	amuser; musers
MURID	–; murids		
MURINE	–; murines	MUSERS	amusers; –
MURING	–; –	MUSES	amuses; –

MUSETTE	–; musettes	**MUSTH**	–; musths
MUSEUM	–; museums	**MUSTIER**	–; –
MUSH	–; mushy	**MUSTILY**	–; –
MUSHED	–; –	**MUSTING**	–; –
MUSHER	–; mushers	**MUT**	smut; mute,
MUSHES	–; –		muts, mutt
MUSHIER	–; –		
MUSHILY	–; –	**MUTABLE**	–; –
MUSHING	–; –	**MUTABLY**	–; –
MUSIC	–; musics	**MUTAGEN**	–; mutagens
MUSICAL	–; musicals	**MUTANT**	–; mutants
MUSING	amusing;	**MUTASE**	–; mutases
	musings	**MUTATE**	–; mutated,
MUSJID	–; musjids		mutates
MUSK	–; musks,	**MUTCH**	smutch; –
	musky	**MUTCHES**	smutches;
MUSKEG	–; muskegs	**MUTE**	–; muted,
MUSKET	–; muskets		muter, mutes
MUSKIE	–; muskier,		
	muskies	**MUTEDLY**	–; –
MUSKIES	–; muskiest	**MUTELY**	–; –
MUSKILY	–; –	**MUTES**	–; mutest
MUSKIT	–; muskits	**MUTINE**	–; mutined,
MUSKRAT	–; muskrats		mutines
MUSLIN	–; muslins	**MUTING**	–; –
MUSPIKE	–; muspikes	**MUTINY**	–; –
MUSS	–; mussy	**MUTISM**	–; mutisms
MUSSED	–; –	**MUTS**	smuts; –
MUSSEL	–; mussels	**MUTT**	–; mutts
MUSSES	–; –	**MUTTER**	–; mutters
MUSSIER	–; –	**MUTTON**	–; muttons,
MUSSILY	–; –		muttony
MUSSING	–; –	**MUTUAL**	–; –
MUST	–; musth,	**MUTUEL**	–; mutuels
	musts, musty	**MUTULAR**	–; –
MUSTANG	–; mustangs	**MUTULE**	–; mutules
MUSTARD	–; mustards	**MUUMUU**	–; muumuus
MUSTED	–; –	**MUZHIK**	–; muzhiks
MUSTEE	–; mustees	**MUZJIK**	–; muzjiks
MUSTER	–; musters	**MUZZIER**	–; –
		MUZZILY	–; –
		MUZZLE	–; muzzled,

	muzzler,	**MYOMA**	–; myomas
	muzzles	**MYOPE**	–; myopes
MUZZLER	–; muzzlers	**MYOPIA**	–; myopias
MUZZY	–; –	**MYOPIC**	–; –
MY	–; –	**MYOPIES**	–; –
MYALGIA	–; myalgias	**MYOPY**	–; –
MYALGIC	–; –	**MYOSES**	–; –
MYASES	–; –	**MYOSIN**	–; myosins
MYASIS	–; –	**MYOSIS**	–; –
MYCELE	–; myceles	**MYOSOTE**	–; myosotes
MYCELIA	–; mycelial,	**MYOTIC**	–; myotics
	mycelian	**MYOTOME**	–; myotomes
MYCOSES	–; –	**MYRIAD**	–; myriad
MYCOSIS	–; –	**MYRICA**	–; myrica
MYCOTIC	–;	**MYRRH**	–; myrrhs
MYELIN	–; myeline,	**MYRRHIC**	–; –
	myelins	**MYRTLE**	–; myrtles
MYELINE	–; myelines	**MYSELF**	–; –
MYELOID	–; –	**MYSOST**	–; mysosts
MYELOMA	–; myelomas	**MYSTERY**	–; –
MYIASES	–; –	**MYSTIC**	–; mystics
MYIASIS	–; –	**MYSTIFY**	–; –
MYNA	–; mynah,	**MYTH**	–; myths
	mynas	**MYTHIC**	–; –
MYNAH	–; mynahs	**MYTHOI**	–; –
MYNHEER	–; mynheers	**MYTHOS**	–; –
MYOID	–; –	**MYXOID**	–; –
MYOLOGY	–; –	**MYXOMA**	–; myxomas

N

N	an, en, in,	**NABBING**	–; –
	on, un; na,	**NABIS**	–; –
	ne, no, nu	**NABOB**	–; nabobs
NA	ana; nab,	**NACELLE**	–; nacelles
	nae, nag,	**NACRE**	–; nacred,
	nap, nay		nacres
NAB	–; nabs	**NADIR**	–; nadirs
NABBED	–; –	**NADIRAL**	–; –

NAEVI	–; –	NANISM	onanism; nanisms
NAEVOID	–; →		
NAEVUS	–; –	NANISMS	onanisms; –
NAG	snag; nags	NANKEEN	–; nankeens
NAGANA	–; naganas	NANKIN	–; nankins
NAGGED	snagged; –	NANNIE	–; nannies
NAGGER	–; naggers	NANNY	–; –
NAGGING	snagging; –	NAOI	–; –
NAGS	snags; –	NAOS	–; –
NAIAD	–; naiads	NAP	knap, snap; nape, naps
NAIADES	–; –		
NAIF	–; naifs	NAPALM	–; napalms
NAIL	snail; nails	NAPE	–; napes
NAILED	snailed; –	NAPERY	–; –
NAILER	–; nailers	NAPHTHA	–; naphthas
NAILING	snailing; –	NAPHTOL	–; naphtols
NAILS	snails; –	NAPKIN	–; napkins
NAILSET	–; nailsets	NAPLESS	snapless; –
NAIVE	–; naiver, naives	NAPPE	–; napped, napper nappes
NAIVELY	–; –		
NAIVES	–; naivest	NAPPED	knapped snapped; –
NAIVETE	–; naivetes		
NAIVETY	–; –	NAPPER	knapper, snapper; nappers
NAKED	snaked; –		
NAKEDER	–; –	NAPPERS	knappers, snappers; –
NAKEDLY	–; –		
NALED	–; naleds	NAPPIE	–; nappies
NAMABLE	–; –	NAPPIER	snappier; –
NAME	–; named, namer, names	NAPPING	knapping, snapping; –
NAMELY	–; –	NAPPY	snappy; –
NAMER	–; namers	NAPS	knaps, snaps; –
NAMING	–; –		
NANA	jnana; nanas	NARC	–; narco, narcs
NANAS	jnanas; –		
NANCE	–; nances	NARCEIN	–; narceine, narceins
NANDIN	–; nandins		
		NARCISM	–; narcisms

NARCIST	–; narcists	**NATIVE**	–; natives
NARCO	–; narcos	**NATRIUM**	–; natriums
NARCOS	–; narcose	**NATRON**	–; natrons
NARD	–; nards	**NATTER**	–; natters
NARDINE	–; –	**NATTIER**	gnattier; –
NARES	snares; –	**NATTILY**	–; –
NARGILE	–; nargileh, nargiles	**NATTY**	gnatty; –
NARIAL	–; –	**NATURAL**	–; naturals
NARIC	–; –	**NATURE**	–; natured, natures
NARINE	–; –		
NARIS	–; –	**NAUGHT**	–; naughts, naughty
NARK	snark; narks	**NAUSEA**	–; nauseas
NARKED	–; –	**NAUTCH**	–; –
NARKING	–; –	**NAUTILI**	–; –
NARKS	snarks; –	**NAVAID**	–; navaids
NARRATE	–; narrated, narrater, narrates	**NAVAL**	–; –
		NAVALLY	–; –
		NAVAR	–; navars
NARROW	–; narrows	**NAVE**	knave; navel, naves
NARTHEX	–; –		
NARWAL	–; narwals	**NAVEL**	–; navels
NARWHAL	–; narwhale, narwhals	**NAVES**	knaves; –
		NAVETTE	–; navettes
NARY	unary; –	**NAVIES**	–; –
NASAL	–; nasals	**NAVVY**	–; –
NASALLY	–; –	**NAVY**	–; –
NASCENT	–; –	**NAWAB**	–; nawabs
NASIAL	–; –	**NAY**	–; nays
NASION	–; nasions	**NAZI**	–; nazis
NASTIC	–; –	**NAZIFY**	–; –
NASTIER	–; –	**NE**	ane, one; neb, nee, net, new
NASTILY	–; –		
NASTY	–; –		
NATAL	–; –	**NEAP**	sneap; neaps
NATANT	–; –		
NATES	enates; –	**NEAPS**	sneaps; –
NATION	enation; nations	**NEAR**	anear; nears
		NEARBY	–; –
NATIONS	enations; –	**NEARED**	–; –

NEARER	–; –
NEAREST	–; –
NEARING	–; –
NEARLY	–; –
NEARS	anears; –
NEAT	–; neath, neats
NEATEN	uneaten; neatens
NEATER	–; –
NEATEST	–; –
NEATLY	–; –
NEB	–; nebs
NEBBISH	–; –
NEBULA	–; nebulae, nebular, nebulas
NEBULE	–; –
NEBULY	–; –
NECK	sneck; necks
NECKED	–; –
NECKING	–; neckings
NECKS	snecks; –
NECKTIE	–; neckties
NECROSE	–; necrosed, necroses
NECTAR	–; nectars, nectary
NEE	knee; need, neem, neep
NEED	kneed; needs, needy
NEEDED	–; –
NEEDER	–; needers
NEEDFUL	–; needfuls
NEEDIER	–; –
NEEDILY	–; –
NEEDING	–; –
NEEDLE	; needled, needler, needles
NEEDLER	–; needlers
NEEM	–; neems
NEEP	–; neeps
NEGATE	–; negated, negater, negates
NEGATER	–; negaters
NEGATON	–; negatons
NEGATOR	–; negators
NEGLECT	–; neglects
NEGLIGE	–; negligee, negliges
NEGRO	–; –
NEGROES	–; –
NEGROID	–; negroids
NEGUS	–; –
NEGUSES	–; –
NEIF	–; neifs
NEIGH	–; neighs
NEIGHED	–; –
NEIST	–; –
NEITHER	–; –
NEKTON	–; nektons
NELSON	–; nelsons
NELUMBO	–; nelumbos
NEMA	enema; nemas
NEMAS	enemas; -
NEMATIC	–; –
NEMESES	–; –
NEMESIS	–; –
NENE	–; –
NEOLITH	–; neoliths
NEOLOGY	–; –
NEON	–; neons
NEONATE	–; neonates
NEONED	–; –
NEOTENY	–; –

NEOTYPE	-; neotypes
NEPHEW	-; nephews
NEPHRIC	-; -
NEPHRON	-; nephrons
NEREID	-; nereids
NEREIS	-; -
NERITIC	-; -
NEROL	-; neroli, nerols
NEROLI	-; nerolis
NERTS	inerts; -
NERTZ	-; -
NERVATE	enervate; -
NERVE	-; nerved, nerves
NERVIER	-; -
NERVILY	-; -
NERVINE	-; nervines
NERVING	-; nervings
NERVOUS	-; -
NERVULE	-; nervules
NERVURE	-; nervures
NERVY	-; -
NESS	-; -
NESSES	-; -
NEST	-; nests
NESTED	-; -
NESTER	-; nesters
NESTING	-; -
NESTLE	-; nestled, nestler, nestles
NESTLER	-; nestlers
NESTOR	-; nestors
NET	-; nets, nett
NETHER	-; -
NETLESS	-; -
NETLIKE	-; -
NETOP	-; netops
NETSUKE	-; netsukes

NETT	-; netts, netty
NETTED	-; -
NETTER	-; netters
NETTIER	-; -
NETTING	-; nettings
NETTLE	-; nettled, nettler, nettles
NETTLER	-; nettlers
NETTLY	-; -
NETWORK	-; networks
NEUM	-; neume, neums
NEUME	-; neumes
NEUMIC	-; -
NEURAL	-; -
NEUROID	-; -
NEUROMA	-; neuromas
NEURON	-; neurone, neurons
NEURONE	-; neurones
NEUSTON	-; neustons
NEUTER	-; neuters
NEUTRAL	-; neutrals
NEUTRON	-; neutrons
NEVE	-; never, neves
NEVI	-; -
NEVOID	-; -
NEVUS	-; -
NEW	anew, knew; news, newt
NEWBORN	-; newborns
NEWEL	-; newels
NEWER	-; -
NEWEST	-; -
NEWISH	-; -
NEWLY	-; -
NEWMOWN	-; -

NEWNESS	–; –	**NICKS**	snicks; –
NEWS	–; newsy	**NICOL**	–; nicols
NEWSBOY	–; newsboys	**NICOTIN**	–; nicotine,
NEWSIER	–; –		nicotins
NEWSIES	–; newsiest	**NICTATE**	–; nictated,
NEWSMAN	–; –		nictates
NEWSMEN	–; –	**NIDAL**	–; –
NEWT	–; newts	**NIDE**	snide; nided
NEWTON	–; newtons		nides
NEXT	–, –	**NIDGET**	–; nidgets
NEXUS	–; –	**NIDI**	–; –
NEXUSES	–; –	**NIDIFY**	–; –
NGWEE	–; –	**NIDING**	–; –
NIACIN	–; niacins	**NIDUS**	–; –
NIB	snib; nibs	**NIDUSES**	–; –
NIBBED	snibbed; –	**NIECE**	–; nieces
NIBBING	snibbing; –	**NIELLI**	–; –
NIBBLE	–; nibbled,	**NIELLO**	–; niellos
	nibbler,	**NIEVE**	–; nieves
	nibbles	**NIFFER**	sniffer;
NIBBLER	–; nibblers		niffers
NIBLICK	–; niblicks	**NIFFERS**	sniffers; –
NIBLIKE	–; –	**NIFTIER**	–; niftier
NIBS	snibs; –	**NIFTIES**	–; niftiest
NICE	–; nicer	**NIFTY**	–; –
NICELY	–; –	**NIGGARD**	–; niggards
NICEST	–; –	**NIGGER**	snigger;
NICETY	–; –		niggers
NICHE	–; niched,	**NIGGERS**	sniggers; –
	niches	**NIGGLE**	sniggle;
NICHING	–; –		niggled,
NICK	snick; nicks		niggler,
NICKED	snicked; –		niggles
NICKEL	–; nickels	**NIGGLED**	sniggled; –
NICKER	snicker;	**NIGGLER**	sniggler;
	nickers		nigglers
NICKERS	knickers,	**NIGGLES**	sniggles; –
	snickers; –	**NIGH**	–; nighs,
NICKING	snicking; –		night
NICKLE	–; nickles	**NIGHED**	–; –

NIGHER	–; –
NIGHEST	–; –
NIGHING	;
NIGHT	knight; nights, nighty
NIGHTIE	–; nighties
NIGHTLY	knightly; –
NIGHTS	knights; –
NIGRIFY	–; –
NIHIL	–; nihils
NIL	anil; nill, nils
NILGAI	–; nilgais
NILGAU	–; nilgaus
NILGHAI	–; nilghais
NILGHAU	–; nilghaus
NILL	–; nills
NILLED	–; –
NILLING	–; –
NILS	anils; –
NIM	–; nims
NIMBI	–; –
NIMBLE	–; nimbler
NIMBLY	–; –
NIMBUS	–; –
NIMIETY	–; –
NIMIOUS	–; –
NIMMED	–; –
NIMMING	–; –
NIMROD	–; nimrods
NINE	–; nines
NINEPIN	–; ninepins
NINETY	–; –
NINNIES	–; –
NINNY	–; –
NINON	–; ninons
NINTH	–; ninths
NINTHLY	–; –
NIOBIC	–; –
NIOBIUM	–; niobiums
NIOBOUS	–; –

NIP	snip; nipa, nips
NIPA	–; nipas
NIPPED	snipped; –
NIPPER	snipper; nippers
NIPPERS	snippers; –
NIPPIER	snippier; –
NIPPILY	–; –
NIPPING	snipping; –
NIPPLE	–; nipples
NIPPY	snippy; –
NIPS	snips; –
NIRVANA	–; nirvanas
NISEI	–; niseis
NISI	–; –
NISUS	–; –
NIT	knit, snit, unit; nits
NITCHIE	–; nitchies
NITER	uniter; niters
NITERS	uniters; –
NITID	–; –
NITON	–; nitons
NITPICK	–; nitpicks
NITRATE	–; nitrated, nitrates
NITRE	–; nitres
NITRIC	–; –
NITRID	–; nitride, nitrids
NITRIDE	–; nitrides
NITRIFY	–; –
NITRIL	–; nitrile, nitrils
NITRILE	–; nitriles
NITRITE	–; nitrites
NITRO	–; nitros
NITROSO	–; –
NITROUS	–; –

NITS	knits, snits, units; –	**NOCTUID**	–; noctuids
		NOCTULE	–; noctules
NITTIER	–; –	**NOCTURN**	–; nocturne
NITTY	–; –		nocturns
NITWIT	–; nitwits	**NOCUOUS**	–; –
NIVAL	–; –	**NOD**	anode;
NIVEOUS	–; –		node, nodi,
NIX	–; nixy		nods
NIXED	–; –	**NODAL**	anodal; –
NIXES	–; –	**NODALLY**	anodally; –
NIXIE	–; nixies	**NODDED**	–; –
NIXING	–; –	**NODDER**	–; nodders
NIZAM	–; nizams	**NODDIES**	–; –
NO	–; nob, nod,	**NODDING**	–; –
	nog, noh,	**NODDLE**	–; noddled,
	nom, noo,		noddles
	nor, nos,	**NODDY**	–; –
	not, now	**NODE**	anode;
NOB	knob, snob;		nodes
	nobs	**NODES**	anodes; –
NOBBIER	snobbier; –	**NODI**	–; –
NOBBILY	snobbily; –	**NODICAL**	–; –
NOBBLE	–; nobbled,	**NODOSE**	–; –
	nobbler,	**NODOUS**	–; –
	nobbles	**NODULAR**	–; –
NOBBLER	–; nobblers	**NODULE**	–; nodules
NOBBY	knobby,	**NODUS**	–; –
	snobby; –	**NOEL**	–; noels
NOBLE	–; nobler,	**NOES**	–; –
	nobles	**NOESIS**	–; –
NOBLES	–; noblest	**NOETIC**	–; –
NOBLY	–; –	**NOG**	–; nogg,
NOBODY	–; –		nogs
NOBS	knobs,	**NOGG**	–; noggs
	snobs; –	**NOGGIN**	–; nogging,
NOCENT	–; –		noggins
NOCK	knock; nocks	**NOGGING**	–; noggings
NOCKED	knocked; –	**NOH**	–; –
NOCKING	knocking; -	**NOHOW**	–; –
NOCKS	knocks; –		

NOIL	–; noils, noily	**NONEGO**	–; nonegos
NOIR	–; –	**NONFARM**	–; –
NOISE	–; noised, noises	**NONFAT**	–
		NONFOOD	–; –
NOISING	–; –	**NONGAME**	–; –
NOISIER	–; –	**NONHERO**	–; –
NOISILY	–; –	**NONLIFE**	–; –
NOISY	–; –	**NONMAN**	–; –
NOLO	–; nolos	**NONMEN**	–; –
NOM	–; noma, nome, noms	**NONPAR**	–; –
		NONPLUS	–; –
NOMA	–; nomad, nomas	**NONPROS**	–; –
		NONSKED	–; nonskeds
NOMAD	–; nomads	**NONSKID**	–; –
NOMADIC	–; –	**NONSLIP**	–; –
NOMARCH	–; nomarchs, nomarchy	**NONSTOP**	–; –
		NONSUCH	–; –
NOMBLES	–; –	**NONSUIT**	–; nonsuits
NOMBRIL	–; nombrils	**NONTAX**	–; –
NOME	gnome; nomen, nomes	**NONUPLE**	–; nonuples
		NONUSE	–; nonuser, nonuses
NOMES	gnomes; –	**NONUSER**	–; nonusers
NOMINA	–; nominal	**NONZERO**	–; –
NOMINAL	–; nominals	**NOO**	–; nook, noon
NOMINEE	–; nominees	**NOODLE**	–; noodled, noodles
NOMISM	–; nomisms		
NOMOI	–; –	**NOOK**	snook; nooks, nooky
NOMOS	–; –		
NONA	–; nonas	**NOOKIES**	–; –
NONACID	–; nonacids	**NOOKS**	snooks; –
NONAGE	–; nonages	**NOON**	–; noons
NONAGON	–; nonagons	**NOONDAY**	–; noondays
NONBANK	–; –	**NOONING**	–; noonings
NONBOOK	–; nonbooks	**NOOSE**	–; noosed, nooser, nooses
NONCASH	–; –		
NONCE	–; nonces		
NONCOM	–; noncoms	**NOOSER**	–; noosers
NONE	–; nones	**NOPAL**	–; nopals

NOPE	–; –	**NOTATE**	–; notated, notates
NOR	–; norm		
NORIA	–; norias	**NOTCH**	–; –
NORITE	–; norites	**NOTCHED**	–; –
NORITIC	–; –	**NOTCHER**	–; notchers
NORLAND	–; norlands	**NOTCHES**	–; –
NORM	enorm; norms	**NOTE**	–; noted, noter, notes
NORMAL	–; normals	**NOTEDLY**	–; –
NORMED	–; –	**NOTER**	–; noters
NORTH	–; norths	**NOTHING**	–; nothings
NORTHER	–; northern, northers	**NOTICE**	–; noticed, notices
NOS	–; nose, nosy	**NOTIFY**	–; –
		NOTING	–; –
NOSE	–; nosed, noses, nosey	**NOTION**	–; notions
		NOTUM	–; –
NOSEBAG	–; nosebags	**NOUGAT**	–; nougats
NOSEGAY	–; nosegays	**NOUGHT**	–; noughts
NOSES	gnoses; –	**NOUN**	–; nouns
NOSEY	–; –	**NOUNAL**	–; –
NOSH	–; –	**NOURISH**	–; –
NOSHED	–; –	**NOUS**	–; –
NOSHER	–; noshers	**NOUSES**	–; –
NOSHES	–; –	**NOVA**	–; novae, novas
NOSHING	–; –		
NOSIER	–; –	**NOVEL**	–; novels
NOSIEST	–; –	**NOVELLA**	–; novellas
NOSILY	–; –	**NOVELLE**	–; –
NOSING	–; nosings	**NOVELLY**	–; –
NOSTOC	–; nostocs	**NOVELTY**	–; –
NOSTRIL	–; nostrils	**NOVENA**	–; novenae, novenas
NOSTRUM	–; nostrums		
NOT	knot, snot; nota, note	**NOVICE**	–; novices
		NOW	enow, know, snow; nows, nowt
NOTA	–; notal		
NOTABLE	–; notables		
NOTABLY	–; –	**NOWAY**	–; noways
NOTARY	–; –	**NOWHERE**	–; nowheres
		NOWISE	–; –

NOWS	enows, knows, anows,	**NUDGING**	–; –
		NUDIE	–; nudies
		NUDISM	–; nudisms
NOWT	–; nowts	**NUDIST**	–; nudists
NOXIOUS	–; –	**NUDITY**	–; –
NOYADE	–; noyades	**NUDNICK**	–; nudnicks
NOZZLE	–; nozzles	**NUDNIK**	–; nudniks
NTH	–; –	**NUGGET**	–; nuggets,
NU	gnu; nub,		nuggety
	nun, nus, nut	**NUKE**	–; nukes
NUANCE	–; nuanced,	**NULL**	–; nulls
	nuances	**NULLAH**	–; nullahs
NUB	snub; nubs	**NULLED**	–; –
NUBBIER	snubbier; –	**NULLIFY**	–; –
NUBBIN	–; nubbins	**NULLING**	–; –
NUBBLE	–; nubbles	**NULLITY**	–; –
NUBBLY	–; –	**NUMB**	–; numbs
NUBBY	snubby; –	**NUMBED**	–; –
NUBIA	–; nubias	**NUMBER**	–; numbers
NUBILE	–; –	**NUMBEST**	–; –
NUBS	snubs; –	**NUMBING**	–; –
NUCHA	–; nuchae,	**NUMBLES**	–; –
	nuchal	**NUMBLY**	–; –
NUCHAL	–; nuchals	**NUMEN**	–; –
NUCLEAL	–; –	**NUMERAL**	–; numerals
NUCLEAR	–; –	**NUMERIC**	–; numerics
NUCLEI	–; nuclein	**NUMINA**	–; –
NUCLEIN	–; nucleins	**NUMMARY**	–; –
NUCLEON	–; nucleons	**NUN**	–; nuns
NUCLEUS	–; –	**NUNCIO**	–; nuncios
NUCLIDE	–; nuclides	**NUNCLE**	–; nuncles
NUDE	–; nuder,	**NUNLIKE**	–; –
	nudes	**NUNNERY**	–; –
NUDELY	–; –	**NUNNISH**	–; –
NUDES	–; nudest	**NUPTIAL**	–; nuptials
NUDGE	–; nudged,	**NURL**	knurl; nurls
	nudger,	**NURLED**	knurled; –
	nudges	**NURLING**	knurling; –
NUDGER	–; nudgers	**NURLS**	knurls; –
		NURSE	–; nursed,

nurser,
nurses
NURSER —; nursers,
nursery
NURSING —; nursings
NURTURE —; nurtured,
nurturer,
nurtures
NUS anus, gnus,
onus; —
NUT —; nuts
NUTANT —; —
NUTATE —; nutated,
nutates
NUTGALL —; nutgalls
NUTLET —; nutlets
NUTLIKE —; —
NUTMEAT —; nutmeats
NUTMEG —; nutmegs
NUTPICK —; nutpicks
NUTRIA —; nutrias

NUTTED —; —
NUTTER —; nutters
NUTTIER —; —
NUTTILY —; —
NUTTING —; —
NUTTY —; —
NUTWOOD —; nutwoods
NUZZLE —; nuzzled,
nuzzles
NYALA —; nyalas
NYLGHAI —; nylghais
NYLGHAU —; nylghaus
NYLON —; nylons
NYMPH —; nympha,
nympho,
nymphs
NYMPHA —; nymphae,
nymphal
NYMPHET —; nymphets
NYMPHO —; nymphos

O

O bo, do, go,
ho, jo, lo,
mo, no, so,
to, wo; od,
oe, of, oh,
om, on, op,
or, os, ow,
ox, oy
OAF loaf; oafs
OAFISH —; —
OAFS loafs
OAK soak; oaks
OAKEN —; —
OAKLIKE —; —

OAKMOSS —; —
OAKS soaks; —
OAKUM —; oakums
OAR boar, hoar,
roar, soar;
oars
OARED roared,
soared; —
OARFISH —; —
OARING roaring,
soaring; —
OARLESS —; —
OARLIKE —; —
OARLOCK —; oarlocks

OARS	boars, hoars, roars, soars; –	**OBELIAS**	lobelias; –
		OBELISE	–; obelised obelises
OARSMAN	–; –	**OBELISK**	–; obelisks
OARSMEN	–; –	**OBELISM**	–; obelisms
OASES	–; –	**OBELIZE**	–; obelized, obelizes
OASIS	–; –		
OAST	boast, coast, roast, toast; oasts	**OBELUS**	–; –
		OBES	lobes, robes; obese
OASTS	boasts, coasts, roasts, toasts; –	**OBESELY**	–; –
		OBESITY	–; –
		OBEY	–; obeys
OAT	boat, coat, doat, goat, moat; oath, oats	**OBEYED**	–; –
		OBEYER	, obeyers
		OBEYING	–; –
		OBI	–; obia, obis, obit
OATCAKE	–; oatcakes	**OBIA**	cobia; obias
OATEN	–; –	**OBIAS**	cobias; –
OATER	boater, coater; oaters	**OBIISM**	–; obiisms
		OBIT	–; obits
		OBJECT	–; objects
OATERS	boaters, coaters; –	**OBLAST**	–; oblasti, oblasts
OATH	loath; oaths	**OBLATE**	–; oblates
OATLIKE	–; –	**OBLIGE**	–; obliged, obligee, obliger, obliges
OATMEAL	–; oatmeals		
OATS	boats, coats, doats, goats, moats; –		
		OBLIGEE	–; obligees
		OBLIGER	–; obligers
OAVES	loaves, soaves; –	**OBLIGOR**	–; obligors
OBE	lobe, robe; obes, obey	**OBLIQUE**	–; obliqued, obliques
		OBLONG	–; oblongs
OBEAH	–; obeahs	**OBLOQUY**	–; –
OBELI	–; obelia	**OBOE**	–; oboes
OBELIA	lobelia; obelias	**OBOES**	goboes; –
		OBOIST	–; oboists

OBOL	–; obole, oboli, obols	**OCEANIC**	–; –
		OCELLAR	–; –
OBOLE	–; oboles	**OCELLI**	–; –
OBOLUS	–; –	**OCELLUS**	–; –
OBOVATE	–; –	**OCELOID**	–; –
OBOVOID	–; –	**OCELOT**	–; ocelots
OBSCENE	–; obscener	**OCHER**	–; ochers, ochery
OBSCURE	–; obscured, obscurer, obscures		
		OCHERED	–; –
		OCHONE	–; –
OBSEQUY	–; –	**OCHRE**	–; ochrea, ochred, ochres
OBSERVE	–; observed, observer, observes		
		OCHREA	–; ochreae
OBSESS	–; –	**OCHRING**	–; –
OBTAIN	–; obtains	**OCHROID**	–; –
OBTECT	–; –	**OCHROUS**	–; –
OBTEST	–; obtests	**OCHRY**	–; –
OBTRUDE	–; obtruded, obtruder, obtrudes	**OCREA**	–; ocreae
		OCREATE	–; –
		OCTAD	–; octads
OBTUND	–; obtunds	**OCTADIC**	–; –
OBTUSE	–; obtuser	**OCTAGON**	–; octagons
OBVERSE	–; obverses	**OCTAL**	–; –
OBVERT	–; obverts	**OCTANE**	–; octanes
OBVIATE	–; obviated, obviates	**OCTANT**	–; octants
		OCTAVAL	–; –
OBVIOUS	–; –	**OCTAVE**	–; octaves
OCA	coca, loca; ocas	**OCTAVO**	–; octavos
		OCTET	–; octets
OCARINA	–; ocarinas	**OCTETTE**	–; octettes
OCAS	cocas; –	**OCTOPI**	–; –
OCCIPUT	–; occiputs	**OCTOPOD**	–; octopods
OCCLUDE	–; occluded, occludes	**OCTOPUS**	–; –
		OCTROI	–; octrois
OCCULT	–; occults	**OCTUPLE**	–; octupled, octuples, octuplet, octuplex
OCCUPY	–; –		
OCCUR	–; occurs		
OCEAN	–; oceans		

OCTUPLY	–; –		sodium;
OCTYL	–; octyls		odiums
OCULAR	locular, jocular; oculars	ODIUMS	podiums, sodiums; –
OCULIST	–; oculists	ODONATE	–; odonates
OD	bod, cod, god, hod, mod, nod, pod, rod, sod, tod, yod; odd, ode, ods	ODOR	–; odors
		ODORANT	–; odorants
		ODORED	–; –
		ODORFUL	–; –
		ODORIZE	–; odorized, odorizes
		ODOROUS	–; –
ODALISK	–; odalisks	ODOUR	–; odours
ODD	–; odds	ODS	bods, cods, gods, hods, mods, nods, pods, rods, sods, tods, yods; –
ODDBALL	–; oddballs		
ODDER	codder, fodder, dodder, nodder; –		
		ODYL	–; odyle, odyls
ODDEST	–; –		
ODDISH	–; –	ODYLE	–; odyles
ODDITY	–; –	ODYSSEY	–; odysseys
ODDLY	–; –	OE	doe, foe, hoe, joe, roe, toe, voe, woe; oes
ODDMENT	–; oddments		
ODDNESS	–; –		
ODE	bode, code, lode, mode, node, rode; odea, odes		
		OEDEMA	–; oedemas
		OEDIPAL	–; –
ODEON	–; odeons	OENOMEL	–; oenomels
ODES	bodes, codes, lodes, modes, nodes; –	OERSTED	–; oersteds
		OES	does, foes, hoes, joes, roes, toes, voes, woes; –
ODEUM	–; –		
ODIC	iodic, sodic; –	OESTRIN	–; oestrins
ODIOUS	–; –	OESTRUM	–; oestrums
ODIUM	podium,	OESTRUS	–; –

OEUVRE	–; oeuvres	**OFTENER**	–; –
OF	–; off, oft	**OFTER**	softer; –
OFAY	–; ofays	**OFTEST**	softest; –
OFF	boff, coff,	**OFTS**	lofts, softs,
	doff, toff;		tofts; –
	offs	**OGAM**	–; ogams
OFFAL	–; offals	**OGDOAD**	–; ogdoads
OFFBEAT	–; offbeats	**OGEE**	–; ogees
OFFCAST	–; offcasts	**OGEES**	yogees; –
OFFED	doffed; –	**OGHAM**	–; oghams
OFFENCE	–; offences	**OGHAMIC**	–; –
OFFEND	–; offends	**OGIVAL**	–; –
OFFENSE	–; offenses	**OGIVE**	–; ogives
OFFER	coffer,	**OGLE**	bogle;
	doffer,		ogled, ogler
	goffer; offers		ogles
OFFERED	coffered,	**OGLER**	–; oglers
	goffered; –	**OGLES**	bogles; –
OFFERER	–; offerers	**OGLING**	–; –
OFFEROR	–; offerors	**OGRE**	–; ogres
OFFERS	coffers,	**OGREISH**	–; –
	doffers,	**OGREISM**	–; ogreisms
	goffers; –	**OGRESS**	–; –
OFFHAND	–; –	**OGRISH**	–; –
OFFICE	–; officer,	**OGRISM**	–; ogrisms
	offices	**OH**	foh, noh,
OFFICER	–; officers		ooh, poh;
OFFING	coffing,		ohm, oho,
	doffing;		ohs
	offings	**OHED**	–; –
OFFISH	–; –	**OHIA**	–; ohias
OFFLOAD	–; offloads	**OHING**	–; –
OFFS	boffs, coffs,	**OHM**	–; ohms
	doffs,	**OHMAGE**	–; ohmages
	toffs; –	**OHMIC**	–; –
OFFSET	–; offsets	**OHO**	coho; –
OFFSIDE	–; –	**OHS**	nohs; –
OFT	coft, loft,	**OIDIA**	–; –
	soft, toft; –	**OIDIUM**	–; –
OFTEN	soften; –	**OIL**	boil, coil,

foil, moil,
noil, roil,
soil, toil; oils,
oily

OILBIRD —; oilbirds
OILCAMP —; oilcamps
OILCAN —; oilcans
OILCUP —; oilcups
OILED boiled,
coiled,
doiled,
foiled,
moiled,
roiled,
soiled,
toiled; —
OILER boiler, coiler,
moiler, toiler;
oilers
OILERS boilers,
coilers,
moilers,
toilers; —
OILHOLE —; oilholes
OILIER roilier; —
OILIEST —; —
OILILY —; —
OILING boiling,
coiling,
foiling,
moiling,
roiling,
soiling,
toiling; —
OILMAN —; —
OILMEN —; —
OILS boils, coils,
foils, moils,
noils, roils,
soils, toils; —

OILSEED —; oilseeds
OILSKIN —; oilskins
OILWAY —; oilways
OILY doily, noily,
roily; —
OINK —; oinks
OINKED —; —
OINKING —; —
OINOMEL —; oinomels
OKA —; okas,
okay
OKAPI —; okapis
OKAY tokay; okays
OKAYED —; —
OKAYING —; —
OKAYS tokays; —
OKE coke, hoke,
joke, moke,
poke, soke,
toke, woke,
yoke; okeh,
okes
OKEH —; okehs
OKES cokes,
hokes, jokes,
mokes,
pokes,
sokes, tokes,
yokes; —
OKRA —; okras
OLD bold, cold,
fold, gold,
hold, mold,
sold, told,
wold; olds
OLDEN golden,
holden; —
OLDER bolder,
colder,
folder,

	golder, holder, molder, polder, solder; –
OLDEST	boldest, coldest, goldest; –
OLDIE	–; oldies
OLDISH	coldish; –
OLDNESS	–; –
OLDS	colds, folds, golds, holds, molds, wolds; –
OLDSTER	–; oldsters
OLDWIFE	–; –
OLE	bole, cole, dole, hole, jole, mole, pole, role, sole, tole, vole; olea, oleo, oles
OLEATE	–; oleates
OLEFIN	–; olefine, olefins
OLEFINE	–; olefines
OLEIC	–; –
OLEIN	–; oleine, oleins
OLEINE	–; oleines
OLEO	–; oleos
OLES	boles, coles, doles, holes, joles, moles, poles, roles, soles, toles, voles; –
OLEUM	–; oleums

OLIO	folio, polio; olios
OLIOS	folios, polios; –
OLIVARY	–; –
OLIVE	–; olives
OLIVINE	–; olivines
OLLA	holla; ollas
OLLAS	hollas; –
OLOGIES	–; –
OLOGIST	–; ologists
OLOGY	–; –
OM	dom, mom, nom, tom, yom; oms
OMASA	–; –
OMASUM	–; –
OMBER	bomber, comber, somber; ombers
OMBERS	bombers, combers; –
OMBRE	hombre, sombre; ombres
OMBRES	hombres; –
OMEGA	–; omegas
OMELET	–; omelets
OMEN	homen, nomen, women; omens
OMENED	–; –
OMENING	–; –
OMENS	homens; –
OMENTA	–; omental
OMENTUM	–; omentums
OMER	comer, homer,

	vomer;
	omers
OMERS	comers,
	homers,
	vomers; –
OMICRON	–; omicrons
OMIKRON	–; omikrons
OMINOUS	–; –
OMIT	vomit; omits
OMITS	vomits; –
OMITTED	vomitted; –
OMNIBUS	–; –
OMNIFIC	–; –
OMPHALI	–; –
OMS	doms, moms,
	noms, toms; –
ON	con, don,
	eon, fon,
	ion, mon,
	son, ton,
	von, won,
	yon; one,
	ons
ONAGER	–; onagers
ONANISM	–; onanisms
ONANIST	–; onanists
ONCE	nonce,
	ponce;
	onces
ONCES	nonces,
	ponces; –
ONE	bone, cone,
	done, gone,
	hone, lone,
	none, pone,
	sone, tone,
	zone; ones
ONEFOLD	–; –
ONEIRIC	–; –
ONENESS	–;

ONEROUS	–; –
ONERY	–; –
ONES	bones,
	cones,
	hones,
	nones,
	pones,
	sones,
	tones,
	zones; –
ONESELF	–; –
ONETIME	–; –
ONGOING	–; –
ONION	gonion,
	ronion,
	onions
ONIONS	ronions; –
ONIUM	conium,
	gonium,
	ionium; –
ONLY	sonly; –
ONRUSH	–; –
ONS	cons, dons,
	eons, fons,
	ions, mons,
	pons, sons,
	tons,
	wons; –
ONSET	–; onsets
ONSHORE	–; –
ONSIDE	–; –
ONSTAGE	–; –
ONTIC	–; –
ONTO	conto; –
ONUS	bonus,
	conus,
	tonus; –
ONUSES	bonuses,
	nonuses,
	tonuses; –

ONWARD	–; onwards	foot, hoot,
ONYX	–; –	loot, moot,
ONYXES	–; –	root, soot,
OOCYST	–; oocysts	toot; oots
OOCYTE	–; oocytes	**OOTHECA** –; oothecae,
OODLES	boodles,	oothecal
	doodles,	**OOTID** –; ootids
	noodles; –	**OOTS** boots, coots,
OODLINS	–; –	foots, hoots,
OOGAMY	–; –	loots, moots,
OOGENY	–; –	roots, soots,
OOGONIA	–; oogonial	toots; –
OOH	pooh; oohs	**OOZE** booze;
OOHED	poohed; –	oozed,
OOHING	poohing; –	oozes
OOHS	poohs; –	**OOZED** boozed; –
OOLITE	–; oolites	**OOZES** boozes; –
OOLITH	–; oliths	**OOZIER** boozier,
OOLITIC	–; –	woozier; –
OOLOGIC	–; –	**OOZIEST** booziest; –
OOLOGY	zoology; –	**OOZILY** boozily,
OOLONG	–; oolongs	woozily; –
OOMIAC	–; oomiack,	**OOZING** boozing; –
	oomiacs	**OOZY** boozy,
OOMIACK	–; oomiacks	doozy,
OOMIAK	–; oomiaks	woozy; –
OOMPH	–; oomphs	**OP** bop, cop,
OOPHYTE	–; oophytes	fop, hop,
OOPS	coops,	kop, lop,
	goops,	mop, pop,
	hoops,	sop, top,
	loops,	wop; ope,
	poops,	ops, opt
	woops; –	**OPACIFY** –; –
OORALI	woorali;	**OPACITY** –; –
	ooralis	**OPAH** –; opahs
OORIE	–; –	**OPAL** copal,
OOSPERM	– oosperms	nopal; opals
OOSPORE	–; oospores	**OPALINE** –; opalines
OOT	boot, coot,	

OPALS   copals, nopals; –

OPAQUE   –; opaqued, opaquer, opaques

OPAQUES   –; opaquest

OPE   cope, dope, hope, lope, mope, nope, pope, rope, tope; oped, open, opes

OPED   coped, doped, hoped, loped, moped, roped, toped; –

OPEN   copen; opens

OPENED   –; –

OPENER   –; openers

OPENEST   –; –

OPENING   –; openings

OPENLY   –; –

OPENS   copens; –

OPERA   –; operas

OPERAND   –; operands

OPERANT   –; operants

OPERATE   –; operated, operates

OPERON   –; operons

OPEROSE   –; –

OPES   copes, dopes, hopes, lopes, mopes, popes, ropes, topes; –

OPHITE   – ophites

OPHITIC   –; –

OPIATE   –; opiated, opiates

OPINE   –; opined, opines

OPING   coping, doping, hoping, loping, moping, roping, toping; –

OPINING   –; –

OPINION   –; opinions

OPIUM   –; opiums

OPOSSUM   –; opossums

OPPIDAN   –; oppidans

OPPOSE   –; opposed, opposer, opposes

OPPOSER   –; opposers

OPPRESS   –; –

OPPUGN   –; oppugns

OPS   bops, cops, fops, hops, kops, lops, mops, pops, sops, tops, wops; –

OPSIN   –; opsins

OPSONIC   –; –

OPSONIN   –; opsonins

OPT   –; opts

OPTED   –; –

OPTIC   –; optics

OPTICAL   –; –

OPTIMA   –; optimal

OPTIME	–; optimes	orated,
OPTIMUM	–; optimums	orates
OPTING	–; –	**ORATED**	borated; –
OPTION	–; options	**ORATES**	borates; –
OPULENT	–; –	**ORATING**	–; –
OPUNTIA	–; opuntias	**ORATION**	–; orations
OPUS	–; –	**ORATOR**	–; orators,
OPUSES	–; –		oratory
OQUASSA	–; oquassas	**ORATRIX**	–; –
OR	dor, for,	**ORB**	forb, sorb;
	gor, kor,		orbs
	mor, nor,	**ORBED**	sorbed; –
	tor; ora, orb,	**ORBING**	sorbing; –
	orc, ore, ors,	**ORBIT**	forbit; orbits
	ort	**ORBITAL**	–; orbitals
ORA	bora, fora,	**ORBITED**	–; –
	hora, mora,	**ORBITER**	–; orbiters
	sora, tora;	**ORBS**	forbs,
	oral, oras		sorbs; –
ORACH	–; orache	**ORC**	–; orca, orcs
ORACHE	–; oraches	**ORCA**	–; orcas
ORACLE	coracle;	**ORCEIN**	–; orceins
	oracles	**ORCHARD**	–; orchards
ORACLES	coracles; –	**ORCHID**	–; orchids
ORAL	coral, goral,	**ORCHIL**	–; orchils
	horal, loral,	**ORCHIS**	–; –
	moral; orals	**ORCIN**	–; orcins
ORALITY	–; –	**ORCINOL**	–; orcinols
ORALLY	–; –	**ORDAIN**	–; ordains
ORALS	corals,	**ORDEAL**	–; ordeals
	gorals,	**ORDER**	border,
	morals; –		corder;
ORANG	–; orange,		orders
	orangs,	**ORDERED**	bordered; –
	orangy	**ORDERER**	borderer;
ORANGE	–; oranges,		orderers
	orangey	**ORDERLY**	–; –
ORAS	boras,	**ORDERS**	borders,
	horas; –		corders; –
ORATE	borate;	**ORDINAL**	–; ordinals

ORDINES	sordines; –	**ORIGAN**	–; origans
ORDO	fordo; ordos	**ORIGIN**	–; origins
ORDURE	bordure,	**ORIOLE**	–; orioles
	ordures	**ORISON**	–; orisons
ORDURES	bordures; –	**ORLE**	–; orles
ORE	bore, core,	**ORLOP**	–; orlops
	fore, gore,	**ORMER**	dormer,
	lore, more,		former,
	pore, sore,		wormer;
	tore, wore,		ormers
	yore; ores	**ORMERS**	dormers,
OREAD	–; oreads		formers; –
ORECTIC	–; –	**ORMOLU**	–; ormolus
OREGANO	–; oreganos	**ORNATE**	–; –
OREIDE	–; oreides	**ORNERY**	–; –
ORES	bores, cores,	**ORNIS**	–; –
	fores, gores,	**OROGENY**	–; –
	lores, mores,	**OROIDE**	–; oroides
	pores, sores,	**OROLOGY**	–; –
	tores,	**OROTUND**	–; –
	yores; –	**ORPHAN**	–; orphans
ORFRAY	–; orfrays	**ORPHIC**	–; –
ORGAN	–; organa,	**ORPHREY**	–; orphreys
	organs	**ORPIN**	–; orpine,
ORGANDY	–; –		orpins
ORGANIC	–; organics	**ORPINE**	–; orpines
ORGANON	–; organons	**ORRA**	–; –
ORGANUM	–; organums	**ORRERY**	–; –
ORGANZA	–; organzas	**ORRICE**	–; orrices
ORGASM	–; orgasms	**ORRIS**	–; –
ORGEAT	–; orgeats	**ORRISES**	–; –
ORGIAC	–; –	**ORS**	dors, kors,
ORGIC	–; –		mors, tors; –
ORGIES	porgies; –	**ORT**	bort, fort,
ORGY	porgy; –		mort, port,
ORIBI	–; oribis		sort, tort,
ORIEL	–; oriels		wort; orts
ORIENT	–; orients	**ORTHO**	–; –
ORIFICE	–; orifices	**ORTOLAN**	–; ortolans
ORIGAMI	–; origamis	**ORTS**	borts, forts,

	morts, ports, sorts, torts, worts; –	**OSMUND**	–; osmunda, osmunds
ORYX	–; –	**OSMUNDA**	–; osmundas
ORYXES	–; –	**OSPREY**	–; ospreys
OS	bos, cos, dos, kos, nos, wos; ose	**OSSA**	fossa; –
		OSSEIN	–; osseins
		OSSEOUS	–; –
		OSSIA	–; –
OSAR	–; –	**OSSICLE**	–; ossicles
OSCINE	–; oscines	**OSSIFIC**	–; –
OSCULA	–; oscular	**OSSIFY**	–; –
OSCULE	–; oscules	**OSSUARY**	–; –
OSCULUM	–; –	**OSTEAL**	–; –
OSE	dose, hose, lose, nose, pose, rose; oses	**OSTEOID**	–; osteoids
		OSTEOMA	–; osteomas
		OSTIA	–; –
		OSTIARY	–; –
OSES	doses, hoses, loses, noses, poses, roses; –	**OSTIOLE**	–; ostioles
		OSTIUM	–; –
		OSTLER	hostler, jostler; ostlers
OSIER	cosier, hosier, nosier, rosier; osiers	**OSTLERS**	hostlers, jostlers; –
		OSTMARK	–; ostmarks
OSIERS	hosiers; –	**OSTOMY**	–; –
OSMATIC	–; –	**OSTOSES**	–; –
OSMIC	cosmic; –	**OSTOSIS**	–; –
OSMIOUS	–; –	**OSTRICH**	–; –
OSMIUM	–; osmiums	**OTALGIA**	–; otalgias
OSMOL	–; osmols	**OTALGIC**	–; –
OSMOLAL	–; –	**OTALGY**	–; –
OSMOLAR	–; –	**OTHER**	bother, mother, pother, tother; others
OSMOSE	–; osmosed, osmoses		
OSMOSES	cosmoses; –	**OTHERS**	bothers, mothers; –
OSMOSIS	–; –		
OSMOTIC	–; –		
OSMOUS	–; –	**OTIC**	lotic; –

OTIOSE	–; –	**OUGHT**	bought,
OTITIC	–; –		dought,
OTITIS	–; –		fought,
OTOCYST	–; otocysts		nought,
OTOLITH	–; otoliths		sought;
OTOLOGY	–; –		oughts
OTTAR	cottar; ottars	**OUGHTED**	–; –
OTTARS	cottars	**OUGHTS**	noughts; –
OTTAVA	–; ottavas	**OUNCE**	bounce,
OTTER	cotter,		jounce,
	dotter,		pounce;
	hotter,		ounces
	potter,	**OUNCES**	bounces,
	rotter, totter;		jounces,
	otters		pounces; –
OTTERS	cotters,	**OUPH**	–; ouphe,
	dotters,		ouphs
	potters,	**OUPHE**	–; ouphes
	rotters,	**OUR**	dour, four,
	totters; –		hour, lour,
OTTO	lotto, motto,		pour, sour,
	potto; ottos		tour, your;
OTTOMAN	–; ottomans		ours
OTTOS	lottos,	**OURANG**	–; ourangs
	mottos,	**OURARI**	–; ouraris
	pottos; –	**OUREBI**	–; ourebis
OUABAIN	–; ouabains	**OURIE**	–; –
OUCH	couch,	**OURS**	fours, hours,
	mouch,		lours, pours,
	pouch,		sours, tours,
	touch,		yours; –
	vouch; –	**OURSELF**	yourself; –
OUCHES	couches,	**OUSEL**	housel;
	douches,		ousels
	mouches,	**OUSELS**	housels; –
	pouches,	**OUST**	joust, roust;
	rouches,		ousts
	touches,	**OUSTED**	jousted,
	vouches; –		rousted; –
OUD	loud; ouds	**OUSTER**	iouster,

	rouster; ousters	**OUTDATE**	–; outdated outdates
OUSTERS	jousters, rousters; –	**OUTDO**	–; –
OUSTING	jousting, rousting; –	**OUTDOES**	–; –
		OUTDONE	–; –
OUSTS	jousts, rousts; –	**OUTDID**	–; –
		OUTDOER	–; outdoers
OUT	bout, gout, lout, pout, rout, tout; outs	**OUTDOOR**	–; outdoors
		OUTDRAW	–; outdrawn, outdraws
OUTACT	–; outacts	**OUTDREW**	–; –
OUTADD	–; outadds	**OUTDROP**	–; outdrops
OUTAGE	–; outages	**OUTEAT**	–; outeats
OUTASK	–; outasks	**OUTECHO**	–; –
OUTATE	–; –	**OUTED**	louted, pouted, routed, touted; –
OUTBACK	–; outbacks		
OUTBAKE	–; outbaked, outbakes	**OUTER**	couter, pouter, router, souter, touter; outers
OUTBARK	–; outbarks		
OUTBAWL	–; outbawls		
OUTBEAM	–; outbeams		
OUTBEG	–; outbegs		
OUTBID	–; outbids	**OUTERS**	couters, pouters, routers, souters, touters; –
OUTBOX	–; –		
OUTBRAG	–; outbrags		
OUTBURN	–; outburns, outburnt		
OUTBY	–; outbye	**OUTFACE**	–; outfaced, outfaces
OUTCAST	–; outcaste, outcasts	**OUTFALL**	–; outfalls
OUTCOME	–; outcomes	**OUTFAST**	–; outfasts
OUTCOOK	–; outcooks	**OUTFAWN**	–; outfawns
OUTCROP	–; outcrops	**OUTFEEL**	–; outfeels
OUTCROW	–; outcrows	**OUTFELT**	–; –
OUTCRY	–; –	**OUTFIND**	–; outfinds
OUTDARE	–; outdared, outdares	**OUTFIRE**	–; outfired, outfires
		OUTFIT	–; outfits

OUTFLEW	–; –	**OUTKISS**	–; –
OUTFLOW	–; outflown, outflows	**OUTLAID**	–; –
		OUTLAIN	–; –
OUTFLY	–; –	**OUTLAND**	–; outlands
OUTFOOL	–; outfools	**OUTLAST**	–; outlasts
OUTFOOT	–; outfoots	**OUTLAW**	–; outlaws
OUTFOX	–; –	**OUTLAY**	–; outlays
OUTGAIN	–; outgains	**OUTLEAP**	–; outleaps, outleapt
OUTGAS	–; –		
OUTGAVE	–; –	**OUTLET**	–; outlets
OUTGIVE	–; outgiven, outgives	**OUTLIE**	–; outlier, outlies
OUTGLOW	–; outglows	**OUTLIER**	–; outliers
OUTGNAW	–; outgnawn, outgnaws	**OUTLINE**	–; outlined, outlines
OUTGO	–; –	**OUTLIVE**	–; outlived, outliver, outlives
OUTGOES	–; –		
OUTGONE	–; –	**OUTLOOK**	–; outlooks
OUTGREW	–; –	**OUTLOVE**	–; outloved, outloves
OUTGRIN	–; outgrins		
OUTGROW	–; outgrown, outgrows	**OUTMAN**	–; outmans
		OUTMODE	–; outmoded, outmodes
OUTGUN	–; outguns		
OUTGUSH	–; –	**OUTMOST**	–; –
OUTHAUL	–; outhauls	**OUTMOVE**	–; outmoved, outmoves
OUTHEAR	–; outheard, outhears		
OUTHIT	–; outhits	**OUTPACE**	–; outpaced, outpaces
OUTHOWL	–; outhowls		
OUTING	louting, pouting, routing, touting; outings	**OUTPASS**	–; –
		OUTPITY	–; –
		OUTPLAN	–; outplans
		OUTPLAY	–; outplays
OUTJINX	–; –	**OUTPLOD**	–; outplods
OUTJUMP	–; outjumps	**OUTPOLL**	–; outpolls
OUTJUT	–; outjuts	**OUTPORT**	–; outports
OUTKEEP	–; outkeeps	**OUTPOST**	–; outposts
OUTKICK	–; outkicks	**OUTPOUR**	–; outpours

OUTPRAY	–; outprays	**OUTSIN**	–; outsing outsins
OUTPULL	–; outpulls		
OUTPUSH	–; –	**OUTSING**	–; outsings
OUTPUT	–; outputs	**OUTSIT**	–; outsits
OUTRACE	–; outraced, outraces	**OUTSIZE**	–; outsizea, outsizes
OUTRAGE	–; outraged, outrages	**OUTSOAR**	–; outsoars
		OUTSOLD	–; –
OUTRAN	–; outrang, outrank	**OUTSOLE**	–; outsoles
		OUTSPAN	–; outspans
OUTRANK	–; outranks	**OUTSTAY**	–; outstays
OUTRAVE	–; outraved, outraves	**OUTSULK**	–; outsulks
		OUTSUNG	–; –
OUTRE	–; –	**OUTSWAM**	–; –
OUTREAD	–; outreads	**OUTSWIM**	–; outswims
OUTRIDE	–; outrides	**OUTTAKE**	–; outtakes
OUTRING	–; outrings	**OUTTALK**	–; outtalks
OUTROAR	–; outroars	**OUTTASK**	–; outtasks
OUTROCK	–; outrocks	**OUTTELL**	–; outtells
OUTRODE	–; –	**OUTTOLD**	–; –
OUTROLL	–; outrolls	**OUTTROT**	–; outtrots
OUTROOT	–; outroots	**OUTTURN**	–; outturns
OUTRUN	–; outrung, outruns	**OUTVOTE**	–; outvotea outvotes
OUTRUSH	–; –	**OUTWAIT**	–; outwaits
OUTS	bouts, gouts, louts, pouts, routs, touts; –	**OUTWALK**	–; outwalks
		OUTWAR	–; outward, outwars
OUTSAIL	–; outsails	**OUTWARD**	–; outwards
OUTSANG	–; –	**OUTWEAR**	–; outwears outweary
OUTSAT	–; –		
OUTSAW	–; –	**OUTWEEP**	–; outweeps
OUTSEE	–; outseen, outsees	**OUTWENT**	–; –
		OUTWEPT	–; –
OUTSELL	–; outsells	**OUTWILE**	–; outwiled outwiles
OUTSERT	–; outserts	**OUTWILL**	–; outwills
OUTSET	–; outsets	**OUTWIND**	–; outwinds
OUTSIDE	–; outsider, outsides	**OUTWIT**	–; outwits
		OUTWORE	–; –

OUTWORK	–; outworks	**OVERBID**	–; overbids
OUTWORN	–; –	**OVERBIG**	–; –
OUTYELL	–; outyells	**OVERBUY**	–; overbuy
OUTYELP	–; outyelps	**OVERCOY**	–; –
OUZEL	–; ouzels	**OVERDID**	–; –
OUZO	–; ouzos	**OVERDO**	–; –
OVA	nova; oval	**OVERDRY**	–; –
OVAL	–; ovals	**OVERDUE**	–; –
OVALITY	–; –	**OVERDYE**	–; overdyed,
OVALLY	–; –		overdyes
OVARIAL	–; –	**OVEREAT**	–; overeats
OVARIAN	–, –	**OVERED**	covered,
OVARIES	–; –		hovered; –
OVARY	–; –	**OVERFAR**	–; –
OVATE	–; –	**OVERFAT**	–; –
OVATELY	–; –	**OVERFED**	–; –
OVATION	–; ovations	**OVERFLY**	–; –
OVEN	coven,	**OVERHOT**	–; –
	doven,	**OVERING**	covering,
	roven,		hovering; –
	woven;	**OVERJOY**	–; overjoys
	ovens	**OVERLAP**	–; overlaps
OVENS	covens,	**OVERLAX**	–; –
	dovens; –	**OVERLAY**	·, overlays
OVER	cover, hover,	**OVERLET**	–; overlets
	lover, mover,	**OVERLIE**	–; overlies
	rover; overs,	**OVERLY**	loverly; –
	overt	**OVERMAN**	–;
OVERACT	–; overacts		overmans,
OVERAGE	coverage;		overmany
	overages	**OVERMIX**	–; –
OVERALL	coverall;	**OVERNEW**	–; –
	overalls	**OVERPAY**	–; overpays
OVERAPT	–; –	**OVERPLY**	–; –
OVERARM	–; –	**OVERRAN**	–; overrank
OVERATE	–; –	**OVERRUN**	–; overruns
OVERAWE	–; overawed,	**OVERS**	covers,
	overawes		hovers,
OVERBET	·; overbets		lovers,

	movers,		dow, how,
	rovers; −		jow, low,
OVERSAD	−; −		mow, now,
OVERSAW	−; −		pow, row,
OVERSEA	−; overseas		sow, tow,
OVERSEE	−; overseed,		vow, wow,
	overseen,		yow; owe,
	overseer,		owl, own
	oversees	**OWE**	howe, lowe,
OVERSET	−; oversets		yowe; owed,
OVERSEW	−; oversewn,		owes
	oversews	**OWED**	bowed,
OVERSUP	−; oversups		cowed,
OVERT	covert; −		jowed,
OVERTAX	−; −		lowed,
OVERTLY	covertly; −		mowed,
OVERTOP	−; overtops		rowed,
OVERUSE	−; overused,		sowed,
	overuses		towed,
OVERWET	−; overwets		vowed,
OVIBOS	−; −		woved; −
OVICIDE	−; ovicides	**OWES**	howes,
OVIDUCT	−; oviducts		lowes; −
OVIFORM	−; −	**OWING**	bowing,
OVINE	bovine;		cowing,
	ovines		jowing,
OVINES	bovines; −		lowing,
OVIPARA	−; −		mowing,
OVISAC	−; ovisacs		rowing,
OVOID	−; ovoids		sowing,
OVOIDAL	−; −		towing,
OVOLI	−; −		vowing,
OVOLO	−; ovolos		wowing,
OVONIC	−; −		yowing; −
OVULAR	−; ovulary	**OWL**	bowl, cowl,
OVULATE	−; ovulated,		fowl, howl,
	ovulates		jowl, yowl;
OVULE	−; ovules		owls
OVUM	−; −	**OWLET**	howlet,
OW	bow, cow,		owlets

OWLETS	howlets; –	**OXES**	boxes,
OWLISH	– ;		oslies,
OWLLIKE	–; –		foxes,
OWLS	bowls,		goxes, loxes,
	cowls, fowls,		poxes; –
	howls, jowls,	**OXFORD**	–; oxfords
	yowls; –	**OXHEART**	–; oxhearts
OWN	down, gown,	**OXID**	–; oxide,
	lown, sown,		oxids
	town; owns	**OXIDANT**	–; oxidants
OWNABLE	–; –	**OXIDASE**	–; oxidases
OWNED	gowned,	**OXIDATE**	–; oxidated,
	downed; –		oxidates
OWNER	downer;	**OXIDE**	–; oxides
	owners	**OXIDIC**	–; –
OWNERS	downers; –	**OXIDISE**	–; oxidised,
OWNING	downing,		oxidiser,
	gowning; –		oxidises
OWNS	downs,	**OXIDIZE**	–; oxidized,
	gowns,		oxidizer,
	towns; –		oxidizes
OWSE	bowse,	**OXIM**	–; oxime,
	dowse,		oxims
	lowse;	**OXIME**	–; oximes
	owsen	**OXLIP**	–; oxlips
OX	box, cox,	**OXTAIL**	foxtail;
	fox, gox,		oxtails
	lox, pox,	**OXTAILS**	foxtails; –
	sox, vox;	**OXTER**	–; oxters
	oxy	**OXY**	boxy, doxy,
OXALATE	–; oxalated,		foxy; –
	oxalates	**OXYACID**	–; oxyacids
OXALIC	–; –	**OXYGEN**	–; oxygens
OXALIS	–; –	**OXYPHIL**	–; oxyphile,
OXAZINE	–; oxazines		oxyphils
OXBLOOD	–; oxbloods	**OXYSALT**	–; oxysalts
OXBOW	–; oxbows	**OXYSOME**	–; oxysomes
OXCART	–; oxcarts	**OXYTONE**	–; oxytones
OXEN	–; –	**OY**	boy, coy,
OXEYE	–; oxeyes		foy, goy,

	hoy, joy,	OYSTERS	roysters; –
	soy, toy; –	OZONE	–; ozones
OYER	coyer, foyer,	OZONIC	–; –
	toyer; oyers	OZONIDE	–; ozonides
OYERS	foyers,	OZONISE	–; ozonised,
	toyers; –		ozonises
OYES	–; –	OZONIZE	–; ozonized,
OYESSES	–; –		ozonizer,
OYEZ	–; –		ozonizes
OYSTER	royster;	OZONOUS	–; –
	oysters		

P

P	op, up; pa,	PACHA	–; pachas
	pe, pi	PACHISI	–; pachisis
PA	spa; pac,	PACHUCO	–; pachocos
	pad, pah,	PACIFIC	–; –
	pal, pam,	PACIFY	opacify; –
	pan, pap,	PACING	spacing; –
	par, pas,	PACK	–; packs
	pat, paw,	PACKAGE	–;
	pax, pay		packaged,
PABULAR	–; –		packager,
PABULUM	–; pabulums		packages
PAC	–; paca,	PACKED	–; –
	pace, pack,	PACKER	–; packers
	pacs, pact	PACKET	–; packets
PACA	–; pacas	PACKING	–; packings
PACE	apace,	PACKLY	–; –
	space;	PACKMAN	–; –
	paced,	PACKMEN	–; –
	pacer,	PACKWAX	–; –
	paces	PACT	epact; pacts
PACED	spaced; –	PACTION	–; pactions
PACER	spacer;	PACTS	epacts; –
	pacers	PAD	–; pads
PACERS	spacers; –	PADAUK	–; padauks
PACES	spaces; –	PADDED	–; –

PADDIES	–; –	**PAIN**	–; pains,
PADDING	–; paddings		paint
PADDLE	–; paddled,	**PAINCH**	–; –
	paddler,	**PAINED**	–; –
	paddles	**PAINFUL**	–; –
PADDLER	–; paddlers	**PAINING**	–; –
PADDOCK	–; paddocks	**PAINT**	–; paints,
PADDY	–; –		painty
PADLE	–; padles	**PAINTED**	–; –
PADLOCK	–; padlocks	**PAINTER**	–; painters
PADNAG	–; padnags	**PAIR**	–; pairs
PADOUK	–; padouks	**PAIRED**	–; –
PADRE	–; padres	**PAIRING**	–; –
PADRI	–; –	**PAISA**	–; paisan,
PADRONE	–; padrones		paisas
PADRONI	–; –	**PAISAN**	–; paisano,
PADSHAH	–; padshahs		paisans
PAEAN	–; paeans	**PAISE**	–; –
PAELLA	–; paellas	**PAISLEY**	–; paisleys
PAEON	–; paeons	**PAJAMA**	–; pajamas
PAGAN	–; pagans	**PAL**	opal; pale,
PAGE	–; paged,		pall, palm,
	pages		palp, pals,
			paly
PAGEANT	–; pageants		
PAGEBOY	–; pageboys	**PALABRA**	–; palabras
PAGINAL	–; –	**PALACE**	–; palaced,
PAGING	–; –		palaces
PAGOD	–; pagoda,	**PALADIN**	–; paladins
	pagods	**PALAIS**	–; –
PAGODA	–; pagodas	**PALATAL**	–; palatals
PAGURID	–; pagurids	**PALATE**	–; palates
PAH	opah; –	**PALAVER**	–; palavers
PAHLAVI	–; pahlavis	**PALE**	–; palea,
PAID	–; –		paled, paler,
PAIK	–; paiks		pales, palet
PAIKED	–; –	**PALEA**	–; paleae,
PAIKING	–; –		paleal
PAIL	spail; pails	**PALELY**	–; –
PAILFUL	–; pailfuls	**PALES**	spales;
PAILS	spails; –		palest

PALET	–; palets	**PALTER**	–; palters
PALETOT	–; paletots	**PALTRY**	–; –
PALETTE	–; palettes	**PALUDAL**	–; –
PALFREY	–; palfreys	**PAM**	spam; pams
PALIER	–; –	**PAMPA**	–; pampas
PALIEST	–; –	**PAMPEAN**	–;
PALIKAR	–; palikars		pampeans
PALING	–; palings	**PAMPER**	–; pampero,
PALISH	–; –		pampers
PALL	spall; palls,	**PAMPERO**	–; pamperos
	pally	**PAN**	span; pane,
PALLED	spalled; –		pang, pans,
PALLET	–; pallets		pant
PALLIA	–; pallial	**PANACEA**	–;
PALLID	–; –		panacean,
PALLIER	–; –		panaceas
PALLING	–; –	**PANACHE**	–; panaches
PALLIUM	–; palliums	**PANADA**	–; panadas
PALLOR	–; pallors	**PANAMA**	–; panamas
PALLS	spalls; –	**PANCAKE**	–;
PALM	–; palms,		pancaked,
	palmy		pancakes
PALMAR	–; palmary	**PANCHAX**	–; –
PALMATE	–; palmated	**PANDA**	–; pandas
PALMED	–; –	**PANDECT**	–; pandects
PALMER	–; palmers	**PANDER**	–; panders
PALMIER	–; –	**PANDIED**	–; –
PALMING	–; –	**PANDIES**	–; –
PALMIST	–; palmists	**PANDIT**	–; pandits
PALMYRA	–; palmyras	**PANDOOR**	–; pandoors
PALOOKA	–; palookas	**PANDORA**	–; pandoras
PALP	–; palps	**PANDORE**	–; pandores
PALPAL	–; –	**PANDOUR**	–; pandours
PALPATE	–; palpated,	**PANDURA**	–; panduras
	palpates	**PANDY**	–; –
PALPI	–; –	**PANE**	–; paned,
PALPUS	–; –		panel, panes
PALS	opals; palsy	**PANEL**	–; panels
PALSIED	–;	**PANFISH**	–; –
PALSIES	–; –	**PANFUL**	–; panfuls

PANG	spang; panga, pangs	**PAPAIN**	–; papains
		PAPAL	–; –
		PAPALLY	–; –
PANGA	–; pangas	**PAPAW**	–; papaws
PANGED	–; –	**PAPAYA**	–; papayan, papayas
PANGEN	–; pangens		
PANGING	–; –	**PAPER**	–; papers, papery
PANIC	–; panics		
PANICKY	–; –	**PAPERED**	–; –
PANICLE	–; panicled, panicles	**PAPERER**	–; paperers
		PAPHIAN	–; paphians
PANICUM	–; panicums	**PAPILLA**	–; papilae, papilar
PANIER	–; paniers		
PANNE	–; panned, pannes	**PAPIST**	–; papists
		PAPOOSE	–; papooses
PANNED	spanned; –	**PAPPI**	–; –
PANNIER	–; panniers	**PAPPIER**	–; –
PANNING	spanning; –	**PAPPIES**	–; pappiest
PANOCHA	–; panochas	**PAPPOSE**	–; –
PANOCHE	–; panoches	**PAPPOUS**	–; –
PANOPLY	–; –	**PAPPUS**	–; –
PANPIPE	–; panpipes	**PAPPY**	–; –
PANSIES	–; –	**PAPRICA**	–; papricas
PANS	spans; pansy	**PAPRIKA**	–; paprikas
PANT	–; pants, panty	**PAPULA**	–; papulae, papulan, papular
PANTED	–; –		
PANTHER	–; panthers	**PAPULE**	–; papules
PANTIE	–; panties	**PAPYRI**	–; –
PANTING	–; –	**PAPYRUS**	–; –
PANTILE	–; pantiled, pantiles	**PAR**	spar; para, pard, pare, park, parr, pars, part
PANTOUM	; pantoums		
PANTRY	–; –		
PANZER	–; panzers	**PARA**	–; paras
PAP	–; papa, paps	**PARABLE**	sparable; parables
PAPA	–; papal, papas	**PARADE**	–; paraded, parader, parades
PAPACY	–; –		

PARADER	−; paraders		parged,
PARADOS	−; −		parges,
PARADOX	−; −		parget
PARAGON	−; paragons	**PARGED**	sparged; −
PARAMO	−; paramos	**PARGES**	sparges; −
PARANG	−; parangs	**PARGET**	−; pargets
PARAPET	−; parapets	**PARGING**	sparging; −
PARAPH	−; paraphs	**PARGO**	−; pargos
PARASOL	−; parasols	**PARIAH**	−; pariahs
PARBOIL	−; parboils	**PARIAN**	−; parians
PARCEL	−; parcels	**PARIES**	−; −
PARCH	eparch; −	**PARING**	sparing;
PARCHED	−; −		parings
PARCHES	−; −	**PARIS**	−; parish
PARD	−; pardi,	**PARITY**	−; −
	pards, pardy	**PARK**	spark;
PARDAH	−; pardahs		parka, parks
PARDEE	−; −	**PARKA**	−; parkas
PARDI	−; pardie	**PARKED**	sparked; −
PARDINE	−; −	**PARKER**	sparker;
PARDNER	−; pardners		parkers
PARDON	−; pardons	**PARKERS**	sparkers; −
PARE	spare;	**PARKING**	−; parkings
	pared,	**PARKS**	sparks; −
	parer, pares,	**PARKWAY**	−; parkways
	pareu	**PARLAY**	−; parlays
PARED	spared; −	**PARLE**	−; parled,
PAREIRA	−; pareiras		parles,
PARENT	−; parents		parley
PARER	sparer;	**PARLEY**	−; parleys
	parers	**PARLING**	−; −
PARERS	sparers; −	**PARLOR**	−; parlors
PARES	spares; −	**PARLOUR**	−; parlours
PARESES	−; −	**PARLOUS**	−; −
PARESIS	−; −	**PARODIC**	−; −
PARETIC	−; paretics	**PARODOI**	−; −
PAREU	−; pareus	**PARODOS**	−; −
PAREVE	−; −	**PARODY**	−; −
PARFAIT	−; parfaits	**PAROL**	−; parole,
PARGE	sparge;		parols

PAROLE	–; paroled, parolee, paroles	PARTIAL	–; partials
PAROLEE	–; parolees	PARTIED	–; –
PARONYM	–; paronyms	PARTIES	–; –
PAROTIC	–; –	PARTING	–; partings
PAROTID	–; parotids	PARTITA	–; partitas
PAROUS	–; –	PARTITE	–; –
PARQUET	–; parquets	PARTLET	–; partlets
PARR	–; parrs, parry	PARTLY	–; –
PARRAL	–; parrals	PARTNER	–; partners
PARRED	sparred; –	PARTON	–; partons
PARREL	–; parrels	PARTOOK	–; –
PARRIED	–; –	PARTWAY	–; –
PARRIES	–; –	PARURA	–; paruras
PARRING	sparring; –	PARURE	–; parures
PARROT	–; parrots, parroty	PARVE	–; –
PARRY	sparry; –	PARVENU	–; parvenue, parvenus
PARS	spars; parse	PARVIS	–; parvise
PARSE	sparse; parsec, parsed, parser, parses	PARVISE	–; parvises
		PAS	spas, upas; pase, pash, past, pass
PARSEC	–; parsecs	PASCHAL	–; paschals
PARSER	sparser; parsers	PASE	–; paseo, pases
PARSING	–; –	PASEO	–; paseos
PARSLEY	–; parsleys	PASES	upases; –
PARSNIP	–; parsnips	PASH	–; pasha
PARSON	–; parsons	PASHA	–; pashas
PART	apart; parts, party	PASHED	–; –
PARTAKE	–; partaken, partaker, partakes	PASHES	–; –
		PASHING	–; –
		PASQUIL	–; pasquils
		PASS	–; passe
		PASSADE	–; passades
		PASSADO	–; passados
		PASSAGE	–; passaged, passages
PARTAN	–; partans	
PARTED	–; –	PASSANT	–; –

PASSE	–; passed, passee, passel, passer, passes	**PATAMAR**	–; patamars
		PATCH	–; patchy
		PATCHED	–; –
		PATCHER	–; patchers
		PATCHES	–; –
PASSEL	–; passels	**PATE**	spate; pated, paten, pater, pates
PASSER	–; passers		
PASSIM	–; –		
PASSING	–; passings		
PASSION	–; passions	**PATELLA**	–; patellae, patellar, patellas
PASSIVE	–; passives		
PASSKEY	–; passkeys		
PASSUS	–; –	**PATEN**	–; patens, patent
PAST	–; pasta, paste, pasts, pasty		
		PATENCY	–; –
PASTA	–; pastas	**PATENT**	–; patents
PASTE	–; pasted, pastel, paster, pastes	**PATER**	–; paters
		PATES	spates; –
		PATH	–; paths
PASTEL	–; pastels	**PATHOS**	–; –
PASTER	–; pastern, pasters	**PATHWAY**	–; pathways
		PATIENT	–; patients
PASTERN	–; pasterns	**PATIN**	–; patina, patine, patins
PASTIER	–; –		
PASTIES	–; pastiest		
PASTIL	–; pastils	**PATINA**	–; patinae, patinas
PASTIME	–; pastimes		
PASTINA	–; pastinas	**PATINE**	–; patined, patines
PASTING	–; –		
PASTOR	–; pastors	**PATIO**	–; patios
PASTRY	–; –	**PATLY**	–; –
PASTURE	–; pastured, pasturer, pastures	**PATNESS**	–; –
		PATOIS	–; –
		PATRIOT	–; patriots
		PATROL	–; patrols
PASTY	–; –	**PATRON**	–; patrons
PAT	spat; pate, pats, paty	**PATROON**	–; patroons
		PATS	spats; patsy
		PATSIES	–; –
PATACA	–; patacas	**PATTED**	spatted; –

PATTEE	–; –	**PAW**	–; pawl,
PATTEN	–; pattens		pawn, paws
PATTER	spatter;	**PAWED**	–; –
	pattern,	**PAWER**	–; pawers
	patters	**PAWING**	–; –
PATTERN	–; patterns	**PAWKIER**	–; –
PATTERS	spatters; –	**PAWKILY**	–; –
PATTIE	–; patties	**PAWKY**	–; –
PATTING	spatting; –	**PAWL**	–; pawls
PATTY	–; –	**PAWN**	spawn;
PAUCITY	–; –		pawns
PAUGHTY	–; –	**PAWNAGE**	–;
PAULIN	–; paulins		pawnages
PAUNCH	–; paunchy	**PAWNED**	spawned; –
PAUPER	–; paupers	**PAWNEE**	–; pawnees
PAUSAL	–; –	**PAWNER**	spawner;
PAUSE	–; paused,		pawners
	pauser,	**PAWNERS**	spawners; –
	pauses	**PAWNING**	spawning; –
PAUSER	–; pausers	**PAWNOR**	–; pawnors
PAUSING	–; –	**PAWNS**	spawns; –
PAVAN	–; pavane,	**PAWPAW**	–; pawpaws
	pavans	**PAX**	–; –
PAVANE	–; pavanes	**PAXES**	–; –
PAVE	–; paved,	**PAXWAX**	–; –
	paver, paves	**PAY**	spay; pays
PAVER	–; pavers	**PAYABLE**	–; –
PAVID	–; –	**PAYABLY**	–; –
PAVIN	spavin;	**PAYDAY**	–; paydays
	paving,	**PAYED**	spayed; –
	pavins	**PAYEE**	–; payees
PAVING	–; pavings	**PAYER**	–; payers
PAVINS	spavins; –	**PAYING**	spaying; –
PAVIOR	–; paviors	**PAYLOAD**	–; payloads
PAVIOUR	–; paviours	**PAYMENT**	–; payments
PAVIS	–; pavise	**PAYNIM**	–; paynims
PAVISE	–; paviser,	**PAYOFF**	–; payoffs
	pavises	**PAYOLA**	–; payolas
PAVISER	–; pavisers	**PAYOR**	–; payors
		PAYROLL	–; payrolls

PAYS	spays; –	PEANUT	–; peanuts
PE	ape, ope;	PEAR	spear; pearl,
	pea, ped,		pears, peart
	pee, peg,	PEARL	–; pearls,
	pen, pep,		pearly
	per, pes,	PEARLED	–; –
	pet, pew	PEARLER	–; pearlers
PEA	–; peag,	PEARS	spears; –
	peak, peal,	PEART	–; –
	pean, pear,	PEARTER	–; –
	peas, peat	PEARTLY	–; –
PEACE	–; peaced,	PEAS	–; pease
	peaces	PEASANT	–; peasants
PEACH	–; peachy	PEASCOD	–; peascods
PEACHER	–; peachers	PEASE	–; peasen,
PEACING	–; –		peases
PEACOAT	–; peacoats	PEAT	–; peats,
PEACOCK	–; peacocks,		peaty
	peacocky	PEATIER	–; –
PEAFOWL	–; peafowls	PEAVEY	–; peaveys
PEAG	–; peage,	PEAVY	–; –
	peags	PEBBLE	–; pebbled,
PEAGE	–; peages		pebbles
PEAHEN	–; peahens	PEBBLY	–; –
PEAK	apeak,	PECAN	–; pecans
	speak;	PECCANT	–; –
	peaks,	PECCARY	–; –
	peaky	PECCAVI	–; peccavis
PEAKED	–; –	PECH	–; pechs
PEAKIER	–; –	PECHAN	–; pechans
PEAKING	speaking; –	PECHED	–; –
PEAKISH	–; –	PECHING	–; –
PEAKS	speaks; –	PECK	apeck,
PEAL	–; peals		speck;
PEALED	–; –		pecks, pecky
PEALIKE	–; –	PECKED	specked; –
PEALING	–; –	PECKER	–; peckers
PEAN	spean;	PECKIER	–; –
	peans	PECKING	specking; –
PEANS	speans; –	PECKS	specks; –

PECTASE	–; pectases	**PEEK**	apeek; peeks
PECTATE	spectate; pectates	**PEEKED**	–; –
PECTEN	–; pectens	**PEEKING**	–; –
PECTIC	–; –	**PEEL**	speel; peels
PECTIN	–; pectins	**PEELED**	speeled; –
PECTIZE	–; pectized, pectizes	**PEELER**	–; peelers
		PEELERS	speelers; –
PECULIA	–; peculiar	**PEELING**	speeling; peelings
PED	aped, oped, sped; peds	**PEELS**	speels; –
PEDAGOG	–; pedagogs, pedagogy	**PEEN**	–; peens
		PEENED	–; –
		PEENING	–; –
PEDAL	–; pedals	**PEEP**	–; peeps
PEDANT	–; pedants	**PEEPED**	–; –
PEDATE	–; –	**PEEPER**	–; peepers
PEDDLE	–; peddled, peddler, peddles	**PEEPING**	–; –
		PEEPUL	–; peepuls
		PEER	speer; peers, peery
PEDDLER	–; peddlers, peddlery	**PEERAGE**	–; peerages
PEDES	–; –	**PEERED**	speered; –
PEDICAB	–; pedicabs	**PEERIE**	–; peeries
PEDICEL	–; pedicels	**PEERING**	speering; –
PEDICLE	–; pedicled, pedicles	**PEERS**	speers; –
		PEES	epees; –
PEDLAR	–; pedlars, pedlary	**PEEVE**	–; peeved, peeves
PEDLER	–; pedlers	**PEEVING**	–; –
PEDOCAL	–; pedocals	**PEEVISH**	–; –
PEDRO	–; pedros	**PEEWEE**	–; peewees
PEE	epee; peed, peek, peel, peen, peep, peer, pees	**PEEWIT**	–; peewits
		PEG	–; pegs
		PEGBOX	–; –
		PEGGED	–; –
PEEBEEN	–; peebeens	**PEGGING**	–; –
PEED	speed; –	**PEGLESS**	–; –
PEEING	–; –	**PEGLIKE**	–; –
		PEH	–; pehs

PEIN	–; peins	**PEMBINA**	–; pembinas
PEINED	–; –	**PEMICAN**	–; pemicans
PEINING	–; –	**PEMPHIX**	–; –
PEISE	speise; peised, peises	**PEN**	open; pend, pens, pent
PEISES	speises; –	**PENAL**	–; –
PEISING	–; –	**PENALLY**	–; –
PEKAN	–; pekans	**PENALTY**	–; –
PEKE	–; pekes	**PENANCE**	–;
PEKIN	–; pekins		penanced, penances
PEKOE	–; pekoes	**PENANG**	–; penangs
PELAGE	–; pelages	**PENATES**	–; –
PELAGIC	–; –	**PENCE**	spence; pencel
PELE	–; peles		
PELF	–; pelfs	**PENCEL**	–; pencels
PELICAN	–; pelicans	**PENCIL**	–; pencils
PELISSE	–; pelisses	**PEND**	spend, upend; pends
PELITE	–; pelites		
PELITIC	–; –		
PELLET	–; pellets	**PENDANT**	–; pendants
PELON	–; –	**PENDED**	upended; –
PELORIA	–; pelorian, pelorias	**PENDENT**	–; pendents
PELORIC	–; –	**PENDING**	spending, upending; –
PELORUS	–; –	**PENDS**	spends, upends; –
PELOTA	–; pelotas		
PELT	spelt; pelts	**PENES**	–; –
PELTAST	–; peltasts	**PENGO**	–; pengos
PELTATE	–; –	**PENGUIN**	–; penguins
PELTED	–; –	**PENIAL**	–; –
PELTER	spelter; pelters	**PENICIL**	–; penicils
		PENILE	–; –
PELTERS	spelters; –	**PENIS**	–; –
PELTING	–; –	**PENISES**	–; –
PELTRY	–; –	**PENLITE**	–; penlites
PELTS	spelts; –	**PENMAN**	–; –
PELVES	–; –	**PENMEN**	–; –
PELVIC	–; pelvics	**PENNA**	–; pennae
PELVIS	–; –	**PENNAME**	–; pennames

PENNANT	–; pennants	PEPLA	–; –
PENNATE	–; pennated	PEPLOS	–; –
PENNED	–; –	PEPLUM	; peplums
PENNER	–; penners	PEPLUS	–; –
PENNI	–; pennia, pennis	PEPO	–; pepos
		PEPPED	–; –
PENNIES	–; –	PEPPER	–; peppers, peppery
PENNINE	–; pennines		
PENNING	–; –	PEPPIER	–; –
PENNON	–; pennons	PEPPILY	–; –
PENNY	–; –	PEPPING	–; –
PENOCHE	–; penoches	PEPPY	–; –
PENS	opens; –	PEPSIN	–; pepsine, pepsins
PENSEE	–; pensees		
PENSIL	–; pensile, pensils	PEPSINE	–; pepsines
		PEPTIC	–; peptics
PENSION	–; pensione, pensions	PEPTID	–; peptide, peptids
PENSIVE	–; –	PEPTIDE	–; peptides
PENSTER	–; pensters	PEPTIZE	–; peptized, peptizer, peptizes
PENT	spent; –		
PENTAD	–; pentads		
PENTANE	–; pentanes	PEPTONE	–; peptones
PENTOSE	–; pentoses	PER	aper; pere, peri, perk, perm, pert
PENTYL	–; pentyls		
PENUCHE	; penuches		
PENUCHI	–; penuchis	PERACID	–; peracids
PENULT	–; penults	PERCALE	–; percales
PENURY	–; –	PERCENT	–; percents
PEON	–; poons, peony	PERCEPT	–; percepts
		PERCH	–; –
PEONAGE	–; peonages	PERCHED	–; –
PEONES	–; –	PERCHER	–; perchers
PEONIES	–; –	PERCHES	–; –
PEONISM	–; peonisms	PERCOID	–; percoids
PEOPLE	–; peopled, peopler, peoples	PERCUSS	–; –
		PERDIE	–; –
		PERDU	–; perdue, perdus
PEP	–; pepo, peps	PERDUE	–; perdues

PERDY	–; –	**PERM**	sperm; perms
PERE	–; peres		
PERFECT	–; perfecta, perfecto, perfects	**PERMIT**	–; permits
		PERMS	sperms; –
PERFIDY	–; –	**PERMUTE**	–; permuted, permutes
PERFORM	–; performs	**PERORAL**	–; –
PERFUME	–; perfumed, perfumer, perfumes	**PEROXID**	–; peroxide, peroxids
PERFUSE	–; perfused, perfuses	**PERPEND**	–; perpends
		PERPENT	–; perpents
PERGOLA	–; pergolas	**PERPLEX**	–; –
PERHAPS	–; –	**PERRIES**	–; –
PERI	–; peril, peris	**PERRON**	–; perrons
		PERRY	–; –
PERIAPT	–; periapts	**PERSALT**	–; persalts
PERIDOT	–; peridots	**PERSE**	–; perses
PERIGEE	–; perigees	**PERSIST**	–; persists
PERIGON	–; perigons	**PERSON**	–; persona, persons
PERIL	–; perils		
PERILLA	–; perillas	**PERSONA**	–; personae, personal, personas
PERINEA	–; perineal		
PERIOD	–; periods		
PERIQUE	–; periques	**PERT**	–; –
PERISH	–; –	**PERTAIN**	–; pertains
PERIWIG	–; periwigs	**PERTER**	–; –
PERJURE	–; perjured, perjurer, perjures	**PERTEST**	–; –
		PERTLY	–; –
		PERTURB	–; perturbs
		PERUKE	–; perukes
PERJURY	–; –	**PERUSAL**	–; perusals
PERK	–; perks, perky	**PERUSE**	–; perused, peruser, peruses
PERKED	–; –		
PERKIER	–; –	**PERUSER**	–; perusers
PERKILY	–; –	**PERVADE**	–; pervaded, pervader, pervades
PERKING	–; –		
PERKISH	–; –		
PERLITE	–; perlites		
		PERVERT	–; perverts

PES	apes, opes; peso, pest	**PETTO**	–; –
		PETTY	–; –
PESADE	, pesades	**PETUNIA**	–; petunias
PESETA	–; pesetas	**PEW**	spew; pews
PESEWA	–; pesewas	**PEWEE**	–; pewees
PERKIER	–; –	**PEWIT**	–; pewits
PESKILY	–; –	**PEWS**	spews; –
PESKY	–; –	**PEWTER**	–; pewters
PESO	–; pesos	**PEYOTE**	–; peyotes
PESSARY	–; –	**PEYOTL**	–; peyotls
PEST	–; pests	**PEYTRAL**	–; peytrals
PESTER	–; pesters	**PEYTREL**	–; peytrels
PESTLE	–; pestled, pestles	**PFENNIG**	–; pfennige, pfennigs
PET	–; pets	**PHAETON**	–; phaetons
PETAL	–; petals	**PHAGE**	–; phages
PETALED	–; –	**PHALLI**	–; phallic
PETARD	–; petards	**PHALLUS**	–; –
PETASOS	–; –	**PHANTOM**	–; phantoms
PETASUS	–; –	**PHARAOH**	–; pharaohs
PETCOCK	–; petcocks	**PHAROS**	–; –
PETER	–; peters	**PHARYNX**	–; –
PETERED	–; –	**PHASE**	–; phased, phases
PETIOLE	–; petioled, petioles		
		PHASEAL	–; –
PETIT	–; petite	**PHASIC**	aphasic; –
PETITE	, petites	**PHASIS**	–; –
PETREL	–; petrels	**PHASING**	–; –
PETRIFY	–; –	**PHASMID**	, phasmids
PETROL	–; petrols	**PHAT**	–; –
PETROUS	–; –	**PHATIC**	–; –
PETTED	–; –	**PHELLEM**	–; phellems
PETTER	–; petters	**PHENIX**	–; –
PETTI	–; –	**PHENOL**	–; phenols
PETTIER	–; –	**PHENOM**	–; phenoms
PETTILY	–; –	**PHENYL**	–; phenyls
PETTING	–; –	**PHEW**	–; –
PETTISH	–; –	**PHI**	–; phis, phi
PETTLE	–; pettled, pettles	**PHIAL**	–; phials
		PHILTER	–; philters

PHILTRE	–; philtred, philtres	**PHOT**	–; photo, phots
PHIZ	–; –	**PHOTIC**	aphotic; photics
PHIZES	–; –		
PHLEGM	–; phlegms, phlegmy	**PHOTO**	–; photog, photon, photos
PHLOEM	–; phloems		
PHLOX	–; –	**PHOTOED**	–; –
PHLOXES	–; –	**PHOTOG**	–; photogs
PHOBIA	–; phobias	**PHOTON**	–; photons
PHOBIC	–; –	**PHPHT**	–; –
PHOCINE	–; –	**PHRASAL**	–; –
PHOEBE	–; phoebes	**PHRASE**	–; phrased, phrases
PHOENIX	–; –		
PHON	–; phone, phono, phons, phony	**PHRATRY**	–; –
		PHRENIC	–; –
		PHRENSY	–; –
PHONAL	–; –	**PHT**	–; –
PHONATE	–; phonated, phonates	**PHTALIC**	–; –
		PHYLA	–; phylae, phylar
PHONE	–; phoned, phones, phoney	**PHYLE**	–; –
		PHYLIC	–; –
		PHYLON	–; –
PHONEME	–; phonemes	**PHYLUM**	–; –
PHONEY	–; phoneys	**PHYSES**	–; –
PHONIC	aphonic; phonics	**PHYSIC**	–; physics
		PHYSIS	–; –
PHONIER	–; –	**PHYTANE**	–; phytanes
PHONIES	–; phoniest	**PHYTIN**	–; phytins
PHONILY	–; –	**PHYTOID**	–; –
PHONING	–; –	**PHYTON**	–; phytons
PHONO	–; phonon, phonos	**PI**	–; pia, pic, pie, pig, pin, pip, pis, pit, piu, pix
PHONON	–; phonons		
PHONY	–; –		
PHOOEY	–; –	**PIA**	–; pial, pian pias
PHORATE	ephorate; ohorates		
		PIAFFE	·; piaffed,

	piaffer, piaffes	**PICKET**	–; pickets
		PICKIER	–; –
PIAFFER	–; piaffers	**PICKING**	–; pickings
PIAL	–; –	**PICKLE**	–; pickled, pickles
PIAN	apian; piano, pians		
PIANIC	–; –	**PICKOFF**	–; pickoffs
PIANISM	–; pianisms	**PICKS**	spicks; –
PIANIST	–; pianists	**PICKUP**	–; pickups
PIANO	–; pianos	**PICNIC**	–; picnics
PIASABA	–; piasabas	**PICOLIN**	–; picoline, picolins
PIASAVA	–; piasavas		
PIASTER	–; piasters	**PICOT**	–; picots
PIASTRE	–; piastres	**PICOTED**	–; –
PIAZZA	–; piazzas	**PICOTEE**	–; picotees
PIAZZE	–; –	**PICQUET**	–; picquets
PIBROCH	–; pibrochs	**PICRATE**	–; picrated, picrates
PIC	epic, spic; pica, pice, pick, pics		
		PICRIC	–; –
		PICRITE	–; picrites
		PICS	epics, spics; –
PICA	spica; pical, picas		
		PICTURE	–; pictured, pictures
PICACHO	–; picachos		
PICADOR	–; picadors	**PICUL**	–; piculs
PICAL	apical, epical; –	**PIDDLE**	–; piddled, piddler, piddles
PICARA	–; picaras		
PICARO	–; picaros		
PICAS	spicas; –	**PIDDLER**	–; piddlers
PICCOLO	–; piccolos	**PIDDOCK**	–; piddocks
PICE	spice; –	**PIDGIN**	–; pidgins
PICEOUS	–; –	**PIE**	–; pied, pier, pies
PICK	spick; picks, picky		
		PIEBALD	–; piebalds
PICKAX	–; pickaxe	**PIECE**	apiece; pieced, piecer, pieces
PICKAXE	–; pickaxed, pickaxes		
PICKED	–; –	**PIECER**	–; piecers
PICKEER	–; pickeers	**PIECING**	–; piecings
PICKER	–; pickers	**PIED**	spied; –

PIEFORT	-; pieforts	**PIGWEED**	-; pigweeds
PIEING	-; -	**PIING**	-; -
PIER	spier; piers	**PIKA**	-; pikas
PIERCE	-; pierced,	**PIKAKE**	-; pikakes
	piercer,	**PIKE**	spike; piked,
	pierces		piker, pikes
PIERCER	-; piercers	**PIKED**	spiked; -
PIERROT	-; pierrots	**PIKER**	spiker; pikers
PIERS	spiers; -	**PIKERS**	spikers; -
PIES	spies; -	**PIKES**	spikes; -
PIETA	-; pietas	**PIKING**	spiking; -
PIETIES	-; -	**PILAF**	-; pilaff,
PIETISM	-; pietisms		pilafs
PIETIST	-; pietists	**PILAFF**	-; pilaffs
PIETY	-; -	**PILAR**	-; -
PIFFLE	-; piffled,	**PILAU**	-; pilaus
	piffles	**PILAW**	-; pilaws
PIG	-; pigs	**PILE**	spile; pilea,
PIGBOAT	-; pigboats		piled, pilei,
PIGEON	-; pigeons		piles
PIGFISH	-; -	**PILEATE**	-; pileated
PIGGED	-; -	**PILED**	spiled; -
PIGGERY	-; -	**PILEOUS**	-; -
PIGGIE	-; piggies	**PILES**	spiles; -
PIGGIN	-; pigging,	**PILEUM**	-; -
	piggins	**PILEUP**	-; pileups
PIGGISH	-; -	**PILEUS**	-; -
PIGGY	-; -	**PILFER**	-; pilfers
PIGLET	-; piglets	**PILGRIM**	-; pilgrims
PIGMENT	-; pigments	**PILI**	-; pilis
PIGMIES	-; -	**PILING**	spiling;
PIGMY	-; -		pilings
PIGNORA	-; -	**PILINGS**	spilings; -
PIGNUS	-; -	**PILL**	spill; pills
PIGNUT	-; pignuts	**PILLAGE**	-; pillaged,
PIGPEN	-; pigpens		pillager,
PIGSKIN	-; pigskins		pillages
PIGSNEY	-; pigsneys	**PILLAR**	-; pillars
PIGSTY	-; -	**PILLBOX**	-; -
PIGTAIL	-; pigtails		

PILLED	spilled; –	pined, pines,
PILLING	spilling; –	piney
PILLION	–; pillions	**PINEAL**	–; –
PILLORY	–; –	**PINENE**	–; pinenes
PILLOW	–; pillows,	**PINED**	opined,
	pillowy		spined; –
PILLS	spills; –	**PINERY**	–; –
PILOSE	–; –	**PINES**	opines,
PILOT	–; pilots		spines; –
PILOTED	–; –	**PINESAP**	–; pinesaps
PILOUS	–; –	**PINETA**	–; –
PILSNER	–; pilsners	**PINETUM**	–; –
PILULAR	–; –	**PINFISH**	–; –
PILULE	–; pilules	**PINFOLD**	–; pinfolds
PILUS	–; –	**PING**	aping,
PILY	–; –		oping;
PIMA	–; pimas		pingo, pings
PIMENTO	–; pimentos	**PINGER**	–; pingers
PIMP	–; pimps	**PINGO**	–; pingos
PIMPED	–; –	**PINGUID**	–; –
PIMPING	–; –	**PINHEAD**	–; pinheads
PIMPLE	–; pimpled,	**PINHOLE**	–; pinholes
	pimples	**PINIER**	spinier; –
PIMPLY	–; –	**PINIEST**	–; –
PIN	spin; pina,	**PINING**	opining; –
	pine, ping,	**PINION**	opinion;
	pink, pins,		pinions
	pint, piny	**PINIONS**	opinions; –
PINA	–; pinas	**PINITE**	–; pinites
PINANG	–; pinangs	**PINK**	–; pinko,
PINATA	–; pinatas		pinks, pinky
PINBALL	–; pinballs	**PINKED**	–; –
PINBONE	–; pinbones	**PINKER**	–; –
PINCER	–; pincers	**PINKEST**	–; –
PINCH	–; –	**PINKEYE**	–; pinkeyes
PINCHED	–; –	**PINKIE**	–; pinkies
PINCHER	–; pinchers	**PINKING**	–; pinkings
PINCHES	–; –	**PINKISH**	–; –
PINDER	–; pinders	**PINKLY**	–; –
PINE	opine, spine;	**PINKO**	–; pinkos

PINKOES	–; –	**PIOSITY**	–; –
PINNA	–; pinnae, pinnal, pinnas	**PIOUS**	–; –
		PIOUSLY	–; –
		PIP	–; pipe, pips, pipy
PINNACE	–; pinnaces		
PINNATE	–; pinnated	**PIPAGE**	–; pipages
PINNED	–; –	**PIPAL**	–; pipals
PINNER	spinner; pinners	**PIPE**	–; piped, piper, pipes, pipet
PINNERS	spinners; –		
PINNING	spinning; –	**PIPEAGE**	–; pipeages
PINNULA	–; pinnulae, pinnular	**PIPEFUL**	–; pipefuls
		PIPER	–; pipers
PINNULE	–; pinnules	**PIPET**	–; pipets
PINOCLE	–; pinocles	**PIPETTE**	–; pipetted, pipettes
PINOLE	–; pinoles		
PINON	–; pinons	**PIPIER**	–; –
PINONES	–; –	**PIPIEST**	–; –
PINS	spins; –	**PIPING**	–; pipings
PINT	–; pinta, pinto, pints	**PIPIT**	–; pipits
		PIPKIN	–; pipkins
PINTA	–; pintas	**PIPPED**	–; –
PINTADA	–; pintadas	**PIPPIN**	–; pipping, pippins
PINTADO	–; pintados		
PINTAIL	–; pintails	**PIQUANT**	–; –
PINTANO	–; pintanos	**PIQUE**	–; piqued, piques, piquet
PINTLE	–; pintles		
PINTO	–; pintos		
PINTOES	–; –	**PIQUET**	–; piquets
PINUP	–; pinups	**PIQUING**	–; –
PINWALE	–; pinwales	**PIRACY**	–; –
PINWEED	–; pinweeds	**PIRAGUA**	–; piraguas
PINWORK	–; pinworks	**PIRANA**	–; piranas
PINWORM	–; pinworms	**PIRANHA**	–; piranhas
PINY	spiny; –	**PIRATE**	–; pirated, pirates
PINYON	–; pinyons		
PIOLET	–; piolets	**PIRATIC**	–; –
PION	–; pions	**PIRAYA**	–; pirayas
PIONIC	–; –	**PIRN**	–; pirns
PIONEER	–; pioneers	**PIROG**	–; pirogi

PIROGEN	–; –	**PITHEAD**	–; pitheads
PIROGHI	–; –	**PITHIER**	–; –
PIROGUE	–; pirogues	**PITHILY**	–; –
PIROQUE	–; piorques	**PITHING**	–; –
PIS	–; piss	**PITIED**	–; –
PISCARY	–; –	**PITIER**	–; –
PISCINA	–; piscinae, piscinal, piscinas	**PITIES**	–; –
		PITIFUL	–; –
PISCINE	–; –	**PITMAN**	–; pitmans
PISH	apish; –	**PITMEN**	–; –
PISHED	–; –	**PITON**	–; pitons
PISHES	–; –	**PITS**	spits; –
PISHING	–; –	**PITSAW**	–; pitsaws
PISMIRE	–; pismires	**PITTED**	spitted; –
PISS	–; –	**PITTING**	spitting; pittings
PISSANT	–; pissants		
PISSED	–; –	**PIU**	–; –
PISSES	–; –	**PIVOT**	–; plvots
PISSING	–; –	**PIVOTAL**	–; –
PISSOIR	–; pissoirs	**PIVOTED**	–; –
PISTIL	–; pistils	**PIX**	–; pixy
PISTOL	–; pistole, pistols	**PIXES**	–; –
		PIXIE	–; pixies
PISTOLE	–; pistoled, pistoles	**PIXYISH**	–; –
		PIZAZZ	–; –
PISTON	–; pistons	**PIZZA**	–; pizzas
PIT	spit; pita, pith, pits, pity	**PIZZAZZ**	–; –
		PIZZLE	–; pizzles
PITA	–; pitas	**PLACARD**	–; placards
PITAPAT	–; pitapats	**PLACATE**	–; placated placater, placates
PITCH	–; pitchy		
PITCHED	–; –	**PLACE**	–; placed, placer, places, placet
PITCHER	–; pitchers		
PITCHES	–; –		
PITFALL	–; pitfalls		
PITH	–; piths, pithy	**PLACEBO**	–; placebos
		PLACER	–; placers
PITHED	–; –	**PLACET**	; placets
		PLACID	–;

PLACING	–; –
PLACK	–; placks
PLACKET	–; plackets
PLACOID	–; placoids
PLAFOND	–; plafonds
PLAGAL	–; –
PLAGE	–; plages
PLAGUE	–; plagued, plaguer, plagues, plaguey
PLAGUER	–; plaguers
PLAGUY	–; –
PLAICE	–; plaices
PLAID	–; plaids
PLAIDED	–; –
PLAIN	–; plains, plaint
PLAINED	–; –
PLAINER	–; –
PLAINLY	–; –
PLAINT	–; plaints
PLAIT	–; plaits
PLAITED	–; –
PLAITER	–; plaiters
PLAN	–; plane, plank, plans, plant
PLANAR	–; –
PLANATE	–; –
PLANCH	–; planche
PLANCHE	–; planches, planchet
PLANE	–; planed, planer, planes, planet
PLANED	–; –
PLANER	–; planers
PLANET	–; planets

PLANING	–; –
PLANISH	–; –
PLANK	–; planks
PLANKED	–; –
PLANNED	–; –
PLANNER	–; planners
PLANT	–; plants
PLANTAR	–; –
PLANTED	–; –
PLANTER	–; planters
PLANULA	–; planulae, planular
PLAQUE	–; plaques
PLASH	splash; plashy
PLASHED	splashed; –
PLASHER	–; plashers
PLASHES	splashes; –
PLASHY	splashy; –
PLASM	–; plasma, plasms
PLASMA	–; plasmas
PLASMIC	–; –
PLASMID	–; plasmids
PLASMIN	–; plasmins
PLASMON	–; plasmons
PLASTER	–; plasters, plastery
PLASTIC	aplastic; plastics
PLASTID	–; plastids
PLAT	splat; plate, plats, platy
PLATAN	–; platane, platans
PLATANE	–; platanes
PLATE	–; plated, platen, plater, plates

PLATEAU	–; plateaus, plateaux	**PLEASER**	–; pleasers
		PLEAT	–; pleats
PLATEN	–; platens	**PLEATED**	–; –
PLATER	–; platers	**PLEATER**	–; pleaters
PLATIER	–; –	**PLEB**	–; plebe, plebs
PLATIES	–; platiest		
PLATINA	–; platinas	**PLEBE**	–; plebes
PLATING	–; platings	**PLED**	–; –
PLATOON	–; platoons	**PLEDGE**	–; pledged, pledgee, pledger, pledges, pledget
PLATS	splats; –		
PLATTED	–; –		
PLATTER	splatter; platters		
PLATY	–; platys	**PLEDGEE**	–; pledgees
PLAUDIT	–; plaudits	**PLEDGER**	–; pledgers
PLAY	splay; pluya, plays	**PLEDGET**	–; pledgets
		PLEDGOR	–; pledgors
PLAYA	–; playas	**PLEIAD**	–; pleiads
PLAYACT	–; playacts	**PLENA**	–; –
PLAYBOY	–; playboys	**PLENARY**	–; –
PLAYDAY	–; playdays	**PLENISH**	–; –
PLAYED	splayed; –	**PLENISM**	–; plenisms
PLAYER	–; players	**PLENIST**	–; plenists
PLAYERS	splayers; –	**PLENTY**	aplenty; –
PLAYFUL	–; –	**PLENUM**	–; plenums
PLAYING	splaying; –	**PLEOPOD**	–; pleopods
PLAYLET	–; playlets	**PLESSOR**	–; plessors
PLAYOFF	–; playoffs	**PLEURA**	–; pleurae, pleural, pleuras
PLAYPEN	–; playpens		
PLAYS	splays; –		
PLAZA	–; plazas	**PLEURON**	–; –
PLEA	–; plead, pleas, pleat	**PLEXOR**	–; plexors
		PLEXUS	–; –
PLEACH	–; –	**PLIABLE**	–; –
PLEAD	–; pleads	**PLIABLY**	–; –
PLEADED	–; –	**PLIANCY**	–; –
PLEADER	–; pleaders	**PLIANT**	–; –
PLEASE	–; pleased, pleaser, pleases	**PLICA**	–; plicae, plical
		PLICATE	–; plicated

PLIE	–; plied, plier, plies	PLUCK	–; plucks, plucky
PLIER	–; pliers	PLUCKED	–; –
PLIGHT	–; plights	PLUCKER	–; pluckers
PLIMSOL	–; plimsole, plimsoll, plimsols	PLUG	–; plugs
		PLUGGED	–; –
		PLUGGER	–; pluggers
PLINK	–; plinks	PLUM	–; plumb, plume, plump, plums, plumy
PLINKED	–; –		
PLINKER	–; plinkers		
PLINTH	–; plinths		
PLISKIE	–; pliskies	PLUMAGE	–; plumaged, plumages
PLISKY	–; –		
PLISSE	–; plisses		
PLOD	–; plods	PLUMATE	–; –
PLODDED	–; –	PLUMB	–; plumbs
PLODDER	–; plodders	PLUMBED	–; –
PLOIDY	–; –	PLUMBER	–; plumbers, plumbery
PLONK	–; plonks		
PLONKED	–; –	PLUMBIC	–; –
PLOP	–; plops	PLUMBUM	–; plumbums
PLOPPED	–; –	PLUME	–; plumed, plumes
PLOSION	–; plosions		
PLOSIVE	–; plosives	PLUMIER	–; –
PLOT	–; plots	PLUMING	–; –
PLOTTED	–; –	PLUMMET	–; plummets
PLOTTER	–; plotters	PLUMMY	–; –
PLOTTY	–; –	PLUMOSE	–; –
PLOUGH	–; ploughs	PLUMP	–; plumps
PLOVER	–; plovers	PLUMPED	–; –
PLOW	–; plows	PLUMPEN	–; plumpens
PLOWBOY	–; plowboys	PLUMPER	–; plumpers
PLOWED	–; –	PLUMPLY	–; –
PLOWER	–; plowers	PLUMULE	–; plumules
PLOWING	–; –	PLUNDER	–; plunders
PLOWMAN	–; –	PLUNGE	–; plunged, plunger, plunges
PLOWMEN	–; –		
PLOY	–; ploys		
PLOYED	–; –	PLUNGER	–; plungers
PLOYING	–; –	PLUNK	–; plunks

PLUNKED	–; –	PODIA	–; –
PLUNKER	–; plunkers	PODITE	–; podites
PLURAL	, plurals	PODITIC	–; –
PLUS	–; plush	PODIUM	–; podiums
PLUSES	–; –	PODSOL	–; podsols
PLUSH	–; plushy	PODZOL	–; podzols
PLUSHER	–; –	POEM	–; poems
PLUSHES	–; plushest	POESIES	–; –
PLUSHLY	–; –	POESY	–; –
PLUSSES	–; –	POET	–; poets
PLUTON	–; plutons	POETIC	–; poetics
PLUVIAL	–; pluvials	POETISE	–; poetised, poetiser, poetises
PLY	–; –		
PLYER	–; plyers		
PLYING	–; –	POETIZE	–; poetized, poetizer, poetizes
PLYWOOD	–; plywoods		
PNEUMA	–; pneumas		
POACH	–; poachy	POETRY	–; –
POACHED	–; –	POGEY	–; pogeys
POACHER	–; poachers	POGIES	–; –
POACHES	–; –	POGONIA	–; pogonias
POCHARD	–; pochards	POGONIP	–; pogonips
POCK	–; pocks, pocky	POGROM	–; pogroms
		POGY	–; –
POCKED	–; –	POH	–; –
POCKET	–; pockets	POI	–; pois
POCKIER	–; –	POILU	–; poilus
POCKILY	–; –	POIND	–; poinds
POCKING	–; –	POINDED	–; –
POCO	–; –	POINT	–; pointe, points, pointy
POCOSIN	–; pocosins		
POD	–; pods		
PODAGRA	–; podagral, podagras	POINTE	–; pointed, pointer, pointes
PODDED	–; –		
PODDING	–; –	POINTER	–; pointers
PODESTA	–; podestas	POISE	–; poised, poiser, poises
PODGIER	–; –		
PODGILY	–; –		
PODGY	–; –	POISER	–; poisers

POISING	–; –	**POLIS**	–; polish
POISON	–; poisons	**POLITE**	–; politer
POITREL	–; poitrels	**POLITIC**	–; politick,
POKE	spoke;		politics
	poked,	**POLITY**	–; –
	poker,	**POLKA**	–; polkas
	pokes,	**POLKAED**	–; –
	pokey	**POLL**	–; polls
POKED	spoked; –	**POLLACK**	–; pollacks
POKER	–; pokers	**POLLARD**	–; pollards
POKES	spokes; –	**POLLED**	–; –
POKEY	–; pokeys	**POLLEE**	–; pollees
POKIER	–; –	**POLLEN**	–; pollens
POKIES	–; pokiest	**POLLER**	–; pollers
POKILY	–; –	**POLLEX**	–; –
POKING	spoking; –	**POLLING**	–; –
POKY	–; –	**POLLIST**	–; pollists
POL	–; pole,	**POLLOCK**	–; pollocks
	poll, polo,	**POLLUTE**	–; polluted,
	pols, poly		polluter,
POLAR	–; polars		pollutes
POLARON	–; polarons	**POLO**	–; polos
POLDER	–; polders	**POLOIST**	–; poloists
POLE	–; poled,	**POLY**	–; polyp,
	poler, poles		polys
POLEAX	–; poleaxe	**POLYCOT**	–; polycots
POLEAXE	–;	**POLYENE**	–; polyenes
	poleaxed,	**POLYGON**	–; polygons,
	poleaxes		polygony
POLECAT	–; polecats	**POLYMER**	–; polymers
POLEIS	–; –	**POLYNYA**	–; polynyas
POLEMIC	–; polemics	**POLYP**	–; polypi,
POLENTA	–; polentas		polyps
POLER	–; polers	**POLYPOD**	–; polypods,
POLEYN	–; poleyns		polypody
POLICE	–; policed,	**POLYPUS**	–; –
	polices	**POMACE**	–; pomaces
POLICY	–; –	**POMADE**	–;
POLING	–; –		pomaded,
POLIO	–; polios		pomades

POMATUM	−; pomatums	**POOLING**	spooling; −
POME	−; pomes	**POOLS**	spools; −
POMELO	−; pomelos	**POON**	spoon,
POMMEE	−; −		poons
POMMEL	−; pommels	**POONS**	spoons; −
POMP	−; pomps	**POOP**	−; poops
POMPANO	−;	**POOPED**	−; −
	pompanos	**POOPING**	−; −
POMPOM	−; pompoms	**POOR**	spoor; poori
POMPON	−; pompons	**POORER**	−; −
POMPOUS	−; −	**POOREST**	−; −
PONCE	−; ponces	**POORI**	−; pooris
PONCHO	−; ponchos	**POORIS**	−; poorish
POND	−; ponds	**POORLY**	−; −
PONDER	−; ponders	**POORS**	spoors; −
PONE	; pones	**POP**	−; pope,
PONENT	−; −		pops
PONGEE	−; pongees	**POPCORN**	−; popcorns
PONGID	−; pongids	**POPE**	−; popes
PONIARD	−; poniards	**POPEDOM**	−;
PONIED	−; −		popedoms
PONIES	−; −	**POPERY**	−; −
PONS	−; −	**POPEYED**	−; −
PONTES	−; −	**POPGUN**	−; popguns
PONTIFF	−; pontiffs	**POPISH**	−; −
PONTIL	−; pontils	**POPLAR**	−; poplars
PONTINE	−; −	**POPLIN**	−; poplins
PONTON	−; pontons	**POPOVER**	−; popovers
PONTOON	spontoon;	**POPPA**	−; poppas
	pontoons	**POPPED**	−; −
PONY	−; −	**POPPER**	−; poppers
POOCH	−; −	**POPPET**	−; poppets
POOCHES	−; −	**POPPIED**	−; −
POOD	−; poods	**POPPIES**	−; −
POODLE	−; poodles	**POPPING**	−; −
POOH	−; poohs	**POPPLE**	−; poppled,
POOHED	−; −		popples
POOHING	−; −	**POPPY**	−; −
POOL	spool; pools	**POPULAR**	−; −
POOLED	spooled; −	**PORCH**	−; −

PORCHES	–; –	POSE	–; posed,
PORCINE	–; –		poser, poses
PORE	spore;	POSER	–; posers
	pored, pores	POSEUR	–; poseurs
PORED	spored; –	POSH	–; –
PORES	spores; –	POSHER	–; –
PORGIES	–; –	POSHEST	–; –
PORGY	–; –	POSIES	–; –
PORING	sporing; –	POSING	–; –
PORISM	–; porisms	POSIT	–; posits
PORK	–; porks,	POSITED	–; –
	porky	POSSE	–; posses,
PORKER	–; porkers		posset
PORKIER	–; –	POSSES	–; possess
PORKIES	–; porkiest	POSSET	–; possets
PORKPIE	–; porkpies	POSSUM	opossum;
PORN	–; porno,		possums
	porns	POSSUMS	opossums; –
PORNO	–; pornos	POST	–; posts
POROSE	–; –	POSTAGE	–; postages
POROUS	–; –	POSTAL	–; postals
PORT	aport, sport;	POSTBAG	–; postbags
	ports	POSTBOX	–; –
PORTAGE	–; portaged,	POSTBOY	–; postboys
	portages	POSTED	–; –
PORTAL	–; portals	POSTEEN	–; posteens
PORTED	sported; –	POSTER	–; postern,
PORTEND	–; portends		posters
PORTENT	–; portents	POSTFIX	–; –
PORTER	sporter,	POSTIN	–; posting,
	porters		postins
PORTERS	sporters; –	POSTING	–; postings
PORTICO	–; porticos	POSTMAN	–; –
PORTING	sporting; –	POSTMEN	–; –
PORTION	–; portions	POSTURE	–; postured,
PORTLY	–; –		posturer,
PORTRAY	–; portrays		postures
PORTS	sports; –	POSTWAR	–; –
POSADA	–; posadas	POSY	–; –
		POT	spot; pots

POTABLE	–; potables	**POTTO**	–; pottos
POTAGE	–; potages	**POTTY**	spotty; –
POTASH	–; –	**POUCH**	–; pouchy
POTATO	–; –	**POUCHED**	–; –
POTBOIL	–; potboils	**POUCHES**	–; –
POTBOY	–; potboys	**POUF**	–; pouff,
POTEEN	–; poteens		poufs
POTENT	–; –	**POUFED**	–; –
POTFUL	–; potfuls	**POUFF**	–; pouffe,
POTHEAD	–; potheads		pouffs
POTHEEN	–; potheens	**POUFFE**	–; pouffed,
POTHER	–; potherb,		pouffes
	pothers	**POULARD**	–; poularde,
POTHERB	–; potherbs		poulards
POTHOLE	–; potholed,	**POULT**	–; poults
	potholes	**POULTRY**	–; –
POTHOOK	–; pothooks	**POUNCE**	–; pounced,
POTICHE	–; potiches		pouncer,
POTION	–; potions		pounces
POTLACH	–; potlache	**POUNCER**	–; pouncers
POTLIKE	–; –	**POUND**	–; pounds
POTLUCK	–; potlucks	**POUNDAL**	–; poundals
POTMAN	–; –	**POUNDED**	–; –
POTMEN	–; –	**POUNDER**	–; pounders
POTPIE	–; potpies	**POUR**	–; pours
POTS	spots; –	**POURED**	–; –
POTSHOT	–; potshots	**POURER**	–; pourers
POTSIE	–; potsies	**POURING**	–; –
POTSY	–; –	**POUSSIF**	–; poussies
POTTAGE	–; pottages	**POUT**	spout; pouts,
POTTED	spotted; –		pouty
POTTEEN	–; potteens	**POUTED**	spouted; –
POTTER	spotter;	**POUTER**	spouter;
	potters,		pouters
	pottery	**POUTERS**	spouters; –
POTTERS	spotters; –	**POUTFUL**	–; –
POTTIER	–; –	**POUTIER**	–; –
POTTIES	–; pottiest	**POUTING**	spouting; –
POTTING	spotting; –	**POUTS**	spouts; –
POTTLE	–; pottles	**POUTY**	–; –

POVERTY	–; –	**PRAT**	sprat; prate, prats
POW	–; pows		
POWDER	–; powders, powdery	**PRATE**	–; prated, prater, prates
POWER	–; powers		
POWERED	–; –	**PRATER**	–; praters
POWTER	–; powters	**PRATING**	–; –
POWWOW	–; powwows	**PRATS**	sprats; –
POX	–; –	**PRATTLE**	sprattle; prattled, prattler, prattles
POXED	–; –		
POXES	–; –		
POXING	–; –		
POYOU	–; poyous	**PRAU**	–; praus
PRAAM	–; praams	**PRAWN**	–; prawns
PRACTIC	–; practice	**PRAWNED**	–; –
PRAETOR	–; praetors	**PRAWNER**	–; prawners
PRAHU	–; prahus	**PRAXES**	–; –
PRAIRIE	–; prairies	**PRAXIS**	–; –
PRAISE	upraise; praised, praiser, praises	**PRAY**	spray; prays
		PRAYED	sprayed; –
		PRAYER	sprayer; prayers
PRAISED	upraised; –		
PRAISER	upraiser; praisers	**PRAYERS**	sprayers; –
		PRAYING	spraying; –
PRAISES	upraises; –	**PRAYS**	sprays; –
PRALINE	–; pralines	**PREACH**	upreach; preachy
PRAM	–; prams		
PRANCE	–; pranced, prancer, prances	**PREACT**	–; preacts
		PREAMP	–; preamps
		PREANAL	–; –
		PREARM	–; prearms
PRANCER	–; prancers	**PREAVER**	–; preavers
PRANG	sprang; prangs	**PREBEND**	–; prebends
		PREBILL	–; prebills
PRANGED	–; –	**PREBIND**	–; prebinds
PRANK	–; pranks	**PREBOIL**	–; preboils
PRANKED	–; –	**PRECAST**	–; precasts
PRAO	–; praos	**PRECAVA**	–; precavae, precaval
PRASE	–; prases		

PRECEDE	–; preceded, precedes	**PRELATE**	–; prelates
		PRELECT	–; prelects
		PRELIM	–; prelims
PRECENT	–; precents	**PRELUDE**	–; preluded, preluder, preludes
PRECEPT	–; precepts		
PRECESS	–; –		
PRECIPE	–; precipes	**PREMAN**	–; –
PRECIS	–; precise	**PREMED**	–; premeds
PRECISE	–; precised, preciser, precises	**PREMEN**	–; –
		PREMIE	–; premier, premies
PRECOOK	–; precooks	**PREMIER**	–; premiere, premiers
PRECOOL	–; precools		
PRECURE	–; precured, precures	**PREMISE**	–; premised, promises
PREDATE	–; predated, predates	**PREMISS**	–; –
		PREMIUM	–; premiums
PREDAWN	–; predawns	**PREMIX**	–; –
PREDIAL	–; –	**PREMUNE**	–; –
PREDICT	–; predicts	**PRENAME**	–; prenames
PREDUSK	–; predusks	**PREP**	–; preps
PREE	spree; preed, preen, prees	**PREPACK**	–; prepacks
		PREPAID	–; –
PREEING	–; –	**PREPARE**	–; prepared, preparer, prepares
PREEMIE	–; preemies		
PREEMPT	–; preempts		
PREEN	–; preens	**PREPAY**	–; prepays
PREENER	–; preeners	**PREPLAN**	–; preplans, preplant
PREES	sprees; –		
PREFAB	–; prefabs	**PREPPED**	–; –
PREFACE	–; prefaced, prefacer, prefaces	**PREPPIE**	–; preppies
		PREPUCE	–; prepuces
		PRESA	–; –
PREFECT	–; prefects	**PRESAGE**	–; presaged, presager, presages
PREFER	–; prefers		
PREFIX	–; –		
PREFORM	–; preforms		
PREGAME	–; –	**PRESE**	–; preset
PREHEAT	–; preheats	**PRESELL**	–; presells
PRELACY	–; –	**PRESENT**	–; presents

PRESET	–; presets	PREWARM	–; prewarms
PRESHOW	–; preshown, preshows	PREWARN	–; prewarns
		PREWASH	–; –
		PREWRAP	–; prewraps
PRESIDE	–; presided, presider, presides	PREX	–; prexy
		PREXES	–; –
		PREXIES	–; –
PRESIFT	–; presifts	PREY	–; preys
PRESOAK	–; presoaks	PREYED	–; –
PRESOLD	–; –	PREYER	–; preyers
PRESS	–; –	PREYING	–; –
PRESSED	–; –	PRIAPI	–; priapic
PRESSER	–; pressers	PRIAPUS	–; –
PRESSES	–;	PRICE	–; priced, pricer, prices, pricey
PRESSOR	–; –		
PREST	–; presto, prests		
		PRICER	–; pricers
PRESTER	–; presters	PRICIER	–; –
PRESTO	–; prestos	PRICING	–; –
PRESUME	–; presumed, presumer, presumes	PRICK	–; pricks, pricky
		PRICKED	–; –
PRETAX	–; –	PRICKER	–; prickers
PRETEEN	–; preteens	PRICKET	–; prickets
PRETEND	–; pretends	PRICKLE	–; prickled, prickles
PRETEST	–; pretests		
PRETEXT	–; pretexts		
PRETOR	–; pretors	PRICKLY	–; –
PRETTY	–; –	PRICY	–; –
PRETZEL	–; pretzels	PRIDE	–; pridea, prides
PREVAIL	–; prevails		
PREVENT	–; prevents	PRIDING	–; –
PREVIEW	–; previews	PRIED	–; –
PREVISE	–; prevised, previses	PRIER	sprier; priers
		PRIES	–; priest
		PRIEST	–; priests
PREVUE	–; prevued, prevues	PRIG	sprig; prigs
		PRIGGED	sprigged; –
PREWAR	–; prewarm, orewarn	PRIGS	sprigs; –
		PRILL	–; prills

PRILLED	–; –	**PRIORLY**	–; –
PRIM	–; prima, prime, primi, primo, primp, prims	**PRISE**	uprise, prised, prises
PRIMA	–; primal, primas	**PRISERE**	–; priseres
		PRISES	uprises; –
PRIMACY	–; –	**PRISING**	–; –
PRIMAGE	–; primages	**PRISM**	–; prisms
PRIMARY	–; –	**PRISON**	–; prisons
PRIMATE	–; primates	**PRISS**	–; prissy
PRIME	–; primed, primer, primes	**PRISSES**	–; –
		PRITHEE	–; –
		PRIVACY	–; –
PRIMER	, primero, primers	**PRIVATE**	–; privater, privates
PRIMERO	–; primeros	**PRIVET**	–; privets
PRIMINE	–; primines	**PRIVIER**	–; –
PRIMING	–; primings	**PRIVIES**	–; priviest
PRIMLY	–; –	**PRIVILY**	–; –
PRIMMED	–; –	**PRIVITY**	–; –
PRIMMER	–; –	**PRIVY**	–; –
PRIMO	–; primos	**PRIZE**	–; prized, prizer, prizes
PRIMP	–; primps		
PRIMPED	–; –	**PRIZER**	–; prizers
PRIMSIE	–; –	**PRIZING**	–; –
PRIMULA	–; primulas	**PRO**	–; proa, prod, prof, prog, prom, prop, pros, prow
PRIMUS	–; –		
PRINCE	–; princes		
PRINCES	–; princess		
PRINK	–; prinks	**PROA**	–; proas
PRINKED	–; –	**PROBAND**	–; probands
PRINKER	–; prinkers	**PROBANG**	–; probangs
PRINT	sprint; prints	**PROBATE**	–; probated, probates
PRINTED	sprinted; –		
PRINTER	sprinter; printers, printery	**PROBE**	–; probed, prober, probes
PRIOR	–; priors, priory	**PROBER**	–; probers
		PROBING	–; –

PROBIT	–; probits, probity	**PROLATE**	–; –
PROBLEM	–; problems	**PROLE**	–; proles
PROCARP	–; procarps	**PROLEG**	–; prolegs
PROCEED	–; proceeds	**PROLINE**	–; prolines
PROCESS	–; –	**PROLIX**	–; –
PROCTOR	–; proctors	**PROLOG**	–; prologs
PROCURE	–; procured, procurer, procures	**PROLONG**	–; prolonge, prolongs
PROD	–; prods	**PROM**	–; proms
PRODDED	–; –	**PROMISE**	–; promised, promisee, promiser, promises
PRODDER	–; prodders		
PRODIGY	–; –		
PRODUCE	–; produced, producer, produces	**PROMOTE**	–; promoted, promoter, promotes
PRODUCT	–; products	**PROMPT**	–; prompts
PROEM	–; proems	**PRONATE**	–; pronated, pronates
PROETTE	–; proettes		
PROF	–; profs	**PRONE**	–; –
PROFANE	–; profaned, profaner, profanes	**PRONELY**	–; –
		PRONG	–; prongs
		PRONGED	–; –
PROFESS	–; –	**PRONOUN**	–; pronouns
PROFFER	–; proffers	**PRONTO**	–; –
PROFILE	–; profiled, profiler, profiles	**PROOF**	–; proofs
		PROOFED	–; –
		PROOFER	–; proofers
PROFIT	–; profits	**PROP**	–; props
PROFUSE	–; –	**PROPANE**	–; propanes
PROG	–; progs	**PROPEL**	–; propels
PROGENY	–; –	**PROPEND**	–; propends
PROGGED	–; –	**PROPENE**	–; propenes
PROGGER	–; proggers	**PROPER**	–; propers
PROGRAM	–; programs	**PROPHET**	–; prophets
PROJECT	–; projects	**PROPINE**	–; propined, propines
PROJET	–; projets		
PROLAN	–; prolans	**PROPJET**	–; propjets
		PROPMAN	–; –

PROPMEN	–; –	**PROTEIN**	–; proteins
PROPONE	–;	**PROTEND**	, protends
	proponed,	**PROTEST**	–; protests
	propones	**PROTEUS**	–; –
PROPOSE	–;	**PROTIST**	–; protists
	proposed,	**PROTIUM**	–; protiums
	proposer,	**PROTON**	–; protons
	proposes	**PROTYL**	–; protyle,
PROPPED	–; –		protyls
PROPYL	–; propyls	**PROTYLE**	–; protyles
PRORATE	–; prorated,	**PROUD**	–; –
	prorates	**PROUDER**	–; –
PROS	–; prose,	**PROUDLY**	–; –
	proso, prost,	**PROVE**	–; proved,
	prosy		proven,
PROSAIC	–; –		prover,
PROSE	uprose;		proves
	prosed,		
	proser,	**PROVER**	–; proverb,
	proses		provers
PROSECT	–; prosects	**PROVERB**	–; proverbs
PROSER	–; prosers	**PROVIDE**	–; provided,
PROSIER	–; –		provider,
PROSILY	–; –		provides
PROSING	–; –	**PROVING**	–; –
PROSIT	–; –	**PROVISO**	–; provisos
PROSO	–; prosos	**PROVOKE**	–; provoked,
PROSODY	–; –		provoker,
PROSOMA	–; prosomal,		provokes
	prosomas	**PROVOST**	–; provosts
PROSPER	–; prospers	**PROW**	–; prowl,
PROTEA	–; protean,		prows
	proteas	**PROWAR**	–; –
PROTECT	–; protects	**PROWER**	–; –
PROTEGE	–; protegee,	**PROWESS**	–; –
	proteges	**PROWEST**	–; –
PROTEI	–; proteid,	**PROWL**	–; prowls
	protein	**PROWLED**	–; –
PROTEID	–; proteide,	**PROWLER**	–; prowlers
	proteids	**PROXIES**	–; –
		PROXIMO	–; –

PROXY	–; –	**PSYCHE**	–; psyched, psyches
PRUDE	–; prudes		
PRUDENT	–; –	**PSYCHIC**	–; psychics
PRUDERY	–; –	**PSYCHO**	–; psychos
PRUDISH	–; –	**PSYLLA**	–; psyllas
PRUNE	–; pruned, pruner, prunes	**PSYLLID**	–; psyllids
		PTERIN	–; pterins
		PTERYLA	–; pterylae
PRUNER	–; pruners	**PTISAN**	–; ptisans
PRUNING	–; –	**PTOMAIN**	–; ptomaine, ptomains
PRURIGO	–; prurigos		
PRUSSIC	–; –	**PTOSES**	–; –
PRUTA	–; prutah	**PTOSIS**	–; –
PRUTOT	–; prutoth	**PTOTIC**	–; –
PRY	spry; –	**PTYALIN**	–; ptyalins
PRYER	spryer; pryers	**PUB**	–; pubs
		PUBERAL	–; –
PRYING	–; –	**PUBERTY**	–; –
PRYTHEE	–; –	**PUBES**	–; –
PSALM	–; psalms	**PUBIC**	–; –
PSALMED	–; –	**PUBIS**	–; –
PSALMIC	–; –	**PUBLIC**	–; publics
PSALTER	–; psalters, psaltery	**PUBLISH**	–; –
		PUCCOON	–; puccoons
PSALTRY	–; –	**PUCE**	–; puces
PSCHENT	–; pschents	**PUCK**	–; pucka, pucks
PSEUDO	–; –		
PSHAW	–; pshaws	**PUCKER**	–; puckers, puckery
PSHAWED	–; –		
PSI	–; psis	**PUCKISH**	–; –
PSIS	apsis; –	**PUD**	spud; puds
PSOAE	–; –	**PUDDING**	–; puddings
PSOAI	–; –	**PUDDLE**	–; puddled, puddler, puddles
PSOAS	–; –		
PSOCID	–; psocids		
PSST	–; –	**PUDDLER**	–; puddlers
PSYCH	–; psyche, psycho, psychs	**PUDDLY**	–; –
		PUDENCY	–; –
		PUDGIER	–; –
		PUDGILY	–; –

PUDGY	-; -	PULL	-; pulls
PUDIC	-; -	PULLED	-; -
PUDS	spuds; -	PULLER	-; pullers
PUEBLO	-; pueblos	PULLET	-; pullets
PUERILE	-; -	PULLEY	-; pulleys
PUFF	-; puffs, puffy	PULLING	-; -
		PULLMAN	-; pullmans
PUFFED	-; -	PULLOUT	-; pullouts
PUFFER	-; puffers, puffery	PULP	-; pulps, pulpy
PUFFIER	-; -	PULPAL	-; -
PUFFILY	-; -	PULPED	-; -
PUFFIN	-; puffing, puffins	PULPER	-; pulpers
		PULPIER	-; -
PUG	-; pugh, pugs	PULPILY	-; -
		PULPING	-; -
PUGAREE	-; pugarees	PULPIT	-; pulpits
PUGGED	-; -	PULPOUS	-; -
PUGGIER	-; -	PULQUE	-; pulques
PUGGING	-; -	PULSANT	-; -
PUGGISH	-; -	PULSAR	-; pulsars
PUGGREE	-; puggrees	PULSATE	-; pulsated pulsates
PUGGRY	-; -		
PUGGY	-; -	PULSE	-; pulsed, pulser, pulses
PUGMARK	-; pugmarks		
PUGREE	-; pugrees		
PUISNE	-; puisnes	PULSER	-; pulsers
PUKE	-; puked, pukes	PULSING	-; -
		PULSION	-; pulsions
PUKING	-; -	PUMA	-; pumas
PUKKA	-; -	PUMELO	-; pumelos
PUL	-; pule, puli, pull, pulp, puls	PUMICE	-; pumiced, pumicer, pumices
PULE	-; puled, puler, pules	PUMICER	-; pumicers
		PUMMEL	-; pummels
PULER	-; pulers	PUMP	-; pumps
PULI	-; pulik, pulis	PUMPED	-; -
		PUMPER	-; pumpers
PULING	; pulings	PUMPING	-; -

PUMPKIN	–; pumpkins	**PUNTED**	–; –
PUN	spun; puna, pung, punk, puns, punt, puny	**PUNTER**	–; punters
		PUNTIES	–; –
		PUNTING	–; –
		PUNTO	–; puntos
PUNA	–; punas	**PUP**	–; pupa, pups
PUNCH	–; punchy		
PUNCHED	–; –	**PUPA**	–; pupae, pupal, pupas
PUNCHER	–; punchers		
PUNCHES	–; –	**PUPATE**	–; pupated, pupates
PUNDIT	–; pundits		
PUNG	–; pungs	**PUPFISH**	–; –
PUNGENT	–; –	**PUPIL**	–; pupils
PUNIER	–; –	**PUPILAR**	–; pupilary
PUNIEST	–; –	**PUPPED**	–; –
PUNILY	–; –	**PUPPET**	–; puppets
PUNISH	–; –	**PUPPIES**	–; –
PUNK	spunk; punka, punks, punky	**PUPPING**	–; –
		PUPPY	–; –
		PUR	spur; pure, puri, purl, purr, purs
PUNKA	–; punkah, punkas		
PUNKAH	–; punkahs	**PURANA**	–; puranas
PUNKEY	–; punkeys	**PURANIC**	–; –
PUNKIE	spunkie; punkier, punkies	**PURDA**	–; purdah, purdas
		PURDAH	–; purdahs
PUNKIER	spunkier; –	**PURE**	–; puree, purer
PUNKIES	spunkies; punkiest		
		PUREE	–; pureed, purees
PUNKIN	–; punkins		
PUNKS	spunks; –	**PURELY**	–; –
PUNKY	spunky; –	**PUREST**	–; –
PUNNED	–; –	**PURFLE**	–; purfled, purfles
PUNNER	–; punners		
PUNNING	–; –	**PURGE**	spurge; purged, purger, purges
PUNNY	–; –		
PUNSTER	–; punsters		
PUNT	–; punts, punty		
		PURGER	–; purgers

PURGES	spurges; –	**PURSING**	–; –
PURGING	–; purgings	**PURSUE**	–; pursued,
PURI	–; purin,		pursuer,
	puris		pursues
PURIFY	–; –	**PURSUER**	–; pursuers
PURIN	–; purine,	**PURSUIT**	–; pursuits
	purins	**PURVEY**	–; purveys
PURINE	–; purines	**PURVIEW**	–; purviews
PURISM	–; purisms	**PUS**	opus; push,
PURIST	–; purists		puss
PURITAN	–; puritans	**PUSES**	opuses; –
PURITY	–; –	**PUSH**	–; pushy
PURL	–; purls	**PUSHED**	–; –
PURLED	–; –	**PUSHER**	–; pushers
PURLIEU	–; purlieus	**PUSHES**	;
PURLIN	–; purline,	**PUSHFUL**	–; –
	purling,	**PUSHIER**	–; –
	purlins	**PUSHILY**	–; –
PURLOIN	–; purloins	**PUSHING**	–; –
PURPLE	–; purpled,	**PUSHPIN**	–; pushpins
	purpler,	**PUSHUP**	–; pushups
	purples	**PUSLEY**	–; pusleys
PURPLES	–; purplest	**PUSLIKE**	–; –
PURPLY	–; –	**PUSS**	–; pussy
PURPORT	–; purports	**PUSSES**	–; –
PURPOSE	–; purposed,	**PUSSIER**	–; –
	purposes	**PUSSIES**	–; pussiest
PURPURA	–; purpuras	**PUSSLEY**	–; pussleys
PURPURE	–; purpures	**PUSSLY**	–; –
PURR	–; purrs	**PUSTULE**	–; pustuled,
PURRED	spurred; –		pustules
PURRING	spurring; –	**PUT**	–; puts, putt
PURS	spurs; purse,	**PUTAMEN**	–; –
	pursy	**PUTLOG**	–; putlogs
PURSE	–; pursed,	**PUTOFF**	–; putoffs
	purser,	**PUTON**	–; putons
	purses	**PUTOUT**	–; putouts
PURSER	–; pursers	**PUTREFY**	–; –
PURSIER	–; –	**PUTRID**	–; –
PURSILY	–; –	**PUTSCH**	–; –

PUTT	–; putts, putty	**PYOID**	–; –
		PYOSES	–; –
PUTTED	–; –	**PYOSIS**	–; –
PUTTEE	–; puttees	**PYRALID**	–; pyralids
PUTTER	sputter; putters	**PYRAMID**	–; pyramids
		PYRAN	–; pyrans
PUTTERS	sputters; –	**PYRE**	–; pyres
PUTTIED	–; –	**PYRENE**	–; pyrenes
PUTTIER	–; –	**PYRETIC**	–; –
PUTTIES	–; –	**PYREXIA**	–; pyrexial, pyrexias
PUTTING	–; –		
PUZZLE	–; puzzled, puzzler, puzzles	**PYREXIC**	–; –
		PYRIC	–; –
		PYRITE	–; pyrites
PUZZLER	–; puzzlers	**PYRITIC**	–; –
PYA	–; pyas	**PYROGEN**	–; pryogens
PYAEMIA	–; pyaemias	**PYROLA**	–; pyrolas
PYAEMIC	–; –	**PYRONE**	–; pyrones
PYE	–; pyes	**PYROPE**	–; pyropes
PYEMIA	–; pyemias	**PYROSIS**	–; –
PYEMIC	–; –	**PYRRHIC**	–; pyrrhics
PYGMEAN	–; –	**PYRROL**	–; pyrrole, pyrrols
PYGMIES	–; –		
PYGMOID	–; –	**PYRROLE**	–; pyrroles
PYGMY	–; –	**PYTHON**	–; pythons
PYIC	–; –	**PYURIA**	–; pyurias
PYIN	–; pyins	**PYX**	–; –
PYJAMAS	–; –	**PYXES**	–; –
PYKNIC	–; pyknics	**PYXIDES**	–; –
PYLON	–; pylons	**PYXIDIA**	–; –
PYLORI	–; pyloric	**PYXIE**	–; pyxies
PYLORUS	–; –	**PYXIS**	–; –

Q

QAID	–; qaids	**QINDAR**	–; qindars
QANAT	–; qanats	**QINTAR**	–; qintars
QAT	–; qats	**QIVIUT**	–; qiviuts

QOPH	–; qophs	QUALM	–; qualms,
QUA	aqua; quad,		qualmy
	quag, quai,	QUAMASH	–; –
	quay	QUANT	–; quanta,
QUACK	–; quacks		quants
QUACKED	–; –	QUANTA	–; quantal
QUAD	squad;	QUANTED	–; –
	quads	QUANTIC	–; quantics
QUADDED	squadded; –	QUANTUM	–; –
QUADRAT	–; quadrate,	QUARE	square; –
	quadrats	QUARK	–; quarks
QUADRIC	–; quadrics	QUARREL	–; quarrels
QUADS	squads; –	QUARRY	–; –
QUAERE	–; quaeres	QUART	–; quarte,
QUAFF	–; quaffs		quarto,
QUAFFED	–; –		quarts,
QUAFFER	–; quaffers		quartz
QUAG	–; quags		
QUAGGA	–; quaggas	QUARTAN	–; quartans
QUAGGY	–; –	QUARTE	–; quarter,
QUAHAUG	–; quahaugs		quartes
QUAHOG	–; quahogs	QUARTER	–; quartern,
QUAI	–; quail,		quarters
	quais	QUARTET	–; quartets
QUAICH	–; quaichs	QUARTIC	–; quartics
QUAIGH	–; quaighs	QUARTO	–; quartos
QUAIL	–; quails	QUARTZ	–; –
QUAILED	–; –	QUASAR	–; quasars
QUAINT	–; –	QUASH	squash; –
QUAKE	–; quaked,	QUASHED	squashed; –
	quaker,	QUASHES	squashes; –
	quakes	QUASI	–; –
		QUASS	–; –
QUAKER	–; quakers	QUASSES	–; –
QUAKIER	–; –	QUASSIA	–; quassias
QUAKILY	–; –	QUASSIN	–; quassins
QUAKY	–; –	QUATE	equate; –
QUALE	–; –	QUATRE	–; quatres
QUALIA	–; –	QUAVER	–; quavers,
QUALIFY	–; –		quavery
QUALITY	equality; –	QUAY	–; quays

QUAYAGE	–; quayages	QUICKIE	–; quickies
QUEAN	–; queans	QUICKLY	–; –
QUEASY	–; –	QUID	squid; quids
QUEAZY	–; –	QUIDS	squids; –
QUEEN	–; queens	QUIET	–; quiets
QUEENED	–; –	QUIETED	–; –
QUEENLY	–; –	QUIETEN	–; quietens
QUEER	–; queers	QUIETER	–; quieters
QUEERED	–; –	QUIETLY	–; –
QUEERER	–; –	QUIETUS	–; –
QUEERLY	–; –	QUIFF	–; quiffs
QUELL	–; quells	QUILL	squill; quills
QUELLED	–; –	QUILLAI	–; quillais
QUELLER	–; quellers	QUILLED	–; –
QUENCH	–; –	QUILLET	–; quillets
QUERIDA	–; queridas	QUILLS	squills; –
QUERIED	–; –	QUILT	–; quilts
QUERIER	–; queriers	QUILTED	–; –
QUERIES	–; –	QUILTER	–; quilters
QUERIST	–; querists	QUINARY	–; –
QUERN	–; querns	QUINATE	–; –
QUERY	–; –	QUINCE	–; quinces
QUEST	–; quests	QUINIC	–; –
QUESTED	–; –	QUININ	–; quinina
QUESTER	–; questers		quinine,
QUESTOR	–; questors		quinins
QUETZAL	–; quetzals	QUININA	–; quininas
QUEUE	–; queued,	QUININE	–; quinines
	queuer,	QUINNAT	–; quinnats
	queues	QUINOA	–; quinoas
QUEUER	–; queuers	QUINOID	–; quinoids
QUEY	–; queys	QUINOL	–; quinols
QUEZAL	–; quezals	QUINONE	–; quinones
QUIBBLE	–; quibbled,	QUINSY	–; –
	quibbler,	QUINT	squint; quints
	quibbles	QUINTAL	–; quintals
QUICHE	–; quiches	QUINTAN	–; quintans
QUICK	–; quicks	QUINTAR	–; quintars
QUICKEN	–; quickens	QUINTET	–; quintets
QUICKER	–; –	QUINTIC	–; quintics

QUINTIN	–; quintins	quivers,
QUINTS	squints; –	quivery
QUIP	equip; quips, quipu	**QUIXOTE**	–; quixotes
		QUIZ	–; –
QUIPPED	equipped; –	**QUIZZED**	–; –
QUIPS	equips; –	**QUIZZER**	–; quizzers
QUIPPU	–; quippus	**QUIZZES**	–; –
QUIPU	–; quipus	**QUOD**	–; quods
QUIRE	squire; quired, quires	**QUOIN**	–; quoins
		QUOINED	–; –
QUIRED	squired; –	**QUOIT**	–; quoits
QUIRES	squires; –	**QUOITED**	–; –
QUIRING	squiring; –	**QUOMODO**	–;
QUIRK	–; quirks, quirky	quomodos
		QUONDAM	–; –
QUIRKED	–; –	**QUORUM**	–; quorums
QUIRT	squirt; quirts	**QUOTA**	–; quotas
QUIRTED	squirted; –	**QUOTE**	–; quoted,
QUIRTS	squirts; –	quoter,
QUIT	–; quite, quits	quotes
		QUOTER	–; quoters
QUITCH	–; –	**QUOTH**	–; quotha
QUITTED	–; –	**QUOTING**	–; –
QUITTER	–; quitters	**QURSH**	–; –
QUITTOR	–; quittors	**QURSHES**	–; –
QUIVER	aquiver;	**QURUSH**	–; –

R

R	ar, er, or; re	**RABBIN**	–; rabbins
RABATO	–; rabatos	**RABBIT**	–; rabbits
RABBET	drabbet; rabbets	**RABBLE**	brabble, drabble, grabble; rabbled, rabbler, rabbles
RABBI	–; rabbin, rabbis, rabbit	
RABBIES	–; –	
		RABBLED	brabbled,

	drabbled, grabbled; –	**RACIEST**	–; –
		RACILY	–; –
RABBLER	brabbler, grabbler; rabblers	**RACING**	bracing, gracing, tracing; racings
RABBLES	brabbles, drabbles, grabbles; –	**RACISM**	–; racisms
		RACIST	–; racists
RABBONI	–; rabbonis	**RACK**	crack, track, wrack; racks
RABIC	–; –		
RABID	–; –	**RACKED**	cracked, tracked, wracked; –
RABIDLY	–; –		
RABIES	–; –		
RACCOON	–; raccoons	**RACKER**	cracker, tracker; rackers
RACE	brace, grace, trace; raced, racer, races		
		RACKERS	crackers, trackers; –
RACED	braced, graced, traced; –	**RACKET**	bracket; rackets, rackety
RACEME	–; racemed, racemes	**RACKETS**	brackets; –
		RACKING	cracking, tracking, wracking; –
RACEMIC	–; –		
RACER	bracer, tracer; racers	**RACKLE**	crackle, grackle; –
RACERS	bracers, tracers; –	**RACKS**	cracks, tracks, wracks; –
RACES	braces, graces, traces; –		
		RACON	–; racons
		RACOON	–; racoons
RACEWAY	–; raceways	**RACQUET**	–; racquets
RACHET	brachet; rachets	**RACY**	–; –
		RAD	brad, grad, trad; rads
RACHETS	brachets; –		
RACHIAL	–; –	**RADAR**	–; radars
RACHIS	–; –	**RADDED**	bradded; –
RACIAL	–; –	**RADDING**	bradding; –
RACIER	–; –		

RADDLE	–; raddled, raddles	**RAFTED**	crafted, drafted, grafted; –
RADIAL	–; radiale, radials	**RAFTER**	drafter, grafter; rafters
RADIAN	–; radians, radiant		
RADIANT	–; radiants	**RAFTERS**	drafters, grafters; –
RADIATE	eradiate; radiated, radiates	**RAFTING**	crafting, drafting, grafting; –
RADICAL	–; radicals	**RAFTS**	crafts, drafts, grafts, kratts; –
RADICEL	–; radicels		
RADICES	–; –		
RADICLE	–; radicles		
RADII	–; –	**RAG**	brag, crag, drag, frag, trag; raga, rage, ragi, rags
RADIO	–; radios		
RADIOED	–; –		
RADISH	–; –		
RADIUM	–; radiums		
RADIUS	–; –		
RADIX	–; –	**RAGA**	–; ragas
RADIXES	–; –	**RAGBAG**	–; ragbags
RADOME	–; radomes	**RAGE**	–; raged, ragee, rages
RADON	–; radons		
RADULA	–; radulae, radular, radulas	**RAGEE**	dragee; ragees
RADS	brads, grads; –	**RAGEES**	dragees; –
RAFF	draff; raffs	**RAGGED**	bragged, cragged, dragged, fragged; raggedy
RAFFIA	–; raffias		
RAFFISH	draffish; –		
RAFFLE	–; raffled, raffler, raffles	**RAGGING**	bragging, dragging, fragging; –
RAFFLER	–; rafflers	**RAGGLE**	draggle; raggles
RAFFS	draffs; –		
RAFT	craft, draft, graft, kraft; rafts	**RAGGLES**	–; draggles
		RAGGY	braggy,

	craggy,	**RAIMENT**	–; raiments
	draggy; –	**RAIN**	brain, drain,
RAGI	tragi; ragis		grain, train;
RAGING	–; –		rains, rainy
RAGLAN	–; raglans	**RAINBOW**	–; rainbows
RAGMAN	–; –	**RAINED**	brained,
RAGMEN	–; –		drained,
RAGOUT	–; ragouts		grained,
RAGS	brags,		trained; –
	crags,	**RAINIER**	grainier; –
	drags,	**RAINILY**	–; –
	frags; –	**RAINING**	braining,
RAGTIME	–; ragtimes		draining,
RAGTAG	–; ragtags		graining,
RAGWEED	–; ragweeds		training; –
RAGWORT	–; ragworts	**RAINOUT**	–; rainouts
RAH	–; –	**RAINS**	brains,
RAIA	–; raias		drains,
RAID	braid; raids		grains,
RAIDED	braided; –		trains; –
RAIDER	braider;	**RAINY**	brainy,
	raiders		grainy; –
RAIDERS	braiders; –	**RAISE**	braise,
RAIDING	braiding; –		fraise,
RAIDS	braids; –		praise;
RAIL	brail, drail,		raised,
	frail, grail,		raiser, raises
	trail; rails	**RAISED**	braised,
RAILED	brailed,		praised; –
	trailed; –	**RAISER**	praiser;
RAILER	frailer,		raisers
	trailer; railers	**RAISERS**	praisers; –
RAILERS	trailers; –	**RAISES**	braises,
RAILING	brailing,		fraises,
	trailing;		praises; –
	railings	**RAISIN**	braising;
RAILS	brails, drails,		raising,
	frails, grails,		raisins
	trails; –	**RAISING**	praising;
RAILWAY	–; railways		raisings

RAJ	–; raja	**RAMEKIN**	–; ramekins
RAJA	–; rajah rajas	**RAMET**	–; ramets
		RAMI	–; ramie
RAJAH	–; rajahs	**RAMIE**	–; ramies
RAJES	–; –	**RAMIFY**	–; –
RAKE	brake, crake, drake; raked, rakee, raker, rakes	**RAMILIE**	–; ramilies
		RAMJET	–; ramjets
		RAMMED	crammed, drammed, trammed; –
RAKED	braked; –	**RAMMER**	crammer; rammers
RAKEE	–; rakees	
RAKEOFF	–; rakeoffs	**RAMMERS**	crammers; –
RAKER	–; rakers	**RAMMIER**	–; –
RAKES	brakes, crakes, drakes; –	**RAMMING**	cramming, dramming, tramming; –
RAKI	–; rakis	**RAMMISH**	–; –
RAKING	braking; –	**RAMMY**	–; –
RAKIS	–; rakish	**RAMOSE**	–; –
RALE	–; rales	**RAMOUS**	–; –
RALLIED	–; –	**RAMP**	cramp, gramp, tramp; ramps
RALLIER	–; ralliers	
RALLIES	–; –	
RALLINE	–; –	**RAMPAGE**	–; rampaged, rampager, rampages
RALLY	orally; rallye	
RALLYE	–; rallyes	
RAM	cram, dram, gram, pram, tram; rami, ramp, rams	
		RAMPANT	–; –
		RAMPART	–; ramparts
RAMATE	–; –	**RAMPED**	cramped, tramped; –
RAMBLE	bramble; rambled, rambler, rambles	
		RAMPING	cramping, tramping; –
		RAMPIKE	–; rampikes
		RAMPION	–; rampions
RAMBLED	brambled; –	**RAMPOLE**	–; rampoles
RAMBLER	–; ramblers	**RAMPS**	cramps, gramps, tramps; –
RAMBLES	brambles; –	
RAMEE	–; ramees	

RAMROD	–; ramrods	**RANEE**	–; ranees
RAMS	crams,	**RANG**	orang,
	drams,		prang,
	grams,		wrang;
	prams,		range,
	trams; –		rangy
RAMSON	–; ramsons	**RANGE**	grange,
RAMTIL	–; ramtils		orange;
RAMUS	–; –		ranged,
RAN	bran; rand,		ranger,
	rang, rani,		ranges
	rank, rant	**RANGED**	pranged; –
RANCE	prance,	**RANGER**	granger;
	trance;		rangers
	rances	**RANGERS**	grangers; –
RANCES	prances,	**RANGES**	granges,
	trances; –		oranges; –
RANCH	branch,	**RANGIER**	orangier; –
	cranch;	**RANGING**	–; –
	rancho	**RANGY**	orangy; –
RANCHED	branched,	**RANI**	–; ranid,
	cranched; –		ranis
RANCHER	–; ranchero,	**RANID**	–; ranids
	ranchers	**RANK**	brank, crank,
RANCHES	branches,		drank, frank,
	cranches; –		prank; ranks
RANCHO	–; ranchos	**RANKED**	cranked,
RANCID	–; –		franked,
RANCOR	–; rancors		pranked; –
RANCOUR	–; rancours	**RANKER**	cranker,
RAND	brand,		franker;
	grand;		rankers
	rands, randy	**RANKERS**	frankers; –
RANDAN	–; randans	**RANKEST**	crankest,
RANDIES	–; –		frankest; –
RANDOM	–; randoms	**RANKING**	cranking,
RANDS	brands,		franking,
	grands; –		pranking; –
RANDY	brandy; –	**RANKISH**	prankish; –

RANKLE	crankle; rankled, rankler, rankles	grapes, trapes; –
		RAPHAE	–; –
		RAPHE	–; raphes
RANKLED	crankled; –	**RAPHES**	graphes; –
RANKLES	crankles; –	**RAPHIA**	–; raphias
RANKLY	crankly, frankly; –	**RAPHIDE**	–; raphides
		RAPHIS	–; –
RANPIKE	–; ranpikes	**RAPID**	–; rapids
RANKS	branks, cranks, franks, pranks; –	**RAPIDER**	–; –
		RAPIDLY	–; –
		RAPIER	grapier; rapiers
RANSACK	–; ransacks	
RANSOM	–; ransoms	**RAPINE**	–; rapines
RANT	brant, grant; rants	**RAPING**	craping, draping; –
RANTED	granted; –	**RAPIST**	–; rapists
RANTER	granter; ranters	**RAPPED**	crapped, frapped, trapped, wrapped; –
RANTERS	granters; –	
RANTING	–; –	
RANTS	brants, grants; –	**RAPPEE**	–; rappees
		RAPPEL	–; rappels
RANULA	–; ranulas	**RAPPEN**	;
RAP	crap, frap, trap, wrap; rape, raps, rapt	**RAPPER**	crapper, trapper, wrapper; rappers
RAPE	crape, drape, grape; raped, raper, rapes	**RAPPERS**	crappers, trappers, wrappers; –
		RAPPING	crapping, frapping, trapping, wrapping; –
RAPED	craped, draped; –	
RAPER	draper; rapers	**RAPPINI**	–; –
		RAPPORT	–; rapports
RAPERS	drapers; –	**RAPS**	craps, fraps, traps, wraps; –
RAPES	crapes, drapes,	

RAPT	trapt, wrapt; –		trashes; rashest
RAPTLY	–; –	**RASHEST**	brashest; –
RAPTOR	–; raptors	**RASHLY**	brashly; –
RAPTURE	–; raptured, raptures	**RASING**	erasing; –
RARE	urare; rarer	**RASP**	grasp; rasps, raspy
RAREBIT	–; rarebits	**RASPED**	grasped; –
RAREFY	–; –	**RASPER**	grasper; raspers
RARELY	–; –		
RAREST	–; –	**RASPERS**	graspers; –
RARIFY	–; –	**RASPIER**	–; –
RARING	–; –	**RASPING**	grasping; –
RARITY	–; –	**RASPISH**	–; –
RAS	bras, eras; rase, rash, rasp	**RASPS**	grasps; –
		RASSLE	–; rassled, rassles
RASBORA	–; rasboras	**RASTER**	–; rasters
RASCAL	–; rascals	**RASURE**	erasure; rasures
RASE	erase, prase, urase; rased, raser, rases		
		RASURES	erasures; –
		RAT	brat, drat, frat, grat, prat; rate, rath, rato, rats
RASED	erased; –		
RASER	eraser; rasers		
RASERS	erasers; –	**RATABLE**	–; –
RASES	crases, erases, prases, urases; –	**RATABLY**	–; –
		RATAFEE	–; ratafees
		RATAFIA	–; ratafias
		RATAL	–; ratals
RASH	brash, crash, trash; –	**RATAN**	–; ratans, ratany
RASHER	brasher, crasher; rashers	**RATATAT**	–; ratatats
		RATCH	cratch; –
		RATCHES	cratches; –
RASHERS	crashers; –	**RATCHET**	–; ratchets
RASHES	brashes, crashes,	**RATE**	crate, grate, irate, orate,

	prate, urate;	**RATLIKE**	–; –
	rated, ratel	**RATLIN**	–; ratline,
	rater, rates		ratlins
RATED	crated,	**RATLINE**	–; ratlines
	grated,	**RATO**	–; ratos
	orated,	**RATOON**	–; ratoons
	prated; –	**RATS**	brats, drats,
RATEL	–; ratels		frats,
RATER	crater, frater,		prats; –
	grater, irater,	**RATTAIL**	–; rattails
	krater, prater;	**RATTAN**	–; rattans
	raters	**RATTED**	dratted; –
RATERS	craters,	**RATTEEN**	–; ratteens
	fraters,	**RATTEN**	–; rattens
	graters,	**RATTER**	–; ratters
	kraters,	**RATTIER**	brattier; –
	praters; –	**RATTING**	dratting; –
RATES	crates,	**RATTISH**	–; –
	grates,	**RATTLE**	brattle,
	orates,		prattle;
	prates,		rattled,
	urates; –		rattler,
RATFINK	–; ratfinks		rattles
RATFISH	–; –	**RATTLED**	brattled,
RATH	wrath; rathe		prattled; –
RATHE	–; rather	**RATTLER**	prattler;
RATHOLE	–; ratholes		rattlers
RATIFY	–; –	**RATTLES**	brattles,
RATINE	–; ratines		prattles; –
RATING	crating,	**RATTLY**	–; –
	grating,	**RATTON**	–; rattons
	orating,	**RATTOON**	–; rattoons
	prating;	**RATTRAP**	–; rattraps
	ratings	**RATTY**	bratty; –
RATIO	–; ration,	**RAUCITY**	–; –
	ratios	**RAUCOUS**	–; –
RATION	oration;	**RAUNCHY**	–; –
	rations	**RAVAGE**	–; ravaged,
RATIONS	orations; –		ravager,
RATITE	–; ratites		ravages

RAVAGER	–; ravagers	**RAVING**	braving,
RAVE	brave,		craving,
	crave,		graving;
	drave,		ravings
	grave, trave;	**RAVINGS**	cravings; –
	raved, ravel,	**RAVIOLI**	–; raviolis
	raven, raver,	**RAVISH**	–; –
	raves	**RAW**	braw, craw,
RAVED	braved,		draw; raws
	craved,	**RAWER**	brawer,
	graved; –		drawer; –
RAVEL	gravel,	**RAWEST**	brawest; –
	travel; ravels	**RAWHIDE**	–; rawhided,
RAVELED	graveled,		rawhides
	traveled; –	**RAWISH**	–; –
RAVELER	traveler;	**RAWLY**	brawly,
	ravelers		crawly,
RAVELIN	–; raveling,		drawly; –
	ravelins	**RAWNESS**	–; –
RAVELLY	gravelly; –	**RAWS**	braws,
RAVELS	gravels,		craws,
	travels; –		draws; –
RAVEN	craven,	**RAX**	–; –
	graven;	**RAXED**	–; –
	ravens	**RAXES**	praxes; –
RAVENED	–; –	**RAXING**	–; –
RAVENER	–; raveners	**RAY**	bray, dray,
RAVER	braver,		fray, gray,
	craver,		pray, tray;
	graver;		raya, rays
	ravers	**RAYA**	–; rayah,
RAVERS	bravers,		rayas
	gravers; –	**RAYAH**	–; rayahs
RAVES	braves,	**RAYED**	brayed,
	craves,		drayed,
	graves,		frayed,
	traves; –		grayed,
RAVIN	–; ravine,		prayed; –
	raving, ravins	**RAYING**	braying,
RAVINE	–; ravines		draying,

	fraying,		rec, red,
	graying,		ree, ref, rei,
	praying; –		rem, res, ret,
RAYLESS	–; –		rev, rex
RAYON	crayon;	**REACH**	breach,
	rayons		preach; –
RAYS	brays, drays,	**REACHED**	breached,
	frays, grays,		preached; –
	prays,	**REACHER**	breacher,
	trays; –		preacher;
RAZE	braze,		reachers
	craze,	**REACHES**	preaches; –
	graze;	**REACT**	preact;
	razed,		reacts
	razee, razer,	**REACTED**	preacted; –
	razes	**REACTOR**	–; reactors
RAZED	brazed,	**REACTS**	preacts; –
	crazed,	**READ**	bread,
	grazed; –		dread,
RAZEE	–; razeed,		oread,
	razees		tread;
RAZER	brazer,		readd,
	grazer;		reads, ready
	razers	**READAPT**	preadapt;
RAZERS	brazers,		readapts
	grazers; –	**READD**	–; readds
RAZES	brazes,	**READER**	treader;
	crazes,		readers
	grazes; –	**READERS**	treaders; –
RAZING	brazing,	**READIED**	–; –
	crazing,	**READIER**	–; –
	grazing; –	**READIES**	–; readiest
RAZOR	–; razors	**READILY**	–; –
RAZORED	–; –	**READING**	breading,
RAZZ	–; –		dreading;
RAZZED	–; –		readings
RAZZES	–; –	**READMIT**	preadmit;
RAZZING	–; –		readmits
RE	are, ere, ire,	**READOPT**	preadopt;
	ore; reb,		readopts

READORN	–; readorns	**REAMERS**	creamers,
READOUT	–; readouts		dreamers; –
READS	breads,	**REAMING**	breaming,
	dreads,		creaming,
	oreads,		dreaming; –
	treads; –	**REAMS**	breams,
REAFFIX	–; –		creams,
REAGENT	–; reagents		dreams; –
REAGIN	–; reagins	**REAP**	–; reaps
REAL	–; reals	**REAPED**	–; –
REALER	–; –	**REAPER**	–; reapers
REALES	–; realest	**REAPING**	–; –
REALGAR	–; realgars	**REAPPLY**	–; –
REALIA	–; –	**REAR**	drear; rears
REALIGN	–; realigns	**REARED**	–; –
REALISE	–; realised,	**REARER**	–; rearers
	realiser,	**REARGUE**	–; reargued,
	realises		reargues
REALISM	–; realisms	**REARING**	–; –
REALIST	–; realists	**REARM**	prearm;
REALITY	–; –		rearms
REALIZE	–; realized,	**REARMED**	–; –
	realizer,	**REARMS**	prearms; –
	realizes	**REASON**	treason;
REALLOT	–; reallots		reasons
REALLY	–; –	**REASONS**	treasons; –
REALM	–; realms	**REATA**	–; reatas
REALTER	–; realters	**REAVE**	greave;
REALTY	–; –		reaved,
REAM	bream,		reaver,
	cream,		reaves
	dream;	**REAVED**	greaved; –
	reams	**REAVER**	preaver;
REAMED	breamed,		reavers
	creamed,	**REAVERS**	preavers; –
	dreamed; –	**REAVES**	greaves; –
REAMER	creamer,	**REAVING**	–; –
	dreamer;	**REAVOW**	–; reavows
	reamers	**REAWAKE**	–;
			reawaked,

	reawaken,	**REBUKER**	–; rebukers
	reawakes	**REBURY**	–; –
REAWOKE	–; reawoken	**REBUS**	–; –
REB	–; rebs	**REBUSES**	–; –
REBAIT	–; rebaits	**REBUT**	–; rebuts
REBATE	–; rebated,	**REC**	–; reck, recs
	rebater,	**RECALL**	–; recalls
	rebates	**RECANE**	–; recaned,
REBATER	–; rebaters		recanes
REBATO	–; rebatos	**RECANT**	–; recants
REBBE	–; rebbes	**RECAP**	–; recaps
REBEC	–; rebeck,	**RECARRY**	–; –
	rebecs	**RECAST**	precast;
REBECK	–; rebecks		recasts
REBEL	–; rebels	**RECASTS**	precasts; –
REBID	–; rebids	**RECEDE**	precede;
REBILL	prebill; rebills		receded,
REBILLS	prebills; –		recedes
REBIND	prebind;	**RECEDED**	preceded; –
	rebinds	**RECEDES**	precedes; –
REBINDS	prebinds; –	**RECEIPT**	–; receipts
REBIRTH	–; rebirths	**RECEIVE**	–; received,
REBLOOM	–; reblooms		receiver,
REBOANT	–; –		receives
REBOARD	–; reboards	**RECENCY**	–; –
REBOIL	preboil;	**RECENT**	–; –
	reboils	**RECEPT**	precept;
REBOILS	preboils; –		recepts
REBOP	–; rebops	**RECEPTS**	precepts; –
REBORN	–; –	**RECESS**	precess; –
REBOUND	prebound;	**RECHART**	–; recharts
	rebounds	**RECHEAT**	–; recheats
REBOZO	–; rebozos	**RECHECK**	precheck;
REBUFF	–; rebuffs		rechecks
REBUILD	–; rebuilds	**RECIPE**	precipe;
REBUILT	–; –		recipes
REBUKE	–; rebuked,	**RECIPES**	precipes; –
	rebuker,	**RECITAL**	–; recitals
	rebukes	**RECITE**	–; recited,

	reciter, recites	**RECRATE**	–; recrated, recrates
RECITED	precited; –	**RECROSS**	–; –
RECITER	–; reciters	**RECROWN**	–; recrowns
RECK	dreck, wreck; recks	**RECRUIT**	–; recruits
		RECTA	–; rectal
RECKED	wrecked; –	**RECTI**	–; –
RECKING	wrecking; –	**RECTIFY**	–; –
RECKON	–; reckons	**RECTO**	–; rector, rectos
RECKS	drecks, wrecks; –	**RECTOR**	erector; rectors, rectory
RECLAD	–; –	
RECLAIM	–; reclaims	
RECLAME	–; reclames	**RECTORS**	erectors; –
RECLASP	–; reclasps	**RECTRIX**	–; –
RECLEAN	preclean; recleans	**RECTUM**	–; rectums
		RECTUS	–; –
RECLINE	–; reclined, recliner, reclines	**RECUR**	–; recurs
		RECURVE	–; recurved, recurves
RECLUSE	–; recluses	**RECUSE**	–; recused, recuses
RECOAL	–; recoals	
RECOCK	–; recocks	**RECUT**	–; recuts
RECOIL	–; recoils	**RECYCLE**	–; recycled, recycles
RECOIN	–; recoins	
RECOLOR	–; recolors	**RED**	bred, ired, ored; redd, rede, redo, reds
RECOMB	–; recombs	
RECON	–; recons	
RECOOK	precook; recooks	
		REDACT	–; redacts
RECOOKS	precooks; –	**REDAN**	–; redans
RECOPY	–; –	**REDATE**	predate; redated, redates
RECORD	–; records	
RECOUNT	–; recounts	
RECOUP	–; recoupe, recoups	**REDATED**	predated; –
		REDATES	predates; –
RECOUPE	–; recouped	**REDBAIT**	–; redbaits
RECOVER	–; recovers, recovery	**REDBAY**	–; redbays
		REDBIRD	–; redbirds
		REDBONE	–; redbones

REDBUD	–; redbuds	**REDO**	credo,
REDBUG	–; redbugs		uredo;
REDCAP	–; redcaps		redos, redox
REDCOAT	–; redcoats	**REDOCK**	–; redocks
REDD	–; redds	**REDOES**	–; –
REDDED	–; –	**REDOING**	–; –
REDDEN	–; reddens	**REDONE**	–; –
REDDER	–; redders	**REDOS**	credos,
REDDEST	–; –		uredos; –
REDDING	–; –	**REDOUBT**	–; redoubts
REDDISH	–; –	**REDOUND**	–; redounds
REDDLE	treddle;	**REDOUT**	–; redouts
	reddled,	**REDOWA**	–; redowas
	reddles	**REDOX**	–; –
REDDLED	treddled; –	**REDOXES**	–; –
REDDLES	treddles; –	**REDPOLL**	–; redpolls
REDE	brede;	**REDRAFT**	–; redrafts
	reded, redes	**REDRAW**	–; redrawn,
REDEAR	–; redears		redraws
REDEEM	–; redeems	**REDRESS**	–; –
REDEFY	–; –	**REDREW**	–; –
REDENY	–; –	**REDRIED**	–; –
REDES	bredes; –	**REDRIES**	–; –
REDEYE	–; redeyes	**REDRILL**	–; redrills
REDFIN	–; redfins	**REDRIVE**	–; redriven,
REDFISH	–; –		redrives
REDHEAD	–; redheads	**REDROOT**	–; redroots
REDIA	uredia;	**REDROVE**	–; –
	rediae,	**REDRY**	–; –
	redial, redias	**REDSKIN**	–; redskins
REDIAL	predial,	**REDTOP**	–; redtops
	uredial; –	**REDUCE**	–; reduced,
REDID	–; –		reducer,
REDING	–; –		reduces
REDIP	–; redips,	**REDUCER**	–; reducers
	redipt	**REDWARE**	–; redwares
REDLEG	–; redlegs	**REDWING**	–; redwings
REDLY	–; –	**REDWOOD**	–; redwoods
REDNECK	–; rednecks	**REDYE**	–; redyed,
REDNESS	–; –		redyes

REE	bree, dree, free, gree, pree, tree; reed, reef, reek, reel, rees	**REEL**	creel; reels
		REELED	–; –
		REELER	–; reelers
		REELECT	preelect; reelects
		REELING	–; –
REEARN	–; reearns	**REELS**	creels; –
REECHO	–; –	**REEMIT**	–; reemits
REED	breed, creed, dreed, freed, greed, preed, treed; reeds, reedy	**REENACT**	preenact; reenacts
		REENDOW	–; reendows
		REENJOY	–; reenjoys
		REENTER	–; reenters
		REENTRY	–; –
		REEQUIP	–; reequips
		REERECT	–; reerects
REEDED	–; –	**REES**	brees, drees, frees, grees, prees, trees; reest
REEDIER	greedier; –		
REEDIFY	–; –		
REEDING	breeding; readings		
		REEST	freest; reests
REEDIT	–; reedits	**REESTED**	–; –
REEDS	breeds, creeds, greeds; –	**REEVE**	–; reeved, reeves
		REEVING	–; –
REEDY	greedy; –	**REEVOKE**	–; reevoked, reevokes
REEF	–; reefs, reefy		
		REEXPEL	–; reexpels
REEFED	–; –	**REF**	tref; refs, reft
REEFER	–; reefers	**REFACE**	preface; refaced, refaces
REEFIER	–; –		
REEFING	–; –		
REEK	creek, greek; reeks, reeky	**REFACED**	prefaced; –
		REFACES	prefaces; –
REEKED	–; –	**REFALL**	–; refalls
REEKER	–; reekers	**REFECT**	prefect; refects
REEKIER	–; –		
REEKING	–; –		
REEKS	breeks, creeks; –	**REFECTS**	prefects; –
		REFED	–; –

REFEED	–; refeeds	**REFORGE**	–; reforged,
REFEL	–; refell,		reforges
	retels	**REFORM**	preforms;
REFER	prefer; refers		reforms
REFEREE	–; refereed,	**REFORMS**	preforms; –
	referees	**REFOUND**	–; refounds
REFERS	prefers; –	**REFRAME**	–; reframed,
REFFED	–; –		reframes
REFFING	–; –	**REFRACT**	–; refracts
REFIGHT	–; refights	**REFRAIN**	–; refrains
REFILE	–; refiled,	**REFRESH**	–; –
	refiles	**REFRIED**	–; –
REFILL	–; refills	**REFRIES**	–; –
REFILM	–; refilms	**REFRONT**	–; refronts
REFIND	–; refinds	**REFRY**	; –
REFINE	–; refined,	**REFT**	, –
	refiner,	**REFUEL**	–; refuels
	refines	**REFUGE**	–; refuged,
REFINER	–; refiners,		refugee,
	refinery		refuges
REFIRE	–; refired,	**REFUGEE**	–; refugees
	refires	**REFUND**	–; refunds
REFIT	–; refits	**REFUSAL**	–; refusals
REFIX	prefix; –	**REFUSE**	–; refused,
REFIXED	prefixed; –		refuser,
REFIXES	prefixes; –		refuses
REFLATE	–; reflated,	**REFUSER**	–; refusers
	reflates	**REFUTAL**	–; refutals
REFLECT	–; reflects	**REFUTE**	–; refuted,
REFLET	–; reflets		refuter,
REFLEW	–; –		refutes
REFLEX	–; –	**REFUTER**	–; refuters
REFLIES	–; –	**REGAIN**	–; regains
REFLOAT	–; refloats	**REGAL**	–; regale
REFLOOD	–; refloods	**REGALE**	–; regaled,
REFLOW	–; reflown,		regales
	reflows	**REGALIA**	–; –
REFLUX	–; –	**REGALLY**	–; –
REFOCUS	prefocus; –	**REGARD**	–; regards
REFOLD	–; refolds	**REGATTA**	–; regattas

REGAUGE	–; regauged, regauges	**REGRATE**	–; regrated, regrates
REGAVE	–; –	**REGREET**	–; regreets
REGEAR	–; regears	**REGRESS**	–; –
REGENCY	–; –	**REGRET**	–; regrets
REGENT	–; regents	**REGREW**	–; –
REGES	–; –	**REGRIND**	–; regrinds
REGILD	–; regilds,	**REGROUP**	–; regroups
REGILT	–; regilts	**REGROW**	–; regrown, regrows
REGIME	–; regimen, regimes	**REGULAR**	–; regulars
REGIMEN	–; regimens, regiment	**REGULI**	–; –
		REGULUS	–; –
REGINA	–; reginae, reginal, reginas	**REHANG**	–; rehangs
		REHASH	–; –
		REHEAR	–; reheard, rehears
REGION	–; regions	**REHEAT**	preheat;
REGIUS	–; –		reheats
REGIVE	–; regiven, regives	**REHEATS**	preheats; –
		REHEEL	–; reheels
REGLAZE	–; reglazed, reglazes	**REHEM**	–; rehems
		REHINGE	–; rehinged, rehinges
REGLET	–; reglets		
REGLOSS	–; –	**REHIRE**	–; rehired, rehires
REGLOW	–; reglows		
REGLUE	–; reglued, reglues	**REHOUSE**	–; rehoused, rehouses
REGMA	bregma; –	**REHUNG**	–; –
REGMATA	bregmata; –	**REI**	–; reif, rein, reis
REGNA	–; regnal		
REGNANT	–; –	**REIF**	–; reifs, reify
REGNUM	–; –	**REIFIED**	–; –
REGORGE	–; regorged, regorges	**REIFIER**	–; reifiers
		REIFIES	–; –
REGOSOL	–; regosols	**REIGN**	–; reigns
REGRADE	–; regarded, regrades	**REIGNED**	–; –
		REIMAGE	–; reimaged, reimages
REGRAFT	–; regrafts		
REGRANT	–; regrants	**REIN**	–; reins

REINCUR	–; reincurs	RELAXIN	–; relaxing,
REINDEX	–; –		relaxins
REINED	–; –	RELAY	–; relays
REINING	–; –	RELAYED	–; –
REINTER	–; reinters	RELEARN	–; relearns,
REISSUE	–; reissued,		relearnt
	reissues	RELEASE	–; released,
REITBOK	–; reitboks		releaser,
REIVE	–; reived,		releases
	reiver, reives	RELEND	–; relends
REIVER	–; reivers	RELENT	–; relents
REJECT	–; rejects	RELET	–; relets
REJOICE	–; rejoiced,	RELIANT	–; –
	rejoicer,	RELIC	–; relics,
	rejoices		relict
REJOIN	–; rejoins	RELICT	–; relicts
REJUDGE	prejudge;	RELIED	–; –
	rejudged,	RELIEF	–; reliefs
	rejudges	RELIER	–; reliers
REKEY	–; rekeys	RELIES	–; –
REKEYED	–; –	RELIEVE	–; relieved,
REKNIT	–; reknits		reliever,
RELABEL	–; relabels		relieves
RELACE	–; relaced,	RELIEVO	–; relievos
	relaces	RELIGHT	–; relights
RELAID	–; –	RELINE	–; relined,
RELAPSE	–; relapsed,		relines
	relapser,	RELIQUE	–; reliques
	relapses	RELISH	–; –
RELATE	prelate;	RELIST	–; relists
	related,	RELIT	–; –
	relater,	RELIVE	–; relived,
	relates		relives
RELATER	–; relaters	RELOAD	–; reloads
RELATES	prelates; –	RELOAN	–; reloans
RELATOR	–; relators	RELUCT	–; relucts
RELAX	–; –	RELUME	–; relumed,
RELAXED	–; –		relumes
RELAXER	–; relaxers	RELY	–; –
RELAXES	–; –	RELYING	–; –

REM	–; rems	**REMOLD**	–; remolds
REMADE	–; –	**REMORA**	–; remoras
REMAIL	–; remails	**REMORID**	–; –
REMAIN	cremain; remains	**REMORSE**	premorse; remorses
REMAINS	cremains; –	**REMOTE**	–; remoter
REMAKE	–; remakes	**REMOUNT**	–; remounts
REMAN	preman; remand, remans	**REMOVAL**	–; removals
		REMOVE	–; removed, remover, removes
REMAND	–; remands		
REMAP	–; remaps	**REMOVER**	–; removers
REMARK	–; remarks	**REMUDA**	–; remudas
REMARRY	–; –	**RENAL**	–; –
REMATCH	–; –	**RENAME**	prename; renamed, renames
REMEDY	–; –		
REMEET	–; remeets		
REMELT	–; remelts	**RENAMES**	prenames; –
REMEND	–; remends	**REND**	trend; rends
REMERGE	–; remerged, remerges	**RENDED**	trended; –
		RENDER	–; renders
		RENDING	trending; –
REMET	–; –	**RENDS**	trends; –
REMEX	–; –	**RENEGE**	–; reneged reneger, reneges
REMIGES	–; –		
REMIND	–; reminds		
REMINT	–; remints	**RENEGER**	–; renegers
REMISE	premise; remised, remises	**RENEW**	–; renews
		RENEWAL	–; renewals
		RENEWED	–; –
REMISED	premised; –	**RENEWER**	–; renewers
REMISES	premises; –	**RENIG**	–; renigs
REMISS	premiss; –	**RENIN**	–; renins
REMIT	–; remits	**RENNASE**	–; rennases
REMIX	premix; remixt	**RENNET**	–; rennets
		RENNIN	–; rennins
REMIXED	premixed; –	**RENOWN**	–; renowns
REMIXES	premixes; –	**RENT**	brent; rente, rents
REMNANT	–; remnants		
REMODEL	–; remodels	**RENTAL**	–; rentals

RENTE	–; rented, renter, rentes	**REPINER**	–; repiners
		REPLACE	preplace; replaced, replacer, replaces
RENTER	–; renters		
RENTIER	–; rentiers		
RENTS	brents; –	**REPLAN**	preplan; replans, replant
RENVOI	–; renvois		
REOCCUR	–; reoccurs		
REOFFER	–; reoffers	**REPLANS**	preplans; –
REOIL	–; reoils	**REPLANT**	preplant; replants
REOILED	–; –		
REOPEN	–; reopens	**REPLATE**	–; replated, replates
REORDER	–; reorders		
REP	prep; repp, reps	**REPLAY**	–; replays
		REPLETE	–; –
REPACK	prepack; repacks	**REPLEVY**	–; –
		REPLICA	–; replicas
REPACKS	prepacks; –	**REPLIED**	–; –
REPAID	prepaid; –	**REPLIER**	–; repliers
REPAINT	–; repaints	**REPLIES**	–; –
REPAIR	–; repairs	**REPLY**	–; –
REPAND	–; –	**REPORT**	–; reports
REPAPER	–; repapers	**REPOSAL**	–; reposals
REPASS	–; –	**REPOSE**	–; reposed, reposer, reposes
REPAST	–; repasts		
REPAVE	–; repaved, repaves		
		REPOSER	–; reposers
REPAY	prepay; repays	**REPOSIT**	–; reposits
		REPOUR	–; repours
REPAYS	prepays; –	**REPOWER**	–; repowers
REPEAL	–; repeals	**REPP**	–; repps
REPEAT	–; repeats	**REPPED**	prepped; –
REPEL	–; repels	**REPRESS**	–; –
REPENT	–; repents	**REPRICE**	–; repriced, reprices
REPERK	–; reperks		
REPIN	–; repine, repins	**REPRINT**	–; reprints
		REPRISE	–; reprised, reprises
REPINE	–; repined, repiner, repines		
		REPRO	–; repros

REPROBE	–; reprobed, reprobes	**RESAW**	–; resawn, resaws
REPROOF	–; reproofs	**RESAWED**	–; –
REPROVE	–; reproved, reprover, reproves	**RESAY**	–; resays
		RESCALE	–; rescaled, rescales
REPS	preps; –	**RESCIND**	–; rescinds
REPTANT	–; –	**RESCORE**	prescore; rescored, rescores
REPTILE	–; reptiles		
REPUGN	–; repugns		
REPULSE	–; repulsed, repulser, repulses	**RESCUE**	–; rescued, rescuer, rescues
REPUTE	–; reputed, reputes	**RESCUER**	–; rescuers
REQUEST	–; requests	**RESEAL**	–; reseals
REQUIEM	–; requiems	**RESEAT**	–; reseats
REQUIN	–; requins	**RESEAU**	–; reseaus, reseaux
REQUIRE	–; required, requirer, requires	**RESECT**	–; resects
		RESEDA	–; resedas
REQUITE	–; requited, requiter, requites	**RESEE**	–; reseed, reseek, reseen, resees
RERAN	–; –	**RESEED**	–; reseeds
REREAD	–; rereads	**RESEEK**	–; reseeks
REREDOS	–; –	**RESEIZE**	–; reseized, reseizes
RERISE	–; rerisen, rerises		
REROLL	–; rerolls	**RESELL**	presell; resells
REROSE	–; –	**RESELLS**	presells; –
REROUTE	–; rerouted, reroutes	**RESEND**	–; resends
RERUN	–; reruns	**RESENT**	present; resents
RES	ares, ires, ores; resh, rest	**RESENTS**	presents; –
		RESERVE	preserve; reserved, reserver, reserves
RESAID	–; –		
RESAIL	–; resails		
RESALE	–; resales		

RESET	preset; resets	**RESIN**	–; resins, resiny
RESETS	presets;	**RESINED**	–; –
RESEW	–; resewn, resews	**RESIST**	–; resists
RESEWED	–; –	**RESIZE**	–; resized, resizes
RESH	fresh; –	**RESMELT**	–; resmelts
RESHAPE	preshape; reshaped, reshapes	**RESOJET**	–; resojets
		RESOLD	presold; –
RESHES	freshes; –	**RESOLE**	–; resoled, resoles
RESHIP	–; reships	**RESOLVE**	–; resolved, resolver, resolves
RESHOD	–; –		
RESHOE	–; reshoes		
RESHOOT	–; reshoots	**RESORB**	–; resorbs
RESHOT	–; –	**RESORT**	–; resorts
RESHOW	preshow; reshown, reshows	**RESOUND**	–; resounds
		RESOW	–; resown, resows
RESHOWN	preshown; –	**RESOWED**	–; –
RESHOWS	preshows; –	**RESPECT**	–; respects
RESID	–; reside, resids	**RESPELL**	–; respells
		RESPELT	–; –
RESIDE	preside; resided, resider, resides	**RESPIRE**	–; respired, respires
		RESPITE	–; respited, respites
RESIDED	presided; –	**RESPOND**	; responds
RESIDER	presider; residers	**REST**	crest, drest, prest, wrest; rests
RESIDES	presides; –		
RESIDUA	–; residual	**RESTACK**	; restacks
RESIDUE	–; residues	**RESTAFF**	–; restaffs
RESIFT	presift; resifts	**RESTAGE**	–; restaged, restages
RESIFTS	presifts; –	**RESTAMP**	prestamp; restamps
RESIGN	–; resigns		
RESILE	–; resiled, resiles	**RESTART**	–; restarts
		RESTATE	–; restated, restates

RESTED	crested, wrested; –	retaker, retakes
RESTER	prester, wrester; resters	**RETARD**	–; retards
		RETASTE	pretaste; retasted, retastes
RESTERS	presters, wresters; –	
		RETCH	wretch; –
RESTFUL	–; –	**RETCHED**	wretched; –
RESTING	cresting, wresting; –	**RETCHES**	wretches; –
		RETE	arete; retem
RESTIVE	–; –	**RETEACH**	–; –
RESTOCK	–; restocks	**RETELL**	–; retells
RESTORE	–; restored, restorer, restores	**RETEM**	–; retems
		RETENE	–; retenes
		RETEST	pretest; retests
RESTS	crests, prests, wrests; –	
		RETESTS	pretests; –
RESTUDY	–; –	**RETHINK**	–; rethinks
RESTUFF	–; restuffs	**RETIA**	–; retial
RESTYLE	–; restyled, restyles	**RETIARY**	–; –
		RETICLE	–; reticles
RESULT	–; results	**RETIE**	–; retied, reties
RESUME	presume; resumed, resumer, resumes	
		RETIME	–; retimed, retimes
		RETINA	–; retinae, retinal, retinas
RESUMED	presumed; –	
RESUMER	presumer; resumers	
		RETINAL	–; retinals
RESUMES	presumes; –	**RETINOL**	–; retinols
RESURGE	–; resurged, resurges	**RETINT**	–; retints
		RETINUE	–; retinued, retinues
RET	fret, tret; rete, rets	**RETIRE**	–; retired, retiree, retirer, retires
RETABLE	–; retables	
RETAIL	–; retails	
RETAIN	–; retains	**RETIREE**	–; retirees
RETAKE	–; retaken,	**RETIRER**	–; retirers

RETITLE	–; retitled, retitles	REUSE	–; reused, reuses
RETOLD	–; –	REUTTER	–; reutters
RETOOK	–; –	REV	–; revs
RETOOL	–; retools	REVALUE	–; revalued, revalues
RETORT	–; retorts		
RETOUCH	–; –	REVAMP	–; revamps
RETRACE	–; retraced, retraces	REVEAL	–; reveals
		REVEL	–; revels
RETRACK	–; retracks	REVELED	–; –
RETRACT	–; retracts	REVELER	–; revelers
RETRAIN	–; retrains	REVELRY	–; –
RETRAL	–; –	REVENGE	–; revenged, revenger, revenges
RETREAD	–; retreads		
RETREAT	pretreat; retreats		
		REVENUE	–; revenued, revenuer, revenues
RETRIAL	–; retrials		
RETRIED	–; –		
RETRIES	–; –	REVERB	–; reverbs
RETRIM	–; retrims	REVERE	–; revered, reverer, reveres
RETRY	–; –		
RETS	frets, trets; –		
RETSINA	–; retsinas	REVERER	–; reverers
RETTED	fretted; –	REVERIE	; reveries
RETTING	fretting; –	REVERS	–; reverse, reverso
RETUNE	–; retuned, retunes		
		REVERSE	–; reversed, reverser, reverses
RETURN	–; returns		
RETUSE	–; –		
RETWIST	–; retwists	REVERSO	–; reversos
RETYING	–; –	REVERT	–; reverts
RETYPE	–; retyped, retypes	REVERY	–; –
		REVEST	–; revests
REUNIFY	–; –	REVET	brevet, trevet; revets
REUNITE	preunite; reunited, reunites		
		REVETS	brevets, trevets; –
REUNION	preunion; reunions	REVIEW	preview; reviews
		REVIEWS	previews; –

REVILE	–; reviled, reviler, reviles	rewaken, rewakes
		REWAKEN –; rewakens
REVILER	–; revilers	**REWAN** –; –
REVISAL	–; revisals	**REWARD** –; rewards
REVISE	previse; revised, reviser, revises	**REWARM** prewarms; rewarms
		REWARMS prewarms; –
		REWASH prewash; –
REVISED	prevised; –	**REWAX** –; –
REVISER	–; revisers	**REWAXED** –; –
REVISES	previses; –	**REWAXES** –; –
REVISOR	previsor; revisors, revisory	**REWEAVE** –; reweaved, reweaves
REVISIT	–; revisits	**REWED** –; reweds
REVIVAL	–; revivals	**REWEIGH** –; reweighs
REVIVE	–; revived, reviver, revives	**REWELD** –; rewelds
		REWIDEN –; rewidens
		REWIN –; rewind, rewins
REVIVER	–; revivers	
REVOICE	–; revoiced, revoices	**REWIND** –; rewinds
		REWIRE –; rewired, rewires
REVOKE	–; revoked, revoker, revokes	
		REWOKE –; rewoken
		REWON –; –
REVOKER	–; revokers	**REWORD** –; rewords
REVOLT	–; revolts	**REWORK** –; reworks
REVOLVE	–; revolved, revolver, revolves	**REWOUND** –; –
		REWOVE –; rewoven
		REWRAP prewrap; rewraps, rewrapt
REVOTE	–; revoted, revotes	
REVUE	prevues; revues	**REWRAPS** –; –
		REWRITE –; rewrites
REVUES	prevues; –	**REWROTE** –; –
REVUIST	–; revuists	**REX** prex; –
REVVED	–; –	**REXES** prexes; –
REVVING	–; –	**REYNARD** –; reynards
REWAKE	–; rewaked,	

REZONE	–; rezoned, rezones			rhymer, rhymes
RHABDOM	–; rhabdome, rhabdoms	RHYMER	–; rhymers	
		RHYTA	–; –	
		RHYTHM	–; rhythms	
RHACHIS	–; –	RHYTON	–; –	
RHAMNUS	–; –	RIAL	trial; rials	
RHAPHAE	–; –	RIALS	trials; –	
RHAPHE	–; rhaphes	RIALTO	–; rialtos	
RHATANY	–; –	RIANT	–; –	
RHEA	–; rheas	RIANTLY	–; –	
RHEBOK	–; rheboks	RIATA	–; riatas	
RHENIUM	–; rheniums	RIB	crib, drib; ribs	
RHESUS	–; –			
RHETOR	–; rhetors	RIBALD	–; ribalds	
RHEUM	–; rheums, rheumy	RIBAND	–; ribands	
		RIBBAND	–; ribbands	
RHEUMIC	–; –	RIBBED	cribbed, dribbed; –	
RHINAL	–; –			
RHINO	–; rhinos	RIBBER	cribber; ribbers	
RHIZOID	–; rhizoids			
RHIZOMA	–; –	RIBBERS	cribbers; –	
RHIZOME	–; rhizomes	RIBBIER	–; –	
RHO	–; rhos	RIBBING	cribbing, dribbing; ribbings	
RHODIC	–; –			
RHODIUM	–; rhodiums			
RHODORA	–; rhodoras	RIBBON	–; ribbons, ribbony	
RHOMB	–; rhombi, rhombs			
		RIBBY	–; –	
RHOMBI	–; rhombic	RIBES	bribes, tribes; –	
RHOMBUS	–; –			
RHONCHI	–; –	RIBLESS	–; –	
RHUBARB	–; rhubarbs	RIBLET	–; riblets	
RHUMB	–; rhumba, rhumbs	RIBLIKE	–; –	
		RIBOSE	–; riboses	
RHUMBA	–; rhumbas	RIBS	cribs, dribs; –	
RHUS	–; –			
RHUSES	–; –	RIBWORT	–; ribworts	
RHYME	–; rhymed,	RICE	price, trice;	

	riced, ricer, rices	**RICRAC**	–; ricracs
		RICTAL	–; –
RICED	priced, triced; –	**RICTUS**	–; –
		RID	arid, grid; ride, rids
RICER	pricer; ricers		
RICERS	pricers; –	**RIDABLE**	–; –
RICES	prices, trices; –	**RIDDED**	–; –
		RIDDEN	–; –
RICH	–; –	**RIDDER**	–; ridders
RICHEN	–; richens	**RIDDING**	–; –
RICHER	–; –	**RIDDLE**	griddle; riddled, riddler, riddles
RICHES	–; richest		
RICHLY	–; –		
RICIN	–; ricing, ricins		
		RIDDLED	griddled; –
RICING	pricing, tricing; –	**RIDDLER**	–; riddlers
		RIDDLES	griddles; –
RICINUS	–; –	**RIDE**	bride, cride, gride, pride; rider, rides
RICK	prick, trick; ricks		
RICKED	bricked, cricked, pricked, tricked; –	**RIDENT**	trident; –
		RIDER	arider; riders
		RIDES	brides, grides, irides, prides; –
RICKETS	crickets, prickets, rickets; –		
		RIDGE	bridge, fridge; ridged, ridgel, ridges
RICKETY	–; –		
RICKEY	–; rickeys		
RICKING	bricking, cricking, pricking, tricking; –	**RIDGED**	bridged; –
		RIDGEL	–; ridgels
		RIDGES	bridges, fridges; –
RICKS	bricks, cricks, pricks, tricks; –		
		RIDGIER	–; –
RICKSHA	–; rickshas, rickshaw	**RIDGIL**	–; ridgils
		RIDGING	bridging; –
RICOTTA	–; ricottas	**RIDGY**	–; –
		RIDING	griding,

	priding; ridings		grig, prig, tria; rias
RIDLEY	–; ridleys	**RIGGED**	frigged,
RIDOTTO	–; ridottos		prigged,
RIDS	arids,		trigged; –
	grids; –	**RIGGER**	trigger;
RIEL	ariel, oriel;		riggers
	riels	**RIGGERS**	triggers; –
RIELS	ariels,	**RIGGING**	frigging,
	oriels; –		prigging,
RIEVER	griever;		trigging;
	rievers		riggings
RIEVERS	–; grievers	**RIGHT**	aright,
RIFE	–; rifer		bright, fright,
RIFELY	–; –		wright;
RIFEST	–; –		righto, rights,
RIFF	griff; riffs		righty
RIFFED	–; –	**RIGHTED**	frighted; –
RIFFING	–; –	**RIGHTER**	brighter;
RIFFLE	–; riffled,		righters
	riffler, riffles	**RIGHTLY**	–; –
RIFFLER	–; rifflers	**RIGHTS**	brights,
RIFFS	griffs; –		frights,
RIFLE	trifle; rifled,		wrights; –
	rifler, rifles	**RIGID**	frigid; –
RIFLER	trifler; riflers,	**RIGIDLY**	–; –
	riflery	**RIGOR**	–; rigors
RIFLERS	triflers; –	**RIGOUR**	–; rigours
RIFLES	trifles; –	**RIGS**	brigs, frigs,
RIFLING	trifling;		grigs, prigs,
	riflings		trigs; –
RIFT	drift, grift;	**RIKISHA**	–; rikishas
	rifts	**RIKSHAW**	–; rikshaws
RIFTED	drifted,	**RILE**	–; riled,
	grifted; –		riles, riley
RIFTING	drifting,	**RILED**	ariled; –
	grifting; –	**RILIEVI**	–; –
RIFTS	drifts,	**RILIEVO**	–; –
	grifts; –	**RILING**	–; –
RIG	brig, frig,	**RILL**	brill, drill,

	frill, grill, krill, prill, trill; rille, rills	**RIMING**	griming, priming; –
RILLE	grille; rilled, rilles, rillet	**RIMLAND**	–; rimlands
		RIMLESS	–; –
RILLED	drilled, frilled, grilled, prilled, trilled; –	**RIMMED**	brimmed, primmed, trimmed; –
		RIMMER	brimmer, crimmer, grimmer, krimmer, primmer, trimmer; rimmers
RILLES	grilles; –		
RILLET	–; rillets		
RILLING	drilling, frilling, grilling, prilling, trilling; –		
RILLS	brills, drills, frills, grills, krills, prills, trills; –	**RIMMERS**	brimmers, crimmers, krimmers, trimmers; –
		RIMMING	brimming, primming, trimming; –
RIM	brim, grim, prim, trim; rime, rims, rimy	**RIMOSE**	–; –
		RIMOUS	–; –
		RIMPLE	crimple; rimpled, rimples
RIME	crime, grime, prime; rimed, rimer, rimes		
		RIMPLED	crimpled; –
		RIMPLES	crimples; –
RIMED	grimed, primed; –	**RIMROCK**	–; rimrocks
		RIMS	brims, prims, trims; –
RIMER	primer, trimer; rimers	**RIMY**	grimy; –
		RIN	brin, grin; rind, ring, rink, rins
RIMERS	primers, trimers; –		
RIMES	crimes, grimes, primes; –		
		RIND	grind; rinds
		RINDED	brinded, grinded; –
RIMFIRE	–; –		
RIMIER	grimier; –	**RINDS**	grinds; –
RIMIEST	grimiest; –		

RING	bring, iring, wring; rings	RIPCORD	–; ripcords
RINGED	cringed, fringed, wringed; –	RIPE	gripe, tripe; riped, ripen, riper, ripes
RINGENT	–; –	RIPED	griped; –
RINGER	bringer, cringer, wringer; ringers	RIPELY	–; –
		RIPEN	–; ripens
		RIPENED	–; –
		RIPER	griper; –
RINGERS	bringers, cringers, wringers; –	RIPES	gripes, tripes; ripest
		RIPIENI	–; –
		RIPIENO	–; ripienos
RINGING	bringing, fringing, wringing; –	RIPING	griping; –
		RIPOST	–; riposte, riposts
RINGLET	–; –	RIPOSTE	–; riposted, ripostes
RINGS	brings, wrings; –	
RINGTAW	–; ringtaws	RIPPED	dripped, gripped, tripped; –
RINK	brink, drink, prink; rinks	
		RIPPER	dripper, gripper, tripper; rippers
RINKS	brinks, drinks, prinks; –	
		RIPPERS	drippers, grippers, trippers; –
RINNING	–; –	
RINS	brins, grins; rinse	RIPPING	dripping, gripping, tripping; –
RINSE	–; rinsed, rinser, rinses	
		RIPPLE	cripple, gripple; rippled, rippler, ripples
RINSER	–; rinsers	
RINSING	–; rinsings	
RIOT	–; riots	
RIOTED	–; –	
RIOTER	–; rioters	RIPPLED	crippled; –
RIOTING	–; –	RIPPLER	crippler; ripplers
RIOTOUS	–; –	
RIP	drip, grip, trip; ripe rips	
		RIPPLET	–; ripplets

RIPPLY	–; –	RISUS	–; –
RIPRAP	–; ripraps	RISUSES	–; –
RIPS	drips, grips, trips; –	RITARD	–; ritards
		RITE	trite, write; rites
RIPSAW	–; ripsaws		
RIPT	gript; –	RITES	writes; –
RIPTIDE	–; riptides	RITTER	critter, fritter; ritters
RISE	arise, frise, prise; risen, riser, rises	RITTERS	critters, fritters; –
RISEN	arisen; –	RITTS	britts, fritts; –
RISER	–; risers		
RISES	arises, crises, frises, irises, krises, prises; –	RITUAL	–; rituals
		RITZ	–; ritzy
		RITZIER	–; –
		RITZILY	–; –
RISHI	–; rishis	RIVAGE	–; rivages
RISIBLE	–; –	RIVAL	–; rivals
RISING	arising, irising, prising; risings	RIVALED	–; –
		RIVALRY	–; –
		RIVE	drive; rived, riven, river, rives, rivet
RISK	brisk, frisk; risks, risky		
		RIVEN	driven; –
RISKED	brisked, frisked; –	RIVER	driver; rivers
		RIVERS	drivers; –
RISKER	brisker, frisker; riskers	RIVES	drives; –
		RIVET	grivet, privet, trivet; rivets
RISKERS	friskers; –	RIVETED	–; –
RISKIER	–; –	RIVETER	–; reviters
RISKILY	–; –	RIVETS	grivets, privets, trivets; –
RISKING	brisking, frisking; –		
RISKS	brisks, frisks; –	RIVIERA	–; rivieras
		RIVIERE	–; rivieres
RISKY	frisky; –	RIVING	driving; –
RISOTTO	–; risottos	RIVULET	–; rivulets
RISQUE	–; –	RIYAL	–; riyals
RISSOLE	–; rissoles	ROACH	broach; –

ROACHED	broached; –	**ROBOTRY**	–; –
ROACHES	broaches; –	**ROBUST**	–; –
ROAD	broad; roads	**ROC**	–; rock, rocs
		ROCHET	crochet; rochets
ROADBED	–; roadbeds		
ROADS	broads; –	**ROCHETS**	crochets; –
ROADWAY	–; roadways	**ROCK**	brock, crock, frock, trock; rocks, rocky
ROAM	–; roams		
ROAMED	–; –		
ROAMER	–; roamers	**ROCKABY**	–; rockabye
ROAMING	–; –	**ROCKED**	crocked, frocked, trocked; –
ROAN	groan; roans		
ROANS	groans; –		
ROAR	–; roars	**ROCKER**	–; rockers, rockery
ROARED	–; –		
ROARER	–; roarers	**ROCKERY**	crockery; –
ROARING	–; roarings	**ROCKET**	brocket, crocket; rockets
ROAST	–; roasts		
ROASTED	–; –		
ROASTER	–; roasters	**ROCKETS**	brockets, crockets; –
ROB	–; robe, robs		
		ROCKIER	–; –
ROBALO	–; robalos	**ROCKING**	crocking, frocking, trocking; –
ROBAND	proband; robands		
ROBANDS	probands; –	**ROCKOON**	–; rockoons
ROBBED	–; –	**ROCKS**	brocks, crocks, frocks, trocks; –
ROBBER	–; robbers, robbery		
ROBBIN	–; robbing, robbins	**ROCOCO**	–; rococos
		ROD	prod, trod; rode, rods
ROBE	probe; robed, robes		
ROBED	probed; –	**RODDED**	prodded; –
ROBES	probes; –	**RODDING**	prodding; –
ROBIN	–; robing, robins	**RODE**	erode, trode; rode ›
ROBING	probing; –	**RODENT**	erodent; rodents
ROBLE	–; robles		
ROBOT	–; robots	**RODEO**	–; rodeos

RODLESS	–; –		trolling;
RODLIKE	–; –		rollings
RODMAN	–; –	**ROLLMOP**	–; rollmops
RODMEN	–; –	**ROLLOUT**	–; rollouts
RODSMAN	–; –	**ROLLS**	drolls, trolls; –
RODSMEN	–; –	**ROLLTOP**	–; –
RODS	prods; –	**ROLLWAY**	–; rollways
ROE	froe; roes	**ROMAINE**	–; romaines
ROEBUCK	–; roebucks	**ROMAN**	–; romano,
ROES	froes; –		romans
ROGER	–; rogers	**ROMANCE**	–;
ROGUE	brogue,		romanced,
	drogue;		romancer,
	rogued,		romances
	rogues	**ROMANO**	–; romanos
ROGUERY	broguery; –	**ROMAUNT**	–; romaunts
ROGUES	brogues,	**ROMP**	tromp; romps
	drogues; –	**ROMPED**	tromped; –
ROGUING	–; –	**ROMPER**	–; rompers
ROGUISH	broguish; –	**ROMPING**	tromping; –
ROIL	broil; roils,	**ROMPISH**	–; –
	roily	**ROMPS**	tromps; –
ROILED	broiled; –	**RONDEAU**	–; rondeaux
ROILIER	–; –	**RONDEL**	–; rondels
ROILING	broiling; –	**RONDO**	–; rondos
ROILS	broils; –	**RONDURE**	–; rondures
ROISTER	–; roisters	**RONION**	–; ronions
ROLE	prole; roles	**RONNEL**	–; ronnels
ROLES	proles; –	**RONTGEN**	–; rontgens
ROLL	droll, troll;	**RONYON**	–; ronyons
	rolls	**ROOD**	brood;
ROLLED	drolled,		roods
	trolled; –	**ROODS**	broods; –
ROLLER	droller,	**ROOF**	proof; roofs
	troller;	**ROOFED**	proofed; –
	rollers	**ROOFER**	proofer;
ROLLERS	trollers; -		roofers
ROLLICK	–; rollicks,	**ROOFERS**	proofers; –
	rollicky	**ROOFING**	proofing;
ROLLING	drolling,		roofings

ROOFS	proofs; –	**ROOSING**	–; –
ROOFTOP	–; rooftops	**ROOST**	–; roosts
ROOK	brook,	**ROOSTED**	–; –
	crook; rooks,	**ROOSTER**	–; roosters
	rooky	**ROOT**	–; roots,
ROOKED	brooked,		rooty
	crooked; –	**ROOTAGE**	–; rootages
ROOKERY	–; –	**ROOTED**	–; –
ROOKIE	–; rookier,	**ROOTER**	–; rooters
	rookies	**ROOTIER**	–; –
ROOKIES	–; rookiest	**ROOTING**	–; –
ROOKING	brooking,	**ROOTLET**	–; rootlets
	crooking; –	**ROPABLE**	–; –
ROOKS	brooks,	**ROPE**	grope,
	crooks; –		trope;
ROOM	broom,		roped,
	groom,		roper, ropes
	vroom;	**ROPED**	groped; –
	rooms,	**ROPER**	groper,
	roomy		proper;
ROOMED	broomed,		ropers,
	groomed,		ropery
	vroomed; –	**ROPERS**	gropers,
ROOMER	groomer;		propers; –
	roomers	**ROPES**	gropes,
ROOMERS	groomers; –		tropes; –
ROOMFUL	–; roomfuls	**ROPEWAY**	–; ropeways
ROOMIER	broomier; –	**ROPIER**	–; –
ROOMILY	–; –	**ROPIEST**	–; –
ROOMING	brooming,	**ROPILY**	–; –
	grooming,	**ROPING**	groping; –
	vrooming; –	**ROPY**	–; –
ROOMS	brooms,	**ROQUE**	–; roques,
	grooms,		roquet
	vrooms; –	**ROQUET**	croquet;
ROOMY	broomy; –		roquets
ROOSE	–; roosed,	**ROQUETS**	croquets; –
	rooser,	**RORQUAL**	–; rorquals
	rooses	**ROSARIA**	–; rosarian
ROOSER	–; roosers	**ROSARY**	–; –

ROSCOE	–; roscoes	**ROTARY**	–; –
ROSE	arose,	**ROTATE**	–; rotated,
	brose,		rotates
	erose,	**ROTATOR**	–; rotators,
	prose;		rotatory
	rosed, roses,	**ROTCH**	crotch;
	roset		rotche
ROSEATE	–; –	**ROTCHE**	–; rotches
ROSEBAY	–; rosebays	**ROTCHES**	crotches; –
ROSEBUD	–; rosebuds	**ROTE**	wrote; rotes
ROSED	prosed; –	**ROTGUT**	–; rotguts
ROSELLE	–; roselles	**ROTIFER**	–; rotifers
ROSEOLA	–; roseolar,	**ROTL**	–; rotls
	roseolas	**ROTO**	–; rotor,
ROSERY	–; –		rotos
ROSES	broses,	**ROTOR**	–; rotors
	eroses,	**ROTS**	grots,
	proses; –		trots; –
ROSET	–; rosets	**ROTTED**	trotted; –
ROSETTE	–; rosettes	**ROTTEN**	–; –
ROSIER	crosier,	**ROTTER**	trotter;
	prosier; –		rotters
ROSIEST	prosiest; –	**ROTTERS**	trotters; –
ROSILY	prosily; –	**ROTTING**	trotting; –
ROSIN	–; rosing,	**ROTUND**	–; rotunda
	rosins, rosiny	**ROTUNDA**	–; rotundas
ROSINED	–; –	**ROUBLE**	trouble;
ROSING	prosing; –		roubles
ROSOLIO	–; rosolios	**ROUBLES**	troubles; –
ROSTER	–; rosters	**ROUCHE**	–; rouches
ROSTRA	–; rostral	**ROUCHES**	crouches,
ROSTRUM	–; rostrums		grouches; –
ROSY	brosy,	**ROUE**	–; rouen,
	prosy,		roues
	trosy; –	**ROUEN**	–; rouens
ROT	grot, trot;	**ROUGE**	–; rouged,
	rota, rote,		rouges
	rotl, roto,	**ROUGH**	trough;
	rots		roughs
ROTA	–; rotas	**ROUGHED**	–; –

ROUGHEN	–; roughens		grouser,
ROUGHER	–; roughers		trouser,
ROUGHLY	–; –		rousers
ROUGHS	troughs; –	**ROUSERS**	arousers,
ROUGING	–; –		grousers,
ROULADE	–; roulades		trousers; –
ROULEAU	–; rouleaus,	**ROUSES**	arouses,
	rouleaux		grouses; –
ROUND	around,	**ROUSING**	arousing,
	ground;		grousing; –
	rounds	**ROUST**	–; rousts
ROUNDED	grounded; –	**ROUSTED**	–; –
ROUNDEL	–; roundels	**ROUSTER**	–; rousters
ROUNDER	grounder;	**ROUT**	grout, trout;
	rounders		route, routh,
ROUNDLY	–; –		routs
ROUNDS	grounds; –	**ROUTE**	–; routed,
ROUNDUP	–; roundups		router,
ROUP	croup,		routes
	group;	**ROUTED**	grouted; –
	roups, roupy	**ROUTER**	grouter;
ROUPED	grouped,		routers
	trouped; –	**ROUTERS**	grouters; –
ROUPET	–; –	**ROUTH**	drouth,
ROUPIER	croupier; –		rouths
ROUPILY	croupily;	**ROUTHS**	drouths; –
ROUPING	grouping,	**ROUTINE**	–; routines
	trouping; –	**ROUTING**	grouting; –
ROUPS	croups,	**ROUTS**	grouts,
	groups; –		trouts; –
ROUPY	croupy; –	**ROUX**	–; –
ROUSE	arouse,	**ROVE**	drove,
	crouse,		grove,
	grouse;		prove, trove;
	roused,		roved,
	rouser,		roven, rover,
	rouses		roves
ROUSED	aroused,	**ROVED**	droved,
	groused; –		groved,
ROUSER	arouser,		proved; –

ROVEN	proven; –	**ROWING**	crowing, growing, trowing; rowings
ROVER	drover, prover, trover; rovers		
		ROWLOCK	–; rowlocks
ROVERS	drovers, provers, trovers; –	**ROWS**	brows, crows, frows, grows, prows, trows, vrows; –
ROVES	droves, groves, proves, troves; –		
		ROWTH	growth, trowth; rowths
ROVING	droving, proving; rovings		
		ROWTHS	growths, trowths; –
ROW	brow, crow, frow, grow, prow, trow, vrow; rows	**ROYAL**	–; royals
		ROYALLY	–; –
ROWABLE	growable; –	**ROYALTY**	–; –
ROWAN	–; rowans	**ROYSTER**	–; roysters
ROWBOAT	–; rowboats	**ROZZER**	–; rozzers
ROWDIER	–; –	**RUB**	drub, grub; rube, rubs, ruby
ROWDIES	crowdies; rowdiest		
ROWDILY	–; –	**RUBABOO**	–; rubaboos
ROWDY	crowdy; –	**RUBACE**	–; rubaces
ROWED	crowed, trowed; –	**RUBASSE**	–; rubasses
		RUBATO	–; rubatos
ROWEL	trowel; rowels	**RUBBED**	drubbed, grubbed; –
ROWELED	–; –	**RUBBER**	drubber, grubber; rubbers, rubbery
ROWELS	trowels; –		
ROWEN	–; rowens		
ROWER	crower, grower, prower; rowers	**RUBBERS**	drubbers, grubbers; ·
		RUBBING	drubbing, grubbing; rubbings
ROWERS	crowers, growers; -		

RUBBISH	–; rubbishy	**RUDELY**	crudely; –
RUBBLE	–; rubbled, rubbles	**RUDER**	cruder; –
		RUDERAL	–; ruderals
RUBBLY	–; –	**RUDESBY**	–; –
RUBDOWN	–; rubdowns	**RUDEST**	crudest; –
RUBE	–; rubes	**RUE**	true; rued, ruer, rues
RUBELLA	–; rubellas		
RUBEOLA	–; rubeolar, rubeolas	**RUED**	trued; –
		RUEFUL	–; –
RUBIDIC	–; –	**RUER**	truer; ruers
RUBIED	–; –	**RUES**	trues; –
RUBIER	–; –	**RUFF**	gruff; ruffe, ruffs
RUBIES	–; rubiest		
RUBIGO	–; rubigos	**RUFFE**	truffe; ruffed, ruffes
RUBIOUS	–; –		
RUBLE	–; rubles	**RUFFED**	gruffed; –
RUBRIC	–; rubrics	**RUFFES**	truffes; –
RUBS	drubs, grubs; –	**RUFFIAN**	–; ruffians
RUBUS	–; –	**RUFFING**	–; –
RUBY	–; –	**RUFFLE**	truffle; ruffled, ruffler, ruffles
RUBYING	–; –		
RUCHE	–; ruches		
RUCHING	–; ruchings	**RUFFLED**	truffled; –
RUCK	truck; rucks	**RUFFLER**	–; rufflers
RUCKED	trucked; –	**RUFFLES**	truffles; –
RUCKING	trucking; –	**RUFFLY**	gruffly; –
RUCKS	trucks; –	**RUFFS**	gruffs; –
RUCKUS	–; –	**RUFOUS**	–; –
RUCTION	–; ructions	**RUG**	drug, frug; ruga, rugs
RUDD	–; rudds, ruddy		
		RUGA	–; rugae, rugal
RUDDER	–; rudders		
RUDDIER	–; –	**RUGAL**	frugal; –
RUDDILY	–; –	**RUGATE**	–; –
RUDDLE	–; ruddled, ruddles	**RUGBIES**	–; –
		RUGBY	–; –
RUDDOCK	–; ruddocks	**RUGGED**	drugged, frugged; –
RUDDY	cruddy; –		
RUDE	crude, prude; ruder	**RUGGER**	–; ruggers

RUGGING	drugging, frugging; –	**RUMBLY**	crumbly, grumbly; –
RUGLIKE	–; –	**RUMEN**	–; rumens
RUGOSE	–; –	**RUMINA**	–; ruminal
RUGOUS	–; –	**RUMMAGE**	–;
RUGS	drugs, frugs; –		rummaged, rummager, rummages
RUIN	bruin; ruing, ruins	**RUMMER**	drummer, grummer; rummers
RUINATE	–; ruinated, ruinates		
RUINED	–; –	**RUMMERS**	drummers; –
RUINER	–; ruiners	**RUMMEST**	grummest; –
RUING	truing; –	**RUMMIER**	–; –
RUINING	–; –	**RUMMIES**	–; rummiest
RUINOUS	–; –	**RUMMY**	crummy; –
RUINS	bruins; –	**RUMOR**	–; rumors
RULE	–; ruled, ruler, rules	**RUMORED**	–; –
		RUMOUR	–; rumours
RULER	–; rulers	**RUMP**	crump, frump, grump, trump; rumps
RULING	–; rulings		
RUM	arum, drum, grum; rump, rums		
		RUMPLE	crumple; rumpled, rumples
RUMBA	–; rumbas		
RUMBAED	–; –	**RUMPLED**	crumpled; –
RUMBLE	crumble, drumble, grumble; rumbled, rumbler, rumbles	**RUMPLES**	crumples; rumpless
		RUMPLY	crumply; –
		RUMPS	crumps, frumps, grumps, trumps; –
RUMBLED	crumbled, drumbled, grumbled; –		
		RUMPUS	–; –
RUMBLER	grumbler; rumblers	**RUMS**	arums, drums; –
RUMBLES	crumbles, drumbles, grumbles; –	**RUN**	rune, rung, runs, runt; –
		RUNAWAY	–; runaways

RUNBACK	–; runbacks	**RUSE**	cruse, druse;
RUNDLE	trundle;		ruses
	rundles,	**RUSES**	cruses,
	rundlet		druses,
RUNDLES	trundles; –		uruses;
RUNDLET	–; rundlets	**RUSH**	brush, crush;
RUNDOWN	–; rundowns		rushy
RUNE	prune; runes	**RUSHED**	brushed,
RUNES	prunes; –		crushed; –
RUNG	wrung; rungs	**RUSHEE**	–; rushees
RUNIC	–; –	**RUSHER**	brusher,
RUNKLE	–; runkled,		crusher;
	runkles		rushers
RUNLESS	–; –	**RUSHERS**	brushers,
RUNLET	–; runlets		crushers; –
RUNNEL	trunnel;	**RUSHES**	brushes,
	runnels		crushes; –
RUNNELS	trunnels; –	**RUSHIER**	brushier; –
RUNNER	–; runners	**RUSHING**	brushing,
RUNNIER	–; –		crushing;
RUNNING	–; runnings		rushings
RUNNY	–; –	**RUSHY**	brushy; –
RUNOFF	–; runoffs	**RUSINE**	–; –
RUNOUT	–; runouts	**RUSK**	brusk; rusks
RUNOVER	–; runovers	**RUSSET**	–; russets,
RUNT	brunt, grunt;		russety
	runts, runty	**RUSSIFY**	–; –
RUNTIER	–; –	**RUST**	crust, trust;
RUNTISH	–; –		rusts, rusty
RUNTS	brunts,	**RUSTED**	crusted,
	grunts; –		trusted; –
RUNWAY	–; runways	**RUSTIC**	–; rustics
RUPEE	–; rupees	**RUSTIER**	trustier; –
RUPIAH	–; rupiahs	**RUSTILY**	–; –
RUPTURE	–; ruptured,	**RUSTING**	crusting,
	ruptures		trusting; –
RURAL	crural; –	**RUSTLE**	–; rustled,
RURALLY	–; –		rustler,
RURBAN	–; –		rustles
		RUSTLER	–; rustlers

RUSTS	crusts, trusts; –	**RUTTILY**	–; –
RUSTY	crusty, trusty; –	**RUTTING**	–; –
		RUTTISH	–; –
RUT	brut; ruth, ruts	**RUTTY**	–; –
		RYA	–; ryas
RUTH	truth; ruths	**RYE**	–; ryes
RUTHFUL	–; –	**RYKE**	–; ryked, rykes
RUTHS	truths; –		
RUTILE	–; rutiles	**RYKING**	–; –
RUTTED	–; –	**RYND**	–; rynds
RUTTIER	–; –	**RYOT**	–; ryots

S

S	as, es, is, os, us; sh, si, so	**SABRE**	–; sabred, sabres
SAB	–; sabs, sabe	**SAC**	–; sack, sacs
		SACATON	–; sacatons
SABATON	–; sabatons	**SACBUT**	–; sacbuts
SABBAT	–; sabbath, sabbats	**SACCADE**	–; saccades
		SACCATE	–; –
SABBATH	–; sabbaths	**SACCULE**	–; saccules
SABBED	–; –	**SACCULI**	–; –
SABBING	–; –	**SACHEM**	–; sachems
SABE	–; sabed, saber, sabes	**SACHET**	–; sachets
		SACK	–; sacks
SABEING	–; –	**SACKBUT**	–; sackbuts
SABER	–; sabers	**SACKED**	–; –
SABERED	–; –	**SACKER**	–; sackers
SABIN	–; sabine, sabins	**SACKFUL**	–; sackfuls
		SACKING	–; sackings
SABINE	–; sabines	**SACLIKE**	–; –
SABIR	–; sabirs	**SACQUE**	–; sacques
SABLE	usable; sables	**SACRA**	–; sacral
		SACRAL	–; sacrals
SABOT	–; sabots	**SACRED**	–; –
SABRA	–; sabras	**SACRIST**	–; sacrists, sacristy

SACRUM	–; –	SAGE	usage;
SAD	–; sade,		sager, sages
	sadi	SAGELY	–; –
SADDEN	–; saddens	SAGES	usages;
SADDER	–; –		sagest
SADDEST	–; –	SAGGAR	–; saggard,
SADDHU	–; saddhus		saggars
SADDLE	–; saddled,	SAGGARD	–; saggards
	saddler,	SAGGED	–; –
	saddles	SAGGER	–; saggers
SADDLER	–; saddlers,	SAGGING	–; –
	saddlery	SAGIER	–; –
SADE	tsade; sades	SAGIEST	–; –
SADHE	–; sadhes	SAGO	–; sagos
SADHU	–; sadhus	SAGUARO	–; saguaros
SADI	tsadi; sadis	SAGUM	–; –
SADIRON	–; sadirons	SAHIB	–; sahibs
SADIS	tsadis; –	SAHIWAL	–; sahiwals
SADISM	–; sadisms	SAHUARO	–; sahuaros
SADIST	–; sadists	SAICE	–; saices
SADLY	–; –	SAID	–; saids
SADNESS	–; –	SAIGA	–; saigas
SAE	–; –	SAIL	–; sails
SAFARI	–; safaris	SAILED	–; –
SAFE	–; safer,	SAILER	–; sailers
	safes	SAILING	–; sailings
SAFELY	–; –	SAILOR	–; sailors
SAFES	–; safest	SAIN	–; sains,
SAFETY	–; –		saint
SAFFRON	–; saffrons	SAINED	–; –
SAFROL	–; safrole,	SAINING	–; –
	safrols	SAINT	–; saints
SAFROLE	–; safroles	SAINTED	–; –
SAG	–; saga,	SAINTLY	–; –
	sage, sago,	SAITH	–; saithe
	sags, sagy	SAIYID	–; saiyids
SAGA	; sagas	SAJOU	–; sajous
SAGAMAN	–; –	SAKE	–; saker,
SAGAMEN	–; –		sakes
SAGBUT	–; sagbuts	SAKER	–; sakers

SAKI	–; sakis	SALT	–; salts, salty
SAL	–; sale, sall, salp, sals, salt	SALTANT	–; –
		SALTBOX	–; –
SALAAM	–; salaams	SALTED	–; –
SALABLE	–; –	SALTER	psalter; saltern, salters
SALABLY	–; –		
SALAD	–; salads	SALTERN	–; salterns
SALAMI	–; salamis	SALTERS	psalters; –
SALARY	–; –	SALTEST	–; –
SALE	–; salep, sales	SALTIE	–; saltier, salties
SALEP	–; saleps	SALTIES	–; saltiest
SALIC	–; –	SALTILY	–; –
SALICIN	–; salicine, salicins	SALTINE	–; saltines
		SALTING	–; –
SALIENT	–; salients	SALTIRE	–; saltires
SALIFY	–; –	SALTISH	–; –
SALINA	–; salinas	SALTPAN	–; saltpans
SALINE	–; salines	SALUKI	–; salukis
SALIVA	–; salivas	SALUTE	–; saluted, saluter, salutes
SALL	–; sally		
SALLET	–; sallets		
SALLIED	–; –		
SALLIER	–; salliers	SALUTER	–; saluters
SALLOW	–; sallows, sallowy	SALVAGE	–; salvaged, salvagee, salvager, salvages
SALMI	–; salmis		
SALMON	–; salmons		
SALOL	–; salols	SALVE	–; salved, salver, salves
SALON	–; salons		
SALOON	–; saloons		
SALOOP	–; saloops	SALVER	–; salvers
SALP	–; salpa, salps	SALVIA	–; salvias
		SALVING	–; –
SALPA	–; salpae, salpas	SALVO	–; salvor, salvos
SALPIAN	–; salpians	SALVOED	–; –
SALPID	–; salpids	SALVOES	–; –
SALSIFY	–; –	SALVOR	–; salvors

SAMARA	–; samaras	SANDER	–; sanders
SAMBA	–; sambar, sambas	SANDFLY	–; –
		SANDHI	–; sandhis
SAMBAR	–; sambars	SANDHOG	–; sandhogs
SAMBHAR	–; sambhars	SANDIER	–; –
SAMBHUR	–; sambhurs	SANDING	–; –
SAMBO	–; sambos	SANDLOT	–; sandlots
SAMBUCA	–; sambucas	SANDMAN	–; –
SAMBUKE	–; sambukes	SANDMEN	–; –
SAMBUR	–; samburs	SANDPIT	–; sandpits
SAME	–; samek	SANE	–; saned, saner, sanes
SAMECH	–; samechs		
SAMEK	–; samekh, sameks	SANELY	–; –
		SANES	–; sanest
SAMEKH	–; samekhs	SANG	–; sanga, sangh
SAMIEL	–; samiels		
SAMISEN	–; samisens	SANGA	–; sangar, sangas
SAMITE	–; samites		
SAMLET	–; samlets	SANGAR	–; sangars
SAMOVAR	–; samovars	SANGER	–; sangers
SAMP	–; samps	SANGH	–; sanghs
SAMPAN	–; sampans	SANGRIA	–; sangrias
SAMPLE	–; sampled, sampler, samples	SANICLE	–; sanicles
		SANIES	–; –
		SANING	–; –
SAMPLER	–; samplers	SANIOUS	–; –
SAMSARA	–; samsaras	SANITY	–; –
SAMSHU	–; samshus	SANJAK	–; sanjaks
SAMURAI	–; samurais	SANK	–; –
SANCTA	–; –	SANNOP	–; sannops
SANCTUM	–; sanctums	SANNUP	–; sannups
SAND	–; sands, sandy	SANS	–; –
		SANSAR	–; sansars
SANDAL	–; sandals	SANSEI	–; sanseis
SANDBAG	–; sandbags	SANTIMI	–; –
SANDBAR	–; sandbars	SANTIMS	–; –
SANDBOX	–; –	SANTIR	–; santirs
SANDBUR	–; sandburr, sandburs	SANTOL	–; santols
		SANTOUR	–; santours
SANDED	–; –	SAP	–; saps

SAPAJOU	–; sapajous	SARMENT	–; sarmenta, sarments
SAPHEAD	–; sapheads		
SAPHENA	–; saphenae	SAROD	–; sarode, sarods
SAPID	–; –		
SAPIENS	–; –	SARODE	–; sarodes
SAPIENT	–; –	SARONG	–; sarongs
SAPLESS	–; –	SARSAR	–; sarsars
SAPLING	–; saplings	SARSEN	–; sarsens
SAPONIN	–; saponine, saponins	SARTOR	–; sartors
		SASH	–; –
SAPOR	–; sapors	SASHAY	–; sashays
SAPOTA	–; sapotas	SASHED	–; –
SAPOUR	–; sapours	SASHES	–; –
SAPPED	–; –	SASHIMI	–; sashimis
SAPPER	–; sappers	SASHING	–; –
SAPPHIC	–; sapphics	SASIN	–; sasins
SAPPIER	–; –	SASS	–; sassy
SAPPILY	–; –	SASSABY	–; –
SAPPING	–; –	SASSED	–; –
SAPPY	–; –	SASSES	–; –
SAPROBE	–; saprobes	SASSIER	–; –
SAPSAGO	–; sapsagos	SASSIES	–; sassiest
SAPWOOD	–; sapwoods	SASSILY	–; –
		SASSING	–; –
SARAN	–; sarans	SAT	–; sate, sati
SARAPE	–; sarapes	SATANG	–; satangs
SARCASM	–; sarcasms	SATANIC	–; –
SARCOID	–; sarcoids	SATARA	–; sataras
SARCOMA	–; sarcomas	SATCHEL	–; satchels
SARCOUS	–; –	SATE	–; sated, satem, sates
SARD	–; sards		
SARDAR	–; sardars	SATEEN	–; sateens
SARDINE	–; sardines	SATEM	–; –
SARDIUS	–; –	SATI	–; satin, satis
SAREE	–; sarees		
SARGE	–; sarges	SATIATE	–; satiated, satiates
SARI	–; sarin, saris		
		SATIETY	–; –
SARIN	–; sarins	SATIN	isatin; sating, satins, satiny
SARK	–; sarks		

SATINET	–; satinets	savager,
SATINS	isatins; –	savages
SATIRE	–; satires	**SAVAGER** –; savagery
SATIRIC	–; –	**SAVAGES** –; savagest
SATISFY	–; –	**SAVANNA** –; savannah,
SATORI	–; satoris	savannas
SATRAP	–; satraps,	**SAVANT** –; savants
	satrapy	**SAVATE** –; savates
SATYR	–; satyrs	**SAVE** –; saved,
SATYRID	–; satyrids	saver, saves
SAU	–; saul	**SAVELOY** –; saveloys
SAUCE	–; sauces,	**SAVER** –; savers
	saucer,	**SAVIN** –; savine,
	sauces	saving,
SAUCER	–; saucers	savins
SAUCH	; sauchs	**SAVINE** –; savines
SAUCIER	–; –	**SAVING** –; savings
SAUCILY	–; –	**SAVIOR** –; saviors
SAUCING	–; –	**SAVIOUR** –; saviours
SAUCY	–; –	**SAVOR** –; savors,
SAUGER	–; saugers	**SAVORED** –; –
SAUGH	–; saughs	**SAVORER** –; savorers
SAUL	–; sauls,	**SAVOUR** –; savours,
	sault	savoury
SAULT	–; saults	**SAVOY** –; savoys
SAUNA	–; saunas	**SAVVIED** –; –
SAUNTER	–; saunters	**SAVVIES** –; –
SAUREL	–; saurels	**SAVVY** –; –
SAURIAN	–; saurians	**SAW** –; sawn, saws
SAURIES	–; –	**SAWBILL** –; sawbills
SAURY	–; –	**SAWBUCK** –; sawbucks
SAUSAGE	–; sausages	**SAWDUST** –; sawdusts
SAUTE	–; sauted,	**SAWED** –; –
	sautes	**SAWER** –; sawers
SAUTEED	–; –	**SAWFISH** –; –
SAUTOIR	–; sautoire,	**SAWFLY** –; –
	sautoirs	**SAWING** –; –
SAVABLE	–; –	**SAWLIKE** –; –
SAVAGE	–; savaged,	**SAWLOG** –; sawlogs

SAWMILL	–; sawmills	**SCALL**	–; scalls
SAWNEY	–; sawneys	**SCALLOP**	–; scallops
SAWYER	–; sawyers	**SCALP**	–; scalps
SAX	–; –	**SCALPED**	–; –
SAXES	–; –	**SCALPEL**	–; scalpels
SAXHORN	–; saxhorns	**SCALPER**	–; scalpers
SAXONY	–; –	**SCALY**	–; –
SAXTUBA	–; saxtubas	**SCAM**	–; scamp,
SAY	–; says		scams
SAYABLE	–; –	**SCAMP**	–; scampi,
SAYER	–; sayers		scamps
SAYEST	–; –	**SCAMPED**	–; –
SAYID	–; sayids	**SCAMPER**	–; scampers
SAYING	–; sayings	**SCAN**	–; scans,
SAYS	–; sayst		scant
SAYYID	–; sayyids	**SCANDAL**	–; scandals
SCAB	–; scabs	**SCANDIA**	–; scandias
SCABBED	–; –	**SCANDIC**	–; –
SCABBLE	scabbled,	**SCANNED**	–; –
	scabbles	**SCANNER**	–; scanners
SCABBY	–; –	**SCANT**	–; scants,
SCABIES	–; –		scanty
SCAD	–; scads	**SCANTED**	–; –
SCAG	–; scags	**SCANTER**	–; –
SCALADE	–; scalades	**SCANTLY**	–; –
SCALADO	–; scalados	**SCAPE**	escape;
SCALAGE	–; scalages		scaped,
SCALAR	–; scalare,		scapes
	scalars	**SCAPED**	escaped; –
SCALARE	–; scalares	**SCAPES**	escapes; –
SCALD	–; scalds	**SCAPING**	escaping; –
SCALDED	–; –	**SCAPOSE**	–; –
SCALDIC	–; –	**SCAPULA**	–; scapulae,
SCALE	–; scaled,		scapular,
	scaler,		scapulas
	scales	**SCAR**	escar, oscar;
SCALENE	–; –		scare, scarf,
SCALER	–; scalers		scarp, scars,
SCALIER	–; –		scart, scary
SCALING	–; –	**SCARAB**	–; scarabs

SCARCE	–; scarcer	SCENDS	ascends; –
SCARE	–; scared,	SCENE	–; –
	scarer,	SCENERY	–; –
	scares,	SCENIC	–; –
	scarey	SCENT	ascent;
SCARER	–; scarers		scents
SCARF	–; scarfs	SCENTED	–; –
SCARFED	–; –	SCENTS	ascents; –
SCARIER	–; –	SCEPTER	–; scepters
SCARIFY	–; –	SCEPTIC	–; sceptics
SCARING	–; –	SCEPTRE	–; sceptred,
SCARLET	–; scarlets		sceptres
SCARP	escarp;	SCHAPPE	–; schappes
	scarph,	SCHAV	–; schavs
	scarps	SCHEMA	–; –
SCARPED	–; –	SCHEME	–; schemed,
SCARPER	–; scarpers		schemer,
SCARPH	–; scarphs		schemes
SCARPS	escarps; –	SCHEMER	–; schemers
SCARRED	–; –	SCHERZI	–; –
SCARRY	–; –	SCHERZO	–; scherzos
SCART	–; scarts	SCHISM	–; schisms
SCARTED	–; –	SCHIST	–; schists
SCARVES	–; –	SCHIZO	–; schizos
SCAT	–; scats,	SCHLEP	–; schlepp,
	scatt		schleps
SCATHE	–; scathed,	SCHLEPP	–; schlepps
	scathes	SCHLOCK	–; schlocks
SCATT	–; scatts,	SCHMALZ	–; schmalzy
	scatty	SCHMEER	–; schmeers
SCATTED	–; –	SCHMO	–; schmoe
SCATTER	–; scatters	SCHMOE	–; schmoes
SCATTY	–; –	SCHMOOS	–; schmoose
SCAUP	–; scaups	SCHMUCK	–; schmucks
SCAUPER	–; scaupers	SCHNAPS	–; –
SCAUR	–; scaurs	SCHNOOK	–; schnooks
SCENA	–; scenas	SCHOLAR	–; scholars
SCEND	ascend;	SCHOLIA	–; –
	scends	SCHOOL	–; schools
SCENDED	–; –	SCHORL	–; schorls

SCHRIK	–; schriks	scorer,
SCHTICK	–; schticks	scores
SCHUIT	–; schuits	**SCORER** –; scorers
SCHUL	–; schuln	**SCORIA** –; scoriae
SCHUSS	–; –	**SCORIFY** –; –
SCHWA	–; schwas	**SCORING** –; –
SCIATIC	–; sciatica,	**SCORN** –; scorns
	sciatics	**SCORNED** –; –
SCIENCE	–; sciences	**SCORNER** –; scorners
SCILLA	–; scillas	**SCOT** ascot, escot;
SCION	–; scions	scots
SCISSOR	–; scissors	
SCLAFF	–; sclaffs	**SCOTCH** –; –
SCLERA	–; sclerae,	**SCOTER** –; scoters
	scleral,	**SCOTIA** –; scotias
	scleras	**SCOTOMA** –; scotomas
		SCOTS ascots,
SCOFF	–; scoffs	escots;–
SCOFFED	–; –	**SCOTTIE** –; scotties
SCOFFER	–; scoffers	**SCOUR** –; scours
SCOLD	–; scolds	**SCOURED** –; –
SCOLDED	–; –	**SCOURER** –; scourers
SCOLDER	–; scolders	**SCOURGE** –; scourged,
SCOLEX	–; –	scourger,
SCOLLOP	–; scollops	scourges
SCONCE	–; sconced,	
	sconces	**SCOUSE** –; scouses
SCONE	–; scones	**SCOUT** –; scouth,
SCOOP	–; scoops	scouts
SCOOPED	–; –	**SCOUTED** –; –
SCOOPER	–; scoopers	**SCOUTER** –; scouters
SCOOT	–; scoots	**SCOUTH** –; scouths
SCOOTED	–; –	**SCOW** –; scowl,
SCOOTER	–; scooters	scows
SCOP	–; scope,	**SCOWDER** –; scowders
	scops	**SCOWED** –; –
SCOPE	–; scopes	**SCOWING** –; –
SCOPULA	–; scopulae,	**SCOWL** –; scowls
	scopulas	**SCOWLED** –; –
SCORCH	–; –	**SCOWLER** –; scowlers
SCORE	–; scored,	**SCRAG** –; scrags
		SCRAGGY –; –

SCRAICH	-; scraichs	SCRIMP	-; scrimps, scrimpy
SCRAIGH	-; scraighs		
SCRAM	-; scrams	SCRIP	-; scrips, script
SCRAP	-; scrape, scraps		
		SCRIPT	-; scripts
SCRAPE	-; scraped, scraper, scrapes	SCRIVE	-; scrived, scrives
		SCROD	-; scrods
SCRAPER	-; scrapers	SCROGGY	-; -
SCRAPIE	-; scrapies	SCROLL	-; scrolls
SCRAPPY	-; -	SCROOGE	-; scrooges
SCRATCH	-; scratchy	SCROOP	-; scroops
SCRAWL	-; scrawls, scrawly	SCROTA	-; scrotal
		SCROTUM	-; scrotums
SCRAWNY	-; -	SCROUGE	-; scrouged, scrouges
SCREAK	-; screaks, screaky		
		SCRUB	-; scrubs
SCREAM	-; screams	SCRUBBY	-; -
SCREE	-; screed, screen, screes	SCRUFF	-; scruffs, scruffy
		SCRUM	-; scrums
SCREECH	-; screechy	SCRUNCH	-; -
SCREED	-; screeds	SCRUPLE	-; scrupled, scruples
SCREEN	-; screens		
SCREW	-; screws, screwy	SCUBA	-; scubas
		SCUD	-; scudi, scudo, scuds
SCREWED	-; -		
SCREWER	-; screwers	SCUDDED	-; -
SCRIBAL	-; -	SCUDO	escudo; -
SCRIBE	ascribe; scribed, scriber, scribes	SCUFF	-; scuffs
		SCUFFED	-; -
		SCUFFLE	-; scuffled, scuffler, scuffles
SCRIBED	ascribed; -		
SCRIBER	-; scribers	SCULK	-; sculks
SCRIBES	ascribes; -	SCULKED	-; -
SCRIEVE	-; scrieved, scrieves	SCULKER	-; sculkers
		SCULL	-; sculls
SCRIM	-; scrimp, scrims	SCULLED	-; -

SCULLER	–; scullers, scullery	**SEACOCK**	–; seacocks
SCULP	–; sculps, sculpt	**SEADOG**	–; seadogs
		SEAFOOD	–; seafoods
		SEAFOWL	–; seafowls
SCULPED	–; –	**SEAGRIT**	–; –
SCULPIN	–; sculpins	**SEAL**	–; seals
SCULPT	–; sculpts	**SEALANT**	–; sealants
SCUM	–; scums	**SEALED**	–; –
SCUMBLE	–; scumbled, scumbles	**SEALER**	–; sealers, sealery
SCUMMED	–; –	**SEALING**	–; –
SCUMMER	–; scummers	**SEAM**	–; seams, seamy
SCUMMY	–; –		
SCUNNER	–; scunners	**SEAMAN**	–; –
SCUP	–; scups	**SEAMARK**	–; seamarks
SCUPPER	–; scuppers	**SEAMED**	–; –
SCURF	–; scurfs, scurfy	**SEAMEN**	–; –
		SEAMER	–; seamers
SCURRIL	–; scurrile	**SEAMIER**	–; –
SCURRY	–; –	**SEAMING**	–; –
SCURVY	–; –	**SEANCE**	–; seances
SCUT	–; scuta, scute, scuts	**SEAPORT**	–; seaports
		SEAR	–; sears
SCUTAGE	–; scutages	**SEARCH**	–; –
SCUTATE	–; –	**SEARED**	–; –
SCUTCH	–; –	**SEARER**	–; –
SCUTE	–; scutes	**SEAREST**	–; –
SCUTTER	–; scutters	**SEARING**	–; –
SCUTTLE	–; scuttled, scuttles	**SEASICK**	–; –
		SEASIDE	–; seasides
SCUTUM	–; –	**SEASON**	–; seasons
SCYTHE	–; scythed, scythes	**SEAT**	–; seats
		SEATED	–; –
SEA	asea; seal, seam, sear, seas, seat	**SEATER**	–; seaters
		SEATING	–; seatings
		SEAWALL	–; seawalls
SEABAG	–; seabags	**SEAWAN**	–; seawans, seawant
SEABED	–; seabeds		
SEABIRD	–; seabirds	**SEAWANT**	–; seawants
SEABOOT	–; seaboots	**SEAWARD**	–; seawards

SEAWARE	–; seawares	SECURES	–; securest
SEAWAY	–; seaways	SEDAN	; sedans
SEAWEED	–; seaweeds	SEDARIM	–; –
SEBACIC	–; –	SEDATE	–; sedated,
SEBASIC	–; –		sedater,
SEBUM	–; sebums		sedates
SEC	–; secs, sect	SEDATES	–; sedatest
SECANT	–; secants	SEDER	–; seders
SECCO	–; seccos	SEDGE	–; sedges
SECEDE	–; seceded,	SEDGIER	–; –
	seceder,	SEDGY	–; –
	secedes	SEDILE	–; –
SECEDER	–; seceders	SEDILIA	–; –
SECERN	–; secerns	SEDUCE	–; seduced,
SECLUDE	–; secluded,		seducer,
	secludes		seduces
SECOND	–; seconde,	SEDUCER	–; seducers
	secondi,	SEDUM	–; sedums
	secondo,	SEE	–; seed,
	seconds		seek, seel,
SECONDE	–; seconder,		seem, seen,
	secondes		seep, seer,
SECPAR	–; secpars		sees
SECRECY	–; –	SEEABLE	–; –
SECRET	–; secrete,	SEED	–; seeds,
	secrets		seedy
SECRETE	; secreted,	SEEDBED	–; seedbeds
	secreter,	SEEDED	–; –
	secretes	SEEDER	–; seeders
SECT	–; sects	SEEDIER	–; –
SECTARY	–; –	SEEDILY	–; –
SECTILE	–; –	SEEDING	–; –
SECTION	–; sections	SEEDMAN	–; –
SECTOR	–; sectors	SEEDMEN	–; –
SECULAR	–; seculars	SEEDPOD	–; seedpods
SECUND	–; –	SEEING	–; seeings
SECURE	–; secured,	SEEK	–; seeks
	securer,	SEEKER	–; seekers
	secures	SEEKING	–; –
SECURER	–; securers		

SEEL	–; seels, seely	**SEISIN**	–; seising, seisins
SEELED	–; –	**SEISING**	–; seisings
SEELING	–; –	**SEISM**	–; seisms
SEEM	–; seems	**SEISMAL**	–; –
SEEMED	–; –	**SEISMIC**	–; –
SEEMER	–; seemers	**SEISOR**	–; seisors
SEEMING	–; seemings	**SEISURE**	–; seisures
SEEMLY	–; –	**SEIZE**	–; seized, seizer, seizes
SEEP	–; seeps, seepy		
SEEPAGE	–; seepages	**SEIZER**	–; seizers
SEEPED	–; –	**SEIZIN**	–; seizing, seizins
SEEPIER	–; –		
SEEPING	–; –	**SEIZING**	–; seizings
SEER	–; seers	**SEIZOR**	–; seizors
SEERESS	–; –	**SEIZURE**	–; seizures
SEESAW	–; seesaws	**SEJANT**	–; –
SEETHE	–; seethed, seethes	**SEL**	–; self, sell, sels
SEGETAL	–; –	**SELAH**	–; selahs
SEGGAR	–; seggars	**SELDOM**	–; –
SEGMENT	–; segments	**SELECT**	–; selects
SEGNI	–; –	**SELENIC**	–; –
SEGNO	–; segnos	**SELF**	–; selfs
SEGO	–; segos	**SELFDOM**	–; selfdoms
SEGUE	–; segued, segues	**SELFED**	–; –
		SELFING	–; –
SEI	–; seis	**SELFISH**	–; –
SEICHE	–; seiches	**SELL**	–; selle, sells
SEIDEL	–; seidels	**SELLE**	–; seller, selles
SEINE	–; seined, seiner, seines		
		SELLER	–; sellers
SEINER	–; seiners	**SELLING**	–; –
SEINING	–; –	**SELLOUT**	–; sellouts
SEISE	–; seised, seiser, seises	**SELSYN**	–; selsyns
		SELTZER	–; seltzers
SEISER	–; seisers	**SELVAGE**	–; selvaged, selvages
		SELVES	–; –

SEMATIC	–; –	SENNIT	–; sennits
SEME	, semen, semes	SENOPIA	–; senopias
		SENOR	–; senora, senors
SEMEME	–; sememes		
SEMEN	–; semens	SENORA	–; senoras
SEMI	–; semis	SENORES	–; –
SEMIDRY	–; –	SENSA	–; –
SEMIFIT	–; –	SENSATE	–; sensated, sensates
SEMILOG	–; –		
SEMIMAT	–; semimatt	SENSE	–; sensed, senses
SEMINA	–; seminal, seminar		
		SENSING	–; –
SEMINAR	–; seminars, seminary	SENSOR	–; sensors, sensory
SEMIPRO	–; semipros	SENSUAL	–; –
SEMIRAW	–; –	SENSUM	–; –
SEMISES	–; –	SENT	–; senti
SEMPLE	–; –	SENTRY	–; –
SEMPRE	–; –	SEPAL	–; sepals
SEN	–; send, sent	SEPALED	–; –
SENARY	–; –	SEPIA	–; sepias
SENATE	–; senates	SEPIC	–; –
SENATOR	–; senators	SEPOY	–; sepoys
SEND	–; sends	SEPPUKU	–; seppukus
SENDAL	–; sendals	SEPSES	asepses; –
SENDER	–; senders	SEPSIS	asepsis; –
SENDING	–; –	SEPT	–; septa, septs
SENDOFF	–; sendoffs		
SENECA	–; senecas	SEPTA	–; septal
SENECIO	–; senecios	SEPTATE	–; –
SENEGA	–; senegas	SEPTET	–; septets
SENGI	–; –	SEPTIC	–; septics
SENHOR	–; senhora, senhors	SEPTIME	–; septimes
		SEPTUM	–; –
SENHORA	–; senhoras	SEQUEL	–; sequela, sequels
SENILE	–; seniles		
SENIOR	–; seniors	SEQUELA	–; sequelae
SENITI	–; –	SEQUENT	–; sequents
SENNA	–; sennas	SEQUIN	–; sequins
SENNET	–; sennets	SEQUOIA	–; sequoias

SER	user; sera, sere, serf, sers	**SERMON**	–; sermons
		SEROSA	–; serosae, serosal, serosas
SERA	–; serac, serai, seral		
SERAC	–; seracs	**SEROUS**	–; –
SERAI	–; serail, serais	**SEROW**	–; serows
		SERPENT	–; serpents
		SERPIGO	–; –
SERAIL	–; serails	**SERRATE**	–; serrated, serrates
SERAPE	–; serapes		
SERAPH	–; seraphs	**SERRIED**	–; –
SERDAB	–; serdabs	**SERRIES**	–; –
SERE	–; sered, serer, seres	**SERRY**	–; –
		SERS	users; –
SEREIN	–; sereins	**SERUM**	–; serums
SERENE	–; serener, serenes	**SERUMAL**	–; –
		SERVAL	–; servals
SERENES	–; serenest	**SERVANT**	–; servants
SERES	–; serest	**SERVE**	–; served, server, serves
SERF	–; serfs		
SERFAGE	–; serfages		
SERFDOM	–; serfdoms	**SERVER**	–; servers
SERFISH	–; –	**SERVICE**	–; serviced, servicer, services
SERGE	–; serges		
SERGING	–; sergings		
SERIAL	–; serials	**SERVILE**	–; –
SERIATE	–; seriated, seriates	**SERVING**	–; servings
		SERVO	–; servos
SERICIN	–; sericins	**SESAME**	–; sesames
SERIEMA	–; seriemas	**SESSILE**	–; –
SERIES	–; –	**SESSION**	–; sessions
SERIF	–; serifs	**SESTET**	–; sestets
SERIN	–; serine, sering, serins	**SESTINA**	–; sestinas
		SESTINE	–; sestines
SERINE	eserine; serines	**SET**	–; seta, sets
		SETA	–; setae, setal
SERINES	eserines; –		
SERING	–; seringa	**SETBACK**	–; setbacks
SERINGA	–; seringas	**SETLINE**	–; setlines
SERIOUS	–; –	**SETOFF**	–; setoffs

SETON	–; setons	SEXT	–; sexto,
SETOSE	,		sexis
SETOUS	–; –	SEXTAIN	–; sextains
SETOUT	–; setouts	SEXTAN	–; sextans,
SETTEE	–; settees		sextant
SETTER	–; setters		
SETTING	–; settings	SEXTANT	–; sextants
SETTLE	–; settled,	SEXTET	–; sextets
	settler,	SEXTILE	–; sextiles
	settles	SEXTO	–; sexton,
			sextos
SETTLER	–; settlers	SEXTON	–; sextons
SETTLOR	–; settlors	SEXUAL	asexual; –
SETUP	–; setups	SFERICS	–; –
SEVEN	–; sevens	SFUMATO	–; sfumatos
SEVENTH	–; sevenths	SH	ash; she,
SEVENTY	–; –		shh, shy
SEVER	–; severe,		
	severs	SHABBY	–; –
SEVERAL	–; severals	SHACK	–; shacko,
SEVERE	–; severed,		shacks
	severer	SHACKLE	–; shackled,
SEW	–; sewn,		shackler,
	sews		shackles
		SHACKO	–; shackos
SEWAGE	–; sewages	SHAD	–, shade,
SEWAN	–; sewans		shads,
SEWAR	–; sewars		shady
SEWED	–; –	SHADE	–; shaded,
SEWER	–; sewers		shader,
SEWING	–; sewings		shades
SEX	–; sext, sexy	SHADER	–; shaders
SEXED	–; –	SHADFLY	–; –
SEXES	–; –	SHADIER	–; –
SEXIER	–; –	SHADILY	–; –
SEXIEST	–; –	SHADING	–; shadings
SEXILY	–; –	SHADOOF	–; shadoofs
SEXING	–; –	SHADOW	–; shadows,
SEXISM	–; sexisms		shadowy
SEXIST	–; sexists	SHADUF	–; shadufs
SEXLESS	–; –	SHAFT	–; shafts
SEXPOT	–; sexpots	SHAFTED	–; –

SHAG	–; shags	**SHAMMAS**	–;
SHAGGED	–; –		shammash
SHAGGY	–; –	**SHAMMED**	–; –
SHAH	–; shahs	**SHAMMER**	–; shammers
SHAHDOM	–; shahdoms	**SHAMMES**	–; –
SHAIRD	–; shairds	**SHAMMOS**	–; –
SHAIRN	–; shairns	**SHAMMY**	–; –
SHAITAN	–; shaitans	**SHAMOIS**	–; –
SHAKE	–; shaken,	**SHAMOY**	–; shamoys
	shaker,	**SHAMPOO**	–; shampoos
	shakes	**SHAMUS**	–; –
SHAKER	–; shakers	**SHANDY**	–; –
SHAKEUP	–; shakeups	**SHANK**	–; shanks
SHAKIER	–; –	**SHANKED**	–; –
SHAKILY	–; –	**SHANTEY**	–; shanteys
SHAKING	–; –	**SHANTI**	–; shantih,
SHAKO	–; shakos		shantis
SHAKOES	–; –	**SHANTIH**	–; shantihs
SHAKY	–; –	**SHANTY**	–; –
SHALE	–; shaled,	**SHAPE**	–; shaped,
	shales		shapen,
SHALIER	–; –		shaper,
SHALL	–; –		shapes
SHALLOP	–; shallops	**SHAPELY**	–; –
SHALLOT	–; shallots	**SHAPER**	–; shapers
SHALLOW	–; shallows	**SHAPEUP**	–; shapeups
SHALOM	–; –	**SHAPING**	–; –
SHALT	–; –	**SHARD**	–; shards
SHALY	–; –	**SHARE**	–; shared,
SHAM	–; shame,		sharer,
	shams		shares
SHAMAN	–; shamans	**SHARER**	–; sharers
SHAMBLE	–;	**SHARIF**	–; sharifs
	shambled,	**SHARING**	–; –
	shambles	**SHARK**	–; sharks
SHAME	–; shamed,	**SHARKED**	–; –
	shames	**SHARKER**	–; sharkers
SHAMED	ashamed; –	**SHARN**	–; sharns,
SHAMING	–; –		sharny

SHARP	–; sharps, sharpy	SHEARED	–; –
SHARPED	–; –	SHEATH	–; sheathe, sheaths
SHARPEN	–; sharpens	SHEATHE	–; sheathed, sheather
SHARPER	–; sharpers		
SHARPIE	–; sharpies	SHEAVE	–; sheaved, sheaves
SHARPLY	–; –		
SHASLIK	–; shasliks	SHEBANG	–; shebangs
SHATTER	–; shatters	SHEBEAN	–; shebeans
SHAUGH	–; shaughs	SHEBEEN	–; shebeens
SHAUL	–; shauls	SHED	ashed; sheds
SHAULED	–; –	SHEDDED	–; –
SHAVE	–; shaved, shaven, shaver, shaves	SHEDDER	–; shedders
		SHEEN	–; sheens, sheeny
SHAVER	–; shavers	SHEENED	–; –
SHAVIE	–; shavies	SHEENEY	–; sheeneys
SHAVING	–; shavings	SHEENIE	–; sheenies
SHAW	pshaw; shawl, shawn, shaws	SHEEP	–; –
		SHEER	–; sheers
		SHEERED	–; –
		SHEERER	–; –
		SHEERLY	–; –
SHAWED	pshawed; –	SHEET	–; sheets
SHAWING	–; –	SHEETED	–; –
SHAWL	–; shawls	SHEETER	–; sheeters
SHAWLED	–; –	SHEEVE	–; sheeves
SHAWM	–; shawms	SHEGETZ	–; –
SHAWS	pshaws; –	SHEIK	–; sheikh, sheiks
SHAY	–; shays		
SHE	shea, shed, shes, shew; –	SHEIKH	–; sheikhs
		SHEITAN	–; sheitans
		SHEKEL	–; shekels
SHEA	–; sheaf, sheal, shear, sheas	SHELF	–; –
		SHELL	–; shells, shelly
SHEAF	–; sheafs		
SHEAFED	–; –	SHELLAC	–; shellack, shellacs
SHEAL	–; sheals		
SHEAR	–; shears	SHELLED	–; –
		SHELLER	–; shellers

SHELTER	–; shelters	**SHIFTED**	–; –
SHELTIE	–; shelties	**SHIFTER**	–; shifters
SHELTY	–; –	**SHIKAR**	–; shikari,
SHELVE	–; shelved,		shikars
	shelver,	**SHIKARI**	–; shikaris
	shelves	**SHIKSA**	–; shiksas
SHELVER	–; shelvers	**SHIKSE**	–; shikses
SHELVY	–; –	**SHILL**	–; shills
SHEND	–; shends	**SHILLED**	–; –
SHENT	–; –	**SHILPIT**	–; –
SHEOL	–; sheols	**SHILY**	–; –
SHERBET	–; sherbets	**SHIM**	–; shims
SHERD	–; sherds	**SHIMMED**	–; –
SHEREEF	–; shereefs	**SHIMMER**	–; shimmers,
SHERIF	–; sheriff,		shimmery
	sherifs	**SHIMMY**	–; –
SHERIFF	–; sheriffs	**SHIN**	–; shine,
SHEROOT	–; sheroots		shins, shiny
SHERRIS	–; –	**SHINDIG**	–; shindigs
SHERRY	–; –	**SHINDY**	–; shindys
SHES	ashes; –	**SHINE**	–; shined,
SHEUCH	–; sheuchs		shiner, shines
SHEUGH	–; sheughs	**SHINER**	–; shiners
SHEW	–; shewn,	**SHINGLE**	–; shingled
	shews		shingler,
SHEWED	–; –		shingles
SHEWER	–; shewers	**SHINGLY**	–; –
SHEWING	–; –	**SHINIER**	–; –
SHH	–; –	**SHINILY**	–; –
SHIBAH	–; shibahs	**SHINING**	–; –
SHICKSA	–; shicksas	**SHINNED**	–; –
SHIED	–; –	**SHINNEY**	–; shinney
SHIEL	–; shield,	**SHINNY**	–; –
	shiels	**SHIP**	–; ships
SHIELD	–; shields	**SHIPLAP**	–; shiplaps
SHIER	ashier; shiers	**SHIPMAN**	–; –
SHIES	–; shiest	**SHIPMEN**	–; shipmen
SHIEST	ashiest; –	**SHIPPED**	–; –
SHIFT	–; shifts,	**SHIPPEN**	–; shippens
	shifty	**SHIPPER**	–; shippers

SHIPPON	–; shippons	shoepack,
SHIPWAY	–; shipways	shoepacs
SHIRE	–; shires	**SHOER**	–; shoers
SHIRK	–; shirks	**SHOEING**	–; –
SHIRKED	–; –	**SHOFAR**	–; shofars
SHIRKER	–; shirkers	**SHOG**	–; shogs
SHIRR	–; shirrs	**SHOGGED**	–; –
SHIRRED	–; –	**SHOGUN**	–; shoguns
SHIRT	–; shirts,	**SHOJI**	–; shojis
	shirty	**SHOLOM**	–; –
SHIST	–; shists	**SHONE**	–; –
SHITTAH	–; shittahs	**SHOO**	–; shook,
SHITTIM	–; shittims		shool,
SHIV	–; shiva,		shoon,
	shive, shivs		shoos, shoot
SHIVA	–; shivah,	**SHOOED**	–; –
	shivas	**SHOOFLY**	–; –
SHIVAH	–; shivahs	**SHOOK**	–; shooks
SHIVE	–; shiver,	**SHOOL**	–; shools
	shives	**SHOOLED**	–; –
SHIVER	–; shivers,	**SHOOT**	–; shoots
	shivery	**SHOOTER**	–; shooters
SHLOCK	–; shlocks	**SHOP**	–; shops
SHMO	–; –	**SHOPBOY**	–; shopboys
SHMOES	–; –	**SHOPHAR**	–; shophars
SHNAPS	–; –	**SHOPMAN**	–; –
SHOAL	–; shoals,	**SHOPMEN**	–; –
	shoaly	**SHOPPE**	–; shopped,
SHOALED	–; –		shopper,
SHOALER	–; –		shoppes
SHOAT	–; shoats	**SHOPPER**	–; shoppers
SHOCK	–; shocks	**SHORAN**	–; shorans
SHOCKED	–; –	**SHORE**	ashore;
SHOCKER	–; shockers		shored,
SHOD	–; –		shores
SHODDEN	–; –	**SHORING**	–; shorings
SHODDY	–; –	**SHORL**	–; shorls
SHOE	–; shoed,	**SHORN**	–; –
	shoer, shoes	**SHORT**	–; shorts
SHOEPAC	–;		shorty

SHORTED	–; –	**SHRI**	–; shris
SHORTEN	–; shortens	**SHRIEK**	–; shrieks,
SHORTIA	–; shortias		shrieky
SHORTIE	–; shorties	**SHRIEVE**	–; shrieved,
SHORTLY	–; –		shrieves
SHOT	–; shote,	**SHRIFT**	–; shrifts
	shots, shott	**SHRIKE**	–; shrikes
SHOTE	–; shotes	**SHRILL**	–; shrills,
SHOTGUN	–; shotguns		shrilly
SHOTT	–; shotts	**SHRIMP**	–; shrimps.
SHOTTED	–; –		shrimpy
SHOTTEN	–; –	**SHRINE**	–; shrined,
SHOULD	–; –		shrines
SHOUT	–; shouts	**SHRINK**	–; shrinks
SHOUTED	–; –	**SHRIVE**	–; shrivel,
SHOUTER	–; shouters		shriven,
SHOVE	–; shoved,		shriver,
	shovel,		shrives
	shover,	**SHRIVEL**	–; shrivels
	shoves	**SHRIVER**	–; shrivers
SHOVEL	–; shovels	**SHROFF**	–; shroffs
SHOVER	–; shovers	**SHROUD**	–; shrouds
SHOVING	–; –	**SHROVE**	–; –
SHOW	–; shown,	**SHRUB**	–; shrubs
	shows,	**SHRUBBY**	–; –
	showy	**SHRUG**	–; shrugs
SHOWED	–; –	**SHRUNK**	–; –
SHOWER	–; showers,	**SHTETEL**	–; –
	showery	**SHTETL**	–; –
SHOWIER	–; –	**SHTICK**	–; shticks
SHOWILY	–; –	**SHUCK**	–; shucks
SHOWING	–; showings	**SHUCKED**	–; –
SHOWMAN	–; –	**SHUCKER**	–; shuckers
SHOWMEN	–; –	**SHUDDER**	–; shudders
SHOWOFF	–; showoffs		shuddery
SHRANK	–; –	**SHUFFLE**	–; shuffled
SHRED	–; shreds		shuffler,
SHREW	–; shrewd,		shuffles
	shrews	**SHUL**	–; shuln,
SHREWED	–; –		shuls

SHUN	–; shuns, shunt	**SIBYL**	–; sibyls
		SIBYLIC	–; –
SHUNNED	–; –	**SIC**	–; sice, sick, sics
SHUNNER	–; shunners		
SHUNT	–; shunts	**SICCAN**	–; –
SHUNTED	–; –	**SICE**	–; sices
SHUNTER	–; shunters	**SICK**	–; sicks
SHUSH	–; –	**SICKBAY**	–; sickbays
SHUSHED	–; –	**SICKBED**	–; sickbeds
SHUSHES	–; –	**SICKED**	–; –
SHUT	–; shute, shuts	**SICKEN**	–; sickens
		SICKER	–; –
SHUTE	–; shuted, shutes	**SICKEST**	–; –
		SICKING	–; –
SHUTEYE	–; shuteyes	**SICKISH**	–; –
SHUTOFF	–; shutoffs	**SICKLE**	–; sickled, sickles
SHUTOUT	–; shutouts		
SHUTTER	–; shutters	**SICKLY**	–; –
SHUTTLE	–; shuttled, shuttles	**SIDDUR**	–; siddurs
		SIDE	aside; sided, sides
SHY	ashy; –		
SHYER	–; shyers	**SIDEARM**	–; –
SHYEST	–; –	**SIDECAR**	–; sidecars
SHYING	–; –	**SIDES**	asides; –
SHYLOCK	–; shylocks	**SIDEWAY**	–; sideways
SHYLY	–; –	**SIDING**	–; sidings
SHYNESS	–; –	**SIDLE**	–; sidled, sidler, sidles
SHYSTER	–; shysters		
SI	psi; sib, sic, sim, sin, sip, sir, sis, sit, six	**SIDLER**	–; sidlers
		SIDLING	–; –
		SIEGE	–; sieged, sieges
SIAL	–; sials	**SIEGING**	–; –
SIALIC	–; –	**SIENITE**	–; sienites
SIALOID	–; –	**SIENNA**	–; siennas
SIAMANG	–; siamangs	**SIERRA**	–; sierran, sierras
SIAMESE	–; siameses		
SIB	–; sibb, sibs	**SIESTA**	–; siestas
SIBB	–; sibbs	**SIEUR**	–; sieurs
SIBLING	–; siblings		

SIEVE	–; sieved, sieves	**SILAGE**	–; silages
SIEVING	–; –	**SILANE**	–; silanes
SIFT	–; sifts	**SILD**	–; silds
SIFTED	–; –	**SILENCE**	–; silenced, silencer, silences
SIFTER	–; sifters		
SIFTING	–; siftings		
SIGANID	–; siganids	**SILENI**	–; –
SIGH	–; sighs, sight	**SILENT**	–; silents
		SILENUS	–; –
SIGHED	–; –	**SILESIA**	–; silesias
SIGHER	–; sighers	**SILEX**	–; –
SIGHING	–; –	**SILEXES**	–; –
SIGHT	–; sights	**SILICA**	–; silicas
SIGHTED	–; –	**SILICIC**	–; –
SIGHTER	–; sighters	**SILICLE**	–; silicles
SIGHTLY	–; –	**SILICON**	–; silicone, silicons
SIGIL	–; sigils		
SIGLOI	–; –	**SILIQUA**	–; siliquae
SIGLOS	–; –	**SILIQUE**	–; siliques
SIGMA	–; sigmas	**SILK**	–; silks, silky
SIGMATE	–; –	**SILKED**	–; –
SIGMOID	–; sigmoids	**SILKEN**	–; –
SIGN	–; signs	**SILKIER**	–; –
SIGNAL	–; signals	**SILKILY**	–; –
SIGNED	–; –	**SILKING**	–; –
SIGNER	–; signers	**SILL**	–; sills, silly
SIGNET	–; signets	**SILLER**	–; sillers
SIGNIFY	–; –	**SILLIER**	–; –
SIGNING	–; –	**SILLIES**	–; silliest
SIGNIOR	–; signiors, signiory	**SILLILY**	–; –
		SILO	–; silos
SIGNOR	–; signora, signore, signori, signors, signory	**SILOED**	–; –
		SILOING	–; –
		SILT	–; silts, silty
		SILTED	–; –
		SILTIER	–; –
SIGNORA	–; signoras	**SILTING**	–; –
SIKE	–; siker, sikes	**SILURID**	–; silurids
		SILVA	–; silvae, silvan, silvas

SILVAN	–; silvans	**SINFUL**	–; –
SILVER	–; silvern, silvers, silvery	**SING**	using; singe, sings
SILVICS	–; –	**SINGE**	–; singed, singer, singes
SIM	–; sima, simp, sims	**SINGER**	–; singers
SIMA	–; simar, simas	**SINGING**	–; –
SIMAR	–; simars	**SINGLE**	–; singled, singles, singlet
SIMIAN	–; simians		
SIMILAR	–; –	**SINGLET**	–; singlets
SIMILE	–; similes	**SINGLY**	–; –
SIMIOID	–; –	**SINH**	–; sinhs
SIMIOUS	–; –	**SINK**	–; sinks
SIMITAR	–; simitars	**SINKAGE**	–; sinkages
SIMLIN	–; simlins	**SINKER**	–; sinkers
SIMMER	–; simmers	**SINKING**	–; –
SIMNEL	–; simnels	**SINLESS**	–; –
SIMONY	–; –	**SINNED**	–; –
SIMOOM	–; simooms	**SINNER**	–; sinners
SIMOON	–; simoons	**SINNING**	–; –
SIMP	–; simps	**SINOPIA**	–; sinopias
SIMPER	–; simpers	**SINOPIE**	–; –
SIMPLE	; simpler, simples, simplex	**SINSYNE**	–; –
		SINTER	–; sinters
SIMPLES	–; simplest	**SINUATE**	–; sinuated, sinuates
SIMPLY	–; –		
SIMULAR	–; simulars	**SINUOUS**	–; –
SIN	–; sine, sing, sinh, sink, sins	**SINUS**	–; –
		SINUSES	–; –
		SIP	–; sipe, sips
SINCE	–; –	**SIPE**	–; siped, sipes
SINCERE	–; sincerer		
SINE	–; sines, sinew	**SIPHON**	–; siphons
		SIPING	–; –
SINEW	–; sinews, sinewy	**SIPPED**	–; –
		SIPPER	–; sippers
		SIPPET	–; sippets
SINEWED	–; –	**SIPPING**	–; –

SIR	–; sire, sirs	**SITUS**	–; –
SIRDAR	–; sirdars	**SITUSES**	–; –
SIRE	–; sired, siree, siren, sires	**SIVER**	–; sivers
		SIX	–; –
		SIXES	–; –
SIREE	–; sirees	**SIXFOLD**	–; –
SIREN	–; sirens	**SIXMO**	–; sixmos
SIRING	–; –	**SIXTE**	–; sixtes
SIRLOIN	–; sirloins	**SIXTEEN**	–; sixteens
SIROCCO	–; siroccos	**SIXTH**	–; sixths
SIRRA	–; sirrah, sirras	**SIXTHLY**	–; –
		SIXTIES	–; –
SIRRAH	–; sirrahs	**SIXTY**	–; –
SIRREE	–; sirrees	**SIZABLE**	–; –
SIRUP	–; sirups, sirupy	**SIZABLY**	–; –
		SIZAR	–; sizars
SIS	psis; –	**SIZE**	–; sized, sizer, sizes
SISAL	–; sisals		
SISES	–; –	**SIZER**	–; sizers
SISKIN	–; siskins	**SIZIER**	–; –
SISSIER	–; –	**SIZIEST**	–; –
SISSIES	–; sissiest	**SIZING**	–; sizings
SISSY	–; –	**SIZY**	–; –
SISTER	–; sisters	**SIZZLE**	–; sizzled, sizzler, sizzles
SISTRA	–; –		
SISTRUM	–; sistrums		
SIT	–; sita, site, sith, siti, sits	**SIZZLER**	–; sizzlers
		SKAG	–; skags
SITAR	–; sitars	**SKALD**	–; skalds
SITE	–; sited, sites	**SKALDIC**	–; –
		SKAT	–; skate, skats
SITH	–; –		
SITHENS	–; –	**SKATE**	–; skated, skater, skates
SITI	–; –		
SITING	–; –		
SITTEN	–; –	**SKATER**	–; skaters
SITTER	–; sitters	**SKATING**	–; skatings
SITTING	–; sittings	**SKATOL**	–; skatole, skatols
SITUATE	–; situated, situates		
		SKATOLE	–; skatoles

SKEAN	–; skeane, skeans	**SKIED**	–; –
		SKIER	–; skiers
SKEANF	, skeaneu	**SKIES**	–; –
SKEE	–; skeed, skeen, skees, skeet	**SKIEY**	–; –
		SKIFF	–; skiffs
		SKIFFLE	–; skiffled, skiffles
SKEEING	–; –		
SKEEN	–; skeens	**SKIING**	–; skiings
SKEET	–; skeets	**SKILFUL**	–; –
SKEETER	–; skeeters	**SKILL**	–; skills
SKEG	–; skegs	**SKILLED**	–; –
SKEIGH	–; –	**SKILLET**	–; skillets
SKEIN	–; skeins	**SKIM**	–; skimo, skimp, skims
SKEINED	–; –		
SKELLUM	–; skellums		
SKELP	–; skelps	**SKIMMED**	–; –
SKELPED	–; –	**SKIMMER**	–; skimmers
SKELPIT	–; –	**SKIMO**	–; skimos
SKELTER	–; skelters	**SKIMP**	–; skimps, skimpy
SKENE	–; skenes		
SKEP	–; skeps	**SKIMPED**	–; –
SKEPSIS	–; –	**SKIN**	–; skink, skins, skint
SKEPTIC	–; skeptics		
SKERRY	–; –	**SKINFUL**	–; skinfuls
SKETCH	–; sketchy	**SKINK**	–; skinks
SKEW	askew; skews	**SKINKED**	–; –
SKEWED	,	**SKINKER**	–; skinkers
SKEWER	–; skewers	**SKINNED**	–; –
SKEWING	–; –	**SKINNER**	–; skinners
SKI	–; skid, skip, skin, skis, skit	**SKINNY**	–; –
		SKIP	–; skips
SKIABLE	–; –	**SKIPPED**	–; –
SKIBOB	–; skibobs	**SKIPPER**	–; skippers
SKID	–; skids	**SKIPPET**	–; skippets
SKIDDED	–; –	**SKIRL**	–; skirls
SKIDDER	–; skidders	**SKIRLED**	–; –
SKIDDOO	–; skiddoos	**SKIRR**	–; skirrs
SKIDDY	–; –	**SKIRRED**	–; –
SKIDOO	–; skidoos	**SKIRRET**	–; skirrets
SKIDWAY	–; skidways	**SKIRT**	–; skirts
		SKIRTED	–; –

SKIRTER	–; skirters	**SKYMAN**	–; –
SKIT	–; skite, skits	**SKYMEN**	–; –
SKITE	–; skited, skiter	**SKYPHOI**	–; –
		SKYPHOS	–; –
SKITTER	–; skitters, skittery	**SKYSAIL**	–; skysails
		SKYWARD	–; skywards
SKITING	–; –	**SKYWAY**	–; skyways
SKITTLE	–; skittles	**SLAB**	–; slabs
SKIVE	–; skived, skiver, skives	**SLABBED**	–; –
		SLABBER	–; slabbers, slabbery
SKIVER	–; skivers		
SKIVING	–; –	**SLACK**	–; slacks
SKIVVY	–; –	**SLACKED**	–; –
SKIWEAR	–; skiwears	**SLACKEN**	–; slackens
SKLENT	–; sklents	**SLACKER**	–; slackers
SKOAL	–; skoals	**SLACKLY**	–; –
SKOALED	–; –	**SLAG**	–; slags
SKOOKUM	–; –	**SLAGGED**	–; –
SKREEGH	–; skreeghs	**SLAGGY**	–; –
SKREIGH	–; skreighs	**SLAIN**	–; –
SKUA	–; skuas	**SLAKE**	–; slaked, slaker, slakes
SKULK	–; skulks		
SKULKED	–; –	**SLAKER**	–; slakers
SKULKER	–; skulkers	**SLAKING**	–; –
SKULLED	–; –	**SLALOM**	–; slaloms
SKULL	–; skull	**SLAM**	–; slams
SKUNK	–; skunks	**SLAMMED**	–; –
SKUNKED	–; –	**SLANDER**	islander; slanders
SKY	–; –		
SKYCAP	–; skycaps	**SLANG**	–; slangs, slangy
SKYDIVE	–; skydived, skydiver, skydives		
		SLANGED	–; –
		SLANK	–; –
SKYED	–; –	**SLANT**	aslant; slants
SKYEY	–; –	**SLANTED**	–; –
SKYHOOK	–; skyhooks	**SLAP**	–; slaps
SKYING	–; –	**SLAPPED**	–; –
SKYJACK	–; skyjacks	**SLAPPER**	–; slappers
SKYLARK	–; skylarks	**SLASH**	–; –
SKYLINE	–; skylines	**SLASHED**	–; –

SLASHER	–; slashers	**SLEEP**	asleep;
SLASHES	–; –		sleeps,
SLAT	–; slate,		sleepy
	slats, slaty	**SLEEPER**	–; sleepers
SLATCH	–; –	**SLEET**	–; sleets,
SLATE	–; slated,		sleety
	slater, slates	**SLEETED**	–; –
SLATER	–; slaters	**SLEEVE**	–; sleeved,
SLATHER	–; slathers		sleeves
SLATIER	–; –	**SLEIGH**	–; sleighs,
SLATING	–; slatings		sleight
SLATTED	–; –	**SLEIGHT**	–; sleights
SLAVE	–; slaved,	**SLENDER**	–; –
	slaver,	**SLEPT**	–; –
	slaves,	**SLEUTH**	–; sleuths
	slavey	**SLEW**	–; slews
SLAVER	–; slavers,	**SLEWED**	–; –
	slavery	**SLEWING**	–; –
SLAVEY	–; slaveys	**SLICE**	–; sliced,
SLAVING	–; –		slicer, slices
SLAVISH	–; –	**SLICER**	–; slicers
SLAW	–; slaws	**SLICING**	–; –
SLAY	–; slays	**SLICK**	–; slicks
SLAYER	–; slayers	**SLICKED**	–; –
SLAYING	–; –	**SLICKER**	–; slickers
SLEAVE	–; sleaved,	**SLICKLY**	–; –
	sleaves	**SLID**	–; slide
SLEAZY	–; –	**SLIDDEN**	–; –
SLED	isled; sleds	**SLIDE**	–; slider,
SLEDDED	–; –		slides
SLEDDER	–; sledders	**SLIDER**	–; sliders
SLEDGE	–; sledged,	**SLIDING**	–; –
	sledges	**SLIER**	–; –
SLEEK	–; sleeks,	**SLIEST**	–; –
	sleeky	**SLIGHT**	–; slights
SLEEKED	–; –	**SLILY**	–; –
SLEEKEN	–; sleekens	**SLIM**	–; slime,
SLEEKER	–; –		slims, slimy
SLEEKIT	–; –	**SLIME**	–; slimed,
SLEEKLY	–; –		slimes

SLIMER	–; slimers	**SLOOP**	–; sloops
SLIMIER	–; –	**SLOP**	–; slope,
SLIMILY	–; –		slops
SLIMING	–; –	**SLOPE**	aslope;
SLIMLY	–; –		sloped,
SLIMMED	–; –		sloper,
SLIMMER	–; –		slopes
SLIMPSY	–; –	**SLOPER**	–; slopers
SLING	isling; slings	**SLOPPED**	–; –
SLINGER	–; slingers	**SLOPPY**	–; –
SLINK	–; slinks,	**SLOSH**	–; sloshy
	slinky	**SLOSHED**	–; –
SLIP	–; slipe,	**SLOSHES**	–; –
	slips, slipt	**SLOT**	–; sloth,
SLIPE	–; sliped,		slots
	slipes	**SLOTH**	–; sloths
SLIPING	–; –	**SLOTTED**	–; –
SLIPOUT	–; slipouts	**SLOUCH**	–; slouchy
SLIPPED	–; –	**SLOUGH**	–; sloughs,
SLIPPER	–; slippers,		sloughy
	slippery	**SLOVEN**	–; slovens
SLIPPY	–; –	**SLOW**	–; slows
SLIPUP	–; slipups	**SLOWED**	–; –
SLIPWAY	–; slipways	**SLOWER**	–; –
SLIT	–; slits	**SLOWING**	–; –
SLITHER	–; slithers,	**SLOWISH**	–; –
	slithery	**SLOWLY**	–; –
SLITTED	–; –	**SLOYD**	–; sloyds
SLITTER	–; slitters	**SLUB**	–; slubs
SLIVER	–; slivers	**SLUBBED**	–; –
SLOB	–; slobs	**SLUBBER**	–; slubbers
SLOBBER	–; slobbers,	**SLUDGE**	–; sludges
	slobbery	**SLUDGY**	–; –
SLOE	–; sloes	**SLUE**	–; slued,
SLOG	–; slogs		slues
SLOGAN	–; slogans	**SLUFF**	–; sluffs
SLOGGED	–; –	**SLUFFED**	–; –
SLOGGER	–; sloggers	**SLUG**	–; slugs
SLOID	–; sloids	**SLUGGED**	–; –
SLOJD	–; slojds	**SLUGGER**	–; sluggers

SLUICE	–; sluiced, sluices	smalto, smalts
SLUICY	–; –	
SLUING	–; –	**SMALTO**	–; smaltos
SLUM	–; slump, slums	**SMARAGD**	–; smaragde, smaragds
SLUMBER	–; slumbers, slumbery	**SMARM**	–; smarms, smarmy
SLUMGUM	–; slumgums	**SMART**	–; smarts, smarty
SLUMMED	–; –	
SLUMMER	–; slummers	**SMARTED**	–; –
SLUMMY	–; –	**SMARTEN**	–; smartens
SLUMP	–; slumps	**SMARTER**	–; –
SLUMPED	–; –	**SMARTIE**	–; smarties
SLUNG	–; –	**SMARTLY**	–; –
SLUNK	–; –	**SMASH**	–; –
SLUR	–; slurb, slurp, slurs	**SMASHED**	–; –
		SMASHER	–; smashers
SLURB	–; slurbs	**SMASHES**	–; –
SLURBAN	–; –	**SMASHUP**	–; smashups
SLURP	–; slurps	**SMATTER**	–; smatters
SLURPED	–; –	**SMAZE**	–; smazes
SLURRED	–; –	**SMEAR**	–; smears, smeary
SLURRY	–; –	
SLUSH	–; slushy	**SMEARED**	–; –
SLUSHED	–; slushed	**SMEARER**	–; smearers
SLUSHES	–; –	**SMECTIC**	–; –
SLUT	–; sluts	**SMEDDUM**	–; smeddums
SLY	–; –	
SLYER	–; –	**SMEEK**	–; smeeks
SLYEST	–; –	**SMEEKED**	–; –
SLYLY	–; –	**SMEGMA**	–; smegmas
SLYNESS	–; –	**SMELL**	–; smells, smelly
SLYPE	–; slypes	
SMACK	–; smacks	**SMELLED**	–; –
SMACKED	–; –	**SMELLER**	–; smellers
SMACKER	–; smackers	**SMELT**	–; smelts
SMALL	–; smalls	**SMELTED**	–; –
SMALLER	–; –	**SMELTER**	–; smelters, smeltery
SMALT	–; smalti,	

SMERK	–; smerks	**SMOOTH**	–; smooths, smoothy
SMERKED	–; –		
SMEW	–; smews	**SMOTE**	–; –
SMIDGEN	–; smidgens	**SMOTHER**	–; smothers, smothery
SMIDGIN	–; smidgins		
SMILAX	–; –	**SMUDGE**	–; smudged, smudges
SMILE	–; smiled, smiler, smiles	**SMUDGY**	–; –
SMILER	–; smilers	**SMUG**	–; –
SMILING	–; –	**SMUGGER**	–; –
SMIRCH	–; –	**SMUGGLE**	–; smuggled, smuggler, smuggles
SMIRK	–; smirks, smirky		
SMIRKED	–; –	**SMUGLY**	–; –
SMIRKER	–; smirkers	**SMUT**	–; smuts
SMIT	–; smite	**SMUTCH**	–; smutchs, smutchy
SMITE	–; smiter, smites		
SMITER	–; smiters	**SMUTTED**	–; –
SMITH	–; smiths, smithy	**SMUTTY**	–; –
		SNACK	–; snacks
SMITING	–; –	**SNACKED**	–; –
SMITTEN	–; –	**SNAFFLE**	–; snaffled, snaffles
SMOCK	–; smocks		
SMOCKED	–; –	**SNAFU**	–; snafus
SMOG	–; smogs	**SNAFUED**	–; –
SMOGGY	–; –	**SNAG**	–; snags
SMOKE	–; smoked, smoker, smokes, smokey	**SNAGGED**	–; –
		SNAGGY	–; –
		SNAIL	–; snails
		SNAILED	–; –
SMOKER	–; smokers	**SNAKE**	–; snaked, snakes
SMOKIER	–; –		
SMOKILY	–; –	**SNAKIER**	–; –
SMOKING	–; –	**SNAKILY**	–; –
SMOKY	–; –	**SNAKING**	–; –
SMOLDER	–; smolders	**SNAKY**	–; –
SMOLT	–; smolts	**SNAP**	–; snaps
SMOOCH	–; smoochy	**SNAPPED**	–; –
		SNAPPER	–; snappers
		SNAPPY	–; –

SNARE	–; snared, snarer snares	SNIB	–; snibs
SNARER	–; snarers	SNIBBED	–; –
SNARING	–; –	SNICK	–; snicks
SNARK	–; snarks	SNICKED	–; –
SNARL	–; snarls, snarly	SNICKER	–; snickers, snickery
SNARLED	–; –	SNIDE	–; snider
SNARLER	–; snarlers	SNIDELY	–; –
SNASH	–; –	SNIDEST	–; –
SNASHES	–; –	SNIFF	–; sniffs, sniffy
SNATCH	–; snatchy	SNIFFED	–; –
SNATH	–; snathe, snaths	SNIFFER	–; sniffers
SNATHE	–; snathes	SNIFFLE	–; sniffled, sniffler, sniffles
SNAW	–; snaws		
SNAWED	–; –	SNIFTER	–; snifters
SNAWING	–; –	SNIGGER	–; sniggers
SNAZZY	–; –	SNIGGLE	–; sniggled, sniggler, sniggles
SNEAK	–; sneaks, sneaky		
SNEAKED	–; –	SNIP	–; snipe, snips
SNEAKER	–; sneakers	SNIPE	–; sniped, sniper, snipes
SNEAP	–; sneaps		
SNEAPED	–; –		
SNECK	–; snecks	SNIPER	–; snipers
SNED	–; sneds	SNIPPED	–; –
SNEDDED	–; –	SNIPPER	–; snippers
SNEER	–; sneers	SNIPPET	–; snippets, snippety
SNEERED	–; –		
SNEERER	–; sneerers	SNIPPY	–; –
SNEESH	–; –	SNIT	–; snits
SNEEZE	–; sneezed, sneezer, sneezes	SNITCH	–; –
		SNIVEL	–; snivels
		SNOB	–; snobs
SNEEZER	–; sneezers	SNOBBY	–; –
SNEEZY	–; –	SNOOD	–; snoods
SNELL	–; snells	SNOODED	–; –
SNELLER	–; –	SNOOK	–; snooks

SNOOKED	–; –	SNOWMEN	–; –
SNOOKER	–; snookers	SNUB	–; snubs
SNOOL	–; snools	SNUBBED	–; –
SNOOLED	–; –	SNUBBER	–; snubbers
SNOOP	–; snoops, snoopy	SNUBBY	–; –
		SNUCK	–; –
SNOOPED	–; –	SNUFF	–; snuffs, snuffy
SNOOPER	–; snoopers		
SNOOT	–; snoots, snooty	SNUFFED	–; –
		SNUFFER	–; snuffers
SNOOTED	–; –	SNUFFLE	–; snuffled, snuffler, snuffles
SNOOZE	–; snoozed, snoozer, snoozes		
		SNUFFLY	–; –
SNOOZER	–; snoozers	SNUG	–; snugs
SNOOZLE	–; snoozled, snoozles	SNUGGED	–; –
		SNUGGER	–; –
SNOOZY	–; –	SNUGGLE	–; snuggled, snuggles
SNORE	–; snored, snorer, snores		
		SNUGLY	–; –
		SNYE	–; snyes
SNORER	–; snorers	SO	–; sob, sod,
SNORING	–; –		sol, son,
SNORKEL	–; snorkels		sop, sot,
SNORT	–; snorts		sou, sos,
SNORTED	–; –		sow, sox,
SNORTER	–; snorters		soy
SNOT	–; snots	SOAK	–; soaks
SNOTTY	–; –	SOAKAGE	–; soakages
SNOUT	–; snouts, snouty	SOAKED	–; –
		SOAKER	–; soakers
SNOUTED	–; –	SOAP	–; soaps, soapy
SNOW	–; snows, snowy		
		SOAPBOX	–; –
SNOWCAP	–; snowcaps	SOAPED	–; –
SNOWED	–; –	SOAPIER	–; –
SNOWIER	–; –	SOAPILY	–; –
SNOWILY	–; –	SOAPING	–; –
SNOWING	–; –	SOAR	–; soars
SNOWMAN	–; –	SOARED	–; –

SOARER	–; soarers	SODIUM	–; sodiums
SOARING	–; soarings	SODOMY	–;
SOAVE	–; soaves	SOEVER	–; –
SOB	–; sobs	SOFA	–; sofar,
SOBBED	–; –		sofas
SOBBER	–; sobbers	SOFAR	–; sofars
SOBBING	–; –	SOFFIT	–; soffits
SOBEIT	–; –	SOFT	–; softa,
SOBER	–; sobers		softs, softy
SOBERED	–; –	SOFTA	–; softas
SOBERER	–; –	SOFTEN	–; softens
SOBERLY	–; –	SOFTER	–; –
SOBFUL	–; –	SOFTEST	–; –
SOCAGE	–; socager,	SOFTIE	–; softies
	socages	SOFTLY	–; –
SOCAGER	–; socagers	SOGGED	–; –
SOCCAGE	–; soccages	SOGGIER	–; –
SOCCER	–; soccers	SOGGILY	–; –
SOCIAL	asocial;	SOGGY	–; –
	socials	SOIGNE	–; soignee
SOCIETY	–; –	SOIL	–; soils
SOCK	–; socks	SOILAGE	–; soilages
SOCKED	–; –	SOILED	–; –
SOCKET	–; sockets	SOILING	–; –
SOCKEYE	–; sockeyes	SOILURE	–; soilures
SOCKING	–; –	SOIREE	–; soirees
SOCKMAN	–; –	SOJA	–; sojas
SOCKMEN	–; –	SOJOURN	–; sojourns
SOCLE	–; socles	SOKE	–; sokes
SOCMAN	–; –	SOKEMAN	–; –
SOCMEN	–; –	SOKEMEN	–; –
SOD	–; soda,	SOL	–; sola,
	sods		sold, sole,
SODA	–; sodas		soll, solo,
SODDED	–; –		sols
SODDEN	–; soddens	SOLA	–; solan,
SODDIES	–;		solar
SODDING	–; –	SOLACE	–; solaced,
SODDY	–; –		solacer,
SODIC	–; –		solaces

SOLACER	–; solacers	**SOLOED**	; –
SOLAN	–; soland,	**SOLOING**	–; –
	solano,	**SOLOIST**	–; soloists
	solans	**SOLON**	–; solons
SOLAND	–; solands	**SOLUBLE**	–; solubles
SOLANIN	–; solanine,	**SOLUBLY**	–; –
	solanins	**SOLUM**	–; solums
SOLANO	–; solanos	**SOLUS**	–; –
SOLANUM	–; solanums	**SOLUTE**	–; solutes
SOLARIA	–; –	**SOLVATE**	–; solvated,
SOLATE	isolate;		solvates
	solated,	**SOLVE**	–; solved,
	solates		solver,
SOLATED	isolated; –		solves
SOLATES	isolates; –	**SOLVENT**	–; solvents
SOLATIA	–; –	**SOLVER**	–; solvers
SOLD	–; soldi,	**SOLVING**	–; –
	soldo	**SOMA**	–; somas
SOLDAN	–; soldans	**SOMATA**	–; –
SOLDER	–; solders	**SOMATIC**	–; –
SOLDIER	–; soldiers,	**SOMBER**	–; –
	soldiery	**SOMBRE**	–; –
SOLE	–; soled,	**SOME**	–; –
	soles	**SOMEDAY**	–; –
SOLELY	–; –	**SOMEHOW**	–; –
SOLEMN	–; –	**SOMEONE**	–; someones
SOLERET	–; solerets	**SOMEWAY**	–;
SOLFEGE	–; solfeges		someways
SOLGEL	–; –	**SOMITAL**	–; –
SOLI	–; solid	**SOMITE**	–; somites
SOLICIT	–; solicits	**SOMITIC**	–; –
SOLID	–; solidi,	**SON**	–; sone,
	solids		song, sons
SOLIDER	–; –	**SONANCE**	–; sonances
SOLIDLY	–; –	**SONANT**	–; sonants
SOLIDUS	–; –	**SONAR**	–; sonars
SOLING	–; –	**SONATA**	–; sonatas
SOLION	–; solions	**SONDE**	–; sonder,
SOLO	–; solon,		sondes
	solos	**SONDER**	–; sonders

SONE	–; sones	SOPITE	–; sopited, sopites
SONG	–; songs		
SONGFUL	–; –	SOPOR	–; sopors
SONIC	–; sonics	SOPPED	–; –
SONLESS	–; –	SOPPIER	–; –
SONLIKE	–; –	SOPPING	–; –
SONLY	–; –	SOPPY	–; –
SONNET	–; sonnets	SOPRANI	–; –
SONNIES	–; –	SOPRANO	–; sopranos
SONNY	–; –	SORA	–; soras
SONOVOX	–; –	SORB	–; sorbs
SONS	–; sonsy	SORBATE	–; sorbates
SONSHIP	–; sonships	SORBED	–; –
SONSIE	–; sonsier	SORBENT	–; sorbents
SOOEY	–; –	SORBET	–; sorbets
SOON	–; –	SORBIC	–; –
SOONER	–; sooners	SORBING	–; –
SOONEST	–; –	SORBOSE	–; sorboses
SOOT	–; sooth, soots, sooty	SORCERY	–; –
		SORD	–; sords
SOOTED	–; –	SORDID	–; –
SOOTH	–; soothe, sooths	SORDINE	–; sordines
		SORDINI	–; –
SOOTHE	–; soothed, soother, soothes	SORDINO	–; –
		SORE	–; sorel, sorer, sores
SOOTHER	–; soothers	SOREL	–; sorels, sorely
SOOTHES	–; soothest		
SOOTHLY	–; –	SORES	–; sorest
SOOTIER	–; –	SORGHO	–; sorghos
SOOTILY	–; –	SORGHUM	–; sorghums
SOOTING	–; –	SORGO	–; sorgos
SOP	–; soph, sops	SORI	–; –
		SORITES	–; –
SOPH	–; sophs, sophy	SORITIC	–; –
		SORN	–; sorns
SOPHIES	–; –	SORNED	–; –
SOPHISM	–; sophisms	SORNER	–; sorners
SOPHIST	–; sophists	SORNING	–; –
		SOROCHE	–; soroches

SORORAL	–; –	**SOUPCON**	–; soupcons
SOROSES	–; –	**SOUPED**	–; –
SOROSIS	–; –	**SOUPIER**	–; –
SORREL	–; sorrels	**SOUPING**	–; –
SORRIER	–; –	**SOUR**	–; sours
SORRILY	–; –	**SOURCE**	–; sources
SORROW	–; sorrows	**SOURED**	–; –
SORRY	–; –	**SOURER**	–; –
SORT	–; sorts	**SOUREST**	–; –
SORTED	–; –	**SOURING**	–; –
SORTER	–; sorters	**SOURISH**	–; –
SORTIE	–; sortied, sorties	**SOURLY**	–; –
		SOURSOP	–; soursops
SORTING	–; –	**SOUSE**	–; soused, souses
SORUS	–; –		
SOT	–; soth, sots	**SOUSING**	–; –
SOTH	–; soths	**SOUTANE**	–; soutanes
SOTOL	–; sotols	**SOUTER**	–; souters
SOTTISH	–; –	**SOUTH**	–; souths
SOU	–; soul, soup, sour, sous	**SOUTHED**	–; –
		SOUTHER	–; southern, southers
SOUARI	–; souaris	**SOVIET**	–; soviets
SOUBISE	–; soubises	**SOVKHOZ**	–; sovkhozy
SOUCAR	–; soucars	**SOVRAN**	–; sovrans
SOUDAN	–; soudans	**SOW**	–; sown, sows
SOUDING	–; soudings		
SOUFFLE	–; souffles	**SOWABLE**	–; –
SOUGH	–; soughs, sought	**SOWANS**	–; –
		SOWAR	–; sowars
SOUGHED	–; –	**SOWCAR**	–; sowcars
SOUL	–; souls	**SOWED**	–; –
SOULED	–; –	**SOWENS**	–; –
SOULFUL	–; –	**SOWER**	–; sowers
SOUND	–; sounds	**SOWING**	–; –
SOUNDED	–; –	**SOX**	–; –
SOUNDER	–; sounders	**SOY**	–; soya, soys
SOUNDLY	–; –		
SOUP	–; soups, soupy	**SOYA**	–; soyas
		SOYBEAN	–; soybeans

SOZIN	–; sozine, sozins	SPANK	–; spanks
SOZINE	–; sozines	SPANKED	–; –
SPA	–; spae, span, spar, spas, spat, spay	SPANKER	–; spankers
		SPANNED	–; –
		SPANNER	–; spanners
		SPAR	–; spare, spark, spars
SPACE	–; spaced, spacer, spaces	SPARE	–; spared, sparer, spares
SPACER	–; spacers	SPARELY	–; –
SPACIAL	–; –	SPARER	–; sparers
SPACING	–; spacings	SPARES	–; sparest
SPADE	–; spaded, spader, spades	SPARGE	–; sparged, sparger, sparges
SPADER	–; spaders	SPARGER	–; spargers
SPADING	–; –	SPARID	–; sparids
SPADIX	–; –	SPARING	–; –
SPADO	–; –	SPARK	–; sparks, sparky
SPAE	–; spaed, spaes		
		SPARKED	–; –
SPAEING	–; spaeings	SPARKER	–; sparkers
SPAHEE	–; spahees	SPARKLE	–; sparkled, sparkler, sparkles
SPAHI	–; spahis		
SPAIL	–; spails		
SPAIT	–; spaits	SPAROID	–; sparoids
SPAKE	–; –	SPARRED	–; –
SPALE	–; spales	SPARROW	–; sparrows
SPALL	–; spalls	SPARRY	–; –
SPALLED	–; –	SPARSE	–; sparser
SPALLER	–; spallers	SPASM	–; spasms
SPAN	–; spang, spank, spans	SPASTIC	–; spastics
		SPAT	–; spate, spats
SPANCEL	–; spancels		
SPANG	–; –	SPATE	–; spates
SPANGLE	–; spangled, spangles	SPATHAL	–; –
		SPATHE	–; spathed, spathes
SPANGLY	–; –		
SPANIEL	–; spaniels	SPATHIC	–;

SPATIAL	–; –	SPEER	–; speers
SPATTED	–; –	SPEERED	–; –
SPATTER	–; spatters	SPEIL	–; speils
SPATULA	–; spatular, spatulas	SPEILED	–; –
		SPEIR	–; speirs
SPAVIE	–; spavies, spaviet	SPEIRED	–; –
		SPEISE	–; speises
SPAVIN	–; spavins	SPEISS	–; –
SPAWN	–; spawns	SPELEAN	–; –
SPAWNED	–; –	SPELL	–; spells
SPAWNER	–; spawners	SPELLED	–; –
SPAY	–; spays	SPELLER	–; spellers
SPAYED	–; –	SPELT	–; spelts, speltz
SPAYING	–; –		
SPEAK	–; speaks	SPELTER	–; spelters
SPEAKER	–; speakers	SPELUNK	–; spelunks
SPEAN	–; speans	SPENCE	–; spencer, spences
SPEANED	–; –		
SPEAR	–; spears	SPENCER	–; spencers
SPEARED	–; –	SPEND	–; spends
SPEARER	–; spearers	SPENDER	–; spenders
SPECIAL	–; specials	SPENT	–; –
SPECIE	–; species	SPERM	–; sperms
SPECIFY	–; –	SPERMIC	–; –
SPECK	–; specks	SPEW	–; spews
SPECKED	–; –	SPEWED	–; –
SPECKLE	–; speckled, speckles	SPEWER	–; spewers
		SPEWING	–; –
SPECS	–; –	SPHENE	–; sphenes
SPECTER	–; specters	SPHENIC	–; –
SPECTRA	–; spectral	SPHERAL	–; –
SPECTRE	–; spectres	SPHERE	–; sphered, spheres
SPECULA	–; specular		
SPED	–; –	SPHERIC	–; spherics
SPEECH	–; –	SPHERY	–; –
SPEED	–; speeds, speedy	SPHINX	–; –
		SPIC	aspic; spica, spice, spics, spicy
SPEEDER	–; speeders	
SPEEDUP	–; speedups	
SPEEL	–; speels	

SPICA	–; spicae, spicas	**SPILING**	–; spilings
		SPILL	–; spills
SPICATE	–; spicated	**SPILLED**	–; –
SPICE	–; spiced, spicer, spices, spicey	**SPILLER**	–; spillers
		SPILT	–; spilth
		SPILTH	–; spilths
		SPIN	–; spine, spins, spiny
SPICER	–; spicers, spicery		
		SPINACH	–; –
SPICIER	–; –	**SPINAGE**	–; spinages
SPICILY	–; –	**SPINAL**	–; spinals
SPICING	–; –	**SPINATE**	–; –
SPICK	–; spicks	**SPINDLE**	–; spindled, spindler, spindles
SPICS	aspics; –		
SPICULA	–; spiculae, spicular		
		SPINDLY	–; –
SPICULE	–; spicules	**SPINE**	–; spined, spinel, spines, spinet
SPICY	–; –		
SPIDER	–; spiders, spidery		
		SPINEL	–; spinels
SPIED	espied; –	**SPINET**	–; spinets
SPIEGEL	–; spiegels	**SPINIER**	–; –
SPIEL	–; spiels	**SPINNER**	–; spinners, spinnery
SPIELED	–; –		
SPIELER	–; spielers		
SPIER	–; spiers	**SPINNEY**	–; spinneys
SPIERED	–; –	**SPINNY**	–; –
SPIES	espies; –	**SPINOFF**	–; spinoffs
SPIFFY	–; –	**SPINOR**	–; spinors
SPIGOT	–; spigots	**SPINOSE**	–; –
SPIK	–; spike, spiks, spiky	**SPINOUS**	–; –
		SPINOUT	–; spinouts
SPIKE	–; spiked, spiker, spikes	**SPINULA**	–; spinulae
		SPINULE	–; spinules
SPIKER	–; spikers	**SPIRAEA**	–; spiraeas
SPIKIER	–; –	**SPIRAL**	–; spirals
SPIKILY	–; –	**SPIRANT**	aspirant; spirants
SPIKING	–; –		
SPILE	–; spiled, spiles	**SPIRE**	aspire; spirea,

	spired,	**SPLICER**	–; splicers
	spirem, spires	**SPLINE**	–; splined,
SPIREA	–; spireas		splines
SPIRED	aspired; –	**SPLINT**	–; splints
SPIRES	aspires; –	**SPLIT**	–; splits
SPIREM	–; spireme,	**SPLORE**	–; splores
	spirems	**SPLOSH**	–; –
SPIREME	–; spiremes	**SPLOTCH**	–; splotchy
SPIRING	aspiring; –	**SPLURGE**	–; splurged,
SPIRIT	–; spirits		splurges
SPIROID	–; –	**SPLURGY**	–; –
SPIRT	–; spirts	**SPODE**	–; spodes
SPIRTED	–; –	**SPOIL**	–; spoils,
SPIRULA	–; spirulae,		spoilt
	spirulas	**SPOILED**	–; –
SPIRY	–; –	**SPOILER**	–; spoilers
SPIT	–; spite,	**SPOKE**	–; spoked,
	spits, spitz		spoken,
SPITAL	–; spitals		spokes
SPITE	–; spited,	**SPOKING**	–; –
	spites	**SPONDEE**	–; spondees
SPITING	–; –	**SPONGE**	–; sponged,
SPITTED	–; –		sponger,
SPITTER	–; spitters		sponges
SPITTLE	–; spittles	**SPONGER**	–; spongers
SPITZ	–; –	**SPONGIN**	–; sponging,
SPIV	–; spivs		spongins
SPLAKE	–; splakes	**SPONGY**	–; –
SPLASH	–; splashy	**SPONSAL**	–; –
SPLAT	–; splats	**SPONSON**	–; sponsons
SPLAY	–; splays	**SPONSOR**	–; sponsors
SPLAYED	–; –	**SPOOF**	–; spoofs
SPLEEN	–; spleens,	**SPOOFED**	–; –
	spleeny	**SPOOK**	–; spooks,
SPLENIA	–; splenial		spooky
SPLENIC	–; –	**SPOOKED**	–; –
SPLENT	–; splents	**SPOOL**	–; spools
SPLICE	–; spliced,	**SPOOLED**	–; –
	splicer,	**SPOON**	–; spoons,
	splices		spoony

SPOONED	–; –	SPRIEST	–; –
SPOONEY	–; spooneys	SPRIG	–; sprigs
SPOOR	–; spoors	SPRIGGY	–; –
SPORAL	–; –	SPRIGHT	–; sprights
SPOORED	–; –	SPRING	–; springs,
SPORE	–; spored,		springy
	spores	SPRINGE	–; springed,
SPORING	–; –		springer,
SPOROID	–; –		springes
SPORRAN	–; sporrans	SPRINT	–; sprints
SPORT	–; sports,	SPRIT	esprit; sprite,
	sporty		sprits
SPORTED	–; –	SPRITE	–; sprites
SPORTER	–; sporters	SPROUT	–; sprouts
SPORULE	–; sporules	SPRUCE	–; spruced,
SPOT	–; spots		sprucer,
SPOTTED	–; –		spruces
SPOTTER	–; spotters	SPRUCY	–; –
SPOTTY	–; –	SPRUE	–; sprues
SPOUSAL	–; spousals	SPRUG	–; sprugs
SPOUSE	espouse;	SPRUNG	–; –
	spoused,	SPRY	–; –
	spouses	SPRYER	–; –
SPOUT	–; spouts	SPRYEST	–; –
SPOUTED	–; –	SPRYLY	–; –
SPOUTER	; spouters	SPUD	–; spuds
SPRAG	–; sprags	SPUDDED	–; –
SPRAIN	–; sprains	SPUDDER	–; spudders
SPRANG	–; –	SPUE	–; spued,
SPRAT	–; sprats		spues
SPRAWL	–; sprawls,	SPUING	–; –
	sprawly	SPUME	–; spumed,
SPRAY	–; sprays		spumes
SPRAYED	–; –	SPUMIER	–; –
SPRAYER	–; sprayers	SPUMING	–; –
SPREAD	–; spreads	SPUMONE	–; spumones
SPREE	–; sprees	SPUMONI	–; spumonis
SPRENT	–; –	SPUMOUS	–; –
SPRIER	–; –	SPUMY	–; –

SPUN	–; spunk	SQUATTY	–; –
SPUNK	–; spunks, spunky	SQUAW	–; squawk squaws
SPUNKIE	–; spunkier, spunkies	SQUAWK	–; squawks
		SQUEAK	–; squeaks,
SPUR	–; spurn, spurs, spurt		squeaky
		SQUEAL	–; squeals
SPURGE	–; spurges	SQUEEZE	–;
SPURN	–; spurns		squeezed,
SPURNED	–; –		squeezer,
SPURNER	–; spurners		squeezes
SPURRED	–; –	SQUEG	–; squegs
SPURRER	–; spurrers	SQUELCH	–; squelchy
SPURREY	–; spurreys	SQUIB	–; squibs
SPURRY	–; –	SQUID	–; squids
SPURT	–; spurts	SQUIFFY	–; –
SPURTED	–; –	SQUILL	–; squilla,
SPURTLE	–; spurtles		squills
SPUTA	–; –	SQUILLA	–; squillae,
SPUTNIK	–; sputniks		squillas
SPUTTER	–; sputters	SQUINCH	–; –
SPUTUM	–; –	SQUINNY	–; –
SPY	espy; –	SQUINT	asquint;
SPYING	–; –		squints,
SQUAB	–; squabs		squinty
SQUABBY	–; –	SQUIRE	esquired;
SQUAD	–; squads		squired,
SQUALID	–; –		squires
SQUALL	–; squalls, squally	SQUIRED	esquired; –
		SQUIRES	esquires; –
SQUALOR	–; squalors	SQUIRM	–; squirms,
SQUAMA	–; squamae		squirmy
SQUARE	–; squared, squarer, squares	SQUIRT	–; squirts
		SQUISH	–; squishy
		SQUOOSH	–; –
SQUARER	–; squarers	SQUUSH	–; –
SQUARES	–; squarest	SRADDHA	–; sraddhas
SQUASH	–; squashy	SRADHA	–; sradhas
SQUAT	–; squats	SRI	–; sris
SQUATLY	–; –	STAB	–; stabs

STABBED	–; –	STAIN	–; stains
STABBER	–; stabbers	STAINED	–; –
STABILE	–; stabiles	STAINER	–; stainers
STABLE	–; stabled, stabler, stables	STAIR	–; stairs
		STAKE	–; staked, stakes
STABLER	–; stablers	STAKING	–; –
STABLES	–; stablest	STALAG	–; stalags
STABLY	–; –	STALE	–; staled, staler, stales
STACK	–; stacks		
STACKED	–; –	STALELY	–; –
STACKER	–; stackers	STALES	–; stalest
STACTE	–; stactes	STALING	–; –
STADDLE	–; staddles	STALK	–; stalks, stalky
STADE	–; stades		
STADIA	–; stadias	STALKED	–; –
STADIUM	–; stadiums	STALKER	–; stalkers
STAFF	–; staffs	STALL	–; stalls
STAFFED	–; –	STALLED	–; –
STAFFER	–; staffers	STAMEN	–; stamens
STAG	–; stage, stags, stagy	STAMINA	–; staminal, staminas
STAGE	–; staged, stager, stages, stagey	STAMMEL	–; stammels
		STAMMER	–; stammers
		STAMP	–; stamps
		STAMPED	, stampede
STAGER	–; stagers	STAMPER	–; stampers
STAGGED	–; –	STANCE	–; stances
STAGGER	–; staggers, staggery	STANCH	–; –
		STAND	–; stands
STAGGIE	–; staggier, staggies	STANDBY	–; standbys
		STANDEE	–; standees
STAGGY	–; –	STANDER	–; standers
STAGIER	–; –	STANDUP	–; –
STAGILY	–; –	STANE	–; staned, stanes
STAGING	–; stagings		
STAID	–; –	STANG	–; stangs
STAIDER	–; –	STANGED	–; –
STAIDLY	–; –	STANING	–; –
STAIG	–; staigs	STANK	–; stanks

STANNIC	–; –	**STASHES**	–; –
STANNUM	–; stannums	**STASIS**	–; –
STANZA	–; stanzas	**STATAL**	–; –
STAPES	–; –	**STATANT**	–; –
STAPH	–; staphs	**STATE**	estate;
STAPLE	–; stapled,		stated,
	stapler,		stater, states
	staples	**STATED**	estated; –
STAPLER	–; staplers	**STATELY**	–; –
STAR	–; stare,	**STATER**	–; staters
	stark, stars,	**STATES**	estates; –
	start	**STATIC**	astatic;
STARCH	–; starchy		statics
STARDOM	–; stardoms	**STATICE**	–; statices
STARE	–; stared,	**STATING**	–; –
	starer, stares	**STATION**	–; stations
STARER	–; starers	**STATISM**	–; statisms
STARETS	–; –	**STATIST**	–; statists
STARING	–; –	**STATIVE**	–; statives
STARK	–; –	**STATOR**	–; stators
STARKER	–; –	**STATUE**	–; statued,
STARKLY	–; –		statues
STARLET	–; starlets	**STATURE**	–; statures
STARLIT	–; –	**STATUS**	–; –
STARRED	–; –	**STATUTE**	–; statutes
STARRY	–; –	**STAUNCH**	–; –
START	–; starts	**STAVE**	–; staved,
STARTED	–; –		staves
STARTER	–; starters	**STAVING**	–; –
STARTLE	–; startled,	**STAW**	–; –
	startler,	**STAY**	–; stays
	startles	**STAYED**	–; –
STARTS	–; startsy	**STAYER**	–; stayers
STARVE	–; starved,	**STAYING**	–; –
	starver,	**STEAD**	–; steads,
	starves		steady
STARVER	–; starvers	**STEADED**	–; –
STASES	–; –	**STEAK**	–; steaks
STASH	–; –	**STEAL**	osteal; steals
STASHED	–; –	**STEALER**	–; stealers

STEALTH	–; stealth, stealthy	**STEMMER**	–; stemmers, stemmery
STEAM	–; steams, steamy	**STEMMY**	–; –
		STEMSON	–; stemsons
STEAMED	–; –	**STENCH**	–; stenchy
STEAMER	–; steamers	**STENCIL**	–; stencils
STEARIC	–; –	**STENGAH**	–; stengahs
STEARIN	–; stearine, stearins	**STENO**	–; stenos
		STENTOR	–; stentors
STEED	–; steeds	**STEP**	–; steps
STEEK	–; steeks	**STEPPE**	–; stepped, stepper, steppes
STEEKED	–; –		
STEEL	–; steels, steely		
		STEPPER	–; steppers
STEELED	–; –	**STEPSON**	–; stepsons
STEELIE	–; steelies	**STERE**	–; stereo, steres
STEEP	–; steeps		
STEEPED	–; –	**STEREO**	–; stereos
STEEPEN	–; steepens	**STERIC**	–; –
STEEPER	–; steepers	**STERILE**	–; –
STEEPLE	–; steepled, steeples	**STERLET**	–; sterlets
		STERN	astern; sterna, sterns
STEEPLY	–; –		
STEER	–; steers		
STEERED	–; –	**STERNA**	–; sternal
STEERER	–; steerers	**STERNER**	–; –
STEEVE	–; steeved, steeves	**STERNLY**	–; –
		STERNUM	–; sternums
STEIN	–; steins	**STEROID**	–; steroids
STELA	–; stelae, stelai, stelar	**STEROL**	–; sterols
		STERTOR	–; stertors
STELE	–; steles	**STET**	–; stets
STELIC	–; –	**STETSON**	–; stetsons
STELENE	–; –	**STETTED**	–; –
STELLA	–; stellar, stellas	**STEW**	–; stews
		STEWARD	–; stewards
STEM	–; stems	**STEWBUM**	–; stewbums
STEMMA	–; stemmas	**STEWED**	–; –
STEMMED	–; –	**STEWING**	–; –
		STEWPAN	–; stewpans

STEY	–; –	**STING**	–; stingo, stings, stingy
STHENIA	–; sthenias		
STHENIC	–; –	**STINGER**	–; stingers
STIBIAL	–; –	**STINGO**	–; stingos
STIBINE	–; stibines	**STINK**	–; stinko, stinks, stinky
STIBIUM	–; stibiums		
STICH	–; stichs	**STINKER**	–; stinkers
STICHIC	–; –	**STINT**	–; stints
STICK	–; sticks, sticky	**STINTED**	–; –
		STINTER	–; stinters
STICKED	–; –	**STIPE**	–; stiped, stipel, stipes
STICKER	–; stickers		
STICKIT	–; –	**STIPEL**	–; stipels
STICKLE	–; stickled, stickler, stickles	**STIPEND**	–; stipends
		STIPPLE	–; stippled stippler, stipples
STICKUM	–; stickums		
STICKUP	–; stickups	**STIPULE**	–; stipuled, stipules
STIED	–; –		
STIES	–; –	**STIR**	astir; stirk, stirp, stirs
STIFF	–; stiffs		
STIFFEN	–; stiffens	**STIRK**	–; stirks
STIFFER	–; –	**STIRP**	–; stirps
STIFFLY	–; –	**STIRPES**	–; –
STIFLE	–; stifled, stifler, stifles	**STIRRED**	–; –
		STIRRER	–; stirrers
STIFLER	–; stiflers	**STIRRUP**	–; stirrups
STIGMA	–; stigmal, stigmas	**STITCH**	–; –
		STITHY	–; –
STILE	–; stiles	**STIVER**	–; stivers
STILL	–; stills, stilly	**STOA**	–; stoae, stoai, stoas, stoat
STILLED	–; –		
STILLER	–; –		
STILT	–; stilts	**STOAT**	–; stoats
STILTED	–; –	**STOB**	–; stobs
STIME	–; stimes	**STOBBED**	–; –
STIMIED	–; –	**STOCK**	–; stocks, stocky
STIMIES	–; –		
STIMY	–; –	**STOCKED**	–; –
		STOCKER	–; stockers

STODGE	–; stodged, stodger	**STOOKED**	–; –
STODGY	–; –	**STOOKER**	–; stookers
STOGEY	–; stogeys	**STOOL**	–; stools
STOGIE	–; stogies	**STOOLED**	–; –
STOGY	–; –	**STOOLIE**	–; stoolies
STOIC	–; stoics	**STOOP**	–; stoops
STOICAL	–; –	**STOOPED**	–; –
STOKE	–; stoked, stoker, stokes	**STOOPER**	–; stoopers
		STOP	estop; stope, stops, stopt
STOKER	–; stokers	**STOPE**	–; stoped, stoper, stopes
STOKING	–; –		
STOLE	–; stoled, stolen, stoles	**STOPER**	–; stopers
STOLID	–; –	**STOPGAP**	–; stopgaps
STOLLEN	–; stollens	**STOPING**	–; –
STOLON	–; stolons	**STOPPED**	–; –
STOMA	–; stomal, stomas	**STOPPER**	–; stoppers
		STOPPLE	–; stoppled, stopples
STOMACH	–; stomachy	**STOPS**	estops; –
STOMATA	–; stomatal	**STORAGE**	–; storages
STOMATE	–; stomates	**STORAX**	–; –
STOMP	–; stomps	**STORE**	–; stored, stores, storey
STOMPED	–; –		
STOMPER	–; stompers		
STONE	–; stoned, stoner, stones, stoney	**STOREY**	–; storeys
		STORIED	–; –
		STORIES	–; –
		STORING	–; –
STONER	–; stoners	**STORK**	–; storks
STONIER	–; –	**STORM**	–; storms, stormy
STONILY	–; –		
STONING	–; –	**STORMED**	–; –
STONISH	–; –	**STORY**	–; –
STONY	astony; –	**STOSS**	–; –
STOOD	–; –	**STOUND**	astound; stounds
STOOGE	–; stooged, stooges		
		STOUNDS	astounds; –
STOOK	–; stooks	**STOUP**	–; stoups

STOUR	–; stoure, stours, stoury	estray; strays
		STRAYED	–; –
STOURE	–; stoures	**STRAYER**	–; strayers
STOURIE	–; –	**STRAYS**	estrays; –
STOUT	–; stouts	**STREAK**	–; streaks, streaky
STOUTEN	–; stoutens		
STOUTER	–; –	**STREAM**	–; streams, streamy
STOUTLY	–; –		
STOVE	–; stover, stoves	**STREEK**	–; streeks
		STREET	–; streets
STOVER	–; stovers	**STREP**	–; streps
STOW	–; stowp, stows	**STRESS**	–; –
		STRETCH	–; stretchy
STOWAGE	–; stowages	**STRETTA**	–; strettas
STOWED	–; –	**STRETTE**	–; –
STOWP	–; stowps	**STRETTI**	–; –
STRAFE	–; strafed, strafer, strafes	**STRETTO**	–; strettos
		STREW	–; strewn, strews
STRAFER	–; strafers	**STREWED**	–; –
STRAIN	–; strains	**STREWER**	–; strewers
STRAIT	–; straits	**STRIA**	–; striae
STRAKE	–; straked, strakes	**STRIATE**	–; striated, striates
STRAND	–; strands	**STRICK**	–; stricks
STRANG	–; strange	**STRICT**	astrict; –
STRANGE	–; stranger	**STRID**	–; stride
STRAP	–; straps	**STRIDE**	astride; strider, strides
STRASS	–; –		
STRATA	–; stratal, stratas		
		STRIDER	–; striders
STRATH	–; straths	**STRIDOR**	–; stridors
STRATI	–; –	**STRIFE**	–; strifes
STRATUM	–; stratums	**STRIGIL**	–; strigils
STRATUS	–; –	**STRIKE**	–; striker, strikes
STRAW	–; straws, strawy		
		STRIKER	–; strikers
STRAWED	–; –	**STRING**	–; strings, stringy
STRAY	astray,		

STRIP	–; stripe, strips, stript, simpy		struma, strums
STRIPE	–; striped, striper, stripes	**STRUMA**	–; strumae, strumas
STRIPER	–; stripers	**STRUMS**	estrums; –
STRIVE	–; strived, striven, striver, strives	**STRUNG**	–; –
		STRUNT	–; strunts
		STRUT	–; struts
		STUB	–; stubs
STRIVER	–; strivers	**STUBBED**	–; –
STROBE	–; strobes	**STUBBLE**	–; stubbled, stubbles
STROBIC	–; –		
STROBIL	–; strobila, strobile, strobili, strobils	**STUBBLY**	–; –
		STUBBY	–; –
		STUCCO	–; stuccos
		STUCK	–; –
		STUD	–; studs, study
STRODE	–; –		
STROKE	–; stroked, stroker, strokes	**STUDDED**	–; –
		STUDDIE	–; studdies
		STUDENT	–; students
		STUDIED	–; –
STROKER	–; strokers	**STUDIER**	–; studiers
STROLL	–; strolls	**STUDIES**	–; –
STROMA	–; stromal	**STUDIO**	–; studios
STRONG	–; –	**STUDY**	–; –
STROOK	–; –	**STUFF**	–; stuffs, stuffy
STROP	–; strops		
STROPHE	–; strophes	**STUFFED**	–; –
STROUD	–; strouds	**STUFFER**	–; stuffers
STROVE	–; –	**STUIVER**	–; stuivers
STROW	–; strown, strows	**STULL**	–; stulls
		STUM	–; stump, stums
STROWED	–; –		
STROY	–; stroys	**STUMBLE**	–; stumbled, stumbler, stumbles
STROYED	–; –		
STROYER	–; stroyers		
STRUCK	–; –	**STUMMED**	–; –
STRUDEL	–; strudels	**STUMP**	–; stumps, stumpy
STRUM	estrum;		

STUMPED	–; –	**STYLUS**	–; –
STUMPER	–; stumpers	**STYMIE**	–; stymied,
STUN	–; stung,		stymies
	stunk, stuns,	**STYMY**	–; –
	stunt.	**STYPSES**	–; –
STUNNED	–; –	**STYPSIS**	–; –
STUNNER	–; stunners	**STYPTIC**	–; styptics
STUNT	–; stunts	**STYRAX**	–; –
STUPA	–; stupas	**STYRENE**	–; styrenes
STUPE	–; stupes	**SUABLE**	–; –
STUPEFY	–; –	**SUABLY**	–; –
STUPID	–; stupids	**SUASION**	–; suasions
STUPOR	–; stupors	**SUASIVE**	–; –
STURDY	–; –	**SUASORY**	–; –
STURT	–; sturts	**SUAVE**	–; suaver
STUTTER	–; stutters	**SUAVELY**	–; –
STY	–; stye	**SUAVEST**	–; –
STYE	–; styed,	**SUAVITY**	–; –
	styes	**SUB**	–; suba, subs
STYGIAN	–; –	**SUBA**	tsuba;
STYING	–; –		subah, subas
STYLAR	astylar; –		
STYLATE	–; –	**SUBACID**	–; –
STYLE	–; styled,	**SUBADAR**	–; subadars
	styler, styles,	**SUBAH**	–; subahs
	stylet	**SUBALAR**	–; –
STYLER	–; stylers	**SUBAREA**	–; subareas
STYLET	–; stylets	**SUBARID**	–; –
STYLI	–; –	**SUBATOM**	–; subatoms
STYLING	–; stylings	**SUBBASE**	–; subbases
STYLISE	–; stylised,	**SUBBASS**	–; –
	styliser,	**SUBBED**	–; –
	stylises	**SUBBING**	–; subbings
STYLISH	–; –	**SUBCELL**	–; subcells
STYLIST	–; stylists	**SUBCLAN**	–; subclans
STYLITE	–; stylites	**SUBCOOL**	–; subcools
STYLIZE	–; stylized,	**SUBDEAN**	–; subdeans
	stylizer,	**SUBDEB**	–; subdebs
	stylizes	**SUBDUAL**	–; subduals
STYLOID	–; –	**SUBDUCE**	–; subduced,
			subduces

SUBDUCT	-; subducts	SUBSERE	-; subseres
SUBDUE	-; subdued,	SUBSET	-; subsets
	subduer,	SUBSIDE	-; subsided,
	subdues		subsider,
SUBDUER	-; subduers		subsides
SUBECHO	-; -	SUBSIDY	-; -
SUBEDIT	-; subedits	SUBSIST	-; subsists
SUBER	-; subers	SUBSOIL	-; subsoils
SUBERIC	-; -	SUBSUME	-;
SUBERIN	-; suberins		subsumed,
SUBFIX	-; -		subsumes
SUBGUM	-; -	SUBTEEN	-; subteens
SUBHEAD	-; subheads	SUBTEND	-; subtends
SUBIDEA	-; subideas	SUBTEXT	-; subtexts
SUBITEM	-; subitems	SUBTILE	-; subtiler
SUBITO	-; -	SUBTLE	-; subtler
SUBJECT	-; subjects	SUBTLY	-; -
SUBJOIN	-; subjoins	SUBTONE	-; subtones
SUBLATE	-; sublated,	SUBTYPE	-; subtypes
	sublates	SUBUNIT	-; subunits
SUBLET	-; sublets	SUBURB	-; suburbs
SUBLIME	-; sublimed,	SUBVENE	-; subvened,
	sublimer,		subvenes
	sublimes	SUBVERT	-; subverts
SUBMISS	-; -	SUBWAY	-; subways
SUBMIT	-; submits	SUBZONE	-; subzones
SUBORAL	-; -	SUCCAH	-; succahs
SUBORN	-; suborns	SUCCEED	-; succeeds
SUBOVAL	-; -	SUCCESS	-; -
SUBPAR	-; subpart	SUCCOR	-; succors,
SUBPART	-; subparts		succory
SUBPENA	-; subpenas	SUCCOTH	-; -
SUBPLOT	-; subplots	SUCCOUR	-; succours
SUBRACE	-; subraces	SUCCUBA	-; succubae
SUBRENT	-; subrents	SUCCUMB	-; succumbs
SUBRING	-; subrings	SUCCUSS	-; -
SUBRULE	-; subrules	SUCH	-; -
SUBSALE	-; subsales	SUCK	-; sucks
SUBSECT	-; subsects	SUCKED	-; -

SUCKER	–; suckers	**SUGAR**	–; sugars, sugary
SUCKING	–; –		
SUCKLE	–; suckled, suckler, suckles	**SUGARED**	–; –
		SUGGEST	–; suggests
		SUGH	–; sughs
SUCKLER	–; sucklers	**SUGHED**	–; –
SUCKLES	–; suckless	**SUGHING**	–; –
SUCRASE	–; sucrases	**SUICIDE**	–; suicided, suicides
SUCRE	–; sucres		
SUCROSE	–; sucroses	**SUING**	–; –
SUCTION	–; suctions	**SUINT**	–; suints
SUDARIA	–; –	**SUIT**	–; suite, suits
SUDARY	–; –	**SUITE**	–; suited, suites
SUDD	–; sudds		
SUDDEN	–; suddens	**SUITING**	–; suitings
SUDOR	–; sudors	**SUITOR**	–; suitors
SUDORAL	–; –	**SUKKAH**	–; sukkahs
SUDS	–; sudsy	**SUKKOTH**	–; –
SUDSED	–; –	**SULCATE**	–; sulcated
SUDSER	–; sudsers	**SULCI**	–; –
SUDSES	–; –	**SULCUS**	–; –
SUDSIER	–; –	**SULDAN**	–; suldans
SUDSING	–; –	**SULFA**	–; sulfas
SUE	–; sued, suer, sues, suet	**SULFATE**	–; sulfated, sulfates
		SULFID	–; sulfide, sulfids
SUEDE	–; sueded, suedes		
		SULFIDE	–; sulfides
SUEDING	–; –	**SULFITE**	–; sulfites
SUER	–; suers	**SULFO**	–; –
SUET	–; suets, suety	**SULFONE**	–; sulfones
		SULFUR	–; sulfurs, sulfury
SUFFARI	–; suffaris		
SUFFER	–; suffers	**SULFURY**	–; sulfuryl
SUFFICE	–; sufficed, sufficer, suffices	**SULK**	–; sulks, sulky
		SULKED	–; –
SUFFIX	–; –	**SULKER**	–; sulkers
SUFFUSE	–; suffused, suffuses	**SULKING**	–; –

SULKIER	–; –	sunk, sunn,
SULKIES	–; sulkiest	suns
SULKILY	–; –	
SULLAGE	–; sullages	**SUNBACK** –; –
SULLEN	–; –	**SUNBATH** –; sunbathe,
SULLIED	–; –	sunbaths
SULLIES	–; –	**SUNBEAM** –; sunbeams
SULLY	–; –	**SUNBIRD** –; sunbirds
SULPHA	–; sulphas	**SUNBOW** –; sunbows
SULPHID	–; sulphide,	**SUNBURN** –; sunburns,
	sulphids	sunburnt
SULPHUR	–; sulphurs,	**SUNDAE** –; sundaes
	sulphury	**SUNDER** asunder;
SULTAN	–; sultana,	sunders
	sultans	**SUNDEW** –; sundews
SULTANA	–; sultanas	**SUNDIAL** –; sundials
SULTRY	–; –	**SUNDOG** –; sundogs
SUM	–; sumo,	**SUNDOWN** –; sundowns
	sump, sums	**SUNDRY** –; –
SUMAC	–; sumach,	**SUNFAST** –; –
	sumacs	**SUNFISH** –; –
		SUNGLOW –; sunglows
SUMACH	–; sumachs	**SUNK** –; –
SUMLESS	–; –	**SUNKEN** –; –
SUMMA	–; summae,	**SUNKET** –; sunkets
	summas	**SUNLAMP** –; sunlamps
SUMMAND	–; summands	**SUNLAND** –; sunlands
SUMMARY	–; –	**SUNLESS** –; –
SUMMATE	–;	**SUNLIKE** –; –
	summated,	**SUNLIT** –; –
	summates	**SUNN** –; sunna,
SUMMED	–; –	sunns, sunny
SUMMER	–; summers,	**SUNNA** –; sunnas
	summery	**SUNNED** –; –
SUMMING	–; –	**SUNNIER** –; –
SUMMIT	–; summits	**SUNNILY** –; –
SUMMON	–; summons	**SUNNING** –; –
SUMO	–; sumos	**SUNRISE** –; sunrises
SUMP	–; sumps	**SUNROOF** –; sunroofs
SUMPTER	–; sumpters	**SUNROOM** –; sunrooms
SUN	–; sung,	**SUNSET** –; sunsets

SUNSPOT	–; sunspots	**SURF**	–; surfs,
SUNSUIT	–; sunsuits		surfy
SUNTAN	–; suntans	**SURFACE**	–; surfaced,
SUNUP	–; sunups		surfacer,
SUNWARD	–; sunwards		surfaces
SUNWISE	–; –	**SURFEIT**	–; surfeits
SUP	–; supe,	**SURFED**	–; –
	sups	**SURFER**	–; surfers
SUPE	–; super,	**SURFIER**	–; –
	supes	**SURFING**	–; surfings
SUPER	–; superb,	**SURGE**	–; surged,
	supers		surger,
SUPERED	–; –		surges
SUPINE	–; supines	**SURGEON**	–; surgeons
SUPPED	–; –	**SURGER**	–; surgers,
SUPPER	–; suppers		surgery
SUPPING	–; –	**SURGING**	–; –
SUPPLE	–; suppled,	**SURGY**	–; –
	suppler,	**SURILY**	–; –
	supples	**SURLIER**	–; –
SUPPLY	–; –	**SURLY**	–; –
SUPPORT	–; supports	**SURMISE**	–; surmised,
SUPPOSE	–;		surmiser,
	supposed,		surmises
	supposer,	**SURNAME**	–;
	supposes		surnamed,
SUPRA	–; –		surnamer,
SUPREME	–; supremer		surnames
SURA	–; surah,	**SURPASS**	–; –
	sural, suras	**SURPLUS**	–; –
SURAH	–; surahs	**SURRA**	–; surras
SURBASE	–; surbased,	**SURREAL**	–; –
	surbases	**SURREY**	–; surreys
SURCOAT	–; surcoats	**SURTAX**	–; –
SURD	–; surds	**SURTOUT**	–; surtouts
SURE	–; surer	**SURVEIL**	–; surveils
SURELY	–; –	**SURVEY**	–; surveys
SURER	usurer; –	**SURVIVE**	–; survived,
SUREST	–; –		surviver,
SURETY	–; –		survives

SUSLIK	–; susliks		swamp,
SUSPECT	–; suspects		swamy
SUSPEND	; suspends	**SWAMI**	–; swamis
SUSPIRE	–; suspired,	**SWAMIES**	–; –
	suspires	**SWAMP**	–; swamps,
SUSTAIN	–; sustains		swampy
SUTLER	–; sutlers	**SWAMPED**	–; –
SUTRA	–; sutras	**SWAMPER**	–; swampers
SUTTA	–; suttas	**SWAN**	–; swang,
SUTTEE	–; suttees		swank, swans
SUTURAL	–; –	**SWANK**	–; swanks,
SUTURE	–; sutured,		swanky
	sutures	**SWANKED**	–; –
SVARAJ	–; –	**SWANKER**	–; –
SVELTE	–; svelter	**SWANNED**	–; –
SWAB	–; swabs	**SWANPAN**	–; swanpans
SWABBED	–; –	**SWAP**	–; swaps
SWABBER	–; swabbers	**SWAPPED**	–; –
SWABBIE	–; swabbies	**SWAPPER**	–; swappers
SWABBY	–; –	**SWARAJ**	–; –
SWADDLE	–;	**SWARD**	–; swards
	swaddled,	**SWARDED**	–; –
	swaddles	**SWARE**	–; –
SWAG	–; swage,	**SWARF**	–; swarfs
	swags	**SWARM**	aswarm;
SWAGE	–; swaged,		swarms
	swager,	**SWARMED**	–; –
	swages	**SWARMER**	–; swarmers
SWAGER	–; swagers	**SWART**	–; swarth,
SWAGGED	–; –		swarty
SWAGGER	–; swaggers	**SWARTH**	–; swarths,
SWAGING	–; –		swarthy
SWAGMAN	–; –	**SWASH**	–; –
SWAGMEN	–; –	**SWASHED**	–; –
SWAIL	–; swails	**SWASHER**	–; swashers
SWAIN	–; swains	**SWASHES**	–; –
SWALE	–; swales	**SWAT**	–; swath,
SWALLOW	–; swallows		swats
SWAM	–; swami,	**SWATCH**	–; –

SWATH	–; swathe, swaths	SWEVEN	–; swevens
SWATHE	–; swathed, swather, swathes	SWIFT	–; swifts
		SWIFTER	–; swifters
		SWIFTLY	–; –
		SWIG	–; swigs
SWATHER	–; swathers	SWIGGED	–; –
SWATTED	–; –	SWIGGER	–; swiggers
SWATTER	–; swatters	SWILL	–; swills
SWAY	–; sways	SWILLED	–; –
SWAYED	–; –	SWILLER	–; swillers
SWAYER	–; swayers	SWIM	–; swims
SWAYFUL	–; –	SWIMMER	–; swimmers
SWAYING	–; –	SWIMMY	–; –
SWEAR	–; swears	SWINDLE	–; swindled, swindler, swindles
SWEARER	–; swearers		
SWEAT	–; sweats, sweaty	SWINE	–; –
		SWING	–; swinge, swings, swingy
SWEATED	–; –		
SWEATER	–; sweaters		
SWEDE	–; swedes	SWINGE	–; swinged, swinger, swinges
SWEENY	–; –		
SWEEP	–; sweeps, sweepy		
		SWINGER	–; swingers
SWEEPER	–; sweepers	SWINGLE	–; swingled, swingles
SWEER	–; –		
SWEET	–; sweets	SWINISH	–; –
SWEETEN	–; sweetens	SWINK	–; swinks
SWEETER	–; –	SWINKED	–; –
SWEETIE	–; sweeties	SWINNEY	–; swinneys
SWEETLY	–; –	SWIPE	–; swiped, swipes
SWELL	–; swells		
SWELLED	–; –	SWIPING	–; –
SWELLER	–; –	SWIPLE	–; swiples
SWELTER	–; swelters	SWIPPLE	–; swipples
SWELTRY	–; –	SWIRL	aswirl; swirls, swirly
SWEPT	–; –		
SWERVE	–; swerved, swerver, swerves	SWIRLED	–; –
		SWISH	–; swishy
SWERVER	–; swervers	SWISHED	–; –

SWISHER	–; swishers	SWOUN	–; swound,
SWISHES	–; –		swouns
SWISS		SWOUND	–; swounds
SWISSES	–; –	SWOUNED	–; –
SWITCH	–; –	SWUM	–; –
SWITH	–; swithe	SWUNG	–; –
SWITHE	–; swither	SYBO	–; –
SWITHER	–; swithers	SYBOES	–; –
SWITHLY	–; –	SYCE	–; sycee,
SWIVE	–; swived,		syces
	swivel,	SYCEE	–; sycees
	swives,	SYCOSES	–; –
	swivet	SYCOSIS	–; –
SWIVEL	–; swivels	SYENITE	–; syenites
SWIVET	–; swivets	SYKE	–; sykes
SWIVING	–; –	SYLLABI	–; syllabic
SWIZZLE	–; swizzled,	SYLPH	–; sylphs,
	swizzler,		sylphy
	swizzles	SYLPHIC	–; –
SWOB	–; swobs	SYLPHID	–; sylphids
SWOBBED	–; –	SYLVA	–; sylvae,
SWOBBER	–; swobbers		sylvan,
SWOLLEN	–; –		sylvas
SWOON	aswoon;	SYLVAN	–; sylvans
	swoons	SYLVIN	–; sylvine,
SWOONED	–; –		sylvins
SWOONER	–; swooners	SYLVINE	–; sylvines
SWOOP	–; swoops	SYLVITE	–; sylvites
SWOOPED	–; –	SYMBION	–; symbions,
SWOOPER	–; swoopers		symbiont
SWOOSH	–; –	SYMBIOT	–; symbiote,
SWOP	–; swops		symbiots
SWOPPED	–; –	SYMBOL	–; symbols
SWORD	–; swords	SYMPTOM	–; symptoms
SWORE	–; –	SYN	–; sync,
SWORN	–; –		syne
SWOT	–; swots	SYNAGOG	–; synagogs
SWOTTED	–; –	SYNAPSE	–;
SWOTTER	–; swotters		synapsed,
			synapses

SYNC	–; synch, syncs		synonymy
		SYNOVIA	–; synovial, synovias
SYNCARP	–; syncarps, syncarpy	**SYNTAX**	–; –
SYNCED	–; –	**SYNTONY**	–; –
SYNCH	–; synchs	**SYNURA**	–; synurae
SYNCHED	–; –	**SYPHER**	–; syphers
SYNCHRO	–; synchros	**SYPHON**	–; syphons
SYNCING	–; –	**SYREN**	–; syrens
SYNCOM	–; syncoms	**SYRINGA**	–; syringas
SYNCOPE	–; syncopes	**SYRINGE**	–; syringed, syringes
SYNDET	–; syndets		
SYNDIC	–; syndics	**SYRINX**	–; –
SYNESIS	–; –	**SYRPHID**	–; syrphids
SYNGAMY	–; –	**SYRUP**	–; syrups, syrupy
SYNOD	–; synods		
SYNODAL	–; –	**SYSTEM**	–; systems
SYNODIC	–; –	**SYSTOLE**	–; systoles
SYNONYM	–; synonyme, synonyms,	**SYZYGAL**	–; –
		SYZYGY	–;

T

Г	at, et, it, ut; ta, ti, to	**TABBIED**	–; –
TA	eta, uta; tab, tad, tae, tag, taj, tam, tan, tao, tap, tar, tas, tat, tau, tav, taw, tax	**TABBIES**	–; –
		TABBING	stabbing; –
		TABBIS	–; –
		TABBY	–; –
		TABER	–; tabers
		TABERED	–; –
		TABES	–; –
		TABETIC	–; tabetics
TAB	stab; tabs, tabu	**TABID**	–; –
		TABLA	–; tablas
TABANID	–; tabanids	**TABLE**	stable; tabled, tables, tablet
TABARD	–; tabards		
TABARET	–; tabarets		
TABBED	stabbed; –		

TABLEAU	–; tableaus, tableaux
TABLED	tabled, –
TABLES	stables; –
TABLET	–; tablets
TABLING	stabling; –
TABLOID	–; tabloids
TABOO	–; taboos
TABOOED	–; –
TABOR	–; tabors
TABORED	–; –
TABORER	–; taborers
TABORET	–; taborets
TABORIN	–; taborine, taborins
TABOUR	–; tabours
TABS	stabs; –
TABU	–; tabus
TABUED	–; –
TABUING	–; –
TABULAR	–; –
TACE	–; taces, tacet
TACH	–; tache, tachs
TACHE	–; taches
TACHISM	–; tachisms
TACHIST	–; tachiste, tachists
TACIT	–; –
TACITLY	–; –
TACK	stack; tacks, tacky
TACKED	stacked; –
TACKER	stacker; tackers
TACKERS	stackers;
TACKET	–; tackets
TACKEY	–;
TACKIER	–; –

TACKIFY	–; –
TACKILY	– ;
TACKING	stacking; –
TACKLE	–; tackled, tackler, tackles
TACKLER	–; tacklers
TACKLES	–; tackless
TACKS	stacks; –
TACNODE	–; tacnodes
TACO	–; tacos
TACT	–; tacts
TACTFUL	–; –
TACTIC	–; tactics
TACTILE	–; –
TACTION	–; tactions
TACTUAL	–; –
TAD	–; tads
TADPOLE	–; tadpoles
TAE	–; tael
TAEL	–; taels
TAENIA	–; taeniae, taenias
TAFFETA	–; taffetas
TAFFIA	–; taffias
TAFFIES	–; –
TAFFY	–; –
TAFIA	–; tafias
TAG	stag; tags
TAGGED	stagged; –
TAGGER	stagger; taggers
TAGGERS	staggers; –
TAGGING	stagging; -
TAGLIKE	–; –
TAGMEME	–; tagmeme
TAGRAG	–; tagrags
TAGS	stags; -
TAHR	–; tahrs
TAHSIL	–; tahsils

TAIGA	–; taigas	**TALE**	stale; taler, tales
TAIL	–; tails		
TAILED	–; –	**TALENT**	–; talents
TAILER	–; tailers	**TALER**	staler; talers
TAILING	–; tailings	**TALES**	stales; –
TAILLE	–; tailles	**TALI**	–; –
TAILLES	–; tailless	**TALION**	–; talions
TAILOR	–; tailors	**TALIPED**	–; talipeds
TAIN	stain; tains, taint	**TALIPES**	–; –
		TALIPOT	–; talipots
TAINS	stains; –	**TALK**	stalk; talks, talky
TAINT	–; taints		
TAINTED	–; –	**TALKED**	stalked; –
TAIPAN	–; taipans	**TALKER**	stalker; talkers
TAJ	–; –		
TAJES	–; –	**TALKERS**	stalkers; –
TAKAHE	–; takahes	**TALKIE**	–; talkier, talkies
TAKE	stake; taken, taker, takes		
		TALKIER	stalkier; –
TAKABLE	–; –	**TALKIES**	–; talkiest
TAKEOFF	–; takeoffs	**TALKING**	stalking; talkings
TAKEOUT	stakeout; takeouts		
		TALKS	stalks; –
TAKER	–; takers	**TALKY**	stalky; –
TAKES	stakes; –	**TALL**	stall; tally
TAKIN	–; taking, takins	**TALLAGE**	–; tallaged, tallages
TAKING	staking; –	**TALLBOY**	–; tallboys
TALA	–; talar, talas	**TALLER**	–; –
		TALLEST	–; –
TALAR	–; talars	**TALLIED**	–; –
TALARIA	–; –	**TALLIER**	–; talliers
TALC	–; talcs	**TALLIES**	–; –
TALCED	–; –	**TALLISH**	–; –
TALCING	–; –	**TALLITH**	–; –
TALCKED	–; –	**TALLOL**	–; tallols
TALCKY	–; –	**TALLOW**	–; tallows, tallowy
TALCOSE	–; –		
TALCOUS	–; –	**TALLYHO**	–; tallyhos
TALCUM	–; talcums	**TALON**	–; talons

TALONED	–; –	TAMP	stamp; tamps
TALOOKA	–; talookas		
TALUK	–; taluka, taluks	TAMPALA	–; tampalas
		TAMPAN	–; tampans
TALUKA	–; talukas	TAMPED	stamped; –
TALUS	–; –	TAMPER	stamper; tampers
TALUSES	–; –		
TAM	–; tame, tams	TAMPERS	stampers; –
		TAMPING	stamping; –
TAMABLE	–; –	TAMPION	–; tampions
TAMAL	–; tamale, tamals	TAMPON	–; tampons
		TAMPS	stamps; –
TAMALE	–; tamales	TAN	–; tang, tank, tans
TAMANDU	–; tamandua, tamundus	
		TANAGER	–; tanagers
		TANBARK	–; tanbarks
TAMARAO	–; tamaraos	TANDEM	–; tandems
TAMARAU	–; tamaraus	TANG	stang; tangs, tangy
TAMARIN	–; tamarind, tamarins	
		TANGED	stanged; –
TAMASHA	–; tamashas	TANGELO	–; tangelos
TAMBAC	–; tambacs	TANGENT	–; tangents
TAMBALA	–; tambalas	TANGIER	–; –
TAMBOUR	–; tamboura, tambours	TANGING	stanging; –
		TANGLE	–; tangled, tangler, tangles
TAMBUR	–; tambura, tamburs	
TAMBURA	–; tamburas	TANGLER	–; tanglers
TAME	–; tamed, tamer, tames	TANGLY	–; –
		TANGO	–; tangos
TAMEIN	–; tameins	TANGOED	–; –
TAMELY	–; –	TANGRAM	–; tangrams
TAMER	–; tamers	TANGS	stangs; –
TAMES	–; tamest	TANIST	–; tanists
TAMING	–; –	TANK	stank; tanka, tanks
TAMIS	–; –	
TAMISES	–; –	TANKA	–; tankas
TAMMIE	–; tammies	TANKAGE	–; tankages
TAMMY	–; –	TANKARD	–; tankards
		TANKER	–; tankers

TANKFUL	–; tankfuls	**TAPIR**	–; tapirs
TANKS	stanks; –	**TAPIS**	–; –
TANNAGE	–; tannages	**TAPISES**	–; –
TANNATE	–; tannates	**TAPPED**	–; –
TANNED	–; –	**TAPPER**	–; tappers
TANNER	–; tanners, tannery	**TAPPET**	–; tappets
TANNEST	–; –	**TAPPING**	–; tappings
TANNIC	stannic; –	**TAPROOM**	–; taprooms
TANNIN	–; tanning, tannins	**TAPROOT**	–; taproots
TANNING	–; tannings	**TAPSTER**	–; tapsters
TANNISH	–; –	**TAR**	star; tare, tarn, taro, tarp, tart
TANREC	–; tanrecs	**TARBUSH**	–; –
TANSIES	–; –	**TARDIER**	–; –
TANSY	–; –	**TARDIES**	–; tardiest
TANTARA	–; tantaras	**TARDILY**	–; –
TANTIVY	–; –	**TARDO**	–; –
TANTO	–; –	**TARDY**	–; –
TANTRA	–; tantras	**TARE**	stare; tared, tares
TANTRIC	–; –		
TANTRUM	–; tantrums	**TARED**	stared; –
TANYARD	–; tanyards	**TARES**	stares; –
TAO	–; taos	**TARGE**	–; targes, target
TAP	–; tapa, tape, taps	**TARGET**	–; targets
TAPALO	–; tapalos	**TARIFF**	–; tariffs
TAPE	etape; taped, taper, tapes	**TARING**	staring; –
		TARMAC	–; tarmacs
		TARN	–; tarns
TAPER	–; tapers	**TARNAL**	–; –
TAPERED	–; –	**TARNISH**	–; –
TAPERER	–; taperers	**TARO**	–; taroc, tarok, taros, tarot
TAPES	etapes, stapes; –		
TAPETA	–; tapetal	**TAROC**	–; tarocs
TAPETUM	–; –	**TAROK**	–; taroks
TAPHOLE	–; tapholes	**TAROT**	–; tarots
TAPING	–; –	**TARP**	–; tarps
TAPIOCA	–; tapiocas		

TARPAN	–; tarpans		tasses,
TARPON	–; tarpons		tasset
TARRE	–; tarred, tarres	TASSEL	–; tassels
TARRED	starred; –	TASSET	–; tassets
TARRIED	–; –	TASSIE	–; tassies
TARRIER	starrier; tarriers	TASTE	–; tasted, taster, tastes
TARRIES	–; tarriest	TASTER	–; tasters
TARRING	starring; –	TASTIER	–; –
TARRY	starry; –	TASTILY	–; –
TARS	stars; –	TASTING	–; –
TARSAL	–; tarsals	TASTY	–; –
TARSI	–; tarsia	TAT	–; tate, tats
TARSIA	–; tarsias	TATAMI	–; tatamis
TARSIER	–; tarsiers	TATE	state; tater, tates
TARSUS	–; –		
TART	start; tarts	TATER	stater; taters
TARTAN	–; tartana, tartans	TATERS	staters; –
		TATES	states; –
TARTANA	–; tartanas	TATOUAY	–; tatouays
TARTAR	–; tartars	TATTED	–; –
TARTED	started; –	TATTER	–; tatters
TARTER	starter; –	TATTIER	–; –
TARTEST	–; –	TATTING	–; tattings
TARTING	starting; –	TATTLE	–; tattled, tattler, tattles
TARTISH	–; –	TATTLER	; tattlers
TARTLET	–; tartlets	TATTOO	–; tattoos
TARTLY	–; –	TATTY	–; –
TARTS	starts; –	TAU	–; taus, taut
TARTUFE	–; tartufes	TAUGHT	–; –
TARWEED	–; tarweeds	TAUNT	–; taunts
TARZAN	–; tarzans	TAUNTED	–; –
TAS	etas, utas; task, tass	TAUNTER	–; taunters
		TAUPE	–; taupes
TASK	–; tasks	TAURINE	–; taurines
TASKED	–; –	TAUT	–; tauts
TASKING	–; –	TAUTAUG	–; tautaugs
TASS	–; tasse	TAUTED	–; –
TASSE	–; tassel,	TAUTEN	–; tautens

TAUTER	–; –	**TAXIWAY**	–; taxiways
TAUTEST	–; –	**TAXLESS**	–; –
TAUTING	–; –	**TAXMAN**	–; –
TAUTLY	–; –	**TAXMEN**	–; –
TAUTOG	–; tautogs	**TAXON**	–; taxons
TAV	–; tavs	**TAXPAID**	–; –
TAVERN	–; taverns	**TAXUS**	–; –
TAW	staw; taws	**TAXWISE**	–; –
TAWDRY	–; –	**TAXYING**	–; –
TAWED	–; –	**TAZZA**	–; tazzas
TAWER	–; tawers	**TAZZE**	–; –
TAWIE	–; –	**TEA**	–; teak, teal,
TAWING	–; –		team, tear,
TAWNEY	–; tawneys		teas, teat
TAWNIER	–; –	**TEABOWL**	–; teabowls
TAWNIES	–; tawniest	**TEABOX**	–; –
TAWNILY	–; –	**TEACAKE**	–; teacakes
TAWNY	–; –	**TEACART**	–; teacarts
TAWPIE	–; tawpies	**TEACH**	–; –
TAWSE	–; tawsed,	**TEACHER**	–; teachers
	tawses	**TEACHES**	–; –
TAWSING	–; –	**TEACUP**	–; teacups
TAX	–; taxa, taxi	**TEAK**	steak; teaks
TAXABLE	–; taxables	**TEAKS**	steaks; –
TAXABLY	–; –	**TEAL**	steal; teals
TAXED	–; –	**TEALS**	steals; –
TAXEME	–; taxemes	**TEAM**	steam; teams
TAXEMIC	–; –	**TEAMED**	steamed; –
TAXER	–; taxers	**TEAMING**	steaming; –
TAXES	–; –	**TEAMS**	steams; –
TAXI	–; taxis	**TEAPOT**	–; teapots
TAXICAB	–; taxicabs	**TEAPOY**	–; teapoys
TAXIMAN	–; –	**TEAR**	–; tears,
TAXIMEN	–; –		teary
TAXIED	–; –		
TAXIES	ataxies; –	**TEARED**	–; –
TAXIING	–; –	**TEARER**	–; tearers
TAXING	–; –	**TEARFUL**	–; –
TAXITE	–; taxites	**TEARGAS**	–; –
TAXITIC	–; –	**TEARIER**	–; –
		TEARILY	–; –

TEARING	–; –	**TEEMED**	–; –
TEAROOM	–; tearooms	**TEEMER**	; teemers
TEASE	–; teased,	**TEEMING**	–; –
	teasel,	**TEEN**	–; teens,
	teaser,		teeny
	teases	**TEENAGE**	–;
TEASEL	–; teasels		teenaged,
TEASER	–; teasers		teenager
TEASHOP	–; teashops	**TEENER**	–; teeners
TEASING	–; –	**TEENFUL**	–; –
TEAT	–; teats	**TEENIER**	–; –
TEATED	–; –	**TEENS**	–; teensy
TEATIME	–; teatimes	**TEENTSY**	–; –
TEAWARE	–; teawares	**TEEPEE**	–; teepees
TEAZEL	–; teazels	**TEETER**	–; teeters
TEAZLE	–; teazled,	**TEETH**	–; teethe
	teazles	**TEETHE**	–; teethed,
TECHED	–; –		teether,
TECHIER	–; –		teethes
TECHILY	–; –	**TEETHER**	–; teethers
TECHNIC	atechnic;	**TEFF**	–; teffs
	technics	**TEG**	–; tegs
TECHY	–; –	**TEGMEN**	–; –
TECTA	–; tectal	**TEGMINA**	–; –
TECTRIX	–; –	**TEGUA**	–; teguas
TECTUM	–; –	**TEGULAR**	–; –
TED	–; teds	**TEGUMEN**	–; tegument
TEDDED	–; –	**TEIID**	–; teiids
TEDDER	–; tedders	**TEIND**	–; teinds
TEDDIES	–; –	**TEKTITE**	–; tektites
TEDDING	–; –	**TELA**	stela; telae
TEDDY	–; –	**TELAE**	stelae; –
TEDIOUS	–; –	**TELAMON**	–; –
TEDIUM	–; tediums	**TELE**	stele; teles,
TEE	–; teed,		telex
	teem, teen,	**TELEDU**	–; teledus
	tees	**TELEGA**	–; telegas
TEED	steed; –	**TELEMAN**	–; –
TEEING	–; –	**TELEMEN**	–; –
TEEM	–; teems	**TELEOST**	–; teleosts

TELERAN	–; telerans	TEN	–; tend,
TELES	steles; –		tens, tent
TELESES	–; –	TENABLE	–; –
TELESIS	–; –	TENABLY	–; –
TELEX	–; –	TENACE	–; tenaces
TELEXED	–; –	TENAIL	–; tenails
TELEXES	–; –	TENANCY	–; –
TELFER	–; telfers	TENANT	–; tenants
TELFORD	–; telfords	TENCH	stench; –
TELIA	–; telial	TENCHES	stenches; –
TELIC	atelic, stelic; –	TEND	–; tends
TELIUM	–; –	TENDED	–; –
TELL	–; tells, telly	TENDER	–; tenders
TELLER	–; tellers	TENDING	–; –
TELLIES	–; –	TENDON	–; tendons
TELLING	–; –	TENDRIL	–; tendrils
TELOI	–; –	TENET	–; tenets
TELOME	–; telomes	TENFOLD	–; tenfolds
TELOMIC	–; –	TENIA	–; teniae,
TELOS	–; –		tenias
TELPHER	–; telphers	TENNER	–; tenners
TELSON	–; telsons	TENNIS	–; tennist
TEMBLOR	–; temblors	TENNIST	–; tennists
TEMPEH	–; tempehs	TENON	–; tenons
TEMPER	–; tempera,	TENONED	–; –
	tempers	TENONER	–; tenoners
TEMPERA	–; temperas	TENOR	–; tenors
TEMPEST	–; tempests	TENOUR	–; tenours
TEMPI	–; –	TENPIN	–; tenpins
TEMPLAR	–; templars	TENREC	–; tenrecs
TEMPLE	–; templed,	TENSE	–; tensed,
	temples,		tenser,
	templet		tenses
TEMPLET	–; templets	TENSELY	–; –
TEMPO	–; tempos	TENSES	–; tensest
TEMPT	–; tempts	TENSILE	–; –
TEMPTED	–; –	TENSING	–; –
TEMPTER	–; tempters	TENSION	–; tensions
TEMPURA	–; tempuras	TENSITY	–; –
		TENSIVE	–; –

TENSOR	–; tensors	**TERGA**	–; tergal
TENT	–; tenth, tenths, tenty	**TERGITE**	–; torgites
		TERGUM	–; –
TENTAGE	–; tentages	**TERM**	–; terms
TENTED	–; –	**TERMED**	–; –
TENTER	–; tenters	**TERMER**	–; termers
TENTH	–; tenths	**TERMING**	–; –
TENTHLY	–; –	**TERMITE**	–; termites
TENTIE	–; tentier	**TERMLY**	–; –
TENTING	–; –	**TERMOR**	–; termors
TENUIS	–; –	**TERN**	stern; terne, terns
TENUITY	–; –		
TENURE	–; tenured, tenures	**TERNARY**	–; –
		TERNATE	–; –
TENUTI	–; –	**TERNE**	eterne; ternes
TENUTO	–; tenutos		
TEOPAN	–; teopans	**TERNION**	–; ternions
TEPA	–; tepal, tepas	**TERNS**	sterns; –
TEPAL	–; tepals	**TERPENE**	–; terpenes
TEPEE	–; tepees	**TERRA**	–; terrae, terras
TEPEFY	–; –	**TERRACE**	–; terraced, terraces
TEPHRA	–; tephras		
TEPID	–; –	**TERRAIN**	–; terrains
TEPIDLY	–; –	**TERRANE**	–; terranes
TEQUILA	–; tequilas	**TERREEN**	–; terreens
TERAI	–; terais	**TERRENE**	–; terrenes
TERAOHM	–; teraohms	**TERRET**	–; terrets
TERAPH	–; –	**TERRIER**	–; terriers
TERBIA	–; terbias	**TERRIES**	–; –
TERBIC	–; –	**TERRIFY**	–; –
TERBIUM	–; terbiums	**TERRINE**	–; terrines
TERCE	–; tercel, terces, tercet	**TERRIT**	–; territs
		TERROR	–; terrors
TERCEL	–; tercels	**TERRY**	–; –
TERCET	–; tercets	**TERSE**	–; terser
TEREBIC	–; –	**TERSELY**	–; –
TEREDO	–; teredos	**TERSEST**	–; –
TEREFAH	–; –	**TERTIAL**	–; tertials
TERETE	–; –	**TERTIAN**	–; tertians

TESLA	–; teslas	**TEWS**	stews; –
TESSERA	–; tesserae	**TEXAS**	–; –
TEST	–; testa, tests, testy	**TEXASES**	–; –
		TEXT	–; texts
TESTA	–; testae	**TEXTILE**	–; textiles
TESTACY	–; –	**TEXTUAL**	–; –
TESTATE	–; –	**TEXTURE**	–; textured, textures
TESTED	–; –		
TESTEE	–; testees	**THACK**	–; thacks
TESTER	–; testers	**THACKED**	–; –
TESTES	–; –	**THAE**	–; –
TESTIER	–; –	**THAIRM**	–; thairms
TESTIFY	–; –	**THALER**	–; thalers
TESTILY	–; –	**THALLI**	–; thallic
TESTING	–; –	**THALLUS**	–; –
TESTIS	–; –	**THAN**	–; thane, thank
TESTON	–; testons		
TESTOON	–; testoons	**THANAGE**	–; thanages
TESTUDO	–; testudos	**THANE**	ethane; thanes
TETANAL	–; –		
TETANIC	–; tetanics	**THANES**	ethanes; –
TETANUS	–; –	**THANK**	–; thanks
TETANY	–; –	**THANKED**	–; –
TETCHED	–; –	**THANKER**	–; thankers
TETCHY	–; –	**THARM**	–; tharms
TETH	–; teths	**THAT**	–; –
TETHER	–; tethers	**THATCH**	–; thatchy
TETOTUM	–; tetotums	**THAW**	–; thaws
TETRA	–; tetrad, tetras	**THAWED**	–; –
		THAWER	–; thawers
TETRAD	–; tetrads	**THAWING**	–; –
TETRODE	–; tetrodes	**THE**	–; thee, them, then, thew, they
TETRYL	–; tetryls		
TETTER	–; tetters		
TEUCH	–; –	**THEATER**	–; theaters
TEUGH	–; –	**THEATRE**	–; theatres
TEUGHLY	–; –	**THECA**	–; thecae, thecal
TEW	stew; tews		
TEWED	stewed; –	**THECATE**	–; –
TEWING	stewing; –	**THEE**	–; –

THEELIN	–; theelins	**THERMAL**	–; thermals
THEELOL	–; theelols	**THERME**	–; thermal,
THEFT	–; thefts		thermes
THEGN	–; thegns	**THERMEL**	–; thermels
THEGNLY	–; –	**THERMIC**	–; –
THEIN	–; theine,	**THERMIT**	–; thermite,
	theins		thermits
THEINE	–; theines	**THERMOS**	–; –
THEIR	–; theirs	**THEROID**	–; –
THEISM	atheism;	**THESE**	–; theses
	theisms	**THESIS**	–; –
THEISMS	atheisms; –	**THETA**	–; thetas
THEIST	atheist;	**THETIC**	–; –
	theists	**THEURGY**	–; –
THEISTS	atheists; –	**THEW**	–; thews,
THEM	–; theme		thewy
THEME	–; themes	**THIAMIN**	–; thiamine,
THEN	–; thens		thiamins
THENAGE	–; thenages	**THIAZIN**	–; thiazine,
THENAL	–; –		thiazins
THENAR	–; thenars	**THIAZOL**	–; thiazole,
THENCE	–; –		thiazols
THEOLOG	–; theologs,	**THICK**	–; thicks
	theology	**THICKEN**	–; thickens
THEORBO	–; theorbos	**THICKET**	–; thickets,
THEOREM	–; theorems		thickety
THEORY	–; –	**THICKLY**	–; –
THERAPY	–; –	**THIEF**	–; –
THERE	–; theres	**THIEVE**	–; thieved,
THEREAT	–; –		thieves
THEREBY	–; –	**THIGH**	–; thighs
THEREIN	–; –	**THIGHED**	–; –
THEREOF	–; –	**THILL**	–; thills
THEREON	–; –	**THIMBLE**	–; thimbles
THERETO	–; –	**THIN**	–; thine,
THERIAC	–; theriaca,		thing, think,
	theriacs		thins
THERM	–; therme,	**THING**	–; things
	therms	**THINK**	–; thinks
THERMAE	–; –	**THINKER**	–; thinkers

THINLY	–; –	**THORON**	–; thorons
THINNED	–; –	**THORP**	–; thorpe,
THINNER	–; thinners		thorps
THIO	–; thiol	**THORPE**	–; thorpes
THIOL	–; thiols	**THOSE**	–; –
THIOLIC	–; –	**THOU**	–; thous
THIONIC	–; –	**THOUED**	–; –
THIONIN	–; thionine,	**THOUGH**	–; thought
	thionins	**THOUGHT**	–; thoughts
THIONYL	–; thionyls	**THOUING**	–; –
THIR	–; third, thirl	**THRALL**	–; thralls
THIRAM	–; thirams	**THRASH**	–; –
THIRD	–; thirds	**THRAVE**	–; thraves
THIRDLY	–; –	**THRAW**	–; thrawn,
THIRL	–; thirls		throws
THIRLED	–; –	**THRAWED**	–; –
THIRST	athirst;	**THREAD**	–; threads,
	thirsts, thirsty		thready
THIRTY	–; –	**THREAP**	–; threaps
THIS	–; –	**THREAT**	–; threats
THISTLE	–; thistles	**THREE**	–; threep,
THISTLY	–; –		threes
THITHER	–; –	**THREEP**	–; threeps
THO	–; thou	**THRESH**	–; –
THOLE	–; tholed,	**THREW**	–; –
	tholes	**THRICE**	–; –
THOLING	–; –	**THRIFT**	–; thrifts,
THOLOI	–; –		thrifty
THOLOS	–; –	**THRILL**	–; thrills
THONG	–; thongs	**THRIP**	–; thrips
THONGED	–; –	**THRIVE**	–; thrived,
THORAX	–; –		thriven,
THORIA	–; thorias		thriver,
THORIC	–; –		thrives
THORITE	–; thorites	**THRIVER**	–; thrivers
THORIUM	–; thoriums	**THRO**	–; throb,
THORN	–; thorns,		throe, throw
	thorny	**THROAT**	–; throats,
THORNED	–; –		throaty
THORO	–; thoron	**THROB**	–; throbs

THROE	–; throes	**THYMI**	–; thymic
THRONE	–; throned, throngs	**THYMIER**	–; –
		THYMINE	–; thymines
THRONG	–; throngs	**THYMOL**	–; thymols
THROUGH	–; –	**THYMUS**	–; –
THROVE	–; –	**THYMY**	–; –
THROW	–; thrown, throws	**THYROID**	–; thyroids
		THYRSE	–; thyrses
THROWER	–; throwers	**THYRSI**	–; –
THRU	–; thrum	**THYRSUS**	–; –
THRUM	–; thrums	**THYSELF**	–; –
THRUMMY	–; –	**TI**	–; tic, tie, til, tin, tip, tis, tit
THRUPUT	–; thruputs		
THRUSH	–; –	**TIARA**	–; tiaras
THRUST	–; thrusts	**TIARAED**	; –
THRUWAY	–; thruways	**TIBIA**	–; tibiae, tibial, tibias
THUD	–; thuds		
THUDDED	–; –	**TIBIAL**	stibial; –
THUG	–; thugs	**TIC**	otic; tick, tics
THUGGEE	–; thuggees	**TICAL**	–; ticals
THUJA	–; thujas	**TICK**	stick; ticks
THULIA	–; thulias	**TICKED**	sticked; –
THULIUM	–; thuliums	**TICKER**	sticker; tickers
THUMB	–; thumbs		
THUMBED	–; –	**TICKERS**	stickers; –
THUMP	–; thumps	**TICKET**	–; tickets
THUMPED	–; –	**TICKING**	sticking; –
THUMPER	–; thumpers	**TICKLE**	stickle; tickled, tickler, tickles
THUNDER	–; thunders, thundery		
		TICKLED	stickled; –
THURL	–; thurls	**TICKLER**	stickler; ticklers
THUS	–; –		
THUSLY	–; –	**TICKS**	sticks; –
THUYA	–; thuyas	**TICTAC**	–; tictacs
THWACK	–; thwacks	**TICTOC**	–; tictocs
THWART	athwart; thwarts	**TIDAL**	–; –
		TIDALLY	–; –
THY	–; –	**TIDBIT**	–; tidbits
THYME	–; thymes, thymey	**TIDDLY**	–; –

TIDE	–; tided, tides	**TIKE**	–; tikes
		TIKI	–; tikis
TIDERIP	–; tiderips	**TIL**	–; tile, till,
TIDEWAY	–; tideways		tils, tilt
TIDIED	–; –	**TILAPIA**	–; tilapias
TIDIER	–; –	**TILBURY**	–; –
TIDIES	–; tidiest	**TILDE**	–; tildes
TIDILY	–; –	**TILE**	stile, utile;
TIDING	–; tidings		tiled, tiler,
TIDY	–; –		tiles
TIDYING	–; –	**TILER**	–; tilers
TIE	–; tied, tier,	**TILES**	stiles; –
	ties	**TILING**	–; tilings
TIEBACK	–; tiebacks	**TILL**	still; tills
TIED	stied; –	**TILLAGE**	–; tillages
TIEING	–; –	**TILLED**	stilled; –
TIEPIN	–; tiepins	**TILLER**	stiller; tillers
TIER	–; tiers	**TILLING**	stilling; –
TIERCE	–; tierced,	**TILLS**	stills; –
	tiercel,	**TILT**	atilt, stilt;
	tierces		tilth, tilts
TIERCEL	–; tiercels	**TILTED**	stilted; –
TIERED	–; –	**TILTER**	–; tilters
TIERING	–; –	**TILTH**	–; tilths
TIES	sties; –	**TILTING**	stilting; –
TIFF	stiff; tiffs	**TILTS**	stilts; –
TIFFANY	–; –	**TIMARAU**	–; timaraus
TIFFED	–; –	**TIMBAL**	–; timbale,
TIFFIN	–; tiffing,		timbals
	tiffins	**TIMBALE**	–; timbales
TIFFS	stiffs; –	**TIMBER**	–; timbers
TIGER	–; tigers	**TIMBRE**	–; timbrel,
TIGHT	–; tights		timbres
TIGHTEN	–; tightens	**TIMBREL**	–; timbrels
TIGHTER	–; –	**TIME**	stime; timed,
TIGHTLY	–; –		timer, times
TIGLON	–; tiglons	**TIMELY**	–; –
TIGON	–; tigons	**TIMEOUS**	–; –
TIGRESS	–; –	**TIMEOUT**	–; timeouts
TIGRISH	–; –	**TIMER**	–; timers

TIMES	stimes; –	**TINING**	–; –
TIMID	–; –	**TINKER**	stinker·
TIMIDER	,		tinkers
TIMIDLY	–; –	**TINKERS**	stinkers; –
TIMING	–; timings	**TINKLE**	–; tinkled,
TIMOTHY	–; –		tinkles
TIMPANA	–; –	**TINKLY**	–; –
TIMPANI	–; –	**TINLIKE**	–; –
TIMPANO	–; –	**TINMAN**	–; –
TIN	–; tine, ting,	**TINMEN**	–; –
	tins, tint, tiny	**TINNED**	–; –
TINAMOU	–; tinamous	**TINNER**	–; tinners
TINCAL	–; tincals	**TINNIER**	–; –
TINCT	–; tincts	**TINNILY**	–; –
TINCTED	–; –	**TINNING**	–; –
TINDER	–; tinders,	**TINNY**	–; –
	tindery	**TINSEL**	–; tinsels
TINE	–; tinea,	**TINT**	stint; tints
	tined, tines	**TINTED**	stinted; –
TINEA	–; tineal,	**TINTER**	stinter; tinters
	tineas	**TINTERS**	stinters; –
TINEID	–; tineids	**TINTING**	stinting;
TINFOIL	–; tinfoils		tintings
TINFUL	–; tinfuls	**TINTS**	stints; –
TING	sting; tinge,	**TINTYPE**	–; tintypes
	tings	**TINWARE**	–; tinwares
TINGE	–; tinged,	**TINWORK**	–; tinworks
	tinges	**TIP**	–; tipi, tips
TINGING	stinging; –	**TIPCART**	–; tipcarts
TINGLE	atingle;	**TIPCAT**	–; tipcats
	tingled,	**TIPI**	–; tipis
	tingler,	**TIPLESS**	–; –
	tingles	**TIPOFF**	–; tipoffs
TINGLER	–; tinglers	**TIPPED**	–; –
TINGLY	–; –	**TIPPER**	–; tippers
TINGS	stings; –	**TIPPET**	–; tippets
TINHORN	–; tinhorns	**TIPPIER**	–; –
TINIER	–; –	**TIPPING**	–; –
TINIEST	–; –	**TIPPLE**	stipple;
TINILY	–; –		tippled,

	tippler, tipples	**TITIAN**	–; titians
TIPPLED	stippled; –	**TITLARK**	–; titlarks
TIPPLER	stippler; tipplers	**TITLE**	–; titled, titles
TIPPLES	stipples; –	**TITLING**	–; –
TIPPY	–; –	**TITLIST**	–; titlists
TIPS	–; tipsy	**TITMAN**	–; –
TIPSIER	–; –	**TITMEN**	–; –
TIPSILY	–; –	**TITRANT**	–; titrants
TIPSTER	–; tipsters	**TITRATE**	–; titrated,
TIPTOE	–; tiptoed, tiptoes		titrates
		TITRE	–; titres
TIPTOP	–; tiptops	**TITTER**	–; titters
TIRADE	–; tirades	**TITTIE**	–; titties
TIRE	–; tired, tires	**TITTLE**	–; tittles
TIREDER	–; –	**TITTUP**	–; tittups
TIREDLY	–; –	**TITTY**	–; –
TIRING	–; –	**TITUPED**	–; –
TIRL	–; tirls	**TITULAR**	–; titulars, titulary
TIRLED	–; –		
TIRLING	–; –	**TIVY**	–; –
TIRO	–; tiros	**TIZZIES**	–; –
TISANE	–; tisanes	**TIZZY**	–; –
TISSUAL	–; –	**TMESES**	–; –
TISSUE	–; tissued, tissues, tissuey	**TMESIS**	–; –
		TO	–; tod, toe, tog, tom, ton, too, top, tor, tot, tow, toy
TIT	–; titi, tits		
TITAN	–; titans		
TITANIA	–; titanias		
TITANIC	–; –	**TOAD**	–; toads, toady
TITBIT	–; titbits		
TITER	–; titers	**TOADIED**	–; –
TITHE	–; tithed, tither, tithes	**TOADIES**	–; –
		TOADISH	–; –
TITHER	–; tithers	**TOAST**	–; toasts, toasty
TITHING	–; tithings		
TITI	–; titis	**TOASTED**	–; –
TITIS	otitis; –	**TOASTER**	–; toasters
		TOBACCO	–; –

TOBIES	–; –	toggler,
TOBY	–; –	toggles
TOCCATA	–; toccatas	**TOGGLER**	–; togglers
TOCCATE	–; –	**TOGUE**	–; togues,
TOCHER	–; tochers	toguet
TOCSIN	–; tocsins	**TOIL**	–; toile, toils
TOD	–; tods,	**TOILE**	etoile; toiled,
	tody	toiler, toiles,
TODAY	–; todays	toilet
TODDIES	–; –	**TOILER**	–; toilers
TODDLE	–; toddled,	**TOILES**	etoiles; –
	toddler,	**TOILET**	–; toilets
	toddles	**TOILFUL**	–; –
TODDLER	–; toddlers	**TOILING**	–; –
TODDY	–; –	**TOIT**	–; toits
TODIES	–; –	**TOITED**	–; –
TOE	–; toed,	**TOITING**	–; –
	toes	**TOKAY**	–; tokays
TOECAP	–; toecaps	**TOKE**	stoke; token,
TOEHOLD	–; toeholds	tokes
TOELESS	–; –	**TOKEN**	–; tokens
TOELIKE	–; –	**TOKENED**	–; –
TOEING	–; –	**TOKES**	stokes; –
TOENAIL	–; toenails	**TOLA**	–; tolan,
TOESHOE	–; toeshoes	tolas
TOFF	–; toffs, toffy	**TOLAN**	–; tolane,
TOFFEE	–; toffees	tolans
TOFFIES	–; –	**TOLANE**	–; tolanes
TOFT	–; tofts	**TOLD**	–; –
TOFU	–; tofus	**TOLE**	stole; toled,
TOG	–; toga,	toles
	togs	**TOLED**	stoled;
TOGA	–; togae,	toledo
	togas	**TOLEDO**	–; toledos
TOGAE	–; togaed	**TOLES**	stoles; –
TOGATE	–; togated	**TOLIDIN**	–; tolidine,
TOGGED	–; –	tolidins
TOGGERY	–; –	**TOLING**	–; –
TOGGING	–; –	**TOLL**	atoll; tolls
TOGGLE	–; toggled,	**TOLLAGE**	–; tollages

TOLLBAR	–; tollbars	TOMPION	–; tompions
TOLLED	–; –	TOMTIT	–; tomtits
TOLLER	–; tollers	TOMS	atoms; –
TOLLING	–; –	TON	–; tone,
TOLLMAN	–; –		tong, tons,
TOLLMEN	–; –		tony
TOLLWAY	–; tollways	TONAL	atonal; –
TOLLS	atolls; –	TONALLY	atonally; –
TOLU	–; tolus	TONDI	–; –
TOLUATE	–; toluates	TONDO	–; –
TOLUENE	–; toluenes	TONE	atone, stone;
TOLUIC	–; –		toned, toner,
TOLUID	–; toluide,		tones
	toluids	TONED	atoned,
TOLUIDE	–; toluides		stoned; –
TOLUOL	–; toluole,	TONEME	–; tonemes
	toluols	TONEMIC	–; –
TOLUOLE	–; toluoles	TONER	atoner,
TOLUYL	–; toluyls		stoner;
TOLYL	–; tolyls		toners
TOM	atom; tomb,	TONERS	atoners,
	tome, toms		stoners; –
TOMAN	–; tomans	TONES	atones,
TOMATO	–; –		stones; –
TOMB	–; tombs	TONETIC	–; tonetics
TOMBAC	–; tomback,	TONETTE	–; tonettes
	tombacs	TONG	–; tonga,
TOMBACK	–; tombacks		tongs
TOMBAK	–; tombaks	TONGA	–; tongas
TOMBAL	–; –	TONGED	–; –
TOMBED	–; –	TONGER	–; tongers
TOMBING	–; –	TONGING	–; –
TOMBOLO	–; tombolos	TONGMAN	–; –
TOMBOY	–; tomboys	TONGMEN	–; –
TOMCAT	–; tomcats	TONGUE	–; tonguea,
TOMCOD	–; tomcods		tongues
TOME	–; tomes	TONIC	atonic; tonics
TOMFOOL	–; tomfools	TONICS	atonics; –
TOMMIES	–; –	TONIER	stonier; –
TOMMY	–; –	TONIEST	stoniest; –

TONIGHT	-; tonights	**TOOTLE**	-; tootled,
TONING	atoning,		tootler,
	stoning; -		tootles
TONISH	stonish; -	**TOOTLER**	-; tootlers
TONLET	-; tonlets	**TOOTS**	-; tootsy
TONNAGE	-; tonnages	**TOOTSES**	-; -
TONNE	-; tonner,	**TOOTSIE**	-; tootsies
	tonnes	**TOP**	atop, stop;
TONNEAU	-; tonneaus,		tope, toph,
	tonneaux		topi, tops
TONNER	-; tonners	**TOPAZ**	-; -
TONNISH	-; -	**TOPAZES**	-; -
TONSIL	-; tonsils	**TOPCOAT**	-; topcoats
TONSURE	-; tonsured,	**TOPE**	stope;
	tonsures		toped,
TONTINE	-; tontines		topee,
TONUS	-; -		toper, topes
TONUSES	-; -	**TOPED**	stoped; -
TONY	atony,	**TOPEE**	-; topees
	stony; -	**TOPER**	stoper;
TOO	-; took,		topers
	tool, toom,	**TOPERS**	stopers; -
	toon, toot	**TOPES**	stopes; -
TOOK	stook; -	**TOPFUL**	-; topfull
TOOL	stool; tools	**TOPH**	-; tophe,
TOOLBOX	-; -		tophi, tophs
TOOLED	stooled; -	**TOPHE**	-; tophes
TOOLER	-; toolers	**TOPHUS**	-; -
TOOLING	stooling;	**TOPI**	-; topic,
	toolings		topis
TOOLS	stools; -	**TOPIARY**	-; -
TOON	-; toons	**TOPIC**	atopic;
TOOT	-; tooth,		topics
	toots	**TOPICAL**	-; -
TOOTED	-; -	**TOPING**	stoping; -
TOOTER	-; tooters	**TOPKICK**	-; topkicks
TOOTH	-; tooths,	**TOPKNOT**	-; topknots
	toothy	**TOPLESS**	-; -
TOOTHED	-; -	**TOPMAST**	-; topmasts
TOOTING	-; -	**TOPMOST**	-; -

TOPOI	–; –	**TORI**	–; toric, torii
TOPONYM	–; toponyms, toponymy	**TORIES**	stories; –
		TORII	–; –
		TORMENT	–; torments
TOPOS	–; –	**TORN**	–; –
TOPPED	stopped; –	**TORNADO**	–; tornados
TOPPER	stopper; toppers	**TORO**	–; toros
		TOROID	–; toroids
TOPPERS	stoppers; –	**TOROSE**	–; –
TOPPING	stopping; toppings	**TOROUS**	–; –
		TORPEDO	–; torpedos
TOPPLE	stopple; toppled, topples	**TORPID**	–; torpids
		TORPOR	–; torpors
		TORQUE	–; torqued, torquer, torques
TOPPLED	stoppled; –		
TOPPLES	stopples; –		
TOPS	stops; –	**TORQUER**	–; torquers
TOPSAIL	–; topsails	**TORREFY**	–; –
TOPSIDE	–; topsides	**TORRENT**	–; torrents
TOPSOIL	–; topsoils	**TORRID**	–; –
TOPWORK	–; topworks	**TORRIFY**	–; –
TOQUE	–; toques, toquet	**TORSADE**	–; torsades
		TORSE	–; torses
TOQUET	–; toquets	**TORSI**	–; –
TOR	–; tora, torc, tore, tori, torn, toro, torr, tors, tort, tory	**TORSION**	–; torsions
		TORSK	–; torsks
		TORSO	–; torsos
		TORT	–; torte, torts
TORA	–; torah, toras	**TORTE**	–; torten, tortes
TORAH	–; torahs	**TORTILE**	–; –
TORC	–; torch, torcs	**TORTONI**	–; tortonis
		TORTRIX	–; –
TORCHED	–; –	**TORTURE**	–; tortured, torturer, tortures
TORCHES	–; –		
TORCHON	–; torchons		
TORE	store; tores	**TORULA**	–; torulae, torulas
TORERO	–; toreros		
TORES	stores; –	**TORUS**	–; –

TORY	story; –	**TOUGHIE**	–; toughies
TOSH	–;	**TOUGHLY**	–; –
TOSHES	–; –	**TOUPEE**	–; toupees
TOSS	stoss; –	**TOUR**	stour; tours
TOSSED	–; –	**TOURACO**	–; touracos
TOSSER	–; tossers	**TOURED**	–; –
TOSSES	–; –	**TOURER**	–; tourers
TOSSING	–; –	**TOURING**	–; tourings
TOSSPOT	–; tosspots	**TOURISM**	–; tourisms
TOSSUP	–; tossups	**TOURIST**	–; tourists, touristy
TOST	–; –		
TOT	–; tots	**TOURNEY**	–; tourneys
TOTABLE	–; –	**TOURS**	stours; –
TOTAL	–; totals	**TOUSE**	–; toused, touses
TOTALED	–; –		
TOTALLY	–; –	**TOUSING**	–; –
TOTE	–; toted, totem, toter, totes	**TOUSLE**	–; tousled, tousles
		TOUT	stout; touts
TOTEM	–; totems	**TOUTED**	–; –
TOTEMIC	–; –	**TOUTER**	stouter; –
TOTER	–; toters	**TOUTING**	–; –
TOTHER	–; –	**TOUTS**	stouts; –
TOTING	–; –	**TOUZLE**	–; touzled, touzles
TOTTED	–; –		
TOTTER	–; totters, tottery	**TOW**	stow; town, tows, towy
TOTTING	–; –	**TOWAGE**	stowage; towages
TOUCAN	–; toucans		
TOUCH	–; touche, touchy	**TOWAGES**	stowages; –
		TOWARD	–; towards
TOUCHE	–; touched, toucher, touches	**TOWAWAY**	stowaway; towaways
TOUCHER	–; touchers	**TOWBOAT**	–; towboats
TOUCHUP	–; touchups	**TOWED**	stowed; –
TOUGH	–; toughs, toughy	**TOWEL**	–; towels
		TOWELED	–; –
TOUGHEN	–; toughens	**TOWER**	–; towers, towery
TOUGHER	–; –	**TOWERED**	–; –

TOWHEAD	–; towheads		tracheal,
TOWHEE	–; towhees		tracheas
TOWIE	–; towies	**TRACHLE**	–; trachled,
TOWING	stowing; –		trachles
TOWLINE	–; towlines	**TRACING**	–; tracings
TOWMOND	–; towmonds	**TRACK**	–; tracks
TOWMONT	–; towmonts	**TRACKED**	–; –
TOWN	–; towns,	**TRACKER**	–; trackers
	towny	**TRACT**	–; tracts
TOWNEE	–; townees	**TRACTOR**	–; tractors
TOWNIE	–; townies	**TRAD**	–; trade
TOWNISH	–; –	**TRADE**	–; traded,
TOWNLET	–; townlets		trader,
TOWPATH	–; towpaths		trades
TOWROPE	–; towropes	**TRADER**	–; traders
TOWS	stows; –	**TRADING**	–; –
TOXEMIA	–; toxemias	**TRADUCE**	–; traduced,
TOXEMIC	–; –		traducer,
TOXIC	–; –		traduces
TOXICAL	–; –	**TRAFFIC**	–; traffics
TOXIN	–; toxine,	**TRAGEDY**	–; –
	toxins	**TRAGI**	–; tragic
TOXINE	–; toxines	**TRAGUS**	–; –
TOXOID	–; toxoids	**TRAIK**	–; traiks
TOY	–; toyo, toys	**TRAIKED**	–; –
TOYED	–; –	**TRAIL**	–; trails
TOYER	–; toyers	**TRAILED**	–; –
TOYING	–; –	**TRAILER**	–; trailers
TOYISH	–; –	**TRAIN**	strain; trains
TOYLESS	–; –	**TRAINED**	strained; –
TOYLIKE	–; –	**TRAINEE**	–; trainees
TOYO	–; toyon,	**TRAINER**	strainer;
	toyos		trainers
TOYON	–; toyons	**TRAINS**	strains; –
TRACE	–; traced,	**TRAIPSE**	–; traipsed,
	tracer,		traipses
	traces	**TRAIT**	strait; traits
TRACER	–; tracers,	**TRAITS**	straits; –
	tracery	**TRAITOR**	–; traitors
TRACHEA	–; tracheae,	**TRAJECT**	–; trajects

TRAM	–; tramp, trams	**TRAVOIS**	–; travoise
TRAMCAR	–; tramcars	**TRAWL**	–; trawls
TRAMEL	–; tramell, tramels	**TRAWLED**	–; –
TRAMMED	–; –	**TRAWLER**	–; trawlers
TRAMMEL	–; trammels	**TRAWLEY**	–; trawleys
TRAMP	–; tramps	**TRAY**	stray; trays
TRAMPED	–; –	**TRAYFUL**	–; trayfuls
TRAMPER	–; trampers	**TRAYS**	strays; –
TRAMPLE	–; trampled, trampler, tramples	**TREACLE**	–; treacles
		TREACLY	–; –
TRAMWAY	–; tramways	**TREAD**	–; treads
TRANCE	–; tranced, trances	**TREADED**	–; –
		TREADER	–; treaders
TRANGAM	–; trangams	**TREADLE**	–; treadled, treadler, treadles
TRANQ	–; tranqs		
TRANS	–; –	**TREASON**	–; treasons
TRANSIT	–; transits	**TREAT**	–; treats, treaty
TRANSOM	–; transoms		
TRAP	strap; traps, trapt	**TREATED**	–; –
		TREATER	–; treaters
TRAPAN	–; trapans	**TREBLE**	–; trebled, trebles
TRAPES	–; –		
TRAPEZE	–; trapezes	**TREBLY**	–; –
TRAPPED	strapped; –	**TREDDLE**	–; treddled, treddles
TRAPPER	strapper; trappers		
		TREE	–; treed, trees
TRAPS	straps; –		
TRASH	–; trashy	**TREEING**	–; –
TRASHED	–; –	**TREETOP**	–; treetops
TRASHES	–; –	**TREF**	–; –
TRASS	strass; –	**TREFAH**	–; –
TRASSES	strasses; –	**TREFOIL**	–; trefoils
TRAUMA	–; traumas	**TREHALA**	–; trehalas
TRAVAIL	–; travails	**TREK**	–; treks
TRAVE	–; travel, traves	**TREKKED**	–; –
		TREKKER	–; trekkers
TRAVEL	–; travels	**TRELLIS**	–; –
		TREMBLE	atremble; trembled,

	trembler, trembles	**TRICK**	strick; tricks, tricky
TREMBLY	–; –	**TRICKED**	–; –
TREMOLO	–; tremolos	**TRICKER**	–; trickers, trickery
TREMOR	–; tremors		
TRENAIL	–; trenails	**TRICKIE**	–; trickier
TRENCH	–; –	**TRICKLE**	strickle;
TREND	–; trends, trendy		trickled, trickles
TRENDED	–; –	**TRICKLY**	–; –
TREPAN	–; trepang, trepans	**TRICKS**	stricks; tricksy
TREPANG	–; trepangs	**TRICLAD**	–; triclads
TREPID	–; –	**TRICORN**	–; tricorne, tricorns
TRESS	stress; tressy		
TRESSED	stressed; –	**TRICOT**	–; tricots
TRESSEL	–; tressels	**TRIDENT**	–; tridents
TRESSES	stresses; –	**TRIDUUM**	–; triduums
TRESTLE	–; trestles	**TRIED**	–; –
TRET	–; trets	**TRIENE**	–; trienes
TREVET	–; trevets	**TRIENS**	–; –
TREWS	strews; –	**TRIER**	–; triers
TREY	–; treys	**TRIES**	–; –
TRIABLE	–; –	**TRIFID**	–; –
TRIACID	–; triacids	**TRIFLE**	–; trifled, trifler, trifles
TRIAD	–; triads		
TRIADIC	–; triadics	**TRIFLER**	–; triflers
TRIAGE	–; triages	**TRIFOLD**	–; –
TRIAL	atrial; trials	**TRIFORM**	–; –
TRIAZIN	–; triazine, triazins	**TRIG**	–; trigo, trigs
		TRIGGED	–; –
TRIBADE	–; tribades	**TRIGGER**	–; triggers
TRIBAL	–; –	**TRIGLY**	–; –
TRIBE	–; tribes	**TRIGO**	–; trigon, trigos
TRIBUNE	–; tribunes		
TRIBUTE	–; tributes	**TRIGON**	–; trigons
TRICE	–; triced, trices	**TRIJET**	–; trijets
		TRILBY	–; –
TRICEPS	–; –	**TRILL**	–; trills
TRICING	–; –	**TRILLED**	–; –

TRILLER	–; trillers	**TRIPPER**	stripper; trippers
TRILOGY	–; –		
TRIM	–; trims	**TRIPPET**	–; trippets
TRIMER	–; trimers	**TRIPS**	strips; –
TRIMLY	–; –	**TRIREME**	–; triremes
TRIMMED	–; –	**TRISECT**	–; trisects
TRIMMER	–; trimmers	**TRISEME**	–; trisemes
TRINAL	–; –	**TRISMIC**	–; –
TRINARY	–; –	**TRISMUS**	–; –
TRINDLE	–; trindled, trindles	**TRISOME**	–; trisomes
		TRISOMY	–; –
TRINE	–; trined, trines	**TRISTE**	–; –
		TRITE	–; triter
TRINING	–; –	**TRITEST**	–; –
TRINITY	; –	**TRITELY**	–; –
TRINKET	–; trinkets	**TRITIUM**	–; tritiums
TRIO	–; triol, trios	**TRITOMA**	–; tritomas
TRIODE	–; triodes	**TRITON**	–; tritone, tritons
TRIOL	–; triols		
TRIOLET	–; triolets	**TRITONE**	–; tritones
TRIOSE	–; trioses	**TRIUMPH**	–; triumphs
TRIOXID	–; trioxide, trioxids	**TRIUNE**	–; triunes
		TRIVET	–; trivets
TRIP	atrip, strip; tripe, trips	**TRIVIA**	–; trivial
		TRIVIUM	–; –
TRIPACK	–; tripacks	**TROAK**	–; troaks
TRIPART	–; –	**TROAKED**	–; –
TRIPE	stripe; tripes	**TROCAR**	–; trocars
TRIPES	stripes; –	**TROCHAL**	–; –
TRIPLE	–; tripled, triples, triplet, triplex	**TROCHAR**	–; trochars
		TROCHE	–; trochee, troches
TRIPLET	–; triplets	**TROCHEE**	–; trochees
TRIPLY	–; –	**TROCHIL**	–; trochili, trochils
TRIPOD	–; tripods, tripody		
		TROCK	–; trocks
TRIPOLI	–; tripolis	**TROCKED**	–; –
TRIPOS	–; –	**TROD**	–; trode
TRIPPED	stripped; –	**TRODDEN**	–; –
		TRODE	strode; –

TROFFER	–; troffers	**TROPINE**	atropine;
TROGON	–; trogons		tropines
TROIKA	–; troikas	**TROPISM**	atropism;
TROILUS	–; –		tropisms
TROIS	–; –	**TROT**	–; troth,
TROKE	-stroke;		trots
	troked,	**TROTH**	–; troths
	trokes	**TROTHED**	–; –
TROKED	stroked; –	**TROTTED**	–; –
TROKES	strokes; –	**TROTTER**	–; trotters
TROKING	stroking; –	**TROTYL**	–; trotyls
TROLAND	–; trolands	**TROUBLE**	–; troubled
TROLL	stroll; trolls,		troubler,
	trolly		troubles
TROLLED	strolled; –	**TROUGH**	–; troughs
TROLLER	stroller;	**TROUNCE**	–; trounced,
	trollers		trounces
TROLLEY	–; trolleys	**TROUPE**	–; trouped,
TROLLOP	–; trollops,		trouper,
	trollopy		troupes
TROLLS	strolls; –	**TROUPER**	–; troupers
TROMMEL	–; trommels	**TROUSER**	–; trousers
TROMP	–; trompe,	**TROUT**	–; trouts,
	tromps		trouty
TROMPE	–; tromped,	**TROVE**	strove;
	trompes		trover, troves
TRONA	–; tronas	**TROVER**	–; trovers
TRONE	–; trones	**TROW**	strow; trows
TROOP	–; troops	**TROWED**	strowed; –
TROOPED	–; –	**TROWEL**	–; trowels
TROOPER	–; troopers	**TROWING**	strowing; –
TROOZ	–; –	**TROWS**	strows; –
TROP	strop; trope	**TROWTH**	–; trowths
TROPE	–; tropes	**TROY**	stroy; troys
TROPHIC	atrophic; –	**TROYS**	stroys; –
TROPHY	atrophy; –	**TRUANCY**	–; –
TROPIC	–; tropics	**TRUANT**	–; truants
TROPIN	atropin;	**TRUCE**	–; truced,
	tropine,		truces
	tropins	**TRUCK**	struck; trucks

TRUCKED	–; –	**TRUSTEE**	–; trustend,
TRUCKER	–; truckers		trustees
TRUCKLE	–; truckled,	**TRUSTER**	–; trusters
	truckler,	**TRUTH**	–; truths
	truckles	**TRY**	–; –
TRUDGE	–; trudged,	**TRYING**	–; –
	trudgen,	**TRYMA**	–; –
	trudger,	**TRYMATA**	–; –
	trudges	**TRYOUT**	–; tryouts
TRUDGEN	–; trudgens	**TRYPSIN**	–; trypsins
TRUDGER	–; trudgers	**TRYPTIC**	–; –
TRUE	–; trued,	**TRYSAIL**	–; trysails
	truer, trues	**TRYST**	–; tryste,
TRUES	–; truest		trysts
TRUFFE	–; truffes	**TRYSTE**	–; trysted,
TRUFFLE	–; truffled,		tryster,
	truffles		trystes
TRUING	–; –	**TRYSTER**	–; trysters
TRUISM	–; truisms	**TSADE**	–; tsades
TRULL	–; trulls	**TSADI**	–; tsadis
TRULY	–; –	**TSAR**	–; tsars
TRUMEAU	–; trumeaux	**TSARDOM**	–; tsardoms
TRUMP	–; trumps	**TSARINA**	–; tsarinas
TRUMPED	–; –	**TSARISM**	–; tsarisms
TRUMPET	strumpet;	**TSARIST**	–; tsarists
	trumpets	**TSETSE**	–; tsetses
TRUNDLE	–; trundled,	**TSIMMES**	–; –
	trundler,	**TSK**	–; tsks
	trundles	**TSKED**	–; –
TRUNK	–; trunks	**TSKING**	–; –
TRUNKED	–; –	**TSKTSK**	–; tsktsks
TRUNNEL	–; trunnels	**TSUBA**	–; –
TRUSS	–; –	**TSUNAMI**	–; tsunamic,
TRUSSED	–; –		tsunamis
TRUSSER	–; trussers	**TSURIS**	–; –
TRUSSES	–; –	**TUATARA**	–; tuataras
TRUST	–; trusts,	**TUATERA**	–; tuateras
	trusty	**TUB**	stub; tuba,
TRUSTED	–; –		tube, tubs

TUBA	–; tubae, tubal, tubas	**TUGRIK**	–; tugriks
		TUI	etui; tuis
TUBATE	–; –	**TUILLE**	–; tuilles
TUBBED	stubbed; –	**TUIS**	etuis; –
TUBBER	–; tubbers	**TUITION**	–; tuitions
TUBBIER	–; –	**TULADI**	–; tuladis
TUBBING	stubbing; –	**TULE**	–; tules
TUBBY	stubby; –	**TULIP**	–; tulips
TUBE	–; tubed, tuber, tubes	**TULLE**	–; tulles
		TUMBLE	stumble; tumbled, tumbler, tumbles
TUBER	–; tubers		
TUBFUL	–; tubfuls		
TUBIFEX	–; –		
TUBING	–; tubings	**TUMBLED**	stumbled; –
TUBLIKE	–; –	**TUMBLER**	stumbler; tumblers
TUBS	stubs; –		
TUBULAR	–; –	**TUMBLES**	stumbles; –
TUBULE	–; tubules	**TUMBREL**	–; tumbrels
TUCHUN	–; tuchuns	**TUMBRIL**	–; tumbrils
TUCK	stuck; tucks	**TUMEFY**	–; –
TUCKED	–; –	**TUMID**	–; –
TUCKER	–; tuckers	**TUMIDLY**	–; –
TUCKET	–; tuckets	**TUMMIES**	–; –
TUCKING	–; –	**TUMMY**	–; –
TUFA	–; tufas	**TUMOR**	–; tumors
TUFF	stuff; tuffs	**TUMORAL**	–; –
TUFFET	–; tuffets	**TUMOUR**	–; tumours
TUFFS	stuffs; –	**TUMP**	stump; tumps
TUFT	–; tufts, tufty	**TUMPS**	stumps; –
TUFTED	–; –	**TUMULAR**	–; –
TUFTER	–; tufters	**TUMULI**	–; –
TUFTIER	–; –	**TUMULT**	–; tumults
TUFTILY	–; –	**TUMULUS**	–; –
TUFTING	–; –	**TUN**	stun; tuna, tune, tung, tuns
TUG	–; tugs		
TUGBOAT	–; tugboats		
TUGGED	–; –	**TUNA**	–; tunas
TUGGER	–; tuggers	**TUNABLE**	–; –
TUGGING	–; –	**TUNABLY**	–; –
TUGLESS	–;	**TUNDISH**	–; –

TUNDRA	–; tundras	**TUREEN**	–; tureens
TUNE	–; tuned, tuner, tunes	**TURF**	; turfs, turfy
		TURFED	–; –
TUNEFUL	–; –	**TURFIER**	–; –
TUNER	–; tuners	**TURFING**	–; –
TUNG	stung; tungs	**TURFMAN**	–; –
TUNIC	–; tunica, tunics	**TURFMEN**	–; –
		TURFSKI	–; turfskis
TUNICA	–; tunicae	**TURGENT**	–; –
TUNICLE	–; tunicles	**TURGID**	–; –
TUNING	–; –	**TURGITE**	–; turgites
TUNNAGE	–; tunnages	**TURGOR**	–; turgors
TUNNED	stunned; –	**TURKEY**	–; turkeys
TUNNEL	–; tunnels	**TURKOIS**	–; –
TUNNIES	–; –	**TURMOIL**	–; turmoils
TUNNING	stunning; –	**TURN**	–; turns
TUNNY	–; –	**TURNED**	–; –
TUNS	stuns; –	**TURNER**	–; turners, turnery
TUP	–; tups		
TUPELO	–; tupelos	**TURNING**	–; turnings
TUPIK	–; tupiks	**TURNIP**	–; turnips
TUPPED	–; –	**TURNKEY**	–; turnkeys
TUPPING	–; –	**TURNOFF**	–; turnoffs
TUQUE	–; tuques	**TURNOUT**	–; turnouts
TURACO	–; turacos, turacou	**TURNUP**	–; turnups
		TURPETH	–; turpeths
TURACOU	–; turacous	**TURPS**	–; –
TURBAN	–; turbans	**TURRET**	–; turrets
TURBARY	–; –	**TURTLE**	–; turtled, turtler, turtles
TURBETH	–; turbeths		
TURBID	–; –	**TURTLER**	–; turtlers
TURBINE	–; turbines	**TURVES**	–; –
TURBIT	–; turbith, turbits	**TUSCHE**	–; tusches
		TUSH	–; –
TURBITH	–; turbiths	**TUSHED**	–; –
TURBO	–; turbos, turbot	**TUSHES**	–; –
		TUSHING	–; –
TURBOT	–; turbots	**TUSK**	–; tusks
TURD	–; turds	**TUSKED**	–; –
TURDINE	–; –	**TUSKER**	–; tuskers

TUSKING	–; –	twaddler,
TUSSAH	–; tussahs	twaddles
TUSSAL	–; –	**TWAE** –; twaes
TUSSAR	–; tussars	**TWAIN** atwain;
TUSSEH	–; tussehs	twains
TUSSER	–; tussers	
TUSSIS	–; –	**TWANG** –; twangs,
TUSSIVE	–; –	twangy
TUSSLE	–; tussled,	**TWANGED** –; –
	tussles	**TWANGLE** –; twangled,
TUSSOCK	–; tussocks,	twangler,
	tussocky	twangles
TUSSOR	–; tussore,	**TWANKY** –; –
	tussors	**TWASOME** –; twasomes
TUSSORE	–; tussores	**TWATTLE** –; twattled,
TUSSUCK	–; tussucks	twattles
TUSSUR	–; tussurs	**TWEAK** –; tweaks,
TUT	–; tuts, tutu	tweaky
TUTEE	–; tutees	**TWEAKED** –; –
TUTELAR	–; tutelars,	**TWEED** –; tweeds,
	tutelary	tweedy
TUTOR	–; tutors	**TWEEDLE** –; tweedled,
TUTORED	–; –	tweedles
TUTOYER	–; tutoyers	**TWEEN** atween; –
TUTTED	–; –	**TWEET** –; tweets
TUTTI	–; tuttis	**TWEETED** –; –
TUTTIES	–; –	**TWEETER** –; tweeters
TUTTING	–; –	**TWEEZE** –; tweezed,
TUTTY	–; –	tweezer,
TUTU	–; tutus	tweezes
TUX	–; –	**TWEEZER** –; tweezers
TUXEDO	–; tuxedos	**TWELFTH** –; twelfths
TUXES	–; –	**TWELVE** –; twelves
TUYER	–; tuyere,	**TWENTY** –; –
	tuyers	**TWERP** –; twerps
TUYERE	–; tuyeres	**TWIBIL** –; twibill,
TWA	–; twae,	twibils
	twas	**TWIBILL** –; twibills
TWADDLE	–; twaddled,	**TWICE** –; –
		TWIDDLE –; twiddled,

	twiddler, twiddles	**TWO**	–; twos
TWIER	–; twiers	**TWOOFF**	; twoofers
TWIG	–; twigs	**TWOFOLD**	–; twofolds
TWIGGED	–; –	**TWOSOME**	–; twosomes
TWIGGEN	–; –	**TWYER**	–; twyers
TWIGGY	–; –	**TYCOON**	–; tycoons
TWILIT	–; –	**TYE**	stye; tyee, tyes
TWILL	–; twills	**TYEE**	–; tyees
TWILLED	–; –	**TYES**	styes; –
TWIN	–; twine, twins, twiny	**TYING**	stying; –
TWINE	–; twined, twiner, twines	**TYKE**	–; tykes
		TYMBAL	–; tymbals
TWINER	–; twiners	**TYMPAN**	–; tympana, tympani, tympans, tympany
TWINGE	–; twinged, twinges		
TWINIER	–; –	**TYMPANA**	–; tympanal
TWINING	–; –	**TYMPANI**	–; tympanic
TWINKLE	–; twinkled, twinkler, twinkles	**TYNE**	–; tyned, tynes
TWINKLY	–; –	**TYNING**	–; –
TWINNED	–; –	**TYPAL**	–; –
TWIRL	–; twirls, twirly	**TYPE**	–; typed, types, typey
TWIRLED	–; –	**TYPEBAR**	–; typebars
TWIRLER	–; twirlers	**TYPESET**	–; typesets
TWIRP	–; twirps	**TYPHOID**	–; typhoids
TWIST	–; twists	**TYPHON**	–; typhons
TWISTED	–; –	**TYPHOON**	–; typhoons
TWISTER	–; twisters	**TYPHOSE**	–; –
TWIT	–; twits	**TYPHOUS**	–; –
TWITCH	–; twitchy	**TYPHUS**	–; –
TWITTED	–; –	**TYPIC**	atypic; –
TWITTER	atwitter; twitters, twittery	**TYPICAL**	atypical; –
		TYPIER	–; –
		TYPIEST	–; –
		TYPIFY	–; –
		TYPING	–; –
TWIXT	–; –	**TYPIST**	–; typists

TYPO	–; typos	**TZADDIK**	–; –
TYPP	–; typps	**TZAR**	–; tzars
TYPY	–; –	**TZARDOM**	–; tzardoms
TYRANNY	–; –	**TZARINA**	–; tzarinas
TYRANT	–; tyrants	**TZARISM**	–; tzarisms
TYRE	–; tyred, tyres	**TZARIST**	–; tzarists
		TZETZE	–; tzetzes
TYRING	–; –	**TZIGANE**	–; tziganes
TYRO	–; tyros	**TZIMMES**	–; –
TYRONIC	–; –	**TZITZIS**	–; –
TYTHE	–; tythed, tythes	**TZURIS**	–; –
		TZUT	–; tzute, tzuts
TYTHING	–; –		

U

U	mu, nu, xu; uh, um, un, up, us, ut	**UGLIFY**	–; –
		UGLILY	–; –
		UGLY	–; –
UBIETY	dubiety; –	**UGSOME**	–; –
UBIQUE	–; –	**UH**	huh; –
UDDER	budder, judder, mudder, rudder; udders	**UHLAN**	–; uhlans
		UIT	duit, quit, suit; –
		UKASE	–; ukases
		UKE	cuke, duke, juke, nuke, puke; ukes
UDDERS	budders, judders, mudders, rudders; –	**UKELELE**	–; ukeleles
		UKES	cukes, dukes, jukes, nukes, pukes; –
UDO	judo, kudo; udos		
UDOS	judos, kudos; –	**UKULELE**	–; ukuleles
UGH	pugh, sugh, vugh; ughs	**ULAMA**	–; ulamas
		ULAN	yulan; ulans
UGHS	sughs, vughs; –	**ULANS**	yulans; –
		ULCER	–; ulcers
UGLIER	–; –	**ULCERED**	–; –
UGLIEST	–; –		

ULEMA	–; ulemas	jumbo;
ULEXITE	–; ulexites	umbos
ULLAGE	sullage;	
	ullaged,	**UMBONAL**	–; –
	ullages	**UMBONES**	–; –
		UMBONIC	–; –
ULLAGES	sullages; –	**UMBOS**	gumbos,
ULNA	–; ulnae,	jumbos; –
	ulnar, ulnas	**UMBRA**	–; umbrae,
ULSTER	–; ulsters	umbral,
ULTIMA	–; ultimas	umbras
ULTIMO	–; –	**UMBRAGE**	–; umbrages
ULTRA	–; ultras	**UMIAC**	–; umiack,
ULULANT	–; –	umiacs
ULULATE	–; ululated,	**UMIACK**	–; umiacks
	ululates	**UMIAK**	–; umiaks
ULVA	vulva; ulvas	**UMLAUT**	–; umlauts
ULVAS	vulvas; –	**UMP**	bump, dump,
UM	bum, cum,	hump, jump,
	gum, hum,	lump, mump,
	lum, mum,	pump, rump,
	rum, sum;	sump, tump;
	ump	umps
UMBEL	–; umbels	**UMPED**	bumped,
UMBELED	–; –	dumped,
UMBER	cumber,	humped,
	dumber,	jumped,
	lumber;	lumped,
	umbers	mumped,
UMBERED	cumbered,	pumped; –
	lumbered; –	**UMPING**	bumping,
UMBERS	cumbers,	dumping,
	lumbers; –	humping,
UMBLES	bumbles,	jumping,
	fumbles,	lumping,
	humbles,	mumping,
	jumbles,	pumping; –
	mumbles,	**UMPIRE**	–; umpired,
	rumbles,	umpires
	tumbles	**UMPS**	bumps,
UMBO	gumbo,	dumps,

	humps, jumps, lumps, mumps, pumps, rumps, sumps, tumps; –	**UNBEND**	–; unbends
		UNBENT	–; –
		UNBID	–; –
		UNBIND	–; unbinds
		UNBLEST	–; –
		UNBLOCK	–; unblocks
		UNBOLT	–; unbolts
UMPTEEN	–; –	**UNBONED**	–; –
UN	bun, dun, fun, gun, hun, jun, mun, nun, pun, run, sun, tun; uns	**UNBORN**	–; –
		UNBOSOM	–; unbosoms
		UNBOUND	–; –
		UNBOWED	–; –
		UNBOX	–; –
		UNBOXED	–; –
UNAI	–; unais	**UNBOXES**	–; –
UNABLE	tunable; –	**UNBRACE**	–; unbraced, unbraces
UNACTED	–; –		
UNAGED	–; –	**UNBRAID**	–; unbraids
UNAGILE	–; –	**UNBRED**	–; –
UNAGING	–; –	**UNBROKE**	–; unbroken
UNAIDED	–; –	**UNBUILD**	–; unbuilds
UNAIMED	–; –	**UNBUILT**	–; –
UNAIRED	–; –	**UNBURNT**	sunburnt; –
UNALIKE	–; –	**UNCAGE**	–; uncaged, uncages
UNAPT	–; –		
UNAPTLY	–; –	**UNCAKE**	–; uncaked, uncakes
UNARM	–; unarms		
UNARMED	–; –	**UNCANNY**	–; –
UNARY	–; –	**UNCAP**	–; uncaps
UNASKED	–; –	**UNCASE**	–; uncased, uncases
UNAU	–; unaus		
UNAWARE	–; –	**UNCHAIN**	–; unchains
UNAWED	–; –	**UNCHARY**	–; –
UNBAKED	–; –	**UNCHIC**	–; –
UNBAR	–; unbars	**UNCHOKE**	–; unchoked, unchokes
UNBASED	–; –		
UNBATED	–; –	**UNCI**	–; uncia
UNBE	–; –	**UNCIA**	–; unciae, uncial
UNBEAR	–; unbears		
UNBELT	–; unbelts	**UNCIAL**	–; uncials

UNCINAL	–; –	**UNDE**	–; undee,
UNCINI	–; –		undei
UNCINUS	–; –	**UNDER**	sunder; –
UNCIVIL	–; –	**UNDERDO**	–; underdog
UNCLAD	–; –	**UNDERGO**	–; undergod
UNCLAMP	–; unclamps	**UNDID**	–; –
UNCLASP	–; unclasps	**UNDIES**	–; –
UNCLE	nuncle;	**UNDINE**	–; undines
	uncles	**UNDO**	–; –
UNCLEAN	–; –	**UNDOCK**	–; undocks
UNCLEAR	–; –	**UNDOER**	–; undoers
UNCLES	nuncles; –	**UNDOES**	–; –
UNCLOAK	–; uncloaks	**UNDOING**	–; undoings
UNCLOG	–; unclogs	**UNDONE**	–; –
UNCLOSE	–; unclosed,	**UNDRAPE**	–;
	uncloses		undraped,
UNCLOUD	–; unclouds		undrapes
UNCO	bunco,	**UNDRAW**	–; undrawn,
	junco; uncos		undraws
UNCOCK	–; uncocks	**UNDRESS**	–; –
UNCOIL	–; uncoils	**UNDREST**	–; –
UNCOMIC	–; –	**UNDREW**	–; –
UNCOOL	–; –	**UNDRIED**	–; –
UNCORK	–; uncorks	**UNDRUNK**	–; –
UNCOS	buncos,	**UNDUE**	–; –
	juncos;	**UNDULY**	–; –
UNCOUTH	–; –	**UNDY**	–; –
UNCOVER	–; uncovers	**UNDYED**	–; –
UNCRATE	–; uncrated,	**UNDYING**	–; –
	uncrates	**UNEAGER**	–; –
UNCROSS	–; –	**UNEARTH**	–; unearths
UNCROWN	–; uncrowns	**UNEASE**	–; uneases
UNCTION	junction;	**UNEASY**	–; –
	unctions	**UNEATEN**	–; –
UNCURB	–; uncurbs	**UNENDED**	–; –
UNCURED	–; –	**UNEQUAL**	–; unequals
UNCURL	–; uncurls	**UNEVEN**	–; –
UNCUS	–; –	**UNFADED**	–; –
UNCUT	–; –	**UNFAIR**	funfair; –
UNDATED	–; –	**UNFAITH**	–; unfaiths

UNFANCY	–; –	**UNHANG**	–; unhangs
UNFAZED	–; –	**UNHAPPY**	–; –
UNFED	–; –	**UNHASTY**	–; –
UNFELT	–; –	**UNHAT**	–; unhats
UNFENCE	–; unfenced, unfences	**UNHEARD**	–; –
		UNHELM	–; unhelms
UNFIRED	–; –	**UNHEWN**	–; –
UNFIT	–; unfits	**UNHINGE**	–; unhinged, unhinges
UNFITLY	–; –		
UNFIX	–; unfixt	**UNHIP**	–; –
UNFIXED	–; –	**UNHIRED**	–; –
UNFIXES	–; –	**UNHITCH**	–; –
UNFOLD	–; unfolds	**UNHOLY**	–; –
UNFOND	–; –	**UNHOOD**	–; unhoods
UNFOUND	–; –	**UNHOOK**	–; unhooks
UNFREE	–; unfreed, unfrees	**UNHOPED**	–; –
		UNHORSE	–; unhorsed, unhorses
UNFROCK	–; unfrocks		
UNFUNNY	–; –	**UNHOUSE**	–; unhoused, unhouses
UNFURL	–; unfurls		
UNFUSED	–; –	**UNHUMAN**	–; –
UNFUSSY	–; –	**UNHUNG**	–; –
UNGIRD	–; ungirds	**UNHURT**	–; –
UNGIRT	–; –	**UNHUSK**	–; unhusks
UNGLOVE	–; ungloved, ungloves	**UNICORN**	–; unicorns
		UNIDEAL	–; –
UNGLUE	–; unglued, unglues	**UNIFACE**	–; unifaces
		UNIFIC	–; –
UNGODLY	–; –	**UNIFIED**	–; –
UNGOT	–; –	**UNIFIER**	–; unifiers
UNGUAL	–; –	**UNIFIES**	–; –
UNGUARD	–; unguards	**UNIFORM**	cuniform; uniforms
UNGUENT	–; unguents		
UNGUES	–; –	**UNIFY**	–; –
UNGUIS	–; –	**UNION**	bunion; unions
UNGULA	–; ungulae, ungular		
		UNIONS	bunions; –
UNHAIR	–; unhairs	**UNIPOD**	–; unipods
UNHAND	–; unhands, unhandy	**UNIQUE**	–; uniquer, uniques

UNIQUES	–; uniquest	**UNLED**	–; –
UNISEX		**UNLESS**	gunless,
UNISON	–; unisons		runless,
UNIT	–; unite,		sunless; –
	units, unity	**UNLET**	runlet; –
UNITAGE	–; unitages	**UNLEVEL**	–; unlevels
UNITARY	–; –	**UNLIKE**	nunlike,
UNITE	dunite;		sunlike; –
	united,	**UNLINED**	–; –
	uniter, unites	**UNLINK**	–; unlinks
UNITER	–; uniters	**UNLIT**	sunlit; –
UNITES	dunites; –	**UNLIVE**	–; unlived,
UNITIES	–; –		unlives
UNITING	–; –	**UNLOAD**	–; unloads
UNITIVE	–; –	**UNLOBED**	–; –
UNITIZE	–; unitized,	**UNLOCK**	gunlock;
	unitizes		unlocks
UNJADED	–; –	**UNLOCKS**	gunlocks; –
UNJUST	–; –	**UNLOOSE**	–; unloosed,
UNKEMPT	–; –		unloosen,
UNKEND	–; –		unlooses
UNKENT	–; –	**UNLOVED**	–; –
UNKEPT	–; –	**UNLUCKY**	–; –
UNKIND	–; –	**UNMADE**	–; –
UNKNIT	–; unknits	**UNMAKE**	–; unmaker,
UNKNOT	–; unknots		unmakes
UNKNOWN	–; unknowns	**UNMAKER**	–; unmakers
UNLACE	–; unlaced,	**UNMAN**	gunmans;
	unlaces		unmans
UNLADE	–; unladed,	**UNMANLY**	–; –
	unladen,	**UNMASK**	–; unmasks
	unlades	**UNMATED**	–; –
UNLAID	–; –	**UNMEANT**	–; –
UNLASH	–; –	**UNMEET**	–; –
UNLATCH	–; –	**UNMET**	–; –
UNLAY	–; unlays	**UNMEW**	–; unmews
UNLEAD	–; unleads	**UNMEWED**	–; –
UNLEARN	–; unlearns,	**UNMITER**	–; unmiters
	unlearnt	**UNMITRE**	–; unmitred,
UNLEASH	–; –		unmitres

UNMIXED	–; –	**UNREEL**	–; unreels
UNMIXT	–; –	**UNREEVE**	–; unreeved, unreeves
UNMOLD	–; unmolds		
UNMOOR	–; unmoors	**UNRENT**	–; –
UNMORAL	–; –	**UNREST**	–; unrests
UNMOVED	–; –	**UNRIG**	–; unrigs
UNMOWN	–; –	**UNRIMED**	–; –
UNNAIL	–; unnails	**UNRIP**	–; unripe, unrips
UNNAMED	–; –		
UNNERVE	–; unnerved, unnerves	**UNRIPE**	–; unriper
		UNRISEN	–; –
UNNOISY	–; –	**UNROBE**	–; unrobed, unrobes
UNNOTED	–; –		
UNOILED	–; –	**UNROLL**	–; unrolls
UNOPEN	–; –	**UNROOF**	sunroof; unroofs
UNOWNED	–; –		
UNPACK	–; unpacks	**UNROOFS**	sunroofs; –
UNPAGED	–; –	**UNROOT**	–; unroots
UNPAID	–; –	**UNROUGH**	–; –
UNPAVED	–; –	**UNROUND**	–; unrounds
UNPEG	–; unpegs	**UNROVE**	–; unroven
UNPEN	–; unpens, unpent	**UNRULED**	–; –
		UNRULY	–; –
UNPICK	–; unpicks	**UNS**	buns, duns,
UNPILE	–; unpiled, unpiles		fums, guns, huns, muns,
UNPIN	–; unpins		nuns, puns,
UNPLAIT	–; unplaits		runs, suns,
UNPLUG	–; unplugs		tuns; –
UNPOSED	–; –	**UNSAFE**	–; –
UNPURE	–; –	**UNSAID**	–; –
UNQUIET	–; unquiets	**UNSATED**	–; –
UNQUOTE	–; unquoted, unquotes	**UNSAVED**	–; –
		UNSAWED	–; –
UNRAKED	–; –	**UNSAWN**	–; –
UNRATED	–; –	**UNSAY**	–; unsays
UNRAVEL	–; unravels	**UNSCREW**	–; unscrews
UNRAZED	–; –	**UNSEAL**	–; unseals
UNREAD	–; unready	**UNSEAM**	–; unseams
UNREAL	–; –	**UNSEAT**	–; unseats

UNSEEN	–; –	UNSTACK	–; unstacks
UNSENT	–; –	UNSTATE	; unstated,
UNSET	sunset; unsets		unstates
UNSETS	sunsets; –	UNSTEEL	–; unsteels
UNSEW	–; unsewn, unsews	UNSTEP	–; unsteps
		UNSTICK	–; unsticks
UNSEWED	–; –	UNSTOP	–; unstops
UNSEX	–; –	UNSTRAP	–; unstraps
UNSEXED	–; –	UNSTUNG	–; –
UNSEXES	–; –	UNSUNG	–; –
UNSHARP	–; –	UNSUNK	–; –
UNSHED	–; –	UNSURE	–; –
UNSHELL	–; unshells	UNSWEAR	–; unswears
UNSHIFT	–; unshifts	UNSWEPT	–; –
UNSHIP	gunship; unships	UNSWORE	–; –
		UNSWORN	–; –
UNSHIPS	gunships; –	UNTACK	–; untacks
UNSHOD	–; –	UNTAKEN	–; –
UNSHORN	–; –	UNTAME	–; untamed
UNSHUT	–; –	UNTAXED	–; –
UNSIGHT	–; unsights	UNTEACH	–; –
UNSIZED	–; –	UNTHINK	–; unthinks
UNSLING	–; unslings	UNTIDY	–; –
UNSLUNG	–; –	UNTIE	auntie; untied, unties
UNSNAP	–; unsnaps		
UNSNARL	–; unsnarls	UNTIES	aunties, punties; –
UNSOBER	–; –		
UNSOLD	–; –	UNTIL	–; –
UNSOLID	–; –	UNTIRED	–; –
UNSONCY	–; –	UNTO	junto, punto; –
UNSONSY	–; –		
UNSOUND	–; –	UNTOLD	–; –
UNSOWED	–; –	UNTREAD	–; untreads
UNSOWN	–; –	UNTRIED	–; –
UNSPEAK	–; unspeaks	UNTRIM	–; untrims
UNSPENT	–; –	UNTROD	–; –
UNSPILT	–; –	UNTRUE	–; untruer
UNSPLIT	–; –	UNTRULY	–; –
UNSPOKE	–; unspoken	UNTRUSS	–; –
UNSPUN	–; –	UNTRUTH	–; untruths

UNTUCK	–; untucks	hup, pup,
UNTUNE	–; untuned,	sup, tup,
	untunes	yup; upo,
UNTWINE	–; untwined,	ups
	untwines	**UPAS**	pupas; –
UNTWIST	–; untwists	**UPASES**	–; –
UNTYING	–; –	**UPBEAR**	–; upbears
UNURGED	–; –	**UPBEAT**	–; upbeats
UNUSED	–; –	**UPBIND**	–; upbinds
UNUSUAL	–; –	**UPBOIL**	–; upboils
UNVEIL	–; unveils	**UPBORE**	–; –
UNVEXED	–; –	**UPBORNE**	–; –
UNVEXT	–; –	**UPBOUND**	–; –
UNVOCAL	–; –	**UPBRAID**	–; upbraids
UNVOICE	–; unvoiced,	**UPBUILD**	–; upbuilds
	unvoices	**UPBUILT**	–; –
UNWARY	–; –	**UPBY**	–; upbye
UNWAXED	–; –	**UPCAST**	–; upcasts
UNWEARY	–; –	**UPCHUCK**	–; upchucks
UNWEAVE	–; unweaves	**UPCLIMB**	–; upclimbs
UNWED	–; –	**UPCOIL**	–; upcoils
UNWELL	–; –	**UPCURL**	–; upcurls
UNWEPT	–; –	**UPCURVE**	–; upcurved,
UNWIND	–; unwinds		upcurves
UNWISE	sunwise;	**UPDART**	–; updarts
	unwiser	**UPDATE**	–; updated,
UNWISH	–; –		updater,
UNWIT	–; unwits		updates
UNWON	–; –	**UPDATER**	–; updaters
UNWOOED	–; –	**UPDIVE**	–; updived,
UNWORN	–; –		updives
UNWOUND	–; –	**UPDO**	–; updos
UNWOVE	–; unwoven	**UPDOVE**	–; –
UNWRAP	–; unwraps	**UPDRAFT**	–; updrafts
UNWRUNG	–; –	**UPDRIED**	–; –
UNYOKE	–; unyoked,	**UPDRIES**	–; –
	unyokes	**UPDRY**	–; –
UNZIP	–; unzips	**UPEND**	–; upends
UNZONED	–; –	**UPENDED**	–; –
UP	cup, dup,	**UPFIELD**	–; –

UPFLING	–; upflings	**UPPED**	cupped,
UPFLOW	–; upflows		dupped,
UPFLUNG	–; –		pupped,
UPFOLD	–; upfolds		supped,
UPGAZE	–; upgazed,		tupped; –
	upgazes	**UPPER**	cupper,
UPGIRD	–; upgirds		supper;
UPGIRT	–; –		uppers
UPGOING	–; –	**UPPERS**	cuppers,
UPGRADE	–;		suppers; –
	upgraded,	**UPPILE**	–; uppiled,
	upgrades		uppiles
UPGREW	–; –	**UPPING**	cupping,
UPGROW	–; upgrown,		dupping,
	upgrows		pupping,
UPHEAP	–; upheaps		supping,
UPHEAVE	–;		tupping;
	upheaved,		uppings
	upheaver,	**UPPINGS**	cuppings; –
	upheaves	**UPPISH**	–; –
UPHELD	–; –	**UPPITY**	–; –
UPHILL	–; uphills	**UPPROP**	–; upprops
UPHOARD	–; uphoards	**UPRAISE**	–; upraised,
UPHOLD	–; upholds		upraiser,
UPHOVE	–; –		upraises
UPHROE	euphroe;	**UPREACH**	–; –
	uphroes	**UPREAR**	–; uprears
UPHROES	euphroes; –	**UPRIGHT**	–; uprights
UPKEEP	–; upkeeps	**UPRISE**	–; uprisen,
UPLAND	–; uplands		upriser,
UPLEAP	–; upleaps,		uprises
	upleapt	**UPRISER**	–; uprisers
UPLIFT	–; uplifts	**UPRIVER**	–; uprivers
UPLIGHT	–; uplights	**UPROAR**	–; uproars
UPLIT	–; –	**UPROOT**	–; uproots
UPMOST	–; –	**UPROSE**	–; –
UPO	–; upon	**UPROUSE**	–; uproused,
UPON	jupon,		uprouses
	yupon; –	**UPRUSH**	–; –
		UPS	cups, dups,

	pups, sups, tups; –	**UPTOSS**	–; –
UPSEND	–; upsends	**UPTOWN**	–; uptowns
UPSENT	–; –	**UPTREND**	–; uptrends
UPSET	–; upsets	**UPTURN**	–; upturns
UPSHIFT	–; upshifts	**UPWAFT**	–; upwafts
UPSHOOT	–; upshoots	**UPWARD**	–; upwards
UPSHOT	–; upshots	**UPWELL**	–; upwells
UPSIDE	–; upsides	**UPWIND**	–; upwinds
UPSILON	–; upsilons	**URACIL**	–; uracils
UPSOAR	–; upsoars	**URAEI**	–; –
UPSTAGE	–; upstaged, upstages	**URAEMIA**	–; uraemias
		URAEMIC	–; –
		URAEUS	–; –
UPSTAIR	–; upstairs	**URALITE**	–; uralites
UPSTAND	–; upstands	**URANIC**	puranic; –
UPSTARE	–; upstared, upstares	**URANIDE**	–; uranides
		URANISM	–; uranisms
UPSTART	–; upstarts	**URANITE**	–; uranites
UPSTATE	–; upstater, upstates	**URANIUM**	–; uraniums
		URANOUS	–; –
UPSTEP	–; upsteps	**URANYL**	–; uranyls
UPSTIR	–; upstirs	**URARE**	curare; urares
UPSTOOD	–; –		
UPSURGE	–; upsurged, upsurges	**URARES**	curares; –
		URARI	curari, ourari; uraris
UPSWEEP	–; upsweeps		
UPSWELL	–; upswells	**URARIS**	curaris, ouraris; –
UPSWEPT	–; –		
UPSWING	–; upswings	**URASE**	–; urases
UPSWUNG	–; –	**URATE**	aurate, curate; urates
UPTAKE	–; uptakes		
UPTEAR	–; uptears		
UPTHREW	–; –	**URATES**	curates; –
UPTHROW	–; upthrown, upthrows	**URATIC**	–; –
		URBAN	rurban, turban; urbane
UPTIGHT	–; –		
UPTILT	–; uptilts		
UPTIME	–; uptimes	**URBANE**	–; urbaner
UPTORE	–; –	**URCHIN**	–; urchins
UPTORN	–; –	**URD**	burd, curd,

	surd, turd;	**URGES**	burges,
	urds		gurges,
URDS	burds, curds,		purges,
	hurds, surds,		surges; —
	turds; —	**URGING**	gurging,
UREA	—; ureal,		purging,
	ureas		surging; —
UREAS	—; urease	**URIC**	auric; —
UREASE	—; ureases	**URIDINE**	—; uridines
UREDIA	—; uredial	**URINAL**	—; urinals
UREDIUM	—; —	**URINARY**	—; —
UREDO	—; uredos	**URINATE**	—; urinated,
UREIC	—; —		urinates
UREIDE	—; ureides	**URINE**	murine,
UREMIA	—; uremias		purine;
UREMIC	—; —		urines
URETER	—; ureters	**URINES**	murines,
URETHAN	—; urethane,		purines; —
	urethans	**URINOSE**	—; —
URETHRA	—; urethrae,	**URINOUS**	—; —
	urethral,	**URN**	burn, curn,
	urethras		durn, turn;
URETIC	—; —		urns
URGE	gurge,	**URNLIKE**	—; —
	purge,	**URNS**	burns, curns,
	surge;		durns, turns; —
	urged, urger,	**URODELE**	—; urodeles
	urges	**UROLITH**	—; uroliths
URGED	gurged,	**UROLOGY**	—; —
	purged,	**UROPOD**	—; uropods
	surged; —	**URSA**	bursa; ursae
URGENCY	—; —	**URSAE**	bursae; —
URGENT	turgent; —	**URSINE**	—; —
URGER	burger,	**URUS**	gurus, kurus; —
	purger,	**URUSES**	—; —
	surger;	**US**	bus, jus, mus,
	urgers		nus, pus; use
URGERS	burgers,	**USABLE**	—; —
	purgers,	**USABLY**	—; —
	surgers; —	**USAGE**	—; usages

USANCE	-; usances	**USURP**	-; usurps
USAUNCE	-; usaunces	**USURPED**	-; -
USE	fuse, muse, ruse; used, user, uses	**USURPER**	-; usurpers
		USURY	-; -
USEABLE	-; -	**UT**	but, cut, gut, hut, jut, mut, nut, out, put, rut, tut; uta, uts
USEABLY	-; -		
USED	bused, fused, mused; -		
USEFUL	museful; -	**UTA**	-; utas
USELESS	fuseless; -	**UTENSIL**	-; utensils
USER	muser; users	**UTERI**	-; -
USERS	musers; -	**UTERINE**	-; -
USES	buses, fuses, muses, puses, ruses; -	**UTERUS**	-; -
		UTILE	futile, rutile; -
		UTILISE	-; utilised, utiliser, utilises
USHER	busher, gusher, lusher, musher, pusher, rusher; ushers	**UTILITY**	futility; -
		UTILIZE	-; utilized, utilizer, utilizes
		UTMOST	outmost; utmosts
USHERED	-; -	**UTOPIA**	-; utopian, utopias
USHERS	bushers, gushers, mushers, pushers, rushers; -		
		UTOPIAN	-; utopians
		UTOPISM	-; utopisms
		UTOPIST	-; utopists
		UTRICLE	-; utricles
USING	busing, fusing, musing; -	**UTS**	buts, cuts, guts, huts, juts, muts, nuts, outs, puts, ruts, tuts; -
USNEA	-; usneas		
USQUE	-; usques		
USUAL	-; usuals		
USUALLY	-; -	**UTTER**	butter, cutter, gutter,
USURER	-; usurers		
USURIES	-; -		

	mutter,		mutters,
	nutter,		nutters,
	putter; utters		putters; –
UTTERED	buttered,	UVEA	–; uveal,
	muttered,		uveas
	puttered; –	UVEITIC	–; –
UTTERER	mutterer,	UVEITIS	–; –
	putterer;	UVEOUS	–; –
	utterers	UVULA	–; uvulae,
UTTERLY	–; –		uvular,
UTTERS	butters,		uvulas
	cutters,	UVULAR	–; uvulars
	gutters,	UXORIAL	–; –

V

VACANCY	–; –	VAGROM	–; –
VACANT	–; –	VAGUE	–; vaguer
VACATE	–; vacated,	VAGUELY	–; –
	vacates	VAGUEST	–; –
VACCINA	–; vaccinal,	VAGUS	–; –
	vaccinas	VAHINE	–; vahinos
VACCINE	–; vaccines	VAIL	avail; vails
VACUA	–; –	VAILED	availed; –
VACUITY	–; –	VAILING	availing; –
VACUOLE	–; vacuoles	VAILS	avails; –
VACUOUS	–; –	VAIN	–; –
VACUUM	–; vacuums	VAINER	–; –
VADOSE	–; –	VAINEST	–; –
VAGAL	–; –	VAINLY	–; –
VAGALLY	–; –	VAIR	–; vairs
VAGARY	–; –	VAKEEL	–; vakeels
VAGI	–; –	VAKIL	–; vakils
VAGILE	–; –	VALANCE	–; valanced,
VAGINA	vaginae,		valances
	vaginal,	VALE	–; vales,
	vaginas		valet
VAGRANT	–; vagrants	VALENCE	–; valences

VALENCY	–; –	**VAMOSE**	–; vamosed, vamoses
VALERIC	–; –		
VALET	–; valets	**VAMP**	–; vamps
VALETED	–; –	**VAMPED**	–; –
VALGOID	–; –	**VAMPER**	–; vampers
VALGUS	–; –	**VAMPING**	–; –
VALIANT	–; valiants	**VAMPIRE**	–; vampires
VALID	–; –	**VAMPISH**	–; –
VALIDLY	–; –	**VAN**	–; vane, vang, vans
VALINE	–; valines		
VALISE	–; valises	**VANADIC**	–; –
VALKYR	–; valkyrs	**VANDA**	–; vandal, vandas
VALLATE	–; –		
VALLEY	–; valleys	**VANDAL**	–; vandals
VALONIA	–; valonias	**VANDYKE**	–; vandyked, vandykes
VALOR	–; valors		
VALOUR	–; valours		
VALSE	–; valses	**VANE**	–; vaned, vanes
VALUATE	evaluate; valuated, valuates		
		VANG	–; vangs
		VANILLA	–; vanillas
VALUE	–; valued, valuer, values	**VANISH**	evanish; –
		VANITY	–; –
		VANMAN	–; –
VALUER	–; valuers	**VANMEN**	–; –
VALUING	–; –	**VANTAGE**	–; vantages
VALUTA	–; valutas	**VANWARD**	–; –
VALVAL	–; –	**VAPID**	–; –
VALVAR	–; –	**VAPIDLY**	–; –
VALVATE	–; –	**VAPOR**	–; vapors, vapory
VALVE	–; valved, valves		
		VAPORED	–; –
VALVING	–; –	**VAPORER**	–; vaporers
VALVULA	–; valvulae, valvular	**VAPOUR**	–; vapours, vapoury
VALVULE	–; valvules	**VAQUERO**	–; vaqueros
VAMOOSE	–; vamoosed, vamooses	**VARA**	–; varas
		VARIA	–; –
		VARIANT	–; variants

VARIATE	–; variated, variates	**VATFUL**	–; vatfuls
VARICES	avarices; –	**VATIC**	;
VARIED	–; –	**VATICAL**	–; –
VARIER	–; variers	**VATTED**	–; –
VARIES	ovaries; –	**VATTING**	–; –
VARIETY	–; –	**VAU**	–; vaus
VARIOLA	–; variolar, variolas	**VAULT**	–; vaults, vaulty
VARIOLE	ovariole; varioles	**VAULTED**	–; –
		VAULTER	–; vaulters
VARIOUS	–; –	**VAUNT**	avaunt; vaunts, vaunty
VARIX	–; –		
VARLET	–; varlets	**VAUNTED**	–; –
VARMENT	–; varments	**VAUNTER**	–; vaunters
VARMINT	–; varmints	**VAUNTIE**	–; –
VARNA	–; varnas	**VAV**	–; vavs
VARNISH	–; varnishy	**VAVASOR**	–; vavasors
VARSITY	–; –	**VAW**	–; vaws
VARUS	–; –	**VAWARD**	–; vawards
VARUSES	–; –	**VAWNTIE**	–; –
VARVE	–; varved, varves	**VEAL**	uveal; veals, vealy
VARY	ovary; –	**VEALED**	–; –
VARYING	–; –	**VEALER**	–; vealers
VAS	kvas; vasa, vase, vast	**VEALIER**	–; –
		VEALING	–; –
VASA	–; vasal	**VECTOR**	–; vectors
VASCULA	–; vascular	**VEDALIA**	–; vedalias
VASE	–; vases	**VEDETTE**	–; vedettes
VASES	kvases; –	**VEE**	–; veep, veer, vees
VASSAL	–; vassals		
VAST	avast; vasts, vasty	**VEENA**	–; veenas
		VEEP	–; veeps
VASTER	–; –	**VEEPEE**	–; veepees
VASTEST	–; –	**VEER**	–; veers, veery
VASTIER	–; –		
VASTITY	–; –	**VEERED**	–; –
VASTLY	–; –	**VEERIES**	–; –
VAT	–; vats	**VEG**	–; –

VEGAN	–; vegans	**VEND**	–; vends
VEGETAL	–; –	**VENDACE**	–; vendaces
VEGETE	–; –	**VENDED**	–; –
VEHICLE	–; vehicles	**VENDEE**	–; vendees
VEIL	–; veils	**VENDER**	–; venders
VEILED	–; –	**VENDING**	–; –
VEILER	–; veilers	**VENDOR**	–; vendors
VEILING	–; veilings	**VENDUE**	–; vendues
VEIN	–; veins, veiny	**VENEER**	–; veneers
		VENERY	–; –
VEINAL	–; –	**VENGE**	avenge; venged, venges
VEINED	–; –		
VEINER	–; veiners		
VEINIER	–; –	**VENGED**	avenged; –
VEINING	–; veinings	**VENGES**	avenges; –
VEINLET	–; veinlets	**VENGING**	avenging; –
VEINULE	–; veinules, veinulet	**VENIAL**	–; –
		VENIN	–; venine, venins
VELA	–; velar		
VELAMEN	–; –	**VENINE**	–; venines
VELAR	–; velars	**VENIRE**	–; venires
VELATE	–; –	**VENISON**	–; venisons
VELD	–; velds, veldt	**VENOM**	–; venoms
		VENOMED	–; –
VELDT	–; veldts	**VENOMER**	–; venomers
VELIGER	–; veligers	**VENOSE**	–; –
VELITES	–; –	**VENOUS**	–; –
VELLUM	–; vellums	**VENT**	event; vents
VELOCE	–; –	**VENTAGE**	–; ventages
VELOUR	–; velours	**VENTAIL**	aventail; ventails
VELOUTE	–; veloutes		
VELUM	–; –	**VENTED**	–; –
VELURE	–; velured, velures	**VENTER**	–; venters
		VENTING	–; –
VELVET	–; velvets, velvety	**VENTRAL**	–; ventrals
		VENTURE	–; ventured, venturer, ventures
VENA	–; venae, venal		
		VENTURI	–; venturis
VENALLY	–; –		
VENATIC	–; –	**VENTS**	events; –

VENUE	avenue; venues	VERMES	–; –
VENUES	avenues; –	VERMIAN	–; –
VENULAR	–; –	VERMIN	–; –
VENULE	–; venules	VERMIS	–; –
VERA	–; –	VERMUTH	–; vermuths
VERANDA	–; verandah, verandas	VERNAL	–; –
		VERNIER	–; verniers
VERB	–; verbs	VERNIX	–; –
VERBAL	–; verbals	VERRUCA	–; verrucae
VERBENA	–; verbenas	VERSAL	–; –
VERBID	overbid; verbids	VERSANT	–; versants
		VERSE	averse; versed, verser, verses, verset
VERBIDS	overbids; –		
VERBIFY	–; –		
VERBILE	–; verbiles	VERSER	–; versers
VERBOSE	–; –	VERSET	overset; versets
VERDANT	–; –		
VERDICT	–; verdicts	VERSETS	oversets; –
VERDIN	–; verdins	VERSIFY	–; –
VERDURE	–; verdured, verdures	VERSINE	–; versines
		VERSING	–; –
VERGE	–; verged, verger, verges	VERSION	aversion, version; versions
VERGER	–; vergers	VERSO	–; versos
VERGING	–; –	VERST	–; verste, versts
VERGLAS	–; –		
VERIDIC	–; –	VERSUS	–; –
VERIER	–; –	VERT	avert, evert, overt; verts, vertu
VERIEST	–; –		
VERIFY	–; –		
VERILY	–; –	VERTEX	–; –
VERISM	–; verismo, verisms	VERTIGO	–; vertigos
		VERTS	averts, everts; –
VERISMO	–; verismos		
VERIST	–; verists	VERTU	–; vertus
VERITAS	–; –	VERVAIN	–; vervains
VERITY	–; –	VERVE	–; verves, vervet
VERMEIL	–; vermeils		

VERVET	–; vervets	**VEXIL**	–; vexils
VERY	every; –	**VEXILLA**	–; vexillar
VESICA	–; vesicae, vesical	**VEXING**	–; –
		VIA	–; vial
VESICLE	–; vesicles	**VIABLE**	–; –
VESPER	–; vespers	**VIABLY**	–; –
VESPID	–; vespids	**VIADUCT**	–; viaducts
VESPINE	–; –	**VIAL**	–; vials
VESSEL	–; vessels	**VIALED**	–; –
VEST	–; vesta, vests	**VIALING**	–; –
		VIALLED	–; –
VESTA	–; vestal, vestas	**VIAND**	–; viands
		VIATIC	–; viatica
VESTAL	–; vestals	**VIATICA**	–; viatical
VESTED	–; –	**VIATOR**	aviator; viators
VESTEE	–; vestees		
VESTIGE	–; vestiges	**VIATORS**	aviators; –
VESTING	–; vestings	**VIBES**	–; –
VESTRAL	–; –	**VIBIST**	–; vibists
VESTRY	–; –	**VIBRANT**	–; vibrants
VESTURE	–; vestured, vestures	**VIBRATE**	–; vibrated, vibrates
VET	–; veto, vets	**VIBRATO**	–; vibrator, vibratos
VETCH	kvetch; –		
VETCHES	kvetches; –	**VIBRIO**	–; vibrion, vibrios
VETERAN	–; veterans		
VETIVER	–; vetivers	**VIBRION**	–; vibrions
VETO	–; –	**VICAR**	–; vicars
VETOED	–; –	**VICARLY**	–; –
VETOER	–; vetoers	**VICE**	–; viced, vices
VETOES	–; –		
VETOING	–; –	**VICEROY**	–; viceroys
VETTED	–; –	**VICHIES**	–; –
VETTING	–; –	**VICHY**	–; –
VEX	–; vext	**VICINAL**	–; –
VEXED	–; –	**VICING**	–; –
VEXEDLY	–; –	**VICIOUS**	–; –
VEXER	–; vexers	**VICOMTE**	–; vicomtes
VEXES	–; –	**VICTIM**	–; victims
		VICTOR	evictor;

	victors,	**VILLEIN**	–; villeins
	victory	**VILLOSE**	,
VICTORS	evictors; –	**VILLOUS**	–; –
VICTUAL	–; victuals	**VILLUS**	–; –
VICUGNA	–; vicugnas	**VIM**	–; vims
VICUNA	–; vicunas	**VIMEN**	–; –
VIDE	–; video	**VIMINA**	–; viminal
VIDEO	–; videos	**VIN**	–; vina, vine,
VIDETTE	–; videttes		vino, vins,
VIDICON	–; vidicons		viny
VIDUITY	–; –	**VINA**	–; vinal,
VIE	–; vied, vier,		vinas
	vies, view	**VINAL**	–; vinals
VIED	ivied; –	**VINASSE**	–; vinasses
VIER	–; viers	**VINCA**	–; vincas
VIES	ivies; –	**VINE**	ovine; vined,
VIEW	–; views,		vines
	viewy	**VINEAL**	–; –
VIEWED	–; –	**VINEGAR**	–; vinegars,
VIEWER	–; viewers		vinegary
VIEWIER	–; –		
VIEWING	–; viewings	**VINERY**	–; –
VIGIL	–; vigils	**VINES**	ovines; –
VIGOR	–; vigors	**VINIC**	–; –
VIGOUR	–; vigours	**VINIER**	–; –
VIKING	–; vikings	**VINIEST**	–; –
VILAYET	–; vilayets	**VINING**	–; –
VILE	–; viler	**VINO**	–; vinos
VILELY	–; –	**VINOUS**	–; –
VILER	eviler; –	**VINTAGE**	–; vintager,
VILEST	evilest; –		vintages
VILIFY	–; –	**VINTNER**	–; vintners
VILL	–; villa, villi,	**VINY**	–; vinyl
	vills	**VINYL**	–; vinyls
VILLA	–; villae,	**VINYLIC**	–; –
	villas	**VIOL**	–; viola,
VILLAGE	–; villager,		viols
	villages	**VIOLA**	–; violas
VILLAIN	–; villains,	**VIOLATE**	–; violated,
	villainy		violater,
			violates

VIOLENT	–; –	**VISCOID**	–; –
VIOLET	–; violets	**VISCOSE**	–; viscoses
VIOLIN	–; violins	**VISCOUS**	–; –
VIOLIST	–; violists	**VISCUS**	–; –
VIOLONE	–; violones	**VISE**	–; vised, vises
VIPER	–; vipers		
VIRAGO	–; viragos	**VISEED**	–; –
VIRAL	–; –	**VISEING**	–; –
VIRALLY	–; –	**VISIBLE**	–; –
VIRELAI	–; virelais	**VISIBLY**	–; –
VIRELAY	–; virelays	**VISING**	–; –
VIREMIA	–; viremias	**VISION**	–; visions
VIREMIC	–; –	**VISIT**	–; visits
VIREO	–; vireos	**VISITED**	–; –
VIRES	–; –	**VISITER**	–; visiters
VIRGA	–; virgas	**VISITOR**	–; visitors
VIRGATE	–; virgates	**VISIVE**	–; –
VIRGIN	–; virgins	**VISOR**	–; visors
VIRGULE	–; virgules	**VISORED**	–; –
VIRID	–; –	**VISTA**	–; vistas
VIRILE	–; –	**VISUAL**	–; –
VIRION	–; virions	**VITA**	–; vitae, vital
VIRL	–; virls	**VITAL**	–; vitals
VIROSES	–; –	**VITALLY**	–; –
VIROSIS	–; –	**VITAMER**	–; vitamers
VIRTU	–; virtue, virtus	**VITAMIN**	–; vitamine, vitamins
VIRTUAL	–; –	**VITESSE**	–; vitesses
VIRTUE	–; virtues	**VITIATE**	–; vitiated, vitiates
VIRUS	–; –		
VIRUSES	–; –	**VITRIC**	–; –
VIS	–; visa, vise	**VITRIFY**	–; –
VISA	–; visas	**VITRINE**	–; vitrines
VISAED	–; –	**VITRIOL**	–; vitriols
VISAGE	–; visaged, visages	**VITTA**	–; vittae
		VITTATE	–; –
VISAING	–; –	**VITTLE**	–; vittled, vittles
VISARD	–; visards		
VISCERA	–; visceral	**VIVA**	–; vivas
VISCID	–; –	**VIVACE**	–; –

VIVARY	–; –	VOIDERS	avoiders; –
VIVE	;	VOIDING	avoiding; –
VIVERS	–; –	VOIDS	avoids,
VIVID	–; –		ovoids; –
VIVIDER	–; –	VOILE	–; voiles
VIVIDLY	–; –	VOLANT	–; volante
VIVIFIC	–; –	VOLAR	–; –
VIVIFY	–; –	VOLCANO	–; volcanos
VIXEN	–; vixens	VOLE	–; voled,
VIXENLY	–; –		voles
VIZARD	–; vizards	VOLERY	–; –
VIZIER	–; viziers	VOLING	–; –
VIZIR	–; vizirs	VOLLEY	–; volleys
VIZOR	–; vizors	VOLOST	–; volosts
VIZORED	–; –	VOLT	–; volta,
VIZSLA	–; vizslas		volte, volti,
VOCABLE	evocable;		volts
	vocables	VOLTAGE	–; voltages
VOCABLY	–; –	VOLTAIC	–; –
VOCAL	–; vocals	VOLTE	–; voltes
VOCALIC	–; vocalics	VOLUBLE	–; –
VOCALLY	–; –	VOLUBLY	–; –
VOCES	–; –	VOLUME	–; volumed,
VOCODER	–; vocoders		volumes
VODKA	–; vodkas	VOLUTE	evolute;
VODUN	–; voduns		voluted,
VOE	–; voes		volutes
VOGIE	–; –	VOLUTED	evoluted; –
VOGUE	–; vogues	VOLUTES	evolutes; –
VOGUISH	–; –	VOLUTIN	–; volutins
VOICE	–; voiced,	VOLVA	–; volvas
	voicer,	VOLVATE	–; –
	voices	VOLVOX	–; –
VOICER	–; voicers	VOMER	–; vomers
VOICING	–; –	VOMICA	–; vomicae
VOID	avoid, ovoid;	VOMIT	–; vomito,
	voids		vomits
VOIDED	avoided; –	VOMITED	–; –
VOIDER	avoider;	VOMITER	–; vomiters
	voiders	VOMITO	–; vomitos

VOMITUS	–; –	**VOWS**	avows; –
VON	–; –	**VOX**	–; –
VOODOO	–; voodoos	**VOYAGE**	–; voyaged,
VORLAGE	–; vorlages		voyager,
VORTEX	–; –		voyages
VOTABLE	–; –	**VOYAGER**	–; voyagers
VOTARY	–; –	**VOYEUR**	–; voyeurs
VOTE	–; voted,	**VROOM**	–; vrooms
	voter, votes	**VROOMED**	–; –
VOTER	–; voters	**VROUW**	–; vrouws
VOTING	–; –	**VROW**	–; vrows
VOTIVE	–; –	**VUG**	–; vugg,
VOTRESS	–; –		vugh, vugs
VOUCH	avouch; –	**VUGG**	–; vuggs,
VOUCHED	avouched; –		vuggy
VOUCHEE	–; vouchees	**VUGH**	–; vughs
VOUCHER	avoucher;	**VULGAR**	–; vulgars
	vouchers	**VULGATE**	–; vulgates
VOUCHES	avouches; –	**VULGO**	–; –
VOW	avow; vows	**VULGUS**	–; –
VOWED	avowed; –	**VULPINE**	–; –
VOWING	–; –	**VULTURE**	–; vultures
VOWEL	–; vowels	**VULVA**	–; vulvae,
VOWER	avower;		vulval,
	vowers		vulvar, vulvas
VOWERS	avowers; –	**VULVATE**	–; –
VOWING	avowing; –	**VYING**	–; –
VOWLESS	–; –	**VYINGLY**	–; –

W

W	aw, ow; we,	**WABBLY**	–; –
	wo	**WABS**	swabs; –
WAB	swab; wabs	**WACK**	–; wacke,
WABBLE	–; wabbled,		wacks,
	wabbler,		wacky
	wabbles	**WACKE**	–; wackes
WABBLER	–; wabblers	**WACKIER**	–; –

WACKILY	–; –	**WAES**	twaes; –
WAD	–; wade	**WAESUCK**	; waesucks
	wadi, wads,	**WAFER**	–; wafers,
	wady		wafery
WADABLE	–; –	**WAFERED**	–; –
WADDED	–; –	**WAFF**	–; waffs
WADDER	–; wadders	**WAFFED**	–; –
WADDIE	–; waddied,	**WAFFIE**	–; waffies
	waddies	**WAFFING**	–; –
WADDING	–; waddings	**WAFFLE**	–; waffled,
WADDLE	swaddle,		waffles
	twaddle;	**WAFT**	–; wafts
	waddled,	**WAFTAGE**	–; waftages
	waddler,	**WAFTED**	–; –
	waddles	**WAFTER**	–; watters
WADDLED	swaddled,	**WAFTING**	–; –
	twaddled; –	**WAFTURE**	–; waftures
WADDLER	twaddler;	**WAG**	swag; wage,
	waddlers		wags
WADDLES	swaddles,	**WAGE**	swage;
	twaddles; –		waged,
WADDLY	–; –		wager,
WADDY	–; –		wages
WADE	–; waded,	**WAGED**	swaged; –
	wader,	**WAGER**	swager;
	wades		wagers
WADER	–; waders	**WAGERED**	–; –
WADI	–; wadis	**WAGERER**	–; wagerers
WADIES	–; –	**WAGERS**	swagers; –
WADING	–; –	**WAGES**	swages; –
WADMAAL	–; wadmaals	**WAGGED**	swagged; –
WADMAL	–; wadmals	**WAGGER**	swagger;
WADMEL	–; wadmels		waggers,
WADMOL	–; wadmoll,		waggery
	wadmols	**WAGGERS**	swaggers; –
WADMOLL	–; wadmolls	**WAGGING**	swagging; –
WADSET	–; wadsets	**WAGGISH**	–; –
WAE	twae; waes	**WAGGLE**	–; waggled,
WAEFU	–; waeful		waggles
WAENESS	–; –	**WAGGLY**	–; –

WAGGON	–; waggons	**WAIVING**	–; –
WAGING	swaging; –	**WAKANDA**	–; wakandas
WAGON	–; wagons	**WAKE**	awake;
WAGONED	–; –		waked,
WAGONER	–; wagoners		waken,
WAGS	swags; –		waker,
WAGSOME	–; –		wakes
WAGTAIL	–; wagtails	**WAKED**	awaked; –
WAHINE	–; wahines	**WAKEFUL**	–; –
WAHOO	–; wahoos	**WAKEN**	awaken;
WAIF	–; waifs		wakens
WAIFED	–; –	**WAKENED**	awakened; –
WAIFING	–; –	**WAKENER**	awakener;
WAIL	swail; wails		wakeners
WAILED	–; –	**WAKENS**	awakens; –
WAILER	–; wailers	**WAKER**	–; wakers
WAILFUL	–; –	**WAKES**	awakes; –
WAILING	–; –	**WAKIKI**	–; wakikis
WAILS	swails; –	**WAKING**	awaking; –
WAIN	swain, twain;	**WALE**	swale;
	wains		waled,
WAINS	swains,		waler,
	twains; –		wales
WAIR	–; wairs	**WALER**	–; walers
WAIRED	–; –	**WALES**	swales; –
WAIRING	–; –	**WALIES**	–; –
WAIST	–; waists	**WALING**	–; –
WAISTED	–; –	**WALK**	–; walks
WAISTER	–; waisters	**WALKED**	–; –
WAIT	await; waits	**WALKER**	–; walkers
WAITED	awaited; –	**WALKING**	–; walkings
WAITER	awaiter;	**WALKOUT**	–; walkouts
	waiters	**WALKUP**	–; walkups
WAITERS	awaiters; –	**WALKWAY**	–; walkways
WAITING	–; waitings	**WALL**	–; walla,
WAITS	awaits; –		walls, wally
WAIVE	–; waived,	**WALLA**	–; wallah,
	waiver,		wallas
	waives	**WALLABY**	–; –
WAIVER	–; waivers	**WALLAH**	–; wallahs

WALLED	–; –	**WANGLE**	twangle;
WALLET	–; wallets		wangled,
WALLEYE	–; walleyed,		wangler,
	walleyes		wangles
WALLIE	–; wallies	**WANGLED**	twangled; –
WALLING	–; –	**WANGLER**	twangler;
WALLOP	–; wallops		wanglers
WALLOW	swallow;	**WANGLES**	twangles; –
	wallows	**WANGUN**	–; wanguns
WALLOWS	swallows; –	**WANIER**	–; –
WALNUT	–; walnuts	**WANIEST**	–; –
WALRUS	–; –	**WANIGAN**	–; wanigans
WALTZ	–; –	**WANING**	–; –
WALTZED	–; –	**WANION**	–; wanions
WALTZER	–; waltzers	**WANLY**	–; –
WALTZES	–; –	**WANNED**	swanned; –
WALY	–; –	**WANNER**	–; –
WAMBLE	–; wambled,	**WANNESS**	–; –
	wambles	**WANNEST**	–; –
WAMBLY	–; –	**WANNING**	swanning; –
WAME	–; wames	**WANS**	swans; –
WAMEFOU	–; wamefous	**WANT**	–; wants
WAMEFUL	–; wamefuls	**WANTAGE**	–; wantages
WAMMUS	–; –	**WANTED**	–; –
WAMPISH	–; –	**WANTER**	–; wanters
WAMPUM	–; wampums	**WANTING**	–; –
WAMPUS	–; –	**WANTON**	–; wantons
WAMUS	–; –	**WAP**	swap; waps
WAMUSES	–; –	**WAPITI**	–; wapitis
WAN	hwan, swan;	**WAPPED**	swapped; –
	wand, wane,	**WAPPING**	swapping; –
	wans, want,	**WAPS**	swaps; –
	wany	**WAR**	–; ward,
WAND	–; wands		ware, wark,
WANDER	–; wanders		warm, warn,
WANDLE	–; –		warp, wars,
WANE	–; waned,		wart, wary
	wanes,	**WARBLE**	–; warbled,
	waney		warbler,
WANGAN	–; wangans		warbles

WARBLER	–; warblers	WARMISH	–; –
WARD	award,	WARMLY	–; –
	sward;	WARMS	swarms; –
	wards	WARMTH	–; warmths
WARDED	awarded,	WARMUP	–; warmups
	swarded; –	WARN	–; warns
WARDEN	–; wardens	WARNED	–; –
WARDER	awarder;	WARNER	–; warners
	warders	WARNING	–; warnings
WARDERS	awarders; –	WARP	–; warps
WARDING	awarding,	WARPAGE	–; warpages
	swarding; –	WARPATH	–; warpaths
WARDS	awards,	WARPED	–; –
	swards; –	WARPER	–; warpers
WARE	aware,	WARPING	–; –
	sware;	WARRANT	–; warrants,
	wared,		warranty
	wares	WARRED	–; –
WARFARE	–; warfares	WARREN	–; warrens
WARHEAD	–; warheads	WARRING	–; –
WARIER	–; –	WARRIOR	–; warriors
WARIEST	–; –	WARSAW	–; warsaws
WARILY	–; –	WARSHIP	–; warships
WARING	–; –	WARSLE	–; warsled,
WARISON	–; warisons		warsler,
WARK	–; warks		warsles
WARKED	–; –	WARSLER	–; warslers
WARKING	–; –	WARSTLE	–; warstled,
WARLESS	–; –		warstler,
WARLIKE	–; –		warstles
WARLOCK	–; warlocks	WART	swart; warts,
WARLORD	–; warlords		warty
WARM	swarm;	WARTED	–; –
	warms	WARTHOG	–; warthogs
WARMED	swarmed; –	WARTIER	–; –
WARMER	swarmer;	WARTIME	–; wartimes
	warmers	WARWORK	–; warworks
WARMERS	swarmers; –	WARWORN	–; –
WARMEST	–; –	WARTY	swarty; –
WARMING	swarming; –		

WAS	–; wash, woot	**WATCH**	swatch; –
		WATCHED	–; –
WASH	awash, swash; washy	**WATCHER**	–; watchers
		WATCHES	swatches; –
		WATER	–; waters, watery
WASHDAY	–; washdays		
WASHED	swashed; –	**WATERED**	–; –
WASHER	swasher; washers	**WATERER**	–; waterers
		WATS	swats; –
WASHERS	swashers; –	**WATT**	–; watts
WASHES	swashes; –	**WATTAGE**	–; wattages
WASHIER	–; –	**WATTAPE**	–; wattapes
WASHING	swashing; washings	**WATTER**	swatter; –
		WATTEST	–; –
WASHOUT	–; washouts	**WATTLE**	twattle; wattled, wattles
WASHRAG	–; washrags		
WASHTUB	–; washtubs		
WASP	–; wasps, waspy	**WATTLED**	twattled; –
		WATTLES	twattles; wattless
WASPIER	–; –		
WASPILY	–; –	**WAUCHT**	–; wauchts
WASPISH	–; –	**WAUGH**	–; waught
WASSAIL	–; wassails	**WAUGHT**	–; waughts
WAST	–; waste, wasts	**WAUK**	–; wauks
		WAUKED	–; –
WASTAGE	–; wastages	**WAUKING**	–; –
WASTE	–; wasted, waster, wastes	**WAUL**	–; wauls
		WAULED	–; –
		WAULING	–; –
WASTER	–; wasters, wastery	**WAUR**	–; –
		WAVE	–; waved, waver, waves, wavey
WASTING	–; –		
WASTREL	–; wastrels		
WASTRIE	–; wastries		
WASTRY	–; –	**WAVELET**	–; wavelets
WAT	swat; wats, watt	**WAVEOFF**	–; waveoffs
		WAVER	–; wavers, wavery
WATAP	–; watape, wataps		
		WAVERED	–; –
WATAPE	–; watapes	**WAVERER**	–; waverers

WAVEY	–; waveys	WEAK	tweak; –
WAVIER	–; –	WEAKEN	–; weakens
WAVIES	–; waviest	WEAKER	–; –
WAVILY	–; –	WEAKEST	–; –
WAVING	–; –	WEAKISH	–; –
WAVY	–; –	WEAKLY	–; –
WAW	–; wawl, waws	WEAL	–; weald, weals
WAWL	–; wawls	WEALD	–; wealds
WAWLED	–; –	WEALTH	–; wealths, wealthy
WAWLING	–; –		
WAX	–; waxy	WEAN	–; weans
WAXBILL	–; waxbills	WEANED	–; –
WAXED	–; –	WEANER	–; weaners
WAXEN	–; –	WEANING	–; –
WAXER	–; waxers	WEAPON	–; weapons
WAXIER	–; –	WEAR	swear;
WAXIEST	–; –		wears,
WAXILY	–; –		weary
WAXING	–; waxings	WEARER	swearer;
WAXLIKE	–; –		wearers
WAXWEED	–; waxweeds	WEARERS	swearers; –
WAXWING	–; waxwings	WEARIED	–; –
WAXWORK	–; waxworks	WEARIER	–; –
WAXWORM	–; waxworms	WEARIES	–; weariest
		WEARILY	–; –
WAY	away, sway; ways	WEARING	swearing; –
		WEARISH	–; –
WAYBILL	–; waybills	WEARS	swears; –
WAYLAID	–; –	WEARY	aweary; –
WAYLAY	–; waylays	WEASAND	–; weasands
WAYLESS	–; –	WEASEL	–; weasels
WAYSIDE	–; waysides	WEASON	–; weasons
WAYWARD	–; –	WEATHER	aweather; weathers
WAYWORN	–; –		
WAYS	sways; –	WEAVE	–; weaved, weaver, weaves
WE	awe, ewe, owe; web, wed, wee, wen, wet		
		WEAVER	–; weavers
		WEAVING	–; –

WEAZAND	–; weazands	WEEDED	–; –
WEB	–; webs	WEEDER	–; weeders
WEBBED	–; –	WEEDIER	tweedier; –
WEBBIER	–; –	WEEDILY	–; –
WEBBING	–; webbings	WEEDING	–; –
WEBBY	–; –	WEEDS	tweeds; –
WEBER	–; webers	WEEDY	tweedy; –
WEBFED	–; –	WEEK	–; weeks
WEBFEET	–; –	WEEKDAY	–; weekdays
WEBFOOT	–; –	WEEKEND	–; weekends
WEBLESS	–; –	WEEKLY	–; –
WEBLIKE	–; –	WEEL	–; –
WEBSTER	–; websters	WEEN	tween;
WEBWORM	–; webworms		weens,
WECHT	–; wechts		weeny
WED	awed, owed;	WEENED	–; –
	weds	WEENIE	–; weenies
WEDDED	–; –	WEENING	–; –
WEDDER	–; wedders	WEENS	–; weensy
WEDDING	–; weddings	WEENY	sweeny; –
WEDEL	–; wedeln,	WEEP	sweep;
	wedels		weeps,
WEDELED	–; –		weepy
WEDELN	–; wedelns	WEEPER	sweeper;
WEDGE	–; wedged,		weepers
	wedges	WEEPERS	sweepers; –
WEDGIE	–; wedgier,	WEEPIER	sweepier; –
	wedgies	WEEPING	sweeping; –
WEDGIES	–; wedgiest	WEEPS	sweeps; –
WEDGING	–; –	WEEPY	sweepy; –
WEDGY	–; –	WEER	sweer; –
WEDLOCK	–; wedlocks	WEES	–; weest
WEE	awee; weed,	WEET	sweet, tweet;
	week, weel,		weets
	ween, weep,	WEETED	tweeted; –
	weer, wees,	WEETING	tweeting; –
	weet	WEETS	sweets,
WEED	tweed;		tweets; –
	weeds,	WEEVER	–; weevers
	weedy		

WEEVIL	–; weevils, weevily	**WELLED**	dwelled, swelled; –
WEEWEE	–; weeweed, weewees	**WELLING**	dwelling, swelling; –
WEFT	–; wefts	**WELLS**	dwells, swells; –
WEIGELA	–; weigelas	**WELSH**	–; –
WEIGH	aweigh; weighs, weight	**WELSHED**	–; –
		WELSHER	–; welshers
		WELSHES	–; –
WEIGHED	–; –	**WELT**	dwelt; welts
WEIGHER	–; weighers	**WELTED**	–; –
WEIGHT	–; weights, weighty	**WELTER**	swelter; welters
WEINER	–; weiners	**WELTERS**	swelters; –
WEIR	–; weird, weirs	**WELTING**	–; weltings
		WEN	–; wend, wens, went
WEIRD	–; weirdo, weirds, weirdy	**WENCH**	–; –
		WENCHED	–; –
WEIRDIE	–; weirdies	**WENCHER**	–; wenchers
WEIRDLY	–; –	**WENCHES**	–; –
WEIRDO	–; weirdos	**WEND**	–; wends
WEKA	–; wekas	**WENDED**	–; –
WELCH	–; –	**WENDIGO**	–; wendigos
WELCHED	–; –	**WENDING**	–; –
WELCHER	–; welchers	**WENNIER**	–; –
WELCHES	–; –	**WENNISH**	–; –
WELCOME	–; welcomed, welcomer, welcomes	**WENNY**	–; –
		WEPT	swept; –
		WERE	–; –
WELD	–; welds	**WERGELD**	–; wergelds
WELDED	–; –	**WERGELT**	–; wergelts
WELDER	–; welders	**WERGILD**	–; wergilds
WELDING	–; –	**WERT**	–; –
WELDOR	–; weldors	**WERWOLF**	–; –
WELFARE	–; welfares	**WESKIT**	–; weskits
WELKIN	–; welkins	**WESSAND**	–; wessands
WELL	dwell, swell; wells	**WEST**	–; wests

WESTER	−; western, westers	WHAUP	−; whaups
WESTERN	−; westerns	WHEAL	−; wheals
WESTING	−; westings	WHEAT	−; wheats
WET	−; wets	WHEATEN	−; −
WETBACK	−; wetbacks	WHEE	−; wheel, wheen, wheep
WETHER	−; wethers		
WETLAND	−; wetlands		
WETLY	−; −	WHEEDLE	−; wheedled, wheedler, wheedles
WETNESS	−; −		
WETTED	−; −		
WETTER	−; wetters	WHEEL	−; wheels
WETTEST	−; −	WHEELED	−; −
WETTING	−; wettings	WHEELER	−; wheelers
WETTISH	−; −	WHEELIE	−; wheelies
WHA	−; wham, whap, what	WHEEN	−; wheens
		WHEEP	−; wheeps
WHACK	−; whacks, whacky	WHEEPED	−; −
		WHEEPLE	−; wheepled, wheeples
WHACKED	−; −		
WHACKER	−; whackers		
WHALE	−; whaled, whaler, whales	WHEEZE	−; wheezed, wheezer, wheezes
WHALER	−; whalers	WHEEZER	−; wheezers
WHALING	−; whalings	WHEEZY	−; −
WHAM	−; whams	WHELK	−; whelks, whelky
WHAMMED	−; −		
WHAMMY	−; −	WHELM	−; whelms
WHANG	−; whangs	WHELMED	−; −
WHANGED	−; −	WHELP	−; whelps
WHANGEE	−; whangees	WHELPED	−; −
WHAP	−; whaps	WHEN	−; whens
WHAPPED	−; −	WHENAS	−; −
WHAPPER	−; whappers	WHENCE	−; −
WHARF	−; wharfs	WHERE	−; wheres
WHARFED	−; −	WHEREAS	−; −
WHARVE	−; wharves	WHEREAT	−; −
WHAT	−; whats	WHEREBY	−; −
WHATNOT	−; whatnots	WHEREIN	−; −

WHEREOF	–; –		whines,
WHEREON	–; –		whiney
WHERETO	–; –	**WHINER**	–; whiners
WHERRY	–; –	**WHINIER**	–; –
WHERVE	–; wherves	**WHINING**	–; –
WHET	–; whets	**WHINNY**	–; –
WHETHER	–; whethers	**WHINY**	–; –
WHETTED	–; –	**WHIP**	–; whips,
WHETTER	–; whetters		whipt
WHEW	–; whews	**WHIPPED**	–; –
WHEY	–; wheys	**WHIPPER**	–; whippers
WHEYEY	–; –	**WHIPPET**	–; whippets
WHEYISH	–; –	**WHIPPY**	–; –
WHICH	–; –	**WHIPRAY**	–; whiprays
WHICKER	–; whickers	**WHIPSAW**	–;
WHID	–; whids		whipsawn,
WHIDAH	–; whidahs		whipsaws
WHIDDED	–; –	**WHIR**	–; whirl,
WHIFF	–; whiffs		whirr, whirs
WHIFFED	–; –	**WHIRL**	awhirl;
WHIFFER	–; whiffers		whirls, whirly
WHIFFET	–; whiffets	**WHIRLED**	–; –
WHIFFLE	–; whiffled,	**WHIRLER**	–; whirlers
	whiffler,	**WHIRLY**	–; –
	whiffles	**WHIRR**	–; whirrs,
WHILE	awhile;		whirry
	whiled,	**WHIRRED**	–; –
	whiles	**WHISH**	–; whisht
WHILING	–; –	**WHISHED**	–; –
WHILOM	–; –	**WHISHES**	–; –
WHILST	–; –	**WHISHT**	–; whishts
WHIM	–; whims	**WHISK**	–; whisks,
WHIMPER	–; whimpers		whisky
WHIMS	–; whimsy	**WHISKED**	–; –
WHIMSEY	–; whimseys	**WHISKER**	–; whiskers,
WHIN	–; whine,		whiskery
	whins	**WHISKEY**	–; whiskeys
WHINE	–; whined,	**WHISPER**	–; whispers,
	whiner,		whispery

WHIST	–; whists
WHISTED	–; –
WHISTLE	–; whistled, whistler, whistles
WHIT	–; white, whits, whity
WHITE	–; whited, whiten, whiter, whites, whitey
WHITELY	–; –
WHITEN	–; whitens
WHITES	–; whitest
WHITEY	–; whiteys
WHITHER	–; –
WHITIES	–; –
WHITING	–; whitings
WHITISH	–; –
WHITLOW	–; whitlows
WHITTER	–; whitters
WHITTLE	–; whittled, whittler, whittles
WHITY	–; –
WHIZ	–; whizz
WHIZZED	–; –
WHIZZER	–; whizzers
WHIZZES	–; –
WHO	–; whoa, whom, whop
WHOEVER	–; –
WHOLE	–; wholes
WHOLISM	–; wholisms
WHOLLY	–; –
WHOM	–; whomp
WHOMP	–; whomps
WHOMPED	–; –
WHOMSO	–; –

WHOOP	–; whoops
WHOOPED	;
WHOOPEE	–; whoopees
WHOOPER	–; whoopers
WHOOPLA	–; whooplas
WHOOSH	–; –
WHOOSIS	–; –
WHOP	–; whops
WHOPPED	–; –
WHOPPER	–; whoppers
WHORE	–; whored, whores
WHORING	–; –
WHORISH	–; –
WHORL	–; whorls
WHORLED	–; –
WHORT	–; whorts
WHORTLE	–; whortles
WHOSE	–; –
WHOSIS	–; –
WHOSO	–; –
WHUMP	–; whumps
WHUMPED	–; –
WHY	–; whys
WHYDAH	–; whydahs
WICH	–; –
WICHES	–; –
WICK	–; wicks
WICKAPE	–; wickapes
WICKED	–; –
WICKER	–; wickers
WICKET	–; wickets
WICKING	–; wickings
WICKIUP	–; wickiups
WICKYUP	–; wickyups
WICOPY	–; –
WIDDER	–; widders
WIDDIE	–; widdies
WIDDLE	twiddle;

	widdled, widdles	**WIGGLE**	–; wiggled, wiggler, wiggles
WIDDLED	twiddled; –		
WIDDLES	twiddles; –	**WIGGLER**	–; wigglers
WIDDY	–; –	**WIGGLY**	–; –
WIDE	–; widen, wider, wides	**WIGHT**	–; wights
		WIGLESS	–; –
WIDELY	–; –	**WIGLET**	–; wiglets
WIDEN	–; widens	**WIGLIKE**	twiglike; –
WIDENED	–; –	**WIGS**	swigs, twigs; –
WIDENER	–; wideners		
WIDES	–; widest	**WIGWAG**	–; wigwags
WIDGEON	–; widgeons	**WIGWAM**	–; wigwams
WIDGET	–; widgets	**WIKIUP**	–; wikiups
WIDISH	–; –	**WILCO**	–; –
WIDOW	–; widows	**WILD**	–; wilds
WIDOWED	–; –	**WILDCAT**	–; wildcats
WIDOWER	–; widowers	**WILDER**	–; wilders
WIDTH	–; widths	**WILDEST**	–; –
WIELD	–; wields, wieldy	**WILDING**	–; wildings
		WILDISH	–; –
WIELDED	–; –	**WILDLY**	–; –
WIELDER	–; wielders	**WILE**	–; wiled, wiles
WIENER	–; wieners		
WIENIE	–; wienies	**WILFUL**	–; –
WIFE	–; wifed, wifes	**WILIER**	–; –
		WILIEST	–; –
WIFEDOM	–; wifedoms	**WILILY**	–; –
WIFELY	–; –	**WILING**	–; –
WIFING	–; –	**WILL**	swill, twill; wills, willy
WIG	swig, twig; wigs		
		WILLED	swilled, twilled; –
WIGAN	–; wigans		
WIGEON	–; wigeons	**WILLER**	swiller; willers
WIGGED	swigged, twigged; –		
		WILLERS	swillers; –
WIGGERY	–; –	**WILLET**	–; willets
WIGGING	swigging, twigging; wiggings	**WILLFUL**	–; –
		WILLIED	–; –
		WILLIES	–; –

WILLING	swilling, twilling,	**WINDLE**	dwindle, swindle; windled, windles
WILLOW	–; willows, willowy		
		WINDLED	dwindled, swindled; –
WILLS	swills, twills; –	**WINDLES**	dwindles, swindles; windless
WILT	–; wilts		
WILTED	–; –		
WILTING	–; –		
WILY	–; –	**WINDOW**	–; windows
WIMBLE	–; wimbled, wimbles	**WINDROW**	–; windrows
		WINDUP	–; windups
WIMPLE	–; wimpled, wimples	**WINDWAY**	–; windways
		WINE	dwine, swine, twine; wined, wines, winey
WIN	twin; wind, wine, wing, wink, wino, wins, winy		
		WINED	dwined, twined; –
WINCE	–; winced, wincer, winces, wincey	**WINERY**	–; –
		WINES	dwines, swines, twines; –
WINCER	–; wincers		
WINCEY	–; winceys	**WINESOP**	–; winesops
WINCH	–; –	**WING**	awing, owing, swing; wings, wingy
WINCHED	–; –		
WINCHER	–; winchers		
WINCHES	–; –		
WINCING	–; –	**WINGBOW**	–; wingbows
WIND	–; winds, windy	**WINGED**	swinged, twinged; –
WINDAGE	–; windages	**WINGER**	swinger; wingers
WINDBAG	–; windbags		
WINDED	–; –	**WINGERS**	swingers; –
WINDER	–; winders	**WINGIER**	swingier; –
WINDIER	–; –	**WINGING**	swinging, twinging; –
WINDIGO	–; windigos		
WINDILY	–; –	**WINGLET**	–; winglets
WINDING	–; windings	**WINGMAN**	–; –
		WINGMEN	–; –

WINGS	owings, swings; —
WINGY	swingy; —
WINIER	twinier; —
WINIEST	twiniest; —
WINING	dwining, twining; —
WINISH	swinish; —
WINK	swink; winks
WINKED	swinked; —
WINKER	—; winkers
WINKING	swinking; —
WINKLE	twinkle; winkled, winkles
WINKLED	twinkled
WINKLES	twinkles; —
WINKS	swinks; —
WINNED	twinned; —
WINNER	—; winners
WINNING	twinning; winnings
WINNOCK	—; winnocks
WINNOW	—; winnows
WINO	—; winos
WINOES	—; —
WINS	twins; —
WINSOME	—; winsomer
WINTER	—; winters, wintery
WINTLE	—; wintled, wintles
WINTRY	—; —
WINY	twiny; —
WINZE	—; winzes
WIPE	swipe; wiped, wiper, wipes
WIPED	swiped; —
WIPEOUT	—; wipeouts
WIPER	—; wipers
WIPES	swipes; —
WIPING	swiping; —
WIRABLE	—; —
WIRE	—; wired, wirer, wires
WIRER	—; wirers
WIREMAN	—; —
WIREMEN	—; —
WIRETAP	—; wiretaps
WIREWAY	—; wireways
WIRIER	—; —
WIRIEST	—; —
WIRILY	—; —
WIRING	—; wirings
WIRRA	—; —
WIRY	—; —
WIS	iwis, ywis; wise, wish, wisp, wiss, wist
WISDOM	—; wisdoms
WISE	—; wised, wiser, wises
WISELY	—; —
WISENT	—; wisents
WISER	—; —
WISES	—; wisest
WISH	swish; wisha
WISHED	swished; —
WISHER	swisher; wishers
WISHERS	swishers; —
WISHES	swishes; —
WISHFUL	—; —
WISHING	swishing; —
WISING	—; —
WISP	—; wisps, wispy
WISPED	—; —

WISPIER	–; –	**WITHOUT**	–; withouts
WISPILY	–; –	**WITTING**	–; –
WISPING	–; –	**WITLESS**	–; –
WISPISH	–; –	**WITLING**	–; witlings
WISS	swiss; –	**WITLOOF**	–; witloofs
WISSED	–; –	**WITNESS**	–; –
WISSES	swisses; –	**WITNEY**	–; witneys
WISSING	–; –	**WITS**	twits; –
WIST	twist; wists	**WITTED**	twitted; –
WISTED	twisted; –	**WITTIER**	–; –
WISTFUL	–; –	**WITTILY**	–; –
WISTING	twisting; –	**WITTING**	twitting;
WISTS	twists; –		wittings
WIT	twit; wite,	**WITTOL**	–; wittols
	with, wits	**WITTY**	–; –
WITAN	–; –	**WIVE**	swive; wived,
WITCH	switch,		wiver, wives
	twitch;	**WIVED**	swived; –
	witchy	**WIVER**	–; wivern,
WITCHED	switched,		wivers
	twitched; –	**WIVERN**	–; wiverns
WITCHES	switches,	**WIVES**	swives; –
	twitches; –	**WIVING**	swiving; –
WITCHY	twitchy; –	**WIZ**	–; –
WITE	–; wited,	**WIZARD**	–; wizards
	witen, wites	**WIZEN**	–; wizens
WITH	swith; withe,	**WIZENED**	–; –
	withy	**WIZES**	–; –
WITHAL	–; –	**WIZZEN**	–; wizzens
WITHE	swithe;	**WO**	two; woe,
	withed,		wok, won,
	wither, withes		woo, wop,
WITHER	swither;		wos, wot,
	withers		wow
WITHERS	swithers; –	**WOAD**	–; woads
WITHIER	–; –	**WOADED**	–; –
WITHIES	–; withiest	**WOADWAX**	–; –
WITHIN	–; withing,	**WOALD**	–; woalds
	withins	**WOBBLE**	–; wobbled,

	wobbler, wobbles	**WONNED**	–; –
		WONNER	–; wonners
WOBBLER	–; wobblers	**WONNING**	–; –
WOBBLY	–; –	**WONT**	–; wonts
WOE	–; woes	**WONTED**	–; –
WOEFUL	–; –	**WONTING**	–; –
WOENESS	–; –	**WONTON**	–; wontons
WOESOME	–; –	**WOO**	–; wood,
WOFUL	–; –		woof, wool,
WOFULLY	–; –		woos
WOK	–; woke, woks	**WOOD**	–; woods, woody
WOKE	awoke; woken	**WOODBIN**	–; woodbind, woodbine,
WOKEN	awoken; –		woodbins
WOLD	–; wolds	**WOODBOX**	–; –
WOLF	–; wolfs	**WOODCUT**	–; woodcuts
WOLFED	–; –	**WOODED**	–; –
WOLFER	–; wolfers	**WOODEN**	–; –
WOLFING	–; –	**WOODHEN**	–; woodhens
WOLFISH	–; –	**WOODIER**	–; –
WOLFRAM	–; wolframs	**WOODING**	–; –
WOLVER	–; wolvers	**WOODLOT**	–; woodlots
WOLVES	–; –	**WOODMAN**	–; –
WOMAN	–; womans	**WOODMEN**	–; –
WOMANED	–; –	**WOODS**	–; woodsy
WOMANLY	–; –	**WOODSIA**	–; woodsias
WOMB	–; wombs, womby	**WOODWAX**	–; –
		WOOED	–; –
WOMBAT	–; wombats	**WOOER**	–; wooers
WOMBED	–; –	**WOOING**	–; –
WOMBIER	–; –	**WOOF**	–; woofs
WOMEN	–; –	**WOOFED**	–; –
WOMERA	–; womeras	**WOOFER**	–; woofers
WOMMERA	–; wommeras	**WOOFING**	–; –
WON	–; wons, wont	**WOOL**	–; wools, wooly
WONDER	–; wonders	**WOOLED**	–; –
WONKIER	–; –	**WOOLEN**	–; woolens
WONKY	–; –	**WOOLER**	–; woolers

WOOLIE	–; woolier, woolier	**WORKUP**	–; workups
		WORLD	, worlds
WOOLIES	–; wooliest	**WORLDLY**	–; –
WOOLLEN	–; woollens	**WORM**	–; worms, wormy
WOOLLY	–; –		
WOOLMAN	–; –	**WORMED**	–; –
WOOLMEN	–; –	**WORMER**	–; wormers
WOOMERA	–; woomeras	**WORMIER**	–; –
		WORMIL	–; wormils
WOOPS	swoops; –	**WORMING**	–; –
WOORALI	–; wooralis	**WORMISH**	–; –
WOORARI	–; wooraris	**WORN**	sworn; –
WOOSH	swoosh; –	**WORRIED**	–; –
WOOSHED	swooshed; –	**WORRIER**	–; worriers
WOOSHES	swooshes; –	**WORRIES**	–; –
WOOZIER	–; –	**WORRIT**	–; worrits
WOOZILY	–; –	**WORRY**	–; –
WOOZY	–; –	**WORSE**	–; worsen, worser, worses, worset
WOP	swop; wops		
WOPS	swops; –		
WORD	sword; words, wordy	**WORSEN**	–; worsens
		WORSET	–; worsets
WORDAGE	–; wordages	**WORSHIP**	–; worships
WORDED	–; –	**WORST**	–; worsts
WORDIER	–; –	**WORSTED**	–; worsteds
WORDILY	–; –	**WORT**	–; worth, worts
WORDING	–; wordings		
WORDS	swords; –	**WORTH**	–; worths, worthy
WORE	swore; –		
WORK	–; works	**WORTHED**	–; –
WORKBAG	–; workbags	**WOS**	twos; wost
WORKBOX	–; –	**WOT**	swot; wots
WORKDAY	–; workdays	**WOTS**	swots; –
WORKED	–; –	**WOTTED**	swotted; –
WORKER	–; workers	**WOTTETH**	–; –
WORKING	–; workings	**WOTTING**	swotting; –
WORKMAN	–; –	**WOULD**	–; –
WORKMEN	–; –	**WOULDST**	–; –
WORKOUT	–; workouts		

WOUND	swound; wounds	**WREST**	–; wrests
		WRESTED	–; –
WOUNDED	swounded; –	**WRESTER**	–; wresters
WOUNDS	swounds; –	**WRESTLE**	–; wrestled,
WOVE	–; woven		wrestler,
WOW	–; wows		wrestles
WOWED	–; –	**WRETCH**	–; –
WOWING	–; –	**WRIED**	–; –
WOWSER	–; wowsers	**WRIER**	–; –
WRACK	–; wracks	**WRIES**	–; wriest
WRACKED	–; –	**WRIGGLE**	–; wriggled,
WRAITH	–; wraiths		wriggler,
WRANG	–; wrangs		wriggles
WRANGLE	–; wrangled, wrangler, wrangles	**WRIGGLY**	–; –
		WRIGHT	–; wrights
		WRING	–; wrings
WRAP	–; wraps, wrapt	**WRINGED**	–; –
		WRINGER	–; wringers
WRAPPED	–; –	**WRINKLE**	–; wrinkled,
WRAPPER	–; wrappers		wrinkles
WRASSE	–; wrasses	**WRINKLY**	–; –
WRASTLE	–; wrastled, wrastles	**WRIST**	–; wrists, wristy
WRATH	–; wraths, wrathy	**WRIT**	–; write, writs
WRATHED	–; –	**WRITE**	–; writer, writes
WREAK	–; wreaks		
WREAKED	–; –	**WRITER**	–; writers
WREAKER	–; wreakers	**WRITHE**	–; writhed, writhen, writher, writhes
WREATH	–; wreathe, wreaths, wreathy		
		WRITHER	–; writhers
		WRITING	–; writings
WREATHE	–; wreathed, wreathen, wreathes	**WRITTEN**	–; –
		WRONG	–; wrongs
WRECK	–; wrecks	**WRONGED**	–; –
WRECKED	–; –	**WRONGER**	–; wrongers
WRECKER	–; wreckers	**WRONGLY**	–; –
WREN	–; wrens	**WROTE**	–; –
WRENCH	–; –		

WROTH	–; –	WYCH	–; –
WROUGHT	;	WYCHES	–; –
WRUNG	–; –	WYE	–; wyes
WRY	–; –	WYLE	–; wyled,
WRYER	–; –		wyles
WRYEST	–; –	WYLING	–; –
WRYING	–; –	WYND	–; wynds
WRYLY	–; –	WYNN	–; wynns
WRYNECK	–; wrynecks	WYTE	–; wyted,
WRYNESS	–; –		wytes
WUD	–; –	WYTING	–; –
WURST	–; wursts	WYVERN	–; wyverns
WURZEL	–; wurzels		

X

X	ax, ex, ox; xi, xu	XIPHOID	–; xiphoids
		XU	–; –
XANTHIC	–; –	XYLAN	–; xylans
XANTHIN	–; xanthine, xanthins	XYLEM	–; xylems
		XYLENE	–; xylenes
XEBEC	–; xebecs	XYLIDIN	–; xylidine,
XENIA	–; xenial, xenias		xylidins
		XYLOID	–; –
XENIC	axenic; –	XYLOL	–; xylols
XENON	–; xenons	XYLOSE	–; xyloses
XERARCH	–; –	XYLYL	–; xylyls
XERIC	–; –	XYST	–; xysti,
XEROSES	–; –		xysts
XEROSIS	–; –	XYSTER	–; xysters
XEROTIC	–; –	XYSTOI	–; –
XERUS	–; –	XYSTOS	–; –
XERUSES	–; –	XYSTUS	–; –
XI	–; xis		

Y

| Y | ay, by, my, oy; ya, ye | YA | pya, rya; yah, yak, |

	yam, yap, yar, yaw, yay	YARD	lyard; yards
		YARDAGE	–; yardages
YABBER	–; yabbers	YARDARM	–; yardarms
YACHT	–; yachts	YARDMAN	–; –
YACHTED	–; –	YARDMEN	–; –
YACHTER	–; yachters	YARDED	–; –
YACK	kyack; yacks	YARDING	–; –
YACKED	–; –	YARE	–; yarer
YACKING	–; –	YARELY	–; –
YACKS	kyacks; –	YAREST	–; –
YAFF	–; yaffs	YARN	–; yarns
YAFFED	–; –	YARNED	–; –
YAFFING	–; –	YARNING	–; –
YAGER	–; yagers	YARROW	–; yarrows
YAGI	–; yagis	YASHMAC	–; yashmacs
YAH	ayah; –	YASHMAK	–; yashmaks
YAHOO	–; yahoos	YASMAK	–; yasmaks
YAIRD	–; yairds	YATAGAN	–; yatagans
YAK	–; yaks	YAUD	–; yauds
YAKKED	–; –	YAULD	–; –
YAKKING	–; –	YAUP	–; yaups
YALD	–; –	YAUPED	–; –
YAM	–; yams	YAUPER	–; yaupers
YAMEN	–; yamens	YAUPING	–; –
YAMMER	–; yammers	YAUPON	–; yaupons
YAMUN	–; yamuns	YAW	–; yawl, yawn, yawp, yaws
YANG	–; yangs		
YANK	–; yanks		
YANKED	–; –	YAWL	–; yawls
YANKING	–; –	YAWLED	–; –
YANQUI	–; yanquis	YAWLING	–; –
YAP	–; yaps	YAWN	–; yawns
YAPOCK	–; yapocks	YAWNED	–; –
YAPOK	–; yapoks	YAWNER	–; yawners
YAPON	–; yapons	YAWNING	–; –
YAPPED	–; –	YAWP	–; yawps
YAPPER	–; yappers	YAWPED	–; –
YAPPING	–; –	YAWPER	–; yawpers
YAR	kyar; yard, yare, yarn	YAWPING	–; yawpings

YAY	–; –	**YELP**	–; yelps
YCLEPED	–; –	**YELPED**	–; –
YCLEPT	–; –	**YELPER**	–; yelpers
YE	aye, bye,	**YELPING**	–; –
	dye, eye,	**YEN**	eyen; yens
	lye, pye,	**YENNED**	–; –
	rye, tye,	**YENNING**	–; –
	wye; yea,	**YENTA**	–; yentas
	yeh, yen,	**YEOMAN**	–; –
	yep, yes,	**YEOMEN**	–; –
	yet, yew	**YEP**	–; –
YEA	–; yeah,	**YERBA**	–; yerbas
	yean, year,	**YERK**	–; yerks
	yeas	**YERKED**	–; –
YEALING	–; yealings	**YERKING**	–; –
YEAN	–; yeans	**YES**	ayes, byes,
YEANED	–; –		dyes, eyes,
YEANING	–; –		lyes, oyes,
YEAR	–; yearn,		pyes, ryes,
	years		tyes,
YEARLY	–; –		wyes; –
YEARN	–; yearns	**YESHIVA**	–; yeshivah,
YEARNED	–; –		yeshivas
YEARNER	–; yearners	**YESSED**	–; –
YEAST	–; yeasts,	**YESSES**	oyesses;
	yeasty		yessess
YEASTED	–; –	**YESSING**	–; –
YEELIN	–; yeelins	**YESTER**	–; yestern
YEGG	–; yeggs	**YET**	–; yeti, yett
YEGGMAN	–; –	**YETI**	–; yetis
YEGGMEN	–; –	**YETT**	–; yetts
YEH	–; –	**YEUK**	–; yeuks,
YELD	–; –		yeuky
YELK	–; yelks	**YEUKED**	–; –
YELL	–; yells	**YEUKING**	–; –
YELLED	–; –	**YEW**	–; yews
YELLER	–; yellers	**YID**	–; yids
YELLING	–; –	**YIELD**	–; yields
YELLOW	–; yellows,	**YIELDED**	–; –
	yellowy	**YIELDER**	–; yielders

YILL	–; yills	YOKEL	–; yokels
YIN	ayin, pyin; yins	YOKING	–; –
		YOLK	–; yolks, yolky
YINCE	–; –		
YINS	ayins, pyins; –	YOLKED	–; –
		YOLKIER	–; –
YIP	–; yipe, yips	YOM	–; –
YIPE	–; yipes	YOMIM	–; –
YIPPED	–; –	YON	–; yond, yoni
YIPPEE	–; –		
YIPPIE	–; yippies	YONDER	–; –
YIPPING	–; –	YONI	–; yonis
YIRD	–; yirds	YONKER	–; yonkers
YIRR	–; yirrs	YORE	–; yores
YIRRED	–; –	YOU	–; your
YIRRING	–; –	YOUNG	–; youngs
YIRTH	–; yirhts	YOUNGER	–; youngers
YOD	–; yodh, yods	YOUNKER	–; younkers
		YOUPON	–; youpons
YODEL	–; yodels	YOUR	–; yourn, yours
YODELED	–; –		
YODELER	–; yodelers	YOUSE	–; –
YODH	–; yodhs	YOUTH	–; youths
YODLE	–; yodled, yodler, yodles	YOUTHEN	–; youthens
		YOW	–; yowe, yowl, yows
YODLER	–; yodlers	YOWE	–; yowed, yowes
YOGA	–; yogas		
YOGEE	–; yogees	YOWIE	–; yowies
YOGH	–; yoghs	YOWING	–; –
YOGHURT	–; yoghurts	YOWL	–; yowls
YOGI	–; yogic, yogin, yogis	YOWLED	–; –
		YOWLER	–; yowlers
YOGIN	–; yogini, yogins	YOWLING	–; –
		YPERITE	–; yperites
YOGINI	–; yoginis	YTTRIA	–; yttrias
YOGURT	–; yogurts	YTTRIC	–; –
YOICKS	–; –	YTTRIUM	–; yttriums
YOKE	–; yoked, yokel, yokes	YUAN	–; yuans
		YUCCA	–; yuccas

YUGA	–; yugas	YUMMIES	–; yummiest
YUK	–; yuks	YUMMY	,
YUKKED	–; –	YUP	–; –
YUKKING	–; –	YUPON	–; yupons
YULAN	–; yulans	YURT	–; yurta,
YULE	–; yules		yurts
YUMMIER	–; –	YWIS	–; –

Z

ZACATON	–; zacatons	ZAREEBA	–; zareebas
ZADDIK	tzaddik; –	ZARF	–; zarfs
ZAFFAR	–; zaffars	ZARIBA	–; zaribas
ZAFFER	–; zaffers	ZAX	–; –
ZAFFIR	–; zaffirs	ZAXES	–; –
ZAFFRE	–; zaffres	ZAYIN	–; zayins
ZAFTIG	–; –	ZEAL	–; zeals
ZAG	–; zags	ZEALOT	–; zealots
ZAGGED	–; –	ZEATIN	–; zeatins
ZAGGING	–; –	ZEBEC	–; zebeck,
ZAIRE	–; zaires		zebecs
ZAMARRA	–; zamarras	ZEBECK	–; zebecks
ZAMARRO	–; zamarros	ZEBRA	–; zebras,
ZAMIA	–; zamias	ZEBRAS	–; zebrass
ZANANA	–; zananas	ZEBRAIC	–; –
ZANDER	–; zanders	ZEBRINE	–; –
ZANIER	–; –	ZEBROID	–; –
ZANIES	–; zaniest	ZEBU	–; zebus
ZANILY	–; –	ZECCHIN	–; zecchini,
ZANY	–; –		zecchino,
ZANYISH	–; –		zecchins
ZANZA	–; zanzas	ZECHIN	–; zechins
ZAP	–; zaps	ZED	–; zeds
ZAPATEO	–; zapateos	ZEDOARY	–; –
ZAPPED	–; –	ZEE	–; zees
ZAPPING	–; –	ZEIN	–; zeins
ZAPTIAH	–; zaptiahs	ZELKOVA	–; zelkovas
ZAPTIEH	–; zaptiehs	ZEMSTVO	–; zemstvos
ZAREBA	–; zarebas		

ZENANA	–; zenanas	ZING	–; zings, zingy
ZENITH	–; zeniths		
ZEOLITE	–; zeolites	ZINGANI	–; –
ZEPHYR	–; zephyrs	ZINGANO	–; –
ZERO	–; zeros	ZINGARA	–; –
ZEROED	–; –	ZINGARE	–; –
ZEROES	–; –	ZINGARI	–; –
ZEROING	–; –	ZINGARO	–; –
ZEST	–; zests, zesty	ZINGED	–; –
		ZINGIER	–; –
ZESTED	–; –	ZINGING	–; –
ZESTIER	–; –	ZINKIFY	–; –
ZESTFUL	–; –	ZINKY	–; –
ZESTING	–; –	ZINNIA	–; zinnias
ZETA	–; zetas	ZIP	–; zips
ZEUGMA	–; zeugmas	ZIPPED	–; –
ZIBET	–; zibeth, zibets	ZIPPER	–; zippers
		ZIPPIER	–; –
ZIBETH	–; zibeths	ZIPPING	–; –
ZIG	–; zigs	ZIPPY	–; –
ZIGGED	–; –	ZIRAM	–; zirams
ZIGGING	–; –	ZIRCON	–; zircons
ZIGZAG	–; zigzags	ZITHER	–; zithern, zithers
ZIKURAT	–; zikurats		
ZILCH	–; –	ZITHERN	–; zitherns
ZILCHES	–; –	ZITI	–; zitis
ZILLAH	–; zillahs	ZIZITH	–; –
ZILLION	–; zillions	ZIZZLE	–; zizzled, zizzles
ZINC	–; zincs, zincy		
		ZLOTY	–; zlotys
ZINCATE	–; zincates	ZOA	–; –
ZINCED	–; –	ZOARIA	–; zoarial
ZINCIC	–; –	ZODIAC	–; zodiacs
ZINCIFY	–; –	ZOEA	–; zoeae, zoeal, zoeas
ZINCING	–; –		
ZINCITE	–; zincites	ZOFTIG	–; –
ZINCKED	–; –	ZOIC	azoic; –
ZINCKY	–; –	ZOISTE	–; zoistes
ZINCOID	–; –	ZOMBI	–; zombie, zombis
ZINCOUS	–; –		

ZOMBIE	–; zombies	ZOON	–; zoons
ZONAL	ozonal; –	ZOONAL	–; –
ZONALLY	–; –	ZOOTOMY	–; –
ZONARY	–; –	ZORI	–; zoril
ZONATE	–; zonated	ZORIL	–; zorils
ZONE	ozone; zoned, zoner, zones	ZORILLA	–; zorillas
		ZORILLE	–; zorilles
		ZORILLO	–; zorillos
ZONER	–; zoners	ZOSTER	–; zosters
ZONES	ozones; –	ZOUAVE	–; zouaves
ZONING	–; –	ZOUNDS	–; –
ZONKED	–; –	ZOWIE	–; –
ZONULA	–; zonulae, zonular, zonulas	ZOYSIA	–; zoysias
		ZYGOMA	–; zygomas
		ZYGOSE	–; zygoses
ZONULE	–; zonules	ZYGOSIS	–; –
ZOO	–; zoom, zoon, zoos	ZYGOTE	–; zygotes
		ZYGOTIC	–; –
ZOOGLEA	–; zoogleae, zoogleal, zoogleas	ZYMASE	–; zymases
		ZYME	–; zymes
		ZYMOGEN	–; zymogene, zymogens
ZOOID	–; zooids		
ZOOIDAL	–; –	ZYMOSES	–; –
ZOOKS	–; –	ZYMOSIS	–; –
ZOOLOGY	–; –	ZYMOTIC	–; –
ZOOM	–; zooms	ZYMURGY	–; –
ZOOMED	–; –	ZYZZYVA	–; zyzzyvas
ZOOMING	–; –